CODE OF FEDERAL REGULATIONS

Title 27

Alcohol, Tobacco Products and Firearms

Parts 40 to 399

Revised as of April 1, 2016

Containing a codification of documents
of general applicability and future effect

As of April 1, 2016

Published by the Office of the Federal Register
National Archives and Records Administration
as a Special Edition of the Federal Register

U.S. GOVERNMENT OFFICIAL EDITION NOTICE

Legal Status and Use of Seals and Logos

The seal of the National Archives and Records Administration (NARA) authenticates the Code of Federal Regulations (CFR) as the official codification of Federal regulations established under the Federal Register Act. Under the provisions of 44 U.S.C. 1507, the contents of the CFR, a special edition of the Federal Register, shall be judicially noticed. The CFR is prima facie evidence of the original documents published in the Federal Register (44 U.S.C. 1510).

It is prohibited to use NARA's official seal and the stylized Code of Federal Regulations logo on any republication of this material without the express, written permission of the Archivist of the United States or the Archivist's designee. Any person using NARA's official seals and logos in a manner inconsistent with the provisions of 36 CFR part 1200 is subject to the penalties specified in 18 U.S.C. 506, 701, and 1017.

Use of ISBN Prefix

This is the Official U.S. Government edition of this publication and is herein identified to certify its authenticity. Use of the 0–16 ISBN prefix is for U.S. Government Publishing Office Official Editions only. The Superintendent of Documents of the U.S. Government Publishing Office requests that any reprinted edition clearly be labeled as a copy of the authentic work with a new ISBN.

GPO U.S. GOVERNMENT PUBLISHING OFFICE

U.S. Superintendent of Documents • Washington, DC 20402–0001

http://bookstore.gpo.gov

Phone: toll-free (866) 512-1800; DC area (202) 512-1800

Table of Contents

Cite this Code: CFR

To cite the regulations in this volume use title, part and section number. Thus, 27 CFR 40.1 *refers to title 27, part 40, section 1.*

Explanation

The Code of Federal Regulations is a codification of the general and permanent rules published in the Federal Register by the Executive departments and agencies of the Federal Government. The Code is divided into 50 titles which represent broad areas subject to Federal regulation. Each title is divided into chapters which usually bear the name of the issuing agency. Each chapter is further subdivided into parts covering specific regulatory areas.

Each volume of the Code is revised at least once each calendar year and issued on a quarterly basis approximately as follows:

Title 1 through Title 16	as of January 1
Title 17 through Title 27	as of April 1
Title 28 through Title 41	as of July 1
Title 42 through Title 50	as of October 1

The appropriate revision date is printed on the cover of each volume.

LEGAL STATUS

The contents of the Federal Register are required to be judicially noticed (44 U.S.C. 1507). The Code of Federal Regulations is prima facie evidence of the text of the original documents (44 U.S.C. 1510).

HOW TO USE THE CODE OF FEDERAL REGULATIONS

The Code of Federal Regulations is kept up to date by the individual issues of the Federal Register. These two publications must be used together to determine the latest version of any given rule.

To determine whether a Code volume has been amended since its revision date (in this case, April 1, 2016), consult the "List of CFR Sections Affected (LSA)," which is issued monthly, and the "Cumulative List of Parts Affected," which appears in the Reader Aids section of the daily Federal Register. These two lists will identify the Federal Register page number of the latest amendment of any given rule.

EFFECTIVE AND EXPIRATION DATES

Each volume of the Code contains amendments published in the Federal Register since the last revision of that volume of the Code. Source citations for the regulations are referred to by volume number and page number of the Federal Register and date of publication. Publication dates and effective dates are usually not the same and care must be exercised by the user in determining the actual effective date. In instances where the effective date is beyond the cut-off date for the Code a note has been inserted to reflect the future effective date. In those instances where a regulation published in the Federal Register states a date certain for expiration, an appropriate note will be inserted following the text.

OMB CONTROL NUMBERS

The Paperwork Reduction Act of 1980 (Pub. L. 96–511) requires Federal agencies to display an OMB control number with their information collection request.

Many agencies have begun publishing numerous OMB control numbers as amendments to existing regulations in the CFR. These OMB numbers are placed as close as possible to the applicable recordkeeping or reporting requirements.

PAST PROVISIONS OF THE CODE

Provisions of the Code that are no longer in force and effect as of the revision date stated on the cover of each volume are not carried. Code users may find the text of provisions in effect on any given date in the past by using the appropriate List of CFR Sections Affected (LSA). For the convenience of the reader, a "List of CFR Sections Affected" is published at the end of each CFR volume. For changes to the Code prior to the LSA listings at the end of the volume, consult previous annual editions of the LSA. For changes to the Code prior to 2001, consult the List of CFR Sections Affected compilations, published for 1949-1963, 1964-1972, 1973-1985, and 1986-2000.

"[RESERVED]" TERMINOLOGY

The term "[Reserved]" is used as a place holder within the Code of Federal Regulations. An agency may add regulatory information at a "[Reserved]" location at any time. Occasionally "[Reserved]" is used editorially to indicate that a portion of the CFR was left vacant and not accidentally dropped due to a printing or computer error.

INCORPORATION BY REFERENCE

What is incorporation by reference? Incorporation by reference was established by statute and allows Federal agencies to meet the requirement to publish regulations in the Federal Register by referring to materials already published elsewhere. For an incorporation to be valid, the Director of the Federal Register must approve it. The legal effect of incorporation by reference is that the material is treated as if it were published in full in the Federal Register (5 U.S.C. 552(a)). This material, like any other properly issued regulation, has the force of law.

What is a proper incorporation by reference? The Director of the Federal Register will approve an incorporation by reference only when the requirements of 1 CFR part 51 are met. Some of the elements on which approval is based are:

(a) The incorporation will substantially reduce the volume of material published in the Federal Register.

(b) The matter incorporated is in fact available to the extent necessary to afford fairness and uniformity in the administrative process.

(c) The incorporating document is drafted and submitted for publication in accordance with 1 CFR part 51.

What if the material incorporated by reference cannot be found? If you have any problem locating or obtaining a copy of material listed as an approved incorporation by reference, please contact the agency that issued the regulation containing that incorporation. If, after contacting the agency, you find the material is not available, please notify the Director of the Federal Register, National Archives and Records Administration, 8601 Adelphi Road, College Park, MD 20740-6001, or call 202-741-6010.

CFR INDEXES AND TABULAR GUIDES

A subject index to the Code of Federal Regulations is contained in a separate volume, revised annually as of January 1, entitled CFR INDEX AND FINDING AIDS. This volume contains the Parallel Table of Authorities and Rules. A list of CFR titles, chapters, subchapters, and parts and an alphabetical list of agencies publishing in the CFR are also included in this volume.

An index to the text of "Title 3—The President" is carried within that volume.

The Federal Register Index is issued monthly in cumulative form. This index is based on a consolidation of the "Contents" entries in the daily Federal Register.

A List of CFR Sections Affected (LSA) is published monthly, keyed to the revision dates of the 50 CFR titles.

REPUBLICATION OF MATERIAL

There are no restrictions on the republication of material appearing in the Code of Federal Regulations.

INQUIRIES

For a legal interpretation or explanation of any regulation in this volume, contact the issuing agency. The issuing agency's name appears at the top of odd-numbered pages.

For inquiries concerning CFR reference assistance, call 202–741–6000 or write to the Director, Office of the Federal Register, National Archives and Records Administration, 8601 Adelphi Road, College Park, MD 20740-6001 or e-mail *fedreg.info@nara.gov.*

SALES

The Government Publishing Office (GPO) processes all sales and distribution of the CFR. For payment by credit card, call toll-free, 866-512-1800, or DC area, 202-512-1800, M-F 8 a.m. to 4 p.m. e.s.t. or fax your order to 202-512-2104, 24 hours a day. For payment by check, write to: US Government Publishing Office – New Orders, P.O. Box 979050, St. Louis, MO 63197-9000.

ELECTRONIC SERVICES

The full text of the Code of Federal Regulations, the LSA (List of CFR Sections Affected), The United States Government Manual, the Federal Register, Public Laws, Public Papers of the Presidents of the United States, Compilation of Presidential Documents and the Privacy Act Compilation are available in electronic format via *www.ofr.gov.* For more information, contact the GPO Customer Contact Center, U.S. Government Publishing Office. Phone 202-512-1800, or 866-512-1800 (toll-free). E-mail, *ContactCenter@gpo.gov.*

The Office of the Federal Register also offers a free service on the National Archives and Records Administration's (NARA) World Wide Web site for public law numbers, Federal Register finding aids, and related information. Connect to NARA's web site at *www.archives.gov/federal-register.*

The e-CFR is a regularly updated, unofficial editorial compilation of CFR material and Federal Register amendments, produced by the Office of the Federal Register and the Government Publishing Office. It is available at *www.ecfr.gov.*

OLIVER A. POTTS,
Director,
Office of the Federal Register.
April 1, 2016.

THIS TITLE

Title 27—ALCOHOL, TOBACCO PRODUCTS AND FIREARMS is composed of three volumes: Parts 1–39, parts 40–399, and part 400 to end. The contents of these volumes represent all current regulations issued by the Alcohol and Tobacco Tax and Trade Bureau, Department of the Treasury, and the Bureau of Alcohol, Tobacco, Firearms, and Explosives, Department of Justice, as of April 1, 2016.

For this volume, Bonnie Fritts was Chief Editor. The Code of Federal Regulations publication program is under the direction of John Hyrum Martinez, assisted by Stephen J. Frattini.

Title 27—Alcohol, Tobacco Products and Firearms

(This book contains parts 40 to 399)

ABBREVIATIONS USED IN THIS CHAPTER:

ATF = *Alcohol, Tobacco and Firearms*. T.D. = *Treasury Decision*. TTB = *Alcohol and Tobacco Tax and Trade Bureau*.

CHAPTER I—ALCOHOL AND TOBACCO TAX AND TRADE BUREAU, DEPARTMENT OF THE TREASURY (CONTINUED)

EDITORIAL NOTE: Nomenclature changes to chapter I appear by T.D. TTB–44, 71 FR 16920, Apr. 4, 2006.

SUBCHAPTER B—TOBACCO

SUBCHAPTER C—FIREARMS

SUBCHAPTERS D–E [RESERVED]

SUBCHAPTER F—PROCEDURES AND PRACTICES

SUBCHAPTER B—TOBACCO

PART 40—MANUFACTURE OF TOBACCO PRODUCTS, CIGARETTE PAPERS AND TUBES, AND PROCESSED TOBACCO

AUTHORITY: 26 U.S.C. 448, 5701, 5703–5705, 5711–5713, 5721–5723, 5731–5734, 5741, 5751, 5753, 5761–5763, 6061, 6065, 6109, 6151, 6301, 6302, 6311, 6313, 6402, 6404, 6423, 6676, 6806, 7011, 7212, 7325, 7342, 7502, 7503, 7606, 7805; 31 U.S.C. 9301, 9303, 9304, 9306.

SOURCE: 26 FR 8174, Aug. 31, 1961, unless otherwise noted. Redesignated at 40 FR 16835,

Apr. 15, 1975; 54 FR 48839, Nov. 27, 1989, and further redesignated by T.D. ATF–460, 66 FR 39093, July 27, 2001.

EDITORIAL NOTE: Nomenclature changes to part 40 appear by T.D. ATF–460, 66 FR 39094–39096, July 27, 2001; T.D. ATF–464, 66 FR 43479, Aug. 20, 2001; and T.D. TTB–91, 76 FR 5479, Feb. 1, 2011.

Subpart A—Scope of Regulations

§40.1 Manufacture of tobacco products, cigarette papers and tubes, and processed tobacco.

This part contains regulations relating to the manufacture of tobacco products, cigarette papers and tubes, and processed tobacco; the payment by manufacturers of tobacco products and cigarette papers and tubes of internal revenue taxes imposed by 26 U.S.C. chapter 52; and the qualification of and operations by manufacturers of tobacco products, cigarette papers and tubes, and processed tobacco.

[T.D. TTB–78, at 74 FR 29408, June 22, 2009]

§40.2 Territorial extent.

The provisions of the regulations in this part shall apply in the several States of the United States and the District of Columbia.

Subpart B—Definitions

§40.11 Meaning of terms.

When used in this part and in forms prescribed under this part, the following terms shall have the meanings given in this section, unless the context clearly indicates otherwise. Words in the plural form shall include the singular, and vice versa, and words indicating the masculine gender shall include the feminine. The terms "includes" and "including" do not exclude things not listed which are in the same general class.

Administrator. The Administrator, Alcohol and Tobacco Tax and Trade Bureau, Department of the Treasury, Washington, DC.

Appropriate TTB officer. An officer or employee of the Alcohol and Tobacco Tax and Trade Bureau (TTB) authorized to perform any functions relating to the administration or enforcement of this part by TTB Order 1135.40, Delegation of the Administrator's Authorities in 27 CFR Part 40, Manufacture of Tobacco Products and Cigarette Papers and Tubes.

Bank. Any commercial bank.

Banking day. Any day during which a bank is open to the public for carrying on substantially all its banking functions.

CFR. The Code of Federal Regulations.

Chewing tobacco. Any leaf tobacco that is not intended to be smoked.

Cigar. Any roll of tobacco wrapped in leaf tobacco or in any substance containing tobacco (other than any roll of tobacco which is a cigarette within the meaning of paragraph (2) of the definition for cigarette).

Cigarette. (1) Any roll of tobacco wrapped in paper or in any substance not containing tobacco, and

(2) Any roll of tobacco wrapped in any substance containing tobacco which, because of its appearance, the type of tobacco used in the filler, or its packaging and labeling, is likely to be offered to, or purchased by, consumers as a cigarette described in paragraph (1) of this definition.

Cigarette paper. Paper, or any other material except tobacco, prepared for use as a cigarette wrapper.

Cigarette tube. Cigarette paper made into a hollow cylinder for use in making cigarettes.

Commercial bank. A bank, whether or not a member of the Federal Reserve System, which has access to the Federal Reserve Communications System (FRCS) or Fedwire. The "FRCS" or "Fedwire" is a communications network that allows Federal Reserve System member banks to effect a transfer of funds for their customers (or other commercial banks) to the Treasury Account at the Federal Reserve Bank in New York.

Determine. To establish enough information about taxable products at the time of removal to calculate the tax, specifically the quantity (pounds or number) and kind (for example, cigarettes, snuff, paper tubes). Where the tax rate depends on additional information (such as number of cigarette papers to a set before January 1, 2000 or sale price of large cigars), that information must also be established as part of tax determination.

Director of the service center. The Director, Internal Revenue Service Center, in any of the Internal Revenue regions.

District director. A district director of internal revenue.

Electronic fund transfer or EFT. Any transfer of funds effected by a manufacturer's commercial bank, either directly or through a correspondent banking relationship, via the Federal Reserve Communications System (FRCS) or Fedwire to the Treasury Account at the Federal Reserve Bank of New York.

Export warehouse. A bonded internal revenue warehouse for the storage of tobacco products or cigarette papers or tubes or any processed tobacco, upon which the internal revenue tax has not been paid for subsequent shipment to a foreign country, Puerto Rico, the Virgin Islands, or a possession of the United States, or for consumption beyond the jurisdiction of the internal revenue laws of the United States.

Export warehouse proprietor. Any person who operates an export warehouse.

Factory. The premises of a manufacturer of tobacco products or processed tobacco as described in his permit issued under 26 U.S.C. chapter 52, or the premises of a manufacturer of cigarette papers and tubes on which such business is conducted.

Fiscal year. The period which begins October 1 and ends on the following September 30.

In bond. The status of tobacco products and cigarette papers and tubes, which come within the coverage of a bond securing the payment of internal revenue taxes imposed by 26 U.S.C. 5701 or 7652, and in respect to which such taxes have not been determined as provided by regulations in this chapter, including (a) such articles in a factory, (b) such articles removed, transferred, or released, pursuant to 26 U.S.C. 5704, and with respect to which relief from the tax liability has not occurred, and (c) such articles on which the tax has been determined, or with respect to which relief from the tax liability has occurred, which have been returned to the coverage of a bond.

Large cigarettes. Cigarettes weighing more than three pounds per thousand.

Large cigars. Cigars weighing more than three pounds per thousand.

Manufacturer of cigarette papers and tubes. Any person who manufactures cigarette paper, or makes up cigarette paper into tubes, except for his own personal use or consumption.

Manufacturer of processed tobacco. Any person who processes any tobacco other than tobacco products.

Manufacturer of tobacco products. (1) Any person who manufactures cigars, cigarettes, smokeless tobacco, pipe tobacco, or roll-your-own tobacco, other than:

(i) A person who produces tobacco products solely for that person's own consumption or use; or

(ii) A proprietor of a customs bonded manufacturing warehouse with respect to the operation of such warehouse.

(2) The term "Manufacturer of tobacco products" includes any person who for commercial purposes makes available for consumer use (including such consumer's personal consumption or use under paragraph (1)(i) of this definition) a machine capable of making cigarettes, cigars, or other tobacco products. A person making such a machine available for consumer use shall be deemed the person making the removal with respect to any tobacco products manufactured by such machine. A person who sells a machine directly to a consumer at retail for a consumer's personal home use is not making a machine available for commercial purposes if such machine is not used at a retail premises and is designed to produce tobacco products only in personal use quantities.

Package. The immediate container in which tobacco products, processed tobacco, or cigarette papers or tubes are put up by the manufacturer and offered for sale or delivery to the ultimate consumer. For purposes of this definition, a container of processed tobacco, the contents of which weigh 10 pounds or less (including any added non-tobacco ingredients or constituents), that is removed within the meaning of this part, for any purpose other than destruction, export, delivery as a sample to a manufacturer of processed tobacco or tobacco products for the purpose of soliciting orders of processed tobacco, or scientific testing or testing of equipment which results in the destruction of the processed tobacco or the return of the processed tobacco to the factory premises, is deemed to be a package offered for sale or delivery to the ultimate consumer. For appropriate tax rate, see § 40.25a.

Packaging. When used in the context of an action, the act of placing processed tobacco or a tobacco product in a package.

Permit number. The identifying number and/or letters that are assigned to a TTB permit by the appropriate TTB officer.

Person. An individual, partnership, association, company, corporation, estate, or trust.

Pipe tobacco. Any tobacco which, because of its appearance, type, packaging, or labeling, is suitable for use and likely to be offered to, or purchased by, consumers as tobacco to be smoked in a pipe.

Processed tobacco. Processed tobacco is any tobacco that has undergone processing, but does not include tobacco products. For purposes of this definition, the processing of tobacco does not include the farming or growing of tobacco or the handling of tobacco solely for sale, shipment, or delivery to a manufacturer of tobacco products or processed tobacco, nor does the processing of tobacco include curing, baling, or packaging activities. For purposes of this definition, the processing of tobacco includes, but is not limited to, stemming (that is, removing the stem from the tobacco leaf), fermenting, threshing, cutting, or flavoring the tobacco, or otherwise combining the tobacco with non-tobacco ingredients.

Removal or remove. The removal of tobacco products or cigarette papers or tubes, or any processed tobacco from the factory or release from customs custody, including the smuggling of other unlawful importation of such articles into the United States.

Roll-your-own tobacco. Any tobacco which, because of its appearance, type, packaging, or labeling, is suitable for use and likely to be offered to, or purchased by, consumers as tobacco for making cigarettes or cigars, or for use as wrappers of cigars or cigarettes.

Sale price. The price for which large cigars are sold by the U.S. manufacturer, determined in accordance with § 40.22 and used for computation of the tax.

Service center. An Internal Revenue Service Center in any of the Internal Revenue regions.

Service center director. A director of an internal revenue service center.

Sets. Any collection, grouping, or packaging of cigarette papers made up by any person for delivery to the consumer as a unit.

Small cigarettes. Cigarettes weighing not more than three pounds per thousand.

Small cigars. Cigars weighing not more than three pounds per thousand.

Smokeless tobacco. Any snuff or chewing tobacco.

Snuff. Any finely cut, ground, or powdered tobacco that is not intended to be smoked.

Special tax. The special (occupational) tax on manufacturers of tobacco products, manufacturers of cigarette papers and tubes, and export warehouse proprietors, imposed by 26 U.S.C. 5731.

This chapter. Title 27, Code of Federal Regulations, chapter I (27 CFR chapter I).

Tobacco products. Cigars, cigarettes, smokeless tobacco, pipe tobacco, and roll-your-own tobacco.

Treasury Account. The Department of the Treasury's General Account at the Federal Reserve Bank of New York.

TTB. The Alcohol and Tobacco Tax and Trade Bureau, Department of the Treasury

U.S.C. The United States Code.

(26 U.S.C. 7805 (68A Stat. 917), 27 U.S.C. 205 (49 Stat. 981 as amended), (82 Stat. 959), and Sec. 38, Arms Export Control Act (90 Stat. 744) Aug. 16, 1954, ch. 736, 68A Stat. 775, as amended (26 U.S.C. 6301); June 29, 1956, ch. 462, 70 Stat. 391 (26 U.S.C. 6301))

[T.D. ATF–48, 43 FR 13553, Mar. 31, 1978]

EDITORIAL NOTE: For FEDERAL REGISTER citations affecting § 40.11, see the List of CFR Sections Affected, which appears in the Finding Aids section of the printed volume and at *www.fdsys.gov.*

EFFECTIVE DATE NOTE: At 78 FR 38567, June 27, 2013, § 40.11 was amended by revising the definition of "Manufacturer of tobacco products", effective Aug. 26, 2013 through Aug. 26, 2016.

Subpart C—Taxes

§ 40.21 Cigar tax rates.

(a) Cigars are taxed at the following rates under 26 U.S.C. 5701(a):

Type and amount	Tax rate for removals during the following periods:	
	2002 to March 31, 2009	April 1, 2009 and after
Small cigars per thousand	$1.828	$50.33
Large cigars*		
• percentage of sale price.	20.719%	52.750%
• but not to exceed—	$48.75 per thousand.	$0.4026 per cigar.

*For large cigars: Until March 31, 2009, the percentage tax rate applies when the sale price is $235.294 per thousand or less, and the flat tax rate applies when the sale price is more than $235.294 per thousand. On and after April 1, 2009, the percentage tax rate applies when the sale price is $763.222 or less per thousand cigars, and the flat tax rate applies when the sale price is more than $763.222 per thousand cigars.

(b) See § 40.22 of this part for rules concerning determination of sale price of large cigars.

(c) Cigars not exempt from tax under 26 U.S.C. chapter 52 and the provisions of this part which are removed but not intended for sale shall be taxed at the same rate as similar cigars removed for sale.

[T.D. ATF-420, 64 FR 71939, Dec. 22, 1999, as amended by T.D. TTB-75, 74 FR 14481, Mar. 31, 2009]

§ 40.22 Determination of sale price of large cigars.

(a) *General rule.* The tax imposed on large cigars is computed based on the sale price (the price for which the large cigars are sold by the manufacturer). In addition to money, goods or services exchanged for cigars may be considered as part of the sale price.

(b) *Special cases*—(1) *In general.* If there is any question concerning the applicable sale price for tax purposes, the appropriate TTB officer will determine such price, applying rules similar to the constructive sale price rules in 26 U.S.C. 4216(b) and the implementing regulations in 26 CFR 48.4216(b)-1 through 48.4216(b)-4. These constructive sale price rules apply to cigars sold by a manufacturer at retail, sold on consignment, or sold (otherwise than through an arm's length transaction) at less than the fair market price. Sales of cigars between affiliated corporations may be analyzed under the constructive sale price rules. The appropriate TTB officer may make this analysis on his or her own initiative or upon the written request of a manufacturer. If TTB decides it is necessary, we will publish constructive sale price determinations in the TTB Bulletin in accordance with § 70.701(d) of this chapter.

(2) *Adjustments in sale price*—(i) *Reasons for adjustment.* Adjustments to the sale price may occur as a result of a discount or price increase by the manufacturer or as a result of a TTB determination pursuant to paragraph (b)(1) above. In either case, the manufacturer must make conforming changes to the tax that was computed on the sale price before the adjustment.

(ii) *Time of adjustment.* If an adjustment is made before the end of the same tax return period as the original determination of the tax, the adjustment may be made on the same return. If the price is increased or decreased retroactively (during a later return period), either by the manufacturer or by TTB's determination, the manufacturer must make an adjustment on the tax return for the current return period in which the price change was determined.

(iii) *Amount of adjustment.* The taxpayer must compute the adjustment to the tax as the difference between the tax that was paid and the tax that should have been paid, based on the newly determined sale price, together with interest thereon and any applicable penalties. The interest must be computed from the time of payment of the original tax until the time the adjustment was made. Upon request, the appropriate TTB officer will provide information regarding interest rates applicable to specific time periods and any applicable penalties.

(3) *Pricing for different packaging.* If different bona fide sale prices are applicable to different types of packaging (*e. g.*, boxes of 25 and boxes of 50), then the cigars in each type of packaging are taxed on the basis of their respective sale prices.

(4) *Pricing of seconds.* If some of an otherwise identical cigar brand and size:

(i) Are distinctive from other such cigars because of physical imperfections,

(ii) Are offered to the consumer through clear labeling as ''imperfects'', ''seconds'', ''throw-outs'', or a comparable commonly understood term, and

(iii) The manufacturer has a separate sale price for such cigars, then they are taxed on the basis of this separate sale price.

(5) *Combination packages.* If a manufacturer has a sale price for a combination package containing cigars of different sizes, the cigars are taxed based on that combination sale price. If there is no sale price for the combination, then the cigars are taxed based on their individual sale prices.

(6) *Removals for another person.* If a manufacturer makes taxable removals of a brand and size of cigar only for distribution by others who establish the sale price, the tax is based on such sale price even though the manufacturer who makes the removals does not establish the price.

[T.D. ATF–420, 64 FR 71939, Dec. 22, 1999, as amended by T.D. TTB–91, 76 FR 5479, Feb. 1, 2011]

§ 40.23 Cigarette tax rates.

Cigarettes are taxed at the following rates under 26 U.S.C. 5701(b):

Product	Tax rate per thousand for removals during the following periods:	
	2002 to March 31, 2009	April 1, 2009 and after
Small cigarettes	$19.50	$50.33
Large cigarettes up to 6½″ long.	$40.95	$105.69
Large cigarettes over 6½″ long.	Taxed at the rate for small cigarettes, counting each 2¾″ or fraction thereof of the length of each as one cigarette.	

[T.D. TTB–75, 74 FR 14482, Mar. 31, 2009]

§ 40.24 Classification of cigarettes.

For tax purposes, small cigarettes are designated Class A and large cigarettes are designated Class B.

(72 Stat. 1414; 26 U.S.C. 5701)

§ 40.25 Smokeless tobacco tax rates.

Smokeless tobacco products are taxed at the following rates under 26 U.S.C. 5701(e):

Product	Tax rate per pound* for removals during the following periods:	
	2002 to March 31, 2009	April 1, 2009 and after
Snuff	$ 0.585	$ 1.51
Chewing tobacco	$ 0.195	$ 0.5033

* Prorate tax for fractions of a pound.

[T.D. TTB–75, 74 FR 14482, Mar. 31, 2009]

§ 40.25a Pipe tobacco and roll-your-own tobacco tax rates and classification.

(a) *Tax rates.* Pipe tobacco and roll-your-own tobacco are taxed at the following rates under 26 U.S.C. 5701(f) and (g), respectively:

Product	Tax rate per pound* for removals during the following periods:	
	2002 to March 31, 2009	April 1, 2009 and after
Pipe tobacco	$ 1.0969	$ 2.8311
Roll-your-own tobacco	$ 1.0969	$ 24.78

* Prorate tax for fractions of a pound.

(b) *Classification.* (1) Pipe tobacco and roll-your-own tobacco, before removal subject to tax, must be put up in packages that conform to the requirements of §§ 40.211 and 40.212, and of § 40.216a or § 40.216b as appropriate.

(2) Any tobacco that has been processed and that is removed in a package, as that term is defined in § 40.11, that does not bear the notice for smokeless tobacco prescribed in § 40.216 or the notice for pipe tobacco prescribed in § 40.216a is deemed to be roll-your-own tobacco and subject to tax at the rate applicable to roll-your-own tobacco. A container of processed tobacco, the contents of which weigh 10 pounds or less (including any added non-tobacco ingredients or constituents), that is removed within the meaning of this part for any purpose other than destruction, export, delivery as a sample to a manufacturer of processed tobacco or tobacco products for the purpose of soliciting orders of processed tobacco, or scientific testing or testing of equipment which results in the destruction of the processed tobacco or the return of the processed tobacco to the factory

premises, is deemed to be a package offered for sale or delivery to the ultimate consumer.

(3) Subject to paragraph (b)(4) of this section, any tobacco that has been processed and that is removed in a package, as that term is defined in §40.11, is deemed to be roll-your-own tobacco and subject to tax at the rate applicable to roll-your-own tobacco, even though the package bears the notice required for pipe tobacco under §40.216a, if:

(i) The package does not bear the declaration "pipe tobacco" in direct conjunction with, parallel to, and in substantially the same conspicuousness of type and background as the brand name each time the brand name appears on the package; or

(ii) The package or accompanying materials bear any representation that would suggest a use other than as pipe tobacco. (26 U.S.C. 5702 and 5723) The term 'accompanying materials' includes, but is not limited to, any point of sale advertising or other printed product communications issued by the manufacturer or importer of pipe tobacco products. In addition, the inclusion of cigarette papers or tubes in a package bearing a 'pipe tobacco' declaration will suggest a use other than pipe tobacco.

(4) During the period from June 22, 2009, through March 23, 2010, manufacturers may continue to remove products as pipe tobacco in packages that do not bear the declaration "pipe tobacco" in the manner prescribed in paragraph (b)(3)(i) of this section.

[T.D. TTB–75, 74 FR 14482, Mar. 31, 2009, as amended by T.D. TTB–78, 74 FR 29408, June 22, 2009; T.D. TTB–81, 74 FR 48653, Sept. 24, 2009; T.D. TTB–104, 77 FR 37302, June 21, 2012]

§40.26 Persons liable for tax.

The manufacturer of tobacco products shall be liable for the taxes imposed on tobacco products by 26 U.S.C. 5701: *Provided*, That when tobacco products are transferred in bond pursuant to 26 U.S.C. 5704, to the bonded premises of another such manufacturer or an export warehouse proprietor, the transferee shall become liable for the tax upon receipt by him of such products and the transferor shall thereupon be relieved of his liability for the tax. When tobacco products are released in bond from customs custody for transfer to the bonded premises of a manufacturer of tobacco products, the transferee shall become liable for the tax on such products upon release from customs custody. Any person who possesses tobacco products in violation of 26 U.S.C. 5751(a)(1) or (2), shall be liable for a tax equal to the tax on such products.

(Sec. 201, Pub. L. 85–859, 72 Stat 1415, as amended, 1424, as amended (26 U.S.C. 5703, 5751))

[T.D. 6871, 31 FR 32, Jan. 4, 1966. Redesignated at 40 FR 16835, Apr. 15, 1975, and amended by T.D. ATF–48, 44 FR 55854, Sept. 28, 1979; T.D. ATF–232, 51 FR 28080, Aug. 5, 1986; T.D. ATF–243, 52 FR 43194, Dec. 1, 1986]

§40.27 Assessment.

Whenever any person required by law to pay tax on tobacco products fails to pay such tax, the tax shall be ascertained and assessed against such person, subject to the limitations prescribed in 26 U.S.C. 6501. The tax so assessed shall be in addition to the penalties imposed by law for failure to pay such tax when required. Except in cases where delay may jeopardize collection of the tax, or where the amount is nominal or the result of an evident mathematical error, no such assessment shall be made until and after notice has been afforded such person to show cause against assessment. The person will be allowed 45 days from the date of such notice to show cause, in writing, against such assessment.

(Sec. 201, Pub. L. 85–859, 72 Stat. 1415, as amended (26 U.S.C. 5703))

[T.D. 6871, 31 FR 32, Jan. 4, 1966. Redesignated at 40 FR 16835, Apr. 15, 1975, and amended by T.D. ATF–48, 44 FR 55854, Sept. 28, 1979; T.D. ATF–232, 51 FR 28080, Aug. 5, 1986; T.D. ATF–243, 52 FR 43194, Dec. 1, 1986]

Subpart Ca—Special (Occupational) Taxes

SOURCE: T.D. ATF–271, 53 FR 17560, May 17, 1988, unless otherwise noted.

§40.31 Liability for special tax.

(a) *Manufacturer of tobacco products*. Every manufacturer of tobacco products shall pay a special (occupational) tax at a rate specified by § 40.32 of the part. The tax shall be paid on or before the date of commencing the business of manufacturing tobacco products, and thereafter every year on or before July 1. On commencing business, the tax shall be computed from the first day of the month in which liability is incurred, through the following June 30. Thereafter, the tax shall be computed for the entire year (July 1 through June 30).

(b) [Reserved]

(c) *Each place of business taxable.* A manufacturer of tobacco products incurs special tax liability at each place of business in which an occupation subject to special tax is conducted. A place of business means the entire office, plant or area of the business in any one location under the same proprietorship. Passageways, streets, highways, rail crossings, waterways, or partitions dividing the premises are not sufficient separation to require additional special tax, if the divisions of the premises are otherwise contiguous.

(d) *Payment of tax.* Special tax must be paid by return. The prescribed return is TTB Form 5630.5t, Special Tax Registration and Return—Tobacco. Special tax returns, with payment of tax, must be filed with TTB in accordance with the instructions on the form and the requirements of subpart D of part 46 of this chapter.

(26 U.S.C. 5731, 5733)

[T.D. ATF–271, 53 FR 17560, May 17, 1988, as amended by T.D. TTB–79, 74 FR 37419, July 28, 2009]

§ 40.32 Rates of special tax.

(a) *General.* Title 26 U.S.C. 5731(a)(1) imposes a special tax of $1,000 per year on every manufacturer of tobacco products.

(b) *Reduced rate for small proprietors.* Title 26 U.S.C. 5731(b) provides for a reduced rate of $500 per year with respect to any manufacturer of tobacco products whose gross receipts (for the most recent taxable year ending before the first day of the taxable period to which the special tax imposed by § 40.31 relates) are less than $500,000. The "taxable year" to be used for determining gross receipts is the taxpayer's income tax year. All gross receipts of the taxpayer shall be included, not just the gross receipts of the business subject to special tax. Proprietors of new businesses that have not yet begun a taxable year, as well as proprietors of existing businesses that have not yet ended a taxable year, who commence a new activity subject to special tax, qualify for the reduced special (occupational) tax rate, unless the business is a member of a "controlled group"; in that case, the rules of paragraph (c) of this section shall apply.

(c) *Controlled group.* All persons treated as one taxpayer under 26 U.S.C. 5061(e)(3) shall be treated as one taxpayer for the purpose of determining gross receipts under paragraph (b) of this section. "Controlled group" means a controlled group of corporations, as defined in 26 U.S.C. 1563 and implementing regulations in 26 CFR 1.1563–1 through 1.1563–4, except that the words "at least 80 percent" shall be replaced by the words "more than 50 percent" in each place they appear in subsection (a) of 26 U.S.C. 1563, as well as in the implementing regulations. Also, the rules for a "controlled group of corporations" apply in a similar fashion to groups which include partnerships and/or sole proprietorships. If one entity maintains more than 50% control over a group consisting of corporations and one, or more, partnerships and/or sole proprietorships, all of the members of the controlled group are one taxpayer for the purpose of this section.

(d) *Short taxable year.* Gross receipts for any taxable year of less than 12 months shall be annualized by multiplying the gross receipts for the short period by 12 and dividing the result by the number of months in the short period as required by 26 U.S.C. 448(c)(3).

(e) *Returns and allowances.* Gross receipts for any taxable year shall be reduced by returns and allowances made during such year under 26 U.S.C. 448(c)(3).

(26 U.S.C. 448, 5061, 5731)

§ 40.33 Cross reference.

For additional rules pertaining to liability for special tax, filing special tax returns, issuance and examination of special (occupational) tax stamps, and notification of changes to special tax stamps, see subpart D of part 46 of this chapter.

[T.D. TTB–79, 74 FR 37419, July 28, 2009]

§§ 40.34–40.36 [Reserved]

Subpart D—Administrative Provisions

§ 40.41 Forms prescribed.

(a) The appropriate TTB officer is authorized to prescribe all forms required by this part. All of the information called for in each form shall be furnished as indicated by the headings on the form and the instructions on or pertaining to the form. In addition, information called for in each form shall be furnished as required by this part. When a return, form, claim, or other document called for under this part is required by this part, or by the document itself, to be executed under penalties of perjury, it shall be executed under penalties of perjury.

(b) Forms prescribed by this part are available for printing through the TTB Web site (*http://www.ttb.gov*) or by mailing a request to the Alcohol and Tobacco Tax and Trade Bureau, National Revenue Center, 550 Main Street, Room 1516, Cincinnati, OH 45202.

(5 U.S.C. 552(a) (80 Stat. 383, as amended))

[T.D. ATF–92, 46 FR 46921, Sept. 23, 1981, as amended by T.D. ATF–232, 51 FR 28080, Aug. 5, 1986; T.D. ATF–243, 52 FR 43194, Dec. 1, 1986; T.D. ATF–372, 61 FR 20725, May 8, 1996; T.D. TTB–44, 71 FR 16949, Apr. 4, 2006]

§ 40.42 Authority of Appropriate TTB officers to enter premises.

Any appropriate TTB officer may enter in the daytime any premises where tobacco products are produced or kept, so far as it may be necessary for the purpose of examining such products. When such premises are open at night, any appropriate TTB officer may enter them, while so open, in the performance of his official duties. The owner of such premises, or person having the superintendence of the same, who refuses to admit any appropriate TTB officer or permit him to examine such products shall be liable to the penalties prescribed by law for the offense.

(68A Stat. 872, 903; 26 U.S.C. 7342, 7606)

[T.D. 6871, 31 FR 33, Jan. 4, 1966. Redesignated at 40 FR 16835, Apr. 15, 1975; T.D. ATF–232, 51 FR 28080, Aug. 5, 1986; T.D. ATF–243, 52 FR 43194, Dec. 1, 1986; T.D. TTB–91, 76 FR 5479, Feb. 1, 2011]

§ 40.43 Interference with administration.

Whoever, corruptly or by force or threats of force, endeavors to hinder or obstruct the administration of this part, or endeavors to intimidate or impede any TTB officer acting in his official capacity, or forcibly rescues or attempts to rescue or causes to be rescued any property, after it has been duly seized for forfeiture to the United States in connection with a violation of the internal revenue laws, shall be liable to the penalties prescribed by law.

(68A Stat. 855; 26 U.S.C. 7212)

§ 40.44 Disposal of forfeited, condemned, and abandoned tobacco products.

A Federal, State, or local officer shall not sell or cause to be sold for consumption in the United States any forfeited, condemned, or abandoned tobacco products in his custody upon which the Federal tax has not been paid, if in his opinion the sale thereof will not bring a price equal to the tax due and payable thereon and the expenses incident to the sale thereof. Where the products are not sold the officer may deliver them to a Federal or State hospital or institution (if they are fit for consumption) or cause their destruction by burning completely or by rendering them unfit for consumption. Where such products are sold they shall be released by the officer having custody thereof only after they are properly packaged and taxpaid. A receipt from the appropriate TTB officer evidencing payment of tax on such products shall be presented to the officer having custody of the products, which tax shall be considered part of the sales price. Where tobacco products which have been packaged under the provisions of part 44 or part 45 of this chapter are to be released after payment of tax, the purchaser shall appropriately mark each package "Federal Tax Paid (date)" before the officer having custody of the products releases them:

Provided, That if the purchaser is a qualified manufacturer of tobacco products, or for products packaged under part 44 a qualified export warehouse proprietor, the products may be released without such marking of the packages if the manufacturer or proprietor does not intend to place such products on the domestic market for taxable products but will dispose of them otherwise, such as by destruction or return to bond through claim for refund, and files a written statement to that effect, in original only, with the officer having custody of the products. In the case of products forfeited under the internal revenue laws the sale shall be subject to the provisions of part 172 of this chapter.

(68A Stat. 870, as amended, 72 Stat. 1425, as amended; 26 U.S.C. 7325, 5753)

[T.D. 6961, 33 FR 9488, June 28, 1968. Redesignated at 40 FR 16835, Apr. 15, 1975, and amended by T.D. ATF–232, 51 FR 28080, Aug. 5, 1986; T.D. ATF–243, 52 FR 43194, Dec. 1, 1986; T.D. ATF–251, 52 FR 19339, May 22, 1987; T.D. ATF–469, 66 FR 56758, Nov. 13, 2001]

§ 40.45 Alternate methods or procedures.

A manufacturer of tobacco products, on specific approval by the appropriate TTB officer as provided in this section, may use an alternate method or procedure in lieu of a method or procedure specifically prescribed in this part. The appropriate TTB officer may approve an alternate method or procedure, subject to stated conditions, when he finds that—

(a) Good cause has been shown for the use of the alternate method or procedure,

(b) The alternate method or procedure is within the purpose of, and consistent with the effect intended by, the specifically prescribed method or procedure, and affords equivalent security to the revenue, and

(c) The alternate method or procedure will not be contrary to any provision of law, and will not result in an increase in cost to the Government or hinder the effective administration of this part.

No alternate method or procedure relating to the giving of any bond or to the assessment, payment, or collection of tax, shall be authorized under this section. Where a manufacturer desires to employ an alternate method or procedure, he shall submit a written application to do so, in triplicate, to the appropriate TTB officer. The application shall specifically describe the proposed alternate method or procedure, and shall set forth the reasons therefor. Alternate methods or procedures shall not be employed until the application has been approved by the appropriate TTB officer. The manufacturer shall, during the period of authorization of an alternate method or procedure, comply with the terms of the approved application. Authorization for any alternate method or procedure may be withdrawn whenever in the judgment of the appropriate TTB officer the revenue is jeopardized or the effective administration of this part is hindered. The manufacturer shall retain, as part of his records, any authorization of the appropriate TTB officer under this section.

§ 40.46 Emergency variations from requirements.

The appropriate TTB officer may approve methods of operation other than as specified in this part, where he finds that an emergency exists and the proposed variations from the specified requirements are necessary, and the proposed variations—

(a) Will afford the security and protection to the revenue intended by the prescribed specifications.

(b) Will not hinder the effective administration of this part, and

(c) Will not be contrary to any provision of law.

Variations from requirements granted under this section are conditioned on compliance with the procedures, conditions, and limitations set forth in the approval of the application. Failure to comply in good faith with such procedures, conditions, and limitations shall automatically terminate the authority for such variations and the manufacturer thereupon shall fully comply with the prescribed requirements of regulations from which the variations were authorized. Authority for any variations may be withdrawn whenever in the judgment of the appropriate TTB officer the revenue is jeopardized or the effective administration of this part is hindered by the continuation of such variation. Where a manufacturer desires to employ such variation, he shall submit a written application to do so, in triplicate, to the appropriate TTB officer. The application shall describe the proposed variations and set forth the reasons therefor. Variations shall not be employed until the application has been approved. The manufacturer shall retain, as part of his records, any authorization of the appropriate TTB officer under this section.

§40.47 Other businesses within factory.

(a) *General.* The appropriate TTB officer may authorize such other businesses within the factory of a manufacturer of tobacco products as he finds will not jeopardize the revenue, will not hinder the effective administration of this part, and will not be contrary to law. A manufacturer of tobacco products who wishes to engage in another business within the factory must submit a written application to do so to the appropriate TTB officer. Except as otherwise provided in paragraph (b) of this section, a manufacturer of tobacco products may not engage in such other business until the application is approved by the appropriate TTB officer. The manufacturer must retain as part of its records any authorization provided under this section.

(b) *Processed tobacco.* A manufacturer of tobacco products may engage in certain activities related to processed tobacco without an approval under paragraph (a) of this section. Section 40.72(b) specifies the activities and circumstances that do not require authorization to engage in another business as well as those activities and circumstances that do.

[T.D. TTB–78, 74 FR 29408, June 22, 2009, as amended by T.D. TTB–104, 77 FR 37302, June 21, 2012]

§40.48 Penalties and forfeitures.

Anyone who fails to comply with the provisions of this part becomes liable to the civil and criminal penalties, and forfeitures, provided by law.

(72 Stat. 1425, 1426; 26 U.S.C. 5761, 5762, 5763)

§40.49 Delegations of the Administrator.

Most of the regulatory authorities of the Administrator contained in this part are delegated to appropriate TTB officers. These TTB officers are specified in TTB Order 1135.40, Delegation of the Administrator's Authorities in 27 CFR Part 40, Manufacture of Tobacco Products and Cigarette Papers and Tubes. You may obtain a copy of this order by accessing the TTB Web site (*http://www.ttb.gov*) or by mailing a request to the Alcohol and Tobacco Tax and Trade Bureau, National Revenue Center, 550 Main Street, Room 1516, Cincinnati, OH 45202.

[T.D. TTB–44, 71 FR 16949, Apr. 4, 2006]

Subpart E—Qualification Requirements for Manufacturers of Tobacco Products

§40.61 Qualification.

(a) *General.* Except as otherwise provided in paragraph (b) of this section, every person who manufactures tobacco products must qualify for, and obtain, a permit as a manufacturer of tobacco products in accordance with the provisions of this part.

(b) *Exceptions.* The following persons are not considered to be engaged in the business of manufacturing tobacco products for purposes of this part:

(1) A person who produces tobacco products solely for that person's own consumption or use;

(2) A proprietor of a customs bonded manufacturing warehouse with respect to the operation of such warehouse;

(3) A retailer of tobacco products, such as a tobacconist, who takes taxpaid tobacco products out of the package, as that term is defined in §40.11, in front of waiting customers and places the tobacco products into a different container for immediate delivery to those customers; or

(4) A person whose operations are limited to, and who holds a permit as, a manufacturer of processed tobacco.

(c) *Minimum manufacturing and activity requirements.* A permit to manufacture tobacco products will only be granted to those persons whose principal business activity under such permit will be the manufacture of tobacco products. A permit will not be granted to any person whose principal business activity under such permit will be to receive or transfer tobacco products in bond. As a minimum activity requirement, in order to qualify for a permit, the quantity of tobacco products manufactured under the permit must be equivalent to, or exceed, the quantity to be transferred or received in bond under the permit. For the purposes of this section, the activity of packaging processed tobacco may be sufficient to qualify as a manufacturing activity.

[T.D. TTB–78, 74 FR 29409, June 22, 2009]

§ 40.61a Transitional rule.

Any person who:

(a) On August 5, 1997, was engaged in business as a manufacturer of roll-your-own tobacco, and

(b) Before January 1, 2000, submits an application, as provided in this part, to engage in such business, may, continue to engage in such business pending final action on such application. Pending such final action, all provisions of chapter 52 of the Internal Revenue Code of 1986 shall apply to such applicant in the same manner and to the same extent as if such applicant were a holder of a permit to manufacture roll-your-own tobacco under such chapter 52.

[T.D. ATF–424, 64 FR 71931, Dec. 22, 1999]

§ 40.62 Application for permit.

Every person, before commencing business as a manufacturer of tobacco products as defined in § 40.11, shall make application for, and obtain, the permit provided in § 40.75, covering operations at each proposed factory. Such application shall be made on TTB F 5200.3, in duplicate, to the appropriate TTB officer. All documents required under this part to be furnished with such application shall be made a part thereof. Where the applicant for a permit under this section holds a permit or permits authorizing the production of any tobacco products at premises to be covered by the permit applied for, the applicant shall surrender such permit or permits for cancellation, upon the issuance of the permit applied for.

(72 Stat. 1421; 26 U.S.C 5712)

§ 40.63 Corporate documents.

Every corporation, before commencing business as a manufacturer of tobacco products, shall furnish with its application for permit, required by § 40.62, a true copy of the corporate charter or a certificate of corporate existence or incorporation executed by the appropriate officer of the State in which incorporated. The corporation shall likewise furnish duly authenticated extracts of the stockholders' meetings, bylaws, or directors' meetings, listing the offices the incumbents of which are authorized to sign documents or otherwise act in behalf of the corporation in matters relating to 26 U.S.C. chapter 52, and regulations issued thereunder. The corporation shall also furnish evidence, in duplicate, of the identity of the officers and directors and each person who holds more than ten percent of the stock of such corporation. Where any of the information required by this section has previously been filed with the appropriate TTB officer and such information is currently complete and accurate, a written statement to that effect, in duplicate, will be sufficient for the purpose of this section.

(Sec. 201, Pub. L. 85–859, 72 Stat. 1421, as amended (26 U.S.C. 5712))

[T.D. 6840, 30 FR 9310, July 27, 1965. Redesignated at 40 FR 16835, Apr. 15, 1975, and amended by T.D. ATF–48, 44 FR 55854, Sept. 28, 1979]

§ 40.64 Articles of partnership or association.

Every partnership or association, before commencing business as a manufacturer of tobacco products, shall furnish with its application for permit, required by § 40.62, a true copy of the articles of partnership or association, if any, or certificate of partnership or association where required to be filed by any State, county, or municipality.

Where a partnership or association has previously filed such documents with the appropriate TTB officer and such documents are currently complete and accurate, a written statement, in duplicate, to that effect by the partnership or association will be sufficient for the purpose of this section.

(72 Stat. 1421; 26 U.S.C. 5712)

§40.65 Trade name certificate.

Every person, before commencing business under a trade name as a manufacturer of tobacco products, shall furnish with his application for permit, required by §40.62, a true copy of the certificate or other document, if any, issued by a State, county, or municipal authority in connection with the transaction of business under such trade name. If no such certificate or other document is so required, a written statement, in duplicate, to that effect by such person will be sufficient for the purpose of this section.

(72 Stat. 1421; 26 U.S.C. 5712)

§40.66 Bond.

Every person, before commencing business as a manufacturer of tobacco products, shall file, in connection with his application for permit, a bond on TTB F 5200.25 or 5200.26, in duplicate, in accordance with the applicable provisions of subpart G of this part, conditioned upon compliance with the provisions of chapter 52, I.R.C., and regulations thereunder, including, but not limited to, the timely payment of taxes imposed by such chapter and penalties and interest in connection therewith for which he may become liable to the United States: *Provided*, That any person who, on the effective date of this part, October 1, 1961, has on file a valid and adequate bond, Form 2100, "Bond—Manufacturer of Cigars and Cigarettes," may continue, under such bond, the operations with respect to the permit to which that bond relates, in accordance with the provisions of this part.

(72 Stat. 1421, as amended; 26 U.S.C. 5711)

[T.D. 6871, 31 FR 33, Jan. 4, 1966. Redesignated at 40 FR 16835, Apr. 15, 1975]

§40.67 Blanket bond.

Where a manufacturer of tobacco products operates more than one factory he may, in lieu of filing separate bonds, file a blanket bond on TTB F 5200.25 or 5200.26, in duplicate, in accordance with the provisions of §40.134, for any or all of the factories. The total amount of any blanket bond given under this section shall be available for the satisfaction of any liability incurred at any factory covered by the bond.

(72 Stat. 1421; 26 U.S.C. 5711)

[26 FR 8174, Aug. 31, 1961. Redesignated at 40 FR 16835, Apr. 15, 1975; 54 FR 48839, Nov. 27, 1989, and further redesignated by T.D. ATF–460, 66 FR 39093, July 27, 2001, as amended by T.D. TTB–91, 76 FR 5480, Feb. 1, 2011]

§40.68 Power of attorney.

If the application for permit or any report, return, notice, schedule, or other document required to be executed is to be signed by an individual (including one of the partners for a partnership or one of the members of an association) as an attorney in fact for any person, or if an individual is to otherwise officially represent such person, power of attorney on TTB F 5000.8 shall be furnished to the appropriate TTB officer. (For power of attorney in connection with conference and practice requirements see 26 CFR 601.501 through 601.527.) Such power of attorney is not required for persons whose authority is furnished with the corporate documents as required by §40.63. TTB F 5000.8 does not have to be filed again with a appropriate TTB officer where such form has previously been submitted to that appropriate TTB officer and is still in effect.

[T.D. 6840, 30 FR 9310, July 27, 1965. Redesignated at 40 FR 16835, Apr. 15, 1975, as amended by T.D. TTB–91, 76 FR 5480, Feb. 1, 2011]

§40.69 Factory premises.

The premises to be used by a manufacturer of tobacco products as his factory may consist of more than one building, or portions of buildings, which need not be contiguous but must be located in the same city, town, or village: Except that, where the appropriate TTB officer determines that a building or portion of a building which is not within the city, town, or village, is so conveniently and closely situated to the general factory premises as to present no jeopardy to the revenue and as to offer no hindrance to the administration of this part, he may authorize the inclusion of such building or portion of building as part of the factory. The buildings or portions of buildings shall be described in the application for permit and the bond by number, street, and city, town, or village, and State. If any of the following conditions exist a diagram shall also be furnished, in duplicate, showing the information indicated:

(a) Where the factory is in more than one building, and each building is not identifiable by a separate street address—identify each building by a letter, number, or similar designation;

(b) Where the factory consists of a portion of a building or where portions of buildings are part of the factory—show the particular floor or floors, or room or rooms, comprising the factory;

(c) Where there is an adjoining retail store operated by the manufacturer tobacco products including any doors or other openings between the premises.

(72 Stat. 1421; 26 U.S.C. 5712)

[T.D. 6840, 30 FR 9310, July 27, 1965, as amended by T.D. 6871, 31 FR 33, Jan. 4, 1966. Redesignated at 40 FR 16835, Apr. 15, 1975, as amended by T.D. ATF–232, 51 FR 28080, Aug. 5, 1986; T.D. ATF–243, 52 FR 43194, Dec. 1, 1986]

§40.70 Separation of and access to factory.

Where the factory consists of a portion of a building, or where portions of buildings are part of the factory, the factory shall be completely separated by walls from adjoining portions of the building. Such walls shall be securely constructed of substantial materials. The appropriate TTB officer may, wherever he finds that the revenue will not be jeopardized, authorize openings and doors in such walls or means of separation other than walls if such means adequately delineate the factory. The factory shall be accessible directly from a street, yard, common passageway, or other common means of entrance.

(72 Stat. 1421; 26 U.S.C. 5712)

§40.71 Factories established prior to October 1, 1961.

Factories established prior to the effective date of this part, October 1, 1961, shall not be subject to the provisions of §40.70 if, in the opinion of the appropriate TTB officer, the existing premises afford adequate protection to the revenue.

(72 Stat. 1421; 26 U.S.C. 5712)

[T.D. 6871, 31 FR 33, Jan. 4, 1966. Redesignated at 40 FR 16835, Apr. 15, 1975]

§40.72 Use of factory premises.

(a) *General.* Unless otherwise authorized by the appropriate TTB officer as provided in §40.47, the premises used by a manufacturer of tobacco products for his factory shall be used exclusively for the purposes of manufacturing and storing tobacco products; storing materials, equipment, and supplies related thereto or used or useful in the conduct of the business; and carrying on activities in connection with business of the manufacturer of tobacco products.

(b) *Processed tobacco.* (1) A manufacturer of tobacco products that processes tobacco or receives processed tobacco on its factory premises solely for use in the manufacture of tobacco products under its permit, that removes processed tobacco from the factory premises only for purposes related to its business of manufacturing tobacco products as set forth in (b)(2) of this section, and that maintains records sufficient to show the final disposition of any processed tobacco removed from the factory premises may engage in such activities on the factory premises under the authority of its existing permit without prior authorization from TTB under §40.47. If a manufacturer of tobacco products removes processed tobacco for purposes other than those specified in paragraph (b)(2) of this section, that manufacturer must obtain prior authorization from TTB in accordance with §40.47 and must keep records and submit reports as prescribed in §§40.521 and 40.522.

(2) The following activities are considered to be activities related to the manufacture of tobacco products: Removal of samples of processed tobacco for the purpose of soliciting orders of tobacco products; removal of processed

tobacco for destruction; removal of processed tobacco for scientific testing or testing of equipment which results in the destruction of the processed tobacco or the return of the processed tobacco to the factory premises; and transfer of processed tobacco between permitted premises of the same manufacturer. Any removal of processed tobacco other than those listed above requires the manufacturer to first obtain authorization to engage in another business within the factory under §40.47 and to keep records and submit reports under §§40.521 and 40.522, unless the manufacturer can show to the satisfaction of the appropriate TTB officer that the removal is connected with the business of a manufacturer of tobacco products rather than with the business of a manufacturer of processed tobacco.

[T.D. TTB–78, 74 FR 29409, June 22, 2009, as amended by T.D. TTB–104, 77 FR 37302, June 21, 2012]

§40.73 Additional information.

The appropriate TTB officer may require such additional information as he may deem necessary to determine whether the applicant is entitled to a permit under the provisions of this part. The applicant shall, when required by the appropriate TTB officer, furnish as a part of his application for such permit such additional information as may be necessary for the appropriate TTB officer to determine whether the applicant is entitled to a permit.

§40.74 Investigation of applicant.

(a) *Investigation.* The appropriate TTB officer may cause inquiry or investigation to be made to verify the information furnished in connection with an application for permit and to ascertain whether the applicant is eligible for a permit. Any of the following conditions may be grounds for denial of a permit:

(1) The premises on which it is proposed to conduct the business are not adequate to protect the revenue;

(2) The activity proposed to be carried out at such premises does not meet the minimum manufacturing or activity requirements of §40.61(b); or

(3) The applicant (including, in the case of a corporation, any officer, director, or principal stockholder and, in the case of a partnership, a partner)—

(i) Is, by reason of his business experience, financial standing, or trade connections or by reason of previous or current legal proceedings involving a felony violation of any other provision of Federal criminal law relating to tobacco products, processed tobacco, cigarette paper, or cigarette tubes, not likely to maintain operations in compliance with this chapter;

(ii) Has been convicted of a felony violation of any provision of Federal or State criminal law relating to tobacco products, processed tobacco, cigarette paper, or cigarette tubes; or

(iii) Has failed to disclose any material information required or made any material false statement in the application therefor.

(b) *TTB action.* The appropriate TTB officer, if there is reason to believe that the applicant is not entitled to a permit, shall promptly give the applicant notice of the contemplated disapproval of the application and opportunity for hearing thereon in accordance with part 71 of this chapter, which part (including the provisions relating to the recommended decision and to appeals) is applicable to such proceedings. If, after such notice and opportunity for hearing, the appropriate TTB officer finds that the applicant is not entitled to a permit, he shall, by order stating the findings on which his decision is based, deny the permit.

(26 U.S.C. 5712)

[T.D. TTB–75, 74 FR 14482, Mar. 31, 2009]

§40.75 Issuance of permit.

If the application for permit, together with the bond and supporting documents, required under this part is approved by him, the appropriate TTB officer shall issue a permit on TTB F 5200.10 to the applicant as a manufacturer of tobacco products.

(72 Stat. 1421; 26 U.S.C. 5713)

[T.D. 6871, 31 FR 33, Jan. 4, 1966. Redesignated at 40 FR 16835, Apr. 15, 1975]

§40.76 Retention of permit and supporting documents.

The manufacturer shall retain his permit, together with the copy of the application and supporting documents returned to him with the permit, at the same place where the records required by this part are kept and they shall be made available for inspection by any appropriate TTB officer upon his request.

(72 Stat. 1421, 1423; 26 U.S.C. 5712, 5713, 5741)

Subpart F—Changes After Original Qualification of Manufacturers of Tobacco Products

CHANGES IN NAME

§ 40.91 Change in individual name.

Where there is a change in the name of an individual operating as a manufacturer of tobacco products he shall, within 30 days of such change, make application on Form 2098 for an amended permit.

(72 Stat. 1421; 26 U.S.C. 5712)

[26 FR 8174, Aug. 31, 1961. Redesignated at 40 FR 16835, Apr. 15, 1975; 54 FR 48839, Nov. 27, 1989; and further redesignated by T.D. ATF–460, 66 FR 39093, July 27, 2001, as amended by T.D. TTB–91, 76 FR 5480, Feb. 1, 2011]

§ 40.92 Change in trade name.

Where there is a change in, or an addition or discontinuance of, a trade name used by a manufacturer of tobacco products in connection with operations authorized by his permit the manufacturer shall, within 30 days of such change, addition or discontinuance, make application on TTB F 5200.16 for an amended permit to reflect such change. The manufacturer shall also furnish a true copy of any new trade name certificate or document issued to him, or statement in lieu thereof, required by § 40.65.

(72 Stat. 1421; 26 U.S.C. 5712)

[T.D. 6840, 30 FR 9311, July 27, 1965. Redesignated at 40 FR 16835, Apr. 15, 1975]

§ 40.93 Change in corporate name.

Where there is a change in the name of a corporate manufacturer of tobacco products, the manufacturer shall, within 30 days of such change, make application on TTB F 5200.16 for an amended permit. The manufacturer shall also furnish such documents as may be necessary to establish that the corporate name has been changed.

(72 Stat. 1421; 26 U.S.C. 5712)

CHANGES IN OWNERSHIP AND CONTROL

§ 40.101 Fiduciary successor.

If an administrator, executor, receiver, trustee, assignee, or other fiduciary, is to take over the business of a manufacturer of tobacco products, as a continuing operation, such fiduciary shall, before commencing operations, make application for permit and file bond as required by subpart E, of this part, furnish certified copies, in duplicate, of the order of the court, or other pertinent documents, showing his appointment and qualification as such fiduciary, and make a commencing inventory, in accordance with the provisions of § 40.201: *Provided,* That where a diagram has been furnished by the predecessor, in accordance with the provisions of § 40.69, the successor may adopt such diagram if it is currently complete and accurate. However, where a fiduciary intends only to liquidate the business, qualification as a manufacturer of tobacco products will not be required if he promptly files with the appropriate TTB officer a written statement to that effect, in duplicate, together with an extension of coverage of the predecessor's bond, executed by the fiduciary and the surety on such bond, in accordance with the provisions of § 40.137.

(72 Stat. 1421, 1422; 26 U.S.C. 5711, 5712, 5721)

§ 40.102 Transfer of ownership.

If a transfer is to be made in ownership of the business of a manufacturer of tobacco products (including a change of any member of a partnership or association), such manufacturer shall give notice, in writing, to the appropriate TTB officer, naming the proposed successor and the desired effective date of such transfer. The proposed successor shall, before commencing operations, qualify as a manufacturer of tobacco products, in accordance with the applicable provisions of subpart E of this part: *Provided,* That where a diagram has been furnished by the manufacturer in accordance with the provisions of § 40.69, the proposed successor may adopt such diagram if it is currently complete and accurate. The manufacturer shall give such notice of transfer, and the proposed successor shall make application for permit and file bond, as required, in ample time for examination and approval thereof before the desired date of such change. The predecessor shall make a concluding inventory and concluding report, in accordance with the provisions of §§40.201 and 40.202, respectively, and surrender his permit with such inventory and report. The successor shall make a commencing inventory and commencing report, in accordance with the provisions of §§40.201 and 40.202, respectively.

(72 Stat. 1421, 1422; 26 U.S.C. 5711, 5712, 5713, 5721, 5722)

§40.103 Change in officers, directors, or stockholders of a corporation.

Upon election or appointment (excluding successive reelection or reappointment) of any officer or director of a corporation operating the business of a manufacturer of tobacco products, or upon any occurrence which results in a person acquiring ownership or control of more than ten percent in aggregate of the outstanding stock of such corporation, the manufacturer shall, within 30 days of such action, so notify the appropriate TTB officer in writing, giving the identity of such person. When there is any change in the authority furnished under §40.63 for officers to act in behalf of the corporation the manufacturer shall immediately so notify the appropriate TTB officer in writing.

(72 Stat. 1421; 26 U.S.C. 5712)

[T.D. 6840, 30 FR 9311, July 27, 1965. Redesignated at 40 FR 16835, Apr. 15, 1975]

§40.104 Change in control of a corporation.

Where the issuance, sale, or transfer of the stock of a corporation, operating as a manufacturer of tobacco products, results in a change in the identity of the principal stockholders exercising actual or legal control of the operations of the corporation, the corporate manufacturer shall, within 30 days after the change occurs, make application on TTB F 5200.3 for a new permit. Otherwise, the present permit shall be automatically terminated at the expiration of such 30-day period, and the manufacturer shall dispose of all tobacco products on hand, in accordance with this part, make a concluding inventory and concluding report, in accordance with the provisions of §§40.201 and 40.202, respectively, and surrender his permit with such inventory and report. If the application for a new permit is timely made, the present permit shall continue in effect pending final action with respect to such application.

(72 Stat. 1421, 1422; 26 U.S.C. 5712, 5713, 5721, 5722)

[T.D. 6871, 31 FR 33, Jan. 4, 1966. Redesignated at 40 FR 16835, Apr. 15, 1975, as amended by T.D. ATF–232, 51 FR 28081, Aug. 5, 1986; T.D. ATF–243, 51 FR 43194, Dec. 1, 1986]

CHANGES IN LOCATION OF FACTORY

§40.111 Change in location.

Whenever a manufacturer of tobacco products intends to relocate its factory, the manufacturer shall, before commencing operations at the new location, make application on TTB F 5200.16 for, and obtain, an amended permit. The application shall be supported by bond coverage in accordance with the provisions of subpart G of this part.

[T.D. TTB–91, 76 FR 5479, Feb. 1, 2011]

§40.112 Change in address.

Whenever any change occurs in the address, but not the location, of the factory of a manufacturer of tobacco products, as a result of action of local authorities, the manufacturer shall, within 30 days of such change, make application on TTB F 5200.16 for an amended permit.

(72 Stat. 1421; 26 U.S.C. 5712)

§40.114 Extension or curtailment of factory.

Where a tobacco products factory is to be changed to an extent which will make inaccurate the description of the factory as set forth in the last application by the manufacturer for permit, on the diagram, if any, furnished with such application, the manufacturer shall first make an application on TTB F 5200.16 for, and obtain, an amended permit. Such application shall describe the proposed change in the factory and shall be accompanied by a new diagram if required under the provisions of §40.69.

(72 Stat. 1421; 26 U.S.C. 5711, 5712)

Subpart G—Bonds and Extensions of Coverage of Bonds

§40.131 Corporate surety.

(a) Surety bonds required under the provisions of this part may be given only with corporate sureties holding certificates of authority from the Secretary of the Treasury as acceptable sureties on Federal bonds. Each bond and each extension of coverage of bond shall at the time of filing be accompanied by a power of attorney authorizing the agent or officer who executed the bond to so act on behalf of the surety. The appropriate TTB officer who is authorized to approve the bond may, whenever he deems it necessary, require additional evidence of the authority of the agent or officer to execute the bond or extension of coverage of bond. The power of attorney shall be prepared on a form provided by the surety company and executed under the corporate seal of the company. If the power of attorney submitted is other than a manually signed document it shall be accompanied by a certificate of its validity. Limitations concerning corporate sureties are prescribed by the Secretary in Treasury Department Circular No. 570, as revised. The surety shall have no interest whatever in the business covered by the bond.

(b) Treasury Department Circular No. 570 (Companies Holding Certificates of Authority as Acceptable Sureties on Federal Bonds and as Acceptable Reinsuring Companies) is published in the FEDERAL REGISTER annually as of the first workday in July. As they occur, interim revisions of the circular are published in the FEDERAL REGISTER. Copies may be obtained from the Audit Staff, Bureau of Government Financial Operations, Department of the Treasury, Washington, DC 20226.

(61 Stat. 649, 72 Stat. 1421, as amended; 31 U.S.C. 9304, 9306; 26 U.S.C. 5711; 5 U.S.C. 552(a) (80 Stat. 383, as amended))

[T.D. 6961, 33 FR 9488, June 28, 1968. Redesignated at 40 FR 16835, Apr. 15, 1975 and amended by T.D. ATF–92, 46 FR 46921, Sept. 23, 1981]

§40.132 Deposit of securities in lieu of corporate surety.

In lieu of corporate surety the manufacturer of tobacco products may pledge and deposit, as security for his bond, securities which are transferable and are guaranteed as to both interest and principal by the United States, in accordance with the provisions of 31 CFR part 225.

(61 Stat. 650, 72 Stat. 1421; 6 U.S.C.9301, 9303; 26 U.S.C. 5711)

§40.133 Amount of individual bond.

The amount of the bond of a manufacturer of tobacco products shall be not less than the total amount of tax liability on all tobacco products manufactured in his factory, received in bond from other factories and from export warehouses, and released to him in bond from customs custody, during any calendar month. Where the amount of any bond is no longer sufficient and the bond is in less than the maximum amount, the manufacturer shall immediately file a strengthening or superseding bond as required by this subpart. The amount of any such bond (or the total amount including strengthening bonds, if any) need not exceed $250,000 for a manufacturer producing or receiving cigarettes in bond; need not exceed $150,000 for a manufacturer producing or receiving cigars, smokeless tobacco, pipe tobacco, or roll-your-own tobacco in bond; and need not exceed $250,000 for a manufacturer producing or receiving any combination of tobacco products in bond. The bond of a manufacturer of tobacco products shall in no case be less than $1,000.

[T.D. ATF–232, 51 FR 28080, Aug. 5, 1986; T.D. ATF–243, 51 FR 43194, Dec. 1, 1986, as amended by T.D. ATF–289, 54 FR 48839, Nov. 27, 1989; T.D. ATF–424, 64 FR 71931, Dec. 22, 1999]

§40.134 Amount of blanket bond.

In the case of a blanket bond filed under the provisions of §40.67, where the total amount of individual bonds otherwise required for the factories under §40.133 does not exceed $250,000, such blanket bond shall be not less than the total amount of such individual bonds. Where the total amount of such individual bonds required is in excess of $250,000 but not in excess of $500,000, the amount of the blanket bond shall be not less than $250,000 plus 50 percent of such total amount which is in excess of $250,000. Where the total amount of such individual bonds required is in excess of $500,000 the amount of the blanket bond shall be not less than $375,000 plus 25 percent of such total amount which is in excess of $500,000.

(72 Stat. 1421; 26 U.S.C. 5711)

§40.135 Strengthening bond.

Where the amount of any bond is no longer sufficient under the provisions of §40.133 or §40.134, the manufacturer shall immediately file a strengthening bond in an appropriate amount with the same surety as that on the bond already in effect, unless a superseding bond is filed pursuant to §40.136. Strengthening bonds will not be approved where any notation is made thereon which is intended, or which may be construed, as a release of any former bond, or as limiting the amount of either bond to less than its full amount.

(72 Stat. 1421; 26 U.S.C. 5711)

§40.136 Superseding bond.

A manufacturer of tobacco products shall immediately file a new bond to supersede his current bond when

(a) The corporate surety on the current bond becomes insolvent,

(b) The appropriate TTB officer approves a request from the surety on the current bond to terminate his liability under the bond,

(c) Payment of any liability under a bond is made by the surety thereon,

(d) The amount of the bond is no longer sufficient under the provisions of §40.133 or §40.134 and a strengthening bond has not been filed, or

(e) The appropriate TTB officer considers such a superseding bond necessary for the protection of the revenue.

Where a bond is not filed as required under the provisions of this section the manufacturer shall discontinue forthwith the operations to which such bond relates.

(72 Stat. 1421: 26 U.S.C. 5711)

§40.137 Extension of coverage of bond.

An extension of coverage of bond shall be manifested on TTB F 5200.18 by the manufacturer of tobacco products and by the surety on the bond with the same formality and proof of authority as required for the execution of the bond.

(72 Stat. 1421; 26 U.S.C. 5711)

§40.138 Approval of bond and extension of coverage of bond.

No person shall commence operations under any bond, nor extend his operations, until he receives from the appropriate TTB officer notice of his approval of the bond or of an appropriate extension of coverage of the bond required under this part.

(72 Stat. 1421; 26 U.S.C. 5711)

§40.139 Termination of bond.

Any bond required by this part may be terminated by the appropriate TTB officer as to liability for future operations (a) pursuant to application by the surety as provided in the bond, (b) on approval of a superseding bond, or (c) when operations by the manufacturer are permanently discontinued in accordance with subpart J. After a bond is terminated the surety shall remain bound with respect to any liability for unpaid taxes, penalties, and interest, not in excess of the amount of the bond, incurred by the manufacturer prior to the termination date.

(72 Stat. 1421; 26 U.S.C. 5711)

[T.D. 6840, 30 FR 9311, July 27, 1965. Redesignated at 40 FR 16835, Apr. 15, 1975]

§40.140 Release of pledged securities.

Securities of the United States pledged and deposited as provided in §40.132 shall be released only in accordance with the provisions of 31 CFR part

225. Such securities will not be released by the appropriate TTB officer until liability under the bond for which they were pledged has been terminated. When the appropriate TTB officer is satisfied that they may be released, he shall fix the date or dates on which a part or all of such securities may be released. At any time prior to the release of such securities, the appropriate TTB officer may extend the date of release for such additional length of time as he deems necessary.

(61 Stat. 650, 72 Stat. 1421; 31 U.S.C. 9301, 9303, 26 U.S.C. 5711)

Subpart H—Operations by Manufacturers of Tobacco Products

DETERMINATION AND PAYMENT OF TAXES ON TOBACCO PRODUCTS

§ 40.161 Determination of tax and method of payment.

Except for removals in bond and transfers in bond, as authorized by law, the taxes imposed on tobacco products by section 5701, I.R.C., shall be determined at the time of removal of such products and paid on the basis of a return, in accordance with the provisions of this part.

(72 Stat. 1417; 26 U.S.C. 5703)

[T.D. 6929, 32 FR 13866, Oct. 5, 1967. Redesignated at 40 FR 16835, Apr. 15, 1975; T.D. ATF–232, 51 FR 28081, Aug. 5, 1986; T.D. ATF–243, 51 FR 43194, Dec. 1, 1986]

§ 40.162 Semimonthly tax return.

Every manufacturer of tobacco products shall file, for each of his factories, a semimonthly tax return on Form 5000.24 for each return period, including any period during which a manufacturer begins or discontinues business. The return shall be filed with TTB in accordance with the instructions on the form. The manufacturer shall file the return at the time specified in § 40.165 regardless of whether tobacco products are removed or whether tax is due for that particular return period. However, when the manufacturer requests by letter and the appropriate TTB officer grants specific authorization, the manufacturer need not during the term of such authorization file a tax return for which tax is not due or payable.

[T.D. ATF–232, 51 FR 35353, Oct. 3, 1986; T.D. ATF–243, 51 FR 43194, Dec. 1, 1986, as amended by T.D. ATF–251, 52 FR 19339, May 22, 1987]

§ 40.163 Semimonthly tax return periods.

Except as otherwise provided in § 40.164, the periods to be covered by semimonthly tax returns are from the 1st day of each month through the 15th day of that month and from the 16th day of each month through the last day of that month.

[T.D. TTB–89, 76 FR 3513, Jan. 20, 2011]

§ 40.164 Special rule for taxes due for the month of September.

(a) *Division of second semimonthly period.* (1) *General.* Except as otherwise provided in paragraph (a)(2) of this section, the second semimonthly period for the month of September is divided into two payment periods, from the 16th day through the 26th day, and from the 27th day through the 30th day. The manufacturer shall file a return on TTB F 5000.24, and make remittance, for the period September 16–26, no later than September 29. The manufacturer shall file a return on TTB F 5000.24, and make remittance, for the period September 27–30, no later than October 14.

(2) *Taxpayment not by electronic fund transfer.* In the case of taxes for which remittance by electronic fund transfer (EFT) is not required by § 40.165a, the second semimonthly period of September is divided into two payment periods, from the 16th day through the 25th day, and from the 26th day through the 30th day. The manufacturer shall file a return on TTB F 5000.24, and make remittance, for the period September 16–25, no later than September 28. The manufacturer shall file a return on TTB F 5000.24, and make remittance, for the period September 26–30, no later than October 14.

(b) *Amount of payment—Safe harbor rule.* (1) *General.* Taxpayers are considered to have met the requirements of paragraph (a)(1) of this section if the amount paid no later than September 29 is not less than 11/15ths (73.3 percent) of the tax liability incurred for the semimonthly period beginning on September 1 and ending on September 15, and if any underpayment of tax is paid by October 14.

(2) *Taxpayment not by EFT*. Taxpayers are considered to have met the requirements of paragraph (a)(2) of this section if the amount paid no later than September 28 is not less than 2/3rds (66.7 percent) of the tax liability incurred for the semimonthly period beginning on September 1 and ending on September 15, and if any underpayment of tax is paid by October 14.

(c) *Weekends and holidays*. If the required taxpayment due date for the period September 16–25 or September 16–26, as applicable, falls on a Saturday or legal holiday, the return and remittance are due on the immediately preceding day. If the required due date falls on a Sunday, the return and remittance are due on the immediately following day.

(d) *Example: Payment of tax for the month of September*. (1) *Facts*. X, a manufacturer of tobacco products required to pay taxes by electronic fund transfer, incurred tax liability in the amount of $30,000 for the first semimonthly period of September. For the period September 16–26, X incurred tax liability in the amount of $45,000, and for the period September 27–30, X incurred tax liability in the amount of $2,000.

(2) *Payment requirement*. X's payment of tax in the amount of $30,000 for the first semimonthly period of September is due no later than September 29 (§40.165(a)). X's payment of tax for the period September 16–26 is also due no later than September 29 (§40.164(a)(1)). X may use the safe harbor rule to determine the amount of payment due for the period of September 16–26 (§40.164(b)). Under the safe harbor rule, X's payment of tax must not be less than $21,990.00, that is, 11/15ths of the tax liability incurred during the first semimonthly period of September. Additionally, X must pay the tax in the amount of $2,000 for the period September 27–30 no later than October 14 (§40.164(a)(1)). X must also pay the underpayment of tax, $23,010.00, for the period September 16–26, no later than October 14 (§40.164(b)).

[T.D. TTB–89, 76 FR 3513, Jan. 20, 2011]

§40.165 Times for filing semimonthly return.

(a) *General*. Except as otherwise provided in §40.164 and in paragraph (b) of this section, semimonthly returns on TTB F 5000.24 must be filed, for each return period, not later than the 14th day after the last day of the return period. If the due date falls on a Saturday, Sunday, or legal holiday, the return and remittance are due on the immediately preceding day that is not a Saturday, Sunday, or legal holiday, except as otherwise provided in §40.164(c).

(b) *Postmark*. The official postmark of the U.S. Postal Service stamped on the cover in which the return was mailed shall be considered the date of delivery of the tax return and, if the return was accompanied by a remittance, the date of delivery of the remittance. When the postmark is illegible, the manufacturer shall prove when the postmark was made. When the proprietor sends the tax return with or without remittance by registered mail or by certified mail, the date of registry or the date of the postmark on the sender's receipt of certified mail, as the case may be, shall be treated as the date of delivery of the tax return and, if accompanied, of the remittance.

(Approved by the Office of Management and Budget under control number 1512–0467)

[T.D. ATF–246, 52 FR 669, Jan. 8, 1987, as amended by T.D. ATF–251, 52 FR 19339, May 22, 1987; T.D. ATF–365, 60 FR 33675, June 28, 1995; T.D. ATF–446, 66 FR 16602, Mar. 27, 2001; T.D. ATF–446a, 66 FR 19089, Apr. 13, 2001; T.D. TTB–89, 76 FR 3514, Jan. 20, 2011]

§40.165a Payment of tax by electronic fund transfer.

(a) *General*. (1) Each taxpayer who was liable, during a calendar year, for a gross amount equal to or exceeding five million dollars in taxes on tobacco products, cigarette papers, and cigarette tubes combining tax liabilities incurred under this part and part 41 of this chapter, shall use a commercial bank in making payment by electronic fund transfer (EFT) of taxes on tobacco products, cigarette papers, and cigarette tubes during the succeeding calendar year. Payment of taxes on tobacco products by cash, check, or money order, as described in §40.168, is not authorized for a taxpayer who is required, by this section, to make remittances by EFT. For purposes of this section, the dollar amount of tax liability is defined as the gross tax liability on all taxable withdrawals and importations (including tobacco products, cigarette papers, and cigarette tubes brought into the United States from Puerto Rico or the Virgin Islands) during the calendar year, without regard to any drawbacks, credits, or refunds, for all premises from which such activities are conducted by the taxpayer. Overpayments are not taken into account in summarizing the gross tax liability.

(2) For the purposes of this section, a taxpayer includes a controlled group of corporations, as defined in 26 U.S.C. 1563, and implementing regulations in 26 CFR 1.1563–1 through 1.1563–4, except that the words "at least 80 percent" shall be replaced by the words "more than 50 percent" in each place it appears in subsection (a) of 26 U.S.C. 1563, as well as in the implementing regulations. Also, the rules for a "controlled group of corporations" apply in a similar fashion to groups which include partnerships and/or sole proprietorships. If one entity maintains more than 50% control over a group consisting of corporations and one, or more, partnerships and/or sole proprietorships, all of the members of the controlled group are one taxpayer for the purpose of determining who is required to make remittances by EFT.

(3) A taxpayer who is required by this section to make remittances by EFT, shall make a separate EFT remittance and file a separate return, Form 5000.24, for each factory from which tobacco products are withdrawn upon determination of tax.

(b) *Requirements.* (1) On or before January 10 of each calendar year, except for a taxpayer already remitting the tax by EFT, each taxpayer who was liable for a gross amount equal to or exceeding five million dollars in taxes on tobacco products, cigarette papers, and cigarette tubes combining tax liabilities incurred under this part and part 41 of this chapter, during the previous calendar year, shall notify, in writing, the appropriate TTB officer. The notice shall be an agreement to make remittances by EFT.

(2) For each return filed in accordance with this part, the taxpayer shall direct the taxpayer's bank to make an electronic fund transfer in the amount of the tax payment to the Treasury Account as provided in paragraph (e) of this section. The request shall be made to the bank early enough for the transfer to be made to the Treasury Account by no later than the close of business on the last day for filing the return, prescribed in § 40.165 or § 40.167. The request shall take into account any time limit established by the bank.

(3) If a taxpayer was liable for less than five million dollars in taxes on tobacco products, cigarette papers, and cigarette tubes combining tax liabilities incurred under this part and part 41 of this chapter during the preceding calendar year, the taxpayer may choose either to continue remitting the tax as provided in this section or to remit the tax with the return on as prescribed by § 40.168. Upon filing the first return which the taxpayer chooses to discontinue remitting the tax by EFT and to begin remitting the tax with the tax return, the taxpayer shall notify the appropriate TTB officer by attaching a written notification to Form 5000.24, stating that no taxes are due by EFT, because the tax liability during the preceding calendar year was less than five million dollars, and that the remittance shall be filed with the tax return.

(c) *Remittance.* (1) Each taxpayer shall show on the return, Form 5000.24, information about remitting the tax for that return period by EFT and shall file the return with the TTB, in accordance with the instructions on Form 5000.24.

(2) Remittances shall be considered as made when the taxpayment by electronic fund transfer is received by the Treasury Account. For purposes of this section, a taxpayment by electronic fund transfer shall be considered as received by the Treasury Account when it is paid to a Federal Reserve Bank.

(3) When the taxpayer directs the bank to effect an electronic fund transfer message as required by paragraph (b)(2) of this section, any transfer data record furnished to the taxpayer, through normal banking procedures, will serve as the record of payment,

and shall be retained as part of required records.

(d) *Failure to make a taxpayment by EFT.* The taxpayer is subject to a penalty imposed by 26 U.S.C. 5761, 6651, or 6656, as applicable, for failure to make a tax payment by EFT on or before the close of business on the prescribed last day for filing.

(e) *Procedure.* Upon the notification required under paragraph (b)(1) of this section, the appropriate TTB officer will issue to the taxpayer a TTB procedure entitled, Payment of Tax by Electronic Fund Transfer. This publication outlines the procedure a taxpayer is to follow when preparing returns and EFT remittances in accordance with this part. The U.S. Customs Service will provide the taxpayer with instructions for preparing EFT remittances for payments to be made to the U.S. Customs Service.

(Approved by the Office of Management and Budget under control number 1512–0457)

(Act of August 16, 1954, 68A Stat. 775, as amended (26 U.S.C. 6302); sec. 202, Pub. L. 85–859, 72 Stat. 1417, as amended (26 U.S.C. 5703))

[T.D. ATF–198, 49 FR 37582, Sept. 25, 1984]

EDITORIAL NOTE: For FEDERAL REGISTER citations affecting § 40.165a, see the List of CFR Sections Affected, which appears in the Finding Aids section of the printed volume and at *www.fdsys.gov*.

§ 40.166 Default, prepayment of tax required.

Where a check or money order tendered with any return, whether semimonthly or prepayment, for payment of tax on tobacco products is not paid on presentment, where a manufacturer fails to remit with the return the full amount of tax due thereunder, or where a manufacturer is otherwise in default in payment of tax on tobacco products under the internal revenue laws or this chapter, during the period of such default and until the appropriate TTB officer finds that the revenue will not be jeopardized by the deferred payment of tax pursuant to the provisions of this part, no tobacco products shall be removed subject to tax until the tax thereon has first been paid as provided in § 40.167. Any remittance made during the period of a default shall be in cash, or in the form of a certified, cashier's, or treasurer's check drawn on any bank or trust company incorporated under the laws of the United States, or under the laws of any State, Territory, or possession of the United States, or in the form of a U.S. postal money order or other money order, and defined in § 70.61 of this chapter (payment by check or money order), or shall be delivered in the form of an electronic fund transfer message as provided in § 40.165a.

(68A Stat. 777, 72 Stat. 1417; 26 U.S.C. 6311, 5703; Aug. 16, 1954, ch. 736, 68A Stat. 707 (26 U.S.C. 5703); Aug. 16, 1954, ch. 736, 68A Stat. 777 (26 U.S.C. 6311))

[T.D. 6871, 31 FR 34, Jan. 4, 1966. Redesignated at 40 FR 16835, Apr. 15, 1975, and amended by T.D. ATF–48, 44 FR 55855, Sept. 28, 1979; T.D. ATF–77, 46 FR 3008, Jan. 13, 1981; T.D. ATF–232, 51 FR 28081, Aug. 5, 1986; T.D. ATF–243, 51 FR 43194, Dec. 1, 1986; T.D. ATF–301, 55 FR 47658, Nov. 14, 1990]

§ 40.167 Prepayment tax return.

(a) To prepay the tax on tobacco products a manufacturer shall file a prepayment tax return on Form 5000.24 showing the tax to be paid on the tobacco products prior to removal. The return shall be executed and filed, prior to the removal of such products, with TTB, in accordance with the instructions on the form. A manufacturer prepaying the taxes on tobacco products under the provisions of this section shall continue to file semimonthly returns as required by § 40.162.

(b) However, if a manufacturer is required by § 40.165a to pay the tax by electronic fund transfer, the manufacturer shall prepay the tax before any tobacco products can be removed for consumption or sale by completing the return and filing it with TTB, in accordance with the instructions on the form. At the same time, the manufacturer shall direct his bank to effect an EFT.

(Sec. 202, Pub. L. 85–859, 68A Stat. 1417 (26 U.S.C. 5703); sec. 202, Pub. L. 85–859, 72 Stat. 1423, as amended (26 U.S.C. 5741); (Aug. 16, 1954, ch. 736, 68A Stat. 775, as amended (26 U.S.C. 6302)); 26 U.S.C. 7805 (68A Stat. 917, as amended))

[T.D. 6871, 31 FR 34, Jan. 4, 1966. Redesignated at 40 FR 16835, Apr. 15, 1975, and amended by T.D. ATF–77, 46 FR 3008, Jan. 13, 1981; T.D. ATF–219, 50 FR 51390, Dec. 17, 1985; T.D. ATF–232, 51 FR 28081, Aug. 5, 1986; T.D. ATF–243, 51 FR 43194, Dec. 1, 1986; T.D. ATF–251, 52 FR 19340, May 22, 1987]

§40.168 Remittance with return.

Except when an electronic fund transfer has been made under §40.165a for the full amount of tax due, the tax on tobacco products shown to be due and payable on any return shall be paid by remittance in full with the tax return. The remittance may be in the form which the appropriate TTB officer is authorized to accept under §70.61 of this chapter (Payment by check or money order) and which is acceptable to him, except as otherwise specified in §40.166. Checks and money orders shall be made payable to the "Alcohol and Tobacco Tax and Trade Bureau". In paying the tax, a fractional part of a cent shall be disregarded unless it amounts to one-half cent or more, in which case it shall be increased to one cent.

(68A Stat. 778, 72 Stat. 1417; 26 U.S.C. 6313, 5703; Aug. 16, 1954, ch. 736, 68A Stat. 707, as amended (26 U.S.C. 5703))

[T.D. 6871, 31 FR 35, Jan. 4, 1966. Redesignated at 40 FR 16835, Apr. 15, 1975, and amended by T.D. ATF–48, 44 FR 55855, Sept. 28, 1979; T.D. ATF–77, 46 FR 3009, Jan. 13, 1981; T.D. ATF–232, 51 FR 28081, Aug. 5, 1986; T.D. ATF–243, 51 FR 43194, Dec. 1, 1986; T.D. ATF–301, 55 FR 47658, Nov. 14, 1990]

§40.169 Employer identification number.

The employer identification number (defined at 26 CFR 301.7701–12) of a manufacturer of tobacco products who has been assigned such a number shall be shown on each tax return, Form 5000.24. Failure of the manufacturer to include his employer identification number on Form 5000.24 may result in assertion and collection of the penalty specified in §70.113 of this chapter.

[T.D. ATF–219, 50 FR 51390, Dec. 17, 1985, as amended by T.D. ATF–301, 55 FR 47658, Nov. 14, 1990]

§40.170 Application for employer identification number.

Every manufacturer of tobacco products who has neither secured an employer identification number nor made application therefor shall file an application on Form SS–4. Form SS–4 may be obtained from any service center director or from any district director. Such application shall be filed on or before the seventh day after the date on which any tax return under this part is filed. Each manufacturer shall make application for and shall be assigned only one employer identification number for all internal revenue tax purposes.

(75 Stat. 828; 26 U.S.C. 6109)

[T.D. 7055, 35 FR 13515, Aug. 25, 1970. Redesignated at 40 FR 16835, Apr. 15, 1975]

§40.171 Execution and filing of Form SS–4.

The application on Form SS–4, together with any supplementary statement, shall be prepared in accordance with the form, instructions, and regulations applicable thereto, and shall set forth fully and clearly the data therein called for. The application shall be filed with the service center director serving any internal revenue district where the applicant is required to file returns under this part, except that hand-carried applications may be filed with the district director of any such district as provided for in 26 CFR 301.6091–1. The application shall be signed by (a) the individual if the person is an individual; (b) the president, vice president, or other principal officer if the person is a corporation; (c) a responsible and duly authorized member or officer having knowledge of its affairs if the person is a partnership or other unincorporated organization; or

(d) the fiduciary if the person is a trust or estate.

(75 Stat. 828; 26 U.S.C. 6109)

[T.D. 7055, 35 FR 13515, Aug. 25, 1970. Redesignated at 40 FR 16835, Apr. 15, 1975, and amended by T.D. ATF-48, 44 FR 55855, Sept. 28, 1979]

RECORDS

§ 40.181 General.

Every manufacturer of tobacco products must keep records of his operations and transactions which shall reflect, for each day, the information specified in §§ 40.182 and 40.183. For this purpose *day* shall mean calendar day, except that the appropriate TTB officer may, upon application of the manufacturer by letter, in duplicate, authorize as such day for a factory a 24-hour cycle of operation other than the calendar day. A day once so established as other than the calendar day may be changed only by another application approved by the appropriate TTB officer. No specific form is required. The manufacturer may use commercial records from which the required information may be readily ascertained for this purpose. The manufacturer shall keep the auxiliary and supplemental records from which such records are compiled and shall keep supporting records, as specified in §§ 40.184 and 40.186, of tobacco products removed subject to tax and transferred in bond. Except as provided in §§ 40.184 and 40.186, the entries in the commercial records so maintained or kept shall be made not later than the close of the next business day following the day on which the transaction(s) occurred. As used in this section the term *business day* shall mean any day other than Saturday, Sunday, a legal holiday in the District of Columbia, or a statewide legal holiday in the State wherein the factory to which the records relate is located.

(72 Stat. 1423, as amended; 26 U.S.C. 5741)

[T.D. ATF-424, 64 FR 71931, Dec. 22, 1999]

§ 40.182 Record of tobacco and processed tobacco.

(a) Except as provided in paragraph (b) of this section, a manufacturer of tobacco products must maintain a record that shows the total quantity in pounds of all:

(1) Processed tobacco on hand at the beginning of each month;

(2) Processed tobacco received, together with the name and address of the person from whom received and the date of receipt;

(3) Processed tobacco used in the manufacture of tobacco products, together with the date of use;

(4) Processed tobacco lost, together with the date and other circumstances of the loss;

(5) Processed tobacco destroyed, together with the date and other circumstances of the destruction;

(6) Processed tobacco removed, together with the date of the removal and reason for the removal; and

(7) Tobacco (unprocessed) on hand at the beginning of each month and used in the manufacture of tobacco products, lost, destroyed, or removed during each month.

(b) A manufacturer of tobacco products that is required to obtain authorization to engage in another business within the factory under §§ 40.47(b) and 40.72(b) must keep records as prescribed in § 40.521, in addition to those required elsewhere in this part.

(Approved by the Office of Management and Budget under control number 1513-0068)

[T.D. TTB-104, 77 FR 37302, June 21, 2012]

§ 40.183 Record of tobacco products.

The record of a manufacturer of tobacco products must show the date and total quantities of all tobacco products by kind (small cigars; large cigars; small cigarettes; large cigarettes; chewing tobacco; snuff; pipe tobacco; roll-your-own tobacco) that are:

(a) Manufactured;

(b) Received in bond by—

(1) Transfer from other factories,

(2) Release from customs custody,

(3) Transfer from export warehouses, and

(4) Transfer from foreign trade zones;

(c) Received by return to bond;

(d) Disclosed as an overage by inventory;

(e) Removed subject to tax (itemize large cigars by sale price in accordance with § 40.22, except that before April 1, 2009, cigars that cost more than $235.294 may optionally be shown as if the price were $236 per thousand, and on and after April 1, 2009, cigars that cost more than $763.222 may optionally be shown as if the price were $764 per thousand);

(f) Removed, in bond, for—

(1) Export,

(2) Transfer to export warehouses,

(3) Transfer to other factories,

(4) Transfer to foreign trade zones,

(5) Use of the United States, and

(6) Experimental purposes off factory premises;

(g) Otherwise disposed of, without determination of tax, by—

(1) Consumption by employees on factory premises,

(2) Consumption by employees off factory premises, together with the number of employees to whom furnished,

(3) Use for experimental purposes on factory premises,

(4) Loss,

(5) Destruction, and

(6) Reduction to materials;

(h) Disclosed as a shortage by inventory; and

(i) On which the tax has been determined and which are—

(1) Received, and

(2) Disposed of.

(Approved by the Office of Management and Budget under control number 1513–0068.)

[T.D. ATF–421, 64 FR 71923, Dec. 22, 1999, as amended by T.D. ATF–424, 64 FR 71931, Dec. 22, 1999; T.D. ATF–420, 64 FR 71940, Dec. 22, 1999; T.D. TTB–75, 74 FR 14482, Mar. 31, 2009; 78 FR 38567, June 27, 2013]

EFFECTIVE DATE NOTE: At 78 FR 38567, June 27, 2013, § 40.183 was amended by revising the introductory text and paragraphs (a) through (d) and (f) through (i) and the Office of Management and Budget control number referenced at the end of the section, effective Aug. 26, 2013 through Aug. 26, 2016.

§ 40.184 Record of removals subject to tax.

(a) *Requirement.* Every manufacturer of tobacco products must keep a record of tobacco products removed from the factory subject to tax. The manufacturer must make entries in this record at the time of removal. The record for each removal must show:

(1) The date of removal,

(2) The name and address of the person to whom shipped or delivered,

(3) The kind and quantity of tobacco products removed, and

(4) For large cigars, show the sale price (if the sale price is more than $235.294 per thousand before April 1, 2009, or more than $763.222 per thousand on and after April 1, 2009, you may place a note to that effect in the record instead of the actual price).

(b) *Exceptions.* (1) The record of removal may consist of the manufacturer's commercial documents, such as copies of invoices, rather than records prepared expressly to meet the requirements of this section. If commercial documents are used, they must be kept at the factory, contain all the details required by this section, and be clear and accurate. Commercial documents that do not show specifically the tax classification of tobacco products (including sale price of large cigars) are still acceptable if they contain adequate information for an appropriate TTB officer to readily ascertain the applicable tax.

(2) Where tobacco products are delivered within the factory directly to the consumer, the record need not show the name and address of the consumer.

(Sec. 2128(c), Pub. L. 94–455, 90 Stat. 1921 (26 U.S.C. 5741))

[T.D. ATF–420, 64 FR 71941, Dec. 22, 1999, as amended by T.D. TTB–75, 74 FR 14483, Mar. 31, 2009]

§ 40.185 Retention of records.

All records required to be kept under this part, including copies of authorizations, claims, inventories, notices, reports, returns and schedules, shall be retained by the manufacturer for three years following the close of the calendar year in which filed or made, or in the case of an authorization, for three years following the close of the calendar year in which the operation under such authorization is concluded. Such records shall be kept in the factory or a place convenient thereto, and shall be made available for inspection by any appropriate TTB officer upon his request.

(72 Stat. 1423; 26 U.S.C. 5741)

§ 40.186 Record in support of transfers in bond.

Every manufacturer of tobacco products shall keep a supporting record of tobacco products transferred in bond to or received in bond from other factories, and shall make the entries therein at the time of each receipt or removal of such products. Such supporting records shall show the date of receipt or removal, the name of the manufacturer and address of the factory from which received or to which removed or the permit number of such factory, and the kind and quantity of tobacco products. Where the manufacturer keeps, at the factory, copies of invoices or other commercial records containing the information required as to each receipt and removal, in such orderly manner that the information may be readily ascertained therefrom, such copies will be considered the supporting record required by this section.

(Approved by the Office of Management and Budget under control number 1512–0358)

(72 Stat. 1423, as amended; 26 U.S.C. 5741)

[T.D. 6871, 31 FR 35, Jan. 4, 1966. Redesignated at 40 FR 16835, Apr. 15, 1975, and amended by T.D. ATF–172, 49 FR 14943, Apr. 16, 1984; T.D. ATF–232, 51 FR 28081, Aug. 5, 1986; T.D. ATF–243, 51 FR 43194, Dec. 1, 1986]

§ 40.187 Record of sales prices of large cigars.

Every manufacturer of tobacco products who removes large cigars from the factory shall keep such records as are necessary to establish and verify the price for which the cigars are sold, in accordance with § 40.22. The record shall be a continuing one of each brand and size of cigar so that the sale price on which the tax is based may be readily ascertained.

[T.D. ATF–307, 55 FR 52743, Dec. 21, 1990. Redesignated and amended by T.D. ATF–420, 64 FR 71941, Dec. 22, 1999; T.D. ATF–420, 65 FR 1676, Jan. 11, 2000]

INVENTORIES AND REPORTS

§ 40.201 Inventories.

Every manufacturer of tobacco products shall make true and accurate inventories on Form 5210.9, which inventories shall include all tobacco products and processed tobacco on hand required to be accounted for in the records kept under this part. The manufacturer shall make such an inventory at the time of commencing business, which shall be the effective date of the permit issued upon original qualification under this part; at the time of transferring ownership; at the time of changing the location of his factory; at the time of concluding business; and at such other time as any appropriate TTB officer may require. Each inventory shall be prepared in duplicate, and shall be subject to verification by an appropriate TTB officer. The original of each such inventory shall be submitted to the appropriate TTB officer, and the duplicate shall be retained by the manufacturer.

(Approved by the Office of Management and Budget under control number 1512–0358)

(72 Stat. 1422, 1423, as amended; 26 U.S.C. 5721, 5741)

[T.D. 6871, 31 FR 35, Jan. 4, 1966. Redesignated at 40 FR 16835, Apr. 15, 1975, and amended by T.D. ATF–172, 49 FR 14943, Apr. 16, 1984; T.D. ATF–232, 51 FR 28081, Aug. 5, 1986; T.D. ATF–243, 51 FR 43194, Dec. 1, 1986; T.D. ATF–424, 64 FR 71931, Dec. 22, 1999; T.D. TTB–78, 74 FR 29409, June 22, 2009; T.D. TTB–91, 76 FR 5480, Feb. 1, 2011]

§ 40.202 Reports.

(a) *Monthly report.* Every manufacturer of tobacco products shall make a report on Form 5210.5, in duplicate, for each month and for any portion of a month during which he engages in such business. Such report shall be made regardless of whether any operations or transactions occurred during the month or portion of a month covered therein. The report for a month or portion of a month in which business is commenced or is concluded shall be conspicuously marked "Commencing Report" or "Concluding Report," respectively. The original of the report shall be submitted to the appropriate TTB officer not later than the 20th day of the month succeeding the month covered therein, and the duplicate shall be retained by the manufacturer. Each report shall show, for the period covered, the total quantity of tobacco products:

(1) Manufactured,
(2) Received in bond,
(3) Received by return to bond,

(4) Disclosed by inventory as an overage,

(5) Removed subject to tax,

(6) Removed in bond,

(7) Otherwise disposed of without determination of tax,

(8) Disclosed by inventory as a shortage, and

(9) On hand, in bond, beginning of and end of month.

(b) *Report of processed tobacco.* In addition to complying with the requirements set forth in this part relating to the reporting of tobacco products, a manufacturer of tobacco products that is required to obtain authorization to engage in another business within the factory under §§ 40.47(b) and 40.72(b) must also make and submit reports as prescribed in § 40.522.

(Approved by the Office of Management and Budget under control number 1513–0033)

(Sec. 202, Pub. L. 85–859, 72 Stat. 1422 (26 U.S.C. 5722))

[T.D. 6871, 31 FR 36, Jan. 4, 1966. Redesignated at 40 FR 16835, Apr. 15, 1975, and amended by T.D. ATF–40, 42 FR 5001, Jan. 26, 1977; T.D. ATF–232, 51 FR 28081, Aug. 5, 1986; T.D. ATF–243, 51 FR 43194, Dec. 1, 1986; T.D. ATF–307, 55 FR 52743, Dec. 21, 1990; T.D. ATF–424, 64 FR 71931, Dec. 22, 1999; T.D. TTB–78, 74 FR 29409, June 22, 2009; T.D. TTB–104, 77 FR 37302, June 21, 2012]

PACKAGES

§ 40.211 Package.

All tobacco products shall, before removal subject to tax, be put up by the manufacturer in packages which shall be of such construction as will securely contain the products therein and maintain the mark and the notice thereon as required by this part. No package of tobacco products shall have contained therein, attached thereto, or stamped, marked, written, or printed thereon (a) any certificate, coupon, or other device purporting to be or to represent a ticket, chance, share, or an interest in, or dependent on, the event of a lottery, (b) any indecent or immoral picture, print, or representation, or (c) any statement or indication that United States tax has been paid. No person may purchase, receive, possess (except for personal consumption), offer for sale, or sell or otherwise dispose of, after removal, any tobacco products that are not put up in packages bearing the marks, labels, and notices, as required under this part.

(26 U.S.C. 5723 and 5751)

[T.D. 6871, 31 FR 36, Jan. 4, 1966. Redesignated at 40 FR 16835, Apr. 15, 1975, and amended by T.D. ATF–232, 51 FR 28081, Aug. 5, 1986 T.D. ATF–243, 51 FR 43194, Dec. 1, 1986; T.D. TTB–78, 74 FR 29409, June 22, 2009]

§ 40.212 Mark.

Every package of tobacco products packaged in a domestic factory shall, before removal subject to tax, have adequately imprinted thereon, or on a label securely affixed thereto, a mark as specified in this section. The mark may consist of the name of the manufacturer removing the product subject to tax and the location (by city and State) of the factory from which the products are to be so removed, or may consist of the permit number of the factory from which the products are to be so removed. (Any trade name of the manufacturer approved as provided in § 40.65 may be used in the mark as the name of the manufacturer.) As an alternative, where tobacco products are packaged and removed subject to tax by the same manufacturer, either at the same or different factories, the mark may consist of the name of such manufacturer if the factory where packaged is identified on or in the package by a means approved by the appropriate TTB officer. Before using the alternative, the manufacturer shall notify the appropriate TTB officer in writing of the name to be used as the name of the manufacturer and the means to be used for identifying the factory where packaged. If approved by him the appropriate TTB officer shall return approved copies of the notice to the manufacturer. A copy of the approved notice shall be retained as part of the factory records at each of the factories operated by the manufacturer.

(72 Stat. 1422; 26 U.S.C. 5723)

[T.D. 6871, 31 FR 36, Jan. 4, 1966. Redesignated at 40 FR 16835, Apr. 15, 1975; T.D. ATF–232, 51 FR 28081, Aug. 5, 1986; T.D. ATF–243, 52 FR 43194, Dec. 1, 1986]

§40.213 Tobacco products labeled for export.

Tobacco products labeled for export are ineligible for removal from the factory for distribution into the U.S. domestic market. Tobacco products labeled for export may not be sold, transferred, or delivered into the U.S. domestic market by a manufacturer of tobacco products unless the manufacturer repackages the tobacco product by removing it from its original package bearing the export marks and placing it into a new package. The new package, mark, and notice must conform to the requirements of this subpart.

[78 FR 38567, June 27, 2013]

EFFECTIVE DATE NOTE: At 78 FR 38567, June 27, 2013, §40.213 was revised, effective Aug. 26, 2013 through Aug. 26, 2016.

§40.214 Notice for cigars.

Before removal subject to tax, every package of cigars shall have adequately imprinted on it, or on a label securely affixed to it—

(a) The designation "cigars";

(b) The quantity of cigars contained in the package; and

(c) For small cigars, the classification of the product for tax purposes (i.e., either "small" or "little").

(Sec. 202, Pub. L. 85–859, 72 Stat. 1422 (26 U.S.C. 5723))

[T.D. ATF–80, 46 FR 18310, Mar. 24, 1981]

§40.215 Notice for cigarettes.

Every package of cigarettes shall, before removal subject to tax, have adequately imprinted thereon, or on a label securely affixed thereto, the designation "cigarettes", the quantity of such product contained therein, and the classification for tax purposes, i.e., for small cigarettes, either "small" or "Class A", and for large cigarettes, either "large" or "Class B".

(72 Stat. 1422; 26 U.S.C. 5723)

§40.216 Notice for smokeless tobacco.

(a) *Product designation.* Every package of chewing tobacco or snuff shall, before removal subject to tax, have adequately imprinted thereon, or on a label securely affixed thereto, the designation "chewing tobacco" or "snuff." As an alternative, packages of chewing tobacco may be designated "Tax Class C", and packages of snuff may be designated "Tax Class M".

(b) *Product weight.* Every package of chewing tobacco or snuff shall, before removal subject to tax, have adequately imprinted thereon, or on a label securely affixed thereto, a clear statement of the actual pounds and ounces of the product contained therein. As an alternative, the shipping cases containing packages of chewing tobacco or snuff may, before removal, have adequately imprinted thereon, or on a label securely affixed thereto, a clear statement, in pounds and ounces, of the total weight of the product, the tax class of the product, and the total number of the packages of product contained therein.

(Approved by the Office of Management and Budget under control number 1512–0502)

(Sec. 202, Pub. L. 85–859, 72 Stat. 1422 (26 U.S.C. 5723))

[T.D. ATF–243, 51 FR 43194, Dec. 1, 1986, as amended by T.D. ATF–446, 66 FR 16602, Mar. 27, 2001]

§40.216a Notice for pipe tobacco.

(a) *Product designation.* Every package of pipe tobacco shall, before removal subject to tax, have adequately imprinted thereon, or on a label securely affixed thereto, the designation "pipe tobacco."

(b) *Product weight.* Every package of pipe tobacco shall, before removal subject to tax, have adequately imprinted thereon, or on a label securely affixed thereto, a clear statement of the actual pounds and ounces of the product contained therein.

[T.D. ATF–289, 54 FR 48840, Nov. 27, 1989. Redesignated at T.D. ATF–424, 64 FR 71931, Dec. 22, 1999; T.D. TTB–78, 74 FR 29410, June 22, 2009]

§40.216b Notice for roll-your-own tobacco.

(a) *Product designation.* Every package of roll-your-own tobacco, before removal subject to tax, must have adequately imprinted on it, or on a label securely affixed to it, the applicable designation "roll-your-own tobacco", "cigarette tobacco", "cigar tobacco", "cigarette wrapper", or "cigar wrapper".

(b) *Product weight.* Before removal subject to tax, roll-your-own tobacco must have a clear statement of the actual weight in pounds and ounces of the product in the package. This statement must be adequately imprinted on, or on a label securely affixed to, the package.

(Approved by the Office of Management and Budget under control number 1513–0091)

[T.D. ATF–429, 65 FR 57547, Sept. 25, 2000, as amended by T.D. TTB–78, 74 FR 29410, June 22, 2009]

§ 40.216c Package use-up rule.

(a) During the period from June 22, 2009, through March 23, 2010, a manufacturer of tobacco products may remove packages of pipe tobacco or roll-your-own tobacco that do not meet the requirements of § 40.216a(a) or § 40.216b(a), provided that such packages bear the designation "Tax Class L" (to designate pipe tobacco) or "Tax Class J" (to designate roll-your-own tobacco) and were in use prior to June 22, 2009.

(b) During the period from June 22, 2009, through March 23, 2010, a manufacturer may remove roll-your-own tobacco for which the applicable designation is "cigar tobacco," "cigarette wrapper," or "cigar wrapper" even if the packages of such products do not meet the requirements of § 40.216b.

[T.D. TTB–81, 74 FR 48654, Sept. 24, 2009]

§ 40.217 Repackaging.

Where a manufacturer of tobacco products desires to repackage, outside the factory, tobacco products on which the tax has been determined or which were removed for a tax-exempt purpose or transferred in bond to an export warehouse, or to repackage tax determined tobacco products in the factory, he shall make application for authorization to do so, in duplicate, to the appropriate TTB officer. The application shall set forth the location and the number of packages, a description of the contents, the tax status of the tobacco products the reason for wanting to repackage the products (e.g., packages soiled, damaged, or otherwise in a condition making the product unsalable), and a description of the package to be used for repackaging. The packages to be used must comply with the package, mark, and notice provisions of this chapter applicable to the tobacco products being repackaged. The operations authorized under this section are limited solely to repackaging for good cause by a manufacturer, pursuant to an approved application, of the specified tobacco products in the described packages, and do not include any manufacturing processes. If the appropriate TTB officer approves the application, he may assign an appropriate TTB officer to supervise the repackaging or he may authorize the manufacturer to repackage the products without supervision by so stating on a copy of the application returned to the manufacturer. Where the manufacturer is authorized to repackage he shall record the date of repackaging on the approved application and retain it as part of his records.

(72 Stat. 1422; 26 U.S.C. 5723)

[T.D. 6871, 31 FR 36, Jan. 4, 1966. Redesignated at 40 FR 16835, Apr. 15, 1975, and amended by T.D. ATF–232, 51 FR 28082, Aug. 5, 1986; T.D. ATF–243, 51 FR 43194, Dec. 1, 1986]

Exemption From Taxes on Tobacco Products

§ 40.231 Consumption by employees.

A manufacturer of tobacco products may gratuitously furnish tobacco products, without determination and payment of tax, for personal consumption by employees in the factory in such quantities as desired. Each employee may also be gratuitously furnished by the manufacturer, for off-factory personal consumption, not more than 5 large cigars or cigarettes, 20 small cigars or cigarettes, or one retail package of chewing tobacco, snuff, pipe tobacco or roll-your-own tobacco, or a proportionate quantity of each, without determination and payment of tax, on each day the employee is at work. For the purposes of this section, the term "employee" shall mean those persons whose duties require their presence in the factory or whose duties relate to the manufacture, distribution, or sale of tobacco products and who receive compensation from the manufacturer, or a parent, subsidiary, or auxiliary company or corporation of the manufacturer. Such product furnished for off-factory consumption shall be furnished to the employee within the factory and taken from the factory by the employee on the day for which furnished. Employees shall not sell, offer for sale, or give away products so furnished.

[T.D. ATF–232, 51 FR 28082, Aug. 5, 1986; T.D. ATF–243, 51 FR 43194, Dec. 1, 1986, as amended by T.D. ATF–289, 54 FR 48840, Nov. 27, 1989; T.D. ATF–424, 64 FR 71931, Dec. 22, 1999; T.D. TTB–91, 76 FR 5480, Feb. 1, 2011]

§40.232 Experimental purposes.

A manufacturer of tobacco products may use tobacco products for experimental purposes without determination and payment of tax as set forth in this section.

(a) *What are experimental purposes?* Experimental purposes are operations or tests carried out under controlled conditions to discover an unknown scientific principle or fact, to gather or confirm data about a known scientific principle or fact, or to test manufacturing, packaging, or other such equipment. Examples of uses for experimental purposes are:

(1) Use by manufacturers to determine scientific facts relating to tobacco products, such as their chemical content;

(2) Use by producers of packaging machines to test the operation of such machines; and

(3) Use by laboratories, hospitals, medical centers, institutes, colleges, or universities, for scientific, technical, or medical research.

(b) *What purposes are not experimental?* The uses of tobacco products outside the factory premises for advertising or consumer testing or as salespersons' or customers' samples are not experimental purposes.

(c) *Use in factory.* A manufacturer of tobacco products may use tobacco products without determination and payment of tax for experimental purposes in a factory.

(d) *Use outside factory.* A manufacturer may remove tobacco products in bond for experimental purposes outside a factory. When tobacco products are shipped for experimental purposes outside the factory, the proprietor of the factory remains liable for the taxes imposed by 26 U.S.C. 5701 until the occurrence of one of the following events:

(1) The tobacco products are returned to the premises of the factory from which they were shipped; or

(2) The tobacco products are destroyed during or after their use for experimental purposes.

(e) *Record of use.* In addition to the records prescribed by §40.183, a manufacturer who removes tobacco products in bond for experimental purposes outside a factory must prepare and maintain a record containing the following information:

(1) Name and address of the consignee;

(2) Kind and quantity of tobacco products removed;

(3) Description of packaging, if any, of the tobacco products removed;

(4) Description of how and when the consignee will use the tobacco products; and

(5) Disposition of any remaining tobacco products after the consignee's use.

(Approved by the Office of Management and Budget under Control Number 1512–0562)

(72 Stat. 1418, as amended; 26 U.S.C. 5704)

[T.D. ATF–478, 67 FR 19333, Apr. 19, 2002]

§40.233 Transfer in bond.

A manufacturer of tobacco products may transfer tobacco products in bond, to the factory of any manufacturer of tobacco products. The transfer of tobacco products in bond to the premises of an export warehouse proprietor shall be in accordance with the provisions of part 44 of this chapter. However, tobacco products are eligible for transfer in bond to a manufacturer of tobacco products or to an export warehouse only if they bear the required marks, labels, and notices.

(72 Stat. 1418, as amended; 26 U.S.C. 5704)

[T.D. 6871, 31 FR 37, Jan. 4, 1966. Redesignated at 40 FR 16835, Apr. 15, 1975, and amended by T.D. ATF–232, 51 FR 28082, Aug. 5, 1986; T.D. ATF–243, 51 FR 43194, Dec. 1, 1986; T.D. ATF–421, 64 FR 71924, Dec. 22, 1999; 78 FR 38567, June 27, 2013]

EFFECTIVE DATE NOTE: At 78 FR 38567, June 27, 2013, § 40.233 was amended by revising the last sentence, effective Aug. 26, 2013 through Aug. 26, 2016.

§ 40.234 Removal for use of the United States.

The removal of tobacco products in bond, for use of the United States, shall be in accordance with the provisions of part 45 of this chapter.

(72 Stat. 1418, as amended; 26 U.S.C. 5704)

[T.D. 6871, 31 FR 37, Jan. 4, 1966. Redesignated at 40 FR 16835, Apr. 15, 1975; T.D. ATF–232, 51 FR 28082, Aug. 5, 1986; T.D. ATF–243, 51 FR 43194, Dec. 1, 1986; T.D. ATF–469, 66 FR 56758, Nov. 13, 2001]

§ 40.235 Removal for export purposes.

The removal of tobacco products in bond, for shipment to a foreign country, Puerto Rico, the Virgin Islands, or a possession of the United States, or for consumption beyond the jurisdiction of the internal revenue laws of the United States, shall be in accordance with the provisions of part 44 of this chapter.

(72 Stat. 1418, as amended; 26 U.S.C. 5704)

[T.D. 6871, 31 FR 37, Jan. 4, 1966. Redesignated at 40 FR 16835, Apr. 15, 1975, and amended by T.D. ATF–232, 51 FR 28082, Aug. 5, 1986; T.D. ATF–243, 51 FR 43194, Dec. 1, 1986]

§ 40.236 Release from customs custody.

The release of tobacco products from customs custody, in bond, for transfer to the premises of a tobacco products factory, shall be in accordance with the provisions of part 41 of this chapter.

(72 Stat. 1418, as amended; 26 U.S.C. 5704)

[T.D. 6871, 31 FR 37, Jan. 4, 1966. Redesignated at 40 FR 16835, Apr. 15, 1975, and amended by T.D. ATF–232, 51 FR 28082, Aug. 5, 1986; T.D. ATF–243, 51 FR 43194, Dec. 1, 1986; T.D. TTB–16, 69 FR 52423, Aug. 26, 2004]

OTHER PROVISIONS RELATING TO OPERATIONS

§ 40.251 Emergency storage.

In cases of emergency, the appropriate TTB officer may authorize, for a stated period, the temporary storage of tobacco products at a place outside the factory without the application for amended permit required under § 40.114, where such action will not hinder the effective administration of this part, is not contrary to law, and will not jeopardize the revenue. Application for authorization to so store tobacco products shall be submitted to the appropriate TTB officer by letter, in duplicate. All tobacco products so stored outside the factory shall be accounted for in the records and reports required under §§ 40.183 and 40.202 the same as products within the factory.

(72 Stat. 1422, 1423, as amended; 26 U.S.C. 5722, 5741)

[T.D. 6871, 31 FR 37, Jan. 4, 1966. Redesignated at 40 FR 16835, Apr. 15, 1975; T.D. ATF–232, 51 FR 28082, Aug. 5, 1986; T.D. ATF–243, 51 FR 43194, Dec. 1, 1986]

§ 40.252 Reduction of tobacco products to materials.

A manufacturer may reduce tobacco products to materials without supervision. If the tobacco products have been entered in the factory record as manufactured or received, an entry shall be made in such record of the quantity of pipe tobacco or roll-your-own tobacco and the kind and quantity of cigars, cigarettes, and smokeless tobacco reduced to materials and of the quantity of tobacco resulting from the reduction. Where the manufacturer intends to file claims for credit allowance, or refund of tax on such tobacco products, he shall comply with the provisions of §§ 40.311 and 40.313.

[T.D. ATF–232, 51 FR 28082, Aug. 5, 1986; T.D. ATF–243, 51 FR 43194, Dec. 1, 1986, as amended by T.D. ATF–289, 54 FR 48840, Nov. 27, 1989; T.D. ATF–424, 64 FR 71931, Dec. 22, 1999]

§ 40.253 Destruction.

When a manufacturer of tobacco products desires to destroy tobacco products which have been entered in the factory record as manufactured or received, without salvaging the tobacco, he shall notify the appropriate TTB officer by letter, in duplicate, of the kind and quantity of tobacco products to be destroyed, the intended method of destruction, and the date on which he desires to destroy such products. The appropriate TTB officer may assign an appropriate TTB officer to supervise destruction of the tobacco products or he may authorize the manufacturer to destroy such products without supervision by so stating on a copy of the manufacturer's notice returned to the manufacturer. When so authorized by the appropriate TTB officer, the manufacturer shall destroy the tobacco products by burning completely or by rendering them unfit for consumption. Upon completion of the destruction, the manufacturer shall make an entry of such destruction in his factory record, and where destruction without supervision is authorized, shall record the date and method of destruction on the notice returned to him by the appropriate TTB officer, which notice the manufacturer shall retain. Where the manufacturer intends to file claim for credit, allowance, or refund of tax on such products he shall comply with the provisions of §§40.311 and 40.313.

(72 Stat. 1423, as amended; 26 U.S.C. 5741)

[T.D. 6871, 31 FR 37, Jan. 4, 1966. Redesignated at 40 FR 16835, Apr. 15, 1975, and amended by T.D. ATF–232, 51 FR 28082, Aug. 5, 1986; T.D. ATF–243, 51 FR 43194, Dec. 1, 1986]

§40.254 Receipt into factory.

A manufacturer of tobacco products may receive in bond into his factory tobacco products and may also receive into his factory tobacco products on which the tax has been determined (including products on which the tax has been paid). Cigars and cigarettes on which the tax has been determined which are so received shall be segregated and identified as products on which the tax has been determined. If tax determined products received into the factory are so handled that they cannot be identified both physically and in the records as tax determined products they shall be accounted for as returned to bond and upon subsequent removal shall be tax determined. Where returned tax determined tobacco products are to be repackaged without being returned to bond the manufacturer shall make application for authorization to do so to the appropriate TTB officer in accordance with §40.217. Where the manufacturer intends to file claim for credit, allowance, or refund of tax on tax determined products he shall comply with the provisions of §§40.311 and 40.313.

[T.D. 6871, 31 FR 37, Jan. 4, 1966. Redesignated at 40 FR 16835, Apr. 15, 1975, and amended by T.D. ATF–232, 51 FR 28082, Aug. 5, 1986; T.D. ATF–243, 52 FR 43194, Dec. 1, 1986]

§40.255 Shortages and overages in inventory.

Whenever a manufacturer of tobacco products makes a physical inventory of packaged tobacco products in bond, either as part of normal operations or when required by an appropriate TTB officer, and such inventory discloses a shortage or overage in such products by kind as recorded and reported (*i.e.*, small cigars, large cigars, chewing tobacco, snuff, pipe tobacco, or roll-your-own tobacco), the manufacturer shall enter such shortage or overage in the records required by §40.183. Shortages or overages in inventories made at different times may not be used to offset each other, but shall be recorded and reported separately. Unless the manufacturer establishes that a shortage was not caused by a removal subject to the tax the manufacturer shall determine the tax on any shortage, make an adjustment in Schedule A of his next semimonthly tax return and pay the tax thereon. If, after paying the tax on a shortage, the manufacturer satisfactorily establishes that the shortage was not caused by a removal subject to tax, then such payment would be an overpayment of tax which the manufacturer may recover as provided in §40.286. Where the manufacturer can establish prior to paying the tax on a shortage, that the shortage was not the result of a removal subject to tax he shall submit an explanation of such shortage with his report for the month in which the shortage was disclosed and, if appropriate, he may file claim for remission of tax liability as provided in §40.287. When an overage is disclosed which the manufacturer can explain, he shall include such explanation in his monthly report and refund of any overpayment may be recovered as provided in §40.286. Whenever a physical inventory discloses a shortage or overage of tobacco products which have not been packaged the manufacturer shall appropriately enter such shortage or overage in his records and shall, at the time required by the appropriate TTB officer, furnish an explanation in the form of a claim for remission of tax liability as provided in § 40.287. The manufacturer shall pay the tax on any shortage or portion thereof for which he is unable to furnish an explanation acceptable to the appropriate TTB officer.

[T.D. ATF–232, 51 FR 28082, Aug. 5, 1986; T.D. ATF–243, 51 FR 43194, Dec. 1, 1986, as amended by T.D. ATF–289, 54 FR 48840, Nov. 27, 1989; T.D. ATF–424, 64 FR 71931, Dec. 22, 1999]

§ 40.256 Minimum manufacturing and activity requirements.

The minimum manufacturing and activity requirement prescribed in § 40.61(c) of this part is a continuing condition of a manufacturer's permit, that is, a permit to manufacture tobacco products is conditioned upon a person's principal business activity being the manufacture of tobacco products. A permit may be suspended, and subsequently revoked, if the person's principal business activity under such permit is to receive or transfer tobacco products in bond, or if the person has no activity under such permit for a period of one year. As a minimum activity requirement, the quantity of tobacco products manufactured under the permit must be equivalent to, or exceed, the quantity transferred or received in bond under the permit.

[T.D. TTB–78, 74 FR 29410, June 22, 2009, as amended by T.D. TTB–80, 74 FR 37552, July 29, 2009; T.D. TTB–104, 77 FR 37303, June 21, 2012]

§ 40.257 Processed tobacco.

A manufacturer of tobacco products may be required to obtain authorization from the appropriate TTB officer with regard to the activities involving processed tobacco. See § 40.72. Such manufacturers also must maintain records and may be required to submit reports regarding such activities. See §§ 40.182 and 40.202.

[T.D. TTB–78, 74 FR 29410, June 22, 2009]

Subpart I—Claims by Manufacturers

GENERAL

§ 40.281 Abatement of assessment.

A claim for abatement of the unpaid portion of the assessment of any tax on tobacco products or any liability in respect thereof, may be allowed to the extent that such assessment is excessive in amount, is assessed after expiration of the applicable period of limitation, or is erroneously or illegally assessed. Any claim under this section shall be prepared on TTB F 5620.8, in duplicate, and shall set forth the particulars under which the claim is filed. The original of the claim, accompanied by such evidence as is necessary to establish to the satisfaction of the appropriate TTB officer that the claim is valid, shall be filed with the appropriate TTB officer, and the duplicate of the claim shall be retained by the manufacturer.

(68A Stat. 792; 26 U.S.C. 6404)

[T.D. 6871, 31 FR 38, Jan. 4, 1966. Redesignated at 40 FR 16835, Apr. 15, 1975, and amended by T.D. ATF–232, 51 FR 28083, Aug. 5, 1986; T.D. ATF–243, 51 FR 43194, Dec. 1, 1986; T.D. ATF–251, 52 FR 19340, May 22, 1987]

§ 40.282 Allowance of tax.

Relief from the payment of tax on tobacco products may be extended to a manufacturer by allowance of the tax where the tobacco products after removal from the factory upon determination of tax and prior to the payment of such tax, are lost (otherwise than by theft) or destroyed, by fire, casualty, or act of God, while in the possession or ownership of the manufacturer who removed such products, or are withdrawn by him from the market. Any claim for allowance under this section shall be filed on TTB F 5620.8, in duplicate, with the appropriate TTB officer, and shall show the date the tobacco products were removed from the factory. A claim relating to products lost or destroyed shall be supported as prescribed in § 40.301. In the case of a claim relating to tobacco products withdrawn from the market the schedule prescribed in § 40.311 shall be filed with the appropriate TTB officer. The manufacturer may not anticipate allowance of his claim by making the adjusting entry in a tax return pending consideration and action on the claim. Tobacco products to which such a claim relates must be shown as removed on determination of tax in the return covering the period during which such products were so removed. Upon action on the claim by the appropriate TTB officer he will return the copy of TTB F 5620.8 to the manufacturer as notice of such action, which copy, with the copy of any verified supporting schedules, shall be retained by the manufacturer. When such notification of allowance of the claim or any part thereof is received prior to the time the return covering the tax on the tobacco products to which the claim relates is to be filed, the manufacturer may make an adjusting entry and explanatory statement in that tax return. Where the notice of allowance is received after the filing of the return and taxpayment of the tobacco products to which the claim relates, the manufacturer may make an adjusting entry and explanatory statement in the next tax return(s) to the extent necessary to take credit in the amount of the allowance.

(72 Stat. 1419, as amended; 26 U.S.C. 5705)

[T.D. 6961, 33 FR 9488, June 28, 1968. Redesignated at 40 FR 16835, Apr. 15, 1975, and amended by T.D. ATF-232, 51 FR 28083, Aug. 5, 1986; T.D. ATF-243, 51 FR 43194, Dec. 1, 1986]

§ 40.283 Credit or refund of tax.

The taxes paid on tobacco products may be credited or refunded (without interest) to a manufacturer on proof satisfactory to the appropriate TTB officer that the claimant manufacturer paid the tax on tobacco products lost (otherwise than by theft) or destroyed, by fire, casualty, or act of God, while in the possession or ownership of such manufacturer, or withdrawn by him from the market. Any claim for credit or refund under this section shall be prepared on TTB F 5620.8, in duplicate. Claims shall include a statement that the tax imposed on tobacco products by 26 U.S.C. 7652 or chapter 52, was paid in respect to the tobacco products covered by the claim, and that the products were lost, destroyed, or withdrawn from the market within 6 months preceding the date the claim is filed. A claim for credit or refund relating to products lost or destroyed shall be supported as prescribed in § 40.301, and a claim relating to products withdrawn from the market shall be accompanied by a schedule prepared and verified as prescribed in §§ 40.311 and 40.313. The original and one copy of TTB F 5620.8, claim for credit, or the original of TTB F 5620.8, claim for refund, shall be filed with the appropriate TTB officer. Upon action by the appropriate TTB officer on a claim for credit he will return the copy of TTB F 5620.8 to the manufacturer as notification of allowance or disallowance of the claim or any part thereof, which copy, with the copy of any verified supporting schedules, shall be retained by the manufacturer. When the manufacturer is notified of allowance of the claim for credit or any part thereof he shall make an adjusting entry and explanatory statement in the next tax return(s) to the extent necessary to take credit in the amount of the allowance. Prior to consideration and action on his claim the manufacturer may not anticipate allowance of his claim by taking credit in his tax return. The duplicate of a claim for refund, with the copy of any verified supporting schedules, shall be retained by the manufacturer.

(Sec. 201, Pub. L. 85-859, 72 Stat. 1419)

[T.D. 6961, 33 FR 9489, June 28, 1968. Redesignated at 40 FR 16835, Apr. 15, 1975, and amended by T.D. ATF-48, 44 FR 55855, Sept. 28, 1979; T.D. ATF-219, 50 FR 51389, Dec. 17, 1985; T.D. ATF-232, 51 FR 28083, Aug. 5, 1986; T.D. ATF-243, 51 FR 43194, Dec. 1, 1986; T.D. ATF-251, 52 FR 19340, May 22, 1987]

§ 40.284 Remission of tax liability.

Remission of the tax liability on tobacco products may be extended to the manufacturer liable for the tax where tobacco products in bond are lost (otherwise than by theft) or destroyed, by fire, casualty, or act of God, while in the possession or ownership of such manufacturer. Where tobacco products are so lost or destroyed the manufacturer shall report promptly such fact, and the circumstances, to the appropriate TTB officer. If the manufacturer wishes to be relieved of the tax liability thereon he shall also prepare a claim on TTB F 5620.8, in duplicate, setting forth the nature, date, place, and extent of the loss or destruction. Both copies of the claim, accompanied by such evidence as is necessary to establish to the satisfaction of the appropriate TTB officer that the claim is valid, shall be filed with the appropriate TTB officer. Upon action on the claim by the appropriate TTB officer he will return the copy of TTB F 5620.8 to the manufacturer as notice of such action, which copy shall be retained by the manufacturer.

(72 Stat. 1419, as amended; 26 U.S.C. 5705)

[T.D. 6961, 33 FR 9489, June 28, 1968. Redesignated at 40 FR 16835, Apr. 15, 1975, and amended by T.D. ATF–232, 51 FR 28083, Aug. 5, 1986; T.D. ATF–243, 51 FR 43194, Dec. 1, 1986]

§40.285 [Reserved]

§40.286 Refund of overpayment.

Where an error in computation of the quantity of tobacco products or in computation of the amount of tax due results in an overpayment and such error is specifically identified and supported by records, the manufacturer may file claim for refund or may make an adjustment in his semimonthly tax return as provided in §40.164. (Section 6511, 26 U.S.C., provides that, in most cases, any adjustment of claim for refund of an overpayment of tax on tobacco products must be made or filed within three years after the tax is paid.) If the manufacturer elects to file a claim for refund of an overpayment resulting from such a computational error, he shall do so on TTB F 5620.8, in duplicate. The original shall be filed with the appropriate TTB officer, and the duplicate retained by the manufacturer. Where an overpayment of tax on tobacco products results from other than a computational error any claim for refund or credit shall be made in accordance with subpart A of part 46 of this chapter.

(68A Stat. 791, 72 Stat. 9; 26 U.S.C. 6402, 6423)

[T.D. 6871, 31 FR 39, Jan. 4, 1966. Redesignated at 40 FR 16835, Apr. 15, 1975, and amended by T.D. ATF–48, 44 FR 55855, Sept. 28, 1979; T.D. ATF–232, 51 FR 28083, Aug. 5, 1986; T.D. ATF–243, 51 FR 43194, Dec. 1, 1986; T.D. ATF–251, 52 FR 19340, May 22, 1987; T.D. ATF–457, 66 FR 32220, June 14, 2001]

§40.287 Remission of tax liability on shortage.

Whenever a manufacturer of tobacco products desires to submit a claim for remission of tax liability on shortages of tobacco products in bond, disclosed by physical inventory as set forth in §40.255, he shall prepare such claim on TTB F 5620.8, in duplicate. Both copies of the claim shall be filed with the appropriate TTB officer. The claim shall specify the quantities of tobacco products on which claim is made and the tax liability in respect thereof, and shall set forth the circumstances surrounding the shortage and the reason the manufacturer believes tax is not due or payable. The appropriate TTB officer will, after such investigation as he deems appropriate, allow the claim to the extent he is satisfied the shortage was due to operating losses such as damage during grading, sorting, or packaging, and was not caused by theft or other unlawful or improper removal. Upon action on the claim by the appropriate TTB officer he will return the copy of TTB F 5620.8 to the manufacturer as notice of such action, which copy shall be retained by the manufacturer.

(72 Stat. 1414, as amended, 1417, 1419, as amended; 26 U.S.C. 5701, 5703, 5705)

[T.D. 6961, 33 FR 9489, June 28, 1968. Redesignated at 40 FR 16835, Apr. 15, 1975, and amended by T.D. ATF–232, 51 FR 28083, Aug. 5, 1986; T.D. ATF–243, 51 FR 43194, Dec. 1, 1986]

TOBACCO PRODUCTS LOST OR DESTROYED

§40.301 Action by claimant.

Where tobacco products are lost (otherwise than by theft) or destroyed, by fire, casualty, or act of God, and the manufacturer desires to file a claim for the tax on such products under the provisions of § 40.282 or § 40.283, he shall indicate on the claim the nature, date, place, and extent of such loss or destruction. The claim shall be accompanied by such evidence as is necessary to establish to the satisfaction of the appropriate TTB officer that the claim is valid.

(72 Stat. 1419, as amended; 26 U.S.C. 5705)

[T.D. 6871, 31 FR 39, Jan. 4, 1966. Redesignated at 40 FR 16835, Apr. 15, 1975, and amended by T.D. ATF–232, 51 FR 28083, Aug. 5, 1986; T.D. ATF–243, 52 FR 43194, Dec. 1, 1986]

TOBACCO PRODUCTS WITHDRAWN FROM THE MARKET

§ 40.311 Action by claimant.

(a) *General.* Where tobacco products are withdrawn from the market and the manufacturer desires to file claim under the provisions of § 40.282 or § 40.283, he shall assemble the products in or adjacent to a factory if they are to be returned to bond or at any suitable place if they are to be destroyed or reduced to materials. The manufacturer shall group the products according to the rates of tax applicable to the products, and shall prepare a schedule of the products, on TTB Form 5200.7, in triplicate. All copies of the schedule shall be forwarded to the appropriate TTB officer.

(b) *Large cigars.* Refund or credit of tax on large cigars withdrawn from the market is limited to the lowest tax paid on that brand and size of cigar during the required record retention period (see § 40.185), except where the manufacturer establishes that a greater amount was actually paid. For each claim involving large cigars withdrawn from the market, the manufacturer must include a certification on either Form 5200.7 or TTB F 5620.8 to read as follows:

The amounts claimed relating to large cigars are based on the lowest sale price applicable to the cigars during the required record retention period, except where specific documentation is submitted with the claim to establish that any greater amount of tax claimed was actually paid.

(See 26 U.S.C. 5705)

[T.D. ATF–80, 46 FR 18310, Mar. 24, 1981, as amended by T.D. ATF–232, 51 FR 28083, Aug. 5, 1986; T.D. ATF–243, 51 FR 43194, Dec. 1, 1986; T.D. ATF–251, 52 FR 19340, May 22, 1987; T.D. ATF–307, 55 FR 52743, Dec. 21, 1990; T.D. ATF–424, 64 FR 71932, Dec. 22, 1999; T.D. ATF–420, 64 FR 71941, Dec. 22, 1999]

§ 40.312 Action by the appropriate TTB officer.

Upon receipt of a schedule of tobacco products withdrawn from the market, the appropriate TTB officer may assign a TTB officer to verify the schedule and supervise disposition of the tobacco products (and destruction of the stamps, if any), or he may authorize the manufacturer to dispose of the products (and destroy the stamps, if any) without supervision by so stating on the original and one copy of the schedule returned to the manufacturer.

[T.D. 6871, 31 FR 39, Jan. 4, 1966. Redesignated at 40 FR 16835, Apr. 15, 1975, as amended by T.D. ATF–232, 51 FR 28083, Aug. 5, 1986; T.D. ATF–243, 51 FR 43194, Dec. 1, 1986]

§ 40.313 Disposition of tobacco products and schedule.

When so authorized, as evidenced by the appropriate TTB officer's statement on the schedule, the manufacturer shall dispose of the tobacco products (and destroy the stamps, if any) as specified in the schedule. After the manufacturer has disposed of the products (and destroyed the stamps, if any), he shall execute a certificate on both copies of the schedule returned to him by the appropriate TTB officer, to show the disposition and the date of disposition of the products (and stamps, if any). In connection with a claim for allowance the manufacturer then shall return the original of the schedule to the appropriate TTB officer who authorized such disposition, who will cause such schedule to be associated with the claim, TTB F 5620.8, filed under § 40.282. In connection with a claim for credit or refund the manufacturer shall attach the original of the schedule to his claim for credit, TTB F 5620.8, or claim for refund, TTB F 5620.8, filed under § 40.283. When an appropriate TTB officer is assigned to verify the schedule and supervise disposition of the tobacco products, such officer shall, upon completion of his assignment, execute a certificate on all copies of the schedule to show the disposition and the date of disposition of the products. In connection with a claim for allowance the officer shall return one copy of the schedule to be included in the manufacturers records, and in connection with a claim for credit or refund, the officer shall return the original and one copy of the schedule to the manufacturer, the original of which the manufacturer shall attach to the claim, TTB F 5620.8, filed under § 40.283.

(72 Stat. 1419, as amended; 26 U.S.C. 5705)

[T.D. 6871, 31 FR 39, Jan. 4, 1966. Redesignated at 40 FR 16835, Apr. 15, 1975, and amended by T.D. ATF–232, 51 FR 28083, Aug. 5, 1986; T.D. ATF–243, 51 FR 43194, Dec. 1, 1986; T.D. ATF–251, 52 FR 19340, May 22, 1987]

Subpart J—Suspension and Discontinuance of Operations by Manufacturers

§ 40.331 Discontinuance of operations.

Every manufacturer of tobacco products who desires to discontinue operations under this part shall dispose of all tobacco products on hand, in accordance with this part, and make a concluding inventory and concluding report in accordance with the provisions of § 40.201 and § 40.202, respectively. The manufacturer shall surrender his permit, with such inventory and report, to the appropriate TTB officer as notice of such discontinuance. The appropriate TTB officer may then terminate the liability of the surety on the bond of the manufacturer.

(72 Stat. 1422; 26 U.S.C. 5721, 5722)

[T.D. 6871, 37 FR 40, Jan. 4, 1966. Redesignated at 40 FR 16835, Apr. 15, 1975, and amended by T.D. ATF–232, 51 FR 28083, Aug. 5, 1986; T.D. ATF–243, 51 FR 43194, Dec. 1, 1986]

§ 40.332 Suspension and revocation of permit.

Where the appropriate TTB officer has reason to believe that a manufacturer of tobacco products has not in good faith complied with the provisions of 26 U.S.C. chapter 52, and regulations thereunder, or with any other provision of 26 U.S.C. with intent to defraud, or has violated any condition of his permit, or has failed to disclose any material information required or made any material false statement in the application for the permit, or has failed to maintain his premises in such manner as to protect the revenue, or is, by reason of previous or current legal proceedings involving a felony violation of any other provision of Federal criminal law relating to tobacco products, processed tobacco, cigarette paper, or cigarette tubes, not likely to maintain operations in compliance with 26 U.S.C. chapter 52, or has been convicted of a felony violation of any provision of Federal or State criminal law relating to tobacco products, processed tobacco, cigarette paper, or cigarette tubes, the appropriate TTB officer shall issue an order, stating the facts charged, citing such person to show cause why his permit should not be suspended or revoked. Such citation shall be issued and opportunity for hearing afforded in accordance with part 71 of this chapter, which part is applicable to such proceedings. If, after hearing, the hearing examiner, or on appeal, the Administrator, finds that such person has not shown cause why his permit should not be suspended or revoked, such permit shall be suspended for such period as the appropriate TTB officer deems proper or shall be revoked.

(72 Stat 1421, as amended; 26 U.S.C. 5713)

[T.D. TTB–75, 74 FR 14483, Mar. 31, 2009]

Subpart K—Manufacture of Cigarette Papers and Tubes

SOURCE: T.D. ATF–384, 61 FR 54085, Oct. 17, 1996, unless otherwise noted.

TAXES

§ 40.351 Cigarette papers.

Cigarette papers are taxed at the following rates under 26 U.S.C. 5701(c):

Product	Tax rate for each 50 papers* for removals during the following periods:	
	2002 to March 31, 2009	April 1, 2009 and after
Cigarette papers up to 6½″ long.	$ 0.0122	$ 0.0315

Product	Tax rate for each 50 papers* for removals during the following periods:	
	2002 to March 31, 2009	April 1, 2009 and after
Cigarette papers over 6½″ long.	Use rates above, but count each 2¾ inches, or fraction thereof, of the length of each as one cigarette paper.	

*Tax rate for less than 50 papers is the same. The tax is not prorated.

(72 Stat. 1414; 26 U.S.C. 5701)

[T.D. TTB–75, 74 FR 14483, Mar. 31, 2009]

§40.352 Cigarette tubes.

Cigarette tubes are taxed at the following rates under 26 U.S.C. 5701(d):

Product	Tax rate for each 50 tubes* for removals during the years:	
	2002 to March 31, 2009	April 1, 2009 and after
Cigarette tubes up to 6½″ long.	$ 0.0244	$ 0.0630
Cigarette tubes over 6½″ long.	Use rates above, but count each 2¾ inches, or fraction thereof, of the length of each as one cigarette tube.	

*Tax rate for less than 50 tubes is the same. The tax is not prorated.

(72 Stat. 1414; 26 U.S.C. 5701)

[T.D. TTB–75, 74 FR 14483, Mar. 31, 2009]

§40.353 Persons liable for tax.

The manufacturer of cigarette papers and tubes shall be liable for the taxes imposed on such articles by 26 U.S.C. 5701. When a manufacturer of cigarette papers and tubes transfers such papers and tubes without payment of tax, pursuant to 26 U.S.C. 5704 to the bonded premises of another such manufacturer, a manufacturer of tobacco products, or an export warehouse proprietor, the transferee shall become liable for the tax upon receipt of such papers and tubes and the transferor shall thereupon be relieved of liability for the tax. When cigarette papers and tubes are released in bond from customs custody for transfer to the bonded premises of a manufacturer of such papers and tubes or a manufacturer of tobacco products, the transferee shall become liable for the tax on the papers and tubes upon release from customs custody. Any person who possesses cigarette papers and tubes in violation of 26 U.S.C. 5751(a) (1) or (2), shall be liable for a tax equal to the rate of tax applicable to such articles.

(72 Stat. 1417, 1424; 26 U.S.C. 5703, 5751)

§40.354 Determination of tax and method of payment.

Except for removals without payment of tax and transfers in bond, as authorized by law, no cigarette papers and tubes shall be removed until the taxes imposed by section 5701, I.R.C., have been determined. The payment of taxes on cigarette papers and tubes which are removed on determination of tax shall be made by return in accordance with the provisions of this subpart.

(72 Stat. 1417; 26 U.S.C. 5703)

§40.355 Return of manufacturer.

(a) *Requirement for filing.* A manufacturer of cigarette papers and tubes shall file, for each factory, a semimonthly tax return on TTB Form 5000.24. A return shall be filed for each semimonthly return period regardless of whether cigarette papers and tubes were removed subject to tax or whether tax is due for that particular return period.

(b) *Waiver from filing.* The manufacturer need not file a return for each semimonthly return period if cigarette papers and tubes were not removed subject to tax during the period and the appropriate TTB officer has granted a waiver from filing in response to a written request from the manufacturer.

(c) *Semimonthly return periods.* Except as otherwise provided in paragraph (g) of this section, semimonthly return periods run from the 1st day of the month through the 15th day of that month, and from the 16th day of the month through the last day of that month.

(d) *Preparation and filing.* The return shall be executed and filed with TTB in accordance with the instructions on the form.

(e) *Remittance of tax.* Except as provided in §40.357, remittance of the tax, if any, shall accompany the return.

(f) *Time for filing.* Except as otherwise provided in paragraph (g) of this section, for each semimonthly return period, the return shall be filed not later than the 14th day after the last day of the return period. If the due date falls on a Saturday, Sunday, or legal holiday, the return and remittance are due on the immediately preceding day that is not a Saturday, Sunday or legal holiday.

(g) *Special rule for taxes due for the month of September.* (1) *Division of second semimonthly period.* (i) *General.* Except as otherwise provided in paragraph (g)(1)(ii) of this section, the second semimonthly period for the month of September is divided into two payment periods, from the 16th day through the 26th day, and from the 27th day through the 30th day. The manufacturer shall file a return on TTB F 5000.24, and make remittance, for the period September 16–26, no later than September 29. The manufacturer shall file a return on TTB F 5000.24, and make remittance, for the period September 27–30, no later than October 14.

(ii) *Taxpayment not by electronic fund transfer.* In the case of taxes for which remittance by electronic fund transfer (EFT) is not required by § 40.357, the second semimonthly period of September is divided into two payment periods, from the 16th day through the 25th day, and from the 26th day through the 30th day. The manufacturer shall file a return on TTB F 5000.24, and make remittance, for the period September 16–25, no later than September 28. The manufacturer shall file a return on TTB F 5000.24, and make remittance, for the period September 26–30, no later than October 14.

(2) *Amount of payment—Safe harbor rule.* (i) *General.* Taxpayers are considered to have met the requirements of paragraph (g)(1)(i) of this section if the amount paid no later than September 29 is not less than 11/15ths (73.3 percent) of the tax liability incurred for the semimonthly period beginning on September 1 and ending on September 15th, and if any underpayment of tax is paid by October 14th.

(ii) *Taxpayment not by EFT.* Taxpayers are considered to have met the requirements of paragraph (g)(1)(ii) of this section if the amount paid no later than September 28 is not less than 2/3rds (66.7 percent) of the tax liability incurred for the semimonthly period beginning on September 1 and ending on September 15, and if any underpayment of tax is paid by October 14.

(3) *Weekends and holidays.* If the required taxpayment due date for the period September 16–25 or September 16–26, as applicable, falls on a Saturday, or legal holiday, the return and remittance are due on the immediately preceding day. If the required due date falls on a Sunday, the return and remittance are due on the immediately following day.

(Approved by the Office of Management and Budget under Control Number 1512–0467)

[T.D. ATF–384, 61 FR 54085, Oct. 17, 1996, as amended by T.D. TTB–89, 76 FR 3514, Jan. 20, 2011]

§ 40.356 Adjustments in the return of manufacturer.

Adjustments may be made in Schedules A and B of the manufacturer's semimonthly tax return, TTB Form 5000.24, as provided in this section. Schedule A of the return will be used where an unintentional error in a previous return resulted in an underpayment of tax. Schedule B of the return will be used where an unintentional error in a previous return resulted in an overpayment of tax, or where notice has been received from the appropriate TTB officer that a claim for allowance of tax has been approved. In the case of an overpayment, the manufacturer shall have the option of filing a claim on TTB TTB F 5620.8 for refund or taking credit in Schedule B of the return, both subject to the period of limitations prescribed in 26 U.S.C. 6511. Any adjustment made in a return must be fully explained in the appropriate schedule or in a statement attached to and made a part of the return in which such adjustment is made.

(72 Stat. 1417, 68A Stat. 791; 26 U.S.C. 5703, 6402)

§ 40.357 Payment of tax by electronic fund transfer.

(a) *General.* (1) Each taxpayer who was liable, during a calendar year, for a gross amount equal to or exceeding five million dollars in taxes on tobacco products, cigarette papers, and cigarette tubes combining tax liabilities incurred under this part and part 41 of this chapter, shall use a commercial bank in making payment by electronic fund transfer (EFT) of taxes on tobacco products, cigarette papers, and cigarette tubes during the succeeding calendar year. Payment of taxes on tobacco products, cigarette papers, and cigarette tubes in any other form of remittance, as authorized in §40.355, is not authorized for a taxpayer who is required, by this section, to make remittances by EFT. For purposes of this section, the dollar amount of tax liability is defined as the gross tax liability on all taxable withdrawals and importations (including tobacco products, cigarette papers, and cigarette tubes brought into the United States from Puerto Rico or the Virgin Islands) during the calendar year, without regard to any drawbacks, credits, or refunds, for all premises from which such activities are conducted by the taxpayer. Overpayments are not taken into account in summarizing the gross tax liability.

(2) For the purposes of this section, a taxpayer includes a controlled group of corporations, as defined in 26 U.S.C. 1563, and implementing regulations in 26 CFR §§1.563–1 through 1.1563–4. Also, the rules for a "controlled group of corporations" apply in a similar fashion to groups which include partnerships and/or sole proprietorships. If one entity maintains more than 50% control over a group consisting of corporations and one, or more, partnerships and/or sole proprietorships, all of the members of the controlled group are one taxpayer for the purpose of determining who is required to make remittances by EFT.

(3) A taxpayer who is required by this section to make remittances by EFT shall make a separate EFT remittance and file a separate return, TTB Form 5000.24, for each factory from which cigarette papers or cigarette tubes are withdrawn upon determination of tax.

(b) *Requirements.* (1) On or before January 10 of each calendar year, except for a taxpayer already remitting the tax by EFT, each taxpayer who was liable for a gross amount equal to or exceeding five million dollars in taxes on tobacco products, cigarette papers, and cigarette tubes combining tax liabilities incurred under this part and part 41 of this chapter during the previous calendar year, shall notify, in writing, the appropriate TTB officer. The notice shall be an agreement to make remittances by EFT.

(2) For each return filed in accordance with this part, the taxpayer shall direct the taxpayer's bank to make an electronic fund transfer in the amount of the taxpayment to the Department of the Treasury's General Account or the Federal Reserve Bank of New York as provided in paragraph (e) of this section. The request shall be made to the bank early enough for the transfer to be made to the Treasury Account by no later than the close of business on the last day for filing the return, prescribed in §40.355. The request shall take into account any time limit established by the bank.

(3) If a taxpayer was liable for less than five million dollars in taxes on tobacco products, cigarette papers, and cigarette tubes combining tax liabilities incurred under this part and part 41 of this chapter during the preceding calendar year, the taxpayer may choose either to continue remitting the tax as provided in this section or to remit the tax with the return as prescribed by §40.355. Upon filing the first return on which the taxpayer chooses to discontinue remitting the tax by EFT and to begin remitting the tax with the tax return, the taxpayer shall notify the appropriate TTB officer by attaching a written notification to TTB Form 5000.24, stating that no taxes are due by EFT, because the tax liability during the preceding calendar year was less than five million dollars, and that the remittance shall be filed with the tax return.

(c) *Remittance.* (1) Each taxpayer shall show on the return, TTB Form 5000.24, information about remitting the tax for that return period by EFT and shall file the return with TTB, in accordance with the instructions of TTB Form 5000.24.

(2) Remittances shall be considered as made when the taxpayment by EFT is received by the Treasury Account. For purposes of this section, a taxpayment by EFT shall be considered as received by the Treasury Account when it is paid to a Federal Reserve Bank.

(3) When the taxpayer directs the bank to effect an EFT message as required by paragraph (b)(2) of this section, any transfer data record furnished to the taxpayer, through normal banking procedures, will serve as the record of payment, and shall be retained as part of required records.

(d) *Failure to make a taxpayment by EFT.* The taxpayer is subject to a penalty imposed by 26 U.S.C. 5761, 6651, or 6656, as applicable, for failure to make a taxpayment by EFT on or before the close of business on the prescribed last day for filing.

(e) *Procedure.* Upon the notification required under paragraph (b)(1) of this section, the appropriate TTB officer will issue to the taxpayer an TTB Procedure entitled Payment of Tax by Electronic Fund Transfer. This publication outlines the procedure a taxpayer is to follow when preparing returns and EFT remittances in accordance with this part. The U.S. Customs Service will provide the taxpayer with instructions for preparing EFT remittances for payments to be made to the U.S. Customs Service.

(Approved by the Office of Management and Budget under control number 1512–0457)

(Act of August 16, 1954, 68A Stat. 775, as amended (26 U.S.C. 6302); sec. 202, Pub. L. 85–859, 72 Stat. 1417, as amended (26 U.S.C. 5703))

[T.D. ATF–384, 61 FR 54085, Oct. 17, 1996, as amended by T.D. TTB–16, 69 FR 52423, Aug. 26, 2004; T.D. TTB–91, 76 FR 5480, Feb. 1, 2011]

§ 40.358 Assessment.

Whenever any person required by law to pay tax on cigarette papers and tubes fails to pay such tax, the tax shall be ascertained and assessed against such person, subject to the limitations prescribed in 26 U.S.C. 6501. The tax so assessed shall be in addition to the penalties imposed by law for failure to pay such tax when required. Except in cases where delay may jeopardize collection of the tax, or where the amount is nominal or the result of an evident mathematical error, no such assessment shall be made until and after notice has been afforded such person to show cause against assessment. The person will be allowed 45 days from the date of such notice to show cause, in writing, against such assessment.

(72 Stat. 1417; 26 U.S.C. 5703)

§ 40.359 Employer identification number.

The employer identification number (EIN) (defined at 26 CFR 301.7701–12) of a manufacturer of cigarette papers and/or tubes who has been assigned such a number shall be shown on each semimonthly tax return, TTB Form 5000.24, and special tax return (including amended returns), TTB Form 5630.5, filed under this subpart. Failure of the taxpayer to include the EIN on TTB Form 5000.24 may result in assertion and collection of the penalty specified in § 70.113 of this chapter. Failure of the taxpayer to include the EIN on TTB Form 5630.5 may result in the imposition of the penalty specified in 27 CFR 70.113 of this chapter.

(75 Stat. 828; 26 U.S.C. 6109, 6676)

§ 40.360 Application for employer identification number.

Each manufacturer of cigarette papers and tubes who has neither secured an EIN nor made application therefor shall file an application on IRS Form SS–4. IRS Form SS–4 may be obtained from any service center director or from any district director. Such application shall be filed on or before the seventh day after the date on which any tax return under this subpart is filed. Each manufacturer shall make application for and shall be assigned only one EIN for all internal revenue purposes.

(75 Stat. 828; 26 U.S.C. 6109)

§ 40.361 Execution and filing of Form SS–4.

The application on IRS form SS–4, together with any supplementary statement, shall be prepared in accordance with the applicable form, instructions, and regulations, and the data called for shall be set forth fully and clearly. The application shall be filed with the service center director serving the internal revenue district where the applicant is required to file returns under this subpart, except that hand-carried applications may be filed with the district director of any such district as provided for in 26 CFR § 301.6091–1. The application shall be signed by:

(a) The individual if the person is an individual;

(b) The president, vice president, or other principal officer if the person is a corporation;

(c) A responsible and duly authorized member or officer having knowledge of its affairs if the person is a partnership or other unincorporated organization; or

(d) The fiduciary if the person is a trust or estate.

(75 Stat. 828; 26 U.S.C. 6109)

SPECIAL (OCCUPATIONAL) TAXES

§ 40.371 Liability for special tax.

(a) *Manufacturer of cigarette papers and tubes.* Every manufacturer of cigarette papers and tubes shall pay a special (occupational) tax at a rate specified by § 40.372 of this part. The tax shall be paid on or before July 1. On commencing business, the tax shall be computed from the first day of the month in which liability is incurred, through the following June 30. Thereafter, the tax shall be computed for the entire year (July 1 through June 30).

(b) *Each place of business taxable.* A manufacturer of cigarette papers and tubes incurs special tax liability at each place of business in which an occupation subject to special tax is conducted. A place of business means the entire office, plant or area of the business in any one location under the same proprietorship. Passageways, streets, highways, rail crossings, waterways, or partitions dividing the premises are not sufficient separation to require additional special tax, if the divisions of the premises are otherwise contiguous.

(c) *Payment of tax.* Special tax must be paid by return. The prescribed return is TTB Form 5630.5t, Special Tax Registration and Return—Tobacco. Special tax returns, with payment of tax, must be filed with TTB in accordance with the instructions on the form and the requirements of subpart D of part 46 of this chapter.

(26 U.S.C. 5731, 5733)

[T.D. ATF–384, 61 FR 54085, Oct. 17, 1996, as amended by T.D. TTB–79, 74 FR 37419, July 28, 2009]

§ 40.372 Rate of special tax.

(a) *General.* Title 26 U.S.C. 5731(a)(2) imposes a special tax of $1,000 per year on every manufacturer of cigarette papers and tubes.

(b) *Reduced rate for small proprietors.* Title 26 U.S.C. 5731(b) provides for a reduced rate of $500 per year with respect to any manufacturer of cigarette papers and tubes whose gross receipts (for the most recent taxable year ending before the first day of the taxable period to which the special tax imposed by § 40.371 relates) are less than $500,000. The "taxable year" to be used for determining gross receipts is the taxpayer's income tax year. All gross receipts of the taxpayer shall be included, not just the gross receipts of the business subject to special tax. Proprietors of new businesses that have not yet begun a taxable year, as well as proprietors of existing businesses that have not yet ended a taxable year, who commence a new activity subject to special tax, qualify for the reduced special (occupational) tax rate, unless the business is a member of a "controlled group"; in that case the rules of paragraph (c) of this section shall apply.

(c) *Controlled group.* All persons treated as one taxpayer under 26 U.S.C. 5061(e)(3) shall be treated as one taxpayer for the purpose of determining gross receipts under paragraph (b) of this section. "Controlled group" means a controlled group of corporations, as defined in 26 U.S.C. 1563 and implementing regulations in 26 CFR 1.1563–1 through 1.1563–4. Also, the rules for a "controlled group of corporations" apply in a similar fashion to groups which include partnerships and/or sole proprietorships. If one entity maintains more than 50% control over a group consisting of corporations and one, or more, partnerships and/or sole proprietorships, all of the members of the controlled group are one taxpayer for the purpose of this section.

(d) *Short taxable year*. Gross receipts for any taxable year of less than 12 months shall be annualized by multiplying the gross receipts for the short period by 12 and dividing the result by the number of months in the short period as required by 26 U.S.C. 448(c)(3).

(e) *Returns and allowances*. Gross receipts for any taxable year shall be reduced by returns and allowances made during such year under 26 U.S.C. 448(c)(3).

(26 U.S.C. 448, 5061, 5731)

§ 40.373 Cross reference.

For additional rules pertaining to liability for special tax, filing special tax returns, issuance and examination of special tax stamps, and notification of changes to special tax stamps, see subpart D of part 46 of this chapter.

[T.D. TTB–79, 74 FR 37419, July 28, 2009]

§§ 40.374–40.375 [Reserved]

GENERAL

§ 40.382 Authority of TTB officers to enter premises.

The appropriate TTB officer may enter in the daytime any premises where cigarette papers and tubes are produced or kept, so far as it may be necessary for the purpose of examining such articles. When such premises are open at night, the appropriate TTB officer may enter them, while so open, in the performance of his or her official duties. The owner of such premises, or person having the superintendence of the same, who refuses to admit the appropriate TTB officer or permit the appropriate TTB officer to examine such cigarette papers and tubes shall be liable to the penalties prescribed by law for the offense.

(68A Stat. 872; 903 26 U.S.C. 7342, 7606)

§ 40.383 Interference with administration.

Whoever, corruptly or by force or threats of force, endeavors to hinder or obstruct the administration of this subpart, or endeavors to intimidate or impede any TTB officer acting in an official capacity, or forcibly rescues or attempts to rescue or causes to be rescued any property, after it has been duly seized for forfeiture to the United States in connection with a violation or intended violation of this subpart, shall be liable to the penalties prescribed by law.

(68A Stat. 855; 26 U.S.C. 7212)

§ 40.384 Disposal of forfeited, condemned, and abandoned cigarette papers and tubes.

Forfeited, condemned, or abandoned cigarette papers or tubes in the custody of a Federal, State, or local officer upon which the Federal tax has not been paid shall not be sold or caused to be sold for consumption in the United States if, in the opinion of the officer, the sale of such papers and tubes will not bring a price equal to the tax due and payable, and the expenses incident to the sale. Where the cigarette papers or tubes are not sold the officer may deliver them to a Federal or State institution (if they are fit for consumption) or cause their destruction by burning completely or by rendering them unfit for consumption. Where such papers or tubes are sold, release by the officer having custody shall be made only after such papers and tubes are properly packaged and taxpaid. A receipt from the appropriate TTB officer evidencing payment of tax on such papers or tubes shall be presented to the officer having custody of the articles, which tax shall be considered part of the sales price. Where cigarette papers or tubes which have been packaged under the provisions of part 45 of this chapter are to be released after payment of tax, the purchaser shall appropriately mark each package "Federal Tax Paid (date)" before the officer having custody of the papers or tubes releases them. However, the articles may be released without such marking of the packages if the purchaser is a qualified manufacturer of cigarette papers and tubes and does not intend to place such papers or tubes on the domestic market for taxable articles but will otherwise dispose of them. A written statement of notification of disposal by destruction or return to bond through claim for refund, shall be filed, in original only, with the officer having custody of the articles. In the case of cigarette papers and tubes forfeited under the internal revenue laws, the sale shall be subject to the provisions of part 72 of this chapter.

(68A Stat. 870, as amended, 72 Stat. 1425, as amended; 26 U.S.C. 7325, 5753)

[26 FR 8174, Aug. 31, 1961. Redesignated at 40 FR 16835, Apr. 15, 1975, and further redesignated at 54 FR 48839, Nov. 27, 1989, and further redesignated by T.D. ATF-460, 66 FR 39093, July 27, 2001, as amended by T.D. ATF-469, 66 FR 56758, Nov. 13, 2001]

§40.385 Alternate methods or procedures.

A manufacturer of cigarette papers and tubes, on specific approval by the appropriate TTB officer as provided in this section, may use an alternate method or procedure in lieu of a method or procedure specifically prescribed in this subpart. The appropriate TTB officer may approve an alternate method or procedure, subject to stated conditions, when the appropriate TTB officer finds that—

(a) Good cause has been shown for the use of the alternate method or procedure,

(b) The alternate method or procedure is within the purpose of, and consistent with the effect intended by, the specifically prescribed method or procedure, and affords equivalent security to the revenue, and

(c) The alternate method or procedure will not be contrary to any provision of law, and will not result in an increase in cost to the Government or hinder the effective administration of this subpart.

No alternate method or procedure relating to the giving of any bond or to the assessment, payment, or collection of tax, shall be authorized under this section. A manufacturer who desires to employ an alternate method or procedure shall submit a written application, in triplicate, to the appropriate TTB officer. The application shall specifically describe the proposed alternate method or procedure, and shall set forth the reasons therefor. Alternate methods or procedures shall not be employed until the application has been approved by the appropriate TTB officer. The manufacturer shall, during the period of authorization of an alternate method or procedure, comply with the terms of the approved application. Authorization for any alternate method or procedure may be withdrawn whenever, in the judgment of the appropriate TTB officer, the revenue is jeopardized or the effective administration of this part is hindered. Any authorization of the appropriate TTB officer under this section shall be retained as part of the manufacturer's record in accordance with this subpart.

§40.386 Emergency variations from requirements.

The appropriate TTB officer may approve methods of operation other than as specified in this subpart, where it is determined that an emergency exists and the proposed variations from the specified requirements are necessary, and the proposed variations—

(a) Will afford the security and protection to the revenue intended by the prescribed specifications;

(b) Will not hinder the effective administration of this subpart; and

(c) Will not be contrary to any provision of law. Variations from requirements granted under this section are conditioned on compliance with the procedures, conditions, and limitations set forth in the approval of the application. Failure to comply in good faith with such procedures, conditions and limitations shall automatically terminate the authority for such variations and the manufacturer thereupon shall fully comply with the prescribed requirements of regulations from which the variations were authorized. Authority for any variation may be withdrawn whenever in the judgment of the appropriate TTB officer the revenue is jeopardized or the effective administration of this subpart is hindered by the continuation of such variation. Where a manufacturer desires to employ such variation, the manufacturer shall submit a written application to do so (in triplicate) to the appropriate TTB officer. The application shall describe the proposed variations and set forth the reasons therefor. Variations shall not be employed until the application has been approved. In accordance with this subpart, any authorization of the appropriate TTB officer under this section shall be retained as part of the manufacturer's records.

§ 40.387 Penalties and forfeitures.

Anyone who fails to comply with the provisions of this subpart becomes liable to the civil and criminal penalties, and forfeitures, provided by law.

(72 Stat. 1425, 1426; 26 U.S.C. 5761, 5762, 5763)

QUALIFICATION REQUIREMENTS FOR MANUFACTURERS

Original Qualifications

§ 40.391 Persons required to qualify.

Every person who manufactures cigarette paper, or makes up cigarette paper into tubes, except for his own personal use or consumption, must first qualify as a manufacturer of cigarette papers and tubes in accordance with the provisions of this subpart.

[ATF–467, 66 FR 49532, Sept. 28, 2001]

§ 40.392 Bond.

Every person, before commencing business as a manufacturer of cigarette papers and tubes, shall file a bond on TTB F 5200.25 or 5200.26. Such bond shall be filed in accordance with the applicable provisions of §§ 40.401 through 40.410 and conditioned upon compliance with the provisions of 26 U.S.C. Chapter 52, and regulations thereunder, including, but not limited to, the timely payment of taxes imposed by such chapter and penalties and interest in connection therewith for which the manufacturer may become liable to the United States.

(72 Stat. 1421; 26 U.S.C. 5711)

[T.D. ATF–384, 61 FR 54085, Oct. 17, 1996, as amended by T.D. TTB–91, 76 FR 5480, Feb. 1, 2011]

§ 40.393 Power of attorney.

If the bond or any other document required under this part is signed by an attorney in fact for an individual, partnership, association, company, or corporation, by one of the partners for a partnership, or by one of the members of an association, a power of attorney on TTB F 5000.8 shall be furnished to the appropriate TTB officer. If such bond or other document is signed on behalf of a corporation by an officer thereof, it must be supported by duly authenticated extracts of the stockholders' meeting, by-laws, or directors' meeting authorizing such officer to execute such document for the corporation. TTB F 5000.8 or support of authority does not have to be filed again with a appropriate TTB officer where such form or support has previously been submitted to that appropriate TTB officer and is still in effect.

(72 Stat. 1421; 26 U.S.C. 5711)

§ 40.394 Notice of approval of bond.

If the bond required under this subpart is approved by the appropriate TTB officer, a number will be assigned to the factory of the manufacturer of cigarette papers and tubes for internal revenue purposes. The appropriate TTB officer will immediately notify the manufacturer, in writing, of the bond approval, in order that the manufacturer may commence operations.

(72 Stat. 1421; 26 U.S.C. 5711)

Changes after Original Qualifications

§ 40.395 Change in name.

Where there is a change in the individual, trade, or corporate name of a manufacturer of cigarette papers and tubes, the manufacturer shall, within 30 days of the change, furnish the appropriate TTB officer a written notice of such change.

(72 Stat. 1422; 26 U.S.C. 5722)

§ 40.396 Change in proprietorship.

Where there is to be any change in proprietorship (including a change in the identity of the members of a partnership or association, but excluding any change in stock ownership in a corporation) of the business of a manufacturer of cigarette papers and tubes, the proposed successor shall, before commencing operations, qualify as a manufacturer of cigarette papers and tubes, in accordance with this part. If such manufacturer promptly files the required documentation with the appropriate TTB officer, an administrator, executor, receiver, trustee, assignee, or other fiduciary successor may liquidate the business without qualifying as a manufacturer. The manufacturer must promptly file with the appropriate TTB officer a statement of the intent to liquidate and furnish a certified copy of the order of the court, or other pertinent documents. These documents must show the appointment and qualification of any administrator, executor, receiver, trustee, assignee, or other fiduciary, together with an extension of coverage of the predecessor's bond executed by the administrator, executor, receiver, trustee, assignee, or other fiduciary and the surety, in accordance with the provisions of §40.407. The predecessor shall make a closing inventory and closing report in accordance with the provisions of §§40.434 and 40.426, respectively, and the successor shall make an opening inventory and opening report, in accordance with the provision of §§40.432 and 40.423, respectively.

(72 Stat. 1421, 1422; 26 U.S.C. 5711, 5721, and 5722)

§40.397 Change in location.

Whenever a manufacturer of cigarette papers and tubes contemplates a change in location of a factory within the same region, the manufacturer shall, before commencing operations at the new location, file an extension of coverage of bond in accordance with the provisions of §40.407. Whenever a manufacturer of cigarette papers and tubes contemplates changing the location of a factory to another region, the manufacturer shall, before commencing operations at the new location, qualify as a manufacturer in the new region, in accordance with the applicable provisions of this subpart, and make a closing inventory and closing report, in accordance with the provisions of §§40.434 and 40.426, respectively.

(72 Stat. 1421, 1422; 26 U.S.C. 5711, 5721, and 5722)

Bonds and Extensions of Coverage of Bonds

§40.401 Corporate surety.

(a) Surety bonds required by this subpart may be given only with corporate sureties holding certificates of authority from, and subject to any limitations prescribed by the Secretary of the Treasury as set forth in the current revision of Treasury Department Circular No. 570 (Companies Holding Certificates of Authority as Acceptable Sureties on Federal Bonds and as Acceptable Reinsuring Companies). The surety shall have no interest whatever in the business covered by the bond.

(b) Each bond and each extension of coverage of bond shall at the time of filing be accompanied by a power of attorney authorizing the agent or officer who executed the bond to so act on behalf of the surety. The appropriate TTB officer who is authorized to approve the bond may, whenever deemed necessary, require additional evidence of the authority of the agent or officer to execute the bond or extension of coverage of bond. The power of attorney shall be prepared on a form provided by the surety company and executed under the corporate seal of the company. If the power of attorney submitted is other than a manually signed document, it shall be accompanied by a certificate of its validity.

(c) Treasury Department Circular No. 570 is published in the FEDERAL REGISTER annually as of the first workday in July. As they occur, interim revisions of the circular are published in the FEDERAL REGISTER. Copies may be obtained from the Surety Bond Branch, Financial Management Service, Department of the Treasury, Washington, D.C. 20220.

(July 30, 1947, ch. 390, 61 Stat. 648, as amended (31 U.S.C. 9304, 9306); sec. 202. Pub. L. 85–859, 72 Stat. 1421, as amended (26 U.S.C. 5711))

§40.402 Two or more corporate sureties.

A bond executed by two or more corporate sureties shall be the joint and several liability of the principal and the sureties. However, each corporate surety may limit its liability in terms upon the face of the bond in a definite, specific amount, which amount shall not exceed the limitations prescribed for such corporate surety by the Secretary, as set forth in the current revision of Treasury Department Circular 570 (Companies Holding Certificates of Authority as Acceptable Sureties on Federal Bonds and as Acceptable Reinsuring Companies). (See §40.401(c))

When the sureties so limit their liability, the aggregate of such limited liabilities must equal the required amount of the bond.

(July 30, 1947, ch. 390, 61 Stat. 648, as amended (31 U.S.C. 9304, 9306); sec. 202. Pub. L. 85–859, 72 Stat. 1421, as amended (26 U.S.C. 5711))

§40.403 Deposit of securities in lieu of corporate surety.

In lieu of corporate surety, the manufacturer of cigarette papers and tubes may pledge and deposit, as security for the bond, securities which are transferable and are guaranteed as to both interest and principal by the United States, in accordance with the provisions of 31 CFR Part 225—Acceptance of Bonds, Notes or Other Obligations Issued or Guaranteed by the United States as Security in Lieu of Surety or Sureties on Penal Bonds.

(61 Stat. 650, 72 Stat. 1421, 31 U.S.C. 9301, 9303, 26 U.S.C. 5711, 5 U.S.C. 552(a) (80 Stat. 383, as amended))

§40.404 Amount of bond.

The amount of the bond of a manufacturer of cigarette papers and tubes shall be not less than the maximum amount of the tax liability on the cigarette papers and tubes manufactured in the factory, received without payment of tax from other factories, and released without payment of tax from customs custody as provided in §40.452, during any month. In the case of a manufacturer commencing business, the production, receipts from other factories, and releases from customs custody, without payment of tax, shall be estimated for the purpose of this section. The amount of any such bond (or the total amount where strengthening bonds are filed) shall not exceed $20,000, nor be less than $1,000.

(72 Stat. 1421; 26 U.S.C. 5711)

§40.405 Strengthening bond.

Where the appropriate TTB officer determines that the amount of the bond, under which a manufacturer of cigarette papers and tubes is currently carrying on such business, no longer adequately protects the revenue, the appropriate TTB officer may require the manufacturer to file a strengthening bond in an appropriate amount with the same surety as that on the bond already in effect, in lieu of a superseding bond to cover the full liability on the basis of §40.404. The appropriate TTB officer shall refuse to approve any strengthening bond where any notation is made thereon which is intended or which may be construed as a release of any former bond, or as limiting the amount of either bond to less than its full amount.

(72 Stat. 1421; 26 U.S.C. 5711)

§40.406 Superseding bond.

A manufacturer of cigarette papers and tubes shall file a new bond to supersede the current bond immediately when:

(a) The corporate surety on the current bond becomes insolvent,

(b) The appropriate TTB officer approves a request from the surety of the current bond to terminate liability under the bond,

(c) Payment of any liability under a bond is made by the surety thereon, or

(d) The appropriate TTB officer considers such a superseding bond necessary for the protection of the revenue.

(72 Stat. 1421; 26 U.S.C. 5711)

§40.407 Extension of coverage of bond.

An extension of the coverage of bond filed under this subpart shall be manifested on TTB F 5000.18, Extension of Coverage of Bond, by the manufacturer of cigarette papers and tubes and by the surety on the bond with the same formality and proof of authority as required for the execution of the bond.

(72 Stat. 1421; 26 U.S.C. 5711)

§40.408 Approval of bond and extension of coverage of bond.

No person shall commence operations under any bond, nor extend operations, until such person receives from the appropriate TTB officer notice of approval of the bond or an appropriate extension of coverage of the bond required under this subpart. Upon receipt of an approved bond or extension of coverage of bond from the appropriate TTB officer, such bond or extension of coverage of bond shall be retained by the manufacturer of cigarette papers and tubes in factory and shall be made available for inspection by any TTB officer upon request.

(72 Stat. 1421; 26 U.S.C. 5711)

§ 40.409 Termination of liability of surety under bond.

The liability of a surety on any bond required by this subpart shall be terminated only as to operations on and after the effective date of a superseding bond, or the date of approval of the discontinuance of operations by the manufacturer of cigarette papers and tubes, or otherwise in accordance with the termination provisions of the bond. The surety shall remain bound in respect of any liability for unpaid taxes, penalties and interest, not in excess of the amount of the bond, incurred by the manufacturer while the bond is in force.

(72 Stat. 1421; 26 U.S.C. 5711)

§ 40.410 Release of pledged securities.

Securities of the United States pledged and deposited as provided in § 40.403 shall be released only in accordance with the provisions of 31 CFR part 225. Such securities will not be released by the appropriate TTB officer until liability under the bond for which they were pledged has been terminated. When the appropriate TTB officer is satisfied that they may be released, the appropriate TTB officer shall fix the date or dates on which a part or all of such securities may be released. At any time prior to the release of such securities, the appropriate TTB officer may extend the date of release for such additional length of time as is deemed necessary.

(61 Stat. 650, 72 Stat. 1421; 31 U.S.C. 9301, 9303; 26 U.S.C. 5711)

OPERATIONS BY MANUFACTURERS

Records

§ 40.421 General.

(a) Every manufacturer of cigarette papers and tubes must keep records of daily operations and transactions. Records maintained must reflect the date and number of cigarette papers and the date and number of cigarette tubes:

(1) Manufactured;

(2) Received, without payment of tax from another factory, an export warehouse, customs custody, or by withdrawal from the market;

(3) Removed, subject to tax;

(4) Removed, without payment of tax, for export purposes, use of the United States or transfer in bond pursuant to § 40.451; or

(5) Lost or destroyed.

(b) The entries for each day in the records maintained or kept under this subpart must be made by the close of the business day following that on which the operations or transactions occur. No particular form of records is prescribed, but the information required must be readily ascertainable from the records kept.

(c) Records maintained under this section prior to January 1, 2000, must reflect the date and number of books or sets of cigarette papers of each different numerical content and the date and number of cigarette tubes.

(26 U.S.C. 5741.)

[T.D. ATF–240, 64 FR 71941, Dec. 22, 1999]

Reports

§ 40.422 General.

Every manufacturer of cigarette papers and tubes must prepare a report on TTB Form 5230.3 in accordance with instructions for the form. The report must be prepared at the times specified in this subpart and must be prepared whether or not any operations or transactions occurred during the period covered by the report. The manufacturer must retain a copy of each report in accordance with the provisions of this subpart.

(a) *Reports for periods on or after January 1, 2000.* Reports submitted must reflect the total number of cigarette papers and cigarette tubes manufactured, received and lost or destroyed.

(b) *Reports for periods prior to January 1, 2000.* Reports submitted must reflect the number of books or sets of cigarette papers of each different numerical content and the number of cigarette tubes manufactured, received, removed and lost or destroyed.

(26 U.S.C. 5722)

[T.D. ATF–240, 64 FR 71942, Dec. 22, 1999]

§ 40.423 Opening.

An opening report, covering the period from the date of the opening inventory to the end of the month, shall be made on or before the 10th day following the end of the month in which the business was commenced.

(72 Stat. 1422; 26 U.S.C. 5722)

§ 40.424 Monthly.

A report for each calendar month shall be made on or before the 20th day of the next succeeding month.

(72 Stat. 1422; 26 U.S.C. 5722)

§ 40.425 Special.

A special report, covering the unreported period to the day preceding the date of any special inventory required by an appropriate TTB officer, shall be made with such inventory. Another report, covering the period from the date of the special inventory to the end of the month, shall be made on or before the 14th day following the end of the month in which the inventory was made.

(72 Stat. 1422; 26 U.S.C. 5722)

§ 40.426 Closing.

A closing report, covering the period from the first of the month to the date of the closing inventory, shall be made with such inventory.

(72 Stat. 1422; 26 U.S.C. 5722)

Inventories

§ 40.431 General.

Every manufacturer of cigarette papers and tubes must provide a true and accurate inventory on TTB Form 5230.2 in accordance with instructions for the form. Such inventory is subject to verification by the appropriate TTB officer. The manufacturer must retain a copy of each inventory completed on TTB Form 5230.2 in accordance with this subpart.

(a) *Reports of inventory for periods on or after January 1, 2000.* Reports of inventory submitted must reflect the total number of cigarette papers and cigarette tubes held at the times specified in the subpart.

(b) *Reports of inventory for periods prior to January 1, 2000.* Reports of inventory submitted must reflect the number of books or sets of cigarette papers of each different numerical content and the number of cigarette tubes held at the times specified in this subpart.

(26 U.S.C. 5721)

[T.D. ATF–240, 64 FR 71942, Dec. 22, 1999]

§ 40.432 Opening.

An opening inventory shall be made by the manufacturer of cigarette papers and tubes at the time of first commencing business.

(72 Stat. 1422; 26 U.S.C. 5721)

§ 40.433 Special.

A special inventory shall be made by the manufacturer of cigarette papers and tubes when required by the appropriate TTB officer.

(72 Stat. 1422; 26 U.S.C. 5721)

§ 40.434 Closing.

A closing inventory shall be made by the manufacturer of cigarette papers and tubes when a change in proprietorship occurs, or when the manufacturer changes location of the factory to another region, or concludes business. Where a change in proprietorship occurs, the closing inventory shall be made as of the day preceding the date of the opening inventory of the successor.

(72 Stat. 1422; 26 U.S.C. 5721)

Document Retention

§ 40.435 General.

All records and reports required to be kept or maintained under this subpart, including copies of authorizations, inventories, reports, returns, and claims filed with verified supporting schedules, shall be retained by the manufacturer for three years following the close of the calendar year in which filed or made, or in the case of an authorization, for three years following the close of the calendar year in which the operation under such authorization is concluded. Such records shall be made available for inspection by the appropriate TTB officer upon request.

(72 Stat. 1423; 26 U.S.C. 5741)

Packages

§40.441 General.

All cigarette papers and tubes shall, before removal subject to tax, be put up by the manufacturer in packages which shall be of such construction as will securely contain the papers or tubes therein. No package of cigarette papers or tubes shall have contained therein, attached thereto, or stamped, marked, written, or printed thereon:

(a) Any certificate, coupon, or other device purporting to be or to represent a ticket, chance, share, or an interest in, or dependent on, the event of a lottery,

(b) Any indecent or immoral picture, print, or representation, or

(c) Any statement or indication that United States tax has been paid.

(72 Stat. 1422; 26 U.S.C. 5723)

Miscellaneous Operations

§40.451 Transfer in bond.

A manufacturer of cigarette papers and tubes may transfer such papers and tubes, under bond, without payment of tax, to the bonded premises of any manufacturer of cigarette papers and tubes, or to the bonded premises of a manufacturer of tobacco products solely for use in the manufacture of cigarettes. The transfer of cigarette papers and tubes, without payment of tax, to the bonded premises of an export warehouse proprietor shall be in accordance with the provisions of part 44 of this chapter.

(72 Stat. 1418, as amended; 26 U.S.C. 5704)

§40.452 Release from customs custody.

Cigarette papers and tubes which were made in the United States, exported, and subsequently returned to the United States, may be removed from customs custody for transfer to the premises of a manufacturer without payment of the internal revenue tax, upon compliance with part 41 of this chapter.

(72 Stat. 1418; 26 U.S.C. 5704)

[T.D. ATF–384, 61 FR 54085, Oct. 17, 1996, as amended by T.D. TTB–16, 69 FR 52423, Aug. 26, 2004]

§40.453 Use of the United States.

A manufacturer of cigarette papers and tubes may remove cigarette papers and tubes covered under bond, without payment of tax, for use of the United States. Such removal shall be in accordance with the provisions of part 45 of this chapter.

(72 Stat. 1418; 26 U.S.C. 5704)

[26 FR 8174, Aug. 31, 1961. Redesignated at 40 FR 16835, Apr. 15, 1975, and further redesignated at 54 FR 48839, Nov. 27, 1989, and further redesignated by T.D. ATF–460, 66 FR 39093, July 27, 2001, as amended by T.D. ATF–469, 66 FR 56758, Nov. 13, 2001]

§40.454 Removal for export purposes.

The removal of cigarette papers and tubes, without payment of tax, for shipment to a foreign country, Puerto Rico, the Virgin Islands, or a possession of the United States, or for consumption beyond the jurisdiction of the internal revenue laws of the United States, shall be in accordance with the provisions of part 44 of this chapter.

(72 Stat. 1418; 26 U.S.C. 5704)

Permanent Discontinuance of Business

§40.461 Discontinuance of operations.

Every manufacturer of cigarette papers and tubes who desires to discontinue operations and close out a factory shall dispose of all cigarette papers and tubes on hand, in accordance with this subpart, and make a closing inventory and closing report, in accordance with the provisions of §§40.434 and 40.426, respectively.

(72 Stat. 1422; 26 U.S.C. 5721, 5722)

CLAIMS BY MANUFACTURERS

General

§40.471 Abatement.

A claim for abatement of the unpaid portion of the assessment of any tax on cigarette papers and tubes, or any liability in respect thereof, may be allowed to the extent that such assessment is excessive in amount, is assessed after the expiration of the applicable period of limitation, or is erroneously or illegally assessed. Any claim under this section shall be prepared on TTB F 5620.8, in duplicate, and shall set forth the particulars under which the claim is filed. The original of the claim, accompanied by such evidence as is necessary to establish to the satisfaction of the appropriate TTB officer that the claim is valid, shall be filed with the appropriate TTB officer.

(68A Stat. 792, 6404)

§ 40.472 Allowance.

Relief from the payment of tax on cigarette papers and tubes may be extended to a manufacturer by allowance of the tax where the cigarette papers and tubes, after removal from the factory upon determination of tax and prior to the payment of such tax, are lost (otherwise than by theft) or destroyed by fire, casualty, or act of God, while in the possession or ownership of the manufacturer who removed such articles, or are withdrawn by the manufacturer from the market. Any claim for allowance under this section shall be filed on TTB F 5620.8 with the appropriate TTB officer, shall be executed under penalties and perjury and shall show the date the cigarette papers and tubes were removed from the factory. A claim relating to articles lost or destroyed shall be supported as prescribed in § 40.475. In the case of a claim relating to cigarette papers or tubes withdrawn from the market the schedule prescribed in § 40.476 shall be filed with the appropriate TTB officer. The manufacturer may not anticipate allowance of a claim by making the adjusting entry in a tax return pending consideration and action on the claim. Cigarette papers and tubes to which such a claim relates must be shown as removed on determination of tax in the return covering the period during which such articles were so removed. Upon action on the claim by the appropriate TTB officer a copy of TTB F 5620.8 will be returned to the manufacturer as notice of such action. This copy of TTB F 5620.8, with the copy of any verified supporting schedules, shall be retained by the manufacturer. When such notification of allowance of the claim or any part thereof is received prior to the time the return covering the tax on the cigarette papers or tubes to which the claim relates is to be filed, the manufacturer may make an adjusting entry and explanatory statement in that tax return. Where the notice of allowance is received after the filing of the return and taxpayment of the cigarette papers or tubes to which the claim relates, the manufacturer may make an adjusting entry and explanatory statement in the next tax return(s) to the extent necessary to take credit in the amount of the allowance.

(72 Stat. 1419, as amended, 26 U.S.C. 5705)

§ 40.473 Credit or refund.

The taxes paid on cigarette papers and tubes may be credited or refunded (without interest) to a manufacturer on proof satisfactory to the appropriate TTB officer that the claimant manufacturer paid the tax on cigarette papers and tubes lost (otherwise than by theft) or destroyed, by fire, casualty, or act of God, while in the possession or ownership of such manufacturer, or withdrawn by the manufacturer from the market. Any claim for credit or refund under this section shall be prepared on TTB F 5620.8, in duplicate. Claims shall include a statement that the tax imposed on cigarette papers and tubes by 26 U.S.C. 7652 or Chapter 52, was paid in respect to the cigarette papers or tubes covered by the claim, and that the articles were lost, destroyed, or withdrawn from the market within 6 months preceding the date the claim is filed. A claim for credit or refund relating to articles lost or destroyed shall be supported as prescribed in § 40.475, and a claim relating to articles withdrawn from the market shall be accompanied by a schedule prepared and verified as prescribed in §§ 40.476, and 40.477. The original and one copy of TTB F 5620.8, shall be filed with the appropriate TTB officer. Upon action by the appropriate TTB officer on a claim for credit, a copy of TTB F 5620.8 will be returned to the manufacturer as notification of allowance or disallowance of the claim or any part thereof. This copy, with the copy of any verified supporting schedules, shall be retained by the manufacturer. When the manufacturer is notified of allowance of the claim for credit or any part thereof, the manufacturer shall make an adjusting entry and explanatory statement in the next tax return(s) to the extent necessary to take credit in the amount of the allowance. The manufacturer may not anticipate allowance of a claim by taking credit on a tax return prior to consideration and action on such claim. The duplicate of a claim for refund or credit, with a copy of any verified supporting schedules, shall be retained by the manufacturer.

(72 Stat. 1419, as amended, 26 U.S.C. 5705)

§40.474 Remission.

Remission of the tax liability on cigarette papers and tubes may be extended to the manufacturer liable for the tax where cigarette papers and tubes in bond are lost (other than by theft) or destroyed, by fire, casualty, or act of God, while in the possession or ownership of such manufacturer. Where cigarette papers and tubes are so lost or destroyed the manufacturer shall report promptly such fact, and the circumstances, to the appropriate TTB officer. If the manufacturer wishes to be relieved of the tax liability, a claim on TTB F 5620.8, in duplicate, shall also be prepared, setting forth the nature, date, place, and extent of the loss or destruction. The original and one copy of the claim, accompanied by such evidence as is necessary to establish to the satisfaction of the appropriate TTB officer that the claim is valid, shall be filed with the appropriate TTB officer. Upon action on the claim by the appropriate TTB officer, the copy of TTB F 5620.8 will be returned to the manufacturer as notice of such action, which copy shall be retained by the manufacturer.

(72 Stat. 1419, as amended, 26 U.S.C. 5707)

Lost or Destroyed

§40.475 Action by claimant.

Where cigarette papers and tubes are lost (other than by theft) or destroyed, by fire, casualty, or act of God, and the manufacturer desires to file claim under the provisions of §40.472 or §40.473, the manufacturer shall indicate on the claim the nature, date, and extent of such loss or destruction. The claim shall be accompanied by such evidence as necessary to establish to the satisfaction of the appropriate TTB officer that the claim is valid.

(72 Stat. 1419; 26 U.S.C. 5705)

Withdrawn From the Market.

§40.476 Action by claimant.

Where cigarette papers and tubes are withdrawn from the market and the manufacturer desires to file claim under the provisions of §40.472 or §40.473, the manufacturer shall assemble the articles in or adjacent to a factory if they are to be retained in or received into such factory, or at any suitable place if they are to be destroyed. The manufacturer shall group the articles according to the rate of tax applicable thereto, and shall prepare and submit a schedule of the articles, on TTB Form 5200.7 in accordance with the instructions, on the form. All copies of the schedule shall be forwarded to the appropriate TTB officer.

(72 Stat. 1419; 26 U.S.C. 5705)

[T.D. ATF-384, 61 FR 54085, Oct. 17, 1996, as amended by T.D. ATF-424, 64 FR 71932, Dec. 22, 1999]

§40.477 Action by the appropriate TTB officer.

Upon receipt of a schedule of cigarette papers and tubes withdrawn from the market, the appropriate TTB officer may assign a TTB officer to verify the schedule and supervise disposition of the cigarette papers and tubes, or may authorize the manufacturer to dispose of the articles without supervision by so stating on the original and one copy of the schedule returned to the manufacturer.

(72 Stat. 1419; 26 U.S.C. 5705)

§40.478 Disposition of cigarette papers and tubes and schedule.

When so authorized, as evidenced by the appropriate TTB officer's statement on the schedule, the manufacturer shall dispose of the cigarette papers and tubes as specified in the schedule. After the articles are disposed of, the manufacturer shall execute a certificate on both copies of the schedule received from the appropriate TTB officer, to show the disposition and the date of disposition of the articles. In connection with a claim for credit or refund, the manufacturer shall attach the original of the schedule to the claim for credit or refund, TTB F 5620.8, filed under § 40.473. When an appropriate TTB officer is assigned to verify the schedule and supervise disposition of the cigarette papers and tubes, such officer shall, upon completion of the assignment, execute a certificate on all copies of the schedule to show the disposition and the date of disposition of the articles. In connection with a claim for allowance, the officer shall return one copy of the schedule to the manufacturer for the record, and in connection with a claim for credit or refund, the officer shall return the original and one copy of the schedule to the manufacturer, the original of which the manufacturer shall attach to the claim filed under § 40.473.

(72 Stat. 1419, as amended; 26 U.S.C. 26 U.S.C. 5705)

Subpart L—Manufacture of Processed Tobacco

SOURCE: T.D. TTB–78, 74 FR 29410, June 22, 2009, unless otherwise noted.

QUALIFICATION REQUIREMENTS FOR MANUFACTURERS OF PROCESSED TOBACCO

§ 40.491 Persons required to qualify.

(a) *General.* Except as otherwise provided in paragraph (b) of this section, every person who engages in the processing of tobacco must first qualify for and receive a permit as a manufacturer of processed tobacco in accordance with the provisions of this subpart.

(b) *Exceptions.* (1) A person who engages in the processing of tobacco solely for his own personal use or consumption and not for sale or transfer to another person is not engaged in the manufacture of processed tobacco for purposes of this part and, accordingly, is not required to qualify as a manufacturer of processed tobacco.

(2) Any person who holds a TTB permit for the manufacture of tobacco products is thereby authorized to process tobacco solely for use in the manufacture of tobacco products under that permit, so long as the processed tobacco is not removed from the factory for any purpose other than destruction. Such a manufacturer is not required to qualify under this subpart as a manufacturer of processed tobacco.

(3) Any person that holds a TTB permit for the manufacture of tobacco products and that removes processed tobacco from the factory must apply for authorization to engage in that activity, when required to do so under § 40.47.

[T.D. TTB–78, 74 FR 29410, June 22, 2009, as amended by T.D. TTB–104, 77 FR 37304, June 21, 2012]

§ 40.492 Application for permit.

The application for a permit as a manufacturer of processed tobacco must be made on TTB F 5200.3, according to the instructions on the form. All documents required under this subpart to be furnished with the application must be included with the application.

§ 40.493 Transitional rule.

(a) Any person who:

(1) On April 1, 2009, is engaged in business as a manufacturer of processed tobacco; and

(2) On or before June 30, 2009, submits an application for a permit or authorization as provided in this part to engage in such business, may continue to engage in that business pending final action on the application.

(b) Pending final action on an application or request for authorization submitted under paragraph (a) of this section, all provisions of chapter 52 of the Internal Revenue Code of 1986 shall apply to the applicant in the same manner and to the same extent as if the applicant were a holder of a permit to manufacture processed tobacco under chapter 52.

(c) Upon receipt of an application, the appropriate TTB officer will provide the applicant with a written acknowledgement that may be used for a limited period as confirmation of TTB authorization to engage in the business of a manufacturer of processed tobacco.

[T.D. TTB–78, 74 FR 29410, June 22, 2009, as amended by T.D. TTB–80, 74 FR 37552, July 29, 2009]

§ 40.494 Corporate documents.

Every corporation that files an application for a permit as a manufacturer of processed tobacco must furnish with its application for the permit required by §40.492 a true copy of the corporate charter or a certificate of corporate existence or incorporation executed by the appropriate officer of the State in which incorporated. The corporation must likewise furnish duly authenticated extracts of the stockholders' meetings, bylaws, or directors' meetings, listing the offices the incumbents of which are authorized to sign documents or otherwise act in behalf of the corporation in matters relating to 26 U.S.C. chapter 52, and regulations issued thereunder. The corporation must also furnish evidence, in duplicate, of the identity of the officers and directors and each person who holds more than ten percent of the stock of such corporation. Where any of the information required by this section has previously been filed with the appropriate TTB officer and such information is currently complete and accurate, a written statement to that effect, in duplicate, will be sufficient for the purpose of this section.

§40.495 Articles of partnership or association.

Every partnership or association that files an application for a permit as a manufacturer of processed tobacco must furnish with its application for the permit required by §40.492 a true copy of the articles of partnership or association, if any, or certificate of partnership or association where required to be filed by any State, county, or municipality. Where a partnership or association has previously filed such documents with the appropriate TTB officer and such documents are currently complete and accurate, a written statement, in duplicate, to that effect by the partnership or association will be sufficient for the purpose of this section.

§40.496 Trade name certificate.

Every person that files an application for a permit as a manufacturer of processed tobacco operating under a trade name must furnish with the application for the permit required by §40.492 a true copy of the certificate or other document, if any, issued by a State, county, or municipal authority in connection with the transaction of business under such trade name. If no such certificate or other document is so required, a written statement, in duplicate, to that effect by such person will be sufficient for the purpose of this section.

[T.D. TTB–78, 74 FR 29410, June 22, 2009, as amended by T.D. TTB–80, 74 FR 37552, July 29, 2009]

§40.497 Additional information.

The appropriate TTB officer may require such additional information as deemed necessary to determine whether the applicant is entitled to a permit under this subpart. The applicant shall, when required by the appropriate TTB officer, furnish as a part of the application for the permit such additional information as may be necessary for the appropriate TTB officer to determine whether the applicant is entitled to a permit.

§40.498 Investigation of applicant.

Appropriate TTB officers may inquire or investigate to verify the information in connection with an application for a permit. The investigation will ascertain whether the applicant is eligible for a permit. A permit may be denied if the applicant (including, in the case of a corporation, any officer, director, or principal stockholder and, in the case of a partnership, a partner)—

(a) Is, by reason of his business experience, financial standing, or trade connections or by reason of previous or current legal proceedings involving a felony violation of any other provision of Federal criminal law relating to tobacco products, processed tobacco, cigarette paper, or cigarette tubes, not likely to maintain operations in compliance with this chapter;

(b) Has been convicted of a felony violation of any provision of Federal or State criminal law relating to tobacco products, processed tobacco, cigarette paper, or cigarette tubes; or

(c) Has failed to disclose any material information required or made any material false statement in the application therefor.

§ 40.499 Notice of contemplated disapproval.

If the appropriate TTB officer has reason to believe that the applicant is not entitled to a permit, the appropriate TTB officer will promptly give to the applicant notice of the contemplated disapproval of the application and opportunity for hearing thereon in accordance with part 71 of this chapter. If, after such notice and opportunity for hearing, the appropriate TTB officer finds that the applicant is not entitled to a permit, an order will be prepared stating the findings on which the permit request is denied.

§ 40.500 Issuance of permit.

If the application for permit, together with the supporting documents, required under this part is approved, the appropriate TTB officer will issue a permit on TTB F 5200.28 to the applicant as a manufacturer of processed tobacco.

§ 40.501 Retention of permit and supporting documents.

The manufacturer must retain the permit, together with the copy of the application and supporting documents returned with the permit, at the same place where the records required by this subpart are kept. The permit and supporting documents must be made available for inspection by any appropriate TTB officer upon request.

QUALIFICATION REQUIREMENTS FOR MANUFACTURERS OF PROCESSED TOBACCO

§ 40.502 Factory premises.

(a) *General.* The premises used by a manufacturer of processed tobacco to conduct such business must be described on its permit and such premises must include any physical location or building used for: Manufacturing and storing processed tobacco; storing materials, equipment, and supplies related to or used in the manufacturing and storage of processed tobacco; and carrying on activities in connection with the manufacturing and storage of processed tobacco. The premises may consist of more than one building, or portions of buildings, which need not be contiguous or located in the same city, town, village, or State. The manufacturer must designate a central location as a repository for the records required under this subpart. The application for the permit filed under § 40.492 must describe the buildings or portions of buildings by street address (number, street, city or equivalent, and State). The permit application must include a diagram, in duplicate, showing the following information, if applicable:

(1) The identification of each building by a letter, number, or similar designation if the factory is in more than one building and each building is not identifiable by a separate street address; and

(2) The particular floor or floors, or room or rooms, comprising the factory if the factory consists of, or includes, a portion of a building or portions of buildings.

(b) *Permits issued prior to June 21, 2012.* A manufacturer of processed tobacco operating under a permit issued prior to June 21, 2012, must submit the information required under paragraph (a) of this section within 180 days after June 21, 2012.

(c) *Extension or curtailment of factory.* If a manufacturer of processed tobacco wishes to change the premises delineated by its permit to an extent that would be inconsistent with the description or diagram of the premises that was submitted with the manufacturer's last permit application, the manufacturer must submit an application on TTB Form 5200.16 for, and obtain, an amended permit before the change in the premises occurs. The application must describe the proposed change in the premises and must be accompanied by a new diagram if required under paragraph (a) of this section.

[T.D. TTB–104, 77 FR 37303, June 21, 2012]

CHANGES AFTER QUALIFICATION

§ 40.511 Change in name.

(a) *Change in individual name.* When there is a change in the name of an individual operating under a permit as a manufacturer of processed tobacco, the manufacturer must, within 30 days of such change, make application on TTB F 5200.16 for an amended permit.

(b) *Change in trade name.* When there is a change in a trade name used by a manufacturer of processed tobacco in connection with operations authorized by the permit, the manufacturer must, within 30 days of such change, make application on TTB F 5200.16 for an amended permit to reflect such change. This requirement also applies to the addition or discontinuance of a trade name. The manufacturer must also furnish a true copy of any new trade name certificate or document issued to the manufacturer, or statement in lieu thereof, required by § 40.496.

(c) *Change in corporate name.* When there is a change in the corporate name of a manufacturer of processed tobacco, the manufacturer must, within 30 days of such change, make application on TTB F 5200.16 for an amended permit. The manufacturer must also furnish such documents as may be necessary to establish that the corporate name has been changed.

§ 40.512 Change in ownership or control.

(a) *Fiduciary successor.* If an administrator, executor, receiver, trustee, assignee, or other fiduciary is to take over the business of a manufacturer of processed tobacco as a continuing operation, such fiduciary shall, before commencing operations, make application for a permit in accordance with this subpart, furnish certified copies, in duplicate, of the order of the court, or other pertinent documents, showing his appointment and qualification as such fiduciary, and make a commencing inventory in accordance with § 40.523. However, where a fiduciary intends only to liquidate the business, qualification as a manufacturer of processed tobacco will not be required if such fiduciary promptly files with the appropriate TTB officer a written statement to that effect, in duplicate.

(b) *Transfer of ownership.* If a transfer in ownership of the business of a manufacturer of processed tobacco (including a change of any member of a partnership or association) is to be made, such manufacturer shall give notice, in writing, to the appropriate TTB officer, naming the proposed successor and the desired effective date of the transfer. The proposed successor shall, before commencing operations, qualify as a manufacturer of processed tobacco in accordance with this subpart. The manufacturer shall give notice of the transfer, and the proposed successor shall make application for permit, in ample time for examination and approval thereof before the desired date of such change. The predecessor shall make a concluding inventory and concluding report, in accordance with §§ 40.523 and 40.522, respectively, and surrender the permit with such inventory and report. The successor shall make a commencing inventory and first report, in accordance with §§ 40.523 and 40.522, respectively.

(c) *Change in officers, directors, or stockholders of a corporation.* Upon election or appointment (excluding successive reelection or reappointment) of any officer or director of a corporation operating the business of a manufacturer of processed tobacco, or upon any occurrence that results in a person acquiring ownership or control of more than ten percent in aggregate of the outstanding stock of such corporation, the manufacturer shall, within 30 days of such action, so notify the appropriate TTB officer in writing, giving the identity of such person. When there is any change in the authority furnished under § 40.494 for officers to act in behalf of the corporation, the manufacturer shall immediately so notify the appropriate TTB officer in writing.

(d) *Change in control of corporation.* When the issuance, sale, or transfer of the stock of a corporation operating as a manufacturer of processed tobacco results in a change in the identity of the principal stockholders exercising actual or legal control of the operations of the corporation, the corporate manufacturer shall, within 30 days after the change occurs, make application on TTB F 5200.3 for a new permit. Otherwise, the present permit shall be automatically terminated at the expiration of such 30-day period, and the manufacturer shall dispose of all processed tobacco on hand, make a concluding inventory and concluding report, in accordance with the provisions of §§ 40.523 and 40.522, respectively, and surrender the permit with such inventory and report. If the application for a new permit is timely made, the present permit shall continue in effect pending final action with respect to such application.

§ 40.513 Change in location or address of factory.

Whenever a manufacturer of processed tobacco intends to relocate its factory, the manufacturer shall, before commencing operations at the new location, make application on TTB F 5200.16 for, and obtain, an amended permit. Whenever any change occurs in the address, but not the location, of the factory of a manufacturer of processed tobacco as a result of action of local authorities, the manufacturer shall, within 30 days of such change, make application on TTB F 5200.16 for an amended permit.

[T.D. TTB–78, 74 FR 29410, June 22, 2009, as amended by T.D. TTB–80, 74 FR 37552, July 29, 2009]

OPERATIONS BY MANUFACTURERS OF PROCESSED TOBACCO

§ 40.521 Record of tobacco and processed tobacco.

(a) Every manufacturer of processed tobacco and every manufacturer of tobacco products required to obtain authorization to engage in another business within the factory under §§ 40.47(b) and 40.72(b) of this part must keep records of operations and transactions that show the total quantity of all:

(1) Processed tobacco on hand at the beginning of each month;

(2) In the case of a manufacturer of tobacco products, processed tobacco used in the manufacture of tobacco products during each month;

(3) Processed tobacco received, together with the date of receipt and the name and address of the person from whom it was received;

(4) Processed tobacco removed from the factory for shipment to a person holding a TTB permit as a manufacturer of processed tobacco, as a manufacturer of tobacco products, as an importer of processed tobacco, or as an export warehouse proprietor, together with the date of removal and the name and address of the person to whom shipped or delivered;

(5) Processed tobacco removed from the factory for shipment, other than for export, to a person not holding a TTB permit as a manufacturer of processed tobacco, as a manufacturer of tobacco products, as an importer of processed tobacco, or as an export warehouse proprietor, together with the date of removal;

(6) Processed tobacco removed from the factory for export, together with the date of removal;

(7) Processed tobacco removed for any purpose not referred to in paragraphs (a)(4), (5), (6), and (7) of this section, together with the date of removal;

(8) Processed tobacco lost, together with the date and other circumstances of the loss;

(9) Processed tobacco destroyed (either on factory premise or removed from factory premises for destruction), together with the date and other circumstances of the destruction;

(10) Processed tobacco transferred between buildings that are covered under the same permit but that are not located in the same city, town, village, or State; and

(11) Tobacco (unprocessed) on hand at the beginning of each month and used in the manufacture of tobacco products, lost, destroyed, or removed during each month.

(b) Any manufacturer of processed tobacco and any manufacturer of tobacco products that are required to obtain authorization to engage in another business within the factory under §§ 40.47(b) and 40.72(b) and that engage in removals of processed tobacco described in paragraph (a)(5) or (a)(6) of this section must also keep records that show the following information about each such removal:

(1) The full name and business address (including city and State) of the purchaser (if there is a purchaser) and the full name and business address of the recipient, or personal address if the purchaser or recipient is not a business;

(2) The full name, business address (including city and State), and driver's license number of the person picking up the processed tobacco for delivery;

(3) The license number of the vehicle in which the processed tobacco is removed from the manufacturer's premises;

(4) The street address of the destination (not including any in-transit stops) of the processed tobacco; and

(5) The quantity of processed tobacco in the shipment;

(c) The entries in the records of removals required under this section must be made for each day by the close of the business day following the day on which the removal occurs. There is no particular format prescribed for the records required under this section (and commercial records may be used) although the required information must be readily ascertainable from the records kept. In the case of a removal under paragraph (a)(5) or (a)(6) of this section that involves shipment by a common carrier, the appropriate TTB officer may approve an alternate method or procedure pursuant to §§40.45 or 40.531 through which the manufacturer may keep records regarding the common carrier and its means of tracking (including pick up and delivery) of the shipment in lieu of the information required by paragraphs (b)(2) and (b)(3) of this section.

[T.D. TTB–104, 77 FR 37303, June 21, 2012]

§40.522 Reports.

(a) *General.* Every manufacturer of processed tobacco must prepare a monthly report on TTB F 5250.1 in accordance with the instructions for the form. The report must be prepared at the times specified in this section and must be prepared whether or not any operations or transactions occurred during the period covered by the report. The manufacturer must retain a copy of each report in accordance with the provisions of this subpart.

(b) *First report(s).* The first monthly report must be submitted by the 20th day of the month following the month in which the permit or authorization is issued. If the manufacturer is operating as a manufacturer of processed tobacco under the transitional rule set forth in §40.493, the manufacturer must submit the first report by the 20th day of the month following the month in which TTB provides written acknowledgement of the receipt of the application filed under §40.492. In the transitional case, the manufacturer must also submit reports for all previous months back to April 2009. For example, a manufacturer who receives an acknowledgement, dated July 17, 2009, must submit by August 20, 2009, a total of four reports, one each for April, May, June, and July 2009.

(c) *Reports of no activity.* Reports with the notation "No Activity" must be made for those months in which no activity occurs.

(d) *Reports of removals.* (1) Except as otherwise provided in paragraphs (d)(2) or (d)(3) of this section, a manufacturer who removes processed tobacco for export or for shipment to someone other than a person holding a TTB permit as a manufacturer of processed tobacco, as a manufacturer of tobacco products, as an importer of processed tobacco, or as an export warehouse proprietor must report each such removal on TTB F 5250.2 by the close of the next business day following the day of removal, in accordance with the instructions on the form.

(2) In the case of removals for export, as an alternative to the procedure prescribed in paragraph (d)(1) of this section, the manufacturer may submit to TTB a monthly summary report of such removals in a format approved by the appropriate TTB officer. Prior to the use of such an alternate procedure, the manufacturer must obtain written approval from the appropriate TTB officer.

(3) A manufacturer of tobacco products who removes processed tobacco for any of the purposes related to the manufacture of tobacco products set forth under §40.72(b)(2) is not required to report such removals on TTB F 5250.2. Records of such removals must still be kept pursuant to §40.521.

(e) *Concluding report.* A concluding report, covering the period from the first of the month to the date of the concluding inventory, shall be made with such inventory.

(26 U.S.C. 5722)

[T.D. TTB–78, 74 FR 29410, June 22, 2009, as amended by T.D. TTB–80, 74 FR 37552, July 29, 2009; T.D. TTB–104, 77 FR 37304, June 21, 2012]

§40.523 Inventories.

Every manufacturer of processed tobacco must provide a true and accurate inventory on TTB F 5210.9 in accordance with instructions for the form. The manufacturer must make such an inventory at the time of commencing business, at the time of transferring ownership, at the time of changing location of the factory, at the time of concluding business, and at such other time as any appropriate TTB officer may require. In the case of a manufacturer operating under the transitional rule set forth in § 40.493, that manufacturer must make an inventory within 10 days of the date of TTB's written acknowledgement of the receipt of the application filed under § 40.492. Each such inventory is subject to verification by the appropriate TTB officer.

(26 U.S.C. 5721)

§ 40.524 Retention of documents.

Every manufacturer of processed tobacco must retain all records and reports required under this subpart, including copies of permits, authorizations, inventories, and reports, for three years following the close of the calendar year in which filed or made, or in the case of an authorization, for three years following the close of the calendar year in which the operation under such authorization is concluded. Such records shall be made available for inspection by the appropriate TTB officer upon request.

(26 U.S.C. 5741)

§ 40.525 Discontinuance of operations.

Every manufacturer of processed tobacco who desires to discontinue operations and close a factory must dispose of all processed tobacco on hand, make a concluding inventory and concluding report, in accordance with the provisions of §§ 40.523 and 40.522, respectively, and surrender the permit to the appropriate TTB officer.

(26 U.S.C. 5721, 5722)

§ 40.526 Minimum manufacturing and activity requirements.

A permit to manufacture processed tobacco will only be granted to those persons engaged in the processing of tobacco. A permit may be suspended, and subsequently revoked, if the person has no activity under such permit for a period of one year. A person whose permit as a manufacturer of processed tobacco has been revoked for non-use, who wishes to engage in such business, must re-apply for such permit.

(26 U.S.C. 5712)

§ 40.527 Authorization to package processed tobacco.

A permit to manufacture processed tobacco does not authorize packaging of processed tobacco. Packaging of processed tobacco may only occur on the bonded premises of a manufacturer of tobacco products.

§ 40.528 Suspension and revocation of permit.

Where the appropriate TTB officer has reason to believe that a manufacturer of processed tobacco has not in good faith complied with the provisions of 26 U.S.C. chapter 52, and regulations thereunder, or with any other provision of 26 U.S.C. with intent to defraud, or has violated any condition of his permit, or has failed to disclose any material information required or made any material false statement in the application for the permit, or is, by reason of previous or current legal proceedings involving a felony violation of any other provision of Federal criminal law relating to tobacco products, processed tobacco, cigarette paper, or cigarette tubes, not likely to maintain operations in compliance with 26 U.S.C. chapter 52, or has been convicted of a felony violation of any provision of Federal or State criminal law relating to tobacco products, processed tobacco, cigarette paper, or cigarette tubes, the appropriate TTB officer shall issue an order, stating the facts charged, citing such person to show cause why his permit should not be suspended or revoked. Such citation shall be issued and opportunity for hearing afforded in accordance with part 71 of this chapter, which part is applicable to such proceedings. If, after hearing, the hearing examiner, or on appeal, the Administrator, finds that such person has not shown cause why his permit should not be suspended or revoked, such permit shall be suspended for such period as the appropriate TTB officer deems proper or shall be revoked.

[T.D. TTB–78, 74 FR 29410, June 22, 2009, as amended by T.D. TTB–80, 74 FR 37552, July 29, 2009]

OTHER PROVISIONS RELATING TO MANUFACTURERS OF PROCESSED TOBACCO

§40.531 Alternate methods or procedures.

(a) *General.* A manufacturer of processed tobacco, on specific approval by the appropriate TTB officer as provided in this section, may use an alternate method or procedure in lieu of a method or procedure specifically prescribed in this subpart. The appropriate TTB officer may approve an alternate method or procedure, subject to stated conditions, when the appropriate TTB officer finds that—

(1) Good cause has been shown for the use of the alternate method or procedure;

(2) The alternate method or procedure is within the purpose of, and consistent with the effect intended by, the specifically prescribed method or procedure, and

(3) The alternate method or procedure will not be contrary to any provision of law, and will not result in an increase in cost to the Government or hinder the effective administration of this subpart.

(b) *Application.* A manufacturer of processed tobacco who desires to employ an alternate method or procedure must submit a written application to the appropriate TTB officer. The application shall specifically describe the proposed alternate method or procedure, and shall set forth the reasons therefor. An alternate method or procedure shall not be employed until the application has been approved by the appropriate TTB officer. The manufacturer shall, during the period of authorization of an alternate method or procedure, comply with the terms of the approved application. Authorization for any alternate method or procedure may be withdrawn whenever, in the judgment of the appropriate TTB officer, the effective administration of this part is hindered. Any authorization of the appropriate TTB officer under this section shall be retained as part of the manufacturer's records in accordance with this subpart.

[T.D. TTB–78, 74 FR 29410, June 22, 2009, as amended by T.D. TTB–104, 77 FR 37304, June 21, 2012]

§40.532 Emergency variations from requirements.

The appropriate TTB officer may approve methods of operation other than as specified in this subpart, where it is determined that an emergency exists and the proposed variations from the specified requirements are necessary, and provided that the proposed variations will not hinder the effective administration of this subpart and will not be contrary to any provision of law. Variations from requirements granted under this section are conditioned on compliance with the procedures, conditions, and limitations set forth in the approval of the application. Failure to comply in good faith with such procedures, conditions, and limitations will automatically terminate the authority for such variations, and the manufacturer of processed tobacco thereupon must fully comply with the prescribed requirements of the regulations from which the variations were authorized. Authority for any variation may be withdrawn whenever in the judgment of the appropriate TTB officer the effective administration of this subpart is hindered by the continuation of such variation. Where a manufacturer desires to employ such variation, the manufacturer must submit a written application to do so to the appropriate TTB officer. The application must describe the proposed variations and set forth the reasons therefor. Variations may not be employed until the application has been approved. Any authorization of the appropriate TTB officer under this section shall be retained as part of the manufacturer's records, in accordance with this subpart.

§40.533 Penalties and forfeitures.

Anyone who fails to comply with the provisions of this subpart may be liable to the civil and criminal penalties, and forfeitures, provided by law.

§40.534 Power of attorney.

If the application for permit or any report or other document required to be executed under this subpart is to be signed by an individual (including one of the partners for a partnership or one of the members of an association) as an attorney in fact for any person, or if an individual is to otherwise officially represent such person, power of attorney on TTB F 5000.8 shall be furnished to the appropriate TTB officer. Such power of attorney is not required for persons whose authority is furnished with the corporate documents as required by §40.494. TTB F 5000.8 does not have to be filed again with the appropriate TTB officer where such form has previously been submitted to that appropriate TTB officer and is still in effect.

PART 41—IMPORTATION OF TOBACCO PRODUCTS, CIGARETTE PAPERS AND TUBES, AND PROCESSED TOBACCO

AUTHORITY: 26 U.S.C. 5701–5705, 5708, 5712, 5713, 5721–5723, 5741, 5754, 5761–5763, 6301, 6302, 6313, 6402, 6404, 7101, 7212, 7342, 7606, 7651, 7652, 7805; 31 U.S.C. 9301, 9303, 9304, 9306.

SOURCE: Redesignated by T.D. TTB–16, 69 FR 52424, Aug. 26, 2004, unless otherwise noted.

EDITORIAL NOTE: Nomenclature changes to part 41 (formerly part 275) appear at T.D. ATF–460, 66 FR 39093, July 27, 2001.

Subpart A—Scope of Regulations

§ 41.1 Importation of tobacco products, cigarette papers and tubes, and processed tobacco.

This part contains regulations relating to tobacco products, cigarette papers and tubes, and processed tobacco imported into the United States from a foreign country or brought into the United States from Puerto Rico, the Virgin Islands, or a possession of the United States.

[78 FR 38568, June 27, 2013]

EFFECTIVE DATE NOTE: At 78 FR 38568, June 27, 2013, §41.1 was revised, effective Aug. 26, 2013 through Aug. 26, 2016.

Subpart B—Definitions

§ 41.11 Meaning of terms.

When used in this part and in forms prescribed under this part, the following terms shall have the meanings given in this section, unless the context clearly indicates otherwise. Words in the plural form shall include the singular, and vice versa, and words indicating the masculine gender shall include the feminine. The terms "includes" and "including" do not exclude things not listed which are in the same general class.

Administrator. The Administrator, Alcohol and Tobacco Tax and Trade Bureau, Department of the Treasury, Washington, DC.

Appropriate TTB officer. An officer or employee of the Alcohol and Tobacco Tax and Trade Bureau (TTB) authorized to perform any functions relating to the administration or enforcement of this part by TTB Order 1135.41, Delegation of the Administrator's Authorities in 27 CFR Part 41, Importation of Tobacco Products and Cigarette Papers and Tubes.

Bank. Any commercial bank.

Banking day. Any day during which a bank is open to the public for carrying on substantially all its banking functions.

Business day. Any day, other than a Saturday, Sunday, or a legal holiday. (The term legal holiday includes all holidays in the District of Columbia and, in the case of bonded manufacturers in Puerto Rico, all legal holidays in the Commonwealth of Puerto Rico.)

Bonded manufacturer. A manufacturer of tobacco products in Puerto Rico who has an approved bond, in accordance with the provisions of this part, authorizing him to defer the payment in Puerto Rico on the internal revenue tax imposed on such products by 26 U.S.C. 7652(a) as provided in this part.

CFR. The Code of Federal Regulations.

Chewing Tobacco. Any leaf tobacco that is not intended to be smoked.

Cigar. Any roll of tobacco wrapped in leaf tobacco or in any substance containing tobacco (other than any roll of tobacco which is a cigarette within the meaning of paragraph (2) of the definition for cigarette).

Cigarette. (1) Any roll of tobacco wrapped in paper or in any substance not containing tobacco, and

(2) Any roll of tobacco wrapped in any substance containing tobacco which, because of its appearance, the type of tobacco used in the filler, or its packaging and labeling, is likely to be offered to, or purchased by, consumers as a cigarette described in paragraph (1) of this definition.

Cigarette paper. Paper, or any other material except tobacco, prepared for use as a cigarette wrapper.

Cigarette tube. Cigarette paper made into a hollow cylinder for use in making cigarettes.

Commercial bank. A bank, whether or not a member of the Federal Reserve System, which has access to the Federal Reserve Communications System (FRCS) or Fedwire. The "FRCS" or "Fedwire" is a communications network that allows Federal Reserve System member banks to effect a transfer of funds for their customers (or other commercial banks) to the Treasury Account at the Federal Reserve Bank in New York.

Computation or computed. When used with respect to the tax on tobacco products of Puerto Rican manufacture, computation or computed shall mean that the bonded manufacturer has ascertained the quantity and kind (small cigars, large cigars, small cigarettes, large cigarettes, chewing tobacco, snuff, pipe tobacco, or roll-your-own tobacco) of tobacco products and the sale price of large cigars being shipped to the United States; that adequate bond has been posted to cover the payment, in Puerto Rico, of the tax on such products to be deferred under subpart G of this part; that the tax imposed on such products by 26 U.S.C. 7652(a) has been calculated; that the bonded manufacturer has executed an agreement to pay the internal revenue tax which will become due with respect to such products, as provided in this part; and that a TTB officer has verified and executed a certification of such calculation.

Customs officer. An officer of U.S. Customs and Border Protection or any agent or other person authorized by law or designated by the Secretary of the Treasury or the Secretary of Homeland Security to perform the duties of an officer of U.S. Customs and Border Protection.

Determine. To establish enough information about taxable products at the time of removal to calculate the tax, specifically the quantity (pounds or number) and kind (for example, cigarettes, snuff, paper tubes). Where the tax rate depends on additional information (such as number of cigarette papers to a set before 1/1/2000 or sale price of large cigars), that information must also be established as part of tax determination.

Electronic fund transfer or EFT. Any transfer of funds effected by a bonded manufacturer's commercial bank, either directly or through a correspondent banking relationship, via the Federal Reserve Communications System (FRCS) or Fedwire to the Treasury Account at the Federal Reserve Bank of New York.

Export warehouse. A bonded internal revenue warehouse for the storage of tobacco products and cigarette papers and tubes, upon which the internal revenue tax has not been paid or for the storage of processed tobacco, for subsequent shipment to a foreign country, Puerto Rico, the Virgin Islands, or a possession of the United States, or for consumption beyond the jurisdiction of the internal revenue laws of the United States.

Export warehouse proprietor. Any person who operates an export warehouse.

Factory. The premises of a manufacturer of tobacco products, cigarette papers or tubes, or processed tobacco in which he carries on such business.

Fiscal year. The period which begins October 1 and ends on the following September 30.

HTS. The Harmonized Tariff Schedule of the United States, as published by the United States International Trade Commission.

Importer. Any person in the United States to whom non-taxpaid tobacco products or cigarette papers or tubes, or any processed tobacco manufactured in a foreign country, Puerto Rico, the Virgin Islands, or a possession of the United States are shipped or consigned; any person who removes cigars for sale or consumption in the United States from a Customs bonded manufacturing warehouse; and any person who smuggles or otherwise unlawfully brings tobacco products or cigarette papers or tubes, or any processed tobacco into the United States.

Large cigarettes. Cigarettes weighing more than three pounds per thousand.

Large cigars. Cigars weighing more than three pounds per thousand.

Manufacturer of cigarette papers and tubes. Any person who manufactures cigarette paper, or makes up cigarette paper into tubes, except for his own personal use or consumption.

Manufacturer of processed tobacco. Any person who processes any tobacco other than tobacco products.

Manufacturer of tobacco products. (1) Any person who manufactures cigars, cigarettes, smokeless tobacco, pipe tobacco, or roll-your-own tobacco, other than:

(i) A person who produces tobacco products solely for that person's own consumption or use; or

(ii) A proprietor of a customs bonded manufacturing warehouse with respect to the operation of such warehouse.

(2) The term "Manufacturer of tobacco products" includes any person who for commercial purposes makes available for consumer use (including such consumer's personal consumption or use under paragraph (1)(i) of this definition) a machine capable of making cigarettes, cigars, or other tobacco products. A person making such a machine available for consumer use shall be deemed the person making the removal with respect to any tobacco products manufactured by such machine. A person who sells a machine directly to a consumer at retail for a consumer's personal home use is not making a machine available for commercial purposes if such machine is not used at a retail premises and is designed to produce tobacco products only in personal use quantities.

Package. The immediate container in which tobacco products, processed tobacco, or cigarette papers or tubes are put up by the manufacturer or the importer (prior to release from customs custody) and offered for sale or delivery to the ultimate consumer. For purposes of this definition, a container of processed tobacco, the contents of which weigh 10 pounds or less (including any added non-tobacco ingredients or constituents), that is removed within the meaning of this part for any purpose other than destruction, export, delivery as a sample to a manufacturer of processed tobacco or tobacco products for the purpose of soliciting orders of processed tobacco, or for scientific testing or testing of equipment that results in the destruction of the processed tobacco or the return of the processed tobacco, is deemed to be a package offered for sale or delivery to the ultimate consumer. For appropriate tax rate, see §41.30.

Packaging. When used in the context of an action, the act of placing processed tobacco or a tobacco product in a package.

Person. An individual, partnership, association, company, corporation, estate, or trust.

Pipe tobacco. Any tobacco which because of its appearance, type, packaging, or labeling, is suitable for use and likely to be offered to, or purchased by, consumers as tobacco to be smoked in a pipe.

Port Director of Customs. The director of any port or port of entry as defined in 19 CFR 101.1. A list of customs service ports and ports of entry is set forth in 19 CFR 101.3.

Processed tobacco. Processed tobacco is any tobacco that has undergone processing, but does not include tobacco products. For purposes of this definition, the processing of tobacco does not include the farming or growing of tobacco or the handling of tobacco solely for sale, shipment, or delivery to a manufacturer of tobacco products or processed tobacco, nor does the processing of tobacco include curing, baling, or packaging activities. For purposes of this definition, the processing of tobacco includes, but is not limited to, stemming (that is, removing the stem from the tobacco leaf), fermenting, threshing, cutting, or flavoring the tobacco, or otherwise combining the tobacco with non-tobacco ingredients.

Records. The accounts, books, correspondence, declarations, papers, statements, technical data, electronic media and the computer programs necessary to retrieve the stored information in a usable form, and other documents that:

(1) Pertain to any importation of tobacco products, cigarette papers or tubes, or processed tobacco, to the information contained in the documents required by law or regulation under the Tariff Act of 1930, as amended, in connection with the importation or shipment of merchandise into the United States from Puerto Rico; and

(2) Are of the type normally kept in the ordinary course of business; and

(3) Are sufficiently detailed to:

(i) Establish the right to make the importation or shipment into the United States from Puerto Rico;

(ii) Establish the correctness of any importation or shipment into the United States from Puerto Rico;

(iii) Determine the liability of any person for duties and taxes due, or which may be due, to the United States;

(iv) Determine the liability of any person for fines, penalties, and forfeitures; and

(v) Determine whether the person has complied with the laws and regulations administered by TTB and U.S. Customs and Border Protection (CBP) and with any other documents required under laws or regulations administered by TTB and CBP.

Relanding. When used with reference to tobacco products and cigarette papers and tubes, the term "relanding" means importing, bringing, or returning into the jurisdiction of the United States any tobacco products or cigarette papers or tubes that were manufactured in the United States, labeled or shipped for export (including to Puerto Rico) as prescribed in this chapter, and previously exported from the United States.

Removal or remove. When used with reference to tobacco products or cigarette papers or tubes or any processed tobacco, the term "removal" or "removed" means removal from the factory, release from internal revenue bond under 26 U.S.C. 5704, release from customs custody (including conditional release as defined in 19 CFR 141.0a(i)), and also includes the smuggling or other unlawful importation of such articles into the United States.

Roll-your-own tobacco. Any tobacco which, because of its appearance, type, packaging, or labeling, is suitable for use and likely to be offered to, or purchased by, consumers as tobacco for making cigarettes or cigars, or for use as wrappers thereof.

Sale price. The price for which large cigars are sold by the importer or United States manufacturer, determined in accordance with §41.39 and used for computation of the excise tax.

Small cigarettes. Cigarettes weighing not more than three pounds per thousand.

Small cigars. Cigars weighing not more than three pounds per thousand.

Smokeless tobacco. Any chewing tobacco or snuff.

Snuff. Any finely cut, ground, or powdered tobacco that is not intended to be smoked.

This chapter. Chapter I, title 27, Code of Federal Regulations.

Tobacco products. Cigars, cigarettes, smokeless tobacco, pipe tobacco, and roll-your-own tobacco.

Treasury Account. The Department of the Treasury's General Account at the Federal Reserve Bank of New York.

United States. When used in a geographical sense shall include only the States and the District of Columbia.

U.S.C. The United States Code.

(Aug. 16, 1954, ch. 736, 68A Stat. 775, as amended (26 U.S.C. 6301); June 29, 1956, ch. 462, 70 Stat. 391 (26 U.S.C. 6301))

[T.D. ATF–48, 43 FR 13554, Mar. 31, 1978]

EDITORIAL NOTE: For FEDERAL REGISTER citations affecting §41.11, see the List of CFR Sections Affected, which appears in the Finding Aids section of the printed volume and at *www.fdsys.gov*.

EFFECTIVE DATE NOTE: At 78 FR 38568, June 27, 2013, §41.11 was amended by revising the definitions of "Customs officer", "Export warehouse", "Export warehouse proprietor", "Manufacturer of tobacco products", "Port Director of Customs", "Records", "Relanding", and "Removal or remove", effective Aug. 26, 2013 through Aug. 26, 2016.

Subpart C—General

§41.21 Forms prescribed.

(a) The Administrator is authorized to prescribe all forms required by this part. All of the information called for in each form shall be furnished as indicated by the headings on the form and the instructions on or pertaining to the form. In addition, information called for in each form shall be furnished as required by this part. When a return, form, claim, or other document called for under this part is required by this part, or by the document itself, to be executed under penalties of perjury, it shall be executed under penalties of perjury.

(b) Forms prescribed by this part are available for printing through the TTB Web site (*http://www.ttb.gov*) or by mailing a request to the Alcohol and Tobacco Tax and Trade Bureau, National Revenue Center, 550 Main Street, Room 1516, Cincinnati, OH 45202.

(5 U.S.C. 552(a) (80 Stat. 383, as amended)

[T.D. ATF–92, 46 FR 46922, Sept. 23, 1981, as amended by T.D. ATF–232, 51 FR 28084, Aug. 5, 1986; T.D. ATF–243, 51 FR 43194, Dec. 1, 1986; T.D. ATF–372, 61 FR 20725, May 8, 1996; T.D. TTB–16, 69 FR 52424, Aug. 26, 2004]

§ 41.22 Retention of records.

All records required to be kept under this part, including copies of claims and schedules, authorizations, notices of release, reports, and returns, shall be retained for three years following the close of the year in which filed or made, or in the case of an authorization, for three years following the close of the calendar year in which the operation under such authorization is concluded. Such records shall be made available for inspection by any appropriate TTB officer upon his request.

(72 Stat. 1423; 26 U.S.C. 5741)

[26 FR 8189, Aug. 31, 1961. Redesignated at 40 FR 16835, Apr. 15, 1975, and further redesignated and amended by T.D. TTB–16, 69 FR 52424, Aug. 26, 2004]

§ 41.23 Authority of TTB officers to enter premises.

Any appropriate TTB officer may enter in the daytime any premises where tobacco products or cigarette papers or tubes are produced or kept so far as it may be necessary for the purpose of examining such articles. When such premises are open at night, any appropriate TTB officer may enter them, while so open, in the performance of his official duties. The owner of such premises, or person having the superintendence of the same, who refuses to admit any appropriate TTB officer or permit him to examine such articles shall be liable to the penalties prescribed by law for the offense.

(68A Stat. 872, 903; 26 U.S.C. 7342, 7606)

[T.D. 6871, 31 FR 40, Jan. 4, 1966. Redesignated at 40 FR 16835, Apr. 15, 1975, and amended by T.D. ATF–232, 51 FR 28084, Aug. 5, 1986; T.D. ATF–243, 51 FR 43194, Dec. 1, 1986. Redesignated and amended by T.D. TTB–16, 69 FR 52424, Aug. 26, 2004]

§ 41.24 Interference with administration.

Whoever, corruptly or by force or threats of force, endeavors to hinder or obstruct the administration of this part, or endeavors to intimidate or impede any appropriate TTB officer acting in his official capacity, or forcibly rescues or attempts to rescue or causes to be rescued any property, after it has been duly seized for forfeiture to the United States in connection with a violation of the internal revenue laws, shall be liable to the penalties prescribed by law.

(68A Stat. 855; 26 U.S.C. 7212)

[26 FR 8189, Aug. 31, 1961. Redesignated at 40 FR 16835, Apr. 15, 1975, and further redesignated and amended by T.D. TTB–16, 69 FR 52424, Aug. 26, 2004]

§ 41.25 Disposal of forfeited, condemned, and abandoned tobacco products and cigarette papers and tubes.

When any Federal, State, or local officer having custody of forfeited, condemned, or abandoned tobacco products or cigarette papers or tubes, upon which the Federal tax has not been paid, is of the opinion that the sale thereof will not bring a price equal to the tax due and payable thereon, and the expenses incident to the sale thereof, he shall not sell, nor cause to be sold, such articles for consumption in the United States. Where the articles are not sold, the officer may deliver them to a Federal or State hospital or institution (if they are fit for consumption) or cause their destruction by burning completely or by rendering them unfit for consumption. Where such articles are sold, they shall not be released by the officer having custody thereof until they are properly packaged and taxpaid, which tax shall be considered as a portion of the sales price. Except when the tax is to be paid to the Port Director of Customs or other authorized customs officer in accordance with customs regulations (19 CFR part 127) on sales of articles by customs officers, the payment of tax on those articles must be evidenced by presentation, to the officer having custody of the articles, of a receipt from the appropriate TTB officer showing such payment. In the case of such articles held by or for the Federal Government, the sale thereof shall be subject to the applicable provisions of the Regulations of the General Services Administration, Title 1, Personal Property Management.

(68A Stat. 872, 903; 26 U.S.C. 7342, 7606)

[T.D. 6871, 31 FR 40, Jan. 4, 1966. Redesignated at 40 FR 16835, Apr. 15, 1975, and amended by T.D. ATF–232, 51 FR 28084, Aug. 5, 1986; T.D. ATF–243, 51 FR 43194, Dec. 1, 1986; T.D. ATF–422, 64 FR 71948, Dec. 22, 1999. Redesignated and amended by T.D. TTB–16, 69 FR 52424, Aug. 26, 2004; 78 FR 38568, June 27, 2013]

EFFECTIVE DATE NOTE: At 78 FR 38568, June 27, 2013, §41.25 was amended by revising the fourth sentence, effective Aug. 26, 2013 through Aug. 26, 2016.

§41.26 Alternate methods or procedures.

An importer, on specific approval by the appropriate TTB officer as provided in this section, may use an alternate method or procedure in lieu of a method or procedure specifically prescribed in this part. The appropriate TTB officer may approve an alternate method or procedure, subject to stated conditions, when he finds that—

(a) Good cause has been shown for the use of the alternate method or procedure,

(b) The alternate method or procedure is within the purpose of, and consistent with the effect intended by, the specifically prescribed method or procedure, and affords equivalent security to the revenue, and

(c) The alternate method of procedure will not be contrary to any provision of law, and will not result in an increase in cost to the Government or hinder the effective administration of this part.

No alternate method or procedure relating to the giving of any bond or to the assessment, payment, or collection of tax, shall be authorized under this section. When an importer desires to employ an alternate method or procedure, he shall submit a written application to do so, in triplicate, to the appropriate TTB officer. The application shall specifically describe the proposed alternate method or procedure, and shall set forth the reasons therefor. Alternate methods or procedures shall not be employed until the application has been approved by the appropriate TTB officer. The importer shall, during the period of authorization of an alternate method or procedure, comply with the terms of the approved application. Authorization for any alternate method or procedure may be withdrawn whenever in the judgment of the appropriate TTB officer the revenue is jeopardized or the effective administration of this part is hindered. The importer shall retain, as part of his records, any authorization of the appropriate TTB officer under this section.

[26 FR 8190, Aug. 31, 1961. Redesignated at 40 FR 16835, Apr. 15, 1975, and further redesignated and amended by T.D. TTB–16, 69 FR 52424, Aug. 26, 2004]

§41.27 Emergency variations from requirements.

The appropriate TTB officer may approve methods of operation other than as specified in this part, where he finds that an emergency exists and the proposed variations from the specified requirements are necessary, and the proposed variations—

(a) Will afford the security and protection to the revenue intended by the prescribed specifications,

(b) Will not hinder the effective administration of this part, and

(c) Will not be contrary to any provision of law.

Variations from requirements granted under this section are conditioned on compliance with the procedures, conditions, and limitations set forth in the approval of the application. Failure to comply in good faith and with such procedures, conditions, and limitations shall automatically terminate the authority for such variations and the importer thereupon shall fully comply with the prescribed requirements of regulations from which the variations were authorized. Authority for any variations may be withdrawn whenever in the judgment of the appropriate TTB officer the revenue is jeopardized or the effective administration of this part is hindered by the continuation of such variation. Where an importer desires to employ such variation, he shall submit a written application to do so, in triplicate, to the appropriate TTB officer. The application shall describe the proposed variations and set forth the reasons therefor. Variations shall not be employed until the application has been approved. The importer shall retain, as part of his records, any authorization of the appropriate TTB officer under this section.

[26 FR 8190, Aug. 31, 1961. Redesignated at 40 FR 16835, Apr. 15, 1975, and further redesignated and amended by T.D. TTB–16, 69 FR 52424, Aug. 26, 2004]

§41.28 Penalties and forfeitures.

Anyone who fails to comply with the provisions of this part becomes liable to the civil and criminal penalties, and forfeitures, provided by law.

(72 Stat. 1425, 1426; 26 U.S.C. 5761, 5762, 5763)

[26 FR 8190, Aug. 31, 1961. Redesignated at 40 FR 16835, Apr. 15, 1975]

§41.29 Delegations of the Administrator.

The regulatory authorities of the Administrator contained in this part are delegated to appropriate TTB officers. These TTB officers are specified in TTB Order 1135.41, Delegation of the Administrator's Authorities in 27 CFR Part 41, Importation of Tobacco Products and Cigarette Papers and Tubes. You may obtain a copy of this order by accessing the TTB Web site (*http://www.ttb.gov*) or by mailing a request to the Alcohol and Tobacco Tax and Trade Bureau, National Revenue Center, 550 Main Street, Room 1516, Cincinnati, OH 45202.

[T.D. TTB–16, 69 FR 52424, Aug. 26, 2004]

Subpart D—Taxes

TAX RATES

§41.30 Pipe tobacco and roll-your-own tobacco tax rates.

(a) *Tax rates.* Pipe tobacco and roll-your-own tobacco are taxed at the following rates under 26 U.S.C. 5701(f) and (g), respectively:

Product	Tax rate per pound* for removals during the following periods:	
	2002 to March 31, 2009	April 1, 2009 and after
Pipe tobacco	$ 1.0969	$ 2.8311
Roll-your-own tobacco	$ 1.0969	$ 24.78

* Prorate tax for fractions of a pound.

(b) *Classification.* (1) Pipe tobacco and roll-your-own tobacco, before removal subject to tax, must be put up in packages that conform to the requirements of §41.71 and of §41.72a or §41.72b as appropriate.

(2) Any tobacco that has been processed and that is removed in a package, as that term is defined in §41.11, that does not bear the notice for smokeless tobacco prescribed in §41.72 or the notice for pipe tobacco prescribed in §41.72a is deemed to be roll-your-own tobacco and subject to tax at the rate applicable to roll-your-own tobacco. A container of processed tobacco, the contents of which weigh 10 pounds or less (including any added non-tobacco ingredients or constituents), that is removed within the meaning of this part for any purpose other than destruction, export, delivery as a sample to a manufacturer of processed tobacco or tobacco products for the purpose of soliciting orders of processed tobacco, or for scientific testing or testing of equipment that results in the destruction of the processed tobacco or the return of the processed tobacco, is deemed to be a package offered for sale or delivery to the ultimate consumer.

(3) Subject to paragraph (b)(4) of this section, any tobacco that has been processed and that is removed in a package, as that term is defined in §41.11, is deemed to be roll-your-own tobacco and subject to tax at the rate applicable to roll-your-own tobacco, even though the package bears the notice required for pipe tobacco under §41.72a, if:

(i) The package does not bear the declaration "pipe tobacco" in direct conjunction with, parallel to, and in substantially the same conspicuousness of type and background as the brand name each time the brand name appears on the package; or

(ii) The package or accompanying materials bear any representation that would suggest a use other than as pipe tobacco. The term 'accompanying materials' includes, but is not limited to, any point of sale advertising or other printed product communications issued by the manufacturer or importer of pipe tobacco products. In addition, the inclusion of cigarette papers or tubes in a package bearing a 'pipe tobacco' declaration will suggest a use other than pipe tobacco.

(4) During the period from June 22, 2009, through March 23, 2010, importers may continue to remove products as pipe tobacco in packages that do not bear the declaration "pipe tobacco" in the manner prescribed in paragraph (b)(3)(i) of this section.

(26 U.S.C. 5702 and 5723)

[T.D. TTB–75, 74 FR 14483, Mar. 31, 2009, as amended by T.D. TTB–78, 74 FR 29415, June 22, 2009; T.D. TTB–81, 74 FR 48654, Sept. 24, 2009; T.D. TTB–104, 77 FR 37304, June 21, 2012]

§41.31 Cigar tax rates.

(a) Cigars are taxed at the following rates under 26 U.S.C. 5701(a):

Type and amount	Tax rate for removals during the following periods:	
	2002 to March 31, 2009	April 1, 2009 and after
Small cigars per thousand.	$1.828	$50.33
Large cigars*		
• percentage of sale price.	20.719%	52.750%
• but not to exceed—	$48.75 per thousand.	$0.4026 per cigar.

* For large cigars: Until March 31, 2009, the percentage tax rate applies when the sale price is $235.294 per thousand or less, and the flat tax rate applies when the sale price is more than $235.294 per thousand. On and after April 1, 2009, the percentage tax rate applies when the sale price is $763.222 or less per thousand cigars, and the flat tax rate applies when the sale price is more than $763.222 per thousand cigars.

(b) See §41.39 of this part for rules concerning determination of sale price of large cigars.

(c) Cigars not exempt from tax under 26 U.S.C. chapter 52 and the provisions of this part which are removed but not intended for sale shall be taxed at the same rate as similar cigars removed for sale.

[T.D. ATF–420, 64 FR 71942, Dec. 22, 1999. Redesignated and amended by T.D. TTB–16, 69 FR 52424, 52425, Aug. 26, 2004; T.D. TTB–75, 74 FR 14484, Mar. 31, 2009]

§41.32 Cigarette tax rates.

Cigarettes are taxed at the following rates under 26 U.S.C. 5701(b):

Product	Tax rate per thousand for removals during the following periods:	
	2002 to March 31, 2009	April 1, 2009 and after
Small cigarettes	$19.50	$50.33
Large cigarettes up to 6½″ long.	$40.95	$105.69
Large cigarettes over 6½″ long.	Taxed at the rate for small cigarettes, counting each 2¾ or fraction thereof of the length of each as one cigarette.	

[T.D. TTB–75, 74 FR 14484, Mar. 31, 2009]

§41.33 Smokeless tobacco tax rates.

Smokeless tobacco products are taxed at the following rates under 26 U.S.C. 5701(e):

Product	Tax rate per pound* for removals during the following periods:	
	2002 to March 31, 2009	April 1, 2009 and after
Snuff	$0.585	$1.51
Chewing tobacco	$0.195	$0.5033

* Prorate tax for fractions of a pound.

[T.D. TTB–75, 74 FR 14484, Mar. 31, 2009]

§41.34 Cigarette papers.

Cigarette papers are taxed at the following rates under 26 U.S.C. 5701(c):

Product	Tax rate for each 50 papers* for removals during the following periods:	
	2002 to March 31, 2009	April 1, 2009 and after
Cigarette papers up to 6½ long.	$0.0122	$0.0315
Cigarette papers over 6½″ long.	Use rates above, but count each 2¾″ or fraction thereof of the length of each as one cigarette paper.	

* Tax rate for less than 50 papers is the same. The tax is not prorated.

[T.D. TTB–75, 74 FR 14484, Mar. 31, 2009]

§41.35 Cigarette tubes.

Cigarette tubes are taxed at the following rates under 26 U.S.C. 5701(d):

Product	Tax rate for each 50 tubes* for removals during the following periods: 2002 to March 31, 2009	April 1, 2009 and after
Cigarette tubes up to 6½ long.	$0.0244	$ 0.0630
Cigarette tubes over 6½ long.	Use rates above, but count each 2¾ or fraction thereof of the length of each as one cigarette tube.	

*Tax rate for less than 50 tubes is the same. The tax is not prorated.

[T.D. TTB–75, 74 FR 14484, Mar. 31, 2009, as amended by T.D. TTB–85, 75 FR 42607, July 22, 2010]

CLASSIFICATION OF LARGE CIGARS AND CIGARETTES

§41.37 [Reserved]

§41.38 Cigarettes.

For internal revenue tax purposes, small cigarettes are designated Class A and large cigarettes are designated Class B.

(72 Stat. 1414; 26 U.S.C. 5701)

[26 FR 8191, Aug. 31, 1961. Redesignated at 40 FR 16835, Apr. 15, 1975]

§41.39 Determination of sale price of large cigars.

The tax imposed on large cigars is computed based on the sale price (the price for which the large cigars are sold by the importer or United States manufacturer). In addition to money, goods or services exchanged for cigars may be considered as part of the sale price. See §40.22(b) of this chapter for information on determining the sale price in special cases. See §41.40 of this chapter regarding liability for tax on large cigars, not put up in packages, released from customs custody without payment of tax for delivery to a domestic manufacturer of tobacco products.

[T.D. ATF–420, 64 FR 71944, Dec. 22, 1999; T.D. ATF–422, 64 FR 71948, Dec. 22, 1999; T.D. ATF–422a, 65 FR 15058, Mar. 31, 2000; T.D. ATF–460, 66 FR 39093, July 27, 2001; 78 FR 38568, June 27, 2013]

EFFECTIVE DATE NOTE: At 78 FR 38568, June 27, 2013, §41.39 was amended by adding the words "United States" before the word "manufacturer", and by adding a sentence at the end, effective Aug. 26, 2013 through Aug. 26, 2016.

LIABILITY FOR AND PAYMENT OF TAXES

§41.40 Persons liable for tax.

The importer of tobacco products or cigarette papers and tubes is liable for the internal revenue taxes imposed thereon by 26 U.S.C. 5701 or 7652, except when tobacco products or cigarette papers or tubes imported or brought into the United States (other than those previously exported and returned) are released from customs custody, without payment of tax as provided under 26 U.S.C. 5704(c). Under section 5704(c), tobacco products and cigarette papers and tubes, imported or brought into the United States, may be released from customs custody, without payment of tax, for delivery to the proprietor of an export warehouse, or to a manufacturer of tobacco products or cigarette papers and tubes if such articles are not put up in packages. Under these circumstances the transferee will become liable for the internal revenue tax on these articles upon release from customs custody, and the importer will thereupon be relieved from the liability for the tax. However, if the transferee is also the importer, the importer will not be relieved from the liability for the tax.

[78 FR 38568, June 27, 2013]

EFFECTIVE DATE NOTE: At 78 FR 38568, June 27, 2013, §41.40 was revised, effective Aug. 26, 2013 through Aug. 26, 2016.

§41.41 Determination and payment of tax.

Tobacco products and cigarette papers and tubes imported or brought into the United States, on which internal revenue taxes are due and payable, are not eligible for release from customs custody until those taxes have been determined.

[78 FR 38569, June 27, 2013]

EFFECTIVE DATE NOTE: At 78 FR 38569, June 27, 2013, §41.41 was revised, effective Aug. 26, 2013 through Aug. 26, 2016.

EXEMPTIONS FROM TAXES AND PERMITS

§41.50 Exemptions.

The Harmonized Tariff Schedule of the United States (19 U.S.C. 1202) and Customs Regulations, 19 CFR, chapter I, provide for certain exemptions from internal revenue taxes with respect to tobacco products and cigarette papers and tubes imported into the United States. These exemptions include, but are not limited to, certain importations in passengers' baggage, for use of crew members, and by foreign officials. Persons importing tobacco products and cigarette papers and tubes as described in this section are not required to obtain a permit.

[T.D. 6871, 31 FR 41, Jan. 4, 1966. Redesignated at 40 FR 16835, Apr. 15, 1975, and amended by T.D. ATF–232, 51 FR 28084, Aug. 5, 1986; T.D. ATF–243, 52 FR 43194, Dec. 1, 1986; T.D. ATF–284, 54 FR 12190, Mar. 24, 1989; T.D. ATF–422, 64 FR 71949, Dec. 22, 1999; 78 FR 38569, June 27, 2013]

EFFECTIVE DATE NOTE: At 78 FR 38569, June 27, 2013, §41.50 was amended by revising the last two sentences, effective Aug. 26, 2013 through Aug. 26, 2016.

ASSESSMENT OF TAXES

§41.60 Assessment.

Whenever any person required by law to pay internal revenue tax on tobacco products or cigarette papers or tubes fails to pay such tax, the tax shall be ascertained and assessed against such person, subject to the limitations prescribed in 26 U.S.C. 6501. The tax so assessed shall be in addition to the penalties imposed by law for failure to pay such tax when required. Except in cases where delay may jeopardize collection of the tax, or where the amount is nominal or the result of an evident mathematical error, no such assessment shall be made until and after notice has been afforded such person to show cause against assessment. The person will be allowed 45 days from the date of such notice to show cause, in writing, against such assessment.

(72 Stat. 1417; 26 U.S.C. 5703)

[T.D. 6871, 31 FR 41, Jan. 4, 1966. Redesignated at 40 FR 16835, Apr. 15, 1975, and amended by T.D. ATF–48, 44 FR 55855, Sept. 28, 1979; T.D. ATF–232, 51 FR 28084, Aug. 5, 1986; T.D. ATF–243, 51 FR 43194, Dec. 1, 1986]

CUSTOMS' COLLECTION OF TAXES

§41.62 Customs collection of internal revenue taxes on tobacco products and cigarette papers and tubes imported or brought into the United States.

Internal revenue taxes on tobacco products and cigarette papers and tubes imported or brought into the United States, which are to be paid to the Port Director of Customs or other authorized customs officer, in accordance with this part, must be collected, accounted for, and deposited as internal revenue collections by the Port Director of Customs in accordance with customs procedures and regulations.

[78 FR 38569, June 27, 2013]

EFFECTIVE DATE NOTE: At 78 FR 38569, June 27, 2013, §41.62 was revised, effective Aug. 26, 2013 through Aug. 26, 2016.

§41.63 Payment of tax by electronic fund transfer.

(a) Each importer who was liable, during a calendar year, for a gross amount equal to or exceeding five million dollars in taxes on cigars, cigarettes, cigarette papers, and cigarette tubes combining tax liabilities incurred under this part and part 40 of this chapter, shall use a commercial bank in making payment by electronic fund transfer (EFT) of such taxes during the succeeding calendar year. Payment of such taxes by cash, check, or money order is not authorized for an importer who is required, by this section, to make remittances by EFT. For purposes of this section, the dollar amount of tax liability is defined as the gross tax liability on all taxable withdrawals and importations (including similar products brought into the United States from Puerto Rico or the Virgin Islands) during the calendar year, without regard to any drawbacks, credits, or refunds, for all premises from which such activities are conducted by the taxpayer.

(b) For the purposes of this section, a taxpayer includes a controlled group of corporations, as defined in 26 U.S.C. 1563, and implementing regulations in 26 CFR 1.1563–1 through 1.1563–4, except that the words "at least 80 percent" shall be replaced by the words "more than 50 percent" in each place it appears in subsection (a) of 26 U.S.C. 1563, as well as in the implementing regulations. Also, the rules for a "controlled group of corporations" apply in a similar fashion to groups which include partnerships and/or sole proprietorships. If one entity maintains more than 50% control over a group consisting of corporations and one, or more, partnerships and/or sole proprietorships, all of the members of the controlled group are one taxpayer for the purpose of determining who is required to make remittances by EFT.

(c) For the purposes of this section, (1) electronic fund transfer or EFT means any transfer of funds, other than a transaction originated by check, draft, or similar paper instrument, which is initiated through an electronic terminal, telephonic instrument, or computer of magnetic tape, so as to order, instruct, or authorize a financial institution to either debit or credit an account, in accordance with procedures established by the U.S. Customs Service, and (2) electronic fund transfer or EFT does not have the meaning defined in §41.11 for use elswhere in this part.

(d) An importer who is required by this section to make remittances by EFT, shall make the EFT remittance in accordance with the requirements of the U.S. Customs Service.

(Act of August 16, 1954, 68A Stat. 775, as amended (26 U.S.C. 6302); Sec. 202, Pub. L. 85–859, 72 Stat. 1417, as amended (26 U.S.C. 5703))

[T.D. ATF–245, 52 FR 534, Jan. 7, 1987, as amended by T.D. ATF–384, 61 FR 54095, Oct. 17, 1996. Redesignated and amended by T.D. TTB–16, 69 FR 52424, 52425, Aug. 26, 2004]

Subpart E—Packages

§41.71 Package.

All tobacco products, cigarette papers and tubes, except as provided in §41.75, shall, before removal subject to internal revenue tax, be put up in packages which shall be of such construction as will securely contain the articles therein and maintain the notice thereon as required by this subpart. No package of tobacco products or cigarette papers or tubes shall have contained in, attached to, or stamped, marked, written, or printed thereon (a) any certificate, coupon, or other device purporting to be or to represent a ticket, chance, share, or an interest in, or dependent on, the event of a lottery, (b) any indecent or immoral picture, print, or representation, or (c) any statement or indication that United States tax has been paid. No person may purchase, receive, possess (except for personal consumption), offer for sale, or sell or otherwise dispose of, after removal, any tobacco products that are not put up in packages bearing the marks, labels, and notices, as required under this part.

(26 U.S.C. 5723 and 5751)

[T.D. 6871, 31 FR 41, Jan. 4, 1966. Redesignated at 40 FR 16835, Apr. 15, 1975, and amended by T.D. ATF–232, 51 FR 28084, Aug. 5, 1986; T.D. ATF–243, 51 FR 43194, Dec. 1, 1986. Redesignated and amended by T.D. TTB–16, 69 FR 52424, 52425, Aug. 26, 2004; T.D. TTB–78, 74 FR 29415, June 22, 2009]

§41.72 Notice for smokeless tobacco.

(a) *Product designation.* Every package of chewing tobacco or snuff shall, before removal subject to internal revenue tax, have adequately imprinted thereon, or on a label securely affixed thereto, the designation "chewing tobacco" or "snuff." As an alternative, packages of chewing tobacco may be designated "Tax Class C," and packages of snuff may be designated "Tax Class M."

(b) *Product weight.* Every package of chewing tobacco or snuff shall, before removal subject to internal revenue tax, have adequately imprinted thereon, or on a label securely affixed thereto, a clear statement of the actual pounds and ounces of the product contained therein. As an alternative, the shipping cases containing packages of chewing tobacco or snuff may, before removal, have adequately imprinted thereon, or on a label securely affixed thereto, a clear statement, in pounds and ounces, of the total weight of the product, the tax class of the product, and the total number of the packages of product contained therein.

(Approved by the Office of Management and Budget under control number 1512–0502)

(Sec. 202, Pub. L. 85–859, 72 Stat. 1422 (26 U.S.C. 5723))

[T.D. ATF–243, 51 FR 43194, Dec. 1, 1986, as amended by T.D. ATF–446, 66 FR 16602, Mar. 27, 2001]

§41.72a Notice for pipe tobacco.

(a) *Product designation.* Every package of pipe tobacco shall, before removal subject to internal revenue tax, have adequately imprinted thereon, or on a label securely fixed thereto, the designation "pipe tobacco."

(b) *Product weight.* Every package of pipe tobacco shall, before removal subject to internal revenue tax, have adequately imprinted thereon, or on a label securely affixed thereto, a clear statement of the actual pounds and ounces of the product contained therein.

[T.D. ATF–289, 54 FR 48841, Nov. 27, 1989. Redesignated by T.D. ATF–381, 61 FR 37004, July 16, 1996, as amended by T.D. TTB–78, 74 FR 29415, June 22, 2009]

§41.72b Notice for roll-your-own tobacco.

(a) *Product designation.* Every package of roll-your-own tobacco, before removal subject to tax, must have adequately imprinted on it, or on a label securely affixed to it, the applicable designation "roll-your-own tobacco", "cigarette tobacco", "cigarette wrapper", "cigar tobacco" or "cigar wrapper".

(b) *Product weight.* Before removal subject to tax, roll-your-own tobacco must have a clear statement of the actual weight in pounds and ounces of the product in the package. This statement must be adequately imprinted on, or on a label securely affixed to, the package.

(Approved by the Office of Management and Budget under control number 1513–0091)

[T.D. ATF–429, 65 FR 57547, Sept. 25, 2000, as amended by T.D. TTB–78, 74 FR 29415, June 22, 2009]

§41.72c Package use-up rule.

(a) During the period from June 22, 2009, through March 23, 2010, an importer of tobacco products may remove packages of pipe tobacco or roll-your-own tobacco that do not meet the requirements of §41.72a(a) or §41.72b(a), provided that such packages bear the designation "Tax Class L" (to designate pipe tobacco) or "Tax Class J" (to designate roll-your-own tobacco) and were in use prior to June 22, 2009.

(b) During the period from June 22, 2009, through March 23, 2010, an importer may remove roll-your-own tobacco for which the applicable designation is "cigar tobacco," "cigarette wrapper," or "cigar wrapper" even if the packages of such products do not meet the requirements of §41.72b.

[T.D. TTB–81, 74 FR 48654, Sept. 24, 2009]

§41.73 Notice for cigars.

Before removal subject to internal revenue tax, every package of cigars, except as provided in §41.75, shall have adequately imprinted on it, or on a label securely affixed to it—

(a) The designation "cigars";

(b) The quantity of cigars contained in the package; and

(c) For small cigars, the classification of the product for tax purposes (i.e., either "small" or "little").

(Sec. 202, Pub. L. 85–859, 72 Stat. 1422 (26 U.S.C. 5723))

[T.D. ATF–80, 46 FR 18310, Mar. 24, 1981. Redesignated and amended by T.D. TTB–16, 69 FR 52424, 52425, Aug. 26, 2004]

§41.74 Notice for cigarettes.

Every package of cigarettes, except as provided in §41.75, shall, before removal subject to internal revenue tax, have adequately imprinted thereon, or on a label securely affixed thereto, the designation "cigarettes", the quantity of such product contained therein; and the classification for tax purposes, i.e., for small cigarettes either "small" or "Class A", and for large cigarettes, either "large" or "Class B".

(72 Stat. 1422; 26 U.S.C. 5723)

[26 FR 8192, Aug. 31, 1961. Redesignated at 40 FR 16835, Apr. 15, 1975, further redesignated and amended by T.D. TTB–16, 69 FR 52424, 52425, Aug. 26, 2004]

§41.75 Exemptions.

The provisions of this subpart requiring that tobacco products and cigarette papers and tubes be put up in packages and that proper notice be placed on such packages shall not apply to imported tobacco products and cigarette papers and tubes authorized to be released from customs custody, without payment of internal revenue tax, pursuant to §41.50, and shall not apply to tobacco products imported in passengers' baggage, or by mail where the value does not exceed $250, where such products are solely for the personal consumption of the importer or for disposition as his bona fide gift.

(72 Stat. 1422; 26 U.S.C. 5723)

[T.D. 6871, 31 FR 41, Jan. 4, 1966. Redesignated at 40 FR 16835, Apr. 15, 1975, as amended by T.D. ATF–232, 51 FR 28085, Aug. 5, 1986; T.D. ATF–243, 51 FR 43194, Dec. 1, 1986. Redesignated and amended by T.D. TTB–16, 69 FR 52424, 52425, Aug. 26, 2004]

Subpart F—Tobacco Products and Cigarette Papers and Tubes, Imported Into or Returned to the United States

§41.81 Taxpayment.

(a) *General.* This section applies to tobacco products and cigarette papers and tubes upon which internal revenue tax is payable and which are imported into the United States from a foreign country or are brought into the United States from Puerto Rico, the Virgin Islands, or a possession of the United States. For provisions relating to restrictions on the importation of previously exported tobacco products and cigarette papers and tubes, see §41.82.

(b) *Method of payment.* Except for articles imported or brought into the United States as provided in §§41.85 and 41.85a, the internal revenue tax must be determined before the tobacco products, cigarette papers, or cigarette tubes are removed from customs custody. The tax must be paid on the basis of a return on the customs form or by authorized electronic transmission by which the tobacco products, cigarette papers, or cigarette tubes are duty- and tax-paid to customs.

(c) *Required information.* When tobacco products or cigarette papers or tubes enter the United States for consumption, or when they are released from customs custody for consumption, the importer must include the Federal excise tax information specified in paragraphs (c)(1) through (7) of this section on the customs form or on the authorized electronic transmission if the form or electronic transmission allows for the reporting of such information. Whether or not the specified information appears on the form or electronic transmission filed with customs, that information, together with a copy of the customs form or the electronic transmission, must be retained and made available for inspection by the appropriate TTB officer.

(1) *For cigarette papers:* For cigarette papers imported on or after January 1, 2000, the importer will show the total number of cigarette papers, the rate of tax, and the amount of tax due. For cigarette papers imported prior to January 1, 2000, the importer will show the number of books or sets, the number of papers in each book or set, the rate of tax, and the amount of tax due.

(2) *For cigarette tubes:* The importer will show the number of tubes, the rate of tax, and the tax due.

(3) *For cigarettes:* The importer will show whether the cigarettes are small (class A) or large (class B), the number of cigarettes, the rate of tax, and the tax due.

(4) *For cigars.* The importer will show:

(i) The number imported under each HTS item number;

(ii) For large cigars with a sale price of not more than $235.294 per thousand before April 1, 2009, or a sale price of not more than $763.222 per thousand on and after April 1, 2009, the number and total sale price of such cigars;

(iii) For large cigars with a sale price of more than $235.294 per thousand before April 1, 2009, or a sale price of more than $763.222 per thousand on and after April 1, 2009, the number of cigars;

(iv) The applicable tax rate, as specified by §41.31; and

(v) The tax due.

(5) *For smokeless tobacco:* The importer will show whether the product is chewing tobacco or snuff, the number of pounds and ounces, the rate of tax and the tax due.

(6) *For pipe tobacco:* The importer will show the designation "pipe tobacco",

the number of pounds and ounces, the rate of tax, and the tax due.

(7) *For roll-your-own tobacco:* The importer will show the designation "roll-your-own tobacco" or any other acceptable designation ("cigarette tobacco", "cigarette wrapper", "cigar tobacco", or "cigar wrapper"), the number of pounds and ounces, the rate of tax, and the tax due.

(d) *Exceptions.* The provisions of this section shall not apply to:

(1) Tobacco products, cigarette papers, or cigarette tubes released from customs custody and transferred in bond to a U.S. manufacturer of tobacco products or cigarette papers and tubes (see §§41.85, 41.85a, or 41.135);

(2) Puerto Rican products on which the tax is prepaid or deferred (see subpart G); and

(3) Tax payments of cigars from class 6, customs bonded manufacturing warehouses (see §41.151).

(68A Stat. 907, as amended (26 U.S.C. 7652); sec. 202, Pub. L. 85–859, 72 Stat. 1417 (26 U.S.C. 5703))

[T.D. ATF–27, 41 FR 23951, June 14, 1976]

EDITORIAL NOTE: For FEDERAL REGISTER citations affecting §41.81, see the List of CFR Sections Affected, which appears in the Finding Aids section of the printed volume and at *www.fdsys.gov.*

EFFECTIVE DATE NOTE: At 78 FR 38569, June 27, 2013, §41810 was amended by revising paragraphs (a), (b), and (c) introductory text, effective Aug. 26, 2013 through Aug. 26, 2016.

RELEASE FROM CUSTOMS CUSTODY OF TOBACCO PRODUCTS AND CIGARETTE PAPERS AND TUBES WITHOUT PAYMENT OF TAX OR CERTAIN DUTY

§41.82 Restrictions on tobacco products labeled for export.

(a) The provisions of this section apply to tobacco products and cigarette papers and tubes manufactured in the United States and labeled for exportation under parts 44 and 270 of this chapter.

(b) Articles described in paragraph (a) of this section may be transferred to or removed from the premises of a manufacturer or an export warehouse proprietor only if such articles are being transferred or removed without tax as provided in this part.

(c) Articles described in paragraph (a) of this section may only be imported or brought into the United States, after their exportation, under the provisions of 26 U.S.C. 5704(d), by release from Customs custody for delivery to the original manufacturer of such tobacco products or cigarette papers or tubes or to the proprietor of an export warehouse authorized by such manufacturer to receive such articles. These products are transferred in bond and are released from Customs custody without payment of that part of the duty attributable to internal revenue tax.

(d) Articles described in paragraph (a) of this section that are not put up in packages may be imported or brought into the United States under 26 U.S.C. 5704(c) by release from Customs custody without payment of tax for delivery to the original manufacturer of such articles. However, because such articles are also eligible for release under 26 U.S.C. 5704(d), such articles will be treated as though released under section 5704(d), due to the penalty provisions in section 5761(c).

(e) Articles described in paragraph (a) of this section may not be sold or held for sale for domestic consumption in the United States unless such articles are removed from their export packaging and repackaged by the original manufacturer into new packaging that does not contain an export label. The new packages, marks and notices must conform to the requirements of 27 CFR part 270.

(f) The provisions of this section shall apply to articles labeled for export even if the packaging or the appearance of such packaging to the consumer of such articles has been modified or altered by a person other than the original manufacturer so as to remove or conceal or attempt to remove or conceal (including by placement of a sticker over) any export label.

(g) For purposes of this section, an article is labeled for export or contains an export label if it bears the mark, label, or notice required by §44.185 of this chapter.

(h) For purposes of this section, references to exportation shall be treated as including a reference to shipment to the Commonwealth of Puerto Rico.

(i) The provisions of this section do not apply to any person who, when entering U.S. manufactured tobacco products labeled for export under parts 44 and 270 of this chapter, claims and is granted an exemption from duty and tax for such products under chapter 98 of the Harmonized Tariff Schedule of the United States. The quantity of tobacco products entered may not exceed the quantity limit imposed on such products under the applicable tariff provision. A traveler claiming an exemption under this subsection upon arrival at the border may voluntarily relinquish to the U. S. Customs Service at the time of entry any excess of such quantity without incurring the penalty under section §41.83.

(j) For civil penalties and forfeiture provisions related to violations of this section, see §41.83. For a criminal penalty applicable to any violation of this section see 26 U.S.C. 5762(b).

[T.D. ATF–465, 66 FR 45618, Aug. 29, 2001. Redesignated and amended by T.D. TTB–16, 69 FR 52424, 52425, Aug. 26, 2004]

§41.83 Penalties and forfeiture for products labeled or shipped for export.

Except for the return of exported products that are specifically authorized under §41.82(b) and (c):

(a) Every person who sells, relands, or receives within the jurisdiction of the United States any tobacco products or cigarette papers or tubes which have been labeled or shipped for exportation under parts 44 and 270 of this chapter;

(b) Every person who sells or receives such relanded tobacco products or cigarette papers or tubes; and,

(c) Every person who aids or abets in such selling, relanding, or receiving, shall, in addition to the tax and any other penalty provided for in title 26 U.S.C., be liable for a penalty equal to the greater of $1,000 or 5 times the amount of the tax imposed by title 26 U.S.C. All tobacco products and cigarette papers and tubes relanded within the jurisdiction of the United States shall be forfeited to the United States and destroyed. All vessels, vehicles and aircraft used in such relanding or in removing such products, papers, and tubes from the place where relanded, shall be forfeited to the United States.

(d) The provisions of this section do not apply to any person who, when entering U.S. manufactured tobacco products labeled for export, claims and is granted an exemption from duty and tax for such products under chapter 98 of the Harmonized Tariff Schedule of the United States. The quantity of tobacco products entered may not exceed the quantity limit imposed on such products under the applicable tariff provision. A traveler claiming an exemption under this subsection upon arrival at the border may voluntarily relinquish to the U. S. Customs Service at the time of entry any excess of such quantity without incurring the penalty under this section.

(e) For purposes of this section, references to exportation shall be treated as including a reference to shipment to the Commonwealth of Puerto Rico.

[T.D. ATF–465, 66 FR 45619, Aug. 29, 2001. Redesignated and amended by T.D. TTB–16, 69 FR 52424, 52425, Aug. 26, 2004]

§41.85 Release from customs custody of imported tobacco products or cigarette papers or tubes.

(a) *General.* This section applies only to tobacco products and cigarette papers and tubes that are not put up into packages in which they will be sold to consumers. Subject to the requirements of §41.86, the Port Director of Customs or authorized customs officer may release the following articles from customs custody without payment of internal revenue tax under the internal revenue bond of the manufacturer or export warehouse proprietor to whom the articles are released:

(1) Tobacco products manufactured in a foreign country, the Virgin Islands, or a possession of the United States, for transfer to the bonded premises of a manufacturer of tobacco products or to the bonded premises of an export warehouse proprietor; and

(2) Cigarette papers and tubes manufactured in a foreign country, the Virgin Islands, or a possession of the United States, for transfer to the factory of manufacturer of cigarette papers and tubes, to an export warehouse proprietor, or to a manufacturer of tobacco products solely for use in the manufacture of cigarettes.

(b) *Products from the Virgin Islands.* In addition to the documentation required by §41.86, in the case of products exported from the Virgin Islands the manufacturer also must file an extension of coverage of the internal revenue bond on TTB F 5000.18, and receive a notice of approval from the appropriate TTB officer, in order to obtain release under paragraph (a)(1) of this section. The extension of coverage must be executed by the principal and the surety and must be in the following form:

"Whereas the purpose of this extension is to bind the obligors for the purpose of the tax imposed by 26 U.S.C. 7652(b), on tobacco products and cigarette papers and tubes exported from the Virgin Islands and removed from customs custody in the United States without payment of internal revenue tax, for delivery to the principal on said bond."

"Now, therefore, the said bond is further specifically conditioned that the principal named therein must pay all taxes imposed by 26 U.S.C. 7652(b) plus penalties, if any, and interest, for which he may become liable with respect to these products exported from the Virgin Islands and removed from customs custody in the United States without payment of internal revenue tax thereon, and must comply with all provisions of law and regulations with respect thereto."

(c) *Receipt by manufacturer.* Articles received into the factory of a manufacturer under this section are subject to the requirements of part 40 of this chapter.

[78 FR 38569, June 27, 2013]

EFFECTIVE DATE NOTE: At 78 FR 38569, June 27, 2013, §41.85 was revised, effective Aug. 26, 2013 through Aug. 26, 2016.

§41.85a Release from customs custody of returned articles.

(a) Domestically manufactured tobacco products (classifiable under item 9801.00.80 of the Harmonized Tariff Schedule of the United States, 19 U.S.C. 1202) exported from and returned to the United States without change to the product or the shipping container may be released from customs custody in the United States, under the bond of the original manufacturer or of the export warehouse proprietor who has been authorized by the original manufacturer (see §41.82), without payment of that part of the duty attributable to internal revenue tax, for delivery to the bonded premises of the original tobacco products manufacturer or to the bonded premises of the export warehouse proprietor.

(b) Domestically manufactured cigarette papers and tubes (classifiable under item 9801.00.80 of the Harmonized Tariff Schedule of the United States, 19 U.S.C. 1202) exported from and returned to the United States without change to the product or the shipping container may be released from customs custody in the United States, without payment of that part of the duty attributable to internal revenue tax, for delivery to the bonded premises of the original manufacturer of the cigarette papers and tubes or an export warehouse proprietor authorized by the original manufacturer to receive such products.

(c) Releases under this section must be in accordance with the procedures set forth in §41.86. Once released, the tobacco products and cigarette papers and tubes are subject to the tax and other provisions of 26 U.S.C. chapter 52 and, as applicable, to the regulations in part 40 of this chapter as if they had not been exported or otherwise removed from internal revenue bond.

[78 FR 38569, June 27, 2013]

EFFECTIVE DATE NOTE: At 78 FR 38569, June 27, 2013, §41.85a was revised, effective Aug. 26, 2013 through Aug. 26, 2016.

§41.86 Procedure for release.

(a) Every manufacturer of tobacco products or cigarette papers and tubes and every export warehouse proprietor who desires to obtain the release of tobacco products or cigarette papers and tubes from customs custody, without payment of internal revenue tax under its internal revenue bond, as provided in §§41.85 or 41.85a, must prepare a notice of release, TTB F 5200.11 and file the form with the appropriate TTB officer in accordance with the instructions on the form. The appropriate TTB officer will certify TTB F 5200.11 covering the release of the tobacco products or cigarette papers and tubes under 26 U.S.C. 5704(c) or (d) if the manufacturer or export warehouse proprietor is authorized to receive the products.

(b) Importers who are manufacturers of tobacco products or cigarette papers and tubes or export warehouse proprietors, or their authorized agents, who request the release of tobacco products or cigarette papers and tubes from customs custody in the United States under this section, using customs electronic filing procedures, must not request the release until they have received the TTB F 5200.11 certified by the appropriate TTB officer. Once U.S. Customs and Border Protection releases the tobacco products or cigarette papers and tubes in accordance with 19 CFR part 143, customs directives, and any other applicable instructions, the importer must submit a copy of the TTB F 5200.11 along with a copy of the electronic filing and customs release to the appropriate TTB officer at the address shown on TTB F 5200.11. The importer must retain two copies of the TTB F 5200.11, one copy to meet TTB recordkeeping requirements and one copy to meet customs recordkeeping requirements.

(c) Importers or their authorized agents requesting release of tobacco products or cigarette papers or tubes from customs custody in the United States under any authorized procedure other than the electronic filing procedures provided for in paragraph (b) of this section, must submit all copies of the TTB F 5200.11 to the appropriate customs officer along with the request for release. The customs officer will verify that the TTB F 5200.11 has been certified by the appropriate TTB officer and return all copies to the importer or the importer's authorized agent.

(d) Once U.S. Customs and Border Protection releases the tobacco products or cigarette papers and tubes in accordance with 19 CFR part 143, customs directives, and any other applicable instructions, the importer must send a copy of the TTB F 5200.11 along with a copy of the customs release to the appropriate TTB office at the address shown thereon. The importer must retain two copies of the TTB F 5200.11, one copy to meet TTB recordkeeping requirements and one copy to meet customs recordkeeping requirements.

[78 FR 38570, June 27, 2013]

EFFECTIVE DATE NOTE: At 78 FR 38570, June 27, 2013, §41.86 was revised, effective Aug. 26, 2013 through Aug. 26, 2016.

Subpart G—Puerto Rican Tobacco Products and Cigarette Papers and Tubes, Brought Into the United States

§41.101 General.

(a) Tobacco products and cigarette papers and tubes manufactured in Puerto Rico which are brought into the United States and withdrawn for consumption or sale are subject to the tax imposed by 26 U.S.C. 7652(a), at the rates set forth in 26 U.S.C. 5701.

(b) The excise taxes collected on tobacco products and cigarette papers and tubes manufactured in Puerto Rico are covered into the Treasury of Puerto Rico. Tobacco products and cigarette papers and tubes are considered as manufactured in Puerto Rico for purposes of 26 U.S.C. 7652(a)(3) if the sum of the cost or value of the materials produced in Puerto Rico, plus the direct costs of processing operations performed in Puerto Rico, equals or exceeds 50 percent of the value of the product when it is brought into the United States.

(c) The excise tax on tobacco products and cigarette papers and tubes of Puerto Rican manufacture may be prepaid in Puerto Rico prior to shipment of such articles to the United States in accordance with §41.105. In the case of tobacco products such tax may be paid in Puerto Rico on the basis of a semimonthly return in accordance with the applicable provisions of this subpart.

(68A Stat. 907, as amended, 72 Stat. 1417, 1418, as amended (26 U.S.C. 7652, 5703, 5704))

[T.D. ATF–206, 50 FR 15888, Apr. 23, 1985, as amended by T.D. ATF–232, 51 FR 28085, Aug. 5, 1986; T.D. ATF–243, 52 FR 43194, Dec. 1, 1986; T.D. ATF–246, 52 FR 669, Jan. 8, 1987; T.D. ATF–422, 64 FR 71950, Dec. 22, 1999. Redesignated and amended by T.D. TTB–16, 69 FR 52424, 52425, Aug. 26, 2004]

PREPAYMENT OF TAX IN PUERTO RICO ON TOBACCO PRODUCTS AND CIGARETTE PAPERS AND TUBES

§41.105 Prepayment of tax.

To prepay, in Puerto Rico, the internal revenue tax imposed by 26 U.S.C. 7652(a) on tobacco products and cigarette papers and tubes of Puerto Rican manufacture to be shipped to the United States, the shipper must file, or cause to be filed, a tax return, TTB F 5000.25, with full remittance of the tax which will become due on those products.

(Approved by the Office of Management and Budget under control number 1513–0090)

[T.D. ATF–444, 73 FR 16756, Mar. 31, 2008]

§41.106 Record of shipment by taxpayer.

(a) *Shipments other than noncommercial mail shipments.* The taxpayer must ensure that the tax has been prepaid on the tobacco products and cigarette papers and tubes in each shipment. The taxpayer must identify the tobacco products or cigarette papers or tubes by including on the bill of lading or similar record accompanying the shipment the following information:

(1) The marks and numbers on the shipping containers;

(2) The number of containers to be shipped;

(3) The kind of taxable article(s) to be shipped and the rate of tax applicable to each kind of article, as specified in §§41.30 through 41.35;

(4) The number of small cigarettes, large cigarettes, or small cigars to be shipped;

(5) The number and total sale price of large cigars having a sale price of not more than $235.294 per thousand before April 1, 2009, or a sale price of not more than $763.222 per thousand on and after April 1, 2009, to be shipped;

(6) The number of large cigars having a sale price of more than $235.294 per thousand before April 1, 2009, or a sale price of more than $763.222 per thousand on and after April 1, 2009, to be shipped;

(7) The pounds and ounces of chewing tobacco or snuff to be shipped;

(8) The pounds and ounces of pipe tobacco or roll-your-own tobacco to be shipped;

(9) The number of cigarette papers or tubes to be shipped;

(10) The amount of the tax paid for each kind of article under this subpart;

(11) The name and address of the consignee in the United States to whom the products are to be shipped; and

(12) A notation identifying the particular TTB F 5000.25 by which the taxes were prepaid.

(b) *Noncommercial mail shipments.* Noncommercial mail shipments of tobacco products and cigarette papers and tubes to the United States are exempt from the requirements of paragraph (a) of this section, except that the taxpayer must provide a copy of the TTB F 5000.25 upon the request of an appropriate TTB officer.

(Approved by the Office of Management and Budget under control number 1513–0108)

[T.D. ATF–444, 73 FR 16757, Mar. 31, 2008, as amended by T.D. TTB–75, 74 FR 14485, Mar. 31, 2009; T.D. TTB–85, 75 FR 42607, July 22, 2010]

§§41.107–41.108 [Reserved]

DEFERRED PAYMENT OF TAX IN PUERTO RICO ON TOBACCO PRODUCTS

§41.109 Bond required for deferred taxpayment.

Where a manufacturer of tobacco products in Puerto Rico desires to defer payment in Puerto Rico of the internal revenue tax imposed by 26 U.S.C. 7652(a), on tobacco products of Puerto Rican manufacture coming into the United States, he shall file a bond, Form 2986, with the appropriate TTB officer, in accordance with the provisions of this subpart. Such bond shall be conditioned on the payment, at the time and in the manner prescribed in this subpart, of the full amount of tax computed under the provisions of this subpart with respect to tobacco products which are released for shipment to the United States on computation of tax. All taxes which are computed under the provisions of this subpart shall be chargeable against the bond, until such taxes are paid, as provided in §41.112. The bond shall show the location of the factory from which the tobacco products to which it relates are to be shipped.

[T.D. 6871, 31 FR 43, Jan. 4, 1966. Redesignated at 40 FR 16835, Apr. 15, 1975, and amended by T.D. ATF–48, 44 FR 55855, Sept. 28, 1979; T.D. ATF–232, 51 FR 28085, Aug. 5, 1986; T.D. ATF–243, 51 FR 43194, Dec. 1, 1986; T.D. ATF–251, 52 FR 19340, May 22, 1987. Redesignated and amended by T.D. TTB–16, 69 FR 52424, 52425, Aug. 26, 2004]

§ 41.110 Record of tax computation and shipment by bonded manufacturer under deferred taxpayment.

Where tobacco products or cigarette papers or tubes are to be shipped to the United States with deferred taxpayment, the bonded manufacturer must calculate the tax prior to shipment. The tax calculation must conform to the information on the bill of lading or a similar record accompanying the shipment, and the date of completing the bill of lading or similar record accompanying the shipment will be treated as the date of computation of the tax. Tobacco products or cigarette papers or tubes may be shipped to the United States in accordance with the provisions of this section only after computation of the tax. The bill of lading or similar record accompanying the shipment must include the following information:

(a) The marks and numbers on the shipping containers;

(b) The number of containers to be shipped;

(c) The kind of taxable article(s) to be shipped and the rate of tax applicable to each kind of article, as specified in §§ 41.30 through 41.35;

(d) The number of small cigarettes, large cigarettes, or small cigars to be shipped;

(e) The number and total sale price of large cigars having a sale price of not more than $235.294 per thousand before April 1, 2009, or a sale price of not more than $763.222 per thousand on and after April 1, 2009, to be shipped;

(f) The number of large cigars having a sale price of more than $235.294 per thousand before April 1, 2009, or a sale price of more than $763.222 per thousand on and after April 1, 2009, to be shipped;

(g) The pounds and ounces of chewing tobacco or snuff to be shipped;

(h) The pounds and ounces of pipe tobacco or roll-your-own tobacco to be shipped;

(i) The number of cigarette papers or tubes to be shipped;

(j) The amount of the tax to be paid for each kind of article under this subpart; and

(k) The name and address of the consignee in the United States to whom the products are to be shipped.

(Approved by the Office of Management and Budget under control number 1513–0108)

[T.D. ATF–444, 73 FR 16757, Mar. 31, 2008, as amended by T.D. TTB–75, 74 FR 14485, Mar. 31, 2009; T.D. TTB–85, 75 FR 42607, July 22, 2010]

§ 41.111 Verification of bond and agreement to pay tax.

(a) *Verification of bond.* Prior to shipment of tobacco products or cigarette papers or tubes to the United States, the manufacturer must verify:

(1) That there is no default in payment of tax chargeable against the manufacturer's bond on TTB F 2986 (5210.12); and

(2) That the amount of the manufacturer's bond is sufficient or is in the maximum penal sum to cover the tax that will become due on the shipment.

(b) *Agreement to pay tax.* The shipment of tobacco products or cigarette papers or tubes by the bonded manufacturer serves as an agreement by the manufacturer to pay the tax on that shipment.

[T.D. ATF–444, 73 FR 16757, Mar. 31, 2008]

§ 41.112 Tax return.

The internal revenue taxes imposed by 26 U.S.C. 7652(a), with respect to tobacco products manufactured in Puerto Rico and shipped to the United States on computation of tax under the provisions of this subpart shall be paid on the basis of a semimonthly tax return. The bonded manufacturer of such products shall prepare TTB Form 5000.25 in duplicate, and file the original with the appropriate TTB officer, and maintain one copy for the file for each semimonthly return period. The bonded manufacturer shall execute the return, TTB Form 5000.25, under the penalties of perjury. He shall file a return for each return period at the time specified in § 41.114, regardless of whether tax is due for that return period. However, where the appropriate TTB officer, grants specific authorization, the bonded manufacturer need not file a tax return during the term of such authorization for any period in which tax liability was not incurred under the provisions of this subpart.

(Approved by the Office of Management and Budget under control number 1512–0497)

[T.D. ATF–40, 42 FR 5006, Jan. 26, 1977, as amended by T.D. ATF–125, 48 FR 2123, Jan. 18, 1983; T.D. ATF–232, 51 FR 28086, Aug. 5, 1986; T.D. ATF–243, 51 FR 43194, Dec. 1, 1986; T.D. ATF–251, 52 FR 19340, May 22, 1987; T.D. ATF–277, 53 FR 45269, Nov. 9, 1988. Redesignated and amended by T.D. TTB–16, 69 FR 52424, 52425, Aug. 26, 2004]

§41.113 Return periods.

Except as otherwise provided in §41.114, the periods to be covered in the semimonthly tax returns run from the 1st day of the month through the 15th day of that month, and from the 16th day of the month through the last day of that month.

[T.D. TTB–89, 76 FR 3515, Jan. 20, 2011]

§41.114 Time for filing.

(a) *General rule.* Semimonthly tax returns under this subpart shall be filed by the bonded manufacturer, for each return period, not later than the 14th day after the last day of the return period, except as provided by paragraph (b) of this section. The tax shall be paid in full by remittance at the time the return is filed as prescribed in §41.115 or §41.115a.

(b) *Special rule for taxes due for the month of September.* (1) *Division of second semimonthly period.* (i) *General.* Except as otherwise provided in paragraph (b)(1)(ii) of this section, the second semimonthly period for the month of September is divided into two payment periods, from the 16th day through the 26th day, and from the 27th day through the 30th day. The bonded manufacturer shall file a return on TTB F 5000.25, and make remittance, for the period September 16–26, no later than September 29. The bonded manufacturer shall file a return on TTB F 5000.25, and make remittance, for the period September 27–30, no later than October 14.

(ii) *Taxpayment not by electronic fund transfer.* In the case of taxes for which remittance by electronic fund transfer (EFT) is not required by §41.115a, the second semimonthly period of September is divided into two payment periods, from the 16th day through the 25th day, and from the 26th day through the 30th day. The bonded manufacturer shall file a return on TTB F 5000.25, and make remittance, for the period September 16–25, no later than September 28. The bonded manufacturer shall file a return on TTB F 5000.25, and make remittance, for the period September 26–30, no later than October 14.

(2) *Amount of payment—Safe harbor rule.* (i) *General.* Taxpayers are considered to have met the requirements of paragraph (b)(1)(i) of this section if the amount paid no later than September 29 is not less than 11/15ths (73.3 percent) of the tax liability incurred for the semimonthly period beginning on September 1 and ending on September 15, and if any underpayment of tax is paid by October 14.

(ii) *Taxpayment not by EFT.* Taxpayers are considered to have met the requirements of paragraph (b)(1)(ii) of this section if the amount paid no later than September 28 is not less than 2/3rds (66.7 percent) of the tax liability incurred for the semimonthly period beginning on September 1 and ending on September 15, and if any underpayment of tax is paid by October 14.

(3) *Weekend or holiday due date.* If the required taxpayment due date for the period September 16–25 or September 16–26, as applicable, falls on a Saturday or legal holiday, the return and remittance are due on the immediately preceding day. If the required due date falls on a Sunday, the return and remittance are due on the immediately following day.

(c) *Postmark.* If the return, and remittance as the case may be, are delivered by U.S. Mail to the appropriate TTB officer, the date of the official postmark of the U.S. Postal Service stamped on the cover in which the return, and remittance as the case may be, were mailed shall be treated as the date of delivery.

(d) *Weekends and holidays.* Except as otherwise provided in paragraph (b)(3) of this section, if the due date falls on a Saturday, Sunday, or legal holiday, the return and remittance are due on the immediately preceding day that is not a Saturday, Sunday, or legal holiday.

(Approved by the Office of Management and Budget under control number 1512–0467)

[T.D. ATF–246, 52 FR 669, Jan. 8, 1987, as amended by T.D. ATF–251, 52 FR 19340, May 22, 1987; T.D. ATF–365, 60 FR 33675, June 28, 1995; T.D. ATF–444, 66 FR 13851, Mar. 8, 2001. Redesignated and amended by T.D. TTB–16, 69 FR 52424, 52425, Aug. 26, 2004; T.D. TTB–89, 76 FR 3515, Jan. 20, 2011]

§41.114a Qualification for extended deferral.

NOTE: This section applies only to removals made before January 1, 1983.

(a) *Bonded manufacturers with bonds executed before September 1, 1973.* Bonded manufacturers with bonds on Form 2936 executed before September 1, 1973, who desire to file returns under this subpart with benefit of the extended deferral permitted by §41.114 shall file with the appropriate TTB officer an extension of coverage of bond on Form 2105. Such extension of coverage shall identify the particular bond to which it applies and shall contain a statement of purpose as follows:

To continue in effect said bond (including all extensions or limitations of terms and conditions previously consented to and approved) notwithstanding that the time for payment of the tax may be deferred by the extended deferral period permitted by regulations in 27 CFR 41.114.

If the bond on Form 2986 is in an amount insufficient to cover an extended deferral period, according to the requirements of §41.121, the bonded manufacturer must either file a new bond or file a strengthening bond to increase the total amount of the bonds then in force to a sufficient amount.

(b) *Bonded manufacturers with bonds executed after September 1, 1973.* Bonded manufacturers operating under original or superseding bonds executed after September 1, 1973, are automatically qualified for the extended deferral permitted by §41.114 (unless found in default as provided in §41.116). Such bonds must be executed in an amount sufficient to cover an extended deferral period, according to the requirements of §41.121.

(c) *Commencement of extended deferral.* Bonded manufacturers may file returns with benefit of extended deferral only after the applicable bonds and extensions of coverage required by this section have been filed with and approved by the appropriate TTB officer.

(68A Stat. 847, as amended, 907, as amended; 26 U.S.C. 7101, 7652(a); 26 U.S.C. 7805)

[T.D. ATF–5, 38 FR 19688, July 23, 1973. Redesignated at 40 FR 16835, Apr. 15, 1975, and amended by T.D. ATF–48, 44 FR 55855, Sept. 28, 1979; T.D. ATF–125, 48 FR 2123, Jan. 18, 1983; T.D. ATF–251, 52 FR 19340, May 22, 1987. Redesignated and amended by T.D. TTB–16, 69 FR 52424, 52425, Aug. 26, 2004]

§41.115 Remittance with return.

Remittance of the full amount of internal revenue tax computed during the return period shall accompany the return, except as prescribed in §41.115a. Such remittance may be in any form the appropriate TTB officer is authorized to accept under the provisions of §70.61 of this chapter (Payment by check or money order) and which is acceptable to that officer. In paying the tax, a fractional part of a cent shall be disregarded unless it amounts to one-half cent or more, in which case it shall be increased to one cent.

(Aug. 16, 1954, Ch. 736, 68A Stat. 778 (26 U.S.C. 6313) Aug. 16, 1954, ch. 736, 68A Stat. 775 (26 U.S.C. 6301); June 29, 1956, ch. 462, 70 Stat. 391 (26 U.S.C. 6301))

[26 FR 8195, Aug. 31, 1961. Redesignated at 40 FR 16835, Apr. 15, 1975, and amended by T.D. ATF–48, 44 FR 55855, Sept. 28, 1979; T.D. ATF–77, 46 FR 3009, Jan. 13, 1981; T.D. ATF–251, 52 FR 19340, May 22, 1987; T.D. ATF–301, 55 FR 47658, Nov. 14, 1990. Redesignated and amended by T.D. TTB–16, 69 FR 52424, 52425, Aug. 26, 2004]

§41.115a Payment of tax by electronic fund transfer.

(a) *General.* (1) Each taxpayer who was liable, during a calendar year, for a gross amount equal to or exceeding five million dollars in taxes on tobacco products, cigarette papers, and cigarette tubes combining tax liabilities incurred under this part and part 40 of this chapter, shall use a commercial bank in making payment by electronic fund transfer (EFT) of taxes on tobacco products, cigarette papers, and cigarette tubes during the succeeding calendar year. Payment of taxes on tobacco products, cigarette papers, and cigarette tubes by cash, check, or money order, as described in §41.115, is not authorized for a taxpayer who is required, by this section, to make remittances by EFT. For purposes of this section, the dollar amount of tax liability is defined as the gross tax liability of all taxes which are paid in accordance with this subpart, taxable withdrawals from premises in the United States, and importations during the calendar year, without regard to any drawbacks, credits, or refunds, for all premises from which such activities are conducted by the taxpayer. Overpayments are not taken into account in summarizing the gross tax liability.

(2) For the purposes of this section, a taxpayer includes a controlled group of corporations, as defined in 26 U.S.C. 1563, and implementing regulations in 26 CFR 1.1563–1 through 1.1563–4, except that the words "at least 80 percent" shall be replaced by the words "more than 50 percent" in each place it appears in subsection (a) of 26 U.S.C. 1563, as well as in the implementing regulations. Also, the rules for a "controlled group of corporations" apply in a similar fashion to groups which include partnerships and/or sole proprietorships. If one entity maintains more than 50% control over a group consisting of corporations and one, or more, partnerships and/or sole proprietorships, all of the members of the controlled group are one taxpayer for the purpose of determining who is required to make remittances by EFT.

(3) A taxpayer who is required by this section to make remittances by EFT, shall make a separate EFT remittance and file a separate tax return for each factory which tobacco products, or cigarette papers, or cigarette tubes are withdrawn upon determination of tax.

(b) *Requirements.* (1) On or before January 10 of each calendar year, except for a taxpayer already remitting the tax by EFT, each taxpayer who was liable for a gross amount equal to or exceeding five million dollars in taxes on tobacco products, cigarette papers, and cigarette tubes combining tax liabilities incurred under this part and part 40 of this chapter during the previous calendar year, shall notify, in writing, the appropriate TTB officer. The notice shall be an agreement to make remittances by EFT.

(2) For each return filed in accordance with this part, the taxpayer shall direct the taxpayer's bank to make an electronic fund transfer in the amount of the taxpayment to the Treasury Account as provided in paragraph (e) of this section. The request shall be made to the bank early enough for the transfer to be made to the Treasury Account by no later than the close of business on the last day for filing the return, prescribed in §41.105 or §41.114. The request shall take into account any time limit established by the bank.

(3) If a taxpayer was liable for less than five million dollars in taxes on tobacco products, cigarette papers, and cigarette tubes during the preceding calendar year, the taxpayer may choose either to continue remitting the tax as provided in this section or to remit the tax with the return as prescribed by §41.115. On the first return on which the taxpayer chooses to discontinue remitting the tax by EFT and to begin remitting the tax with the tax return, the taxpayer shall notify the appropriate TTB officer by attaching a written notification to the tax return, stating that no taxes are due by EFT, because the tax liability during the preceding calendar year was less than five million dollars, and that the remittance shall be filed with the tax return.

(c) *Remittance.* (1) Each taxpayer shall show on the tax return, information about remitting the tax for that return by EFT and shall file the return with the appropriate TTB officer.

(2) Remittances shall be considered as made when the taxpayment by electronic fund transfer is received by the Treasury Account. For purposes of this section, a taxpayment by electronic fund transfer shall be considered as received by the Treasury Account when it is paid to a Federal Reserve Bank.

(3) When the taxpayer directs the bank to effect an electronic fund transfer message as required by paragraph (b)(2) of this section, any transfer data record furnished to the taxpayer, through normal banking procedures, will serve as the record of payment, and shall be retained as part of required records.

(d) *Failure to make a taxpayment by EFT.* The taxpayer is subject to a penalty imposed by 26 U.S.C. 5761, 6651, or 6656, as applicable, for failure to make a taxpayment by EFT on or before the close of business on the prescribed last day for filing.

(e) *Procedure.* Upon the notification required under paragraph (b)(1) of this section, the appropriate TTB officer will issue to the taxpayer a TTB Procedure entitled, Payment of Tax by Electronic Fund Transfer (EFT). This publication outlines the procedure a taxpayer must follow when preparing returns and EFT remittances under this part.

(Approved by the Office of Management and Budget under Control Number 1512–0457)

(Act of August 16, 1954, 68A Stat. 775, as amended (26 U.S.C. 6302); sec. 202, Pub. L. 85–859, 72 Stat. 1417, as amended (26 U.S.C. 5703))

[T.D. ATF–185, 49 FR 37583, Sept. 25, 1984]

EDITORIAL NOTE: For FEDERAL REGISTER citations affecting §41.115a, see the List of CFR Sections Affected, which appears in the Finding Aids section of the printed volume and at *www.fdsys.gov*.

EFFECTIVE DATE NOTE: At 78 FR 38570, June 27, 2013, §41.115a was amended by revising paragraph (e), effective Aug. 26, 2013 through Aug. 26, 2016.

§41.116 Default.

Where a check or money order tendered with a semimonthly return for payment of internal revenue tax under the provisions of this subpart is not paid on presentment, where a bonded manufacturer fails to remit with the semimonthly return the full amount of tax due thereunder, or where a bonded manufacturer is otherwise in default in payment of tax under the provisions of this subpart, he shall not ship tobacco products to the United States on computation of tax, until the appropriate TTB officer finds that the revenue will not be jeopardized by deferred payment of tax under the provisions of this subpart.

[T.D. 6871, 31 FR 44, Jan. 4, 1966. Redesignated at 40 FR 16835, Apr. 15, 1975, and amended by T.D. ATF–232, 51 FR 28086, Aug. 5, 1986; T.D. ATF–243, 51 FR 43194, Dec. 1, 1986; T.D. ATF–251, 52 FR 19340, May 22, 1987. Redesignated and amended by T.D. TTB–16, 69 FR 52424, 52425, Aug. 26, 2004]

§§41.117–41.118 [Reserved]

§41.119 Corporate surety.

(a) Surety bonds, required under the provisions of this subpart, may be given only with corporate sureties holding certificates of authority from the Secretary of the Treasury as acceptable sureties on Federal bonds. Limitations concerning corporate sureties are prescribed by the Secretary in the current revision of Treasury Department Circular No. 570 (Companies Holding Certificates of Authority as Acceptable Sureties on Federal Bonds and as Acceptable Reinsuring Companies). The surety shall have no interest whatever in the business covered by the bond.

(b) Treasury Department Circular No. 570 is published in the FEDERAL REGISTER annually as of the first workday of July. As they occur, interim revisions of the circular are published in the FEDERAL REGISTER. Copies may be obtained from the Audit Staff, Bureau of Government Financial Operations, Department of the Treasury, Washington, DC 20226.

(July 30, 1947, ch. 390, 61 Stat. 648, as amended (6 U.S.C. 6, 7))

[T.D. ATF–92, 46 FR 46922, Sept. 23, 1981]

§41.120 Deposit of securities in lieu of corporate surety.

In lieu of corporate surety, the manufacturer of tobacco products in Puerto Rico may pledge and deposit, as security for his bond, securities which are transferrable and are guaranteed both as to interest and as to principal by the United States, in accordance with the provisions of 31 CFR part 225.

(61 Stat. 650; 6 U.S.C. 15)

[T.D. 6871, 31 FR 44, Jan. 4, 1966. Redesignated at 40 FR 16835, Apr. 15, 1975, and amended by T.D. ATF–232, 51 FR 28086, Aug. 5, 1986; T.D. ATF–243, 51 FR 43194, Dec. 1, 1986]

§41.121 Amount and account of bond.

(a) *Bond amount.* Except for the maximum and minimum amounts stated in this paragraph, the total amount of the bond or bonds required under this subpart must be in an amount not less than the amount of unpaid tax chargeable at any one time against the bond or bonds. The maximum and minimum amounts of such bond or bonds are as follows:

Taxable article	Bond amount maximum (in dollars)	Bond amount minimum (in dollars)
(1) Cigarettes	250,000	1,000
(2) Any combination of taxable articles	250,000	1,000
(3) One kind of taxable article other than cigarettes	150,000	1,000

(b) *Bond account.* Where the amount of a bonded manufacturer's bond is less than the maximum amount prescribed in paragraph (a) of this section, the bonded manufacturer must maintain an account reflecting all outstanding taxes for which the manufacturer's bond is chargeable. A manufacturer must debit that account with the amount of tax that was agreed to be paid under §41.111 or that is otherwise chargeable against the bond and then must credit the account for the amount paid on TTB F 5000.25 or other TTB-prescribed document, at the time it is filed. A manufacturer who will defer payment of tax for a shipment of tobacco products or cigarette papers or tubes under this subpart must have sufficient credit in this account to cover the taxes prior to making the shipment to the United States.

(Approved by the Office of Management and Budget under control number 1513–0108)

[T.D. ATF–444, 73 FR 16757, Mar. 31, 2008]

§41.122 Strengthening bond.

Where the amount of any bond is no longer sufficient under the provisions of §41.121, the bonded manufacturer shall immediately file a strengthening bond in an appropriate amount with the same surety as that on the bond already in effect, unless a superseding bond is filed pursuant to §41.123. A strengthening bond will not be approved where any notation is made thereon which is intended, or which may be construed, as a release of any former bond, or as limiting the amount of either bond to less than its full amount.

[26 FR 8195, Aug. 31, 1961. Redesignated at 40 FR 16835, Apr. 15, 1975, and further redesignated and amended by T.D. TTB–16, 69 FR 52424, 52425, Aug. 26, 2004]

§41.123 Superseding bond.

A bonded manufacturer shall immediately file a new bond to supersede his current bond when (a) the corporate surety on the current bond becomes insolvent, (b) the appropriate TTB officer approves a request from the surety on the current bond to terminate his liability under the bond, (c) the payment of any liability under a bond is made by the surety thereon, (d) the amount of the bond is no longer sufficient under the provisions of §41.121 and a strengthening bond has not been filed, or (e) the appropriate TTB officer considers a superseding bond necessary for the protection of the revenue.

[26 FR 8195, Aug. 31, 1961. Redesignated at 40 FR 16835, Apr. 15, 1975, and amended by T.D. ATF–251, 52 FR 19341, May 22, 1987. Redesignated and amended by T.D. TTB–16, 69 FR 52424, 52425, Aug. 26, 2004]

§41.124 Extension of coverage of bond.

An extension of coverage of the bond of a bonded manufacturer shall be required (a) as provided in §41.114a, and (b) in the case of any change in the location of the factory as set forth in the bond. Such extension of coverage of the bond shall be manifested on Form 2105 by the bonded manufacturer and by the surety on the bond with the same formality and proof of authority as required for the execution of the bond.

[T.D. ATF–5, 38 FR 19689, July 23, 1973. Redesignated at 40 FR 16835, Apr. 15, 1975, and further redesignated and amended by T.D. TTB–16, 69 FR 52424, 52425, Aug. 26, 2004]

§41.125 Approval of bond and extension of coverage of bond.

The appropriate TTB officer is authorized to approve all bonds and extensions of coverage of bonds (except under §41.136) filed under this subpart. No manufacturer of tobacco products in Puerto Rico shall defer taxes under this subpart until he receives from the appropriate TTB officer notice of approval of the bond or of an appropriate extension of coverage of the bond required under this subpart. Upon receipt of the duplicate copy of an approved bond or extension of coverage of bond from the appropriate TTB officer, such copy of the bond or extension of coverage of bond shall be retained by the bonded manufacturer and shall be made available for inspection by the appropriate TTB officer upon his request.

[T.D. 6871, 31 FR 45, Jan. 4, 1966. Redesignated at 40 FR 16835, Apr. 15, 1975, and amended by T.D. ATF–232, 51 FR 28086, Aug. 5, 1986; T.D. ATF–243, 51 FR 43194, Dec. 1, 1986; T.D. ATF–251, 52 FR 19341, May 22, 1987. Redesignated and amended by T.D. TTB–16, 69 FR 52424, 52425, Aug. 26, 2004]

§ 41.126 Termination of bond.

Any bond given under the provisions of this subpart may be terminated as to future transactions, by the appropriate TTB officer, (a) pursuant to application of surety as provided in § 41.127; (b) on approval of a superseding bond; (c) on notification by the bonded manufacturer to the appropriate TTB officer that he has discontinued the deferral of taxes under the bond; or (d) on notification by the bonded manufacturer to the appropriate TTB officer that he has discontinued business. When any bond is terminated, the appropriate TTB officer shall notify both the bonded manufacturer and surety on such bond, in writing, of such action.

[26 FR 8196, Aug. 31, 1961. Redesignated at 40 FR 16835, Apr. 15, 1975, and amended by T.D. ATF–251, 52 FR 19341, May 22, 1987. Redesignated and amended by T.D. TTB–16, 69 FR 52424, 52425, Aug. 26, 2004]

§ 41.127 Application of surety for relief from bond.

A surety on any bond given under the provisions of this subpart may at any time in writing notify the bonded manufacturer and the appropriate TTB officer that he desires, after a date named, to be relieved of liability under said bond. Such date shall be not less than 10 days after the date the notice is received by the appropriate TTB officer. The surety shall also file with the appropriate TTB officer an acknowledgement or other proof of service on the bonded manufacturer. If such notice is not thereafter in writing withdrawn, the rights of the bonded manufacturer as supported by said bond shall be terminated on the date named in the notice, and the surety shall be relieved from liability to the extent set forth in § 41.128.

[26 FR 8196, Aug. 31, 1961. Redesignated at 40 FR 16835, Apr. 15, 1975, and amended by T.D. ATF–251, 52 FR 19341, May 22, 1987. Redesignated and amended by T.D. TTB–16, 69 FR 52424, 52425, Aug. 26, 2004]

§ 41.128 Relief of surety from bond.

Where the surety on a bond given under the provisions of this subpart has filed application for relief from liability as provided in § 41.127, the surety shall be relieved from liability for transactions occurring wholly subsequent to the date specified in the notice, or the effective date of a new bond, if one is given.

[26 FR 8196, Aug. 31, 1961. Redesignated at 40 FR 16835, Apr. 15, 1975, and further redesignated and amended by T.D. TTB–16, 69 FR 52424, 52425, Aug. 26, 2004]

§ 41.129 Release of pledged securities.

Securities of the United States, pledged and deposited as provided in § 41.120, shall be released only in accordance with the provisions of 31 CFR part 225. Such securities will not be released by the appropriate TTB officer until the liability under the bond for which they were pledged has been terminated. When the appropriate TTB officer is satisfied that they may be released, he shall fix the date or dates on which a part or all of such securities may be released. At any time prior to the release of such securities, the appropriate TTB officer may extend the date of release for such additional length of time as he deems necessary.

(61 Stat. 650; 6 U.S.C. 15)

[26 FR 8196, Aug. 31, 1961. Redesignated at 40 FR 16835, Apr. 15, 1975, and amended by T.D. ATF–251, 52 FR 19341, May 22, 1987. Redesignated and amended by T.D. TTB–16, 69 FR 52424, 52425, Aug. 26, 2004]

§§ 41.135–41.138 [Reserved]

§ 41.139 Records.

Every manufacturer of tobacco products and cigarette papers and tubes in the United States who receives tobacco products or cigarette papers or tubes or Puerto Rican manufacture, without payment of internal revenue tax, under his bond, shall keep separate records of all items received, removed subject to tax, removed for tax-exempt purposes, and otherwise disposed of, showing the following information:

(a) Date, quantity, kind of cigars, cigarettes, smokeless tobacco, pipe tobacco and roll-your-own tobacco (number of small cigars—large cigars; number of small cigarettes—large cigarettes; pounds and ounces of chewing tobacco—snuff; pounds and ounces of pipe tobacco—roll-your-own tobacco).

(b) The sale price of large cigars removed subject to tax, except that if the price is more than $235.294 per thousand, it may be shown as if it were $236 per thousand.

(c) Cigarette papers:

(1) Before January 1, 2000, the date and number of books or sets of cigarette papers of each numerical content.

(2) On and after January 1, 2000, the date and number of cigarette papers.

(d) The date and number of cigarette tubes.

(Approved by the Office of Management and Budget under control number 1512–0362)

(Sec. 2128(c), Pub. L. 94–455, 90 Stat. 1921 (26 U.S.C. 5741))

[T.D. ATF–80, 46 FR 18311, Mar. 24, 1981, as amended by T.D. ATF–172, 49 FR 14943, Apr. 16, 1984; T.D. ATF–243, 51 FR 43194, Dec. 1, 1986; T.D. ATF–289, 54 FR 48841, Nov. 27, 1989; T.D. ATF–307, 55 FR 52745, Dec. 21, 1990; T.D. ATF–424, 64 FR 71933, Dec. 22, 1999; T.D. ATF–420, 64 FR 71944, Dec. 22, 1999]

§41.140 Taxpayment in the United States.

Every manufacturer of tobacco products or cigarette papers or tubes in the United States who receives, under its bond without payment of internal revenue tax, Puerto Rican tobacco products or cigarette papers or tubes not put up in packages, and who subsequently removes such products subject to tax, must pay the tax imposed on these products by 26 U.S.C. 7652(a) at the rates prescribed in 26 U.S.C. 5701 on the basis of a return as prescribed by part 40 of this chapter. Similarly, every manufacturer of cigarette papers and tubes in the United States who receives Puerto Rican cigarette papers and tubes and subsequently removes such articles, shall pay the tax imposed on such articles by 26 U.S.C. 7652(a), at the rates prescribed in 26 U.S.C. 5701, on the basis of a return under the provisions of part 40 of this chapter applicable to taxpayment of cigarette papers and tubes. Such tobacco products and cigarettes papers and tubes shall be separately listed and identified as articles of Puerto Rican manufacture on Form 5000.24. The amount of tax paid on such articles shall be separately stated on Form 5000.24.

[T.D. 6871, 31 FR 45, Jan. 4, 1966. Redesignated at 40 FR 16835, Apr. 15, 1975, and amended by T.D. ATF–48, 44 FR 55855, Sept. 28, 1979; T.D. ATF–232, 51 FR 28086, Aug. 5, 1986; T.D. ATF–243, 51 FR 43194, Dec. 1, 1986; T.D. ATF–384, 61 FR 54095, Oct. 17, 1996; T.D. ATF–424, 64 FR 71933, Dec. 22, 1999; T.D. ATF–422, 64 FR 71951, Dec. 22, 1999; 78 FR 38570, June 27, 2013]

EFFECTIVE DATE NOTE: At 78 FR 38570, June 27, 2013, §41.140 was amended by revising the first sentence, effective Aug. 26, 2013 through Aug. 26, 2016.

§41.141 Reports.

Every manufacturer of tobacco products or cigarette papers or tubes in the United States who receives Puerto Rican tobacco products or cigarette papers or tubes under its bond without payment of internal revenue tax must report the receipt and disposition of such tobacco products and cigarette papers and tubes on supplemental monthly reports. Such supplemental reports shall be made on Form 5210.5 or Form 2138 and shall have inserted thereon the heading, "Cigars and Cigarettes of Puerto Rican Manufacture" or "Cigarette Papers and Tubes of Puerto Rican Manufacture," as the case may be. The original of such supplemental report shall be attached to the manufacturer's regular monthly report when filed.

(72 Stat. 1422; 26 U.S.C. 5722)

[T.D. 6871, 31 FR 46, Jan. 4, 1966. Redesignated at 40 FR 16835, Apr. 15, 1975; T.D. ATF–232, 51 FR 28086, Aug. 5, 1986; T.D. ATF–243, 51 FR 43194, Dec. 1, 1986; T.D. ATF–424, 64 FR 71933, Dec. 22, 1999; T.D. ATF–422, 64 FR 71951, Dec. 22, 1999; 78 FR 38570, June 27, 2013]

EFFECTIVE DATE NOTE: At 78 FR 38570, June 27, 2013, §41.141 was amended by revising the first sentence, effective Aug. 26, 2013 through Aug. 26, 2016.

Subpart H [Reserved]

§§ 41.151–41.153 [Reserved]

Subpart I—Claims

GENERAL

§ 41.161 Abatement of assessment.

A claim for abatement of the unpaid portion of the assessment of any tax on tobacco products and cigarette papers and tubes, or any liability in respect thereof, may be allowed to the extent that such assessment is excessive in amount, is assessed after expiration of the applicable period of limitation, or is erroneously or illegally assessed. Any claim under this section shall be prepared on Form 2635 (5620.8), in duplicate, and shall set forth the particulars under which the claim is filed. The original of the claim, accompanied by such evidence as is necessary to establish to the satisfaction of the appropriate TTB officer that the claim is valid, shall be filed with the appropriate TTB officer, and the duplicate of the claim shall be retained by the claimant.

(68A Stat. 792; 26 U.S.C. 6404)

[T.D. 6871, 31 FR 46, Jan. 4, 1966. Redesignated at 40 FR 16835, Apr. 15, 1975, and amended by T.D. ATF–232, 51 FR 28086, Aug. 5, 1986; T.D. ATF–243, 51 FR 43194, Dec. 1, 1986; T.D. ATF–251, 52 FR 19341, May 22, 1987. Redesignated and amended by T.D. TTB–16, 69 FR 52424, 52425, Aug. 26, 2004]

§ 41.162 Losses caused by disaster occurring after September 2, 1958.

Claims involving internal revenue tax paid or determined and customs duty paid on tobacco products and cigarette papers and tubes removed, which are lost, rendered unmarketable, or condemned by a duly authorized official by reason of a "major disaster" occurring in the United States after September 2, 1958, shall be filed in accordance with the provisions of subpart C of part 46 of this chapter.

(72 Stat. 1420; 26 U.S.C. 5708)

[T.D. 6871, 31 FR 46, Jan. 4, 1966. Redesignated at 40 FR 16835, Apr. 15, 1975, and amended by T.D. ATF–232, 51 FR 28086, Aug. 5, 1986; T.D. ATF–243, 51 FR 43194, Dec. 1, 1986; T.D. ATF–457, 66 FR 32220, June 14, 2001]

§ 41.163 Refund of tax.

The taxes paid on tobacco products and cigarette papers and tubes imported or brought into the United States may be refunded (without interest) to the taxpayer on proof satisfactory to the appropriate TTB officer that the taxpayer has paid the tax on tobacco products and cigarette papers and tubes lost (otherwise than by theft) or destroyed, by fire, casualty, or act of God, while in the possession or ownership of such taxpayer, or withdrawn by him from the market. Any claim for refund of tax under this section shall be prepared on Form 2635 (5620.8), in duplicate, and shall include a statement that the tax imposed on tobacco products and cigarette papers and tubes by 26 U.S.C. 7652 or chapter 52, as applicable, has been paid in respect to the articles covered in the claim, and that the articles were lost, destroyed, or withdrawn from the market, within six months preceding the date the claim is filed and shall be executed under the penalties of perjury. A claim for refund relating to articles lost or destroyed shall be supported as prescribed in § 41.165, and a claim relating to articles withdrawn from the market shall include a schedule prepared and verified as prescribed in §§ 41.170 and 41.171 or §§ 41.172 and 41.173. The original of the claim shall be filed with the appropriate TTB officer. The duplicate of the claim, with the copy of any verified supporting schedules, shall be retained by the claimant.

(68A Stat. 907, as amended, 72 Stat. 1419, as amended; 26 U.S.C. 7652, 5705)

[T.D. 6871, 31 FR 46, Jan. 4, 1966. Redesignated at 40 FR 16835, Apr. 15, 1975, and amended by T.D. ATF–48, 44 FR 55855, Sept. 28, 1979; T.D. ATF–232, 51 FR 28086, Aug. 5, 1986; T.D. ATF–243, 52 FR 43194, Dec. 1, 1986; T.D. ATF–251, 52 FR 19341, May 22, 1987. Redesignated and amended by T.D. TTB–16, 69 FR 52424, 52425, Aug. 26, 2004]

TOBACCO PRODUCTS AND CIGARETTE PAPERS AND TUBES LOST OR DESTROYED

§ 41.165 Action by taxpayer.

Where tobacco products and cigarette papers and tubes which have been imported or brought into the United States are lost (otherwise than by theft) or destroyed, by fire, casualty, or act of God, and the taxpayer desires to file claim for refund of the tax on such articles, he shall, in addition to complying with the requirements of §41.163, indicate on the claim the nature, date, place, and extent of such loss or destruction. The claim shall be accompanied by such evidence as is necessary to establish to the satisfaction of the appropriate TTB officer that the claim is valid.

(72 Stat. 1419, as amended; 26 U.S.C. 5705)

[T.D. 6871, 31 FR 46, Jan. 4, 1966. Redesignated at 40 FR 16835, Apr. 15, 1975, and amended by T.D. ATF–232, 51 FR 28086, Aug. 5, 1986; T.D. ATF–243, 51 FR 43194, Dec. 1, 1986. Redesignated and amended by T.D. TTB–16, 69 FR 52424, 52425, Aug. 26, 2004]

TOBACCO PRODUCTS AND CIGARETTE PAPERS AND TUBES WITHDRAWN FROM THE MARKET

§41.170 Reduction of tobacco products to materials; TTB action.

(a) *General.* Where tobacco products and cigarette papers and tubes which have been imported or brought into the United States are withdrawn from the market and the taxpayer desires to file claim for refund of the tax on the articles, he shall, in addition to the requirements of §41.163, assemble the articles at any suitable place, if they are to be destroyed or reduced to tobacco. The taxpayer shall group the articles according to the rates of tax applicable to the articles, and shall prepare a schedule of the articles on TTB Form 5200.7, in triplicate. All copies of the schedule shall be forwarded to the appropriate TTB officer.

(b) *Large cigars.* Refund or credit of tax on large cigars withdrawn from the market is limited to the lowest tax applicable to that brand and size of cigar during the required record retention period (see §41.22) except where the importer establishes that a greater amount was actually paid. For each claim involving large cigars withdrawn from the market, the importer must include a certification on either TTB Form 5200.7 or TTB Form 2635 (5620.8) to read as follows:

The amounts claimed relating to large cigars are based on the lowest sale price applicable to the cigars during the required record retention period, except where specific documentation is submitted with the claim to establish that any greater amount of tax claimed was actually paid.

(See 26 U.S.C. 5705)

[T.D. ATF–80, 46 FR 18311, Mar. 24, 1981, as amended by T.D. ATF–232, 51 FR 28086, Aug. 5, 1986; T.D. ATF–243, 51 FR 43194, Dec. 1, 1986; T.D. ATF–251, 52 FR 19341, May 22, 1987; T.D. ATF–307, 55 FR 52745, Dec. 21, 1990; T.D. ATF–424, 64 FR 71933, Dec. 22, 1999; T.D. ATF–420, 64 FR 71944, Dec. 22, 1999. Redesignated and amended by T.D. TTB–16, 69 FR 52424, 52425, Aug. 26, 2004]

§41.171 Reduction of tobacco products to materials, action by appropriate TTB officer.

Upon receipt of a schedule of tobacco products and cigarette papers and tubes which have been imported or brought into the United States and which are withdrawn from the market by a taxpayer who desires to destroy such articles or, in the case of tobacco products, reduce them to tobacco, the appropriate TTB officer may verify the schedule and supervise destruction of the articles (and stamps, if any) or the reduction of tobacco products to tobacco, or the appropriate TTB officer may authorize the taxpayer to destroy the articles (and stamps, if any) or reduce tobacco products to tobacco without supervision by so stating on the original and one copy of the schedule returned to the taxpayer.

(72 Stat. 1419, as amended; 26 U.S.C. 5705)

[T.D. 6871, 31 FR 46, Jan. 4, 1966. Redesignated at 40 FR 16835, Apr. 15, 1975, and amended by T.D. ATF–232, 51 FR 28087, Aug. 5, 1986; T.D. ATF–243, 51 FR 43194, Dec. 1, 1986. Redesignated and amended by T.D. TTB–16, 69 FR 52424, 52425, Aug. 26, 2004]

§41.172 Return to nontaxpaid status, action by taxpayer.

(a) *General.* Where tobacco products and cigarette papers and tubes which have been imported or brought into the United States are withdrawn from the market and the taxpayer desires to file a claim for refund of the tax on the articles and return them to a nontaxpaid status, he shall, in addition to the requirements of §41.163, assemble the articles in or adjacent to the factory in which the articles are to be retained or received in a nontaxpaid status. The taxpayer shall group the articles according to the rates of tax applicable to the articles, and shall prepare a schedule of the articles, on Form 5200.7, in triplicate. All copies of the schedule shall be forwarded to the appropriate TTB officer.

(b) *Large cigars.* Refund or credit of tax on large cigars withdrawn from the market is limited to the lowest tax applicable to that brand and size of cigar during the required record retention period (see §41.22) except where the importer establishes that a greater amount was actually paid. For each claim involving large cigars withdrawn from the market, the importer must include a certification on either TTB Form 5200.7 or TTB Form 2635 (5620.8) to read as follows:

The amounts claimed relating to large cigars are based on the lowest sale price applicable to the cigars during the required record retention period, except where specific documentation is submitted with the claim to establish that any greater amount of tax claimed was actually paid.

(See 26 U.S.C. 5705)

[T.D. ATF–80, 46 FR 18311, Mar. 24, 1981, and amended by T.D. ATF–232, 51 FR 28087, Aug. 5, 1986; T.D. ATF–243, 51 FR 43194, Dec. 1, 1986; T.D. ATF–251, 52 FR 19341, May 22, 1987; T.D. ATF–307, 55 FR 52745, Dec. 21, 1990; T.D. ATF–424, 64 FR 71933, Dec. 22, 1999; T.D. ATF–420, 64 FR 71944, Dec. 22, 1999. Redesignated and amended by T.D. TTB–16, 69 FR 52424, 52425, Aug. 26, 2004]

§41.173 Return to nontaxpaid status, action by appropriate TTB officer.

Upon receipt of a schedule of tobacco products and cigarette papers and tubes which have been imported or brought into the United States and which are withdrawn from the market by a taxpayer who desires to return such articles to a nontaxpaid status, the appropriate TTB to officer may verify the schedule and supervise disposition of the articles (and destruction of the stamps, if any) or the appropriate TTB officer may authorize the receiving manufacturer to verify the schedule and disposition of the articles (and destruction of the stamps, if any) covered therein, without supervision, by so stating on the original and one copy of the schedule returned to the manufacturer. Where the receipt in a factory of tobacco products and cigarette papers and tubes has been verified, such articles shall be treated by the receiving manufacturer as nontaxpaid and shall be covered by the manufacturer's bond.

(72 Stat. 1419, as amended; 26 U.S.C. 5705)

[T.D. 6871, 31 FR 47, Jan. 4, 1966. Redesignated at 40 FR 16835, Apr. 15, 1975, and amended by T.D. ATF–232, 51 FR 28087, Aug. 5, 1986; T.D. ATF–243, 51 FR 43194, Dec. 1, 1986. Redesignated and amended by T.D. TTB–16, 69 FR 52424, 52425, Aug. 26, 2004]

§41.174 Disposition of tobacco products and cigarette papers and tubes, and schedule.

When the appropriate TTB officer is assigned to verify the schedule and supervise destruction or other disposition of tobacco products and cigarette papers and tubes which have been imported or brought into the United States, such officer shall, upon completion of his assignment, execute a certificate on all copies of the schedule to show the disposition and the date of disposition of such articles. The appropriate TTB officer shall return the original and one copy of the certified schedule to the taxpayer. When a taxpayer destroys such articles (and stamps, if any) or reduces tobacco products to materials, or a receiving manufacturer verifies the schedule and disposition of such articles (and stamps, if any), he shall execute a certificate on the original and the copy of the schedule returned to him, to show the disposition and the date of disposition of the articles. The taxpayer shall attach the original of the certified schedule to his claim for refund.

(72 Stat. 1419, as amended; 26 U.S.C. 5705)

[T.D. 6871, 31 FR 47, Jan. 4, 1966. Redesignated at 40 FR 16835, Apr. 15, 1975, and amended by T.D. ATF–232, 51 FR 28087, Aug. 5, 1986; T.D. ATF–243, 51 FR 43194, Dec. 1, 1986. Redesignated and amended by T.D. TTB–16, 69 FR 52424, 52425, Aug. 26, 2004]

Subpart J—Records and Reports

SOURCE: T.D. ATF–40, 42 FR 5007, Jan. 26, 1977, unless otherwise noted.

§41.181 Records of large cigars.

Every person who imports large cigars for sale within the United States must keep such records as are necessary to establish and verify the sale price that applies to large cigars removed (entered or withdrawn).

(a) *Basic record.* The importer must keep a record to show each sale price (as determined under §41.39), which is applicable to large cigars removed. No later than the tenth business day in January of each year the importer must prepare such a record to show the sale price in effect on the first day of that year for each brand and size of large cigars. The importer must note any change in a price from that shown in the record within ten business days after such change in price. The record must be a continuing one for each brand and size of cigar (and type of packaging, if pertinent), so that the taxable price on any date may be readily ascertained. If an importer removes new types of large cigars after the beginning of the year, the importer must enter the sale price and its effective date for such large cigars in the basic record within ten business days after such removal.

(b) *Copies of price announcements.* The importer must keep a copy of each general announcement that is issued internally or to the trade about establishment or change of large cigar sale prices. If the copy does not show the actual date when issued it must be annotated to show this information.

(c) *Copies of entry and withdrawal forms.* The importer must keep a copy of each customs entry or withdrawal form on which internal revenue tax for large cigars is declared pursuant to §41.81.

(d) *Alternative record.* If an importer has so few import transactions and/or brands and sizes of large cigars that retention of an appropriate copy of each entry and withdrawal form required under paragraph (c) of this section will provide an adequate record of sale prices, then the record required under paragraph (a) of this section need not be kept. In such case the entry and withdrawal forms must identify the brands and sizes of cigars covered and show the corresponding quantity and sale price for each. If such information was not originally entered on the form it may be included by annotation. Whenever the appropriate TTB officer finds that alternative records being kept pursuant to this paragraph are inadequate for the intended purpose, he or she may so notify the importer in writing, after which time the importer must keep the record required under paragraph (a) of this section.

(Approved by the Office of Management and Budget under control number 1512–0368)

[T.D. ATF–420, 64 FR 71944, Dec. 22, 1999. Redesignated and amended by T.D. TTB–16, 69 FR 52424, 52425, Aug. 26, 2004]

§41.182 Availability of records.

The records required under §41.181 shall be kept by the importer at his usual place of business unless otherwise authorized in writing by the appropriate TTB officer, and shall be made available for inspection by the appropriate TTB officer upon his request. (For retention period, see §41.22.)

[T.D. ATF–40, 42 FR 5007, Jan. 26, 1977. Redesignated and amended by T.D. TTB–16, 69 FR 52424, 52425, Aug. 26, 2004]

§41.183 [Reserved]

Subpart K—Tobacco Products Importers

SOURCE: T.D. ATF–422, 64 FR 71951, Dec. 22, 1999, unless otherwise noted.

§41.190 Persons required to qualify.

Any person who engages in the business as an importer of tobacco products must qualify as an importer of tobacco products in accordance with this part. Any person eligible for an exemption described in §41.50 is not engaged in the business as an importer of tobacco products. A person importing tobacco products for personal use, in such quantities as may be allowed by Customs without payment of tax, is not required to have an importer's permit.

[78 FR 38570, June 27, 2013]

EFFECTIVE DATE NOTE: At 78 FR 38570, June 27, 2013, §41.190 was revised, effective Aug. 26, 2013 through Aug. 26, 2016.

§41.191 Application for permit.

Every person, before commencing business as an importer of tobacco products, must make application for, and obtain, the permit in accordance with this subpart. The permit application must be made on TTB F 5230.4 in accordance with the instructions for the form. All documents required under this part to be furnished with the permit application must be made a part thereof.

[78 FR 38570, June 27, 2013]

EFFECTIVE DATE NOTE: At 78 FR 38570, June 27, 2013, §41.191 was revised, effective Aug. 26, 2013 through Aug. 26, 2016.

§41.192 [Reserved]

§41.193 Corporate documents.

Every corporation that files an application for a permit as an importer of tobacco products must furnish with its application for the permit required by §41.191 a true copy of the corporate charter or a certificate of corporate existence or incorporation executed by the appropriate officer of the State in which incorporated. The corporation must likewise furnish duly authenticated extracts of the stockholders' meetings, bylaws, or directors' meetings, listing the offices that, or the officers who, are authorized to sign documents or otherwise act in behalf of the corporation in matters relating to 26 U.S.C. chapter 52 and the regulations issued thereunder. The corporation must also furnish evidence, in duplicate, of the identity of the officers and directors and each person who holds more than ten percent of the stock of the corporation. Where the corporation has previously filed with the appropriate TTB officer any information required by this section and that information is currently complete and accurate, a written statement to that effect, in duplicate, will be sufficient for purposes of this section.

[78 FR 38571, June 27, 2013]

EFFECTIVE DATE NOTE: At 78 FR 38571, June 27, 2013, §41.193 was revised, effective Aug. 26, 2013 through Aug. 26, 2016.

§41.194 Articles of partnership or association.

Every partnership or association that files an application for a permit as an importer of tobacco products must furnish with its application for the permit required by §41.191 a true copy of the articles of partnership or association, if any, or the certificate of partnership or association where required to be filed by any State, county, or municipality. Where a partnership or association has previously filed these documents with the appropriate TTB officer and the documents are currently complete and accurate, a written statement, in duplicate, to that effect by the partnership or association will be sufficient for purposes of this section.

[78 FR 38571, June 27, 2013]

EFFECTIVE DATE NOTE: At 78 FR 38571, June 27, 2013, §41.194 was revised, effective Aug. 26, 2013 through Aug. 26, 2016.

§41.195 Trade name certificate.

Every person that files an application for a permit as an importer of tobacco products operating under a trade name must furnish with the application for the permit required by §41.191 a true copy of the certificate or other document, if any, issued by a State, county, or municipal authority in connection with the transaction of business under the trade name. If no such certificate or other document is issued by the State, county, or municipal authority, a written statement, in duplicate, to that effect by the person will be sufficient for purposes of this section.

[78 FR 38571, June 27, 2013]

EFFECTIVE DATE NOTE: At 78 FR 38571, June 27, 2013, §41.195 was revised, effective Aug. 26, 2013 through Aug. 26, 2016.

§41.196 Power of attorney.

If the application for a permit or any report or other document required to be executed under this part is to be signed by an individual as an attorney in fact for any person (including one of the partners for a partnership or one of the members of an association), or if an individual is otherwise to officially represent such person, a power of attorney on TTB F 5000.8 must be furnished to the appropriate TTB officer. A power of attorney is not required for individuals whose authority is furnished with the corporate documents required by §41.193. A new TTB F 5000.8

does not have to be filed with the appropriate TTB officer if that form previously was submitted to TTB and is still in effect.

[78 FR 38571, June 27, 2013]

EFFECTIVE DATE NOTE: At 78 FR 38571, June 27, 2013, §41.196 was revised, effective Aug. 26, 2013 through Aug. 26, 2016.

§41.197 Additional information.

The appropriate TTB officer may require the submission of, and the applicant must furnish, as a part of the application for a permit, such additional information the appropriate TTB officer deems necessary to determine whether the applicant is entitled to a permit under this subpart.

[78 FR 38571, June 27, 2013]

EFFECTIVE DATE NOTE: At 78 FR 38571, June 27, 2013, §41.197 was revised, effective Aug. 26, 2013 through Aug. 26, 2016.

§41.198 Investigation of applicant.

Appropriate TTB officers may inquire or investigate to verify the information in connection with an application for a permit. The investigation will ascertain whether the applicant is eligible for a permit. A permit may be denied if the applicant (including, in the case of a corporation, any officer, director, or principal stockholder and, in the case of a partnership, a partner)—

(a) Is, by reason of his business experience, financial standing, or trade connections or by reason of previous or current legal proceedings involving a felony violation of any other provision of Federal criminal law relating to tobacco products, processed tobacco, cigarette paper, or cigarette tubes, not likely to maintain operations in compliance with this chapter;

(b) Has been convicted of a felony violation of any provision of Federal or State criminal law relating to tobacco products, processed tobacco, cigarette paper, or cigarette tubes; or

(c) Has failed to disclose any material information required or made any material false statement in the application therefor.

[T.D. TTB–75, 74 FR 14485, Mar. 31, 2009]

§41.199 Notice of contemplated disapproval.

If the appropriate TTB officer has reason to believe that the applicant is not entitled to a permit, the appropriate TTB officer will promptly provide to the applicant a notice of the contemplated disapproval of the application and an opportunity for hearing thereon in accordance with part 71 of this chapter. If, after the notice and opportunity for hearing, the appropriate TTB officer finds that the applicant is not entitled to a permit, an order will be prepared stating the findings on which the application is denied.

[78 FR 38571, June 27, 2013]

EFFECTIVE DATE NOTE: At 78 FR 38571, June 27, 2013, §41.199 was revised, effective Aug. 26, 2013 through Aug. 26, 2016.

§41.200 Issuance of permit.

If the application for the permit required under this subpart is approved, the appropriate TTB officer will issue the permit on TTB F 5200.24.

[78 FR 38571, June 27, 2013]

EFFECTIVE DATE NOTE: At 78 FR 38571, June 27, 2013, §41.200 was revised, effective Aug. 26, 2013 through Aug. 26, 2016.

§41.201 Duration of permit.

(a) *Permits with an effective date on or after August 26, 2013.* A permit issued under §41.200 bearing an effective date of August 26, 2013 or later will be valid for a period of five years from the effective date shown on the permit. Provided that a timely application for renewal is filed under §41.202, the expiring permit will continue in effect until final action is taken by TTB on the application for renewal.

(b) *Permits with an effective date prior to August 26, 2013.* A person operating as an importer of tobacco products that holds a permit bearing an effective date that is prior to August 26, 2013 and that wishes to continue operations as an importer of tobacco products, must apply for and receive a new permit issued under §41.200. The person must file the application under §41.191 within 150 days after August 26, 2013, or within 30 days prior to the expiration date shown on the existing permit form, whichever is later. If a person timely files an application but that application is not complete (that is, the applicant has not submitted information or documentation sufficient for TTB to take action on the permit), and if the applicant has not provided the missing information within one year of a written request for it or within any shorter time period specified in the written request, the permit application will be deemed abandoned and the applicant will be notified in writing that no permit will be issued in response to the incomplete application. Provided that a timely application is filed, the person may continue operations under the existing permit until TTB takes final action on the application for the new permit.

[78 FR 38571, June 27, 2013]

EFFECTIVE DATE NOTE: At 78 FR 38571, June 27, 2013, §41.201 was revised, effective Aug. 26, 2013 through Aug. 26, 2016.

§41.202 Renewal of permit.

(a) *Permits with an effective date on or after August 26, 2013.* A person operating as an importer of tobacco products that holds a permit required under §41.191 and issued under §41.200 bearing an effective date of August 26, 2013 or later, and that wishes to continue operations beyond the expiration of the permit, must apply for renewal of the permit within 30 days prior to expiration of the permit, in accordance with the instructions provided with the renewal application form. Permits will be renewed only for those persons that have engaged in the importing of tobacco products under the current permit during the one-year period immediately prior to the date of the application to renew.

(b) *Permits with an effective date prior to August 26, 2013.* A person may not obtain renewal of a permit bearing an effective date prior to August 26, 2013. A person operating as an importer of tobacco products that holds a permit bearing an effective date prior to August 26, 2013, and that wishes to continue in operations as an importer of tobacco products, must apply for and receive a new permit for issuance under §41.200 and in accordance with the rules contained in §41.201(b).

[78 FR 38571, June 27, 2013]

EFFECTIVE DATE NOTE: At 78 FR 38571, June 27, 2013, §41.202 was revised, effective Aug. 26, 2013 through Aug. 26, 2016.

§41.203 Retention of permit and supporting documents.

The importer must retain the permit, together with the copy of the application and supporting documents returned with the permit, at the same place where the records required by this subpart are kept. The importer must make the permit and supporting documents available for inspection by any appropriate TTB officer upon request.

[78 FR 38572, June 27, 2013]

EFFECTIVE DATE NOTE: At 78 FR 38572, June 27, 2013, §41.203 was revised, effective Aug. 26, 2013 through Aug. 26, 2016.

§41.203a Suspension and revocation of permit.

When the appropriate TTB officer has reason to believe that an importer of tobacco products has not in good faith complied with the provisions of 26 U.S.C. chapter 52, and regulations thereunder, or with any other provision of 26 U.S.C. with intent to defraud, or has violated any condition of the permit, or has failed to disclose any material information required or made any material false statement in the application for the permit, or is, by reason of previous or current legal proceedings involving a felony violation of any other provision of Federal criminal law relating to tobacco products, processed tobacco, cigarette paper, or cigarette tubes, not likely to maintain operations in compliance with 26 U.S.C. chapter 52, or has been convicted of a felony violation of any provision of Federal or State criminal law relating to tobacco products, processed tobacco, cigarette paper, or cigarette tubes, the appropriate TTB officer shall issue an order, stating the facts charged, citing such person to show cause why the permit should not be suspended or revoked. Such citation shall be issued and opportunity for hearing afforded in accordance with part 71 of this chapter, which part is applicable to such proceedings. If, after hearing, the Administrative Law Judge, or on appeal, the Administrator, finds that such person has not shown cause why the permit should not be suspended or revoked, such permit shall be suspended for such period as the appropriate TTB officer deems proper or shall be revoked.

[T.D. TTB–104, 77 FR 37304, June 21, 2012]

REQUIRED RECORDS AND REPORTS

§41.204 Records and reports in general.

Every tobacco products importer must keep records and, when required by this part, submit reports, of the physical receipt and disposition of tobacco products. Records and reports are not required under this part with respect to tobacco products that are in customs custody.

[78 FR 38572, June 27, 2013]

EFFECTIVE DATE NOTE: At 78 FR 38572, June 27, 2013, §41.204 was revised, effective Aug. 26, 2013 through Aug. 26, 2016.

§41.205 [Reserved]

FILING AND RETENTION OF RECORDS AND REPORTS

§41.206 Reports.

(a) *General.* Importers must file a monthly report on TTB F 5220.6 in accordance with the instructions for the form.

(b) *First report.* The first monthly report must be submitted by the 15th day of the month following the month in which the permit is issued.

(c) *Reports of no activity.* Reports with the notation "No Activity" must be made for those months in which no activity occurs.

(d) *Concluding report.* When a transfer of ownership of the business of an importer of tobacco products described in §41.224, or when a change in control of a corporation described in §41.226 occurs, a concluding report with the notation "Concluding Report" must be made for the month or partial month during which the transfer of ownership or change in control becomes effective. A concluding report must also be made for the month or partial month during which an importer concludes operations under the permit.

[T.D. TTB–78, 74 FR 29415, June 22, 2009]

§41.207 [Reserved]

§41.208 Maintenance and retention of records and reports.

(a) *Maintenance.* All records, reports, and other documents required under this part must be maintained separately, chronologically by transaction or reporting date, at the importer's principal place of business. The appropriate TTB officer may, pursuant to an application by the importer for an approved alternate method or procedure under §41.26, authorize such documents to be maintained at another business location under the control of the importer, if the conditions of §41.26 are met and provided that the use of the alternate location does not cause undue inconvenience to TTB when attempting to examine the files and does not delay the timely transmittal of any document required to be submitted to TTB.

(b) *Retention.* All records and reports and documents or copies of documents supporting these records or reports required by this part to be submitted to TTB or retained by the importer must be retained for not less than three years following the close of the calendar year in which filed or made. Such records, reports, and other documents must be available for inspection by the appropriate TTB officer upon request. Furthermore, the appropriate TTB officer may require these records, reports, and other documents to be kept for an additional period of not more than three years in any case where it is necessary to protect the revenue.

[T.D. TTB–78, 74 FR 29415, June 22, 2009]

Subpart L—Changes After Original Qualification of Importers

SOURCE: 78 FR 38572, June 27, 2013, unless otherwise noted.

EFFECTIVE DATE NOTE: At 78 FR 38572, June 27, 2013, subpart L was revised, effective Aug. 26, 2013 through Aug. 26, 2016.

CHANGES IN NAME

§ 41.220 Change in individual name.

When there is a change in the name of an individual operating under a permit as an importer of tobacco products, the importer must, within 30 days of the change, submit an application on TTB F 5230.5 for an amended permit.

§ 41.221 Change in trade name.

When there is a change in, or an addition or discontinuance of, a trade name used by an importer of tobacco products in connection with operations authorized by the permit, the importer must, within 30 days of the change, apply for an amended permit on TTB F 5230.5 to reflect such change. The importer must also furnish a true copy of any new trade name certificate or document issued to the business, or a statement in lieu thereof, as required by § 41.195.

§ 41.222 Change in corporate name.

When there is a change in the corporate name of an importer of tobacco products, the importer must, within 30 days of such change, apply for an amended permit on TTB F 5230.5. The importer must also furnish such documents as may be necessary to establish that the corporate name has been changed.

CHANGES IN OWNERSHIP OR CONTROL

§ 41.223 Fiduciary successor.

If an administrator, executor, receiver, trustee, assignee, or other fiduciary is to take over the business of an importer of tobacco products as a continuing operation, the fiduciary must, before commencing operations, apply for a permit in accordance with § 41.191 and furnish certified copies, in duplicate, of the order of the court or other pertinent documents, showing his or her appointment and qualification as the fiduciary. Where a fiduciary intends only to liquidate the business, qualification as an importer of tobacco products is not required if the fiduciary promptly files with the appropriate TTB officer a written statement to that effect.

§ 41.224 Transfer of ownership.

If a transfer in ownership of the business of an importer of tobacco products (including a change of any member of a partnership or association) is to be made, the importer must give written notice to the appropriate TTB officer, naming the proposed successor and the desired effective date of the transfer. Before commencing operations, the proposed successor must qualify as an importer of tobacco products in accordance with subpart K of this part. The importer must give notice of the transfer, and the proposed successor must apply for the permit, in sufficient time for examination and approval of the application before the desired date of the transfer. The predecessor importer must make a concluding report in accordance with § 41.206 and must surrender the permit with that report. The successor importer must make a first report in accordance with § 41.206.

§ 41.225 Change in officers, directors, or stockholders of a corporation.

Upon election or appointment (excluding successive reelection or reappointment) of any officer or director of a corporation operating as an importer of tobacco products, or upon any occurrence that results in a person acquiring ownership or control of more than ten percent in aggregate of the outstanding stock of such corporation, the importer must, within 30 days of that action, so notify the appropriate TTB officer in writing, giving the identity of the person. In the event that the acquisition of more than 10 percent in aggregate of the outstanding stock of the corporation results in a change of control of the corporation, the provisions of § 41.226 will apply. When there is any change in the authority furnished under § 41.196 for officers to act on behalf of the corporation, the importer must immediately so notify the appropriate TTB officer in writing.

§ 41.226 Change in control of a corporation.

When the issuance, sale, or transfer of the stock of a corporation operating as an importer of tobacco products results in a change in the identity of the principal stockholders exercising actual or legal control of the operations of the corporation, the corporate importer must, within 30 days after the change occurs, apply for a new permit on TTB F 5230.4. If the application is not timely made, the present permit will automatically terminate at the expiration of that 30-day period, and the importer must dispose of all tobacco products on hand in accordance with this part, make a concluding report in accordance with §41.206, and surrender the permit with that report. If the application for a new permit is timely made, the present permit will continue in effect pending final action with respect to the new application.

CHANGES IN LOCATION OR ADDRESS

§41.227 Change in location.

When an importer of tobacco products intends to relocate its principal business office, the importer must, before commencing operations at the new location, make application on TTB F 5230.5 for, and obtain, an amended permit.

§41.228 Change in address.

When any change occurs in the address, but not the location, of the principal business office of an importer of tobacco products as a result of action by local authorities, the importer must, within 30 days of such change, make application on TTB F 5230.5 for an amended permit.

Subpart M—Importation of Processed Tobacco

SOURCE: T.D. TTB–78, 74 FR 29416, June 22, 2009, unless otherwise noted.

QUALIFICATION REQUIREMENTS FOR IMPORTERS OF PROCESSED TOBACCO

§41.231 Persons required to qualify.

Except as otherwise provided in §41.233, every person, before commencing business as an importer of processed tobacco, must apply for, and obtain, either a permit as an importer of processed tobacco or, if the person holds a TTB permit as an importer of tobacco products, an amendment to the existing permit authorizing the importation of processed tobacco under such permit, in accordance with the provisions of this subpart.

§41.232 Application for permit or amendment of existing permit.

(a) *Application for permit.* Any person who intends to engage in the business of importing processed tobacco, and who is not engaged in the business of importing tobacco products, must apply for a permit by completing and submitting TTB F 5230.4 in accordance with the instructions on that form. All documents required under this subpart to be furnished with the application must be included with the application when it is submitted. If the appropriate TTB officer determines that the application is incomplete and, for that reason, does not include sufficient information for TTB to make a decision on the application, and if the applicant has not provided the missing information within one year of a written request for it or within any shorter time period specified in the written request, the application will be deemed abandoned and the applicant will be notified in writing that no permit will be issued in response to the incomplete application. In the case of an application filed in accordance with §41.233, such notification will constitute the final action on the application and such party will no longer be able to continue as an importer of processed tobacco.

(b) *Application for amendment of existing permit.* Any person who holds a TTB permit as an importer of tobacco products may also qualify to engage in business as an importer of processed tobacco under the same permit by making application on TTB F 5230.5 for an amended permit and receiving TTB authorization.

[T.D. TTB–78, 74 FR 29416, June 22, 2009, as amended by T.D. TTB–104, 77 FR 37304, June 21, 2012]

§41.233 Transitional rule.

(a) Any person who:

(1) On April 1, 2009, had already been engaged in business as an importer of processed tobacco; and

(2) Before June 30, 2009, submits an application for a permit or an amendment of an existing permit, as provided in §41.232, to engage in such business,

may continue to engage in that business pending final action on the application.

(b) Pending final action on the application, all provisions of chapter 52 of the Internal Revenue Code of 1986 shall apply to the applicant in the same manner and to the same extent as if the applicant were a holder of a permit as an importer of processed tobacco or an amended permit authorizing the importation of processed tobacco under chapter 52 and this subpart. Upon receipt of an application, the appropriate TTB officer will provide the applicant with a written acknowledgement that may be used for a limited period as confirmation of TTB authorization to engage in such business of an importer of processed tobacco.

§ 41.234 Corporate documents.

Every corporation that files an application for a permit as an importer of processed tobacco must furnish with its application for the permit required by § 41.231 a true copy of the corporate charter or a certificate of corporate existence or incorporation executed by the appropriate officer of the State in which incorporated. The corporation must likewise furnish duly authenticated extracts of the stockholders' meetings, bylaws, or directors' meetings, listing the offices the incumbents of which are authorized to sign documents or otherwise act in behalf of the corporation in matters relating to 26 U.S.C. chapter 52, and regulations issued thereunder. The corporation must also furnish evidence, in duplicate, of the identity of the officers and directors and each person who holds more than ten percent of the stock of such corporation. Where any of the information required by this section has previously been filed with the appropriate TTB officer and such information is currently complete and accurate, a written statement to that effect will be sufficient for the purpose of this section.

§ 41.235 Articles of partnership or association.

Every partnership or association that files an application for a permit as an importer of processed tobacco must furnish with its application for the permit required by § 41.231 a true copy of the articles of partnership or association, if any, or certificate of partnership or association where required to be filed by any State, county, or municipality. Where a partnership or association has previously filed such documents with the appropriate TTB officer and such documents are currently complete and accurate, a written statement, in duplicate, to that effect by the partnership or association will be sufficient for the purpose of this section.

§ 41.236 Trade name certificate.

Every person that files an application for a permit as an importer of processed tobacco operating under a trade name must furnish with the application for the permit required by § 41.231 a true copy of the certificate or other document, if any, issued by a State, county, or municipal authority in connection with the transaction of business under such trade name. If no such certificate or other document is so required, a written statement, in duplicate, to that effect by such person will be sufficient for the purpose of this section.

§ 41.237 Additional information.

(a) *General.* The appropriate TTB officer may require such additional information as deemed necessary to determine whether the applicant is entitled to obtain either a permit as an importer of tobacco products or, if holding a permit as an importer of processed tobacco, an amended permit authorizing the importation of processed tobacco, under this subpart. The applicant must, when required by the appropriate TTB officer, furnish as a part of the application for the permit or authorization such additional information as may be necessary for the appropriate TTB officer to determine whether the applicant is entitled to a permit or an amended permit.

(b) *Business premises.* Every person that files an application for a permit required by § 41.231 as an importer of processed tobacco must furnish, with its application for the permit, the address to be used as the principal business office where the records and reports required by the subpart must be maintained pursuant to §41.263. The applicant must also include the location (by physical address or other means if there is no physical address) of any premises used for the storage of processed tobacco imported or received. For permits issued prior to June 21, 2012, the permittee has 180 days from June 21, 2012, to submit the information required under this paragraph.

[T.D. TTB–78, 74 FR 29416, June 22, 2009, as amended by T.D. TTB–104, 77 FR 37304, June 21, 2012]

§41.238 Investigation of applicant.

Appropriate TTB officers may inquire or investigate to verify the information in connection with an application for a permit. The investigation will ascertain whether the applicant is eligible for a permit. A permit may be denied if the applicant (including, in the case of a corporation, any officer, director, or principal stockholder and, in the case of a partnership, a partner)—

(a) Is, by reason of his business experience, financial standing, or trade connections or by reason of previous or current legal proceedings involving a felony violation of any other provision of Federal criminal law relating to tobacco products, processed tobacco, cigarette paper, or cigarette tubes, not likely to maintain operations in compliance with this chapter;

(b) Has been convicted of a felony violation of any provision of Federal or State criminal law relating to tobacco products, processed tobacco, cigarette paper, or cigarette tubes; or

(c) Has failed to disclose any material information required or made any material false statement in the application therefor.

§41.239 Notice of contemplated disapproval.

If the appropriate TTB officer has reason to believe that the applicant is not entitled to a permit, the appropriate TTB officer will promptly give to the applicant notice of the contemplated disapproval of the application and opportunity for hearing thereon in accordance with part 71 of this chapter. If, after such notice and opportunity for hearing, the appropriate TTB officer finds that the applicant is not entitled to a permit, an order will be prepared stating the findings on which the application is denied.

§41.240 Issuance of permit.

If the application for the permit required under this subpart is approved, the appropriate TTB officer will issue the permit on TTB F 5200.24.

[78 FR 38573, June 27, 2013]

EFFECTIVE DATE NOTE: At 78 FR 38573, June 27, 2013, §41.240 was revised, effective Aug. 26, 2013 through Aug. 26, 2016.

§41.241 Duration of permit.

(a) *Permits with an effective date on or after August 26, 2013.* A permit issued under §41.240 bearing an effective date of August 26, 2013 or later will be valid for a period of five years from the effective date shown on the permit. Provided a timely application for renewal is filed under §41.242, the expiring permit will continue in effect until final action is taken by TTB on the application for renewal.

(b) *Permits with an effective date prior to August 26, 2013.* A person operating as an importer of processed tobacco that holds a permit bearing an effective date that is prior to August 26, 2013 and that wishes to continue operations as an importer of processed tobacco must apply for and receive a new permit issued under §41.240. The person must file the application under §41.232 within 150 days after August 26, 2013, or within 30 days prior to the expiration date shown on the existing permit form, whichever is later. If a person timely files an application but that application is not complete (that is, the applicant has not submitted information or documentation sufficient for TTB to take action on the permit), and if the applicant has not provided the missing information within one year of a written request for it or within any shorter time period specified in the written request, the permit application will be deemed abandoned and the applicant will be notified in writing that no permit will be issued in response to the incomplete application. Provided that a timely application is filed, the person may continue operations under the existing permit until TTB takes final action on the application for the new permit.

[78 FR 38573, June 27, 2013]

EFFECTIVE DATE NOTE: At 78 FR 38573, June 27, 2013, § 41.241 was revised, effective Aug. 26, 2013 through Aug. 26, 2016.

§ 41.242 Renewal of permit.

(a) *Permits with an effective date on or after August 26, 2013.* A person operating as an importer of processed tobacco that holds a permit issued under § 41.240 bearing an effective date of August 26, 2013 or later, and that wishes to continue operations beyond the expiration of the permit, must apply for renewal of the permit within 30 days prior to expiration of the permit, in accordance with instructions provided with the renewal application form. Permits will be renewed only for those persons that have engaged in the importing of processed tobacco under the current permit during the one year period immediately prior to the date of the application to renew.

(b) *Permits with an effective date prior to August 26, 2013.* A person may not obtain renewal of a permit bearing an effective date prior to August 26, 2013. A person operating as an importer of processed tobacco that holds a permit bearing an effective date prior to August 26, 2013, and that wishes to continue in operations as an importer of processed tobacco, must apply for and receive a new permit for issuance under § 41.240 and in accordance with the rules contained in § 41.241(b).

[78 FR 38573, June 27, 2013]

EFFECTIVE DATE NOTE: At 78 FR 38573, June 27, 2013, § 41.242 was revised, effective Aug. 26, 2013 through Aug. 26, 2016.

§ 41.243 Retention of permit and supporting documents.

The importer of processed tobacco must retain the permit, together with the copy of the application and supporting documents returned with the permit, at the same place where the records required by this subpart are kept. The permit and supporting documents must be made available for inspection by any appropriate TTB officer upon request.

CHANGES AFTER ORIGINAL QUALIFICATION

§ 41.251 Change in name.

(a) *Change in individual name.* When there is a change in the name of an individual operating under a permit as an importer of processed tobacco, the importer must, within 30 days of such change, make application on TTB F 5230.5 for an amended permit.

(b) *Change in trade name.* When there is a change in a trade name used by an importer of processed tobacco in connection with operations authorized by the permit, the importer must, within 30 days of such change, make application on TTB F 5230.5 for an amended permit to reflect such change. This requirement also applies to the addition or discontinuance of a trade name. The importer must also furnish a true copy of any new trade name certificate or document issued to the importer, or statement in lieu thereof, required by § 41.236.

(c) *Change in corporate name.* When there is a change in the corporate name of an importer of processed tobacco, the importer must, within 30 days of such change, make application on TTB F 5230.5 for an amended permit. The importer must also furnish such documents as may be necessary to establish that the corporate name has been changed.

§ 41.252 Change in ownership or control.

(a) *Fiduciary successor.* If an administrator, executor, receiver, trustee, assignee, or other fiduciary is to take over the business of an importer of processed tobacco as a continuing operation, such fiduciary shall, before commencing operations, make application for permit in accordance with § 41.232, furnish certified copies, in duplicate, of the order of the court, or other pertinent documents, showing his appointment and qualification as such fiduciary. However, where a fiduciary intends only to liquidate the business, qualification as an importer of processed tobacco will not be required if he promptly files with the appropriate TTB officer a written statement to that effect.

(b) *Transfer of ownership.* If a transfer in ownership of the business of an importer of processed tobacco (including a change of any member of a partnership or association) is to be made, such importer shall give notice, in writing, to the appropriate TTB officer, naming the proposed successor and the desired effective date of the transfer. The proposed successor must, before commencing operations, qualify as an importer of processed tobacco in accordance with this subpart. The importer must give notice of the transfer, and the proposed successor must make application for permit, in ample time for examination and approval thereof before the desired date of such change. The predecessor must make a concluding report, in accordance with §41.262, and surrender the permit with the report. The successor must make a first report, in accordance with §41.262.

(c) *Change in officers, directors, or stockholders of a corporation.* Upon election or appointment (excluding successive reelection or reappointment) of any officer or director of a corporation operating as an importer of processed tobacco, or upon any occurrence that results in a person acquiring ownership or control of more than ten percent in aggregate of the outstanding stock of such corporation, the importer shall, within 30 days of such action, so notify the appropriate TTB officer in writing, giving the identity of such person. When there is any change in the authority furnished under §41.271 for officers to act on behalf of the corporation, the importer must immediately so notify the appropriate TTB officer in writing.

(d) *Change in control of corporation.* When the issuance, sale, or transfer of the stock of a corporation operating as an importer of processed tobacco results in a change in the identity of the principal stockholders exercising actual or legal control of the operations of the corporation, the corporate manufacturer must, within 30 days after the change occurs, make application on TTB F 5230.4 for a new permit. Otherwise, the present permit shall be automatically terminated at the expiration of such 30-day period, and the importer must make a concluding report, in accordance with §41.262, and surrender the permit with the report. If the application for a new permit is timely made, the present permit will continue in effect pending final action with respect to such application.

§41.253 Change in location or address.

Whenever an importer of processed tobacco intends to relocate the principal business office, the importer must, before commencing operations at the new location, make application on TTB F 5230.5, and obtain an amended permit. Whenever any change occurs in the address, but not the location, of the principal business office of an importer of processed tobacco, as a result of action of local authorities, the importer must, within 30 days of such change, make application on TTB F 5230.5 for an amended permit. Whenever the importer wishes to change the location of the premises used for the storage of processed tobacco imported or received by the importer to an extent that would be inconsistent with the location information submitted with the importer's last permit application, the importer must apply for, and obtain, an amended permit before such a change in premises takes place.

[T.D. TTB–78, 74 FR 29416, June 22, 2009, as amended by T.D. TTB–104, 77 FR 37304, June 21, 2012]

Operations of Importers of Processed Tobacco

§41.261 Records.

(a) Any person who imports, or who knowingly causes to be imported, processed tobacco must make and keep records of operations and transactions. A person purchasing processed tobacco from the importer in a domestic transaction and who does not knowingly cause the processed tobacco to be imported is not required to make and keep records unless the terms and conditions of the importation are controlled by the person placing the order with the importer (for example, the importer is not an independent contractor but the agent of the person placing the order). Records maintained must reflect the date and quantity of processed tobacco:

(1) Imported;

(2) Received otherwise than through importation, together with the name and address of the person from whom it was received;

(3) Returned to customs custody or exported;

(4) Transferred or sold to a person who holds a TTB permit as an importer or manufacturer of tobacco products or of processed tobacco or as an export warehouse proprietor;

(5) Except in the case of returns to customs custody or exportations, transferred or sold to a person who does not hold a TTB permit as an importer or manufacturer of tobacco products or of processed tobacco or as an export warehouse proprietor; and

(6) Lost or destroyed; and

(7) Transferred between buildings that are covered under the same permit but that are not located in the same city, town, village, or State.

(b) The records of any importer who transfers or sells processed tobacco to a person who does not hold a TTB permit as an importer or manufacturer of tobacco products or of processed tobacco or as an export warehouse proprietor must include dated, commercial records that show the following information about each removal:

(1) The full name and business address (including city and State) of the purchaser (if there is a purchaser) or the full name and business address of the recipient (if there is no purchaser), or personal address if the purchaser or recipient is not a business;

(2) The full name, business address (including city and State), and driver's license number of the person picking up the processed tobacco for delivery;

(3) The license number of the vehicle in which the processed tobacco is picked up for delivery to purchaser or transferee;

(4) The street address of the destination of the processed tobacco;

(5) The quantity of processed tobacco in the shipment.

(c) The entries in the records required under this section must be made for each day by the close of the business day following the day on which the transfer or sale occurs. There is no particular format prescribed for the records required under this section (and commercial records may be used), although the required information must be readily ascertainable from the records kept. In the case of a removal under paragraph (a)(5) of this section that involves shipment by a common carrier, the appropriate TTB officer may approve an alternate method or procedure pursuant to § 41.26 of this part through which the importer may keep records regarding the common carrier and its means of tracking (including pick up and delivery) of the shipment in lieu of the information required by paragraphs (b)(2) and (b)(3) of this section. No records are required to be kept under this part regarding processed tobacco within customs custody, although this will not preclude TTB review of records related to such processed tobacco as may be appropriate for purposes of the enforcement of the provisions of this part.

(26 U.S.C. 5741)

[T.D. TTB–78, 74 FR 29416, June 22, 2009, as amended by T.D. TTB–104, 77 FR 37305, June 21, 2012]

§ 41.262 Reports.

(a) *General.* Every importer of processed tobacco must prepare a monthly report on TTB F 5220.6 in accordance with the instructions for the form. The report must be prepared at the times specified in this section and must be prepared whether or not any operations or transactions occurred during the period covered by the report. The importer must retain a copy of each report in accordance with the provisions of this subpart. The importer need not include in the reports under this part information regarding processed tobacco that is in customs custody.

(b) *First report(s).* The first monthly report must be submitted by the 15th day of the month following the month in which the permit is issued. If the importer is operating as an importer of processed tobacco under the transitional rule in accordance with § 41.233, the importer must submit the first report by the 15th day of the month following the month in which TTB provides written acknowledgement of the receipt of the application filed under § 41.232.

(c) *Reports of no activity.* Reports with the notation "No Activity" must be made for those months in which no activity occurs.

(d) *Reports of sales and transfers.* (1) Except as otherwise provided in paragraph (d)(2) of this section, an importer that exports processed tobacco or transfers or sells processed tobacco to someone other than a person holding a permit as an importer or manufacturer of processed tobacco or tobacco products or as an export warehouse proprietor must report each such exportation, sale, or transfer on TTB F 5250.2 by the close of the next business day following the day of exportation, sale, or transfer, in accordance with the instructions on the form.

(2) In the case of removals for export, as an alternative to the procedure prescribed in paragraph (d)(1) of this section, the importer may submit to TTB monthly summary reports of such removals in a format approved by the appropriate TTB officer. Prior to the use of such an alternate procedure, the importer must obtain written approval from the appropriate TTB officer.

(3) An importer that ships or transfers processed tobacco for scientific testing or testing of equipment which results in the destruction of the processed tobacco or the return of the processed tobacco is not required to report such shipment or transfer on TTB F 5250.2.

(e) *Concluding report.* When a transfer of ownership of the business of an importer of processed tobacco described in §41.252(b) occurs, or when a change in control of a corporation described in §41.252(d) occurs, a concluding report with the notation "Concluding Report" must be made for the month or partial month during which the transfer of ownership or change in control becomes effective. A concluding report must also be made for the month or partial month during which an importer concludes operations under the permit or authorization.

(26 U.S.C. 5722)

[T.D. TTB–78, 74 FR 29416, June 22, 2009, as amended by T.D. TTB–104, 77 FR 37305, June 21, 2012]

§41.263 Maintenance of records and reports.

All records and reports required by this subpart must be maintained separately, chronologically by transaction or reporting date, at the importer's principal place of business. The appropriate TTB officer may, pursuant to a written request, authorize files, or an individual file, to be maintained at another business location under the control of the importer, provided that the alternative location does not cause undue inconvenience to TTB when attempting to examine the files and does not delay the timely transmittal of any documents required to be submitted to TTB.

(26 U.S.C. 5741)

§41.264 Inventories.

Every importer of processed tobacco must provide a true and accurate inventory of any processed tobacco stored on premises designated pursuant to §41.237. The importer must make such an inventory at the time of commencing business, at the time of transferring ownership, at the time of changing the location of facilities in which processed tobacco is stored, at the time of concluding business, and at such other time as the appropriate TTB officer may require. A specific format is not prescribed. For permits issued prior to June 21, 2012, the permittee has 180 days from June 21, 2012, to make an inventory as required under this paragraph.

[T.D. TTB–104, 77 FR 37305, June 21, 2012]

Other Provisions Applicable to Importers of Processed Tobacco

§41.271 Power of attorney.

If the application for a permit or authorization or any report or other document required to be executed under this subpart is to be signed by an individual (including one of the partners for a partnership or one of the members of an association) as an attorney in fact for any person, or if an individual is otherwise to officially represent such person, power of attorney on TTB F 5000.8 shall be furnished to the appropriate TTB officer. Such power of attorney is not required for persons whose authority is furnished with the corporate documents as required by §41.234. Form 5000.8 does not have to be filed again with an appropriate TTB officer where such form has previously been submitted to TTB and is still in effect.

§41.272 Cross reference.

For other applicable provisions pertaining to forms prescribed, retention of records, interference with administration, alternate methods or procedures, emergency variations from requirements, penalties and forfeitures, and delegations of the Administrator, see subpart C of this part.

§41.273 Suspension and revocation of permit.

Where the appropriate TTB officer has reason to believe that an importer of processed tobacco has not in good faith complied with the provisions of 26 U.S.C. chapter 52, and regulations thereunder, or with any other provision of 26 U.S.C. with intent to defraud, or has violated any condition of his permit, or has failed to disclose any material information required or made any material false statement in the application for the permit, or is, by reason of previous or current legal proceedings involving a felony violation of any other provision of Federal criminal law relating to tobacco products, processed tobacco, cigarette paper, or cigarette tubes, not likely to maintain operations in compliance with 26 U.S.C. chapter 52, or has been convicted of a felony violation of any provision of Federal or State criminal law relating to tobacco products, processed tobacco, cigarette paper, or cigarette tubes, the appropriate TTB officer shall issue an order, stating the facts charged, citing such person to show cause why his permit should not be suspended or revoked. Such citation shall be issued and opportunity for hearing afforded in accordance with part 71 of this chapter, which part is applicable to such proceedings. If, after hearing, the hearing examiner, or on appeal, the Administrator, finds that such person has not shown cause why his permit should not be suspended or revoked, such permit shall be suspended for such period as the appropriate TTB officer deems proper or shall be revoked.

PART 44—EXPORTATION OF TOBACCO PRODUCTS AND CIGARETTE PAPERS AND TUBES, WITHOUT PAYMENT OF TAX, OR WITH DRAWBACK OF TAX

Subpart A—Scope of Regulations

Subpart B—Definitions

Subpart Ba—Special (Occupational) Taxes

Subpart C—General

VARIATIONS FROM REQUIREMENTS

Subpart D—Qualification Requirements for Export Warehouse Proprietors

Subpart E—Changes Subsequent to Original Qualification of Export Warehouse Proprietors

CHANGES IN NAME

CHANGES IN OWNERSHIP AND CONTROL

CHANGES IN LOCATION AND PREMISES

Subpart F—Bonds and Extensions of Coverage of Bonds

Subpart G—Operations by Export Warehouse Proprietors

INVENTORIES

REPORTS

CLAIMS

Subpart H—Suspension and Discontinuance of Operations

Subpart I [Reserved]

Subpart J—Removal of Shipments of Tobacco Products and Cigarette Papers and Tubes by Manufacturers and Export Warehouse Proprietors

PACKAGING REQUIREMENTS

CONSIGNMENT OF SHIPMENT

NOTICE OF REMOVAL OF SHIPMENT

AUTHORITY: 26 U.S.C. 448, 5701–5705, 5711–5713, 5721–5723, 5731–5734, 5741, 5751, 5754, 6061, 6065, 6151, 6402, 6404, 6806, 7011, 7212, 7342, 7606, 7805; 31 U.S.C. 9301, 9303, 9304, 9306.

EFFECTIVE DATE NOTE: At 78 FR 38573, June 27, 2013, the authority citation to part 44 was revised, effective Aug. 26, 2013, through Aug. 26, 2016.

SOURCE: Redesignated by T.D. ATF–464, 66 FR 43480, Aug. 20, 2001.

EDITORIAL NOTE: Nomenclature changes to part 44 appear by T.D. ATF–464, 66 FR 43480, Aug. 20, 2001, and T.D. ATF–480, 67 FR 30801–30803, May 8, 2002.

Subpart A—Scope of Regulations

§ 44.1 Exportation of tobacco products, and cigarette papers and tubes, without payment of tax, or with drawback of tax.

This part contains the regulations relating to the exportation (including supplies for vessels and aircraft) of tobacco products and cigarette papers and tubes, without payment of tax; the qualification of, and operations by, export warehouse proprietors; and the allowance of drawback of tax paid on tobacco products, and cigarette papers and tubes exported.

[T.D. 6871, 31 FR 48, Jan. 4, 1966. Redesignated at 40 FR 16835, Apr. 15, 1975, and amended by T.D. ATF–232, 51 FR 28087, Aug. 5, 1986; T.D. ATF–243, 51 FR 43194, Dec. 1, 1986]

§ 44.2 Forms prescribed.

(a) The appropriate TTB officer is authorized to prescribe all forms required by this part. All of the information called for in each form shall be furnished as indicated by the headings on the form and the instructions on or pertaining to the form. In addition, information called for in each form shall be furnished as required by this part. The form will be filed in accordance with the instructions for the form.

(b) Forms prescribed by this part are available for printing through the TTB Web site (*http://www.ttb.gov*) or by mailing a request to the Alcohol and Tobacco Tax and Trade Bureau, National Revenue Center, 550 Main Street, Room 1516, Cincinnati, OH 45202.

(5 U.S.C. 552(a) (80 Stat. 383, as amended))

[T.D. ATF–92, 46 FR 46922, Sept. 23, 1981, as amended by T.D. ATF–232, 51 FR 28087, Aug. 5, 1986; T.D. ATF–243, 51 FR 43194, Dec. 1, 1986; T.D. ATF–372, 61 FR 20725, May 8, 1996; T.D. ATF–480, 67 FR 30801, May 8, 2002; T.D. TTB–44, 71 FR 16952, Apr. 4, 2006; T.D. TTB–91, 76 FR 5480, Feb. 1, 2011]

§44.3 Delegations of the Administrator.

Most of the regulatory authorities of the Administrator contained in this part are delegated to appropriate TTB officers. These TTB officers are specified in TTB Order 1135.44, Delegation of the Administrator's Authorities in 27 CFR Part 44, Exportation of Tobacco Products and Cigarette Papers and Tubes, Without Payment of Tax, or With Drawback of Tax. You may obtain a copy of this order by accessing the TTB Web site (*http://www.ttb.gov*) or by mailing a request to the Alcohol and Tobacco Tax and Trade Bureau, National Revenue Center, 550 Main Street, Room 1516, Cincinnati, OH 45202.

[T.D. TTB–44, 71 FR 16952, Apr. 4, 2006]

Subpart B—Definitions

§44.11 Meaning of terms.

When used in this part and in forms prescribed under this part, the following terms shall have the meanings given in this section, unless the context clearly indicates otherwise. Words in the plural form shall include the singular, and vice versa, and words indicating the masculine gender shall include the feminine. The terms "includes" and "including" do not exclude things not listed which are in the same general class.

Administrator. The Administrator, Alcohol and Tobacco Tax and Trade Bureau, Department of the Treasury, Washington, DC.

Appropriate TTB officer. An officer or employee of the Alcohol and Tobacco Tax and Trade Bureau (TTB) authorized to perform any functions relating to the administration or enforcement of this part by TTB Order 1135.44, Delegation of the Administrator's Authorities in 27 CFR Part 44, Exportation of Tobacco Products and Cigarette Papers and Tubes, Without Payment of Tax, or With Drawback of Tax.

Chewing tobacco. Any leaf tobacco that is not intended to be smoked.

Cigar. Any roll of tobacco wrapped in leaf tobacco or in any substance containing tobacco (other than any roll of tobacco which is a cigarette within the definition of "cigarette" given in this section).

Cigarette. (a) Any roll of tobacco wrapped in paper or in any substance not containing tobacco, and

(b) Any roll of tobacco wrapped in any substance containing tobacco which, because of its appearance, the type of tobacco used in the filler, or its packaging and labeling, is likely to be offered to, or purchased by, consumers as a cigarette described in paragraph (a) of this definition.

Cigarette paper. Paper, or other material except tobacco, prepared for use as a cigarette wrapper.

Cigarette tube. Cigarette paper made into a hollow cylinder for use in making cigarettes.

Customs warehouse. A customs bonded manufacturing warehouse, class 6, where cigars are manufactured of imported tobacco.

District director of customs. The district director of customs at a headquarters port of the district (except the district of New York, N.Y.); the area directors of customs in the district of New York, N.Y.; and the port director at a port not designated as a headquarters port.

Exportation or export. A severance of tobacco products or cigarette papers or tubes from the mass of things belonging to the United States with the intention of uniting them to the mass of things belonging to some foreign country. For the purposes of this part, shipment from the United States to Puerto Rico, the Virgin Islands, or a possession of the United States, shall be deemed exportation, as will the clearance from the United States of tobacco products and cigarette papers and tubes for consumption beyond the jurisdiction of the internal revenue laws of the United States, i.e., beyond the 3-mile limit or international boundary, as the case may be.

Export warehouse. A bonded internal revenue warehouse for the storage of tobacco products or cigarette papers or tubes or any processed tobacco, upon which the internal revenue tax has not been paid, for subsequent shipment to a foreign country, Puerto Rico, the Virgin Islands, or a possession of the United States, or for consumption beyond the jurisdiction of the internal revenue laws of the United States.

Export warehouse proprietor. Any person who operates an export warehouse.

Factory. The premises of a manufacturer of tobacco products or cigarette papers and tubes in which he carries on such business.

Foreign-trade zone. A foreign-trade zone established and operated pursuant to the Act of June 18, 1934, as amended.

In bond. The status of tobacco products and cigarette papers and tubes, which come within the coverage of a bond securing the payment of internal revenue taxes imposed by 26 U.S.C. 5701 or 7652, and in respect to which such taxes have not been determined as provided by regulations in this chapter, including (a) such articles in a factory or an export warehouse, (b) such articles removed, transferred, or released, pursuant to 26 U.S.C. 5704, and with respect to which relief from the tax liability has not occurred, and (c) such articles on which the tax has been determined, or with respect to which relief from the tax liability has occurred, which have been returned to the coverage of a bond.

Manufacturer of cigarette papers and tubes. Any person who manufactures cigarette paper, or makes up cigarette paper into tubes, except for his own personal use or consumption.

Manufacturer of tobacco products. (1) Any person who manufactures cigars, cigarettes, smokeless tobacco, pipe tobacco, or roll-your-own tobacco, other than:

(i) A person who produces tobacco products solely for that person's own consumption or use; or

(ii) A proprietor of a customs bonded manufacturing warehouse with respect to the operation of such warehouse.

(2) The term "Manufacturer of tobacco products" includes any person who for commercial purposes makes available for consumer use (including such consumer's personal consumption or use under paragraph (1)(i) of this definition) a machine capable of making cigarettes, cigars, or other tobacco products. A person making such a machine available for consumer use shall be deemed the person making the removal with respect to any tobacco products manufactured by such machine. A person who sells a machine directly to a consumer at retail for a consumer's personal home use is not making a machine available for commercial purposes if such machine is not used at a retail premises and is designed to produce tobacco products only in personal use quantities.

Package. The immediate container in which tobacco products, processed tobacco, or cigarette papers or tubes are put up by the manufacturer and offered for sale or delivery to the ultimate consumer. For purposes of this definition, a container of processed tobacco, the contents of which weigh 10 pounds or less (including any added non-tobacco ingredients or constituents), that is removed within the meaning of this part, is deemed to be a package offered for sale or delivery to the ultimate consumer.

Person. An individual, partnership, association, company, corporation, estate, or trust.

Pipe tobacco. Any tobacco which, because of its appearance, type, packaging, or labeling, is suitable for use and likely to be offered to, or purchased by, consumers as tobacco to be smoked in a pipe.

Processed tobacco. Processed tobacco is any tobacco that has undergone processing, but does not include tobacco products. For purposes of this definition, the processing of tobacco does not include the farming or growing of tobacco or the handling of tobacco solely for sale, shipment, or delivery to a manufacturer of tobacco products or processed tobacco, nor does the processing of tobacco include curing, baling, or packaging activities. For purposes of this definition, the processing of tobacco includes, but is not limited to, stemming (that is, removing the stem from the tobacco leaf), fermenting, threshing, cutting, or flavoring the tobacco, or otherwise combining the tobacco with non-tobacco ingredients.

Removal or remove. The removal of tobacco products or cigarette papers or tubes from either the factory or the export warehouse covered by the bond of the manufacturer or proprietor.

Roll-your-own tobacco. Any tobacco which, because of its appearance, type, packaging, or labeling, is suitable for use and likely to be offered to, or purchased by, consumers as tobacco for making cigarettes or cigars, or for use as wrappers thereof.

Sale price. The price for which large cigars are sold by the manufacturer, determined in accordance with §§40.22 or 41.39.

Smokeless tobacco. Any snuff or chewing tobacco.

Snuff. Any finely cut, ground, or powdered tobacco that is not intended to be smoked.

Special tax. The special (occupational) tax on manufacturers of tobacco products, manufacturers of cigarette papers and tubes, and export warehouse proprietors, imposed by 26 U.S.C. 5731.

State. "State" shall, for the purposes of this part, be construed to include the District of Columbia.

Tobacco products. Cigars, cigarettes, smokeless tobacco, pipe tobacco, and roll-your-own tobacco.

United States. "United States" when used in a geographical sense shall include only the States and the District of Columbia.

U.S.C. The United States Code.

Zone operator. The person to whom the privilege of establishing, operating, and maintaining a foreign-trade zone has been granted by the Foreign-Trade Zones Board created by the Act of June 18, 1934, as amended.

Zone restricted status. The status assigned to tobacco products and cigarette papers and cigarette tubes taken into a foreign trade zone from the customs territory of the United States for the sole purpose of exportation or storage until exported.

[T.D. ATF-48, 43 FR 13556, Mar. 31, 1978]

EDITORIAL NOTE: For FEDERAL REGISTER citations affecting §44.11, see the List of CFR Sections Affected, which appears in the Finding Aids section of the printed volume and at *www.fdsys.gov.*

EFFECTIVE DATE NOTE: At 78 FR 38573, June 27, 2013, §44.11 was amended by revising the definition of "Manufacturer of tobacco products" and of "Zone restricted status", effective Aug. 26, 2013 through Aug. 26, 2016.

Subpart Ba—Special (Occupational) Taxes

SOURCE: T.D. ATF-271, 53 FR 17563, May 17, 1988, unless otherwise noted.

§44.31 Liability for special tax.

(a) *Export warehouse proprietor.* Every export warehouse proprietor shall pay a special (occupational) tax at a rate specified by §44.32. The tax shall be paid on or before the date of commencing the business of an export warehouseman, and thereafter every year on or before July 1. On commencing business, the tax shall be computed from the first day of the month in which liability is incurred, through the following June 30. Thereafter, the tax shall be computed for the entire year (July 1 through June 30).

(b) [Reserved]

(c) *Each place of business taxable.* An export warehouse proprietor under this part incurs special tax liability at each place of business in which an occupation subject to special tax is conducted. A place of business means the entire office, plant or area of the business in any one location under the same proprietorship. Passageways, streets, highways, rail crossings, waterways, or partitions dividing the premises are not sufficient separation to require additional special tax, if the divisions of the premises are otherwise contiguous.

(d) *Payment of tax.* Special tax must be paid by return. The prescribed return is TTB Form 5630.5t, Special Tax Registration and Return—Tobacco. Special tax returns, with payment of tax, must be filed with TTB in accordance with the instructions on the form and the requirements of subpart D of part 46 of this chapter.

(26 U.S.C. 5731, 5733)

[T.D. ATF–271, 53 FR 17563, May 17, 1988, as amended by T.D. TTB–79, 74 FR 37419, July 28, 2009]

§ 44.32 Rate of special tax.

(a) *General.* Title 26 U.S.C. 5731(a)(3) imposes a special tax of $1,000 per year on every export warehouse proprietor.

(b) *Reduced rate for small proprietors.* Title 26 U.S.C. 5731(b) provides for a reduced rate of $500 per year with respect to any export warehouse proprietor whose gross receipts (for the most recent taxable year ending before the first day of the taxable period to which the special tax imposed by § 44.31 relates) are less than $500,000. The "taxable year" to be used for determining gross receipts is the taxpayer's income tax year. All gross receipts of the taxpayer shall be included, not just the gross receipts of the business subject to special tax. Proprietors of new businesses that have not yet begun a taxable year, as well as proprietors of existing businesses that have not yet ended a taxable year, who commence a new activity subject to special tax, qualify for the reduced special (occupational) tax rate, unless the business is a member of a "controlled group"; in that case, the rules of paragraph (c) of this section shall apply.

(c) *Controlled group.* All persons treated as one taxpayer under 26 U.S.C. 5061(e)(3) shall be treated as one taxpayer for the purpose of determining gross receipts under paragraph (b) of this section. "Controlled group" means a controlled group of corporations, as defined in 26 U.S.C. 1563 and implementing regulations in 26 CFR 1.1563–1 through 1.1563–4, except that the words "at least 80 percent" shall be replaced by the words "more than 50 percent" in each place they appear in subsection (a) of 26 U.S.C. 1563, as well as in the implementing regulations. Also, the rules for a "controlled group of corporations" apply in a similar fashion to groups which include partnerships and/or sole proprietorships. If one entity maintains more than 50% control over a group consisting of corporations and one, or more, partnerships and/or sole proprietorships, all of the members of the controlled group are one taxpayer for the purpose of this section.

(d) *Short taxable year.* Gross receipts for any taxable year of less than 12 months shall be annualized by multiplying the gross receipts for the short period by 12 and dividing the result by the number of months in the short period as required by 26 U.S.C. 448(c)(3).

(e) *Returns and allowances.* Gross receipts for any taxable year shall be reduced by returns and allowances made during such year under 26 U.S.C. 448(c)(3).

(26 U.S.C. 448, 5061, 5731)

§ 44.33 Cross reference.

For additional rules pertaining to liability for special (occupational) tax, filing special tax returns, issuance and examination of special tax stamps, and notification of changes to special tax stamps, see subpart D of part 46 of this chapter.

[T.D. TTB–79, 74 FR 37419, July 28, 2009]

§§ 44.34–44.36 [Reserved]

Subpart C—General

§ 44.61 Removals, withdrawals, and shipments authorized.

(a) Tobacco products and cigarette papers and tubes may be removed from a factory or from an export warehouse, and cigars may be withdrawn from a customs bonded warehouse, without payment of tax for direct exportation or for delivery for subsequent exportation, in accordance with the provisions of this part.

(b) Tobacco products and cigarette papers and tubes are eligible for removal or transfer in bond under this part only if they bear the marks, labels, and notices required by this part.

[78 FR 38573, June 27, 2013]

EFFECTIVE DATE NOTE: At 78 FR 38573, June 27, 2013, § 44.61 was revised, effective Aug. 26, 2013 through Aug. 26, 2016.

§44.61a Deliveries to foreign-trade zones—export status.

Tobacco products, and cigarette papers and tubes may be removed from a factory or an export warehouse and cigars may be withdrawn from a customs warehouse, without payment of tax, for delivery to a foreign-trade zone for exportation or storage pending exportation in accordance with the provisions of this part. Such articles delivered to a foreign-trade zone under this part shall be considered exported for the purpose of the statutes and bonds under which removed and for the purposes of the internal revenue laws generally and the regulations thereunder. However, export status is not acquired until an application for admission of the articles into the zone with zone restricted status has been approved by the district director of customs pursuant to the appropriate provisions of 19 CFR chapter I and the required certificate of receipt of the articles in the zone has been made on Form 5200.14 as prescribed in this part.

(48 Stat. 999, as amended, 72 Stat. 1418, as amended; 19 U.S.C. 81c; 26 U.S.C. 5704)

[T.D. 6961, 33 FR 9491, June 28, 1968. Redesignated at 40 FR 16835, Apr. 15, 1975, and amended by T.D. ATF–232, 51 FR 28087, Aug. 5, 1986; T.D. ATF–243, 51 FR 43194, Dec. 1, 1986; T.D. ATF–421, 64 FR 71925, Dec. 22, 1999]

§44.62 Restrictions on deliveries of tobacco products, and cigarette papers and tubes to vessels and aircraft, as supplies.

Tobacco products, and cigarette papers and tubes may be removed from a factory or an export warehouse and cigars may be withdrawn from a customs warehouse, without payment of tax, for delivery to vessels and aircraft, as supplies, for consumption beyond the jurisdiction of the internal revenue laws of the United States, subject to the applicable provisions of this part. Deliveries may be made to vessels actually engaged in foreign, intercoastal, or noncontiguous territory trade (i.e., vessels operating on a regular schedule in trade or actually transporting passengers and/or cargo (a) between a port in the United States and a foreign port; (b) between the Atlantic and Pacific ports of the United States; or (c) between a port on the mainland of the United States and a port in Alaska, Hawaii, Puerto Rico, the Virgin Islands, or a possession of the United States; between a port in Alaska and a port in Hawaii; or between a port in Alaska or Hawaii and a port in Puerto Rico, the Virgin Islands, or a possession of the United States); to vessels clearing through customs for a port beyond the jurisdiction of the internal revenue laws of the United States; to vessels of war or other governmental activity; or to vessels of the United States documented to engage in the fishing business (including the whaling business), and foreign fishing (including whaling) vessels of 5 net tons or over. Such deliveries to vessels shall be subject to lading under customs supervision as provided in §§44.207 and 44.263. As a condition to the lading of the tobacco products, and cigarette papers and tubes, the customs authorities at the port of lading may, if they deem it necessary in order to protect the revenue, require assurances, satisfactory to them, from the master of the receiving vessel that the quantities to be laden are reasonable, considering the number of persons to be carried, the vessel's itinerary, the duration of its intended voyage, etc., and that such articles are to be used exclusively as supplies on the voyage. For this purpose, the customs authorities may require the master of the receiving vessel to submit, prior to lading, customs documentation for permission to lade the articles. Where the customs authorities allow only a portion of a shipment to be laden, the remainder of the shipment shall be returned to the bonded premises of the manufacturer, export warehouse proprietor, or customs warehouse proprietor making the shipment, or otherwise disposed of as approved by the appropriate TTB officer. Deliveries may be made to aircraft that are clearing through customs and that are enroute to a place beyond the jurisdiction of the internal revenue laws of the United States, and to aircraft operating on a regular schedule between U.S. customs areas as defined in the Air Commerce Regulations (19 CFR part 122). Deliveries may not be made to a vessel or aircraft stationed in the United States for an indefinite period and where its schedule does not include operations outside such jurisdiction.

(72 Stat. 1418, as amended; 26 U.S.C. 5704)

[T.D. 6871, 31 FR 48, Jan. 4, 1966. Redesignated at 40 FR 16835, Apr. 15, 1975, and amended by T.D. ATF–232, 51 FR 28088, Aug. 5, 1986; T.D. ATF–243, 51 FR 43194, Dec. 1, 1986; T.D. ATF–421, 64 FR 71925, Dec. 22, 1999; T.D. ATF–480, 67 FR 30801, May 8, 2002; 78 FR 38573, June 27, 2013]

EFFECTIVE DATE NOTE: At 78 FR 38573, June 27, 2013, § 44.62 was amended by revising the fifth and the seventh sentence, effective Aug. 26, 2013 through Aug. 26, 2016.

§ 44.63 Restrictions on disposal of tobacco products, and cigarette papers and tubes on vessels and aircraft.

Tobacco products, and cigarette papers and tubes delivered to a vessel or aircraft, without payment of tax, pursuant to § 44.62, shall not be sold, offered for sale, or otherwise disposed of until the vessel or aircraft is outside the jurisdiction of the internal revenue laws of the United States, i.e., outside the 3-mile limit or international boundary, as the case may be, of the United States. Where the vessel or aircraft returns within the jurisdiction of the internal revenue laws with such articles on board, the articles shall be subject to treatment under the tariff laws of the United States.

(72 Stat. 1418, as amended; 26 U.S.C. 5704; 19 U.S.C. 1317)

[T.D. 6871, 31 FR 49, Jan. 4, 1966. Redesignated at 40 FR 16835, Apr. 15, 1975, and amended by T.D. ATF–232, 51 FR 28088, Aug. 5, 1986; T.D. ATF–243, 51 FR 43194, Dec. 1, 1986]

§ 44.64 Responsibility for delivery or exportation of tobacco products, and cigarette papers and tubes.

Responsibility for compliance with the provisions of this part with respect to the removal under bond of tobacco products, and cigarette papers and tubes, without payment of tax, for export, and for the proper delivery or exportation of such articles, and with respect to the exportation of tobacco products, and cigarette papers and tubes with benefit of drawback of tax, shall rest upon the manufacturer of such articles or the proprietor of an export warehouse or customs warehouse from whose premises such articles are removed for export, and upon the exporter who exports tobacco products, and cigarette papers and tubes with benefit of drawback of tax.

(72 Stat. 1418, as amended; 26 U.S.C. 5704)

[T.D. 6871, 31 FR 49, Jan. 4, 1966. Redesignated at 40 FR 16835, Apr. 15, 1975, and amended by T.D. ATF–232, 51 FR 28088, Aug. 5, 1986; T.D. ATF–243, 51 FR 43194, Dec. 1, 1986]

§ 44.65 Liability for tax on tobacco products, and cigarette papers and tubes.

The manufacturer of tobacco products and cigarette papers and tubes shall be liable for the taxes imposed thereon by 26 U.S.C. 5701: *Provided*, That when tobacco products, and cigarette papers and tubes are transferred, without payment of tax, pursuant to 26 U.S.C. 5704, between the bonded premises of manufacturers and/or export warehouse proprietors, the transferee shall become liable for the tax upon receipt by him of such articles. Any person who possesses tobacco products, or cigarette papers or tubes in violation of 26 U.S.C. 5751(a)(1) or (2), shall be liable for a tax equal to the tax on such articles.

(72 Stat. 1417, 1424; 26 U.S.C. 5703, 5751)

[T.D. 6871, 31 FR 49, Jan. 4, 1966. Redesignated at 40 FR 16835, Apr. 15, 1975, and amended by T.D. ATF–48, 44 FR 55856, Sept. 28, 1979; T.D. ATF–232, 51 FR 28088, Aug. 5, 1986; T.D. ATF–243, 51 FR 43194, Dec. 1, 1986]

§ 44.66 Relief from liability for tax.

A manufacturer of tobacco products or cigarette papers and tubes or an export warehouse proprietor is relieved of the liability for tax on tobacco products, or cigarette papers or tubes upon providing evidence satisfactory to the appropriate TTB officer of exportation or proper delivery. The evidence must comply with this part. Such evidence shall be furnished within 90 days of the date of removal of the tobacco products, or cigarette papers or tubes: *Provided*, That this period may be extended for good cause shown.

(72 Stat. 1417; 26 U.S.C. 5703)

[T.D. 6871, 31 FR 49, Jan. 4, 1966. Redesignated at 40 FR 16835, Apr. 15, 1975; T.D. ATF–232, 51 FR 28088, Aug. 5, 1986; T.D. ATF–243, 51 FR 43194, Dec. 1, 1986; T.D. ATF–480, 67 FR 30801, May 8, 2002]

§44.67 Payment of tax.

(a) *General*. The taxes on tobacco products, and cigarette papers and tubes with respect to which the evidence described in §44.66 is not timely furnished shall become immediately due and payable. The taxes shall be paid to TTB, with sufficient information to identify the taxpayer, the nature and purpose of the payment, and the articles covered by the payment. (TTB Form 5000.24 may be used for this purpose.)

(b) *Large cigars*. The amount of tax liability on large cigars shall be based on the maximum tax rate prescribed in §40.21 of this part, unless the person liable for the tax establishes that a lower tax rate is applicable.

(All recordkeeping requirements have been approved under OMB Control No. 1512–0180)

[T.D. ATF–80, 46 FR 18311, Mar. 24, 1981, as amended by T.D. ATF–232, 51 FR 28088, Aug. 5, 1986; T.D. ATF–243, 51 FR 43194, Dec. 1, 1986; T.D. ATF–251, 52 FR 19341, May 22, 1987; T.D. ATF–307, 55 FR 52745, Dec. 21, 1990; T.D. ATF–460, 66 FR 39093, July 27, 2001]

§44.68 [Reserved]

§44.69 Assessment.

Whenever any person required by law to pay tax on tobacco products, and cigarette papers and tubes fails to pay such tax, the tax shall be ascertained and assessed against such person, subject to the limitations prescribed in 26 U.S.C. 6501. The tax so assessed shall be in addition to the penalties imposed by law for failure to pay such tax when required. Except in cases where delay may jeopardize collection of the tax, or where the amount is nominal or the result of an evident mathematical error, no such assessment shall be made until and after notice has been afforded such person to show cause against assessment. The person will be allowed 45 days from the date of such notice to show cause, in writing, against such assessment.

(72 Stat. 1417; 26 U.S.C. 5703)

[T.D. 6871, 31 FR 49, Jan. 4, 1966. Redesignated at 40 FR 16835, Apr. 15, 1975, and amended by T.D. ATF–48, 44 FR 55856, Sept. 28, 1979; T.D. ATF–232, 51 FR 28088, Aug. 5, 1986; T.D. ATF–243, 51 FR 43194, Dec. 1, 1986]

§44.70 Authority of appropriate TTB officers to enter premises.

Any appropriate TTB officer may enter in the daytime any premises where tobacco products, or cigarette papers or tubes are produced or kept, so far as it may be necessary for the purpose of examining such articles. When such premises are open at night, any appropriate TTB officer may enter them, while so open, in the performance of his official duties. The owner of such premises, or person having the superintendence of the same, who refuses to admit any appropriate TTB officer or permit him to examine such articles shall be liable to the penalties prescribed by law for the offense.

(68A Stat. 872, 903; 26 U.S.C. 7342, 7606)

[T.D. 6871, 31 FR 49, Jan. 4, 1966. Redesignated at 40 FR 16835, Apr. 15, 1975, and amended by T.D. ATF–232, 51 FR 28088, Aug. 5, 1986; T.D. ATF–243, 51 FR 43194, Dec. 1, 1986]

§44.71 Interference with administration.

Whoever, corruptly or by force or threats of force, endeavors to hinder or obstruct the administration of this part, or endeavors to intimidate or impede any appropriate TTB officer acting in his official capacity, or forcibly rescues or attempts to rescue or causes to be rescued any property, after it has been duly seized for forfeiture to the United States in connection with a violation of the internal revenue laws, shall be liable to the penalties prescribed by law.

(68A Stat. 855; 26 U.S.C. 7212)

[25 FR 4716, May 28, 1960. Redesignated at 40 FR 16835, Apr. 15, 1975]

VARIATIONS FROM REQUIREMENTS

§ 44.72 Alternate methods or procedures.

A manufacturer of tobacco products, an export warehouse proprietor, or a customs warehouse proprietor, on specific approval by the appropriate TTB officer as provided in this section, may use an alternate method or procedure in lieu of a method or procedure specifically prescribed in this part. The appropriate TTB officer may approve an alternate method or procedure, subject to stated conditions, when he finds that—

(a) Good cause has been shown for the use of the alternate method or procedure.

(b) The alternate method or procedure is within the purpose of, and consistent with the effect intended by, the specifically prescribed method or procedure, and affords equivalent security to the revenue, and

(c) The alternate method or procedure will not be contrary to any provision of law, and will not result in an increase in cost to the Government or hinder the effective administration of this part. No alternate method or procedure relating to the giving of any bond or to the assessment, payment, or collection of tax, shall be authorized under this section. Where a manufacturer or proprietor desires to employ an alternate method or procedure, he shall submit a written application to the appropriate TTB officer. The application shall specifically describe the proposed alternate method or procedure, and shall set forth the reasons therefor. Alternate methods or procedures shall not be employed until the application has been approved by the appropriate TTB officer. The manufacturer or proprietor shall, during the period of authorization of an alternate method or procedure, comply with the terms of the approved application. Authorization for any alternate method or procedure may be withdrawn whenever in the judgment of the appropriate TTB officer the revenue is jeopardized or the effective administration of this part is hindered. The manufacturer or proprietor shall retain, as part of his records, any authorization of the appropriate TTB officer under this section.

[T.D. 6871, 31 FR 49, Jan. 4, 1966. Redesignated at 40 FR 16835, Apr. 15, 1975; T.D. ATF–480, 67 FR 30801, May 8, 2002]

§ 44.73 Emergency variations from requirements.

The appropriate TTB officer may approve methods of operation other than as specified in this part, where he finds that an emergency exists and the proposed variations from the specified requirements are necessary, and the proposed variations—

(a) Will afford the security and protection to the revenue intended by the prescribed specifications,

(b) Will not hinder the effective administration of this part, and

(c) Will not be contrary to any provision of law. Variations from requirements granted under this section are conditioned on compliance with the procedures, conditions, and limitations set forth in the approval of the application. Failure to comply in good faith with such procedures, conditions, and limitations shall automatically terminate the authority for such variations and the manufacturer, export warehouse proprietor, or customs warehouse proprietor, thereupon shall fully comply with the prescribed requirements of regulations from which the variations were authorized. Authority for any variations may be withdrawn whenever in the judgment of the appropriate TTB officer the revenue is jeopardized or the effective administration of this part is hindered by the continuation of such variation. Where a manufacturer or proprietor desires to employ such variation, he shall submit a written application to the appropriate TTB officer. The application shall describe the proposed variations and set forth the reasons therefor. Variations shall not be employed until the application has been approved. The manufacturer or proprietor shall retain, as part of his records, any authorization of the appropriate TTB officer under this section.

[T.D. 6871, 31 FR 50, Jan. 4, 1966. Redesignated at 40 FR 16835, Apr. 15, 1975; T.D. ATF–480, 67 FR 30801, May 8, 2002]

Subpart D—Qualification Requirements for Export Warehouse Proprietors

SOURCE: 25 FR 4716, May 28, 1960, unless otherwise noted. Redesignated at 40 FR 16835, Apr. 15, 1975.

§44.81 Persons required to qualify.

Every person who intends to engage in business as an export warehouse proprietor, as defined in this part, shall qualify as such in accordance with the provisions of this part.

(72 Stat. 1421; 26 U.S.C. 5711, 5712, 5713)

§44.82 Application for permit.

Every person, before commencing business as an export warehouse proprietor, must apply on TTB Form 2093 (5200.3) and obtain the permit provided for in §44.93. All documents required under this part to be furnished with such application shall be made a part thereof.

(72 Stat. 1421; 26 U.S.C. 5712)

[25 FR 4716, May 28, 1960. Redesignated at 40 FR 16835, Apr. 15, 1975, as amended by T.D. ATF-480, 67 FR 30801, May 8, 2002]

§44.83 Corporate documents.

Every corporation, before commencing business as an export warehouse proprietor, shall furnish with its application for permit required by §44.82, a true copy of the corporate charter or a certificate of corporate existence or incorporation, executed by the appropriate officer of the State in which incorporated. The corporation shall also furnish, in duplicate, evidence which will establish the authority of the officer or other person who executes the application for permit to execute the same; the authority of persons to sign other documents, required by this part, for the corporation; and the identity of the officers and directors, and each person who holds more than ten percent of the stock of such corporation. Where a corporation has previously filed such documents or evidence with the appropriate TTB officer, a written statement by the corporation, in duplicate, to that effect will be sufficient for the purpose of this section.

(72 Stat. 1421; 26 U.S.C. 5712)

§44.84 Articles of partnership or association.

Every partnership or association, before commencing business as an export warehouse proprietor, shall furnish with its application for permit, required by §44.82 a true copy of the articles of partnership or association, if any, or certificate of partnership or association where required to be filed by any State, county, or municipality. Where a partnership or association has previously filed such documents with the appropriate TTB officer, a written statement by the partnership or association, in duplicate, to that effect will be sufficient for the purpose of this section.

(72 Stat. 1421; 26 U.S.C. 5712)

§44.85 Trade name certificate.

Every person, before commencing business under a trade name as an export warehouse proprietor, shall furnish with his application for permit, required by §44.82, a true copy of the certificate or other document, if any, issued by a State, county, or municipal authority in connection with the transaction of business under such trade name. If no such certificate or other document is so required a written statement, in duplicate, to that effect by such person will be sufficient for the purpose of this section.

(72 Stat. 1421; 26 U.S.C. 5712)

[T.D. 6961, 33 FR 9491, June 28, 1968. Redesignated at 40 FR 16835, Apr. 15, 1975]

§44.86 Bond.

Every person, before commencing business as an export warehouse proprietor, shall file, in connection with his application for permit, a bond, Form 2103 (5220.5), in accordance with the applicable provisions of §44.88 and subpart F, conditioned upon compliance with the provisions of chapter 52, I.R.C., and regulations thereunder, including, but not limited to, the timely payment of taxes imposed by such chapter and penalties and interest in connection therewith for which he may become liable to the United States.

(72 Stat. 1421; 26 U.S.C. 5711)

[25 FR 4716, May 28, 1960. Redesignated at 40 FR 16835, Apr. 15, 1975, as amended by T.D. ATF–480, 67 FR 30801, May 8, 2002]

§ 44.87 Power of attorney.

If the application for permit or other qualifying documents are signed by an attorney in fact for an individual, partnership, association, company, or corporation, or by one of the partners for a partnership, or by an officer of an association or company, or, in the case of a corporation, by an officer or other person not authorized to sign by the corporate documents described in § 44.83, power of attorney conferring authority upon the person signing the documents shall be manifested on Form 5000.8 in accordance with its instructions.

[25 FR 4716, May 28, 1960. Redesignated at 40 FR 16835, Apr. 15, 1975, as amended by T.D. ATF–480, 67 FR 30802, May 8, 2002]

§ 44.88 Description and diagram of premises.

The premises to be used by an export warehouse proprietor as his warehouse shall be described, in the application for permit required by § 44.82, and bond required by § 44.86, by number, street, and city, town, or village, and State. Such premises may consist of more than one building, which need not be contiguous: *Provided,* That such premises are located in the same city, town, or village and each located is described in the application for permit and the bond by number and street. Where such premises consist of less than an entire building, a diagram, in duplicate, shall also be furnished showing the particular floor or floors, or room or rooms, comprising the warehouse.

(72 Stat. 1421; 26 U.S.C. 5712)

§ 44.89 Separation of premises.

Where the export warehouse premises consist of less than an entire building, the premises shall be completely separated from adjoining portions of the building, which separation shall be constructed of materials generally used in the construction of buildings and may include any necessary doors or other openings.

(72 Stat. 1421; 26 U.S.C. 5712)

§ 44.90 [Reserved]

§ 44.91 Additional information.

The appropriate TTB officer may require such additional information as may be deemed necessary to determine whether the applicant is entitled to a permit. The applicant shall, when required by the appropriate TTB officer, furnish as a part of his application for permit such additional information as may be necessary for the appropriate TTB officer to determine whether the applicant is entitled to a permit.

§ 44.92 Investigation of applicant.

(a) *Investigation.* The appropriate TTB officer shall promptly cause such inquiry or investigation to be made, as may be necessary, to verify the information furnished in connection with an application for permit and to ascertain whether the applicant is eligible for a permit. Any of the following conditions may be grounds for denial of a permit:

(1) The premises on which it is proposed to conduct the business are not adequate to protect the revenue; or

(2) The applicant (including, in the case of a corporation, any officer, director, or principal stockholder and, in the case of a partnership, a partner)—

(i) Is, by reason of his business experience, financial standing, or trade connections or by reason of previous or current legal proceedings involving a felony violation of any other provision of Federal criminal law relating to tobacco products, processed tobacco, cigarette paper, or cigarette tubes, not likely to maintain operations in compliance with this chapter;

(ii) Has been convicted of a felony violation of any provision of Federal or State criminal law relating to tobacco products, processed tobacco, cigarette paper, or cigarette tubes; or

(iii) Has failed to disclose any material information required or made any material false statement in the application therefor.

(b) *TTB action.* An appropriate TTB officer who has reason to believe that the applicant is not entitled to a permit shall promptly give the applicant notice of the contemplated disapproval of his application and opportunity for hearing thereon in accordance with part 71 of this chapter, which part (including the provisions relating to the recommended decision and to appeals) is made applicable to such proceedings. If, after such notice and opportunity for hearing, the appropriate TTB officer finds that the applicant is not entitled to a permit, he shall, by order stating the findings on which his decision is based, deny the permit.

(72 Stat. 1421; 26 U.S.C. 5712)

[T.D. TTB–75, 74 FR 14485, Mar. 31, 2009, as amended by T.D. TTB–85, 75 FR 42607, July 22, 2010]

§44.93 Issuance of permit.

After the application for permit, bond, and supporting documents, as required under this part, has been approved, the appropriate TTB officer will issue a permit to the export warehouse proprietor. The proprietor must keep such permit at the export warehouse and make it available for inspection by an appropriate TTB officer.

[T.D. ATF–480, 67 FR 30802, May 8, 2002]

Subpart E—Changes Subsequent to Original Qualification of Export Warehouse Proprietors

SOURCE: 25 FR 4717, May 28, 1960, unless otherwise noted. Redesignated at 40 FR 16835, Apr. 15, 1975.

CHANGES IN NAME

§44.101 Change in individual name.

Where there is a change in the name of an individual operating as an export warehouse proprietor he shall, within 30 days of such change, make application on Form 2098 (5200.16) for an amended permit.

(72 Stat. 1421; 26 U.S.C. 5712)

[T.D. 6961, 33 FR 9491, June 28, 1968. Redesignated at 40 FR 16835, Apr. 15, 1975]

§44.102 Change in trade name.

Where there is a change in, or an addition or discontinuance of, a trade name used by an export warehouse proprietor in connection with operations authorized by his permit, the proprietor shall, within 30 days of such change, addition, or discontinuance, make application on Form 2098 (5200.16) for an amended permit to reflect such change. The proprietor shall also furnish a true copy of any new trade name certificate or document issued to him, or statement in lieu thereof, required by §44.85.

(72 Stat. 1421; 26 U.S.C. 5712)

[T.D. 6961, 33 FR 9491, June 28, 1968. Redesignated at 40 FR 16835, Apr. 15, 1975]

§44.103 Change in corporate name.

Where there is a change in the name of a corporate export warehouse proprietor the proprietor shall, within 30 days of such change, make application on Form 2098 (5200.16) for an amended permit. The proprietor shall also furnish such documents as may be necessary to establish that the corporate name has been changed.

(72 Stat. 1421; 26 U.S.C. 5712)

[T.D. 6961, 33 FR 9491, June 28, 1968. Redesignated at 40 FR 16835, Apr. 15, 1975]

CHANGES IN OWNERSHIP AND CONTROL

§44.104 Fiduciary successor.

If an administrator, executor, receiver, trustee, assignee, or other fiduciary, is to take over the business of an export warehouse proprietor, as a continuing operation, such fiduciary shall, before commencing operations, make application for permit and file bond as required by subpart D of this part, furnish certified copies, in duplicate, of the order of the court, or other pertinent documents, showing his appointment and qualification as such fiduciary, and make an opening inventory, in accordance with the provisions of §44.144; *Provided*, That where a diagram has been furnished by the predecessor, in accordance with the provisions of §44.88, the successor may adopt such diagram. However, where a fiduciary intends merely to liquidate the business, qualification as an export warehouse proprietor will not be required if he promptly files with the appropriate TTB officer a statement to that effect, together with an extension of coverage of the predecessor's bond, executed by the fiduciary, also by the surety on such bond, in accordance with the provisions of § 44.126.

(72 Stat. 1421, 1422; 26 U.S.C. 5711, 5712, 5721)

§ 44.105 Transfer of ownership.

If a transfer is to be made in ownership of the business of an export warehouse proprietor (including a change in the identity of the members of a partnership or association), such proprietor shall give notice, in writing, to the appropriate TTB officer, naming the proposed successor and the desired effective date of such transfer. The proposed successor shall, before commencing operations, qualify as a proprietor, in accordance with the applicable provisions of subpart D of this part: *Provided*, That where a diagram has been furnished by the proprietor in accordance with the provisions of § 44.88, the proposed successor may adopt such diagram. The proprietor shall give such notice of transfer, and the proposed successor shall make application for permit and file bond, as required, in ample time for examination and approval thereof before the desired date of such change. The predecessor shall make a closing inventory and closing report, in accordance with the provisions of §§ 44.146 and 44.151, respectively, and surrender, with such inventory and report, his permit, and the successor shall make an opening inventory, in accordance with the provisions of § 44.144.

(72 Stat. 1421, 1422; 26 U.S.C. 5712, 5713, 5721, 5722)

§ 44.106 Change in officers or directors of a corporation.

Where there is any change in the officers or directors of a corporation operating the business of an export warehouse proprietor, the proprietor shall furnish to the appropriate TTB officer notice, in writing, of the election of the new officers or directors within 30 days after such election.

(72 Stat. 1421; 26 U.S.C. 5712)

§ 44.107 Change in stockholders of a corporation.

Where the issuance, sale, or transfer of the stock of a corporation, operating as an export warehouse proprietor, results in a change in the identity of the principal stockholders exercising actual or legal control of the operations of the corporation, the corporate proprietor shall, within 30 days after the change occurs, make application for a new permit; otherwise, the present permit shall be automatically terminated at the expiration of such 30-day period, and the proprietor shall dispose of all cigars, cigarettes, and cigarette papers and tubes on hand, in accordance with this part, make a closing inventory and closing report, in accordance with the provisions of §§ 44.146 and 44.151, respectively, and surrender his permit with such inventory and report. If the application for a new permit is timely made, the present permit shall continue in effect pending final action with respect to such application.

(72 Stat. 1421, 1422; 26 U.S.C. 5712, 5713, 5721, 5722)

[T.D. 6871, 31 FR 50, Jan. 4, 1966. Redesignated at 40 FR 16835, Apr. 15, 1975]

CHANGES IN LOCATION AND PREMISES

§ 44.108 Change in location.

Whenever an export warehouse proprietor contemplates changing the location of his warehouse, the proprietor shall, before commencing operations at the new location, make an application, on Form 2098 (5200.16) for an amended permit. The application shall be supported by an extension of coverage of the bond filed under this part, in accordance with the provisions of § 44.126.

(72 Stat. 1421; 26 U.S.C. 5711, 5712)

[25 FR 4717, May 28, 1960. Redesignated at 40 FR 16835, Apr. 15, 1975, as amended by T.D. ATF–480, 67 FR 30802, May 8, 2002]

§ 44.109 Change in address.

Whenever any change occurs in the address, but not the location, of the warehouse of an export warehouse proprietor, as a result of action of local authorities, the proprietor shall, within 30 days of such change, make application on Form 2098 (5200.16) for an amended permit.

(72 Stat. 1421; 26 U.S.C. 5712)

[T.D. 6961, 33 FR 9492, June 28, 1968. Redesignated at 40 FR 16835, Apr. 15, 1975]

§44.110 [Reserved]

§44.111 Change in export warehouse premises.

Where an export warehouse is to be changed to an extent which will make inaccurate the description of the warehouse as set forth in the last application by the proprietor for permit, or the diagram, if any, furnished with such application, the proprietor shall first make application on Form 2098 (5200.16) for, and obtain, an amended permit. Such application shall describe the proposed change in the warehouse and shall be accompanied by a new diagram if required under §44.88.

(72 Stat. 1421; 26 U.S.C. 5712)

[T.D. 6961 33 FR 9492, June 28, 1968. Redesignated at 40 FR 16835, Apr. 15, 1975]

§44.112 Emergency premises.

In cases of emergency, the appropriate TTB officer may authorize, for a stated period, the temporary use of a place for the temporary storage of tobacco products, and cigarette papers and tubes, without making the application or furnishing the extension of coverage of bond required under §§44.111 and 44.126, or the temporary separation of warehouse premises by means other than those specified in §44.89, where such action will not hinder the effective administration of this part, is not contrary to law, and will not jeopardize the revenue.

[T.D. 6871, 31 FR 50, Jan. 4, 1966. Redesignated at 40 FR 16835, Apr. 15, 1975, and amended by T.D. ATF-232, 51 FR 28088, Aug. 5, 1986; T.D. ATF-243, 51 FR 43194, Dec. 1, 1986]

Subpart F—Bonds and Extensions of Coverage of Bonds

SOURCE: 25 FR 4718, May 28, 1960, unless otherwise noted. Redesignated at 40 FR 16835, Apr. 15, 1975.

§44.121 Corporate surety.

(a) Surety bonds required under the provisions of this part may be given only with corporate sureties holding certificates of authority from the Secretary of the Treasury as acceptable sureties on Federal bonds. Limitations concerning corporate sureties are prescribed by the Secretary in Treasury Department Circular No. 570, as revised (see paragraph (c) of this section). The surety shall have no interest whatever in the business covered by the bond.

(b) Each bond and each extension of coverage of bond shall at the time of filing be accompanied by a power of attorney authorizing the agent or officer who executed the bond to so act on behalf of the surety. The appropriate TTB officer who is authorized to approve the bond may, whenever he deems it necessary, require additional evidence of the authority of the agent or officer to execute the bond or extension of coverage of bond. The power of attorney shall be prepared on a form provided by the surety company and executed under the corporate seal of the company. If the power of attorney submitted is other than a manually signed document, it shall be accompanied by a certificate of its validity.

(c) Treasury Department Circular No. 570 (Companies Holding Certificates of Authority as Acceptable Sureties on Federal Bonds and as Acceptable Reinsuring Companies) is published in the FEDERAL REGISTER annually as of the first workday in July. As they occur, interim revisions of the circular are published in the FEDERAL REGISTER. Copies may be obtained from the Audit Staff, Bureau of Government Financial Operations, Department of the Treasury, Washington, DC 20226.

(July 30, 1947, ch. 390, 61 Stat. 648, as amended (6 U.S.C. 6, 7); sec. 202, Pub. L. 85-859, 72 Stat. 1421, as amended (26 U.S.C. 5711))

[T.D. ATF-92, 46 FR 46923, Sept. 23, 1981]

§44.122 Deposits of bonds, notes, or obligations in lieu of corporate surety.

Bonds or notes of the United States, or other obligations which are unconditionally guaranteed as to both interest and principal by the United States, may be pledged and deposited by the export warehouse proprietor as security in connection with bond to cover his operations, in lieu of the corporate surety, in accordance with the provisions of Treasury Department Circular No. 154, revised (31 CFR part 225). Such bonds or notes which are nontransferable, or the pledging of which will not be recognized by the Treasury Department, are not acceptable as security in lieu of corporate surety.

(72 Stat. 1421, 61 Stat. 650; 26 U.S.C. 5711, 6 U.S.C. 15)

§ 44.123 Amount of bond.

The amount of the bond filed by the export warehouse proprietor, as required by § 44.86, shall be not less than the estimated amount of tax which may at any time constitute a charge against the bond: *Provided*, That the amount of any such bond (or the total amount where original and strengthening bonds are filed) shall not exceed $200,000 nor be less than $1,000. The charge against such bond shall be subject to increase upon receipt of tobacco products, and cigarette papers and tubes into the export warehouse and to decrease as satisfactory evidence of exportation, or satisfactory evidence of such other disposition as may be used as the lawful basis for crediting such bond, is received by the appropriate TTB officer with respect to such articles transferred or removed. When the limit of liability under a bond given in less than the maximum amount has been reached, no additional shipments shall be received into the warehouse until a strengthening or superseding bond is filed, as required by § 44.124 or § 44.125.

(72 Stat. 1421, as amended; 26 U.S.C. 5711)

[T.D. 6871, 31 FR 50, Jan. 4, 1966. Redesignated at 40 FR 16835, Apr. 15, 1975, and amended by T.D. ATF–232, 51 FR 28088, Aug. 5, 1986; T.D. ATF–243, 51 FR 43194, Dec. 1, 1986]

§ 44.124 Strengthening bond.

Where the appropriate TTB officer determines that the amount of the bond, under which an export warehouse proprietor is currently carrying on business, no longer adequately protects the revenue, and such bond is in an amount of less than $200,000, the appropriate TTB officer may require the proprietor to file a strengthening bond in an appropriate amount with the same surety as that on the bond already in effect, in lieu of a superseding bond to cover the full liability on the basis of § 44.123. The appropriate TTB officer shall refuse to approve any strengthening bond where any notation is made thereon which is intended or which may be construed as a release of any former bond, or as limiting the amount of either bond to less than its full amount.

(72 Stat. 1421; 26 U.S.C. 5711)

[25 FR 4718, May 28, 1960. Redesignated at 40 FR 16835, Apr. 15, 1975, as amended by T.D. ATF–480, 67 FR 30802, May 8, 2002]

§ 44.125 Superseding bond.

An export warehouse proprietor shall file a new bond to supersede his current bond, immediately when (a) the corporate surety on the current bond becomes insolvent, (b) the appropriate TTB officer approves a request from the surety on the current bond to terminate his liability under the bond, (c) payment of any liability under a bond is made by the surety thereon, or (d) the appropriate TTB officer considers such a superseding bond necessary for the protection of the revenue.

(72 Stat. 1421; 26 U.S.C. 5711)

§ 44.126 Extension of coverage of bond.

An extension of the coverage of any bond filed under this part shall be manifested on Form 2105 (5000.7) by the export warehouse proprietor and by the surety on the bond with the same formality and proof of authority as required for the execution of the bond.

(72 Stat. 1421; 26 U.S.C. 5711)

[25 FR 4718, May 28, 1960. Redesignated at 40 FR 16835, Apr. 15, 1975, as amended by T.D. ATF–480, 67 FR 30802, May 8, 2002]

§ 44.127 Approval of bond and extension of coverage of bond.

No person shall commence operations under any bond, nor extend his operations, until he receives from the appropriate TTB officer notice of his approval of the bond or of an appropriate extension of coverage of the bond required under this part.

(72 Stat. 1421; 26 U.S.C. 5711)

§ 44.128 Termination of liability of surety under bond.

The liability of a surety on any bond required by this part shall be terminated only as to operations on and after the effective date of a superseding bond, or the date of approval of the discontinuance of operations by the export warehouse proprietor, or otherwise in accordance with the termination provisions of the bond. The surety shall remain bound in respect of any liability for unpaid taxes, penalties, and interest, not in excess of the amount of the bond, incurred by the proprietor while the bond is in force.

(72 Stat. 1421; 26 U.S.C. 5711)

§ 44.129 Release of bonds, notes, and obligations.

(a) Bonds, notes, and other obligations of the United States, pledged and deposited as security in connection with bonds required by this part, shall be released only in accordance with the provisions of Treasury Department Circular No. 154 (31 CFR Part 225—Acceptance of Bonds, Notes or Other Obligations Issued or Guaranteed by the United States as Security in Lieu of Surety or Sureties on Penal Bonds). When the appropriate TTB officer is satisfied that it is no longer necessary to hold such security, he shall fix the date or dates on which a part or all of such security may be released. At any time prior to the release of such security, the appropriate TTB officer may, for proper cause, extend the date of release of such security for such additional length of time as in his judgment may be appropriate.

(b) Treasury Department Circular No. 154 is periodically revised and contains the provisions of 31 CFR part 225 and the forms prescribed in 31 CFR part 225. Copies of the circular may be obtained from the Audit Staff, Bureau of Government Financial Operations, Department of the Treasury, Washington, DC 20226.

(Sec. 202, Pub. L. 85–859, 72 Stat. 1421 (26 U.S.C. 5711); July 30, 1947, ch. 390, 61 Stat. 650 (6 U.S.C. 15))

[T.D. ATF–92, 46 FR 46923, Sept. 23, 1981; 46 FR 48644, Oct. 2, 1981]

Subpart G—Operations by Export Warehouse Proprietors

SOURCE: 25 FR 4719, May 28, 1960, unless otherwise noted. Redesignated at 40 FR 16835, Apr. 15, 1975.

§ 44.141 Sign.

Every export warehouse proprietor shall place and keep, on the outside of the building in which his warehouse is located, or at the entrance of his warehouse, where it can be plainly seen, a sign, in plain and legible letters, exhibiting the name under which he operates and (a) the type of business (''Export Warehouse Proprietor'') or (b) the number of the permit issued to the export warehouse proprietor under this part.

§ 44.141a Use of premises.

Export warehouse premises may only be used for the storage of tobacco products and cigarette papers and tubes, upon which the Internal Revenue tax has not been paid, for subsequent removal under this part, and for the storage of processed tobacco pending export.

[T.D. TTB–78, 74 FR 29419, June 22, 2009]

§ 44.142 Records.

(a) *In general.* Each export warehouse proprietor must keep in the warehouse complete and concise records that show the:

(1) Number of containers;

(2) Unit type (for example: cartons, cases);

(3) Kinds of articles (for example: small cigarettes);

(4) Name of manufacturer and brand; and

(5) Quantity of tobacco products and cigarette papers and tubes, and any processed tobacco received, removed, transferred, destroyed, lost, or returned to manufacturers or to customs bonded warehouse proprietors.

(b) *Other records; form and retention.* In addition to the records specified in paragraph (a) of this section, the export warehouse proprietor must retain a copy of each TTB F 5200.14 from a manufacturer, another export warehouse proprietor, or a customs warehouse proprietor, from whom tobacco products or cigarette papers or tubes were received, as well as a copy of each TTB F 5200.14 covering the tobacco products and cigarette papers and tubes removed from the warehouse. The entries for each day in the records maintained under this section must be made by the close of the business day following the day on which the transactions occur. No particular form of records is prescribed, but the information required must be readily ascertainable. The copies of TTB F 5200.14 and other records must be retained for 3 years following the close of the calendar year in which the shipments were received or removed and must be made available for inspection by any appropriate TTB officer upon request.

[78 FR 38574, June 27, 2013]

EFFECTIVE DATE NOTE: At 78 FR 38574, June 27, 2013, § 44.142 was revised, effective Aug. 26, 2013 through Aug. 26, 2016.

INVENTORIES

§ 44.143 General.

(a) Every export warehouse proprietor shall at the times specified in this subpart make a true and accurate inventory of products held on TTB Form 5220.3 (3373).

(b) This inventory shall be subject to verification by an appropriate TTB officer. A copy of each inventory shall be retained by the export warehouse proprietor for 3 years following the close of the calendar year in which the inventory is made and shall be made available for inspection by any appropriate TTB officer upon request.

[T.D. ATF–289, 54 FR 48841, Nov. 27, 1989, as amended by T.D. ATF–421, 64 FR 71925, Dec. 22, 1999; T.D. ATF–424, 64 FR 71933, Dec. 22, 1999; T.D. ATF–480, 67 FR 30802, May 8, 2002]

§ 44.144 Opening.

An opening inventory shall be made by the export warehouse proprietor at the time of commencing business. The date of commencing business under this part shall be the effective date indicated on the permit issued under § 44.93. A similar inventory shall be made by the export warehouse proprietor when he files a superseding bond. The date of such inventory shall be the effective date of such superseding bond.

(72 Stat. 1422; 26 U.S.C. 5721)

[25 FR 4719, May 28, 1960. Redesignated at 40 FR 16835, Apr. 15, 1975, as amended by T.D. ATF–480, 67 FR 30802, May 8, 2002]

§ 44.145 Special.

A special inventory shall be made by the export warehouse proprietor whenever required by any appropriate TTB officer.

(72 Stat. 1422; 26 U.S.C. 5721)

§ 44.146 Closing.

A closing inventory shall be made by the export warehouse proprietor when he transfers ownership or concludes business. Where the proprietor transfers ownership the closing inventory shall be made as of the day preceding the date of the opening inventory of the successor.

(72 Stat. 1422; 26 U.S.C. 5721)

[25 FR 4719, May 28, 1960. Redesignated at 40 FR 16835, Apr. 15, 1975, as amended by T.D. ATF–480, 67 FR 30802, May 8, 2002]

REPORTS

§ 44.147 General.

Every export warehouse proprietor shall make a report on Form 5220.4 of all tobacco products, cigarette papers and tubes, and any processed tobacco on hand, received, removed, transferred, and lost or destroyed. Such report shall be made at the times specified in this subpart and shall be made whether or not any operations or transactions occurred during the period covered by the report. A copy of each report shall be retained by the export warehouse proprietor at his warehouse for 3 years following the close of the calendar year covered in such reports, and made available for inspection by any appropriate TTB officer upon his request.

(72 Stat. 1422; 26 U.S.C. 5722)

[T.D. 6871, 31 FR 51, Jan. 4, 1966. Redesignated at 40 FR 16835, Apr. 15, 1975; T.D. ATF–232, 51 FR 28088, Aug. 5, 1986; T.D. ATF–243, 51 FR 43194, Dec. 1, 1986; T.D. ATF–421, 64 FR 71925, Dec. 22, 1999; T.D. ATF–424, 64 FR 71933, Dec. 22, 1999; T.D. ATF–480, 67 FR 30802, May 8, 2002; T.D. TTB–78, 74 FR 29419, June 22, 2009]

§ 44.148 Opening.

An opening report, covering the period from the date of the opening inventory, or inventory made in connection with a superseding bond, to the end of the month, shall be made on or before the 20th day following the end of the month in which the business was commenced.

(72 Stat. 1422; 26 U.S.C. 5722)

§44.149 Monthly.

A report for each full month shall be made on or before the 20th day following the end of the month covered in the report.

(72 Stat. 1422; 26 U.S.C. 5722)

§44.150 Special.

A special report, covering the unreported period to the day preceding the date of any special inventory required by an appropriate TTB officer, shall be made with such inventory. Another report, covering the period from the date of such inventory to the end of the month, shall be made on or before the 20th day following the end of the month in which the inventory was made.

(72 Stat. 1422; 26 U.S.C. 5722)

§44.151 Closing.

A closing report, covering the period from the first of the month to the date of the closing inventory, or the day preceding the date of an inventory made in connection with a superseding bond, shall be made with such inventory.

(72 Stat. 1422; 26 U.S.C. 5722)

CLAIMS

§44.152 Claim for remission of tax liability.

Remission of the tax liability on tobacco products, and cigarette papers and tubes may be extended to the export warehouse proprietor liable for the tax where such articles in bond are lost (otherwise than by theft) or destroyed, by fire, casualty, or act of God, while in the possession or ownership of such proprietor. Where articles are so lost or destroyed the proprietor shall report promptly such fact, and the circumstances, to the appropriate TTB officer. If the proprietor wishes to be relieved of the tax liability, the proprietor must prepare and file a claim on TTB Form 5620.8. The nature, date, place, and extent of the loss or destruction must be stated in such claim. The claim must be accompanied by such evidence as is necessary to establish to the satisfaction of the appropriate TTB officer that the claim is valid. When the appropriate TTB officer has acted on the claim, such officer will return a copy of TTB Form 5620.8 to the proprietor as notice of such action. The proprietor must keep the copy of TTB Form 5620.8 for 3 years following the close of the calendar year in which the claim is filed.

(72 Stat. 1419, as amended; 26 U.S.C. 5705)

[T.D. 6961, 33 FR 9492, June 28, 1968. Redesignated at 40 FR 16835, Apr. 15, 1975, and amended by T.D. ATF–232, 51 FR 28088, Aug. 5, 1986; T.D. ATF–243, 51 FR 43194, Dec. 1, 1986; T.D. ATF–421, 64 FR 71925, Dec. 22, 1999; T.D. ATF–480, 67 FR 30802, May 8, 2002]

§44.153 Claim for abatement of assessment.

A claim for abatement of the unpaid portion of the assessment of any tax on tobacco products, and cigarette papers and tubes, or any liability in respect of such tax, alleged to be excessive in amount, assessed after the expiration of the period of limitation applicable thereto, or erroneously or illegally assessed, shall be filed on Form 5620.8. Such claim shall set forth the reasons relied upon for the allowance of the claim and shall be supported by such evidence as is necessary to establish to the satisfaction of the appropriate TTB officer that the claim is valid.

(68A Stat. 792; 26 U.S.C. 6404)

[T.D. 6871, 31 FR 51, Jan. 4, 1966. Redesignated at 40 FR 16835, Apr. 15, 1975, and amended by T.D. ATF–232, 51 FR 28088, Aug. 5, 1986; T.D. ATF–243, 51 FR 43194, Dec. 1, 1986; T.D. ATF–251, 52 FR 19341, May 22, 1987; T.D. ATF–421, 64 FR 71925, Dec. 22, 1999; T.D. ATF–480, 67 FR 30802, May 8, 2002]

§44.154 Claim for refund of tax.

The taxes paid on tobacco products, and cigarette papers and tubes may be refunded (without interest) to an export warehouse proprietor on proof satisfactory to the appropriate TTB officer that the claimant proprietor paid the tax on such articles which were after taxpayment lost (otherwise than by theft) or destroyed, by fire, casualty, or act of God, while in the possession or ownership of such export warehouse proprietor, or withdrawn by him from the market. Any claim for refund under this section shall be prepared on Form 5620.8, in duplicate, and shall include a statement that the tax imposed by 26 U.S.C. 7652 or chapter 52, was paid in respect to the articles covered by the claim, and that the articles were lost, destroyed, or withdrawn from the market within 6 months preceding the date the claim is filed. The claim must be filed on TTB Form 5620.8 and supported by such evidence as is necessary to establish to the satisfaction of the appropriate TTB officer that the claim is valid. The duplicate of the claim shall be retained by the export warehouse proprietor for 3 years following the close of the calendar year in which the claim is filed. Where an export warehouse proprietor has paid the tax on tobacco products, or cigarette papers or tubes, he may file claim for refund of an overpayment of tax under subpart A of part 46 of this chapter if, at the time the tax was paid, these articles had been exported, destroyed, or otherwise disposed of in such a manner that tax was not due and payable.

(68A Stat. 791, 72 Stat. 9, 1419, as amended; 26 U.S.C. 6402, 6423, 5705)

[T.D. 6961, 33 FR 9492, June 28, 1968. Redesignated at 40 FR 16835, Apr. 15, 1975, and amended by T.D. ATF–48, 44 FR 55856, Sept. 28, 1979; T.D. ATF–232, 51 FR 28088, Aug. 5, 1986; T.D. ATF–243, 51 FR 43194, Dec. 1, 1986; T.D. ATF–251, 52 FR 19341, May 22, 1987; T.D. ATF–421, 64 FR 71925, Dec. 22, 1999; T.D. ATF–457, 66 FR 32220, June 14, 2001; T.D. ATF–480, 67 FR 30802, May 8, 2002]

Subpart H—Suspension and Discontinuance of Operations

§ 44.161 Discontinuance of operations.

Every export warehouse proprietor who desires to discontinue operations and close out his warehouse shall dispose of all cigars, cigarettes, and cigarette papers and tubes on hand, in accordance with this part, making a closing inventory and closing report, in accordance with the provisions of §§ 44.146 and 44.151, respectively, and surrender, with such inventory and report, his permit to the appropriate TTB officer as notice of such discontinuance, in order that the appropriate TTB officer may terminate the liability of the surety on the bond of the export warehouse proprietor.

(72 Stat. 1422; 26 U.S.C. 5721, 5722)

[T.D. 6871, 31 FR 51, Jan. 4, 1966. Redesignated at 40 FR 16835, Apr. 15, 1975]

§ 44.162 Suspension and revocation of permit.

Where the appropriate TTB officer has reason to believe that an export warehouse proprietor has not in good faith complied with the provisions of 26 U.S.C. chapter 52, and regulations thereunder, or with any other provision of 26 U.S.C. with intent to defraud, or has violated any condition of his permit, or has failed to disclose any material information required or made any material false statement in the application for permit, or has failed to maintain his premises in such manner as to protect the revenue, or is, by reason of previous or current legal proceedings involving a felony violation of any other provision of Federal criminal law relating to tobacco products, processed tobacco, cigarette paper, or cigarette tubes, not likely to maintain operations in compliance with 26 U.S.C. chapter 52, or has been convicted of a felony violation of any provision of Federal or State criminal law relating to tobacco products, processed tobacco, cigarette paper, or cigarette tubes, the appropriate TTB officer shall issue an order, stating the facts charged, citing such export warehouse proprietor to show cause why the permit should not be suspended or revoked after hearing thereon in accordance with part 71 of this chapter, which part (including the provisions relating to appeals) is made applicable to such proceedings. If, after hearing, the hearing examiner, or on appeal, the Administrator, finds that such person has not shown cause why the permit should not be suspended or revoked, such permit shall be suspended for such period as the appropriate TTB officer deems proper or shall be revoked.

(72 Stat. 1421; 26 U.S.C. 5713)

[T.D. TTB–75, 74 FR 14485, Mar. 31, 2009]

Subpart I [Reserved]

Subpart J—Removal of Shipments of Tobacco Products and Cigarette Papers and Tubes by Manufacturers and Export Warehouse Proprietors

PACKAGING REQUIREMENTS

§44.181 Packages.

All tobacco products and cigarette papers and tubes must, before removal or transfer under this subpart, be put up by the manufacturer in packages that bear the label or notice, tax classification, and mark, as required by this subpart. For purposes of this subpart, the package does not include the cellophane or other transparent exterior wrapping material.

[78 FR 38574, June 27, 2013]

EFFECTIVE DATE NOTE: At 78 FR 38574, June 27, 2013, §44.181 was revised, effective Aug. 26, 2013 through Aug. 26, 2016.

§44.182 Lottery features.

No certificate, coupon, or other device purporting to be or to represent a ticket, chance, share, or an interest in, or dependent on, the event of a lottery shall be contained in, attached to, or stamped, marked, written, or printed on any package of tobacco products, or cigarette papers or tubes.

(72 Stat. 1422; 26 U.S.C. 5723, 18 U.S.C. 1301)

[T.D. 6871, 31 FR 51, Jan. 4, 1966. Redesignated at 40 FR 16835, Apr. 15, 1975, and amended by T.D. ATF–232, 51 FR 28088, Aug. 5, 1986; T.D. ATF–243, 51 FR 43194, Dec. 1, 1986]

§44.183 Indecent or immoral material.

No indecent or immoral picture, print, or representation shall be contained in, attached to, or stamped, marked, written, or printed on any package of tobacco products, or cigarette papers or tubes.

(72 Stat. 1422; 26 U.S.C. 5723)

[T.D. 6871, 31 FR 51, Jan. 4, 1966. Redesignated at 40 FR 16835, Apr. 15, 1975, and amended by T.D. ATF–232, 51 FR 28088, Aug. 5, 1986; T.D. ATF–243, 51 FR 43194, Dec. 1, 1986]

§44.184 Mark.

Every package of tobacco products shall, before removal from the factory under this subpart, have adequately imprinted thereon, or on a label securely affixed thereto, a mark as specified in this section. The mark may consist of the name of the manufacturer removing the product and the location (by city and State) of the factory from which the products are to be so removed, or may consist of the permit number of the factory from which the products are to be so removed. Any trade name of the manufacturer approved as provided in §40.65 of this chapter may be used in the mark as the name of the manufacturer.) As an alternative, where tobacco products are both packaged and removed by the same manufacturer, either at the same or different factories, the mark may consist of the name of such manufacturer if the factory where package is identified on or in the package by a means approved by the appropriate TTB officer. Before using the alternative, the manufacturer shall notify the appropriate TTB officer in writing of the name to be used as the name of the manufacturer and the means to be used for identifying the factory where packaged. If approved by him the appropriate TTB officer shall return approved copies of the notice to the manufacturer. A copy of the approved notice shall be retained as part of the factory records at each of the factories operated by the manufacturer.

(72 Stat. 1422; 26 U.S.C. 5723)

[T.D. 6871, 31 FR 51, Jan. 4, 1966. Redesignated at 40 FR 16835, Apr. 15, 1975, and amended by T.D. ATF–232, 51 FR 28088, Aug. 5, 1986; T.D. ATF–243, 51 FR 43194, Dec. 1, 1986; T.D. ATF–460, 66 FR 39093, July 27, 2001]

§44.185 Label or notice.

Every package of tobacco products shall, before removal from the factory under this subpart, have adequately imprinted thereon, or on a label securely affixed thereto, the words "Tax-exempt. For use outside U.S." or the words "U.S. Tax-exempt. For use outside U.S." except where a stamp, sticker, or notice, required by a foreign country or a possession of the United States, which identifies such country or possession, is so imprinted or affixed.

(26 U.S.C. 5704, 5723)

[T.D. 6871, 31 FR 52, Jan. 4, 1966. Redesignated at 40 FR 16835, Apr. 15, 1975, and amended by T.D. ATF–232, 51 FR 28088, Aug. 5, 1986; T.D. ATF–243, 51 FR 43194, Dec. 1, 1986; T.D. ATF–465, 66 FR 45618, Aug. 29, 2001]

§44.186 Tax classification for cigars.

Before removal from a factory under this subpart, every package of cigars shall have adequately imprinted on it, or on a label securely affixed to it—

(a) The designation "cigars";

(b) The quantity of cigars contained in the package; and

(c) For small cigars, the classification of the product for tax purposes; (i.e., either "small" or "little").

(Sec. 202, Pub. L. 85–859, 72 Stat. 1422 (26 U.S.C. 5723))

[T.D. ATF–80, 46 FR 18312, Mar. 24, 1981]

§44.187 Shipping containers.

Each shipping case, crate, or other container in which tobacco products, or cigarette papers or tubes are to be shipped or removed, under this part, shall bear a distinguishing number, such number to be assigned by the manufacturer or export warehouse proprietor. Removals of tobacco products, and cigarette papers and tubes from an export warehouse shall be made, insofar as practicable, in the same containers in which they were received from the factory.

(72 Stat. 1418, as amended; 26 U.S.C. 5704)

[T.D. 6871, 31 FR 52, Jan. 4, 1966. Redesignated at 40 FR 16835, Apr. 15, 1975, and amended by T.D. ATF–232, 51 FR 28088, Aug. 5, 1986; T.D. ATF–243, 51 FR 43194, Dec. 1, 1986]

Consignment of Shipment

§44.188 General.

Tobacco products, and cigarette papers and tubes transferred or removed from a factory or an export warehouse, under this part, without payment of tax, shall be consigned as required by this subpart.

(72 Stat. 1418, as amended; 26 U.S.C. 5704)

[T.D. 6871, 31 FR 52, Jan. 4, 1966. Redesignated at 40 FR 16835, Apr. 15, 1975, and amended by T.D. ATF–232, 51 FR 28088, Aug. 5, 1986; T.D. ATF–243, 51 FR 43194, Dec. 1, 1986]

§44.189 Transfers between factories and export warehouses.

Where tobacco products, and cigarette papers and tubes are transferred, without payment of tax, from a factory to an export warehouse or between export warehouses, such articles shall be consigned to the export warehouse proprietor to whom such articles are to be delivered.

(72 Stat. 1418, as amended; 26 U.S.C. 5704)

[T.D. 6871, 31 FR 52, Jan. 4, 1966. Redesignated at 40 FR 16835, Apr. 15, 1975, and amended by T.D. ATF–232, 51 FR 28088, Aug. 5, 1986; T.D. ATF–243, 51 FR 43194, Dec. 1, 1986]

§44.190 Return of shipment to a manufacturer or customs warehouse proprietor.

Where tobacco products, and cigarette papers and tubes are returned by an export warehouse proprietor to a manufacturer or where cigars are so returned to a customs warehouse proprietor, such articles shall be consigned to the manufacturer or customs warehouse proprietor to whom the shipment is to be returned.

(72 Stat. 1418, as amended; 26 U.S.C. 5704)

[T.D. 6871, 31 FR 52, Jan. 4, 1966. Redesignated at 40 FR 16835, Apr. 15, 1975, and amended by T.D. ATF–232, 51 FR 28088, Aug. 5, 1986; T.D. ATF–243, 51 FR 43194, Dec. 1, 1986]

§44.191 To officers of the armed forces for subsequent exportation.

Where tobacco products, and cigarette papers and tubes are removed from a factory or an export warehouse for delivery to officers of the armed forces of the United States in this country for subsequent shipment to, and use by, the armed forces outside the United States, the manufacturer or export warehouse proprietor shall consign such articles to the receiving officer at the armed forces base or installation, in this country, to which they are to be delivered.

(72 Stat. 1418, as amended; 26 U.S.C. 5704)

[T.D. 6871, 31 FR 52, Jan. 4, 1966. Redesignated at 40 FR 16835, Apr. 15, 1975, and amended by T.D. ATF–232, 51 FR 28088, Aug. 5, 1986; T.D. ATF–243, 51 FR 43194, Dec. 1, 1986]

§44.192 To vessels and aircraft for shipment to noncontiguous foreign countries and possessions of the United States.

Where tobacco products, and cigarette papers and tubes are removed from a factory or an export warehouse, for direct delivery to a vessel or aircraft for transportation to a noncontiguous foreign country, Puerto Rico, the Virgin Islands, or a possession of the United States, the manufacturer or export warehouse proprietor shall consign the shipment directly to the vessel or aircraft, or to his agent at the port for delivery to the vessel or aircraft.

(72 Stat. 1418, as amended; 26 U.S.C. 5704)

[T.D. 6871, 31 FR 52, Jan. 4, 1966. Redesignated at 40 FR 16835, Apr. 15, 1975, and amended by T.D. ATF–232, 51 FR 28088, Aug. 5, 1986; T.D. ATF–243, 51 FR 43194, Dec. 1, 1986]

§44.193 To a Federal department or agency.

Where tobacco products, and cigarette papers and tubes are removed from a factory or an export warehouse and are destined for ultimate delivery in a noncontiguous foreign country, Puerto Rico, the Virgin Islands, or a possession of the United States, but the shipment is to be delivered in the United States to a Federal department or agency, or to an authorized dispatch agent, transportation officer, or port director of such a department or agency for forwarding on to the place of destination of the shipment, the manufacturer or export warehouse proprietor shall consign the shipment to the Federal department or agency, or to the proper dispatch agent, transportation officer, or port director of such department or agency.

(72 Stat. 1418, as amended; 26 U.S.C. 5704)

[T.D. 6871, 31 FR 52, Jan. 4, 1966. Redesignated at 40 FR 16835, Apr. 15, 1975, and amended by T.D. ATF–232, 51 FR 28088, Aug. 5, 1986; T.D. ATF–243, 51 FR 43194, Dec. 1, 1986]

§44.194 To district director of customs for shipment to contiguous foreign countries.

Where tobacco products, or cigarette papers or tubes are removed from a factory or an export warehouse for export to a contiguous foreign country, the manufacturer or export warehouse proprietor shall consign the shipment to the district director of customs at the border or other port of exit.

(72 Stat. 1418, as amended; 26 U.S.C. 5704)

[T.D. 6961, 33 FR 9492, June 28, 1968. Redesignated at 40 FR 16835, Apr. 15, 1975, and amended by T.D. ATF–232, 51 FR 28089, Aug. 5, 1986; T.D. ATF–243, 51 FR 43194, Dec. 1, 1986]

§44.195 To Government vessels and aircraft for consumption as supplies.

Where tobacco products, and cigarette papers and tubes are removed from a factory or an export warehouse for delivery to a vessel or aircraft engaged in an activity for the Government of the United States or a foreign government, for consumption as supplies beyond the jurisdiction of the internal revenue laws of the United States, the manufacturer or export warehouse proprietor shall consign the shipment to the proper officer on board the vessel or aircraft to which the shipment is to be delivered.

(72 Stat. 1418, as amended; 26 U.S.C. 5704)

[T.D. 6871, 31 FR 52, Jan. 4, 1966. Redesignated at 40 FR 16835, Apr. 15, 1975, and amended by T.D. ATF–232, 51 FR 28089, Aug. 5, 1986; T.D. ATF–243, 51 FR 43194, Dec. 1, 1986]

§44.196 To district director of customs for consumption as supplies on commercial vessels and aircraft.

Where tobacco products, or cigarette papers or tubes are removed from a factory or an export warehouse for consumption as supplies beyond the jurisdiction of the internal revenue laws of the United States, the manufacturer or export warehouse proprietor shall consign the shipment to the district director of customs at the port at which the shipment is to be laden.

(72 Stat. 1418, as amended; 26 U.S.C. 5704)

[T.D. 6961, 33 FR 9493, June 28, 1968. Redesignated at 40 FR 16835, Apr. 15, 1975, and amended by T.D. ATF–232, 51 FR 28089, Aug. 5, 1986; T.D. ATF–243, 51 FR 43194, Dec. 1, 1986]

§ 44.196a To a foreign-trade zone.

Where tobacco products, and cigarette papers and tubes are removed from a factory or an export warehouse for delivery to a foreign-trade zone, under zone restricted status for the purpose of exportation or storage, the manufacturer or export warehouse proprietor shall consign the shipment to the Zone Operator in care of the customs officer in charge of the zone.

(48 Stat. 999, as amended, 72 Stat. 1418, as amended; 19 U.S.C. 81c, 26 U.S.C. 5704)

[T.D. 6871, 31 FR 53, Jan. 4, 1966. Redesignated at 40 FR 16835, Apr. 15, 1975, and amended by T.D. ATF–232, 51 FR 28089, Aug. 5, 1986; T.D. ATF–243, 51 FR 43194, Dec. 1, 1986]

§ 44.197 For export by parcel post.

Tobacco products, and cigarette papers and tubes removed from a factory or an export warehouse, for export by parcel post to a person in a foreign country, Puerto Rico, the Virgin Islands, or a possession of the United States, shall be addressed and consigned to such person when the articles are deposited in the mails. Waiver of his right to withdraw such articles from the mails shall be stamped or written on each shipping container and be signed by the manufacturer or export warehouse proprietor making the shipment.

(72 Stat. 1418, as amended; 26 U.S.C. 5704)

[T.D. 6871, 31 FR 53, Jan. 4, 1966. Redesignated at 40 FR 16835, Apr. 15, 1975, and amended by T.D. ATF–232, 51 FR 28089, Aug. 5, 1986; T.D. ATF–243, 51 FR 43194, Dec. 1, 1986]

NOTICE OF REMOVAL OF SHIPMENT

§ 44.198 Preparation.

For each shipment of tobacco products, and cigarette papers and tubes transferred or removed from his factory, under bond and this part, the manufacturer shall prepare a notice of removal, Form 5200.14, and for each shipment of tobacco products, and cigarette papers and tubes transferred or removed from his export warehouse, under bond and this part, the export warehouse proprietor shall prepare a notice of removal, Form 5200.14. Each such notice shall be given a serial number by the manufacturer or export warehouse proprietor in a series beginning with number 1, with respect to the first shipment removed from the factory or export warehouse under this part and commencing again with number 1 on January 1 of each year thereafter.

(72 Stat. 1418, as amended; 26 U.S.C. 5704)

[T.D. 6871, 31 FR 53, Jan. 4, 1966. Redesignated at 40 FR 16835, Apr. 15, 1975, and amended by T.D. ATF–232, 51 FR 28089, Aug. 5, 1986; T.D. ATF–243, 51 FR 43194, Dec. 1, 1986; T.D. ATF–421, 64 FR 71925, Dec. 22, 1999]

§ 44.199 Disposition.

After actual removal from his factory or export warehouse of the shipment described on the notice of removal, Form 5200.14, the manufacturer or export warehouse proprietor shall, except where the shipment is to be exported by parcel post, promptly forward one copy of the notice of removal to the appropriate TTB officer. A copy of each such notice shall be retained by the manufacturer or export warehouse proprietor as a part of his records, for 3 years following the close of the calendar year in which the shipment was removed and shall be made available for inspection by any appropriate TTB officer upon his request. The manufacturer or export warehouse proprietor shall dispose of the other copies of each notice of removal as required by this subpart.

(72 Stat. 1418; 26 U.S.C. 5704)

[25 FR 4722, May 28, 1960. Redesignated at 40 FR 16835, Apr. 15, 1975; T.D. ATF–421, 64 FR 71926, Dec. 22, 1999; T.D. ATF–480, 67 FR 30802, May 8, 2002]

§44.200 Transfers between factories and export warehouses.

Where tobacco products, and cigarette papers and tubes are transferred from a factory to an export warehouse or between export warehouses, the manufacturer or export warehouse proprietor making the shipment shall forward three copies of the notice of removal, Form 5200.14 to the export warehouse proprietor to whom the shipment is consigned. Immediately upon receipt of the shipment at his warehouse, the export warehouse proprietor shall properly execute the certificate of receipt on each copy of the notice of removal, noting thereon any discrepancy; return one copy to the manufacturer or export warehouse proprietor making the shipment for filing with the appropriate TTB officer; retain one copy at his warehouse as a part of his records; and file the remaining copy with his report, required by §44.147.

(72 Stat. 1418, as amended; 26 U.S.C. 5704)

[T.D. 6871, 31 FR 53, Jan. 4, 1966. Redesignated at 40 FR 16835, Apr. 15, 1975, and amended by T.D. ATF–232, 51 FR 28089, Aug. 5, 1986; T.D. ATF–243, 51 FR 43194, Dec. 1, 1986; T.D. ATF–421, 64 FR 71926, Dec. 22, 1999]

§44.201 Return to manufacturer or customs warehouse proprietor.

Where tobacco products, and cigarette papers and tubes are removed from an export warehouse for return to the factory, or cigars are removed from such a warehouse for return to a customs warehouse, the export warehouse proprietor making the shipment shall forward two copies of the notice of removal, Form 5200.14, to the manufacturer or customs warehouse proprietor to whom the shipment is consigned. Immediately upon receipt of the shipment at his factory or warehouse, the manufacturer or customs warehouse proprietor shall properly execute the certificate of receipt on both copies of the notice of removal, noting thereon any discrepancy, and return one copy to the export warehouse proprietor making the shipment for filing with the appropriate TTB officer. The other copy of the notice of removal shall be retained by the manufacturer or customs warehouse proprietor, as a part of his records, for 3 years following the close of the calendar year in which the shipment was received and shall be made available for inspection by any appropriate TTB officer upon his request.

(72 Stat. 1418, as amended; 26 U.S.C. 5704)

[T.D. 6871, 31 FR 53, Jan. 4, 1966. Redesignated at 40 FR 16835, Apr. 15, 1975, and amended by T.D. ATF–232, 51 FR 28089, Aug. 5, 1986; T.D. ATF–243, 51 FR 43194, Dec. 1, 1986; T.D. ATF–421, 64 FR 71926, Dec. 22, 1999]

§44.202 To officers of the armed forces for subsequent exportation.

Where tobacco products, and cigarette papers and tubes are removed from a factory or an export warehouse for delivery to officers of the armed forces of the United States in this country for subsequent shipment to, and use by, the armed forces outside the United States, the manufacturer or export warehouse proprietor making the removal shall forward a copy of the notice of removal, Form 5200.14, to the officer at the base or installation authorized to receive the articles described on the notice of removal. Upon execution by the armed forces receiving officer of the certificate of receipt on the copy of the notice of removal, he shall return such copy to the manufacturer or export warehouse proprietor making the shipment for filing with the appropriate TTB officer.

(72 Stat. 1418, as amended; 26 U.S.C. 5704)

[T.D. 6871, 31 FR 53, Jan. 4, 1966. Redesignated at 40 FR 16835, Apr. 15, 1975, and amended by T.D. ATF–232, 51 FR 28089, Aug. 5, 1986; T.D. ATF–243, 51 FR 43194, Dec. 1, 1986; T.D. ATF–421, 64 FR 71926, Dec. 22, 1999]

§44.203 To noncontiguous foreign countries and possessions of the United States.

Where tobacco products, or cigarette papers or tubes are removed from a factory or an export warehouse for direct delivery to a vessel or aircraft for transportation to a noncontiguous foreign country, Puerto Rico, the Virgin Islands, or a possession of the United States, the manufacturer or export warehouse proprietor making the shipment shall file two copies of the notice of removal, Form 5200.14, with the office of the district director of customs at the port where the shipment is to be laden. Such copies of the notice of removal should be filed with the related shipper's export declaration, Commerce Form 7525–V. In the event the copies of the notice of removal are not filed with the shipper's export declaration, when the copies of the notice are filed with the district director of customs they shall show all particulars necessary to enable that officer to associate the notice with the related shipper's export declaration and any other documents filed with his office in connection with the shipment. After the vessel or aircraft on which the shipment has been laden clears or departs from the port of lading the customs authority shall execute the certificate of exportation on both copies of the notice of removal, retain one copy for his records, and deliver or transmit the other copy to the manufacturer or export warehouse proprietor making the shipment for filing with the appropriate TTB officer.

(72 Stat. 1418, as amended; 26 U.S.C. 5704)

[T.D. 6961, 33 FR 9493, June 28, 1968. Redesignated at 40 FR 16835, Apr. 15, 1975, and amended by T.D. ATF–232, 51 FR 28089, Aug. 5, 1986; T.D. ATF–243, 51 FR 43194, Dec. 1, 1986; T.D. ATF–421, 64 FR 71926, Dec. 22, 1999]

§ 44.204 To a Federal department or agency.

Where tobacco products, and cigarette papers and tubes are removed from a factory or an export warehouse and are destined for ultimate delivery in a noncontiguous foreign country, Puerto Rico, the Virgin Islands, or a possession of the United States, but the shipment is to be delivered to a Federal department or agency, or to an authorized dispatch agent, transportation officer, or port director of such a department or agency for forwarding on to the place of destination of the shipment, the manufacturer or export warehouse proprietor making the shipment shall furnish a copy of the notice of removal, Form 5200.14, to the Federal department or agency, or an officer thereof at the port, receiving the shipment for ultimate transmittal to the place of destination, in order that such department, agency, or officer can properly execute the certificate of receipt on such notice to evidence receipt of the shipment for transmittal to a place beyond the jurisdiction of the internal revenue laws of the United States. After completing such certificate, the Federal department, agency, or officer shall return the copy of the notice of removal, so executed, to the manufacturer or export warehouse proprietor making the shipment for filing with the appropriate TTB officer.

(72 Stat. 1418, as amended; 26 U.S.C. 5704)

[T.D. 6871, 31 FR 53, Jan. 4, 1966. Redesignated at 40 FR 16835, Apr. 15, 1975, and amended by T.D. ATF–232, 51 FR 28089, Aug. 5, 1986; T.D. ATF–243, 51 FR 43194, Dec. 1, 1986; T.D. ATF–421, 64 FR 71926, Dec. 22, 1999]

§ 44.205 To contiguous foreign countries.

(a) Where tobacco products, or cigarette papers or tubes are removed from a factory or an export warehouse for export to a contiguous foreign country, the manufacturer or export warehouse proprietor making the shipment shall—

(1) Furnish to the district director of Customs at the port of exit two copies of the notice of removal, Form 5200.14, together with the related shipper's export declaration, Commerce Form 7525–V (if required); and,

(2) If copies of the notice of removal are not filed with the shippers export declaration, or if a shipment is for the armed forces of the United States in the contiguous foreign country and a shipper's export declaration is not required, show all the information on the notice of removal when it is filed so that the Customs officer is able to associate the notice with the related shipper's export declaration (if any) or other documents filed with Customs for the shipment.

(b) When a shipment has been cleared by Customs from the United States, and when the Customs officer at the port of exit is satisfied that the products have departed from the United States, he shall—

(1) Complete the certificate of exportation on both copies of the notice of removal;

(2) Retain one copy of the notice of removal for his records; and,

(3) Return the other copy to the manufacturer or export warehouse proprietor making the shipment for filing with the appropriate TTB officer.

(c) The Customs officer may, when he considers it necessary to establish that the merchandise was actually exported, require a landing certificate before he completes the certificate of exportation specified in paragraph (b)(1) of this section. If practical, the Customs officer will give advance notice to the manufacturer or export warehouse proprietor of the type of transactions for which a landing certificate will be required. However, failure to notify the manufacturer or proprietor in advance will not prevent the Customs officer from requiring a landing certificate for specific exportations when he considers it necessary to protect the revenue. In any case, the Customs officer will advise the manufacturer or proprietor before departure of the shipment from the United States as to those exports for which a landing certificate will be required.

(d) The provisions of this section relating to landing certificates also apply when a Form 5200.14 is not required for each transaction (for example: When multiple exportations, individually documented by commercial records, are consolidated on a single Form 5200.14 pursuant to an approved alternate procedure under § 44.72). The provisions apply to each transaction, regardless of the manner in which it is documented, unless specifically provided otherwise in the alternate procedure.

(Sec. 202, Pub. L. 85–859, 72 Stat. 1418; (26 U.S.C. 5704); Sec. 622, Act of June 17, 1930, 49 Stat. 759 (19 U.S.C. 1622))

[T.D. ATF–52, 43 FR 59287, Dec. 19, 1978, as amended by T.D. ATF–232, 51 FR 28089, Aug. 5, 1986; T.D. ATF–243, 51 FR 43194, Dec. 1, 1986; T.D. ATF–421, 64 FR 71926, Dec. 22, 1999]

§ 44.206 To Government vessels and aircraft for consumption as supplies.

Where tobacco products, and cigarette papers and tubes are removed from a factory or an export warehouse for direct delivery to a vessel or aircraft, engaged in an activity for the Government of the United States or a foreign government, for consumption as supplies beyond the jurisdiction of the internal revenue laws of the United States, the manufacturer or export warehouse proprietor making the shipment shall forward a copy of the notice of removal, Form 5200.14, to the officer of the vessel or aircraft authorized to receive the shipment. Upon execution by the receiving officer of the vessel or aircraft of the certificate of receipt on the copy of the notice of removal, he shall return such copy to the manufacturer or export warehouse proprietor making the shipment for filing with the appropriate TTB officer.

(72 Stat. 1418, as amended; 26 U.S.C. 5704)

[T.D. 6871, 31 FR 54, Jan. 4, 1966. Redesignated at 40 FR 16835, Apr. 15, 1975, and amended by T.D. ATF–232, 51 FR 28089, Aug. 5, 1986; T.D. ATF–243, 51 FR 43194, Dec. 1, 1986; T.D. ATF–421, 64 FR 71926, Dec. 22, 1999]

§ 44.207 To commercial vessels and aircraft for consumption as supplies.

Where tobacco products, or cigarette papers or tubes are removed from a factory or an export warehouse for delivery to a vessel or aircraft entitled to receive such articles for consumption as supplies beyond the jurisdiction of the internal revenue laws of the United States, the manufacturer or export warehouse proprietor making the shipment shall file two copies of the notice of removal, Form 5200.14, with the district director of customs at the port where the shipment is to be laden in sufficient time to permit delivery of the two copies of the notice of removal to the customs officer who will inspect the shipment and supervise its lading. After inspection and lading of the shipment the customs officer shall note on the copies of the notice of removal any discrepancy between the shipment inspected and laden under his supervision and that described on the notice of removal or any limitation on the quantity to be laden; complete and sign the certificate of inspection and lading; and return both copies of the notice of removal to the district director of customs. The district director of customs shall execute the certificate of clearance on both copies of the notice of removal, retain one copy for his records, and forward the other copy to the manufacturer or export warehouse proprietor making the shipment for filing with the appropriate TTB officer. Where the vessel or aircraft does not clear from the port at which the shipment is laden, the customs officer supervising the lading of the shipment shall require the person on board the vessel or aircraft authorized to receive the shipment to execute the certificate of receipt on both copies of the notice of removal to indicate the trade or activity in which the vessel or aircraft is engaged.

(72 Stat. 1418, as amended; 26 U.S.C. 5704)

[T.D. 6961, 33 FR 9493, June 28, 1968. Redesignated at 40 FR 16835, Apr. 15, 1975, and amended by T.D. ATF–232, 51 FR 28089, Aug. 5, 1986; T.D. ATF–243, 51 FR 43194, Dec. 1, 1986; T.D. ATF–421, 64 FR 71926, Dec. 22, 1999]

§ 44.207a To a foreign-trade zone.

Where tobacco products, and cigarette papers and tubes are removed from a factory or an export warehouse for delivery to a foreign-trade zone, under zone restricted status for the purpose of exportation or storage, the manufacturer or export warehouse proprietor making the shipment shall forward two copies of the notice of removal, Form 5200.14, to the customs officer in charge of the zone. Upon receipt of the shipment, the customs officer shall execute the certificate of receipt on each copy of the form, noting thereon any discrepancy, retain one copy for his records, and forward the other copy to the manufacturer or export warehouse proprietor making the shipment for filing with the appropriate TTB officer.

(48 Stat. 999, as amended, 72 Stat. 1418, as amended; 19 U.S.C. 81c, 26 U.S.C. 5704)

[T.D. 6871, 31 FR 54, Jan. 4, 1966. Redesignated at 40 FR 16835, Apr. 15, 1975, and amended by T.D. ATF–232, 51 FR 28089, Aug. 5, 1986; T.D. ATF–243, 51 FR 43194, Dec. 1, 1986; T.D. ATF–421, 64 FR 71926, Dec. 22, 1999]

§ 44.208 For export by parcel post.

Where tobacco products, and cigarette papers and tubes are removed from a factory or an export warehouse, for export by parcel post, the manufacturer or export warehouse proprietor shall present one copy of the notice of removal, Form 5200.14, together with the shipping containers, to the postal authorities with the request that the postmaster or his agent execute the certificate of mailing on the form. Where the manufacturer or export warehouse proprietor so desires, he may cover under one notice of removal all the merchandise removed under this part for export by parcel post which is delivered at one time to the postal service for that purpose. The manufacturer or export warehouse proprietor shall immediately file the receipted copy of the notice of removal with the appropriate TTB officer.

(72 Stat. 1418, as amended; 26 U.S.C. 5704)

[T.D. 6871, 31 FR 54, Jan. 4, 1966. Redesignated at 40 FR 16835, Apr. 15, 1975, and amended by T.D. ATF–232, 51 FR 28089, Aug. 5, 1986; T.D. ATF–243, 51 FR 43194, Dec. 1, 1986; T.D. ATF–421, 64 FR 71926, Dec. 22, 1999]

Miscellaneous Provisions

§ 44.209 Diversion of shipment to another consignee.

If, after removal of a shipment from a factory or an export warehouse, the manufacturer or export warehouse proprietor desires to divert the shipment to another consignee, he shall so notify the appropriate TTB officer. The manufacturer or export warehouse proprietor shall describe the shipment, set forth the serial number and date of the notice of removal under which the shipment was removed from his factory or export warehouse, and furnish the name and address of the new consignee, who shall comply with all applicable provisions of this part.

(72 Stat. 1418; 26 U.S.C. 5704)

[25 FR 4723, May 28, 1960. Redesignated at 40 FR 16835, Apr. 15, 1975]

§ 44.210 Return of shipment to factory or export warehouse.

A manufacturer or export warehouse proprietor may return to his factory or export warehouse, without internal revenue supervision when so authorized by the appropriate TTB officer, tobacco products, and cigarette papers and tubes previously removed therefrom, under this part, but not yet exported. The manufacturer or export warehouse proprietor shall, prior to returning the articles to his factory or export warehouse, make application to the appropriate TTB officer for permission so to do, which application shall be accompanied by two copies of the notice of removal, Form 5200.14, under which the articles were originally removed. If less than the entire shipment is intended to be returned to the factory or export warehouse, the application shall set forth accurately the articles to be returned and shall show what disposition was made of the remainder of the original shipment and any other facts pertinent to such shipment. Where the appropriate TTB officer approves the application, he shall so indicate by endorsement to that effect on each of the copies of the notice of removal, set forth the articles for which return is approved, and return both copies of the notice of removal to the manufacturer or export warehouse proprietor concerned. Upon receipt of the copies of the notice of removal bearing the endorsement of the appropriate TTB officer, the manufacturer or export warehouse proprietor shall return the articles to his factory or export warehouse, properly modify and execute the certificate of receipt on each copy of the notice of removal, return one such copy to the appropriate TTB officer, and retain the other copy as a part of his records.

(72 Stat. 1418, as amended; 26 U.S.C. 5704)

[T.D. 6871, 31 FR 54, Jan. 4, 1966. Redesignated at 40 FR 16835, Apr. 15, 1975, and amended by T.D. ATF–232, 51 FR 28089, Aug. 5, 1986; T.D. ATF–243, 51 FR 43194, Dec. 1, 1986; T.D. ATF–421, 64 FR 71926, Dec. 22, 1999]

§ 44.211 [Reserved]

§ 44.212 Delay in lading at port of exportation.

If, on arrival of tobacco products, and cigarette papers and tubes at the port of exportation, the vessel or aircraft for which they are intended is not prepared to receive the articles, they may be properly stored at the port for not more than 30 days. In the event of any further delay, the facts shall be reported by the manufacturer or export warehouse proprietor to the appropriate TTB officer and unless such officer approves an extension of time in which to effect lading and clearance of the shipment it must be returned to the factory or export warehouse.

[T.D. 6871, 31 FR 55, Jan. 4, 1966. Redesignated at 40 FR 16835, Apr. 15, 1975, and amended by T.D. ATF–232, 51 FR 28089, Aug. 5, 1987; T.D. ATF–243, 51 FR 43194, Dec. 1, 1986; T.D. ATF–480, 67 FR 30802, May 8, 2002]

§ 44.213 Destruction of tobacco products, and cigarette papers and tubes.

Where an export warehouse proprietor desires to destroy any of the tobacco products, or cigarette papers or tubes stored in his warehouse, he shall notify the appropriate TTB officer of the kind and quantity of such articles to be destroyed and the date on which he desires the destruction to take place in order that the appropriate TTB officer may assign an appropriate TTB officer to inspect the articles and supervise their destruction. The export warehouse proprietor shall prepare a notice of removal, Form 5200.14, describing the articles to be destroyed. After witnessing the destruction of the articles, the appropriate TTB officer shall certify to their destruction on two copies of the notice of removal and return them to the export warehouse proprietor, who shall retain one copy for his records and file the other copy with the appropriate TTB officer.

[T.D. 6871, 31 FR 55, Jan. 4, 1966. Redesignated at 40 FR 16835, Apr. 15, 1975, and amended by T.D. ATF–232, 51 FR 28089, Aug. 5, 1986; T.D. ATF–243, 51 FR 43194, Dec. 1, 1986; T.D. ATF–421, 64 FR 71926, Dec. 22, 1999]

Subpart K—Drawback of Tax

§ 44.221 Application of drawback of tax.

Allowance of drawback of tax shall apply only to tobacco products, and cigarette papers and tubes, on which tax has been paid, when such articles are shipped to a foreign country, Puerto Rico, the Virgin Islands, or a possession of the United States. Such drawback shall be allowed only to the person who paid the tax on such articles and who files claim and otherwise complies with the provisions of this subpart.

(72 Stat. 1419, 68A Stat. 908; 26 U.S.C. 5706, 7653)

[T.D. 6871, 31 FR 55, Jan. 4, 1966. Redesignated at 40 FR 16835, Apr. 15, 1975, and amended by T.D. ATF–232, 51 FR 28089, Aug. 5, 1986; T.D. ATF–243, 51 FR 43194, Dec. 1, 1986]

§ 44.222 Claim.

Claim for allowance of drawback of tax, under this subpart, must be filed on Form 5620.7. Such claim must be filed in sufficient time to permit the appropriate TTB officer to detail an appropriate TTB officer to inspect the articles and supervise the affixture of a label or notice bearing the legend "For Export With Drawback of Tax." Upon receipt of a claim supported by satisfactory bond, as required by this subpart, an appropriate TTB officer will proceed to the place where the articles involved are held and there perform the functions required in § 44.224.

[T.D. ATF–480, 67 FR 30803, May 8, 2002]

§ 44.223 Drawback bond.

Each claim for allowance of drawback of tax, under this subpart, shall be accompanied by a bond, Form 2148 (5200.17), satisfactory to the appropriate TTB officer with whom the claim is filed. Such bond shall be in an amount not less than the amount of tax for which drawback is claimed, conditioned that the claimant shall furnish, within a reasonable time, evidence satisfactory to the appropriate TTB officer that the tobacco products, and cigarette papers and tubes have been landed at some port beyond the jurisdiction of the internal revenue laws of the United States, or that after clearance from the United States, the articles were lost (otherwise than by theft) or destroyed, by fire, casualty, or act of God, and have not been relanded within the limits of the United States. The provisions of §§ 44.121 and 44.122 are applicable with respect to any drawback bond required under this section.

(72 Stat. 1419; 26 U.S.C. 5706)

[T.D. 6871, 31 FR 55, Jan. 4, 1966. Redesignated at 40 FR 16835, Apr. 15, 1975, and amended by T.D. ATF–232, 51 FR 28089, Aug. 5, 1986; T.D. ATF–243, 51 FR 43194, Dec. 1, 1986; T.D. ATF–480, 67 FR 30803, May 8, 2002]

§ 44.224 Inspection by an appropriate TTB officer.

(a) *Examination.* An appropriate TTB officer will examine the tobacco products, and cigarette papers and tubes listed on TTB Form 5620.7. Such officer will verify the accuracy of the schedule of such articles on TTB Form 5620.7.

(b) *Label or notice.* If the tax on such articles has been paid by return, the appropriate TTB officer must be satisfied that the articles have in fact been taxpaid and each package bears the label or notice required by § 44.222.

(c) *Shipping containers.* The appropriate officer will supervise the packing of such articles in shipping containers. Each container must be numbered and have affixed to it the notice:

Drawback of tax claimed on contents.
Sale, consumption, or use in U.S. prohibited.

(d) *Disposition of TTB Form 5620.7.* After the appropriate TTB officer completes the report of inspection on TTB Form 5620.7, such officer will return two copies to the claimant and send a copy to the TTB office listed on the form.

(e) *Release.* After executing the report of inspection on TTB Form 5620.7, the appropriate TTB office will release the shipment to the claimant for delivery to the port of exportation.

[T.D. ATF–480, 67 FR 30803, May 8, 2002]

§ 44.225 Delivery of tobacco products, or cigarette papers or tubes for export other than by parcel post.

The claimant, upon release of the tobacco products, or cigarette papers or tubes by the appropriate TTB officer for exportation with benefit of drawback of tax under this subpart, shall be responsible for delivery of such articles to the port of exportation for customs inspection, supervision of lading, and clearance of the articles. The claimant shall file with the district director of customs at the port of exportation the two copies of Form 5620.7 returned to the claimant by the appropriate TTB officer in accordance with § 44.224. Such copies shall be filed in sufficient time prior to lading to permit customs inspection and supervision of lading of the tobacco products, or cigarette papers or tubes.

(72 Stat. 1419; 26 U.S.C. 5706)

[T.D. 6961, 33 FR 9493, June 28, 1968. Redesignated at 40 FR 16835, Apr. 15, 1975, and amended by T.D. ATF–232, 51 FR 28089, Aug. 5, 1986; T.D. ATF–243, 51 FR 43194, Dec. 1, 1986; T.D. ATF–424, 64 FR 71933, Dec. 22, 1999]

§44.226 Delivery of tobacco products, and cigarette papers and tubes for export by parcel post.

Where the tobacco products, and cigarette papers and tubes are to be shipped by parcel post to a destination in a foreign country, Puerto Rico, the Virgin Islands, or a possession of the United States, a waiver of his right to withdraw such articles from the mails shall be stamped or written on each shipping container and be signed by the claimant, after which the claimant shall present the shipment to the post office. The claimant shall request the postmaster or his agent to execute the certificate of mailing on the copy of the claim, Form 5620.7, returned to the claimant by the appropriate TTB officer in accordance with §44.224. When so executed by the postal authorities, the Form 5620.7 shall be transmitted at once to the appropriate TTB officer with whom the form was previously filed.

(72 Stat. 1419; 26 U.S.C. 5706)

[T.D. 6871, 31 FR 55, Jan. 4, 1966. Redesignated at 40 FR 16835, Apr. 15, 1975, and amended by T.D. ATF-232, 51 FR 28089, Aug. 5, 1986; T.D. ATF-243, 51 FR 43194, Dec. 1, 1986; T.D. ATF-424, 64 FR 71933, Dec. 22, 1999]

§44.227 Customs procedure.

The customs officer shall satisfy himself that the tobacco products, and cigarette papers and tubes described on the Form 5620.7 and those inspected by him are the same and shall note on the form any discrepancy. After having inspected the articles and supervised the lading thereof on the export carrier, the customs officer shall complete and sign the certificate of inspection and lading on both copies of Form 5620.7 and deliver or transmit such copies to the office of his district director of customs for further processing. After clearance from the port of the export carrier on which the articles are laden, the district director of customs shall execute the certificate of exportation on both copies of Form 5620.7. The district director of customs shall retain one copy of the form for his records and transmit the other copy to the appropriate TTB officer.

(72 Stat. 1419; 26 U.S.C. 5706)

[T.D. 6961, 33 FR 9493, June 28, 1968. Redesignated at 40 FR 16835, Apr. 15, 1975, and amended by T.D. ATF-232, 51 FR 28089, Aug. 5, 1986; T.D. ATF-243, 51 FR 43194, Dec. 1, 1986; T.D. ATF-424, 64 FR 71933, Dec. 22, 1999; T.D. ATF-480, 67 FR 30803, May 8, 2002]

§44.228 Landing certificate.

Each claimant for drawback under this subpart agrees in the bond filed by him that he will furnish, within a reasonable time, evidence satisfactory to the appropriate TTB officer that the tobacco products, and cigarette papers and tubes covered by his claim have been landed at some port beyond the jurisdiction of the internal revenue laws of the United States, or that after shipment from the United States the articles were lost, and have not been relanded within the limits of the United States. The landing certificate shall accurately describe the articles involved, so as to readily identify the drawback claim to which it relates. The landing certificate shall be signed by a revenue officer at the place of destination, unless it is shown that no such officer can furnish such landing certificate, in which case the certificate of landing shall be signed by the consignee, or by the vessel's agent at the place of landing, and shall be sworn to before a notary public or other officer authorized to administer oaths and having an official seal. The landing certificate shall be filed with the appropriate TTB officer, with whom the drawback claim was filed, within 6 months from the date of clearance of the tobacco products, and cigarette papers and tubes from the United States. A landing certificate prepared in a foreign language shall be accompanied by an accurate translation thereof in English.

(72 Stat. 1419; 26 U.S.C. 5706)

[T.D. 6871, 31 FR 56, Jan. 4, 1966. Redesignated at 40 FR 16835, Apr. 15, 1975, and amended by T.D. ATF-232, 51 FR 28089, Aug. 5, 1986; T.D. ATF-243, 51 FR 43194, Dec. 1, 1986]

§ 44.229 Collateral evidence as to landing.

In case of inability to furnish the prescribed evidence of landing, application for relief shall be promptly made by the claimant to the appropriate TTB officer. Such application shall set forth the facts connected with the alleged exportation, and indicate the date of shipment, the kind, quantity, and value of tobacco products and cigarette papers and tubes shipped, the name of the consignee, the name of the vessel, the port or place of destination to which the shipment was made, and the date and amount of the bond covering such shipment. The application shall also state in what particular the provisions of this subpart, respecting the proofs of landing, have not been complied with, and the cause of failure to furnish such proofs; that such failure was not occasioned by any lack of diligence on the part of the claimant, or that of his agents; and that he is unable to furnish any other or better evidence than that furnished with his application. Each such application shall be supported by the best collateral evidence the claimant may be able to submit. The evidence may consist of the original or verified copies of letters from the consignee advising the claimant of the arrival or sale of the tobacco products, and cigarette papers and tubes, with such other statements respecting the failure to furnish the prescribed evidence of landing as may be obtained from the consignee or other persons having knowledge thereof. Such letters and other documents in a foreign language shall be accompanied by accurate translations thereof in English, and, when the letters fail to identify sufficiently the tobacco products, and cigarette papers and tubes, the original sales account must be produced.

(72 Stat. 1419; 26 U.S.C. 5706)

[T.D. 6871, 31 FR 56, Jan. 4, 1966. Redesignated at 40 FR 16835, Apr. 15, 1975, and amended by T.D. ATF–232, 51 FR 28089, Aug. 5, 1986; T.D. ATF–243, 51 FR 43194, Dec. 1, 1986; T.D. ATF–480, 67 FR 30803, May 8, 2002]

§ 44.230 Proof of loss.

When the claimant is unable to procure a certificate of landing, in accordance with the provisions of § 44.228, in consequence of loss of the tobacco products, and cigarette papers and tubes, his application for relief shall set forth the extent of the loss and, if possible, the location and manner of shipwreck or other casualty and the time of its occurrence. When obtainable, affidavits of the vessel's owners should be furnished detailing the manner and extent of the loss and the time and location of the disaster. If the tobacco products, and cigarette papers and tubes were insured, the claimant shall furnish certificates by officers of the insurance companies that the insurance has been paid, and that, to the best of their knowledge and belief, the tobacco products, and cigarette papers and tubes were actually destroyed. The aforesaid proof shall be furnished to the appropriate TTB officer within 6 months from the date of clearance of the tobacco products, and cigarette papers and tubes from the United States.

(72 Stat. 1419; 26 U.S.C. 5706)

[T.D. 6871, 31 FR 56, Jan. 4, 1966. Redesignated at 40 FR 16835, Apr. 15, 1975, and amended by T.D. ATF–232, 51 FR 28089, Aug. 5, 1986; T.D. ATF–243, 51 FR 43194, Dec. 1, 1986]

§ 44.231 Extension of time.

In case the claimant, from causes beyond his control, is unable to furnish the landing certificate or proof of loss, within the time prescribed therefor, he may make an application to the appropriate TTB officer for an extension of time in which to do so. Such application must state specifically the cause of failure to furnish the evidence. Two extensions of three months each may be granted by the appropriate TTB officer, provided the surety on the drawback bond of the claimant assents in writing thereto.

(72 Stat. 1419; 26 U.S.C. 5706)

[25 FR 4725, May 28, 1960. Redesignated at 40 FR 16835, Apr. 15, 1975]

§ 44.232 Allowance of claim.

On receipt of the executed Form 5620.7 from the district director of customs, the appropriate TTB officer will allow or disallow the claim in accordance with existing law and regulations. If the claim is not allowed in full the appropriate TTB officer will notify the claimant, in writing, of the reasons for any disallowance.

(72 Stat. 1419; 26 U.S.C. 5706)

[25 FR 4725, May 28, 1960. Redesignated at 40 FR 16835, Apr. 15, 1975, as amended by T.D. ATF–424, 64 FR 71933, Dec. 22, 1999]

Subpart L—Withdrawal of Cigars From Customs Warehouses

SOURCE: 25 FR 4725, May 28, 1960, unless otherwise noted. Redesignated at 40 FR 16835, Apr. 15, 1975.

§44.241 Shipment restricted.

Cigars produced in a customs warehouse in accordance with customs laws and regulations may be withdrawn under this subpart, without payment of tax, for export or for delivery for subsequent exportation. Duties paid on the tobacco used in the manufacture of such cigars may not be recovered on the exportation of the cigars under this subpart.

§44.242 Responsibility for tax on cigars.

A customs warehouse proprietor who withdraws cigars for export under his bond, without payment of tax, in accordance with the provisions of this part, shall be responsible for payment of such tax until he is relieved of such responsibility by furnishing the appropriate TTB officer evidence satisfactory to the appropriate TTB officer of exportation or proper delivery, as required by this subpart, or satisfactory evidence of such other disposition as may be used as the lawful basis for such relief. Such evidence shall be furnished within 90 days of the date of withdrawal of the cigars: *Provided*, That this period may be extended for good cause shown.

[25 FR 4725, May 28, 1960. Redesignated at 40 FR 16835, Apr. 15, 1975, as amended by T.D. ATF–480, 67 FR 30803, May 8, 2002]

BONDS

§44.243 Bond required.

Where the customs warehouse proprietor desires to withdraw cigars from his warehouse, without payment of tax, under this subpart, he shall, prior to making the first withdrawal, file a bond, Form 2104 (5200.15), conditioned upon compliance with the provisions of 26 U.S.C. chapter 52, and regulations thereunder, including, but not limited to, the timely payment of taxes imposed by such chapter, for which he may be responsible to the United States, and penalties and interest in connection therewith. The provisions of §§44.121 and 44.122 are applicable to the bond required under this section.

[25 FR 4725, May 28, 1960. Redesignated at 40 FR 16835, Apr. 15, 1975, and amended by T.D. ATF–48, 44 FR 55856, Sept. 28, 1979; T.D. ATF–460, 66 FR 39093, July 27, 2001; T.D. ATF–480, 67 FR 30803, May 8, 2002]

§44.244 Amount of bond.

The amount of the bond filed by the customs warehouse proprietor, as required by §44.243, shall be not less than the estimated amount of tax which may at any time constitute a charge against the bond: *Provided*, That the amount of any such bond (or the total amount where original and strengthening bonds are filed) shall not exceed $25,000 nor be less than $1,000. The charges against such bond shall be subject to increase as withdrawals are made and decrease as required evidence of exportation is received by the appropriate TTB officer with respect to cigars withdrawn. When the limit of liability under a bond given in less than the maximum amount has been reached, further withdrawals shall not be made thereunder until a strengthening or superseding bond is filed as required by §44.245 or §44.246.

§44.245 Strengthening bond.

Where the appropriate TTB officer determines that the amount of the bond, under which the customs warehouse proprietor is withdrawing cigars for shipment under this subpart, no longer adequately protects the revenue, and such bond is in an amount of less than $25,000, the appropriate TTB officer may require the proprietor to file a strengthening bond in an appropriate amount with the same surety as that on the bond already in effect, in lieu of a superseding bond to cover the full liability on the basis of §44.244. The appropriate TTB officer shall refuse to approve any strengthening bond where any notation is made thereon which is intended or which may be construed as a release of any former bond, or as limiting the amount of either bond to less than its full amount.

§ 44.246 Superseding bond.

The customs warehouse proprietor shall file a new bond to supersede his current bond, immediately when (a) the corporate surety on the current bond becomes insolvent, (b) the appropriate TTB officer approves a request from the surety on the current bond to terminate his liability under the bond, (c) payment of any liability under a bond is made by the surety thereon, or (d) the appropriate TTB officer considers such a superseding bond necessary for the protection of the revenue.

§ 44.247 Termination of liability of surety under bond.

The liability of a surety on any bond required by this subpart shall be terminated only as to operations on and after the effective date of a superseding bond, or the date of approval of the customs warehouse proprietor's request for termination, or otherwise, in accordance with the termination provisions of the bond. The surety shall remain bound in respect of any liability for unpaid taxes, penalties, and interest, not in excess of the amount of the bond, incurred by the proprietor while the bond is in force.

PACKAGING REQUIREMENTS

§ 44.248 Packages.

Cigars shall, before withdrawal under this part, be put up by the customs warehouse proprietor in packages which shall bear the label or notice, tax classification, and mark, as required by this subpart.

(Sec. 202, Pub. L. 85–859, 72 Stat. 1422 (26 U.S.C. 5723))

[T.D. ATF–40, 42 FR 5009, Jan. 26, 1977]

§ 44.249 Lottery features.

No certificate, coupon, or other device purporting to be or to represent a ticket, chance, share, or an interest in, or dependent on, the event of a lottery shall be contained in, attached to, or stamped, marked, written, or printed on any package of cigars withdrawn under this subpart.

(72 Stat. 1422; 26 U.S.C. 5723; 18 U.S.C. 1301)

§ 44.250 Indecent or immoral material.

No indecent or immoral picture, print, or representation shall be contained in, attached to, or stamped, marked, written, or printed on any package of cigars withdrawn under this subpart.

(72 Stat. 1422; 26 U.S.C. 5723)

§ 44.251 Mark.

Every package of cigars shall, before withdrawal from the customs warehouse under this subpart, have adequately imprinted thereon, or on a label securely affixed thereto, the name and location of the manufacturer. There shall also be adequately stated on each such package the number of cigars contained in the package.

(72 Stat. 1422; 26 U.S.C. 5723)

§ 44.252 Label or notice.

Every package of cigars shall, before withdrawal from the customs warehouse under this subpart, have adequately imprinted thereon, or on a label securely affixed the words "Tax-exempt. For use outside U.S." or the words "U.S. Tax-exempt. For use outside U.S.", except where a stamp, sticker, or notice, required by a foreign country or a possession of the United States, which identifies such country or possession, is so imprinted or affixed.

(72 Stat. 1422; 26 U.S.C. 5723)

§ 44.253 Tax classification for cigars.

Before withdrawal of cigars from a customs warehouse under this subpart, every package of cigars shall have adequately imprinted on it, or on a label securely affixed to it—

(a) The designation "cigars";

(b) The quantity of cigars contained in the package; and

(c) For small cigars, the classification of the product for tax purposes (i.e., either "small" or "little").

(Sec. 202, Pub. L. 85–859, 72 Stat. 1422 (26 U.S.C. 5723))

[T.D. ATF–80, 46 FR 18312, Mar. 24, 1981]

§ 44.254 Shipping containers.

Each shipping case, crate, or other container, in which cigars are to be withdrawn, under this subpart, shall bear a distinguishing number, such number to be assigned by the customs warehouse proprietor.

CONSIGNMENT OF SHIPMENT

§ 44.255 Consignment of cigars.

Cigars withdrawn from a customs warehouse, without payment of tax, under internal revenue bond and this part, shall be consigned in the same manner as provided by subpart J of this part with respect to the removal of tobacco products, and cigarette papers and tubes from a factory or an export warehouse.

[T.D. 6871, 31 FR 56, Jan. 4, 1966. Redesignated at 40 FR 16835, Apr. 15, 1975, and amended by T.D. ATF–232, 51 FR 28089, Aug. 5, 1986; T.D. ATF–243, 51 FR 43194, Dec. 1, 1986]

NOTICE OF REMOVAL OF SHIPMENT

§ 44.256 Preparation.

For each shipment to be withdrawn under this subpart, the customs warehouse proprietor shall prepare a notice of removal, Form 5200.14. Each such notice shall be given a serial number by the proprietor in a series beginning with number 1, with respect to the first shipment withdrawn under this subpart and commencing again with number 1 on January 1 of each year thereafter.

[25 FR 4725, May 28, 1960. Redesignated at 40 FR 16835, Apr. 15, 1975, as amended by T.D. ATF–421, 64 FR 71926, Dec. 22, 1999]

§ 44.257 Disposition.

After actual withdrawal from his warehouse of the shipment described on the notice of removal, Form 5200.14, the customs warehouse proprietor shall, except where the shipment is to be exported by parcel post, promptly forward one copy of the notice of removal to the appropriate TTB officer. A copy of each such notice shall be retained by the customs warehouse proprietor as a part of his records, for 3 years following the close of the calendar year in which the shipment was withdrawn, and shall be made available for inspection by any appropriate TTB officer upon his request. The proprietor shall dispose of the other copies of each notice of removal as required by this subpart.

[25 FR 4725, May 28, 1960. Redesignated at 40 FR 16835, Apr. 15, 1975, as amended by T.D. ATF–421, 64 FR 71926, Dec. 22, 1999; T.D. ATF–480, 67 FR 30803, May 8, 2002]

§ 44.258 To officers of the armed forces for subsequent exportation.

Where cigars are withdrawn from a customs warehouse for delivery to officers of the armed forces of the United States in this country for subsequent shipment to, and use by, the armed forces outside the United States, the customs warehouse proprietor making the shipment shall forward a copy of the notice of removal, Form 5200.14, to the officer at the base or installation authorized to receive the cigars described on the notice of removal. Upon execution by the armed forces receiving officer of the certificate of receipt on the copy of the notice of removal, he shall return such copy to the customs warehouse proprietor making the shipment for filing with the appropriate TTB officer.

[25 FR 4725, May 28, 1960. Redesignated at 40 FR 16835, Apr. 15, 1975, as amended by T.D. ATF–421, 64 FR 71926, Dec. 22, 1999]

§ 44.259 To noncontiguous foreign countries and possessions of the United States.

Where cigars are withdrawn from a customs warehouse for direct delivery to a vessel or aircraft for transportation to a noncontiguous foreign country, Puerto Rico, the Virgin Islands, or a possession of the United States, the customs warehouse proprietor making the withdrawal shall file two copies of the notice of removal, Form 5200.14, with the office of the district director of customs at the port where the shipment is to be laden. Such copies of the notice of removal should be filed with the related shipper's export declaration, Commerce Form 7525–V. In the event the copies of the notice of removal are not filed with the shipper's export declaration, when the copies of the notice are filed with the district director of customs they shall show all particulars necessary to enable that officer to associate the notice with the related shipper's export declaration and any other documents filed with his office in connection with the shipment. After the vessel or aircraft on which the shipment has been laden clears or departs from the port of lading the customs authority shall execute the certificate of exportation on both copies of the notice of removal, retain one copy for his records, and deliver or transmit the other copy to the customs warehouse proprietor making the shipment for filing with the appropriate TTB officer.

[T.D. 6961, 33 FR 9494, June 28, 1968. Redesignated at 40 FR 16835, Apr. 15, 1975, as amended by T.D. ATF–421, 64 FR 71926, Dec. 22, 1999]

§ 44.260 To a Federal department or agency.

Where cigars are withdrawn from a customs warehouse and are destined for ultimate delivery in a noncontiguous foreign country, Puerto Rico, the Virgin Islands, or a possession of the United States, but the shipment is to be delivered to a Federal department or agency, or to an authorized dispatch agent, transportation officer, or port director of such a department or agency for forwarding on to the place of destination of the shipment, the customs warehouse proprietor making the shipment shall furnish a copy of the notice of removal, Form 5200.14, to the Federal department or agency, or an officer thereof at the port, receiving the shipment for ultimate transmittal to the place of destination, in order that such department, agency, or officer, can properly execute the certificate of receipt on such notice to evidence receipt of the shipment for transmittal to a place beyond the jurisdiction of the internal revenue laws of the United States. After completing such certificate, the Federal department, agency, or officer, shall return the copy of the notice of removal, so executed, to the customs warehouse proprietor making the shipment for filing with the appropriate TTB officer.

[25 FR 4725, May 28, 1960. Redesignated at 40 FR 16835, Apr. 15, 1975, as amended by T.D. ATF–421, 64 FR 71926, Dec. 22, 1999]

§ 44.261 To contiguous foreign countries.

Where cigars are withdrawn from a customs warehouse for export to a contiguous foreign country, the customs warehouse proprietor making the shipment shall furnish to the district director of customs at the border or other port of exit two copies of the notice of removal, Form 5200.14, together with the related shipper's export declaration, Commerce Form 7525–V. In the event the copies of the notice of removal are not filed with the shipper's export declaration or, in the case of a shipment for the armed forces of the United States in the contiguous foreign country where no shipper's export declaration is required, the copies of the notice when filed with the district director of customs shall show all particulars necessary to enable that officer to associate the notice with the related shipper's export declaration, if any, and any other documents filed with his office in connection with the shipment. After the shipment has been cleared by customs from the United States, the customs authority at the port of exit shall complete the certificate of exportation on both copies of the notice of removal, retain one copy for his records, and transmit the other copy to the customs warehouse proprietor making the shipment for filing with the appropriate TTB officer.

[T.D. 6961, 33 FR 9494, June 28, 1968. Redesignated at 40 FR 16835, Apr. 15, 1975, as amended by T.D. ATF–421, 64 FR 71926, Dec. 22, 1999]

§ 44.262 To Government vessels and aircraft for consumption as supplies.

Where cigars are withdrawn from a customs warehouse for direct delivery to a vessel or aircraft, engaged in an activity for the Government of the United States or a foreign government, for consumption as supplies beyond the jurisdiction of the internal revenue laws of the United States, the customs warehouse proprietor making the shipment shall forward a copy of the notice of removal, Form 5200.14, to the officer of the vessel or aircraft authorized to receive the shipment. Upon execution by the receiving officer of the vessel or aircraft of the certificate of receipt on the copy of the notice of removal, he shall return such copy to the customs warehouse proprietor making the shipment for filing with the appropriate TTB officer.

[25 FR 4725, May 28, 1960. Redesignated at 40 FR 16835, Apr. 15, 1975, as amended by T.D. ATF–421, 64 FR 71926, Dec. 22, 1999]

§ 44.263 To commercial vessels and aircraft for consumption as supplies.

Where cigars are withdrawn from a customs warehouse for delivery to a vessel or aircraft entitled to receive such articles for consumption as supplies beyond the jurisdiction of the internal revenue laws of the United States, the customs warehouse proprietor making shipment shall file two copies of the notice of removal, Form 5200.14, with the district director of customs at the port where the shipment is to be laden in sufficient time to permit delivery of the two copies of the notice of removal to the customs officer who will inspect the shipment and supervise its lading. After inspection and lading of the shipment the customs officer shall note on the copies of the notice of removal any discrepancy between the shipment inspected and laden under his supervision and that described on the notice of removal or any limitation on the quantity to be laden; complete and sign the certificate of inspection and lading; and return both copies of the notice of removal to the district director of customs. The district director of customs shall execute the certificate of clearance on both copies of the notice of removal, retain one copy for his records, and forward the other copy to the customs warehouse proprietor making the shipment for filing with the appropriate TTB officer. Where the vessel or aircraft does not clear from the port at which the shipment is laden, the customs officer supervising the lading of the shipment shall require the person on board the vessel or aircraft authorized to receive the shipment to execute the certificate of receipt on both copies of the notice of removal to indicate the trade or activity in which the vessel or aircraft is engaged.

[T.D. 6961, 33 FR 9494, June 28, 1968. Redesignated at 40 FR 16835, Apr. 15, 1975, as amended by T.D. ATF–421, 64 FR 71926, Dec. 22, 1999]

§ 44.264 To export warehouses.

Where cigars are withdrawn from a customs warehouse for delivery to an export warehouse, the proprietor of the customs warehouse shall forward to the proprietor of the export warehouse three copies of the notice of removal, Form 5200.14, covering the shipment, for execution and disposition in accordance with procedure similar to that set forth in § 44.200 in connection with a shipment of tobacco products, and cigarette papers and tubes from a factory to an export warehouse. The executed copy of the notice of removal, Form 5200.14, returned to the customs warehouse proprietor by the export warehouse proprietor shall be filed with the appropriate TTB officer.

[T.D. ATF–48, 44 FR 55856, Sept. 28, 1979, as amended by T.D. ATF–232, 51 FR 28089, Aug. 5, 1986; T.D. ATF–243, 51 FR 43194, Dec. 1, 1986; T.D. ATF–421, 64 FR 71926, Dec. 22, 1999; T.D. ATF–480, 67 FR 30803, May 8, 2002]

§ 44.264a To a foreign-trade zone.

Where cigars are withdrawn from a customs warehouse for delivery to a foreign-trade zone, under zone restricted status for the purpose of exportation or storage, the customs warehouse proprietor making the shipment shall forward two copies of the notice of removal, Form 5200.14, to the customs officer in charge of the zone. Upon receipt of the shipment, the customs officer shall execute the certificate of receipt on each copy of the form, noting thereon any discrepancy, retain one copy for his records, and forward the other copy to the customs warehouse proprietor making the shipment for filing with the appropriate TTB officer.

[T.D. 6564, 26 FR 4362, May 19, 1961. Redesignated at 40 FR 16835, Apr. 15, 1975, as amended by T.D. ATF–421, 64 FR 71926, Dec. 22, 1999]

§ 44.265 For export by parcel post.

Where cigars are withdrawn from a customs warehouse for export by parcel post, the customs warehouse proprietor shall present one copy of the notice of removal, Form 5200.14, together with the shipping containers, to the postal authorities with the request that the postmaster or his agent execute the certificate of mailing on the form. Where a customs warehouse proprietor so desires, he may cover under one notice of removal all the cigars removed under this part for export by parcel post which are delivered at one time to the postal service for that purpose. The customs warehouse proprietor shall immediately file the receipted copy of the notice of removal with the appropriate TTB officer.

[25 FR 4725, May 28, 1960. Redesignated at 40 FR 16835, Apr. 15, 1975, as amended by T.D. ATF–421, 64 FR 71926, Dec. 22, 1999]

RETURN OF SHIPMENT

§44.266 Return of cigars from export warehouses.

Where cigars are returned to a customs warehouse from an export warehouse, the officer in charge of the customs warehouse shall execute the certificate of receipt on each of the copies of the related Form 5200.14 received from the export warehouse proprietor, after checking the containers to determine whether all the cigars described on the notice have been received. Thereafter, both copies of the Form 5200.14 shall be turned over to the proprietor of the customs warehouse who shall return one copy to the export warehouse proprietor for disposition as provided in §44.201. The customs warehouse proprietor shall retain the other copy of the notice of removal, as a part of his records, for 3 years following the close of the calendar year in which the shipment was received. Such copy shall be made available for inspection by any appropriate TTB officer upon his request.

[T.D. ATF–48, 44 FR 55856, Sept. 28, 1979, as amended by T.D. ATF–421, 64 FR 71926, Dec. 22, 1999]

§44.267 Return of cigars from other sources.

A customs warehouse proprietor may return to his warehouse cigars previously withdrawn therefrom, under this subpart, provided he promptly files with the appropriate TTB officer a copy of the Form 5200.14 under which the cigars were originally withdrawn, with the certificate of receipt properly modified and executed by the customs officer in charge of the warehouse to show return of the shipment. If less than the entire shipment is returned to the warehouse, the form shall state what disposition was made of the remainder of the original shipment and any other facts pertinent to such shipment. The customs warehouse proprietor shall retain a copy of such form as a part of his records for 3 years after the close of the calendar year in which the shipment was returned. Such copy shall be made available for inspection by any appropriate TTB officer upon request.

[25 FR 4725, May 28, 1960. Redesignated at 40 FR 16835, Apr. 15, 1975, as amended by T.D. ATF–421, 64 FR 71926, Dec. 22, 1999]

PART 45—REMOVAL OF TOBACCO PRODUCTS AND CIGARETTE PAPERS AND TUBES, WITHOUT PAYMENT OF TAX, FOR USE OF THE UNITED STATES

Subpart E—Packaging Requirements

Subpart F—Records

AUTHORITY: 26 U.S.C. 5702–5705, 5723, 5741, 5751, 5762, 5763, 6313, 7212, 7342, 7606, 7805; 44 U.S.C. 3504(h).

SOURCE: Redesignated by T.D. ATF–469, 66 FR 56758, Nov. 13, 2001.

EDITORIAL NOTE: Nomenclature changes to part 45 appear by T.D. ATF–460, 66 FR 39093, July 27, 2001.

Subpart A—Scope of Regulations

§45.1 Removal of tobacco products, and cigarette papers and tubes, without payment of tax, for use of the United States.

This part contains the regulations relating to the removal of tobacco products, and cigarette papers and tubes, without payment of tax, for use of the United States.

[T.D. 6871, 31 FR 57, Jan. 4, 1966. Redesignated at 40 FR 16835, Apr. 15, 1975, and amended by T.D. ATF–232, 51 FR 28090, Aug. 5, 1986; T.D. ATF–243, 51 FR 43194, Dec. 1, 1986]

Subpart B—Definitions

§45.11 Meaning of terms.

When used in this part and in forms prescribed under this part, the following terms shall have the meanings given in this section, unless the context clearly indicates otherwise. Words in the plural form shall include the singular, and vice versa, and words indicating the masculine gender shall include the feminine. The terms "includes" and "including" do not exclude things not listed which are in the same general class.

Administrator. The Administrator, Alcohol and Tobacco Tax and Trade Bureau, Department of the Treasury, Washington, DC.

Appropriate TTB officer. An officer or employee of the Alcohol and Tobacco Tax and Trade Bureau (TTB) authorized to perform any functions relating to the administration or enforcement of this part by TTB Order 1135.45, Delegation of the Administrator's Authorities in 27 CFR Part 45, Removal of Tobacco Products and Cigarette Papers and Tubes, Without Payment of Tax, for Use of the United States.

Armed forces. The Army, Navy (including the Marine Corps), Air Force, and Coast Guard.

Charge of the United States. A patient in a hospital or similar institution, or a Federal prisoner, if the hospital, institution, or prison is operated by a Federal agency and the support or care of such person results in a charge on, or an expense to, the United States Government.

Chewing tobacco. Any leaf tobacco that is not intended to be smoked.

Cigar. Any roll of tobacco wrapped in leaf tobacco or in any substance containing tobacco (other than any roll of tobacco which is a cigarette within the meaning of paragraph (2) of the definition for cigarette).

Cigarette. (1) Any roll of tobacco wrapped in paper or in any substance not containing tobacco, and

(2) Any roll of tobacco wrapped in any substance containing tobacco which, because of its appearance, the type of tobacco used in the filler, or its packaging and labeling, is likely to be offered to, or purchased by, consumers as a cigarette described in paragraph (1) of this definition.

Cigarette paper. Paper, or any other material except tobacco, prepared for use as a cigarette wrapper.

Cigarette tube. Cigarette paper made into a hollow cylinder for use in making cigarettes.

Factory. The premises of a manufacturer of tobacco products or cigarette papers and tubes in which he carries on such business.

Federal agency. A department or agency of the United States Government, including the American National Red Cross, and the U.S. Soldiers Home, Washington, D.C.

Large cigarettes. Cigarettes weighing more than three pounds per thousand.

Large cigars. Cigars weighing more than three pounds per thousand.

Manufacturer of cigarette papers and tubes. Any person who manufactures cigarette paper, or makes up cigarette paper into tubes, except for his own personal use or consumption.

Manufacturer of tobacco products. Any person who manufactures cigars, cigarettes, smokeless tobacco, pipe tobacco, or roll-your-own tobacco but does not include:

(1) A person who produces tobacco products solely for that person's own consumption or use; or

(2) A proprietor of a Customs bonded manufacturing warehouse with respect to the operation of such warehouse.

Package. The immediate container in which tobacco products, processed tobacco, or cigarette papers or tubes are put up by the manufacturer and offered for sale or delivery to the ultimate consumer. For purposes of this definition, a container of processed tobacco, the contents of which weigh 10 pounds or less (including any added non-tobacco ingredients or constituents), that is removed within the meaning of this part, is deemed to be a package offered for sale or delivery to the ultimate consumer.

Person. An individual, partnership, association, company, corporation, estate, or trust.

Pipe tobacco. Any tobacco which, because of its appearance, type, packaging, or labeling, is suitable for use and likely to be offered to, or purchased by, consumers as tobacco to be smoked in a pipe.

Removal or remove. The removal of tobacco products or cigarette papers or tubes from the factory.

Roll-your-own tobacco. Any tobacco which, because of its appearance, type, packaging, or labeling, is suitable for use and likely to be offered to, or purchased by, consumers as tobacco for making cigarettes or cigars, or for use as wrappers thereof.

Sale price. The price for which large cigars are sold by the manufacturer or importer, determined in accordance with §§40.22 or 41.39 and used in computation of the tax.

Small cigarettes. Cigarettes weighing not more than three pounds per thousand.

Small cigars. Cigars weighing not more than three pounds per thousand.

Smokeless tobacco. Any chewing tobacco or snuff.

Snuff. Any finely cut, ground, or powdered tobacco that is not intended to be smoked.

This chapter. Chapter I, title 26, Code of Federal Regulations.

Tobacco products. Cigars, cigarettes, smokeless tobacco, pipe tobacco, and roll-your-own tobacco.

United States. When used in a geographical sense shall include only the States and the District of Columbia.

U.S.C. The United States Code.

[T.D. ATF–48, 43 FR 13557, Mar. 31, 1978]

EDITORIAL NOTE: For FEDERAL REGISTER citations affecting §45.11, see the List of CFR Sections Affected, which appears in the Finding Aids section of the printed volume and at *www.fdsys.gov.*

Subpart C—Administrative Provisions

§45.21 Alternate methods or procedures.

A manufacturer, on specific approval by the appropriate TTB officer as provided in this section, may use an alternate method or procedure in lieu of a method or procedure specifically prescribed in this part. The appropriate TTB officer may approve an alternate method or procedure, subject to stated conditions, when he finds that:

(a) Good cause has been shown for the use of the alternate method or procedure.

(b) The alternate method or procedure is within the purpose of, and consistent with the effect intended by, the specifically prescribed method or procedure, and affords equivalent security to the revenue, and

(c) The alternate method or procedure will not be contrary to any provision of law, and will not result in an increase in cost to the Government or hinder the effective administration of this part.

No alternate method or procedure relating to the giving of any bond or to the assessment, payment, or collection of tax, shall be authorized under this section. Where a manufacturer desires to employ an alternate method or procedure, the manufacturer must submit a written application to the appropriate TTB officer. The application shall specifically describe the proposed alternate method or procedure, and shall set forth the reasons therefor. Alternate methods or procedures shall not be employed until the application has been approved by the appropriate TTB officer. The manufacturer shall, during the period of authorization of an alternate method or procedure, comply with the terms of the approved application. Authorization for any alternate method or procedure may be withdrawn whenever in the judgment of the appropriate TTB officer the revenue is jeopardized or the effective administration of this part is hindered. The manufacturer shall retain, as part of his records, any authorization of the appropriate TTB officer under this section for three years following the close of the calendar year in which the operation under such authorization is concluded.

[Redesignated by T.D. ATF–469, 66 FR 56758, Nov. 13, 2001, as amended by T.D. ATF–472, 67 FR 8880, Feb. 27, 2002]

§ 45.22 Emergency variations from requirements.

The appropriate TTB officer may approve methods of operation other than as specified in this part, where he finds that an emergency exists and the proposed variations from the specified requirements are necessary, and the proposed variations:

(a) Will afford the security and protection to the revenue intended by the prescribed specifications.

(b) Will not hinder the effective administration of this part, and

(c) Will not be contrary to any provision of law.

Variations from requirements granted under this section are conditioned on compliance with the procedures, conditions, and limitations set forth in the approval of the application. Failure to comply in good faith with such procedures, conditions, and limitations shall automatically terminate the authority for such variations and the manufacturer thereupon shall fully comply with the prescribed requirements of regulations from which the variations were authorized. Authority for any variations may be withdrawn whenever in the judgment of the appropriate TTB officer the revenue is jeopardized or the effective administration of this part is hindered by the continuation of such variation. Where a manufacturer desires to employ such variation, the manufacturer must submit a written application to the appropriate TTB officer. The application shall describe the proposed variations and set forth the reasons therefor. Variations shall not be employed until the application has been approved. The manufacturer shall retain, as part of his records, any authorization of the appropriate TTB officer under this section for three years following the close of the calendar year in which the operation under such authorization is concluded.

[27 FR 4476, May 10, 1962. Redesignated at 40 FR 16835, Apr. 15, 1975, as amended by T.D. ATF–472, 67 FR 8880, Feb. 27, 2002]

§ 45.23 Authority of appropriate TTB officers to enter premises.

Any appropriate TTB officer may enter in the daytime any premises where tobacco products, or cigarette papers or tubes removed under this part are kept, so far as it may be necessary for the purpose of examining such articles. When such premises are open at night, any appropriate TTB officer may enter them, while so open, in the performance of his official duties. The owner of such premises, or person having the superintendence of the same, who refuses to admit any appropriate TTB officer or permit him to examine the articles removed under this part shall be liable to the penalties prescribed by law for the offense.

(68A Stat. 872, 903; 26 U.S.C. 7342, 7606)

[T.D. 6871, 31 FR 57, Jan. 4, 1966. Redesignated at 40 FR 16835, Apr. 15, 1975, and amended by T.D. ATF–232, 51 FR 28090, Aug. 5, 1986; T.D. ATF–243, 51 FR 43194, Dec. 1, 1986; T.D. ATF–472, 67 FR 8880, Feb. 27, 2002]

§ 45.24 Interference with administration.

Whoever, corruptly or by force or threats of force, endeavors to hinder or obstruct the administration of this part, or endeavors to intimidate or impede any appropriate TTB officer acting in his official capacity, or forcibly rescues or attempts to rescue or causes to be rescued any property, after it has been duly seized for forfeiture to the United States in connection with a violation of the internal revenue laws, shall be liable to the penalties prescribed by law.

(68A Stat. 855; 26 U.S.C. 7212)

[27 FR 4476, May 10, 1962. Redesignated at 40 FR 16835, Apr. 15, 1975, as amended by T.D. ATF–472, 67 FR 8880, Feb. 27, 2002]

§ 45.25 Unlawful purchase, receipt, possession, or sale of tobacco products, or cigarette papers or tubes, after removal.

Any person who, with intent to defraud the United States, purchases, receives, possesses, offers for sale, or sells or otherwise disposes of tobacco products, or cigarette papers or tubes which, after removal under this part, without payment of tax, have been diverted from the purpose or use specified in this part, shall be subject to the criminal penalties and provisions for forfeiture prescribed by law.

(72 Stat. 1424, 1425, as amended, 1426; 26 U.S.C. 5751, 5762, 5763)

[T.D. 6871, 31 FR 57, Jan. 4, 1966. Redesignated at 40 FR 16835, Apr. 15, 1975, and amended by T.D. ATF–232, 51 FR 28090, Aug. 5, 1986; T.D. ATF–243, 51 FR 43194, Dec. 1, 1986]

§ 45.26 Delegations of the Administrator.

The regulatory authorities of the Administrator contained in this part are delegated to appropriate TTB officers. These TTB officers are specified in TTB Order 1135.45, Delegation of the Administrator's Authorities in 27 CFR Part 45, Removal of Tobacco Products and Cigarette Papers and Tubes, Without Payment of Tax, for Use of the United States. You may obtain a copy of this order by accessing the TTB Web site (*http://www.ttb.gov*) or by mailing a request to the Alcohol and Tobacco Tax and Trade Bureau, National Revenue Center, 550 Main Street, Room 1516, Cincinnati, OH 45202.

[T.D. TTB–44, 71 FR 16955, Apr. 4, 2006]

§ 45.27 Forms prescribed.

(a) The appropriate TTB officer is authorized to prescribe all forms required by this part. You must furnish all of the information required by each form as indicated by the headings on the form and the instructions for the form, and as required by this part. You must file each form in accordance with its instructions.

(b) Forms prescribed by this part are available for printing through the TTB Web site (*http://www.ttb.gov*) or by mailing a request to the Alcohol and Tobacco Tax and Trade Bureau, National Revenue Center, 550 Main Street, Room 1516, Cincinnati, OH 45202.

[T.D. ATF–472, 67 FR 8880, Feb. 27, 2002, as amended by T.D. TTB–44, 71 FR 16955, Apr. 4, 2006]

Subpart D—Removals

SOURCE: T.D. 6871, 31 FR 57, Jan. 14, 1966, unless otherwise noted. Redesignated at 40 FR 16835, Apr. 15, 1975.

§ 45.31 Removals for delivery to a Federal agency.

(a) *Removal of articles.* A manufacturer may remove tobacco products or cigarette papers and tubes without payment of tax, in accordance with this part, for delivery to a Federal agency if:

(1) The removed articles were purchased by the Federal agency with funds appropriated by the Congress of the United States and are for gratuitous distribution under the supervision of the Federal agency;

(2) The removed articles were purchased by a donor from the manufacturer, or donated directly by the manufacturer, for gratuitous distribution under the supervision of the Federal agency to:

(i) Charges of the United States; or

(ii) Patients in a hospital or institution operated by the Government of a State or the District of Columbia where the Federal agency maintains a program for distribution to members or veterans of the armed forces of the United States in the hospital or institution; or

(3) The removed articles are intended for use by the Federal agency in an investigation or other Federal law enforcement activity.

(b) *Sale prohibited.* Except in the case of articles described in paragraph (a)(3) of this section where a sale is incident to the Federal law enforcement activity, tobacco products and cigarette papers and tubes removed under this section may not be sold after their removal.

[T.D. TTB–26, 70 FR 19890, Apr. 15, 2005]

§ 45.32 Under manufacturer's bond.

Removals of tobacco products, and cigarette papers and tubes under this part shall be made under the bond filed by the manufacturer of such articles to cover the operations of his factory as required by section 5711, I.R.C., and regulations issued thereunder.

(72 Stat. 1418, as amended, 1421, as amended; 26 U.S.C. 5704, 5711)

[T.D. 6871, 31 FR 57, as amended by T.D. ATF–243, 51 FR 28090, Aug. 5, 1986; 51 FR 43194, Dec. 1, 1986]

§ 45.33 Return of shipment to factory.

Tobacco products, and cigarette papers and tubes which have been removed, under this part, may be returned to the factory without internal revenue supervision.

(72 Stat. 1418, as amended; 26 U.S.C. 5704)

[T.D. 6871, 31 FR 57, as amended by T.D. ATF–243, 51 FR 28090, Aug. 5, 1986; 51 FR 43194, Dec. 1, 1986]

§ 45.34 Loss or shortage in shipment.

Immediately upon receipt of information of a loss of all or part of a shipment, or of a shortage therein, of tobacco products, or cigarette papers or tubes removed under this part, the manufacturer shall notify the appropriate TTB officer, furnish all pertinent details with respect to the loss or shortage, and either pay the tax due thereon in accordance with the provisions of § 45.36, or file claim for remission of the tax liability under the provisions of part 40 of this chapter, as the case may be.

(72 Stat. 1417, 1419, as amended; 26 U.S.C. 5703, 5705)

[T.D. 6871, 31 FR 57, as amended by T.D. ATF–243, 51 FR 28090, Aug. 5, 1986; 51 FR 43194, Dec. 1, 1986; T.D. ATF–384, 61 FR 54096, Oct. 17, 1996; T.D. ATF–469, 66 FR 56758, Nov. 13, 2001; T.D. ATF–472, 67 FR 8880, Feb. 27, 2002]

§ 45.35 Liability for tax.

The manufacturer who removes tobacco products, or cigarette papers or tubes under this part shall be liable for the taxes imposed thereon by 26 U.S.C. 5701, until such tobacco products, or cigarette papers or tubes are received by the Federal agency. Any person who possesses tobacco products, or cigarette papers or tubes in violation of 26 U.S.C. 5751(a)(1) or (2), shall be liable for a tax equal to the tax on such articles.

(72 Stat. 1417, 1424; 26 U.S.C. 5703, 5751)

[T.D. 6871, 31 FR 57, Jan. 14, 1966. Redesignated at 40 FR 16835, Apr. 15, 1975, and amended by T.D. ATF–48, 44 FR 55856, Sept. 28, 1979; T.D. ATF–232, 51 FR 28090, Aug. 5, 1986; T.D. ATF–243, 51 FR 43194, Dec. 1, 1986]

§ 45.36 Payment of tax.

Any tax which becomes due and payable on tobacco products, and cigarette papers and tubes removed under this part shall be paid to appropriate TTB officer, with sufficient information to identify the taxpayer, the nature and purpose of the payment, and the articles covered by the payment: *Provided,* That a manufacturer of tobacco products or cigarette papers or tubes may pay any tax for which he becomes liable under this part by an appropriate adjustment in his current tax return Form 5000.24. In paying the tax, a fractional part of a cent shall be disregarded unless it amounts to one-half cent or more, in which case it shall be increased to one cent.

[T.D. ATF–232, 51 FR 28090, Aug. 5, 1986; T.D. ATF–243, 51 FR 43194, Dec. 1, 1986, as amended by T.D. ATF–251, 52 FR 19341, May 22, 1987; T.D. ATF–472, 67 FR 8880, Feb. 27, 2002]

§ 45.37 Assessment.

Whenever any person required by law to pay tax on tobacco products, and cigarette papers and tubes fails to pay such tax, the tax shall be ascertained and assessed against such person, subject to the limitations prescribed in 26 U.S.C. 6501. The tax so assessed shall be in addition to the penalties imposed by law for failure to pay such tax when required. Except in cases where delay may jeopardize collection of the tax, or where the amount is nominal or the result of an evident mathematical error, no such assessment shall be made until and after notice has been afforded such person to show cause against assessment. The person will be allowed 45 days from the date of such notice to show cause, in writing, against such assessment.

(72 Stat. 1417; 26 U.S.C. 5703)

[T.D. 6871, 31 FR 57, Jan. 14, 1966. Redesignated at 40 FR 16835, Apr. 15, 1975, and amended by T.D. ATF–48, 44 FR 55856, Sept. 28, 1979; T.D. ATF–232, 51 FR 28090, Aug. 5, 1986; T.D. ATF–243, 51 FR 43194, Dec. 1, 1986]

Subpart E—Packaging Requirements

§ 45.41 Packages.

All tobacco products, and cigarette papers and tubes shall, before removal under this part, be put up by the manufacturer in packages which shall be of such construction as will securely contain the articles therein and maintain the mark, notice, and label thereon, as required by this subpart. No package of tobacco products, or cigarette papers or tubes shall have contained therein, attached thereto, or stamped, marked, written, or printed thereon (a) any certificate, coupon, or other device purporting to be or to represent a ticket, chance, share, or an interest in, or dependent on, the event of a lottery, or (b) any indecent or immoral picture, print, or representation.

(72 Stat. 1422; 26 U.S.C. 5723)

[T.D. 6871, 31 FR 58, Jan. 4, 1966. Redesignated at 40 FR 16835, Apr. 15, 1975 and amended by T.D. ATF–232, 51 FR 28090, Aug. 5, 1986; T.D. ATF–243, 51 FR 43194, Dec. 1, 1986]

§ 45.42 Mark.

Every package of tobacco products shall before removal from the factory under this part, have adequately imprinted thereon, or on a label securely affixed thereto, a mark as specified in this section. The mark may consist of the name of the manufacturer removing the product and the location (by city and State) of the factory from which the products are to be so removed, or may consist of the permit number of the factory from which the products are to be so removed. (Any trade name of the manufacturer approved as provided in § 40.65 of this chapter may be used in the mark as the name of the manufacturer.) As an alternative, where tobacco products are both packaged and removed by the same manufacturer, either at the same or different factories, the mark may consist of the name of such manufacturer if the factory where packaged is identified on or in the package by a means approved by the appropriate TTB officer. Before using the alternative, the manufacturer shall notify the appropriate TTB officer in writing of the name to be used as the name of the manufacturer and the means to be used for identifying the factory where packaged. If approved by him the appropriate TTB officer shall return approved copies of the notice to the manufacturer. A copy of the approved notice shall be retained as part of the factory records at each of the factories operated by the manufacturer.

(72 Stat. 1422; 26 U.S.C. 5723)

[T.D. 6871, 31 FR 58, Jan. 4, 1966. Redesignated at 40 FR 16835, Apr. 15, 1975 and amended by T.D. ATF–232, 51 FR 28090, Aug. 5, 1986; T.D. ATF–243, 51 FR 43194, Dec. 1, 1986; T.D. ATF–472, 67 FR 8880, Feb. 27, 2002]

§ 45.43 Notice for smokeless tobacco.

(a) *Product designation.* Every package of chewing tobacco or snuff shall, before removal under this part, have adequately imprinted thereon, or on a label securely affixed thereto, the designation "chewing tobacco" or "snuff." As an alternative, packages of chewing tobacco may be designated "Tax Class C," and packages of snuff may be designated "Tax Class M."

(b) *Product weight.* Every package of chewing tobacco or snuff shall, before removal under this part, have adequately imprinted thereon, or on a label securely affixed thereto, a clear statement of the actual pounds and ounces of the product contained therein. As an alternative, the shipping cases containing packages of chewing tobacco or snuff may, before removal, have adequately imprinted thereon, or on a label securely affixed thereto, a clear statement, in pounds and ounces, of the total weight of the product, the tax class of the product, and the total number of the packages of product contained therein.

(Approved by the Office of Management and Budget under control number 1512–0502)

(Sec. 202, Pub. L. 85–859, 72 Stat. 1422 (26 U.S.C. 5723))

[T.D. ATF–232, 51 FR 28090, Aug. 5, 1986; T.D. ATF–243, 51 FR 43194, Dec. 1, 1986; T.D. ATF–469, 66 FR 56758, Nov. 13, 2001]

§ 45.44 Notice for cigars.

Before removal under this part, every package of cigars shall have adequately imprinted on it, or on a label securely affixed to it—

(a) The designation "cigars";

(b) The quantity of cigars contained in the package; and

(c) For small cigars, the classification of the product for tax purposes (i.e., either "small" or "little").

(Sec. 202, Pub. L. 85–859, 72 Stat. 1422 (26 U.S.C. 5723))

[T.D. ATF–80, 46 FR 18312, Mar. 24, 1981]

§ 45.45 Notice for cigarettes.

Every package of cigarettes shall, before removal under this part, have adequately imprinted thereon, or on a label securely affixed thereto, the designation "cigarettes", the quantity of such product contained therein, and the classification for tax purposes, i.e., for small cigarettes, either "small" or "Class A", and for large cigarettes, either "large" or "Class B".

(72 Stat. 1422; 26 U.S.C. 5723)

[27 FR 4478, May 10, 1962. Redesignated at 40 FR 16835, Apr. 15, 1975]

§ 45.45a Notice for pipe tobacco.

(a) *Product designation.* Every package of pipe tobacco shall, before removal subject to tax, have adequately imprinted thereon, or on a label securely affixed thereto, the designation "pipe tobacco."

(b) *Product weight.* Every package of pipe tobacco shall, before removal subject to tax, have adequately imprinted thereon, or on a label securely affixed thereto, a clear statement of the actual pounds and ounces of the product contained therein.

[T.D. ATF–289, 54 FR 48842, Nov. 27, 1989, as amended by T.D. TTB–78, 74 FR 29420, June 22, 2009]

§ 45.45b Notice for roll-your-own tobacco.

(a) *Product designation.* Every package of roll-your-own tobacco, before removal subject to tax, must have adequately imprinted on it, or on a label securely affixed to it, the applicable designation "roll-your-own tobacco", "cigarette tobacco", "cigar tobacco", "cigarette wrapper", or "cigar wrapper".

(b) *Product weight.* Before removal subject to tax, roll-your-own tobacco must have a clear statement of the actual weight in pounds and ounces of the product in the package. This statement must be adequately imprinted on, or on a label securely affixed to, the package.

(Approved by the Office of Management and Budget under control number 1513–0091)

[T.D. ATF–429, 65 FR 57547, Sept. 25, 2000, as amended by T.D. TTB–78, 74 FR 29420, June 22, 2009]

§ 45.45c Package use-up rule.

(a) During the period from June 22, 2009, through March 23, 2010, a manufacturer of tobacco products may remove packages of pipe tobacco or roll-your-own tobacco that do not meet the requirements of § 45.45a(a) or § 45.45b(a), provided that such packages bear the designation "Tax Class L" (to designate pipe tobacco) or "Tax Class J" (to designate roll-your-own tobacco)) and were in use prior to June 22, 2009.

(b) During the period from June 22, 2009, through March 23, 2010, a manufacturer may remove roll-your-own tobacco for which the applicable designation is "cigar tobacco," "cigarette wrapper," or "cigar wrapper" even if the packages of such products do not meet the requirements of § 45.45b.

[T.D. TTB–81, 74 FR 48654, Sept. 24, 2009]

§45.46 Tax-exempt label.

Except in the case of articles described in §45.31(a)(3), every package of tobacco products, and cigarette papers and tubes removed under this part shall have the words "Tax-Exempt. For Use of U.S. Not To Be Sold." adequately imprinted on the package or on a label securely affixed thereto.

(72 Stat. 1422; 26 U.S.C. 5723)

[T.D. 6871, 31 FR 58, Jan. 4, 1966. Redesignated at 40 FR 16835, Apr. 15, 1975; and amended by T.D. ATF–232, 51 FR 28090, Aug. 5, 1986; T.D. ATF–243, 51 FR 43194, Dec. 1, 1986; T.D. TTB–26, 70 FR 19890, Apr. 15, 2005]

Subpart F—Records

§45.51 Supporting records.

(a) *Records of removals.* Every manufacturer who removes tobacco products, and cigarette papers and tubes under this part must, in addition to the records kept under part 40 of this chapter, keep a supporting record of such removals and must make appropriate entries therein at the time of removal. The supporting record for each removal must show:

(1) The date of removal;

(2) The name and address of the Federal agency to which shipped or delivered;

(3) The kind and quantity and,

(4) for large cigars, the sale price.

(b) *Records of returns.* If any tobacco products, or cigarette papers or tubes removed under this part are returned to the factory, such returns must be noted in the supporting record.

(c) *Commercial records.* Where the manufacturer keeps, at the factory, copies of invoices or other commercial records containing the information required as to each removal, in such manner that the information may be readily ascertained therefrom, such copies will be considered the supporting record required by this section.

(d) *Retention period.* The manufacturer must retain the supporting record for 3 years following the close of the year covered therein. The record must be made available for inspection by any appropriate TTB officer upon request.

(Approved by the Office of Management and Budget under control number 1512–0363)

(See 26 U.S.C. 5741)

[T.D. ATF–420, 64 FR 71945, Dec. 22, 1999, as amended by T.D. ATF–472, Feb. 27, 2002]

PART 46—MISCELLANEOUS REGULATIONS RELATING TO TOBACCO PRODUCTS AND CIGARETTE PAPERS AND TUBES

Subpart A—Application of 26 U.S.C. 6423, as Amended, to Refund or Credit of Tax on Tobacco Products, and Cigarette Papers and Tubes

GENERAL

CLAIM PROCEDURE

BOND

PENALTIES

Subpart B—Administrative Provisions

Subpart C—Disaster Loss Claims

DEFINITIONS

PAYMENTS

AUTHORITY: 18 U.S.C. 2341–2346, 26 U.S.C. 5061, 5704, 5708, 5731–5734, 5751, 5754, 5761–5763, 6001, 6601, 6621, 6622, 7212, 7342, 7602, 7606, 7805; 44 U.S.C. 3504(h), 49 U.S.C. 782, unless otherwise noted.

SOURCE: Redesignated by T.D. ATF–457, 66 FR 32220, June 14, 2001.

EDITORIAL NOTE: Nomenclature changes to part 46 appear by T.D. ATF–457, 66 FR 32220, 32221, June 14, 2001.

CROSS REFERENCE: For exportation of tobacco materials, tobacco products, and cigarette papers and tubes, without payment of tax, or with drawback of tax, see part 44.

Subpart A—Application of 26 U.S.C. 6423, as Amended, to Refund or Credit of Tax on Tobacco Products, and Cigarette Papers and Tubes

SOURCE: T.D. 6395, 24 FR 599, Jan. 28, 1959, unless otherwise noted. Redesignated at 40 FR 16835, Apr. 15, 1975.

GENERAL

§ 46.1 Scope of regulations in this subpart.

The regulations in this subpart relate to the limitations imposed by 26 U.S.C. 6423, on the refund or credit of tax paid or collected in respect to any article of a kind subject to a tax imposed by 26 U.S.C. chapter 52.

[T.D. ATF–48, 44 FR 55857, Sept. 28, 1979]

§ 46.2 Meaning of terms.

When used in this subpart, where not otherwise distinctly expressed or manifestly incompatible with the intent thereof, terms shall have the meaning ascribed in this section.

Administrator. The Administrator, Alcohol and Tobacco Tax and Trade Bureau, Department of the Treasury, Washington, DC.

Appropriate TTB officer. An officer or employee of the Alcohol and Tobacco Tax and Trade Bureau (TTB) authorized to perform any functions relating to the administration or enforcement of this part by TTB Order 1135.46, Delegation of the Administrator's Authorities in 27 CFR Part 46, Miscellaneous Regulations Relating to Tobacco Products and Cigarette Papers and Tubes.

Article. The commodity in respect to which the amount claimed was paid or collected as a tax.

Claimant. Any person who files a claim for a refund or credit of tax under this subpart.

Owner. A person who, by reason of a proprietary interest in the article, furnished the amount claimed to the claimant for the purpose of paying the tax.

Person. An individual, a trust, estate, partnership, association, company, or corporation.

Tax. Any tax imposed by 26 U.S.C. chapter 52, or by any corresponding provision of prior internal revenue laws, and in the case of any commodity of a kind subject to a tax under such chapter, any tax equal to any such tax, any additional tax, or any floor stocks tax. The term includes an exaction denominated a "tax", and any penalty, addition to tax, additional amount, or interest applicable to any such tax.

[T.D. 6395, 24 FR 599, Jan. 28, 1959. Redesignated at 40 FR 16835, Apr. 15, 1975]

EDITORIAL NOTE: For FEDERAL REGISTER citations affecting § 46.2, see the List of CFR Sections Affected, which appears in the Finding Aids section of the printed volume and at *www.fdsys.gov.*

§ 46.3 Applicability to certain credits or refunds.

The provisions of this subpart apply only where the credit or refund is claimed on the grounds that an amount of tax was assessed or collected erroneously, illegally, without authority, or in any manner wrongfully, or on the grounds that such amount was excessive. This subpart does not apply to:

(a) Any claim for drawback,

(b) Any claim made in accordance with any law expressly providing for credit or refund where an article is withdrawn from the market, returned to bond, lost, or destroyed, and

(c) Any claim based solely on errors in computation of the quantity of an article subject to tax or on mathematical errors in computation of the amount of the tax due, or to any claim in respect of tax collected or paid on an article seized and forfeited, or destroyed, as contraband.

[T.D. 6395, 24 FR 599, Jan. 28, 1959. Redesignated at 40 FR 16835, Apr. 15, 1975, and amended by T.D. ATF–42, 42 FR 8372, Feb. 10, 1977]

§46.4 Ultimate burden.

For the purposes of this subpart, the claimant, or owner, shall be treated as having borne the ultimate burden of an amount of tax only if:

(a) He has not, directly or indirectly, been relieved of such burden or shifted such burden to any other person,

(b) No understanding or agreement exists for any such relief or shifting, and

(c) If he has neither sold nor contracted to sell the articles involved in such claim, he agrees that there will be no such relief or shifting, and furnishes bond as provided in §46.10.

§46.5 Conditions to allowance of credit or refund.

No credit or refund to which this subpart is applicable shall be allowed or made, pursuant to a court decision or otherwise, of any amount paid or collected as a tax unless a claim therefor has been filed, as provided in this subpart, by the person who paid the tax and the claimant, in addition to establishing that he is otherwise legally entitled to credit or refund of the amount claimed, establishes:

(a) That he bore the ultimate burden of the amount claimed, or

(b) That he has unconditionally repaid the amount claimed to the person who bore the ultimate burden of such amount, or

(c) That (1) the owner of the article furnished him the amount claimed for payment of the tax, (2) he has filed with the appropriate TTB officer the written consent of such owner to the allowance to the claimant of the credit or refund, and (3) such owner satisfies the requirements of paragraph (a) or (b) of this section.

[T.D. 6395, 24 FR 599, Jan. 28, 1959. Redesignated at 40 FR 16835, Apr. 15, 1975, as amended by T.D. ATF–472, 67 FR 8880, Feb. 27, 2002]

§46.6 Requirements for persons intending to file claim.

Any person who, having paid the tax with respect to an article, desires to claim refund or credit of any amount of such tax to which the provisions of this subpart are applicable must:

(a) File a claim, as provided in §46.7,

(b) Comply with any other provisions of law or regulations which may apply to the claim, and

(c) If, at the time of filing the claim, neither he nor the owner has sold or contracted to sell the articles involved in the claim, file a bond on TTB Form 5620.10, as provided by §46.10.

[T.D. 6395, 24 FR 599, Jan. 28, 1959. Redesignated at 40 FR 16835, Apr. 15, 1975, as amended by T.D. ATF–472, 67 FR 8880, Feb. 27, 2002]

CLAIM PROCEDURE

§46.7 Execution and filing of claim.

Claims to which this subpart is applicable must be executed on Form 2635 (5620.8) in accordance with instructions for the form. (For provisions relating to hand-carried documents, see §70.304 of this chapter.) The claim shall set forth each ground upon which the claim is made in sufficient detail to apprise the appropriate TTB officer of the exact basis therefor. Allegations pertaining to the bearing of the ultimate burden relate to additional conditions which must be established for a claim to be allowed and are not in themselves legal grounds for allowance of a claim. There shall also be attached to the form and made a part of the claim the supporting data required by §46.8. All evidence relied upon in support of such claim shall be clearly set forth and submitted with the claim.

[T.D. 7008, 34 FR 3672, Mar. 1, 1969. Redesignated at 40 FR 16835, Apr. 15, 1975, and amended by T.D. ATF–48, 44 FR 55857, Sept. 28, 1979; T.D. ATF–251, 52 FR 19342, May 22, 1987; T.D. ATF–301, 55 FR 47658, Nov. 14, 1990; T.D. ATF–472, 67 FR 8880, Feb. 27, 2002]

§ 46.8 Data to be shown in claim.

Claims to which this subpart is applicable, in addition to the requirements of § 46.7, must set forth or contain the following:

(a) A statement that the claimant paid the amount claimed as a "tax" as defined in this subpart.

(b) Full identification (by specific reference to the form number, the date of filing, the place of filing, and the amount paid on the basis of the particular form or return) of the tax forms or returns covering the payments for which refund or credit is claimed.

(c) The written consent of the owner to allow the refund or credit to the claimant (where the owner of the article on which the tax was paid has furnished the claimant the amount claimed for the purpose of paying the tax).

(d) If the claimant or the owner, as the case may be, has neither sold nor contracted to sell the articles involved in the claim, a statement that the claimant or the owner, as the case may be, agrees not to shift, directly or indirectly in any manner whatsoever, the burden of the tax to any other person.

(e) If the claim is for refund of a floor stocks tax, or of an amount resulting from an increase in rate of tax applicable to an article, a statement as to whether the price of the article was increased on or following the effective date of such floor stocks tax or rate increase, and, if so, the date of the increase, together with full information as to the amount of such price increase.

(f) Specific evidence (such as relevant records, invoices, or other documents, or affidavits of individuals having personal knowledge of pertinent facts) which will satisfactorily establish the conditions of allowance set forth in § 46.5.

The appropriate TTB officer may require the claimant to furnish as a part of the claim such additional information as he may deem necessary.

[T.D. ATF–42, 42 FR 8372, Feb. 10, 1977, as amended by T.D. ATF–472a, 67 FR 63544, Oct. 15, 2002]

§ 46.9 Time for filing claim.

No credit or refund of any amount of tax to which the provisions of this subpart apply shall be made unless the claimant files a claim therefor within the time prescribed by law and in accordance with the provisions of this subpart.

[T.D. ATF–42, 42 FR 8373, Feb. 10, 1977]

Bond

§ 46.10 Bond, Form 2490.

Each claim for a refund or credit of tax on articles which the claimant or the owner, as the case may be, has neither sold nor contracted to sell at the time of filing of the claim must be accompanied by a bond on TTB Form 5620.10. The bond shall be executed by the claimant or the owner of the articles, as the case may be, in accordance with the provisions of this subpart and the instructions printed on the form. Such bond shall be conditioned that there will be no relief or shifting of the ultimate burden of the tax to any other person. The penal sum shall not be less than the amount of tax claimed on all articles which have not been sold or contracted for sale at the time of filing of the claim. Bonds required by this subpart shall be given with corporate surety or with collateral security. A separate bond must be filed for each claim.

[T.D. 6395, 24 FR 599, Jan. 28, 1959. Redesignated at 40 FR 16835, Apr. 15, 1975, as amended by T.D. ATF–472, 67 FR 8880, Feb. 27, 2002]

§ 46.11 Corporate surety.

(a) Surety bonds required under the provisions of this subpart may be given only with corporate sureties holding certificates of authority from the Secretary of the Treasury as acceptable sureties on Federal bonds. Limitations concerning corporate sureties are prescribed by the Secretary in the current revision of the Treasury Department Circular No. 570 (refer to paragraph (c) of this section). The surety shall have no interest whatever in the business covered by the bond.

(b) Each bond and each extension of coverage of bond shall at the time of filing be accompanied by a power of attorney authorizing the agent or officer who executed the bond to so act on behalf of the surety. The appropriate TTB officer who is authorized to approve the bond may, whenever he deems it necessary, require additional evidence of the authority of the agent or officer to execute the bond or extension of coverage of bond. The power of attorney shall be prepared on a form provided by the surety company and executed under the corporate seal of the company. If the power of attorney submitted is other than a manually signed document, it shall be accompanied by a certificate of its validity.

(c) Treasury Department Circular No. 570 (Companies Holding Certificates of Authority as Acceptable Sureties on Federal Bonds and as Acceptable Reinsuring Companies) is published in the FEDERAL REGISTER annually as of the first workday in July. As they occur, interim revisions of the circular are published in the FEDERAL REGISTER. Copies may be obtained from the Audit Staff, Bureau of Government Financial Operations, Department of the Treasury, Washington, DC 20226.

(July 30, 1947, ch. 390, 61 Stat. 648, as amended (6 U.S.C. 6, 7); sec. 202, Pub. L. 85–859, 72 Stat. 1421, as amended (26 U.S.C. 5711))

[T.D. ATF–92, 46 FR 46923, Sept. 23, 1981, as amended by T.D. ATF–472, 67 FR 8880, Feb. 27, 2002]

§46.12 Deposit of securities in lieu of corporate surety.

In lieu of corporate surety, the principal may pledge and deposit securities which are transferable and are guaranteed as to both interest and principal by the United States, in accordance with the provisions of 31 CFR part 225.

§46.13 Authority to approve bonds.

An appropriate TTB officer may approve all bonds required by this subpart.

[T.D. ATF–472, 67 FR 8880, Feb. 27, 2002]

§46.14 Termination of liability.

Bonds on TTB Form 5620.10 will be terminated by the appropriate TTB officer on receipt of satisfactory evidence that the person giving the bond has disposed of the articles covered by the bond and that he bore the ultimate burden of the amount claimed and that no understanding or agreement exists whereby he will be relieved of such burden or shift such burden to another person.

[T.D. 6395, 24 FR 599, Jan. 28, 1959. Redesignated at 40 FR 16835, Apr. 15, 1975, as amended by T.D. ATF–472, 67 FR 8880, Feb. 27, 2002]

§46.15 Release of pledged securities.

Securities of the United States, pledged and deposited as provided by §46.12, shall be released only in accordance with the provisions of 31 CFR part 225. When the appropriate TTB officer is satisfied that they may be released, he shall fix the date or dates on which a part or all of such securities may be released. At any time prior to the release of such securities, the appropriate TTB officer may, for proper cause, extend the date of release for such additional length of time as he deems necessary.

[T.D. 6395, 24 FR 599, Jan. 28, 1959. Redesignated at 40 FR 16835, Apr. 15, 1975, as amended by T.D. ATF–472, 67 FR 8880, Feb. 27, 2002]

PENALTIES

§46.16 Penalties.

It is an offense punishable by fine and imprisonment for anyone to make or cause to be made any false or fraudulent claim upon the United States, or to make any false or fraudulent statements, or representations, in support of any claim, or to falsely or fraudulently execute any documents required by the provisions of the internal revenue laws, or any regulations made in pursuance thereof.

Subpart B—Administrative Provisions

SOURCE: T.D. ATF–472, 67 FR 8880, Feb. 27, 2002, unless otherwise noted.

§46.21 Delegations of the Administrator.

The regulatory authorities of the Administrator contained in this part are delegated to appropriate TTB officers. These TTB officers are specified in TTB Order 1135.46, Delegation of the Administrator's Authorities in 27 CFR Part 46, Miscellaneous Regulations Relating to Tobacco Products and Cigarette Papers and Tubes. You may obtain a copy of this order by accessing the TTB Web site (*http://www.ttb.gov*) or by mailing a request to the Alcohol and Tobacco Tax and Trade Bureau, National Revenue Center, 550 Main Street, Room 1516, Cincinnati, OH 45202.

[T.D. TTB–44, 71 FR 16955, Apr. 4, 2006]

§46.22 Forms prescribed.

(a) The appropriate TTB officer is authorized to prescribe all forms required by this part. You must furnish all of the information required by each form as indicated by the headings on the form and the instructions for the form, and as required by this part. You must file each form in accordance with its instructions.

(b) Forms prescribed by this part are available for printing through the TTB Web site (*http://www.ttb.gov*) or by mailing a request to the Alcohol and Tobacco Tax and Trade Bureau, National Revenue Center, 550 Main Street, Room 1516, Cincinnati, OH 45202.

[T.D. ATF–472, 67 FR 8880, Feb. 27, 2002, as amended by T.D. TTB–44, 71 FR 16955, Apr. 4, 2006]

Subpart C—Disaster Loss Claims

§46.71 Scope of subpart.

This subpart prescribes the requirements necessary to implement 26 U.S.C. 5708, concerning payments which may be made by the United States in respect to the internal revenue taxes paid or determined and customs duties paid on tobacco products, and cigarette papers and tubes removed, which were lost, rendered unmarketable, or condemned by a duly authorized official by reason of a disaster occurring in the United States on or after September 3, 1958.

[T.D. 6871, 31 FR 59, Jan. 4, 1966. Redesignated at 40 FR 16835, Apr. 15, 1975, and amended by T.D. ATF–48, 44 FR 55857, Sept. 28, 1979; T.D. ATF–232, 51 FR 28090, Aug. 5, 1986; T.D. ATF–243, 51 FR 43194, Dec. 1, 1986]

DEFINITIONS

§46.72 Meaning of terms.

When used in this subpart, the following terms shall have the meanings given in this section, unless the context clearly indicates otherwise. Words in the plural form shall include the singular, and vice versa, and words indicating the masculine gender shall include the feminine. The terms "includes" and "including" do not exclude things not listed which are in the same general class.

Act. The Excise Tax Technical Changes Act of 1958 (Pub. L. 85–859, 72 Stat. 1275), enacted September 2, 1958.

Appropriate TTB officer. An officer or employee of the Alcohol and Tobacco Tax and Trade Bureau (TTB) authorized to perform any functions relating to the administration or enforcement of this part by TTB Order 1135.46, Delegation of the Administrator's Authorities in 27 CFR Part 46, Miscellaneous Regulations Relating to Tobacco Products and Cigarette Papers and Tubes.

Claimant. The person who held the tobacco products or cigarette papers and tubes for sale at the time of the disaster and who files claim under this subpart.

Commissioner of Customs. The Commissioner of Customs, U.S. Customs Service, The Department of the Treasury, Washington, DC.

Disaster. A flood, fire, hurricane, earthquake, storm, or other catastrophe which has occurred in any part of the United States on and after the day following the date of enactment of the act and which the President of the United States has determined, under the Act of September 30, 1950 (64 Stat. 1109; 42 U.S.C. 1855), was a "major disaster" as defined in such Act.

Duly authorized official. Any Federal, State, or local government official in whom has been vested authority to condemn tobacco products and cigarette papers and tubes made the subject of a claim under this subpart.

Duty or duties. Any duty or duties paid under the customs laws of the United States.

Removal or remove. The removal of tobacco products or cigarette papers or tubes from the factory, or release of such articles from Customs custody.

Sale price. The price for which large cigars are sold by the manufacturer or importer, determined in accordance with §§40.22 or 41.39 and used in computation of the tax.

Tax paid or determined. The internal revenue tax on tobacco products and cigarette papers and tubes which has acutally been paid, or which has been determined pursuant to 26 U.S.C. 5703(b), and regulations thereunder, at the time of their removal subject to tax payable on the basis of a return.

Tobacco Products. Cigars, cigarettes, smokeless tobacco, pipe tobacco, and roll-your-own tobacco.

United States. When used in a geographical sense, includes only the States, and the District of Columbia.

[T.D. 6392, 24 FR 5300, June 30, 1959]

EDITORIAL NOTE: For FEDERAL REGISTER citations affecting §46.72, see the List of CFR Sections Affected, which appears in the Finding Aids section of the printed volume and at *www.fdsys.gov*.

PAYMENTS

§46.73 Circumstances under which payment may be made.

An appropriate TTB officer shall allow payment (without interest) of an amount equal to the amount of tax paid or determined, and the Commissioner of Customs shall allow payment (without interest) of an amount equal to the amount of customs duty paid, on tobacco products, and cigarette papers and tubes removed, which are lost, rendered unmarketable, or condemned by a duly authorized official by reason of a disaster occurring in the United States on and after September 3, 1958. Such payments may be made only if, at the time of the disaster, such tobacco products, or cigarette papers or tubes were being held for sale by the claimant. No payment shall be made under this subpart with respect to any amount of tax or duty claimed or to be claimed under any other provision of law or regulations.

[T.D. 6871, 31 FR 59, Jan. 4, 1966. Redesignated at 40 FR 16835, Apr. 15, 1975 and amended by T.D. ATF–232, 51 FR 28090, Aug. 5, 1986; T.D. ATF–243, 51 FR 43194, Dec. 1, 1986; T.D. ATF–472, 67 FR 8881, Feb. 27, 2002]

CLAIMS PROCEDURE

§46.74 Execution of claims.

Disaster loss claims for tobacco products or cigarette papers or tubes must be executed on TTB Form 2635 (5620.8), Claim—Alcohol, Tobacco and Firearms Taxes, in accordance with the instructions on the form. If a claim involves taxes on both domestic and imported products, the quantities of each must be shown separately in the claim. Prepare a separate claim in respect of customs duties.

[T.D. ATF–420, 64 FR 71945, Dec. 22, 1999]

§46.75 Required information for claim.

The claim should contain the following information:

(a) That the tax on such tobacco products, or cigarette papers or tubes has been paid or determined and customs duty has been paid;

(b) That such tobacco products, or cigarette papers or tubes were lost, rendered unmarketable, or condemned by a duly authorized official, by reason of a disaster;

(c) The type and date of occurrence of the disaster and the location of the tobacco products, or cigarette papers or tubes at that time;

(d) That the claimant was not indemnified by any valid claim of insurance or otherwise in respect of the tax, or tax and duty, on the tobacco products, or cigarette papers or tubes covered by the claim;

(e) That no amount of internal revenue tax or customs duty claimed has been or will be otherwise claimed under any other provision of law or regulations,

(f) That the claimant is entitled to payment under this subpart, and

(g) The claim must set forth the quantity and kind of tobacco products and cigarette papers and tubes in sufficient detail to calculate the amount of tax and duty paid on these products, substantially as shown in the examples below:

[Example using rates for 2002 and After]

Quantity	Article	Rate of tax	Amount
20,000	Small cigars	$1.828 per thousand	36.56
1,000	Large cigars—sale price $100/thousand	20.719% of sale price	20.72
500	Large cigars—sale price $236/thousand	$48.75 per thousand	24.38
10,000	Small cigarettes	$19.50 per thousand	195.00
5,000	Large cigarettes	$40.95 per thousand	204.75
199,975	Cigarette papers	$0.0122 per 50 papers	48.80
1,000	Cigarette tubes	$0.0244 per 50 tubes	0.49
100 lbs	Chewing tobacco	$0.195 per pound	19.50
200 lbs	Snuff	$0.585 per pound	117.00
100 lbs	Pipe tobacco	$1.0969 per pound	109.69
300 lbs	Roll-your-own tobacco	$1.0969 per pound	329.07
Total claimed			1,105.96

EXAMPLE USING RATES FOR APRIL 1, 2009 AND AFTER

Quantity	Article	Rate of tax	Amount
20,000	Small cigars	$50.33 per thousand	$1,006.60
1,000	Large cigars—sale price $100/thousand	52.75% of sale price	52.75
500	Large cigars—sale price $0.77 per cigar	$0.4026 per cigar	201.30
10,000	Small cigarettes	$50.33 per thousand	503.30
5,000	Large cigarettes	$105.69 per thousand	528.45
199,975	Cigarette papers	$0.0315 per 50 papers	126.00
1,000	Cigarette tubes	$0.0630 per 50 tubes	1.26
100 lbs	Chewing tobacco	$0.5033 per pound	50.33
200 lbs	Snuff	$1.51 per pound	302.00
100 lbs	Pipe tobacco	$2.8311 per pound	283.11
300 lbs	Roll-your-own tobacco	$24.78 per pound	7,434.00
Total claimed	10,489.10.		

[T.D. ATF–420, 64 FR 71945, Dec. 22, 1999, as amended by T.D. TTB–75, 74 FR 14485, Mar. 31, 2009]

§ 46.76 Supporting evidence.

The claimant must support the claim with any available evidence (such as inventories, statements, invoices, bills, records, stamps, and labels), relating to the tobacco products or cigarette papers or tubes on hand at the time of the disaster and claimed to have been lost, rendered unmarketable, or condemned as a result thereof. If the claim is for refund of duty, the claimant must furnish, if practicable, the customs entry number, date of entry, and the name of the port of entry.

[T.D. ATF–420, 64 FR 71946, Dec. 22, 1999]

§ 46.77 Time and place of filing.

Disaster loss claims must be filed within 6 months after the date on which the President makes the determination that the disaster has occurred. All forms, including claims for duty on imported products, must be filed with the appropriate TTB officer.

[T.D. ATF–420, 64 FR 71946, Dec. 22, 1999]

§ 46.78 Action by appropriate TTB officer.

The appropriate TTB officer must act upon each claim for payment (without interest) of an amount equal to the tax paid or determined filed under this subpart and must notify the claimant. Claims and supporting data involving customs duties will be forwarded to the Commissioner of Customs with a summary statement of such officer's findings.

[T.D. ATF–472, 67 FR 8881, Feb. 27, 2002]

DESTRUCTION OF TOBACCO PRODUCTS, AND CIGARETTE PAPERS AND TUBES

§46.79 Supervision.

Before payment is made under this subpart in respect of the tax, or tax and duty, on tobacco products, or cigarette papers or tubes rendered unmarketable or condemned by a duly authorized official, such tobacco products, or cigarette papers or tubes must be destroyed by suitable means under the supervision of an appropriate TTB officer who will be assigned for that purpose by another appropriate TTB officer. However, if the destruction of such tobacco products, or cigarette papers or tubes has already occurred, and if the appropriate TTB officer who acts on the claim is satisfied with the supervision of such destruction, TTB supervision will not be required.

[T.D. ATF–472, 67 FR 8881, Feb. 27, 2002]

PENALTIES

§46.80 Penalties.

Penalties are provided in 26 U.S.C. 7206 and 7207 for the execution under the penalties of perjury of any false or fraudulent statement in support of any claim and for the filing of any false or fraudulent document under this subpart. All provisions of law, including penalties, applicable in respect of internal revenue taxes on tobacco products, and cigarette papers and tubes shall, insofar as applicable and not inconsistent with this subpart, be applied in respect of the payments provided for in this subpart to the same extent as if such payments constituted refunds of such taxes.

[T.D. 6871, 31 FR 60, Jan. 4, 1966. Redesignated at 40 FR 16835, Apr. 15, 1975, and amended by T.D. ATF–48, 44 FR 55857, Sept. 28, 1979; T.D. ATF–232, 51 FR 28092, Aug. 5, 1986; T.D. ATF–243, 51 FR 43194, Dec. 1, 1986]

ADMIMISTRATIVE PROVISIONS

§46.81 [Reserved]

Subpart D—Rules for Special (Occupational) Tax

SOURCE: T.D. TTB–79, 74 FR 37420, July 28, 2009, unless otherwise noted.

§46.91 Scope of subpart.

This subpart contains rules relating to special (occupational) taxes that must be paid by manufacturers of tobacco products, manufacturers of cigarette papers and tubes, and export warehouse proprietors.

§46.92 Meaning of terms.

As used in this subpart, the following terms shall have the meanings indicated unless either the context in which they are used requires a different meaning, or a different definition is prescribed for a particular section or portion of this subpart:

Appropriate TTB officer. An officer or employee of the Alcohol and Tobacco Tax and Trade Bureau (TTB) authorized to perform any functions relating to the administration or enforcement of this part by TTB Order 1135.46, Delegation of the Administrator's Authorities in 27 CFR Part 46, Miscellaneous Regulations Relating to Tobacco Products and Cigarette Papers and Tubes.

CFR. The Code of Federal Regulations.

Cigarette paper. Paper, or any other material except tobacco, prepared for use as a cigarette wrapper.

Cigarette tube. Cigarette paper made into a hollow cylinder for use in making cigarettes.

Export warehouse. A bonded internal revenue warehouse for the storage of tobacco products and cigarette papers and tubes, upon which the internal revenue tax has not been paid, for subsequent shipment to a foreign country, Puerto Rico, the Virgin Islands, or a possession of the United States, or for consumption beyond the jurisdiction of the internal revenue laws of the United States.

Export warehouse proprietor. Any person who operates an export warehouse.

Manufacturer of cigarette papers and tubes. Any person who manufactures cigarette paper, or makes up cigarette paper into tubes, except for his own personal use or consumption.

Manufacturer of tobacco products. Any person who manufactures tobacco products.

Person. An individual, a trust, estate, partnership, association or other unincorporated organization, fiduciary, company, or corporation, or the District of Columbia, a State, or a political subdivision thereof (including a city, county, or other municipality).

Special tax. The special (occupational) tax on manufacturers of tobacco products, manufacturers of cigarette papers and tubes, and export warehouse proprietors, imposed by 26 U.S.C. 5731.

Tax year. The period from July 1 of one calendar year through June 30 of the following calendar year.

This chapter. Chapter I of title 27 of the Code of Federal Regulations.

Tobacco products. Cigars, cigarettes, smokeless tobacco, pipe tobacco, and roll-your-own tobacco.

U.S.C. The United States Code.

§46.93 Multiple businesses of same ownership and location.

(a) Where more than one type of taxable business is conducted by the same person at the same place, special tax for each business must be paid at the rates prescribed for each.

(b) Where the same type of taxable business is conducted by the same person in different areas of the same premises, only one special tax payment is required.

(26 U.S.C. 5733)

§46.94 Relation to State and municipal law.

(a) *General.* The payment of special (occupational) tax does not exempt any person from any penalty or punishment provided by the laws of any State for carrying on any trade or business within that State, nor does it authorize the commencement or continuance of any trade or business contrary to State law or in places prohibited by county or municipal law. Payment of this tax does not prohibit any State from placing an additional duty or tax on the same trade or business, for State or other purposes.

(b) *Special tax stamps.* TTB officers are without authority to refuse to issue a special tax stamp to a person engaged in business in violation of State law. The stamp is not a Federal permit or license, but is merely a receipt for the tax. The stamp affords the holder no protection against prosecution for violation of State law.

(26 U.S.C. 5734)

§46.95 Liability of partners.

Any number of persons carrying on one business in partnership at any one place during any tax year are required to pay only one special tax.

(26 U.S.C. 5733)

PAYMENT OF SPECIAL TAX

§46.101 Special tax returns.

(a) *Preparation of TTB Form 5630.5t.* Every manufacturer of tobacco products, manufacturer of cigarette papers and tubes, and export warehouse proprietor is required to pay special (occupational) tax and file a return on TTB Form 5630.5t, "Special Tax Registration and Return—Tobacco." TTB Form 5630.5t must be completed in accordance with the instructions on the form, and all of the information called for on the form must be provided, including the following:

(1) Name of the taxpayer.

(2) Trade name(s) (if any) of the business(es) subject to special (occupational) tax.

(3) Employer identification number (see §46.102).

(4) Exact location of the place of business, by name and number of building or street, or if these do not exist, by some specific description in addition to the post office address. In the case of one return for two or more locations, the address to be shown must be the taxpayer's principal place of business (or principal office, in the case of a corporate taxpayer).

(5) Class(es) of special tax to which the taxpayer is subject.

(6) Ownership and control information. This consists of the name, position, and residence address of every owner of the business and of every person having power to control its management and policies with respect to the activity subject to special tax. "Owner of the business" includes every partner, if the taxpayer is a partnership, and every person owning 10 percent or more of its stock, if the taxpayer is a corporation. However, the

ownership and control information required by this paragraph need not be stated if the same information has been previously provided to TTB in connection with a permit application and that previously provided information is still current.

(b) *Multiple locations and/or classes of tax.* A taxpayer subject to special tax for the same period at more than one location or for more than one class of tax must—

(1) File one special tax return, TTB Form 5630.5t, with payment of tax, to cover all such locations and classes of tax; and

(2) Prepare, in duplicate, a list identified with the taxpayer's name, address (as shown on TTB Form 5630.5t), employer identification number, and period covered by the return. The list must show, by State, the name, address, and tax class of each location for which special tax is being paid. The original of the list must be filed with TTB as an attachment to TTB Form 5630.5t, and the copy must be retained at the taxpayer's principal place of business (or principal office, in the case of a corporate taxpayer) for a period of three years from the date of the return.

(c) *Signing of TTB Form 5630.5t*—(1) *By principal.* The return of an individual proprietor must be signed by the individual. The return of a partnership must be signed by a general partner. The return of a corporation must be signed by an officer. In each case, the person signing the return must designate his or her capacity as "individual owner," "member of firm," or, in the case of a corporation, the officer's title.

(2) *By fiduciary.* A receiver, trustee, assignee, executor, administrator, or other legal representative who continues the business of a bankrupt, insolvent, deceased, or otherwise incapacitated person must indicate the capacity in which the fiduciary acts.

(3) *By agent or attorney in fact.* If a return is signed by an agent or attorney in fact, the signature must be preceded by the name of the principal and followed by the title of the agent or attorney in fact. A return signed by a person as agent will not be accepted unless there is filed, with the TTB office with which the return is required to be filed, a power of attorney authorizing the agent to perform the act.

(d) *Perjury statement.* Each TTB Form 5630.5t must contain, or be verified by, a written declaration that the return has been executed under the penalties of perjury.

(26 U.S.C. 5732, 6061, 6065, 6151, 7011)

(Approved by the Office of Management and Budget under control number 1513–0112)

§ 46.102 Employer identification number.

(a) *Requirement.* The employer identification number (as defined in 26 CFR 301.7701–12) of the taxpayer who has been assigned such a number must be shown on each special tax return, including each amended return, filed under this subpart. Failure of the taxpayer to include the employer identification number may result in the imposition of the penalty specified in § 70.113 of this chapter.

(b) *Application for employer identification number.* Each taxpayer who files a special tax return and who has not already been assigned an employer identification number must file Internal Revenue Service (IRS) Form SS–4 to apply for one. The taxpayer must apply for and be assigned only one employer identification number, regardless of the number of places of business for which the taxpayer is required to file a special tax return. The taxpayer must apply for the employer identification number no later than 7 days after the filing of the taxpayer's first special (occupational) tax return. IRS Form SS–4 may be obtained from the director of an IRS service center, from any IRS district director, or from *http://www.irs.gov/.*

(26 U.S.C. 6109)

§ 46.103 Time for filing return and paying tax.

The return, along with remittance of special tax, must be filed on or before the date of commencing business as a manufacturer of tobacco products, manufacturer of cigarette papers or tubes, or export warehouse proprietor, and thereafter every year on or before July 1. If the return and applicable tax are received in the mail and the U.S. postmark on the cover shows that it was deposited in the mail in the United States within the time prescribed for filing in an envelope or other appropriate wrapper which was properly addressed with postage prepaid, the return will be considered as timely filed. If the postmark is not legible, the sender has the burden of proving the date when the postmark was made. When registered mail is used, the date of registration will be accepted as the postmark date. When certified mail is used, the date of the postmark on the sender's receipt of certified mail is treated as the postmark date.

(26 U.S.C. 5732, 6011, 6071)

§ 46.104 Method of payment.

Payment of special tax must be made in cash, or by check or money order payable to Alcohol and Tobacco Tax and Trade Bureau. If a check or money order so tendered is not honored when presented for payment, the person who tendered the check or money order will remain liable for the payment of the special tax, and for all penalties and additions, to the same extent as if the check or money order had not been tendered. In addition, unless the person who tendered the check or money order can show that the check or money order was issued in good faith, and with reasonable cause to believe that it would be duly paid, there must be paid as penalty an amount equal to 1 percent of the amount of the check or money order, except that if the amount of the check or money order is less than $500, the penalty will be $5, or the amount of the check or money order, whichever is less.

(26 U.S.C. 6311, 6657)

§ 46.105 Receipt for taxes.

Subject to § 46.106, the appropriate TTB officer will issue a receipt to a taxpayer if cash is received as a remittance in payment of special tax (including penalties and interest, if any), or for any type of remittance received if the taxpayer requests a receipt.

§ 46.106 Receipt in lieu of stamp prohibited.

No receipt will be issued in lieu of issuance of a special tax stamp under § 46.116. A receipt may be given only pending the issuance of a stamp, or where the tax liability relates to a prior tax year.

(26 U.S.C. 6314)

§ 46.107 Penalty for failure to file return or to pay tax.

(a) *Failure to file return.* Any person required by this subpart to file a return on TTB Form 5630.5t who fails to file the return on or before the date for filing prescribed in § 46.103 must pay, in addition to the tax, a delinquency penalty, unless it is shown that such failure is due to reasonable cause and not due to willful neglect (see § 46.109). The delinquency penalty for failure to file the return on or before the last date prescribed will be 5 percent of the amount required to be shown as tax on the return if the failure to file is for not more than one month; with an additional 5 percent for each additional month or fraction thereof during which the delinquency continues, but not more than 25 percent in the aggregate.

(b) *Failure to pay tax.* Any person who files a return on TTB Form 5630.5t under this subpart and who fails to pay the amount shown as tax on the return on or before the date prescribed in § 46.103 for payment of such tax, must pay a penalty, in addition to the tax, unless it is shown that such failure is due to reasonable cause and not due to willful neglect (see § 46.109). The penalty for failure to pay the tax on or before the date prescribed for payment is 0.5 percent of the amount shown as tax on the return if the failure to pay is not for more than one month; with an additional 0.5 percent for each additional month or fraction thereof during which the failure continues, but not more than 25 percent in the aggregate. Any person required to pay the special tax who willfully fails to pay the tax shall be fined not more than $5,000, or imprisoned not more than 2 years, or both, for each such offense.

(c) *Limitations.* With respect to any return on Form 5630.5t, the amount of the addition under paragraph (a) of this section will be reduced by the amount of the addition under paragraph (b) of this section for any month to which an addition to tax applies under both paragraph (a) and paragraph (b) of this section. If the amount of tax required to be shown as tax on the return is less than the amount shown as tax on such return, the penalties prescribed in paragraphs (a) and (b) of this section will be applied by substituting that lower amount.

(26 U.S.C. 5731, 6651)

§46.108 Interest on unpaid tax.

(a) *General.* Interest is due on unpaid special tax from the date the tax was required to be paid to the date paid. Interest will be charged for each day at the rate prescribed by law in effect on that day. Interest accruing after December 31, 1982, is compounded daily.

(b) *Adjusted interest rates.* Adjusted interest rates, determined in accordance with the procedure prescribed by 26 U.S.C. 6621(b), are announced quarterly by the Commissioner of Internal Revenue. The appropriate TTB officer will provide information, when requested, regarding interest rates applicable to specific time periods.

(26 U.S.C. 6601, 6621)

§46.109 Waiver of penalties.

In every case where a special tax return is not filed, or the tax is not paid, at the time prescribed in §46.103, the delinquency penalties specified in §46.107 for failure to file a return or for failure to pay the amount shown as tax on the return will be asserted and collected unless a reasonable cause for delay in filing the return or payment of the tax is clearly established. A taxpayer who believes the circumstances that delayed such taxpayer's filing of the return or payment of the tax are reasonable, and who desires to have the penalties waived, must submit with the return a written statement under the penalty of perjury, affirmatively showing all of the circumstances alleged as reasonable causes for delay. If the appropriate TTB officer determines that the delinquency was due to a reasonable cause and not to willful neglect or gross negligence, the addition to the tax will be waived. If the taxpayer exercised ordinary business care and prudence and was nevertheless unable to file the return within the prescribed time, or if the taxpayer made a satisfactory showing that the taxpayer exercised ordinary business care and prudence in providing for payment of the tax liability and was nevertheless either unable to pay the tax or would have suffered an undue hardship if the taxpayer had paid on the due date, then the delay is due to reasonable cause. Mere ignorance of the law will not be considered a reasonable cause.

(26 U.S.C. 6651)

Special Tax Stamps

§46.116 Issuance, distribution, and examination of special tax stamps.

(a) *Issuance of special tax stamps.* Upon filing a properly executed return on TTB Form 5630.5t together with the full tax remittance, the taxpayer will be issued an appropriately designated special tax stamp. If the return covers multiple locations, TTB will send to the taxpayer's principal place of business (or principal office in the case of a corporate taxpayer) one appropriately designated stamp for each location listed on the attachment to TTB Form 5630.5t required by §46.101(b)(2).

(b) *Distribution of special tax stamps for multiple locations.* On receipt of the special tax stamps, the taxpayer must verify that there is one stamp for each location listed on the attachment to TTB Form 5630.5t and that the information on each stamp is correct. The taxpayer must then forward each stamp to the place of business designated on the stamp. Incorrect stamps must be returned to the appropriate TTB officer as provided in §46.120.

(c) *Examination of special tax stamps.* Each stamp denoting payment of special tax must be kept available for inspection by an appropriate TTB officer during business hours at the location for which the stamp is designated.

(26 U.S.C. 5732)

§46.117 Lost or destroyed stamps.

If a special tax stamp has been lost or destroyed, the taxpayer must immediately notify the TTB officer who issued the stamp. A "Certificate in Lieu of Lost or Destroyed Special Tax Stamp" will be issued to the taxpayer who submits an affidavit explaining to the satisfaction of the appropriate TTB officer that the stamp was lost or destroyed. The certificate must be kept available for inspection in the same manner as prescribed for a special tax stamp in § 46.116(c).

§ 46.118 Certificate in lieu of lost or destroyed special tax stamp.

The provisions of this subpart relating to special tax stamps apply as well to certificates in lieu of lost or destroyed special tax stamps issued to taxpayers under § 46.117.

§ 46.119 Errors disclosed by taxpayers.

On receipt of a special tax stamp, the taxpayer must examine it to ensure that the name and address are correctly stated; if not, the taxpayer must return the stamp to the TTB officer who issued it, with a statement showing the nature of the error and the correct name or address. The appropriate TTB officer, on receipt of such stamp and statement, will compare the data on the stamp with that of the Form 5630.5t in TTB files, correct the error if made in the TTB office, and return the stamp to the taxpayer. However, if the error was in the taxpayer's preparation of the Form 5630.5t, the appropriate TTB officer will require the taxpayer to file a new Form 5630.5t, designated "Amended Return," setting forth the taxpayer's correct name and address, and a statement explaining the error on the original Form 5630.5t. On receipt of the amended Form 5630.5t and a satisfactory explanation of the error, the appropriate TTB officer will make the proper correction on the stamp and return it to the taxpayer.

§ 46.120 Errors discovered on inspection.

When a TTB officer discovers on a special tax stamp a material error in the name, ownership, or address of the taxpayer, that officer will require the taxpayer to surrender the erroneous tax stamp and prepare a new Form 5630.5t, designated "Amended Return," showing correctly all of the information required in § 46.101 and containing, in the body of the form or in an attachment thereto, a statement of the reason for requesting correction of the stamp. On receipt of the amended return and an acceptable explanation for the error, the officer will make the proper correction on the stamp and return it to the taxpayer. However, if the error found by the TTB officer is on a special tax stamp issued as a result of a return on Form 5630.5t filed under § 46.101(b), that officer will instruct the taxpayer to return the stamp, with a statement showing the nature of the error and the correct data, to the TTB officer who issued the stamp, for correction in accordance with § 46.119.

CHANGES IN BUSINESSES HOLDING SPECIAL (OCCUPATIONAL) TAX STAMPS

§ 46.126 Change in name or address.

(a) *Change in name.* If there is a change in the corporate or firm name, or in the trade name, as shown on TTB Form 5630.5t, the taxpayer must file an amended special tax return as soon as practicable after the change, covering the new corporate or firm name, or trade name. No new special tax is required to be paid. The taxpayer must attach the special tax stamp for endorsement of the change in name.

(b) *Change in location*—(1) *General.* If there is a change in location of a taxable place of business, the taxpayer must, within 30 days after the change, file with TTB an amended special tax return covering the new location. The taxpayer must attach the special tax stamp or stamps for endorsement of the change in location. No new special tax is required to be paid. However, if the taxpayer does not file the amended return within 30 days, the taxpayer is required to pay a new special tax and obtain a new special tax stamp.

(2) *Procedure.* If the taxpayer's original return on TTB Form 5630.5t covered only one location, the taxpayer may deliver the amended return and the stamp at any TTB office, or to any TTB officer inspecting the business, in lieu of mailing them to TTB. If the taxpayer's original return covered multiple locations under the provisions of § 46.101(b), he or she must forward with the amended return an attachment showing both the old and new address of any place of business which has been relocated, and the special tax stamp covering the location from which the business was removed. The appropriate TTB officer receiving such return or stamp will, if the return is submitted within the 30-day period, enter the

proper endorsement on the stamp and return it to the taxpayer.

(26 U.S.C. 5733, 7011)

§46.127 Change in ownership.

(a) *General.* A special tax stamp is a receipt for tax, personal to the one to whom issued, and is not transferable from one manufacturer of tobacco products, manufacturer of cigarette papers and tubes, or export warehouse proprietor to another. If there is a change in the ownership of a special-tax payer, the successor must pay a new special (occupational) tax and obtain the required special tax stamp(s). Examples of changes in ownership that require payment of a new special tax include, but are not limited to, the following:

(1) Sale of business;

(2) Formation of a partnership by two persons who have paid special tax;

(3) Addition of a partner;

(4) Incorporation of the business;

(5) Creation of a new corporation to replace one or more corporations that have paid special tax; and

(6) Stockholder continuing the business of a corporation after its dissolution.

(b) *Changes that do not require payment of a new special tax.* The following changes do not require payment of a special tax:

(1) Increase in capital stock of a corporation.

(2) Change in ownership of any or all of the capital stock of a corporation.

(c) *Exemption for certain successors.* Persons identified in paragraph (d) of this section as having the right of succession may carry on the business for the remainder of the tax year for which the special tax was paid, without paying a new special tax, if within 30 days after the date on which the successor begins to carry on the business, the successor files with TTB a special tax return on TTB Form 5630.5t showing the basis of succession. A person who is a successor to a business for which special tax has been paid, and who fails to register the succession, is liable for special tax computed from the first day of the calendar month in which the successor began to carry on the business.

(d) *Persons having right of succession.* The right of succession referred to in paragraph (c) of this section will pass to the identified persons in the following circumstances:

(1) *Death.* The surviving spouse or child, or the executor, administrator, or other legal representative, of a deceased taxpayer;

(2) *Succession of spouse.* A husband or wife succeeding to the business of his or her living spouse;

(3) *Insolvency.* A receiver or trustee in bankruptcy, or an assignee for the benefit of creditors;

(4) *Withdrawal from firm.* The partner or partners remaining after the death or withdrawal of a member of a partnership.

(26 U.S.C. 5733)

Stamps for Incorrect Period or Incorrect Liability

§46.131 General.

If a taxpayer through error has filed a return and paid special tax for an incorrect period of liability or for an incorrect class of business, the taxpayer must prepare a corrected TTB Form 5630.5t, designated "Amended Return," for each tax year involved and must submit the amended return, or returns, with remittance for the total applicable tax and additions to the tax (delinquency penalties and interest), to TTB in accordance with the instructions on the Form 5630.5t or, if the error is discovered by a TTB officer inspecting the premises, to that officer. Subject to the limitations imposed by 26 U.S.C. 6511, the incorrectly paid tax (including additions thereto) may be allowed as a credit against the correct tax (including any additions thereto), as provided in §46.132, on surrender of the incorrect stamp or stamps, with the amended return or returns noted to show that credit is requested. Any incorrectly paid tax (including additions thereto) that is not credited as provided in §46.132, including any creditable tax and additions thereto in excess of the correct tax (including additions thereto), may be refunded pursuant to §§46.136 through 46.138 if the taxpayer files a corrected return on Form 5630.5t with remittance of the correct amount of tax (including any additions thereto). A new stamp will be issued only for a current period of liability.

(26 U.S.C. 6011)

§ 46.132 Credit for incorrect stamp.

(a) *General.* The appropriate TTB officer may credit the tax (including additions thereto) paid for an incorrect stamp if the taxpayer has filed an amended return showing the correct tax on TTB Form 5630.5t and has, with the amended return, surrendered the incorrect stamp for credit.

(b) *Underpayment.* Where the correct tax (including any additions thereto) exceeds the incorrect tax paid, the appropriate TTB officer may credit the tax paid against the correct tax upon remittance of the difference between the tax paid and the correct tax plus any additions thereto.

(c) *Overpayment.* Where the tax (and additions thereto) paid for the surrendered incorrect stamp exceeds the amount due, the appropriate TTB officer will advise the taxpayer to file a claim for refund of that excess on TTB Form 5620.8. Sections 46.136 through 46.138 apply to all claims for refund.

(26 U.S.C. 6402, 6511)

ABATEMENT OR REFUND OF SPECIAL TAXES

§ 46.136 Claims.

Claims for abatement of assessment of special tax (including penalties and interest), or for refund of an overpayment of special tax (including interest and penalties), must be filed on TTB Form 5620.8. The claim must be filed with the appropriate TTB officer. Each claim must set forth in detail each ground on which it is based and must contain facts sufficient to explain to the appropriate TTB officer the exact basis for the claim. If the claim is for refund of special tax for which a stamp was issued, either the stamp must be attached to and be made a part of the claim, or the claimant must include in the claim a satisfactory explanation of the reason why the stamp cannot be submitted.

§ 46.137 Time limit on filing of claim for refund.

No claim for the refund of a special tax or penalty will be allowed unless presented within 3 years after the filing of the related tax return or within 2 years after the payment of such tax or penalty, whichever of these periods expires later.

(26 U.S.C. 6511)

§ 46.138 Discontinuance of business.

A dealer who for any reason discontinues business is not entitled to a refund of special tax for the unexpired portion of the tax year for which the special tax stamp was issued.

(26 U.S.C. 5732)

Subparts E–F [Reserved]

Subpart G—Dealers in Tobacco Products

SOURCE: T.D. 6573, 26 FR 8202, Aug. 31, 1961, unless otherwise noted. Redesignated at 40 FR 16835, Apr. 15, 1975.

§ 46.161 Scope of subpart.

The regulations in this subpart relate to the purchase, receipt, possession, offering for sale, or sale or other disposition of tobacco products by dealers in such products.

[T.D. 6871, 81 FR 60, Jan. 4, 1966. Redesignated at 40 FR 16835, Apr. 15, 1975 and amended by T.D. ATF–232, 51 FR 28092, Aug. 5, 1986; T.D. ATF–243, 51 FR 43194, Dec. 1, 1986]

§ 46.162 Territorial extent.

The provisions of the regulations in this subpart shall apply in the several States of the United States and the District of Columbia.

§ 46.163 Meaning of terms.

When used in this subpart, where not otherwise distinctly expressed or manifestly incompatible with the intent thereof, each of the following terms shall have the meaning ascribed in this section. Words in the plural form shall include the singular, words in the singular form shall include the plural, and words importing the masculine gender shall include the feminine. The terms "includes" and "including" do not exclude things not enumerated which are in the same general class.

Appropriate TTB officer. An officer or employee of the Alcohol and Tobacco Tax and Trade Bureau (TTB) authorized to perform any functions relating to the administration or enforcement of this part by TTB Order 1135.46, Delegation of the Administrator's Authorities in 27 CFR Part 46, Miscellaneous Regulations Relating to Tobacco Products and Cigarette Papers and Tubes.

Dealer. Any person who sells, or offers for sale, at wholesale or retail levels, any cigars or cigarettes after removal.

Manufacturer of tobacco products. Any person who manufactures cigars, cigarettes, smokeless tobacco, pipe tobacco, or roll-your-own tobacco but does not include:

(1) A person who produces tobacco products solely for that person's own consumption or use; or

(2) A proprietor of a Customs bonded manufacturing warehouse with respect to the operation of such warehouse.

Package. The container in which tobacco products are put up by the manufacturer or the importer and offered for delivery to the consumer.

Person. An individual, partnership, association, company, corporation, estate, or trust.

Removal or remove. The removal of tobacco products from the factory or release from Customs custody, including the smuggling or other unlawful importation of such articles into the United States.

Tobacco Products. Cigars, cigarettes, smokeless tobacco, pipe tobacco, and roll-your-own tobacco.

U.S.C. The United States Code.

[T.D. 6573, 26 FR 8202, Aug. 31, 1961, as amended by T.D. 6871, 31 FR 60, Jan. 4, 1966. Redesignated at 40 FR 16835, Apr. 15, 1975]

EDITORIAL NOTE: For FEDERAL REGISTER citations affecting §46.163, see the List of CFR Sections Affected, which appears in the Finding Aids section of the printed volume and at *www.fdsys.gov.*

§46.164 Authority of TTB officers to enter premises.

Any appropriate TTB officer may enter in the daytime any premises where tobacco products are kept or stored, so far as it may be necessary for the purpose of examining such products. When such premises are open at night, any appropriate TTB officer may enter them, while so open, in the performance of his official duties. The owner of such premises, or person having the superintendence of the same, who refuses to admit any appropriate TTB officer or permit him to examine such products shall be liable to the penalties prescribed by law for the offense. Operators of vending machines shall make the tobacco products in their machines available for inspection upon the request of any appropriate TTB officer.

(68A Stat. 872, 903; 26 U.S.C. 7342, 7606)

[T.D. 6871, 31 FR 60, Jan. 4, 1966. Redesignated at 40 FR 16835, Apr. 15, 1975 and amended by T.D. ATF-232, 51 FR 28092, Aug. 5, 1986; T.D. ATF-243, 51 FR 43194, Dec. 1, 1986; T.D. ATF-472, 67 FR 8881, Feb. 27, 2002]

§46.165 Interference with administration.

Whoever, corruptly or by force or threats of force, endeavors to hinder or obstruct the administration of this subpart, or endeavors to intimidate or impede any appropriate TTB officer acting in his official capacity, or forcibly rescues or attempts to rescue or causes to be rescued any property, after it has been duly seized for forfeiture to the United States in connection with a violation of the internal revenue laws, shall be liable to the penalties prescribed by law.

(68A Stat. 855; 26 U.S.C. 7212)

[T.D. 6573, 26 FR 8202, Aug. 31, 1961. Redesignated at 40 FR 16835, Apr. 15, 1975, as amended by T.D. ATF-472, Feb. 27, 2002]

§46.166 Dealing in tobacco products.

(a) All tobacco products purchased, received, possessed, offered for sale, sold or otherwise disposed of, by any dealer must be in proper packages which bear the mark or notice as prescribed in parts 40 and 41 of this chapter. Tobacco products may be sold, or offered for sale, at retail from such packages, provided the products remain in the packages until removed by the customer or in the presence of the customer. Where a vending machine is used, tobacco products must similarly be vended in proper packages or directly from such packages.

(b) Tobacco products manufactured in the United States and labeled for exportation under chapter 52 of title 26, U.S.C. may not be sold or held for sale for domestic consumption in the United States unless such articles are removed from their export packaging and repackaged by the original manufacturer into new packaging that does not contain an export label. This applies to articles labeled for export even if the packaging or the appearance of such packaging to the consumer of such articles has been modified or altered by a person other than the original manufacturer so as to remove or conceal or attempt to remove or conceal (including by placement of a sticker over) the export label.

(c) For penalty and forfeiture provisions applicable to the selling, relanding or receipt of articles which have been labeled or shipped for exportation, see § 41.83 of this chapter.

[T.D. ATF–465, 66 FR 45618, Aug. 29, 2001, as amended by T.D. TTB–16, 69 FR 52423, Aug. 26, 2004]

§ 46.167 Liability to tax.

Any dealer who, with intent to defraud the United States, possesses tobacco products (a) upon which the tax has not been paid or determined in the manner and at the time prescribed in parts 40 and 41 of this chapter or (b) which, after removal without payment of tax pursuant to section 5704, I.R.C., and regulations issued thereunder, have been diverted from the applicable purpose or use specified in that section or (c) which are not put up in packages prescribed in parts 40 and 41 of this chapter or are put up in packages not bearing the marks and notices prescribed in such regulations shall be liable for a tax equal to the tax on such products.

(72 Stat. 1424; 26 U.S.C. 5751)

[T.D. 6871, 31 FR 60, Jan. 4, 1966. Redesignated at 40 FR 16835, Apr. 15, 1975, and amended by T.D. ATF–232, 51 FR 28092, Aug. 5, 1986; T.D. ATF–243, 51 FR 43194, Dec. 1, 1986; T.D. ATF–460, 66 FR 390 93, July 27, 2001; T.D. TTB–16, 69 FR 52423, Aug. 26, 2004]

§ 46.168 Liability to penalties and forfeitures.

Any dealer who fails to comply with the provisions of this subpart becomes liable to the civil and criminal penalties, and forfeitures, provided by law.

(72 Stat. 1425, 1426; 26 U.S.C. 5761, 5762, and 5763)

Subpart H [Reserved]

Subpart I—Floor Stocks Tax on Certain Tobacco Products, Cigarette Papers, and Cigarette Tubes Held for Sale on April 1, 2009

AUTHORITY: Section 701, Pub. L. 111–3, unless otherwise noted.

SOURCE: T.D. TTB–75, 74 FR 14486, Mar. 31, 2009, unless otherwise noted.

GENERAL

§ 46.191 Purpose of this subpart.

The regulations in this subpart implement the floor stocks tax on certain tobacco products, cigarette papers, and cigarette tubes held for sale on April 1, 2009.

§ 46.192 Definitions used in this subpart.

As used in this subpart, the following terms have the meanings indicated unless the context in which they are used requires a different meaning or a different definition is prescribed for a particular section or portion of this subpart.

(a) *Appropriate TTB officer.* An officer or employee of the Alcohol and Tobacco Tax and Trade Bureau (TTB) authorized to perform any functions relating to the administration or enforcement of this part by TTB Order 1135.46, Delegation of the Administrator's Authorities in 27 CFR 46, Miscellaneous Regulations Relating to Tobacco Products and Cigarette Papers and Tubes.

(b) *Articles subject to floor stocks tax.* All Federally taxpaid or tax determined tobacco products (other than large cigars described in 26 U.S.C.

5701(a)(2)), cigarette papers, and cigarette tubes that are held for sale on April 1, 2009.

(c) *Cigarette paper.* Paper, or any other material except tobacco, prepared for use as a cigarette wrapper.

(d) *Cigarette tube.* Cigarette paper made into a hollow cylinder for use in making cigarettes.

(e) *Controlled group.* A related group of dealers under common control. Controlled groups include:

(1) *Controlled group of corporations.* The term "controlled group of corporations" has the meaning given to that term by 26 U.S.C. 1563(a) and the implementing regulations in 26 CFR 1.1563–1 through 1.1563–4, except that the phrase "more than 50 percent" shall be substituted for the phrase "at least 80 percent" each time it appears. Controlled groups of corporations include, but are not limited to:

(i) Parent-subsidiary controlled groups as defined in 26 CFR 1.1563–1T(a)(2).

(ii) Brother-sister controlled groups as defined in 26 CFR 1.1563–1T(a)(3).

(iii) Combined groups as defined in 26 CFR 1.1563–1T(a)(4).

(2) *Nonincorporated dealers under common control.* A group of dealers is considered to be a controlled group when the group would qualify as a controlled group of corporations, except for the fact that one or more of the dealers is not incorporated.

(f) *Dealer.* A person or other entity holding articles subject to floor stocks tax for sale on April 1, 2009, including manufacturers, importers, wholesalers, and retailers.

(g) *Floor stocks tax.* A tax imposed on all Federally taxpaid or tax determined tobacco products (other than large cigars described in 26 U.S.C. 5701(a)(2)), cigarette papers, and cigarette tubes held for sale on April 1, 2009. The floor stocks tax is the difference between the previous excise tax rate and the new excise tax rate.

(h) *Foreign trade zone.* A foreign trade zone established and operated pursuant to the Act of June 18, 1934, as amended, 19 U.S.C. 81a.

(i) *Person.* An individual, trust, estate, partnership, association, company, or corporation, any State, including the District of Columbia, or political subdivision thereof, or any agency or instrumentality of a State or political subdivision thereof.

(j) *Tobacco products.* Cigars, cigarettes, snuff, chewing tobacco, pipe tobacco, and roll-your-own tobacco as described in 26 U.S.C. 5702(a), (b), (m)(2), (m)(3), (n) and (o), respectively.

§46.193 Persons liable for floor stocks tax.

A dealer who holds for sale any articles subject to floor stocks tax on April 1, 2009, is liable for floor stocks tax. See §§46.204 and 46.205 regarding articles subject to floor stocks tax that are in transit on April 1, 2009 and §46.206 regarding articles subject to floor stocks tax that are held in a foreign trade zone on April 1, 2009.

§46.194 Persons not liable for floor stocks tax.

A person who does not meet the definition of a dealer is not liable for the floor stocks tax under this subpart.

§46.195 Floor stocks requirements.

(a) *Take inventory.* The dealer must establish the quantity of articles subject to the floor stocks tax held for sale on April 1, 2009. The dealer may take a physical inventory or may use a record (book) inventory, as specified in §46.202 or §46.203.

(b) *Compute tax.* The dealer must compute the amount of tax for the articles held for sale on April 1, 2009. Refer to the table in §46.222. The dealer may apply the tax credit as provided in §46.223.

(c) *File tax return and pay tax.* After computing the floor stocks tax, the dealer must file a return even if no tax is due. See §46.233 for payment methods if tax is due.

(d) *Maintain records.* The dealer must maintain all records used to determine the quantity of articles subject to floor stocks tax and the quantity of articles held for sale on April 1, 2009 that are not subject to floor stocks tax. The dealer must also maintain records of all computations used to determine the amount of tax owed. Refer to §46.241.

(Approved by the Office of Management and Budget under control number 1513–0129)

INVENTORIES

§ 46.201 General.

(a) *Date.* The dealer must take an inventory to establish the quantities of articles subject to the floor stocks tax held for sale on April 1, 2009. The dealer must take the physical inventory or record (book) inventory not earlier than March 26, 2009 and not later than April 10, 2009.

(b) *Reconciliation.* If the dealer takes a physical inventory on any day other than April 1, 2009, the resulting records must be reconciled to reflect the actual quantity of articles held at 12:01 a.m. on April 1, 2009. These records must include all supporting records of receipt and disposition.

(c) *Method.* The dealer may take a physical inventory in accordance with § 46.202 or a record (book) inventory in accordance with § 46.203. The following table lists the taxable articles and the method to use for each to determine quantities:

Article	Inventory method
Small cigarettes	Count the number of cigarettes.
Large cigarettes 6½″ or less in length.	Count the number of large cigarettes.
Large cigarettes more than 6½″ in length.	Keep a separate count for each size of large cigarette. Count each 2¾″, or fraction thereof, as one small cigarette.
Small Cigars	Count the number of small cigars.
Snuff	Count the number of packages at each weight, noting the weight in pounds and ounces. Convert the ounces to pounds.
Chewing tobacco	Count the number of packages at each weight, noting the weight in pounds and ounces. Convert the ounces to pounds.
Pipe tobacco	Count the number of packages at each weight, noting the weight in pounds and ounces. Convert the ounces to pounds.
Roll-your-own tobacco.	Count the number of packages at each weight, noting the weight in pounds and ounces. Convert the ounces to pounds.
Cigarette papers 6½″ or less in length.	Count the number of cigarette papers, divide by 50, and round up if there is any remainder.
Cigarette papers more than 6½″ in length.	Count the number for each size of cigarette paper. Count each 2¾″, or fraction thereof, as new cigarette paper. Divide adjusted total by 50 and round up if there is any remainder.
Cigarette tubes 6½″ or less in length.	Count the number of cigarette tubes, divide by 50, and round up if there is any remainder.
Cigarette tubes more than 6½″ in length.	Count the number for each size of cigarette tube. Count each 2¾″, or fraction thereof, as one cigarette tube. Divide adjusted total by 50 and round up if there is any remainder.

§ 46.202 Physical inventory requirements.

The dealer's physical inventory must result in a written record of:

(a) The quantity and type of each article subject to floor stocks tax recorded in sufficient detail to determine the tax rate as stated in § 46.222. See the table in § 46.201(c) for the information required for each type of article;

(b) The date and time the inventory was taken;

(c) The name of the individual(s) conducting the inventory and the name of the dealer for whom the inventory was taken; and

(d) The location where the inventory was taken (street address, city and State).

(Approved by the Office of Management and Budget under control number 1513–0129)

§ 46.203 Record (book) inventory requirements.

(a) The dealer may use a record (book) inventory if the dealer has source records that show:

(1) The quantities of receipts and dispositions of all articles subject to floor stocks tax;

(2) The types and quantities of articles actually on hand as if a physical inventory had taken place on April 1, 2009. See the table in § 46.201(c) for the information required for each type of article;

(3) The name and address of the consignor and consignee. For over the counter sales by retail dealers, the consignee name and address is not required;

(4) The date of receipt or disposition of the articles; and

(5) The brand name of each product.

(b) If the dealer does not take the inventory as of the close of business on the last business day before April 1, 2009, the records must be reconciled as provided in § 46.201(b).

(Approved by the Office of Management and Budget under control number 1513–0129)

§46.204 Articles in transit.

The dealer must include articles subject to floor stocks tax that are in transit in the inventory if the dealer holds title to those articles. If the dealer has transferred title to the article, the dealer must document the title transfer in writing. For example, the dealer may mark the bill of lading with a written statement that indicates the time and place of the title transfer.

(Approved by the Office of Management and Budget under control number 1513–0129)

§46.205 Guidelines to determine title to articles in transit.

The dealer may use the following guidelines to establish who holds title to articles in transit.

(a) If State law mandates the change in title, then no agreement or contract between seller and buyer can alter it.

(b) In the absence of State law governing the change of title between seller and buyer, the Uniform Commercial Code allows the seller and buyer to agree when title passes.

(c) If there is no State law or agreement between the seller and buyer, the Uniform Commercial Code states that title transfer depends on how the seller ships the articles.

(1) If the shipment is free on board (F.O.B.) destination, the title transfer occurs when the seller completes the physical delivery of the articles.

(2) If the shipment is free on board (F.O.B.) shipping point, the title transfer occurs at the time and place of shipment, which is generally by common carrier.

§46.206 Articles in a foreign trade zone.

If articles subject to floor stocks tax are stored in a foreign trade zone established under the Foreign Trade Zone Act (the Act of June 18, 1934, 48 Stat. 998, 19 U.S.C. 81a *et seq.*), the dealer is liable for the tax and must take an inventory in accordance with §46.207 or when either of the following conditions apply:

(a) Internal revenue taxes have been determined or customs duties liquidated, with respect to the articles pursuant to the first proviso of section 3(a) of the Foreign Trade Zone Act; or

(b) Articles are held by a customs officer pursuant to the second proviso of section 3(a) of the Foreign Trade Zone Act.

§46.207 Articles held in bond.

If the dealer is a manufacturer or an export warehouse proprietor and holds articles in TTB bond on April 1, 2009, the floor stocks tax does not apply to those articles. Likewise, if the dealer holds articles in a customs bonded warehouse on which tax has not been paid or determined, the floor stocks tax does not apply on those articles. However, if the dealer on April 1, 2009, holds articles in a customs bonded warehouse or foreign trade zone on which tax has been paid or determined pursuant to 26 U.S.C. 5703(b)(2)(B), the floor stocks tax applies to those articles.

§46.208 Unmerchantable articles.

Articles that the dealer holds for return to a supplier because of some defect are not subject to the floor stocks tax. However, the dealer must segregate any such unmerchantable articles and include them in a separate section of the inventory record. The dealer cannot include as unmerchantable any items that may be held because of poor market demand or to reduce the dealer's inventory. If, for any reason, the tobacco products or cigarette papers or tubes that were determined to be unmerchantable are not subsequently returned or destroyed, the dealer must file an additional floor stocks tax return and pay tax on such products plus any applicable penalties and interest.

(Approved by the Office of Management and Budget under control number 1513–0129)

§46.209 Articles in vending machines.

There is no exemption for articles in vending machines. They are subject to the floor stocks tax and must be included in the dealer's inventory record.

§46.210 Articles marked "not for sale" or "complimentary".

Articles marked "not for sale" or "complimentary" that are part of a sale (for example, buy two packs and get one pack free) are subject to the floor stocks tax and must be included in the physical or record (book) inventory as provided in §§ 46.202 or § 46.203.

TAX LIABILITY CALCULATION

§ 46.221 Floor stocks tax rates.

Product	Floor stocks tax rate
Small cigars	$48.502 per thousand.
Small cigarettes	30.83 per thousand.
Large cigarettes 6½ inch or less in length.	64.74 per thousand.
Large cigarettes more than 6½ inch in length.	30.83 per thousand units of length.
Snuff	0.925 per pound.
Chewing tobacco	0.3083 per pound.
Pipe tobacco	1.7342 per pound.
Roll-your-own	23.6831 per pound.
Cigarette papers	0.0193 per 50 papers or fraction thereof
Cigarette tubes	0.0386 per 50 tubes or fraction thereof.

§ 46.222 Determination of amount of tax due.

After the dealer has taken the inventory, the dealer must convert the inventory quantities to taxable units using the table below. For tobacco products, round the quantities to two decimal places. The dealer must then apply the applicable tax rate for each type of taxable article using the table in § 46.221 to determine the amount of tax due.

Product	Computation
Small cigars weighing not more than 3 pounds thousand.	Divide number of cigars by 1,000 and multiply by the small cigar tax rate.
Small cigarettes weighing not more than 3 pounds thousand.	Divide number of cigarettes by 1,000 and multiply by the small cigarette tax rate.
Large cigarettes weighing more than 3 pounds thousand, measuring 6½″ or less in length.	Divide number of cigarettes by 1,000 and multiply by the large cigarette tax rate.
Large cigarettes weighing more than 3 pounds thousand, measuring more than 6½″ in length.	Mathematically adjust the number of large cigarettes using the instructions below.* Divide the adjusted number of large cigarettes by 1,000 and multiply by the small cigarette tax rate.
Snuff	Multiply the total in pounds by the snuff tax rate.
Chewing tobacco	Multiply the total in pounds by the chewing tobacco tax rate.
Pipe tobacco	Multiply the total in pounds by the pipe tobacco tax rate.
Roll-your-own	Multiply the total in pounds by the roll-your-own tax rate.
Cigarette papers 6½″ or less in length.	Divide the number of cigarette papers by 50, add 1 if there is a remainder, and multiply that number by the cigarette paper tax rate.
Cigarette papers more than 6½″ in length.	Mathematically adjust the number of cigarette papers using the instructions below.* Divide the adjusted number of cigarette papers by 50, add 1 if there is a remainder, and multiply that number by the cigarette paper tax rate.
Cigarette tubes 6½″ or less in length.	Divide the number of cigarette tubes by 50, add 1 if there is a remainder, and multiply that number by the cigarette tube tax rate.
Cigarette tubes more than 6½″ in length.	Mathematically adjust the number of cigarette tubes using the instructions below.* Divide the adjusted number of cigarette tubes by 50, add 1 if there is a remainder, and multiply that number by the cigarette tube tax rate.

*Large cigarettes, cigarette papers, and cigarette tubes more than 6½ inch in length are counted as multiple units. Each 2¾ inch or fraction of the length is counted as a separate taxable unit. For each different length of product in this category, divide the length by 2¾ inch and add 1 to the result if there is a remainder. Multiply the number of cigarettes, cigarette papers, or tubes of that length by the resulting number.

§ 46.223 Tax credit.

The dealer is allowed a credit of up to $500 against the total floor stocks tax. However, controlled groups are eligible for only one credit for the entire group. The credit may be divided equally among the members or apportioned in any other manner agreeable to the members.

FILING REQUIREMENTS

§ 46.231 Floor stocks tax return.

Form 5000.28T09, 2009 Floor Stocks Tax Return—Tobacco Products and Cigarette Papers and Tubes, is available for printing through the TTB Web site (*http://www.ttb.gov*) or by mailing a request to the Alcohol and Tobacco Tax and Trade Bureau, National Revenue Center, 550 Main Street, Suite 8002, Cincinnati, OH 45202–5215.

§ 46.232 Preparation of floor stocks tax return.

The dealer must complete and file the floor stocks tax return in accordance with the instructions for the form.

§ 46.233 Payment of floor stocks tax.

(a) *Electronic funds transfer.* If the dealer pays any other excise taxes collected by TTB by electronic funds transfer, then the dealer must also send the payment for the floor stocks tax by an electronic funds transfer.

Other dealers may voluntarily elect to pay the floor stocks tax by electronic funds transfer. Electronic funds transfers of floor stocks tax must be received on or before July 31, 2009.

(b) *Check or money order*. Dealers not paying floor stocks tax by electronic fund transfer must pay by a check or money order sent with Form 5000.28T09.

§ 46.234 Tax payment deadline.

Section 701 of Public Law 111–3 specifies a tax payment deadline of August 1, 2009. However, section 5703(b)(2)(E) of the Internal Revenue Code requires that when a due date falls on a Saturday, Sunday or a legal holiday, the preceding day that is not a Saturday, Sunday or legal holiday will be the due date. Therefore, the floor stocks tax is due on July 31, 2009, since August 1, 2009, falls on a Saturday.

§ 46.235 Filing requirements for multiple locations.

The dealer may file a consolidated return if all locations or places of business have the same employer identification number. The dealer also has the option of filing a separate return for each place of business or location.

§ 46.236 Articles in a warehouse.

(a) Articles warehoused at one or more locations must be reported on the tax return representing the location where the articles will be offered for sale.

(b) Articles offered for sale at several locations must be reported on a tax return filed by one or more of the locations. The articles can be reported by a single location or apportioned among several locations.

§ 46.237 Controlled group member.

If the dealer is a member of a controlled group, but has its own employer identification number, the dealer must file a separate floor stocks tax return. The dealer may take the tax credit referred to in § 46.223 if it is apportioned to the dealer as a member of the controlled group.

RECORDS

§ 46.241 Required records.

The dealer must maintain:

(a) Inventory records;

(b) Tax computation records;

(c) Names, addresses and employer identification numbers of all controlled group members, if applicable;

(d) A copy of the tax return, if the dealer filed one;

(e) A list of locations covered by the tax return; and

(f) A copy of any alternate method or procedure approval issued under § 46.263.

(Approved by the Office of Management and Budget under control number 1513–0129)

§ 46.242 Period for maintaining records.

The dealer must maintain the required records for a period of three years from the due date of the tax return or the date the return was filed, whichever is later. However, the appropriate TTB officer may require, in writing, that the dealer keep these records for an additional period of not more than 3 years.

(Approved by the Office of Management and Budget under control number 1513–0129)

§ 46.243 Articles at multiple locations.

The dealer must maintain a list of all places where the dealer holds articles subject to the floor stocks tax. This list must include:

(a) Address;

(b) Name of the proprietor (if different);

(c) The employer identification number (if different); and

(d) Types and quantities of articles held at each location.

(Approved by the Office of Management and Budget under control number 1513–0129)

§ 46.244 Location of records.

The dealer must keep the inventory records at the principal place of business. All records must be made available to an appropriate TTB officer upon demand.

(Approved by the Office of Management and Budget under control number 1513–0129)

§ 46.245 Errors in records.

If the inventory records or tax computation records contain an error that resulted in an overpayment of tax, the dealer may file a claim for refund. If the inventory or tax computation records contain an error that resulted in an underpayment of tax, the dealer must file an additional tax return on which the dealer shows and pays the additional tax, interest and any applicable penalties.

(Approved by the Office of Management and Budget under control number 1513–0129)

CLAIMS

§ 46.251 Payment of tax required.

Before the dealer can file a claim for refund, the dealer must have paid the floor stocks tax and subsequently determined that there was an overpayment of the tax.

§ 46.252 Claim based on error on return.

If the dealer overpaid tax due to an error on the return, the dealer may file a claim for refund. The claim must be filed within 3 years from the date the tax return was filed or 2 years from the time the tax was paid, whichever is later. The dealer's claim must be filed on TTB Form 2635 (5620.8). The claim must include detailed and sufficient evidence explaining why the dealer believes the tax was overpaid. The claim and supporting documentation must be mailed or delivered to the address shown on the form.

(Approved by the Office of Management and Budget under control number 1513–0030)

§ 46.253 Destruction of articles by a Presidentially-declared major disaster.

After the dealer has paid the floor stocks tax, the dealer may file a claim for refund of tax on articles lost, rendered unmarketable, or condemned because of a Presidentially-declared major disaster. Subpart C of this part prescribes the time, evidence, and procedures for filing such a claim.

§ 46.254 Additional reasons for filing a claim.

(a) *Manufacturer.* Subparts I and K of part 40 of this chapter prescribe the times, reasons and procedures for filing other claims for refunds.

(b) *Export warehouse proprietor.* Subpart G of part 44 of this chapter prescribes the time, evidence, and procedures for filing other claims for refunds.

(c) *Exported taxpaid.* If taxpaid articles are shipped from the United States, the dealer may file a claim for drawback of taxes under subpart K of part 44 of this chapter.

(d) *Importer.* An importer may follow the procedures for filing a claim as set forth in subpart I of part 41 of this chapter.

ALTERNATE METHODS OR PROCEDURES

§ 46.261 Purpose of an alternate method or procedure.

For purposes of this subpart, an alternate method or procedure is a different way of meeting a requirement imposed by this subpart. An alternate method or procedure must be approved in writing by TTB.

§ 46.262 Application.

The dealer seeking approval of an alternate method or procedure under this subpart must apply in writing to the National Revenue Center, 550 Main Street, Room 8002, Cincinnati, Ohio 45202–5215. The dealer must describe the alternate method or procedure and reasons the dealer wishes to use it. The dealer cannot use the alternate method until the dealer receives written approval from the appropriate TTB officer.

§ 46.263 Conditions for approval.

The alternate method or procedure may be approved if it meets all of the following conditions:

(a) There is good cause for its use;

(b) It is consistent with the purpose and effect intended by the prescribed method or procedure;

(c) It affords equivalent security to the revenue;

(d) It is not contrary to any provision of law;

(e) It will not result in an increase in cost to the Government;

(f) It will not hinder the effective administration of this subpart such as delaying timely payment of taxes; and

(g) It is not a method or procedure that relates to the payment or collection of tax.

§46.264 Withdrawal of an approval.

The approval will be withdrawn if revenue is jeopardized or administration of this subpart is hindered. The appropriate TTB officer will give the dealer a written notice of the withdrawal.

TTB AUTHORITIES

§46.270 [Reserved]

§46.271 Entry, examination and testimony.

Appropriate TTB officers, in performing official duties, may enter any premises to examine articles subject to floor stocks tax. They may enter the premises during the day or may also enter at night if the premises are open. Appropriate TTB officers may audit and examine all articles, inventory records, books, papers, or other resource data for the purpose of ascertaining, determining, or collecting floor stocks tax. They may take testimony, under oath, of any person when inquiring as to proper payment of floor stocks taxes.

§46.272 Issuance of summons.

Appropriate TTB officers can issue summonses when there is no referral to the Justice Department under the authority stated in §70.22 of this chapter. The summons will state a place and time for such items or person to appear. TTB will issue a summons to require:

(a) Any books of account or other data pertaining to liability for floor stocks tax;

(b) Any person liable for the floor stocks tax or having possession of books of account or other data; and

(c) Any other appropriate person in connection with the books or tax liability.

§46.273 Refusing entry or examination.

If the dealer or another person in charge of the premises refuses to admit any appropriate TTB officer or prevents any appropriate TTB officer from examining the records or articles, the dealer may be liable for the penalties described in 26 U.S.C. 7342 or 7212.

§46.274 Penalties for failure to comply.

If the dealer fails to follow the regulations set forth in this subpart, TTB may apply applicable civil and criminal penalties under the Internal Revenue Code of 1986. For example, failure to file and failure to pay penalties may be assessed against the dealer if the dealer does not timely file the tax return or timely pay the taxes due. In addition, interest under 26 U.S.C. 6621 accrues for any underpayment of tax and on all assessed penalties until paid.

SUBCHAPTER C—FIREARMS

PART 53—MANUFACTURERS EXCISE TAXES—FIREARMS AND AMMUNITION

Subpart A—Introduction

Subpart B—Definitions

Subpart C—Administrative and Miscellaneous Provisions

Subparts D–F [Reserved]

Subpart G—Tax Rates

Subparts H–I [Reserved]

Subpart J—Special Provisions Applicable to Manufacturers Taxes

USE BY MANUFACTURER OR IMPORTER CONSIDERED SALE

APPLICATION OF TAX IN CASE OF SALES BY OTHER THAN MANUFACTURER OR IMPORTER

Subpart K—Exemptions, Registration, Etc.

Subpart L—Refunds and Other Administrative Provisions of Special Application to Manufacturers Taxes

AUTHORITY: 26 U.S.C. 4181, 4182, 4216–4219, 4221–4223, 4225, 6001, 6011, 6020, 6021, 6061, 6071, 6081, 6091, 6101–6104, 6109, 6151, 6155, 6161, 6301–6303, 6311, 6402, 6404, 6416, 7502, 7805.

SOURCE: T.D. ATF–308, 56 FR 303, Jan. 3, 1991, unless otherwise noted.

EDITORIAL NOTE: Nomenclature changes to part 53 appear by T.D. ATF–447, 66 FR 19088, Apr. 13, 2001.

Subpart A—Introduction

§53.1 Introduction.

The regulations in this part (part 53, subchapter C, chapter I, title 27, Code of Federal Regulations) are designated "Manufacturers Excise Taxes—Firearms and Ammunition." The regulations relate to the tax on the sale of firearms and ammunition imposed by section 4181 of the Internal Revenue Code of 1986, and to certain related administrative provisions of chapter 32, subchapter F, of the Code. Chapter 32, subchapter D of the Code imposes taxes on the sale or use by the manufacturer, producer, or importer of certain recreational equipment specified in that chapter. References in the regulations in this part to the "Internal Revenue Code" or the "Code" are references to the Internal Revenue Code of 1986 (United States Code of 1986), as amended, unless otherwise indicated. References to a section or other provision of law are references to a section or other provision of the Internal Revenue Code of 1986, as amended, unless otherwise indicated.

§53.2 Attachment of tax.

(a) For purposes of this part, the manufacturers excise tax generally attaches when the title to the article sold passes from the manufacturer to a purchaser.

(b) When title passes is dependent upon the intention of the parties as gathered from the contract of sale and the attendant circumstances. In the absence of expressed intention, the legal rules of presumption followed in the jurisdiction where the sale is made govern in determining when title passes.

(c) In the case of a sale on credit, the tax attaches whether or not the purchase price is actually collected.

(d) Where a consignor (such as a manufacturer) consigns articles to a consignee (such as a dealer), retaining ownership in them until they are disposed of by the consignee, title does not pass, and the tax does not attach until sale by the consignee. Where the relationship between a manufacturer and a dealer is that of principal and agent, title does not pass, and the tax does not attach, until sale by the dealer.

(e) In the case of a lease, an installment sale, a conditional sale, or a chattel mortgage arrangement or similar arrangement creating a security interest, a proportionate part of the tax attaches to each payment. See section 4217 and §§53.103 and 53.104 for a limitation on the amount of tax payable on lease payments.

(f) In the case of use by the manufacturer, the tax attaches at the time the use begins.

§ 53.3 Exemption certificates.

Several provisions of this part, relating to sales exempt from manufacturers excise tax, require the manufacturer to obtain an exemption certificate from the purchaser to substantiate the exempt character of the sale. Any form of exemption certificate will be acceptable if it includes all the information required by the provisions of this part. These certificates are available as preprinted documents, which may be ordered by mailing a request to the Alcohol and Tobacco Tax and Trade Bureau, National Revenue Center, 550 Main Street, Room 1516, Cincinnati, OH 45202. The preprinted certificates may be reproduced as needed.

[T.D. TTB–44, 71 FR 16957, Apr. 4, 2006]

Subpart B—Definitions

§ 53.11 Meaning of terms.

When used in this part and in forms prescribed under this part, where not otherwise distinctly expressed or manifestly incompatible with the intent thereof, terms shall have the meanings ascribed in this section. Words in the plural form shall include the singular, and vice versa, and words importing the masculine gender shall include the feminine. The terms "includes" and "including" do not exclude other things not enumerated which are in the same general class or are otherwise within the scope thereof.

Administrator. The Administrator, Alcohol and Tobacco Tax and Trade Bureau, Department of the Treasury, Washington, DC.

Appropriate TTB officer. An officer or employee of the Alcohol and Tobacco Tax and Trade Bureau (TTB) authorized to perform any functions relating to the administration or enforcement of this part by TTB Order 1135.53, Delegation of the Administrator's Authorities in 27 CFR Part 53, Manufacturers Excise Taxes—Firearms and Ammunition.

Calendar quarter. A period of 3 calendar months ending on March 31, June 30, September 30, or December 31.

Calendar year. The period which begins January 1 and ends on the following December 31.

Chapter 32. For purposes of this part chapter 32 means section 4181, chapter 32, of the Internal Revenue Code of 1986, as amended.

Code. Internal Revenue Code of 1986, as amended.

Electronic fund transfer (EFT). Any transfer of funds effected by a taxpayer's financial institution, either directly or through a correspondent banking relationship, via the Federal Reserve Communications System (FRCS) or Fedwire to the Treasury Account at the Federal Reserve Bank.

Exportation. The severance of an article from the mass of things belonging within the United States with the intention of uniting it with the mass of things belonging within some foreign country or within a possession of the United States.

Exporter. The person named as shipper or consignor in the export bill of lading.

Financial institution. A bank or other financial institution, whether or not a member of the Federal Reserve System, which has access to the Federal Reserve Communications Systems (FRCS) or Fedwire. The "FRCS" or "Fedwire" is a communications network that allows Federal Reserve System member financial institutions to effect a transfer of funds for their customers (or other financial institutions) to the Treasury Account at the Federal Reserve Bank.

Firearms. Any portable weapons, such as rifles, carbines, machine guns, shotguns, or fowling pieces, from which a shot, bullet, or other projectile may be discharged by an explosive.

Importer. Any person who brings a taxable article into the United States from a source outside the United States, or who withdraws such an article from a customs bonded warehouse for sale or use in the United States. If the nominal importer of a taxable article is not its beneficial owner (for example, the nominal importer is a customs broker engaged by the beneficial owner), the beneficial owner is the "importer" of the article for purposes of chapter 32 of the Code and is liable for tax on his sale or use of the article in the United States. See section 4219 of the Code and 27 CFR 53.121 for the circumstances under which sales by persons other than the manufacturer or importer are subject to the manufacturers excise tax.

Knockdown condition. A taxable article that is unassembled but complete as to all component parts.

Manufacturer. Includes any person who produces a taxable article from scrap, salvage, or junk material, or from new or raw material, by processing, manipulating, or changing the form of an article or by combining or assembling two or more articles. The term also includes a "producer" and an "importer." Under certain circumstances, as where a person manufactures or produces a taxable article for another person who furnishes materials under an agreement whereby the person who furnished the materials retains title thereto and to the finished article, the person for whom the taxable article is manufactured or produced, and not the person who actually manufactures or produces it, will be considered the manufacturer.

A manufacturer who sells a taxable article in a knockdown condition is liable for the tax as a manufacturer. Whether the person who buys such component parts or accessories and assembles a taxable article from them will be liable for tax as a manufacturer of a taxable article will depend on the relative amount of labor, material, and overhead required to assemble the completed article and on whether the article is assembled for business or personal use.

Person. An individual, trust, estate, partnership, association, company, or corporation. When used in connection with penalties, seizures, and forfeitures, the term includes an officer or employee of a partnership, who as an officer, employee or member, is under a duty to perform the act in respect of which the violation occurs.

Pistols. Small projectile firearms which have a short one-hand stock or butt at an angle to the line of bore and a short barrel or barrels, and which are designed, made, and intended to be aimed and fired from one hand. The term does not include gadget devices, guns altered or converted to resemble pistols, or small portable guns erroneously referred to as pistols, as, for example, Nazi belt buckle pistols, glove pistols, or one-hand stock guns firing fixed shotgun or fixed rifle ammunition.

Possession of the United States. Includes Guam, the Midway Islands, Palmyra, the Panama Canal Zone, the Commonwealth of Puerto Rico, American Samoa, the Virgin Islands, and Wake Island.

Purchaser. Includes a lessee where the lessor is also the manufacturer of the article.

Revolvers. Small projectile firearms of the pistol type, having a breechloading chambered cylinder so arranged that the cocking of the hammer or movement of the trigger rotates it and brings the next cartridge in line with the barrel for firing.

Sale. An agreement whereby the seller transfers the property (that is, the title or the substantial incidents of ownership in goods) to the buyer for a consideration called the price, which may consist of money, services, or other things.

Secretary. The Secretary of the Treasury or his delegate.

Shells and cartridges. Include any article consisting of a projectile, explosive, and container that is designed, assembled, and ready for use without further manufacture in firearms, pistols or revolvers. A person who reloads used shell or cartridge casings is a manufacturer of shells or cartridges within the meaning of section 4181 if such reloaded shells or cartridges are sold by the reloader. However, the reloader is not a manufacturer of shells or cartridges if, in return for a fee and expenses, he reloads casings of shells or cartridges submitted by a customer and returns the reloaded shells or cartridges with the identical casings provided by the customer to that customer. Under such circumstances, the customer would be the manufacturer of the shells or cartridges and may be liable for tax on the sale of articles. See section 4218 of the Code and § 53.112.

Taxable article. Any article taxable under section 4181 of the Code.

Treasury Account. The Department of Treasury's General Account at the Federal Reserve Bank of New York.

Vendor. Includes a lessor where the lessor is also the manufacturer of the article.

[T.D. ATF–308, 56 FR 303, Jan. 3, 1991, as amended by T.D. ATF–312, 56 FR 31083, July 9, 1991; T.D. ATF–330, 57 FR 40325, Sept. 3, 1992; T.D. ATF–365, 60 FR 33670, June 28, 1995; T.D. ATF–404, 63 FR 52603, Oct. 1, 1998; T.D. ATF–447, 66 FR 19088, Apr. 13, 2001; T.D. TTB–44, 71 FR 16957, Apr. 4, 2006]

Subpart C—Administrative and Miscellaneous Provisions

§ 53.20 Delegations of the Administrator.

The regulatory authorities of the Administrator contained in this part are delegated to appropriate TTB officers. These TTB officers are specified in TTB Order 1135.53, Delegation of the Administrator's Authorities in 27 CFR Part 53, Manufacturers Excise Taxes—Firearms and Ammunition. You may obtain a copy of this order by accessing the TTB Web site (*http://www.ttb.gov*) or by mailing a request to the Alcohol and Tobacco Tax and Trade Bureau, National Revenue Center, 550 Main Street, Room 1516, Cincinnati, OH 45202.

[T.D. TTB–44, 71 FR 16957, Apr. 4, 2006]

§ 53.21 Forms prescribed.

(a) The appropriate TTB officer is authorized to prescribe all forms required by this part. All of the information called for in each form shall be furnished as indicated by the headings on the form and the instructions on or pertaining to the form. In addition, information called for in each form shall be furnished as required by this part. The form will be filed in accordance with the instructions on the form.

(b) Forms prescribed by this part are available for printing through the TTB Web site (*http://www.ttb.gov*) or by mailing a request to the Alcohol and Tobacco Tax and Trade Bureau, National Revenue Center, 550 Main Street, Room 1516, Cincinnati, OH 45202.

(c) *Signature authorization.* An individual's signature on a return, statement, or other document made by or for a corporation or a partnership shall be prima facie evidence that the individual is authorized to sign the return, statement, or other document.

[T.D. ATF–308, 56 FR 303, Jan. 3, 1991. Redesignated in part by T.D. ATF–365, 60 FR 33670, June 28, 1995, as amended by T.D. 372, 61 FR 20724, May 8, 1996; T.D. ATF–447, 66 FR 19088, Apr. 13, 2001; T.D. TTB–44, 71 FR 16957, Apr. 4, 2006]

§ 53.22 Employer identification number.

(a) *Requirement of application.* (1) Except for one-time or occasional filers, every person who makes a sale or use of an article with respect to which a tax is imposed by section 4181 of the Code, and who has not earlier been assigned an employer identification number or has not applied for one, shall make an application on Form SS–4 for an employer identification number. The application and any supplementary statement accompanying it shall be prepared in accordance with the applicable form, instructions, and regulations and shall set forth fully and clearly the data therein called for. Form SS–4 may be obtained from any internal revenue district office or internal revenue service center. The application shall be filed with the internal revenue officer designated in the instructions applicable to Form SS–4. The application shall be signed by:

(i) The individual if the person is an individual;

(ii) The president, vice-president, or other principal officer, if the person is a corporation;

(iii) A responsible and duly authorized member or officer having knowledge of its affairs, if the person is a partnership or other unincorporated organization; or

(iv) The fiduciary, if the person is a trust or estate.

An employer identification number will be assigned to the person in due course upon the basis of information reported on the application required under this section.

(2) *Time for filing Form SS–4.* The application for an employer identification number shall be filed no later than the seventh day after the date of the first sale or use of an article with respect to which a tax is imposed by chapter 32 of the Code. However, the application should be filed far enough

in advance of the first required use of such number to permit issuance of the number in time for compliance with such requirement.

(3) *One-time or occasional filers.* A person who files a return under the provisions of section 53.151(a)(5) is not required to make application for an employer identification number. Such persons may use their social security number on any return, statement or other document submitted to TTB by that person in lieu of an employer identification number.

(b) *Use of employer identification number.* The employer identification number assigned to a person liable for a tax imposed by chapter 32 of the Code shall be shown on any return, statement, or other document submitted to TTB by the person.

[T.D. ATF-308, 56 FR 303, Jan. 3, 1991, as amended by T.D. ATF-365, 60 FR 33670, June 28, 1995; T.D. ATF-447, 66 FR 19088, Apr. 13, 2001]

§ 53.23 Alternate methods or procedures.

(a) A taxpayer, on specific approval by the appropriate TTB officer as provided in this section, may use an alternate method or procedure in lieu of a method or procedure specifically prescribed in this part. The appropriate TTB officer may approve an alternate method or procedure, subject to stated conditions, when—

(1) Good cause has been shown for the use of the alternate method or procedure;

(2) The alternate method or procedure is within the purpose of, and consistent with the effect intended by, the specifically prescribed method or procedure, and affords equivalent security to the revenue; and

(3) The alternate method or procedure will not be contrary to any provision of law and will not result in an increase in cost to the Government or hinder the effective administration of this part. No alternate method or procedure relating to the assessment, payment, or collection of tax shall be authorized under this paragraph.

(b) Where the taxpayer desires to employ an alternate method or procedure, a written application to do so must be submitted. The application must specifically describe the proposed alternate method or procedure and must set forth the reasons therefor. Alternate methods or procedures must not be employed until the appropriate TTB officer has approved the application. The taxpayer must, during the period of authorization of an alternate method or procedure, comply with the terms of the approved application. Authorization for any alternate method or procedure may be withdrawn whenever, in the judgment of the appropriate TTB officer, the revenue is jeopardized or the effective administration of this part is hindered by the continuation of such authorization.

[T.D. ATF-365, 60 FR 33670, June 28, 1995, as amended by T.D. ATF-447, 66 FR 19088, Apr. 13, 2001]

§ 53.24 Records.

(a) *In general*—(1) *Form of records.* The records required by the regulations in this part shall be kept accurately, but no particular form is required for keeping the records. Such forms and systems of accounting shall be used as will enable appropriate TTB officers to ascertain whether liability for tax is incurred and, if so, the amount thereof.

(2) [Reserved]

(b) *Copies of returns, schedules, and statements.* Every person who is required, by the regulations in this part or by instructions applicable to any form prescribed thereunder, to keep any copy of any return, schedule, statement, or other document, shall keep such copy as a part of the records.

(c) *Records of claimants.* Any person who, pursuant to the regulations in this part, claims a refund, credit, or abatement, shall keep a complete and detailed record with respect to the tax, interest, addition to the tax, additional amount, or assessable penalty to which the claim relates. Such record shall include any records required of the claimant by paragraph (b) of this section and subpart L of this part.

(d) *Place and period for keeping records.* (1) All records required by this part shall be prepared and kept by the person required to keep them, at one or more convenient and safe locations accessible to appropriate TTB officers, and shall at all times be immediately available for inspection by such officers.

(2) Except as otherwise provided in this subparagraph, every person required by the regulations in this part to keep records in respect of a tax shall maintain such records for at least three years after the due date of such tax for the return period to which the records relate, or the date such tax is paid, whichever is later. The records of claimants required by paragraph (c) of this section shall be maintained for a period of at least three years after the date the claim is filed.

(e) *Reproduction of original records.* (1) General books of account, such as cash books, journals, voucher registers, ledgers, etc., shall be maintained and preserved in their original form. However, reproductions of supporting records of details, such as invoices, vouchers, production reports, sales records, certificates, proofs of exportation, etc., may be kept in lieu of the original records. Any process may be used which accurately and timely reproduces the original record, and which forms a durable medium for reproducing and preserving the original record.

(2) *Copies of records treated as original records.* Whenever records are reproduced under this section, the reproduced records shall be preserved in conveniently accessible files, and provisions shall be made for examining, viewing, and using the reproduced records the same as if they were the original record. Such reproduced records shall be treated and considered for all purposes as though they were the original record. All provisions of law and regulations applicable to the original record are applicable to the reproduced record.

[T.D. ATF–365, 60 FR 33670, June 28, 1995, as amended by T.D. ATF–447, 66 FR 19088, Apr. 13, 2001]

Subparts D–F [Reserved]

Subpart G—Tax Rates

§ 53.61 Imposition and rates of tax.

(a) *Imposition of tax.* Section 4181 of the Code imposes a tax on the sale of the following articles by the manufacturer, producer, or importer thereof:

(1) Pistols;

(2) Revolvers;

(3) Firearms (other than pistols and revolvers); and

(4) Shells and cartridges.

(b) *Parts or accessories*—(1) *In general.* No tax is imposed by section 4181 of the Code on the sale of parts or accessories of firearms, pistols, revolvers, shells, and cartridges when sold separately or when sold with a complete firearm for use as spare parts or accessories. The tax does attach, however, to sales of completed firearms, pistols, revolvers, shells, and cartridges, and to sale of such articles that, although in knockdown condition, are complete as to all component parts.

(2) *Component parts.* Component parts are items that would ordinarily be attached to a firearm during use and, in the ordinary course of trade, are packaged with the firearm at the time of sale by the manufacturer or importer. All component parts for firearms are includible in the price for which the article is sold.

(3) *Nontaxable parts.* Parts sold with firearms that duplicate component parts that are not includible in the price for which the article is sold.

(4) *Nontaxable accessories.* Items that are not designed to be attached to a firearm during use or that are not, in the ordinary course of trade, provided with the firearm at the time of the sale by the manufacturer or importer are not includible in the price for which the article is sold.

(5) *Examples*—(i) *In general.* The following examples are provided as guidelines and are not meant to be all inclusive.

(ii) *Component parts.* Component parts include items such as a frame or receiver, breech mechanism, trigger mechanism, barrel, buttstock, forestock, handguard, grips, buttplate, fore end cap, trigger guard, sight or set of sights (iron or optical), sight mount or set of sight mounts, a choke, a flash hider, a muzzle brake, a magazine, a set of sling swivels, and/or an attachable ramrod for muzzle loading firearms when provided by the manufacturer or importer for use with the firearm in the ordinary course of commercial trade. Component parts also include any part provided with the firearm that would affect the tax status of the firearm, such as an attachable shoulder stock.

(iii) *Nontaxable parts.* Nontaxable parts include items such as extra barrels, extra sights, optical sights and mounts (in addition to iron sights), spare magazines, spare cylinders, extra choke tubes, and spare pins.

(iv) *Nontaxable accessories.* Nontaxable accessories include items such as cleaning equipment, slings, slip on recoil pads (in addition to standard buttplate), tools, gun cases for storage or transportation, separate items such as knives, belt buckles, or medallions. Nontaxable accessories also include optional items purchased by the customer at the time of retail sale that do not change the tax classification of the firearm, such as telescopic sights and mounts, recoil pads, slings, sling swivels, chokes, and flash hiders/muzzle brakes of a type not provided by the manufacturer or importer of the firearm in the ordinary course of commercial trade.

(c) *Rates of tax.* Tax is imposed on the sale of the articles specified in section 4181 of the Code at the rates indicated below.

	Percent
(1) Pistols	10
(2) Revolvers	10
(3) Firearms (other than pistols and revolvers)	11
(4) Shells and cartridges	11

(d) *Computation of tax.* The tax is computed by applying to the price for which the article is sold the applicable rate. For definition of the term "price" see section 4216 of the Code and the regulations contained in subpart J of this part.

(e) *Liability for tax.* The tax imposed by section 4181 of the Code is payable by the manufacturer, producer, or importer making the sale.

[T.D. ATF–308, 56 FR 303, Jan. 3, 1991, as amended by T.D. ATF–404, 63 FR 52603, Oct. 1, 1998]

§ 53.62 Exemptions.

(a) *Firearms subject to the National Firearms Act.* Section 4182(a) provides that the tax imposed by section 4181 of the Code shall not attach to the sale of any firearms on which the tax imposed by section 5811 of the Code (relating to tax on the transfer of machine guns, short-barreled firearms, and other weapons) has been paid. Any manufacturer, producer, or importer claiming such an exemption from the tax imposed by section 4181 of the Code must maintain such records and be prepared to produce such evidence as will establish the right to the exemption.

(b) *Sales to Defense Department or to U.S. Coast Guard*—(1) *Military department.* Section 4182(b) of the Code provides that the tax imposed by section 4181 of the Code shall not attach to the sale of firearms, pistols, revolvers, shells, or cartridges that are purchased with funds appropriated for a military department of the United States. For this purpose, the term "military department" means the Department of the Army, the Department of the Navy, and Department of the Air Force. Included in the Department of the Navy are naval aviation and the Marine Corps.

(2) *Coast Guard.* Section 655, title 14, U.S.C., provides that no tax on the sale or transfer of firearms, pistols, revolvers, shells, or cartridges may be imposed on such articles when bought with funds appropriated for the United States Coast Guard.

(3) *Supporting evidence.* Any manufacturer, producer, or importer claiming an exemption from the tax imposed by section 4181 of the Code by reason of section 4182(b) and section 655, title 14 of the Code must maintain such records and be prepared to produce such evidence as will establish the right to the exemption. Generally, clearly identified orders or contracts of a military department signed by an authorized officer of the military department will be sufficient to establish the right to the exemption. In the absence of such orders or contracts, a statement, signed by an authorized officer of a military department or the Coast Guard, that the prescribed articles were purchased with funds appropriated for that military department or

the Coast Guard will constitute satisfactory evidence of the right to an exemption.

(c) *Small manufacturers, producers, and importers*—(1) *Exemption.* Section 4182(c) of the Code provides that the tax imposed by section 4181 of the Code shall not attach to any pistol, revolver, or firearm manufactured, produced, or imported by a person who manufactures, produces, and imports less than an aggregate of 50 of those articles during the calendar year, regardless of when the articles are sold.

(2) *Controlled groups.* All persons treated as a single employer for purposes of subsection (a) or (b) of section 52 of the Code are treated as one person for purposes of paragraph (c)(1) of this section.

(3) *Applicability.* The exemption described in paragraph (c)(1) of this section applies to articles sold by the manufacturer, producer, or importer after September 30, 2005. Application of this exemption is based on the calendar year in which the manufacture, production, or importation of the articles in question took place and does not depend on when the sale occurs. In addition, each calendar year stands alone for purposes of applying the exemption.

[T.D. ATF–308, 56 FR 303, Jan. 3, 1991, as amended by T.D. ATF–344, 58 FR 40354, July 28, 1993; T.D. TTB–62, 72 FR 51711, Sept. 11, 2007]

§ 53.63 Other tax-free sales.

For provisions relating to tax-free sales of firearms and ammunition see:

(a) Section 4221 and 27 CFR 53.131, "Tax-free sales; general rule".

(b) Section 4223 and 27 CFR 53.132, "Tax-free sale of articles to be used for, or resold for, further manufacture".

(c) Section 4222 and 27 CFR 53.140, "Registration".

Subparts H–I [Reserved]

Subpart J—Special Provisions Applicable to Manufacturers Taxes

§ 53.91 Charges to be included in sale price.

(a) *In general.* The "price" for which an article is sold includes the total consideration paid for the article, whether that consideration is in the form of money, services, or other things. However, for purposes of the taxes imposed under chapter 32 of the Code, certain collateral charges made in connection with the sale of a taxable article must be included in the taxable sale price, whereas others may be excluded. Any charge which is required by a manufacturer, producer, or importer to be paid as a condition of its sale of a taxable article and which is not attributable to an expense falling within one of the exclusions provided in section 4216 of the Code or the regulations thereunder is includable in the taxable sale price. It is immaterial for this purpose that the charge may be paid to a person other than the manufacturer, producer, or importer, or that it may be separately billed to the purchaser as a charge earmarked for expenses incurred or to be incurred in his behalf, such as charges for demonstration or display of the article, for sales promotion programs, or otherwise. With respect to the rules relating to exclusion of charges for local advertising of a manufacturer's products, see section 4216(e) of the Code and § 53.100. In the case of sales on credit, a carrying, finance, or service charge is excludable from the sale price if it is reasonably related to the costs of carrying the deferred portion of the sale price (such as interest on the deferred portion of the sale price, expenses of bookkeeping necessary to keep the records of such sales, and expenses of correspondence and other communication in connection with collection).

(b) *Tools and dies.* Separate charges for tools and dies used in the manufacture or production of a taxable article are to be included, in whole or in part, in the sale price on which the tax is based. It is immaterial whether the charges for such items are billed in a lump sum or are amortized or allocated to each of the taxable articles. If, at the termination of a contract to manufacture taxable articles, the tools and dies used in production pass to the purchaser, only the amount of depreciation of the tools and dies incurred in production, computed on a "production output" basis, should be included in the sale price. If the purchaser furnishes the tools and dies, the amount of the cost thereof, to the extent that such cost has been depreciated in the production of the taxable articles (computed on a "production output" basis), shall be included in determining the sale price of the articles for purposes of computing the tax.

(c) *Charges for warranty.* A charge for a warranty of an article which the manufacturer, producer, or importer requires the purchaser to pay in order to obtain the article shall be included in the sale price of the article on which the tax is computed. On the other hand, a charge for a warranty of a taxable article paid at the purchaser's option shall not be included in the sale price for purposes of computing tax thereon.

(d) *Charges for coverings, containers, and packing.* Any charge by the manufacturer, producer, or importer for coverings and containers of whatever nature used to pack an article for shipment shall be included as part of the sale price for the purpose of computing the tax, whether or not the charges are identified as such on the invoice or are billed separately. Even though there is an agreement that the manufacturer, producer, or importer will repay all or a portion of the charge for the coverings or containers upon the return thereof, the full charge nevertheless shall be included in the sale price. It is immaterial whether the charge made at the time of sale is more or less than the actual value of the covering or container. See §53.173(b)(4) for provisions relating to the claiming of a credit or refund in the case of a price readjustment due to the return or repossession of a covering or container. Packing charges are to be included in the sale price whether the charges cover normal packing or special packing services, such as for extra protection of the article or for odd-lot quantities. This rule shall apply whether the packing services are initiated by the manufacturer, producer, or importer or are furnished at the request of the purchaser and whether the packing is performed by the manufacturer, producer, or importer or by another person at his request. If the purchaser supplies packing materials, the fair market value of such materials must be included in the tax base when computing tax liability on the sale of the article.

(e) *Taxable and nontaxable articles sold as a unit.* Where a taxable article and a nontaxable article are sold by the manufacturer as a unit, the tax attaches to that portion of the manufacturer's sale price of the unit which is properly allocable to the taxable article. Normally, the taxable portion of such a unit may be determined by applying to the manufacturer's sale price of the unit the ratio which the manufacturer's separate sale price of the taxable article bears to the sum of the sale prices of both the taxable and nontaxable articles, if such articles are sold separately by the manufacturer. Where the articles (or either one of them) are not sold separately by the manufacturer and do not have established sale prices, the taxable portion is to be determined from a comparison of the actual costs of the articles to the manufacturer. Thus, if the cost of the taxable article represents four-fifths of the total cost of the complete unit, the tax applies to four-fifths of the price charged by the manufacturer for the unit.

[T.D. ATF–308, 56 FR 303, Jan. 3, 1991, as amended by T.D. ATF–312, 56 FR 31083, July 9, 1991]

§53.92 Exclusions from sale price.

(a) *Tax*—(1) *Tax not part of taxable sale price.* The tax imposed by chapter 32 of the Code on the sale of an article is not part of the taxable sale price of the article. Thus, if a manufacturer computes the tax on a sale price which is determined without regard to the tax, and it charges the proper tax as a separate item, the amount of tax so charged does not become a part of the taxable sale price and no tax is due on the tax so charged. Where no separate charge is made as tax, it will be presumed that the price charged to the purchaser for the article includes the proper tax, and the proper percentage of such price will be allocated to the tax.

(2) *Computation of tax.* If an article subject to tax at the rate of 10 percent is sold for $100 and an additional item of $10 is billed as tax, $100 is the taxable selling price and $10 is the amount

of tax due thereon. However, if the article is sold for $100 with no separate billing or indication of the amount of the tax, it will be presumed that the tax is included in the $100, and a computation will be necessary to determine what portion of the total amount represents the sale price of the article and what portion represents the tax. The computation is as follows:

$$\text{Taxable sale price} = \frac{\text{sale price including tax}}{100 + \text{rate of tax}}$$

Thus, if the tax rate is 10 percent and the sale price including tax is $100, the taxable sale price is $90.91 (that is, $100 divided by (100+10)), and the tax is 10 percent of $90.91, or $9.09.

(b) *Transportation, delivery, insurance, or installation charges*—(1) *Charges incurred pursuant to sale.* Charges for transportation, delivery, insurance, installation, and other expenses actually incurred in connection with the delivery of an article to a purchaser pursuant to a bona fide sale shall be excluded from the sale price in computing the tax. Such charges include all items of transportation, delivery, insurance, installation, and similar expense incurred after shipment to a customer begins, in response to the customer's order, pursuant to a bona fide sale. However, costs of such nature incurred by a manufacturer, producer, or importer in transporting, in the normal course of business and for its benefit and convenience, articles from a factory or port of entry to a warehouse or other facility (regardless of the location of such warehouse or facility) are not considered as being incurred in connection with the delivery of an article to a purchaser pursuant to a bona fide sale, and charges therefor cannot be excluded from the sale price in computing tax liability. Similarly, an allowance granted by a manufacturer as reimbursement for expenses incurred by the purchaser in shipping used articles to the manufacturer for credit against the purchase price of taxable articles shall not be excluded from the sale price when computing tax due on the sale of the taxable articles. In any event, no charge may be excluded from the sale price unless the conditions set forth in paragraph (b)(2) of this section are complied with. Said conditions are prescribed under the authority granted the Secretary in section 4216(a) of the Code.

(2) *Only actual expenses to be excluded.* Where a separate charge is made for transportation or other expenses incurred in connection with the delivery of an article to the purchaser pursuant to a bona fide sale, there shall be excluded in arriving at the sale price subject to tax only that portion of the charge which represents the actual expenses incurred for the transportation or other excludable expenses. Where a separate charge is less than the actual expense, the difference is presumed to be included in the billed price. Such difference, together with the separate charge, shall be excluded in arriving at the sale price on which the tax is computed. Similarly, where no separate charge is made but the manufacturer, producer, or importer incurs an expense of the type to which this paragraph has application, the amount of such expense actually incurred shall be excluded from the sale price on which the tax is computed. Where transportation expense is incurred in conjunction with a shipment composed of both taxable and nontaxable articles, only the portion of the expense allocable to the taxable articles shall be excludable. In general, unless the taxpayer establishes to the satisfaction of the appropriate TTB officer that another method reasonably apportions such freight expense between taxable and nontaxable articles, such expense should be apportioned on the basis of the relative weights (or, if available, the relative published tariff rates) applicable to the taxable and nontaxable articles. Where it is not feasible to apportion such expense on the basis of

relative weights or tariff rates, the expense shall be apportioned on another reasonable basis; for example, in the case of a shipment including both taxable and nontaxable articles which are subject to the same tariff rate, it may be appropriate to apportion the transportation expense on the basis of the relative sale prices. A charge for insurance in connection with the delivery of an article to a purchaser is considered to represent an expense actually incurred only to the extent that an amount equivalent to such charge is paid or payable by the manufacturer to a person authorized to assume such insurance risk.

(3) *Transportation, delivery, or installation services performed by manufacturer.* For purposes of computing the taxable sale price of articles, it is immaterial whether the transportation, delivery, or other services of the type to which this paragraph has application are performed by a common carrier or independent agency for or on behalf of the manufacturer, producer, or importer, or are performed by the manufacturer, producer, or importer with the use of its own vehicles or other facilities. Thus, where a manufacturer, producer, or importer performs the transportation, delivery, or other services with its equipment, tools, employees, etc., the cost of such services allocable to the sale of the taxable article shall be excluded. In determining whether an expense is an excludable transportation or delivery expense, only those expenses incurred by reason of the fact that the purchaser accepts delivery at some point other than the manufacturer's place of business shall be considered excludable transportation or delivery expenses. All expenses incurred in placing an article packed, ready for shipment on the loading dock at the manufacturer's factory are not excludable transportation or delivery expenses. An allowance granted by the manufacturer, producer, or importer to the purchaser for transportation, delivery, or other expenses incurred or to be incurred by the purchaser in connection with the sale shall be excluded in computing the taxable sale price, if charges for similar expenses would be excludable if incurred by the manufacturer.

(4) *Records in support of exclusion.* Every manufacturer, producer, or importer making sales of taxable articles shall keep records which will disclose the amount of transportation, delivery, insurance, installation or other expense actually incurred by it in connection with the delivery of a taxable article to a purchaser pursuant to a bona fide sale.

(c) *Other charges.* A charge or expense not within the scope of paragraph (a) or (b) of this section, whether or not separately stated, may not be excluded in computing the taxable sale price unless it can be shown by adequate records that the charge or expense is not properly included as a manufacturing or selling expense or is in no way incidental to placing the article in condition packed ready for shipment. Commissions to manufacturers' agents, or allowances, payments, or adjustments made to, and for the benefit of, persons other than the purchaser may not be excluded or deducted, under any condition, in computing the sale price upon which the tax is computed.

§53.93 Other items relating to tax on sale price.

(a) *Exchanges.* If, in connection with the sale of an article subject to a tax imposed under chapter 32 of the Code on the price for which sold, a manufacturer receives from its vendee another article in exchange, the tax on the manufacturer's sale shall be computed on the basis of the amount allowed for the article received from the vendee, plus any additional amount charged the vendee.

(b) *Replacements under warranty.* If an article, subject to a tax imposed under chapter 32 of the Code on the price for which sold, is returned to the manufacturer by reason of the failure of the article under a warranty as to its quality or service, and a new article is given by the manufacturer, free, or at a reduced price, the tax on the new article shall be computed on the actual amount, if any, to be paid to the manufacturer for the new article. See §53.174(b) for the circumstances under which the allowance made by the manufacturer, producer, or importer upon the return of the first article constitutes a price readjustment of the sale price of the first article and the extent, if any, to which a credit may be allowed, or refund made, of the tax paid by the manufacturer, producer, or importer on the sale of the first article.

(c) *Readjustments in sale price.* Readjustment in sale price (such as allowable discounts, rebates, bonuses, etc.) cannot be anticipated. The tax must be based upon the original price unless the readjustments have actually been made prior to the close of the period for which the tax upon the sale is returned. However, if the price upon which the tax was computed is subsequently readjusted, credit may be taken against the tax due on a subsequent return or a claim for refund filed as provided by section 6416(b)(1) of the Code and §§53.174–53.176.

[T.D. ATF–308, 56 FR 303, Jan. 3, 1991, as amended by T.D. ATF–344, 58 FR 40354, July 28, 1993]

§53.94 Constructive sale price; scope and application.

(a) *In general.* Section 4216(b) of the Code pertains to those taxes imposed under chapter 32 of the Code that are based on the price for which an article is sold, and contains the provisions for constructing a tax base other than the actual sale price of the article, under certain defined conditions.

(b) *Specific applications.* (1) Section 4216(b)(1) of the Code applies to:

(i) Arm's-length sales at retail or on consignment, other than those sales at retail and to retailers to which section 4216(b)(2) of the Code and §53.96 apply; and

(ii) Sales otherwise than at arm's length, and at less than fair market price.

(2) Section 4216(b)(2) of the Code applies generally to arm's-length sales of an article at retail or to retailers, or both, where the manufacturer also sells the same article to wholesale distributors.

(3) Section 4216(b)(3) of the Code provides a formula for determining a constructive sale price for sales of taxable articles between members of an affiliated group of corporations (as "affiliated group" is defined in section 1504(a) of the Code) in those instances where the purchasing corporation regularly resells to retailers but does not regularly resell to wholesale distributors, and except for situations where section 4216(b)(4) of the Code applies.

(4) Section 4216(b)(4) of the Code provides a special method for computing a constructive sale price for sales of taxable articles between affiliated corporations where the purchasing corporation sells only to retailers, and the normal method of selling within the industry is for manufacturers to sell to wholesale distributors.

(c) *Definitions.* For purposes of section 4216(b) of the Code and §§53.94–53.97 and unless otherwise indicated:

(1) *Sale at retail.* A "sale at retail," or a "retail sale", is a sale of an article to a purchaser who intends to use or lease the article rather than resell it. The fact that articles are sold in wholesale lots, or at wholesale prices, will not change the character of such sales as "sales at retail" if the purchaser is not engaged in the business of reselling such articles, and acquires them for the purpose of using them rather than reselling them.

(2) *Retail dealers.* A "retail dealer", or "retailer", is a person engaged in the business of selling articles at retail.

(3) *Wholesale distributor.* The term "wholesale distributor" means a person engaged in the business of selling articles to persons engaged in the business of reselling such articles.

§53.95 Constructive sale price; basic rules.

(a) *In general.* Section 4216(b)(1) of the Code sets forth the conditions that require the Secretary to construct a sale price on which to compute a tax imposed under chapter 32 of the Code on the price for which an article is sold. The section requires a constructive sale price to be established where a taxable article is:

(1) Sold at retail;

(2) Sold while on consignment; or,

(3) Sold otherwise than through an arm's-length transaction at less than fair market price.

(b) *Sales at retail.* Section 4216(b)(1)(A) of the Code relates to the determination of a constructive sale price for sales of taxable articles sold at arm's-length and at retail. In the case of such sales, the constructive sale price is the highest price for which such articles are sold to wholesale distributors, in the ordinary course of trade, by manufacturers or producers thereof, as determined by the Secretary. If the constructive sale price is less than the actual sale price, the constructive sale price shall be used as the tax base. If the constructive sale price is not less than the actual sale price, the actual sale price shall be considered as not less than fair market, and shall be used as the tax base. In determining the highest price for which articles are sold by manufacturers to wholesale distributors, there must be taken into consideration the normal industry practices with respect to inclusions and exclusions under section 4216(a) of the Code. However, once a constructive sale price has been determined by the Secretary, no further adjustment of such price shall be made. The provisions of section 4216(b)(1)(A) of the Code and this paragraph shall not apply in those instances where the provisions of section 4216(b)(2) of the Code and §53.96 apply.

(c) *Sales on consignment.* As in the case of sales at retail, the constructive sale price for sales on consignment shall be the price for which such articles are sold, in the ordinary course for trade, by manufacturers or producers thereof, as determined by the Secretary. For purposes of section 4216(b)(1)(B) of the Code and this paragraph, an article is considered to be sold on consignment if it is sold while it is on consignment to a person which has the right to sell, and does sell, such article in its own name, but never receives title to the article from the manufacturer. Ordinarily, the constructive sale price of an article sold on consignment is the net price received by the manufacturer from the consignee. The provisions of section 4216(b)(1)(B) of the Code and this paragraph shall not apply if the provisions of section 4216(b)(2) of the Code and §53.96 apply.

(d) *Sales not at arm's-length.* For purposes of section 4216(b)(1)(C) of the Code and this paragraph, a sale is considered to be made under circumstances otherwise than at "arm's-length" if:

(1) One of the parties is controlled (in law or in fact) by the other, or there is common control, whether or not such control is actually exercised to influence the sale price, or

(2) The sale is made pursuant to special arrangements between a manufacturer and a purchaser.

In case of an article sold otherwise than at arm's-length, and at less than fair market price, the constructive sale price shall be the price for which such articles are sold, in the ordinary course of trade, by manufacturers or producers thereof, as determined by the Secretary. Once such a constructive sale price has been determined, no further adjustment of such price shall be made. See sections 4216(b) (3) and (4) of the Code, and §53.97, for specific methods for determining constructive sale prices for intercompany sales under certain defined conditions.

§53.96 Constructive sale price; special rule for arm's-length sales.

(a) *In general.* Section 4216(b)(2) of the Code provides a special rule under which a manufacturer shall determine a constructive sale price for this sale of taxable articles at retail, and to retail dealers, under certain conditions. The rule is applicable where:

(1) The manufacturer regularly sells such articles at retail, or to retailers, or both, as the case may be,

(2) The manufacturer also regularly sells such articles to one or more wholesale distributors in arm's-length transactions, and the manufacturer establishes that its prices in such cases are determined without regard to any benefit to be derived under section 4216(b)(2) of the Code, and

(3) The transactions are arm's-length transactions.

(4) A manufacturer meeting the foregoing requirements shall base its tax liability for sales at retail and sales to retailers on the lower of its actual sale price or the highest price for which it sells the same articles under the same conditions to wholesale distributors.

(b) *Definitions.* For purposes of section 4216(b)(2) of the Code and this section:

(1) *Actual sale price.* "Actual sale price" means the actual selling price for an article determined in the same manner as sale price is determined for a taxable sale. Accordingly, such price

must reflect the inclusions and exclusions set forth in sections 4216(a) and (e) of the Code, and any price adjustments described in section 6416(b)(1) of the Code.

(2) *Highest price to wholesale distributors.* The "highest price" charged wholesale distributors for an article by a manufacturer, producer, or importer thereof, is the highest price at which the manufacturer, producer, or importer sells the article to wholesale distributors, determined without regard to quantity. Such price shall be determined in the same manner as sale price is determined for a taxable sale with respect to the inclusions and exclusions under sections 4216(a) and (e) of the Code; however, since the price is to be a "highest" price, no further adjustment may be made for price readjustments under section 6416(b)(1) of the Code.

(3) *Regular sales.* An article is considered to be sold "regularly" at retail or to retailers if sales are made at retail or to retailers periodically and recurringly as a regular part of the seller's business. If a seller makes only isolated or casual sales of an article at retail or to retailers, it is not considered to be selling "regularly" at retail or to retailers. Similarly, a manufacturer is considered to be making regular sales of an article to one or more distributors if it sells the article to at least one distributor periodically and recurringly as a regular part of its business.

(4) *Normal method of sales in industry.* In the absence of a showing to the appropriate TTB officer of a more appropriate manner of determining the normal method of sales within an industry which is practical in application, the normal method of sales within an industry shall be regarded as not being at retail or to retailers, or both, if the industry dollar volume of sales which are at retail or to retailers, or both, is less than half the total industry dollar volume of sales at all levels of distribution by manufacturers, producers, or importers, including sales to other manufacturers, producers, or importers.

[T.D. ATF–308, 56 FR 303, Jan. 3, 1991, as amended by T.D. ATF–312, 56 FR 31083, July 9, 1991; T.D. TTB–91, 76 FR 5481, Feb. 1, 2011]

§53.97 Constructive sale price; affiliated corporations.

(a) *In general.* Sections 4216(b) (3) and (4) of the Code establish procedures for determining a constructive sale price under section 4216(b)(1)(C) of the Code for sales between corporations that are members of the same "affiliated group", as that term is defined in section 1504(a) of the Code.

(b) *Sales to which section 4216(b)(3) of the Code applies.* Section 4216(b)(3) of the Code provides a procedure for determining a constructive sale price under section 4216(b)(1)(C) of the Code in those instances where:

(1) A manufacturer, producer or importer regularly sells a taxable article to a wholesale distributor which is a member of the same affiliated group as the manufacturer, producers or importer, and

(2) The wholesale distributor regularly sells such article to one or more independent retailers, but does not regularly sell to wholesale distributors. Under such circumstances the constructive sale price for the article shall be an amount equal to 90 percent of the lowest price for which the distributor regularly sells the article in arm's-length transactions to such independent retailers. Once the constructive sale price has been determined, no adjustment shall be made for inclusions or exclusions under section 4216(a) of the Code or price readjustments under section 6416(b)(1) of the Code. If both sections 4216(b)(3) and 4216(b)(4) of the Code apply with respect to the sale of an article, the constructive sale price for such article shall be the lower of the prices computed under sections 4216(b)(3) and 4216(b)(4).

(c) *Sales to which section 4216(b)(4) of the Code applies.* Section 4216(b)(4) of the Code provides a procedure for determining a constructive sale price under section 4216(b)(1)(C) of the Code in those instance where:

(1) A manufacturer, producer, or importer regularly sells (except for tax-free sales) a taxable article only to a wholesale distributor which is a member of the same affiliated group as the manufacturer, producer, or importer,

(2) The distributor regularly sells (except for tax-free sales) such article only to retail dealers, and

(3) The normal method of sales for such articles within the industry is to sell such articles in arm's-length transactions to wholesale distributors.

(4) Under section 4216(b)(4) of the Code, the constructive sale price of such article shall be the median price at which the distributor, at the time of the sale by the manufacturer, resells the article to retail dealers, reduced by a percentage of such price equal to the percentage which:

(i) The difference between the median price for which comparable articles are sold to wholesale distributors, in the ordinary course of trade, by manufacturers of producers thereof, and the median price at which such wholesale distributors in arm's-length transactions sell such comparable articles to retailers, is of

(ii) The median price at which such wholesale distributors in arm's-length transactions sell such comparable articles to retailers.

(iii) For purposes of this paragraph, the "median price" for which an article is sold at a particular level of distribution is the price midway between the highest and lowest prices charged vendees at the particular level of distribution. Where only one price is charged at a level of distribution, "median price" is equivalent to "actual price". All sale prices referred to in paragraphs (c) and (d) of this section are prices that must reflect the inclusions and exclusions set forth in section 4216(a) of the Code. However, once a constructive sale price has been determined under these paragraphs, no further adjustment of such price is allowed.

(d) *Application of section 4216(b)(4) of the Code.* The application of section 4216(b)(4) of the Code and paragraph (c) of this section may be illustrated by the following example:

Example. M, a corporation engaged in the manufacture of article X, sold 100 of such articles at $10.00 per article to a wholesale distributor N, a corporation engaged in the business of selling X articles to independent retail dealers. N is a member of the same affiliated group of corporations as M. M sells X articles only to N. The normal method of manufacturers' sales of X articles in the industry is to sell to independent wholesale distributors. N corporation sells X articles to retailers for $15.00 each. The price for which comparable X articles are sold to wholesale distributors in the ordinary course of trade by manufacturers thereof is $12.00 per article. Wholesale distributors sell X articles to retailers in the ordinary course of trade for $16.00 per article. Under the foregoing facts the constructive sale price determined under section 4216(b)(4) of the Code and this paragraph is $11.25, computed as follows:

$$\$15.00-\left(\$15.00\times\frac{\$16.00-\$12.00}{\$16.00}\right)=\$11.25$$

(e) *Determination of "lowest price".* In addition to other considerations, in determining a "lowest price" for purposes of sections 4216(b) (1) and (3) of the Code and §53.97, such price shall be determined:

(1) Without requiring that a given percentage of sales be made at that price (provided that the volume of sales made at that price is great enough to indicate that those sales have not been engaged in primarily to establish a lower tax base), and

(2) Without including any charge for a fixed amount that the purchaser has an unconditional right to recover on the basis of a contractual arrangement existing at the time of sale.

(f) *Definitions.* For purposes of this section and paragraphs (3) and (4) of section 4216(b) of the Code, the term "regularly sells" has the same meaning as that accorded the term "regular sales" in §53.96(b)(3), and the term "normal method of sales in the industry" has the same meaning as accorded that term in §53.96(b)(4).

[T.D. ATF-308, 56 FR 303, Jan. 3, 1991, as amended by T.D. ATF-312, 56 FR 31083, July 9, 1991]

§53.98 Computation of tax on leases and installment sales.

(a) *Leases.* When a taxable article is leased by a manufacturer, producer, or importer, liability for tax is incurred, except as provided by section 4217(b) of the Code and §53.104, on each payment made with respect to such lease. Tax is payable on each lease payment as long as the article is leased by the manufacturer, producer, or importer. The tax payable with respect to each lease payment is a percentage of each payment based on the rate of tax, if any, in effect on the date the lease payment is due. If the article is subsequently sold by the manufacturer, producer, or importer, the tax applies also to such sale, without regard to the tax paid when the article was leased. For definition of the term "lease", see § 53.103.

(b) *Installment sales.* When a taxable article is sold under an installment payment contract with title reserved in the seller, or under a conditional sale contract, chattel mortgage arrangement or other arrangement creating a security interest with payments to be made in installments, tax shall be computed and paid on each payment made by the purchaser. The tax payable with each payment is a percentage of each payment based on the rate of tax, if any, in effect on the date the payment is due. The part of each payment that is subject to tax is that portion of the payment equal to the percentage of the total portion of the payment equal to the percentage of the total charge for the article that is subject to tax. For example, if the total charge for the article is $1,000, and of the total amount charged only 90 percent thereof, or $900, is subject to tax by reason of exclusions, then only 90 percent of the installment payment is subject to tax. If the tax base is a constructive sale price computed under section 4216(b) of the Code that is less than the actual sale price of the article, the portion of each payment subject to tax is the percentage of such payment equal to the percentage that the constructive sale price bears to the actual sale price. For example, if an article is sold at retail for $100, and the constructive sale price for such an article computed under the provisions of section 4216(b)(1)(A) of the Code is $75, the percentage which the constructive sale price bears to the actual sale price is 75 percent. Accordingly, only 75 percent of each installment payment is subject to tax.

(c) *Sales on credit.* Where articles are sold on credit under conditions other than those specified in paragraph (b) of this section, the entire tax shall be reported and paid with the return covering the period in which the sale is made, even though the price may not be paid to the manufacturer, producer, or importer until a later date, or not paid at all.

§ 53.99 Sales of installment accounts.

(a) *In general.* Except as provided in paragraph (d) of this section, in case of a sale or other disposition by a manufacturer, producer, or importer of an installment account of the type specified in section 4216(c) of the Code, the tax shall not apply to subsequent installment payments on such account. Instead, there shall be paid an amount equal to the difference between the tax previously paid on such installment account and the total tax computed by applying:

(1) To each installment due before the sale of the installment account, the rate of tax applicable at the time payment thereof was due, and

(2) To each installment, the time for payment of which has not arrived, the rate of tax which, under the provisions of chapter 32 of the Code as in effect on the date of the sale of the installment account, is (or is to be) in effect on the date such installment is due. However, see paragraph (b) of this section if the sale is made in a bankruptcy or insolvency proceeding. The tax due under this paragraph shall be included in the return for the period in which the account is sold.

(b) *Sale in bankruptcy or insolvency proceeding.* In the case of a sale of an installment account of a manufacturer, producer, or importer pursuant to the order of, or subject to the approval of, a court of competent jurisdiction in a bankruptcy or insolvency proceeding, the amount of tax due shall be computed and paid as provided in paragraph (a) of this section but shall not exceed the amount of tax computed by multiplying:

(1) The proportionate share of the amount for which such accounts are sold which is allocable to each unpaid installment payment, by

(2) The rate of tax which, under the provisions of chapter 32 of the Code as in effect on the date of the sale of the installment account, is (or is to be) in effect on the date such payment is due.

(c) *Collection of installment accounts on behalf of the manufacturer.* Where a manufacturer, producer, or importer retains title to an installment account but turns it over to another person for collection on a fee basis, no sale of such account (or other disposition as contemplated in section 4216(d) of the Code) has been made. The tax shall continue to be paid as provided by section 4216(c) of the Code.

(d) *Returned installment accounts.* Where an installment account which has been sold or otherwise disposed of is returned to the manufacturer, producer, or importer who sold it under an agreement under which the account was sold, and credit or refund has been allowed under section 6416(b)(5) of the Code and §53.183, the manufacturer, producer, or importer shall pay tax as provided by section 4216(c) of the Code and §53.98 on any subsequent payments made on such returned installment account until such time as there shall have been paid the total tax liability with respect to the account as computed under paragraph (a) of this section.

(e) *Limitation.* The sum of the amounts payable under this section and §53.98 or an installment account shall not exceed the total amount of tax which would be payable if such installment account had not been sold or otherwise disposed of (computed as provided in subsection (c)).

§53.100 Exclusion of local advertising charges from sale price.

(a) *In general.* Section 4216(e) of the Code deals with the treatment to be accorded charges made by a manufacturer for, and reimbursements by a manufacturer or expenditures in connection with the advertising of certain articles subject to excise tax under chapter 32 of the Code. Section 4216(e) of the Code provides an exclusion (which is in addition to the exclusions provided by section 4216(a) of the Code and §53.92) in respect of charges for local advertising, as defined in paragraph (b) of this section, for purposes of determining the price for which an article is sold. See paragraph (c) of this section. The exclusion provided by section 4216(e) of the Code and paragraph (c) of this section has application only if the advertising is broadcast over a radio or television station, appears in a newspaper or magazine, or is displayed by means of an outdoor advertising sign or poster. Section 4216(e) of the Code also provides an overall limitation in respect of the sum of the amount of the exclusions from price as charges for local advertising and the amount of the readjustments authorized under section 6416(b)(1) of the Code (relating to credits or refunds for price readjustments) in respect of reimbursements by a manufacturer of expenditures for local advertising. See §53.101. For provisions prohibiting exclusion from price or readjustment of price in respect of charges for, and reimbursements of expenditures for, advertising other than local advertising, see §53.102.

(b) *Definition of local advertising*—(1) *In general.* For purposes of the regulations under sections 4216(e) and 6416(b)(1) of the Code (§§53.100–53.102 and 53.173–53.176), the term "local advertising" means advertising which relates to an article with respect to which tax is imposed under chapter 32 of the Code on the price for which sold and which:

(i) Is initiated or obtained by the purchaser or any subsequent vendee,

(ii) Names the article for which the price is determinable under section 4216 and states the location at which such article may be purchased at retail, and

(iii) Is broadcast over a radio station or television station, appears in a newspaper or magazine, or is displayed by means of an outdoor advertising sign or poster.

(2) *Initiating or obtaining advertising.* For purposes of paragraph (b)(1) of this section, the advertising must be initiated or obtained by one or more of the persons in the chain of distribution of the article (wholesale distributor, jobber, dealer, etc.) who purchased the article for resale. For purposes of this subparagraph, the manufacturer is not considered to be one of the persons in the chain of distribution of the article. In general, advertising of an article is considered to be initiated or obtained by one or more persons in the chain of distribution of the article if any such person:

(i) Takes an active part in the actual planning and development, or in the arrangements or negotiations leading to the development, of the form and content of the advertising, or

(ii) Contracts for the placement of the advertising.

The participation by the manufacturer of the article in the planning, development, or placement of the advertising is immaterial provided the advertising is in fact initiated or obtained by one or more persons in the chain of distribution of the article. Furthermore, it is immaterial whether or not the advertising is subject to the approval of the manufacturer of the article. However, if no person in the chain of distribution of the article takes an active part in the actual planning and development, or in the arrangements or negotiations leading to the development, of the form and content of the advertising, but, rather, all such planning, development, arrangements, and negotiations are accomplished by the manufacturer of the article, then such manufacturer is considered to have initiated the advertising, and if he also contracts for the placement of the advertising, such advertising does not qualify as "local advertising".

(3) *Identification of article and sales location.* To meet the requirements of paragraph (b)(1) of this section, the advertising must identify the article for which the price is determinable under section 4216 of the Code and give the location or locations at which the article may be purchased at retail. All products taxable at the same rate under the same section of chapter 32 of the Code shall be considered to be an "article" for purposes of the preceding sentence. No specific method or means of identification is prescribed. The identification of the article may be made through the use of the name of the manufacturer or the use of an established trade-mark, such as a seal, picture, letter or letters, etc., or a combination thereof. The advertising must identify the particular retail establishment or establishments at which the article may be purchased at retail but need not specify the location of any such establishment in terms of the number by which the premises are designated or the name of the street on which the retail premises are situated. However, the location of the retail premises must be described sufficiently, as, for example, by reference to a particular named shopping area or shopping center, to enable customers to find the retail establishment.

(4) *Determination of costs of local advertising.* Where an advertisement identifies more than one article, and all such articles are not taxable, or are not taxable at the same rate under the same section of chapter 32 of the Code, a reasonable allocation of the cost of the advertisement must be made among:

(i) Articles taxable at the same rate under the same section of the Code, and

(ii) Articles which are not taxable under chapter 32 of the Code.

For example, in the case of a single page newspaper or magazine advertisement, an allocation of costs reflecting the lineage or space devoted to the specified categories will be considered to reflect a reasonable allocation of the cost of advertising the different articles. As a general rule, only the cost of the "spot" portion identifying the retail establishment is considered "local advertising" in the case of national television or radio programs.

(5) *Meaning of "newspaper".* The term *newspaper,* as used in paragraph (b)(1) of this section, is limited to those publications which are commonly understood to be newspapers and which are printed and distributed periodically at daily, weekly, or other short intervals for the dissemination of news of a general character and of a general interest. The term does not include handbills, circulars, flyers, or the like, unless printed and distributed as a part of a publication which constitutes a newspaper within the meaning of this subparagraph. Neither does the term include any publication which is issued to supply information on certain subjects of interest to particular groups unless such publication otherwise qualifies as a newspaper within the meaning of this subparagraph. For purposes of this subparagraph, advertising is not considered to be news of a general character and of a general interest.

(6) *Meaning of "magazine".* The term *magazine,* as used in paragraph (b)(1) of this section, is limited to those publications which are:

(i) Commonly understood to be magazines,

(ii) Printed and distributed periodically at least twice a year, and

(iii) Published for the dissemination of information of a general nature or of special interest to particular groups.

(iv) The term does not include handbills, circulars, flyers or the like, unless printed and distributed as a part of a publication which constitutes a magazine within the meaning of this subparagraph. For purposes of this subparagraph, advertising is not considered to be information of a general nature or information of special interest to particular groups within the contemplation of paragraph (b)(6)(iii) of this section.

(7) *Meaning of "outdoor advertising sign or poster"*. The term "outdoor advertising sign or poster", as used in paragraph (b)(1) of this section, means a sign or poster displaying advertising matter, which is located outside of a roofed enclosure. This term includes both signs or posters on billboards, whether placed on or affixed to land, buildings, or other structures, and those which are displayed on or attached to moving objects, provided the signs or posters are located outside of a roofed enclosure. The term "roofed enclosure" means a roof structure which is enclosed on more than one-half of its sides by walls, fences, or other barriers.

(c) *Exclusion*—(1) *Conditions and limitations.* A charge for local advertising which is required by a manufacturer to be paid as a condition to his sale of an article is not a part of the taxable price of the article, to the extent that such charge meets each of the following conditions and limitations:

(i) Such charge does not exceed 5 percent of the difference between:

(A) An amount which would constitute the taxable price of the article (computed at the time of the sale of the article) if no part of any charge for local advertising were excludable in computing taxable price, and

(B) The amount of any separate charge for local advertising, whatever the amount of such charge may be,

(ii) Such charge is specifically shown as a separate charge for local advertising on the invoice or statement covering the sale of the article.

(iii) Such charge is billed by the manufacturer with the intention on his part of repaying the amount of the charge to the person purchasing the article from him, or to any person who subsequently purchases the article for resale, in reimbursement of costs incurred for local advertising of such article or some other article or articles taxable at the same rate under the same section of the Code. In the absence of evidence to the contrary, the fact of such intention will be assumed in all cases where the manufacturer and his vendees are parties to an advertising plan which calls for such repayments, or the manufacturer can otherwise establish that the vendees to whom he bills such charges understand and expect that such repayments will be made.

(2) *When exclusion ceases to apply.* To the extent that charges for local advertising meet the conditions and limitations stated in paragraph (c)(1) of this section, such charge is excludable in computing the taxable price of the article in respect of which the charge was made. However, the exclusion will cease to apply in respect of any part of such charge which the manufacturer fails to repay before May 1 of the calendar year following the calendar year in which the article was sold, to the person who purchased the article from him, or to some other person who subsequently purchases the article for resale, in reimbursement of costs incurred for local advertising of such article or some other article or articles taxable at the same rate under the same section of the Code. If, before such May 1, any part of the charge so excluded has not been so repaid, the manufacturer becomes liable for tax on such May 1 in the same manner as if an article taxable under such section of the Code had been sold by him on such May 1 at a taxable price equivalent to that part of the charge not so repaid. However, see paragraph (b)(2) of § 53.175, relating to price readjustments in cases where local advertising charges are not repaid before such May 1 but are subsequently paid over by the manufacturer to his vendees in reimbursement of costs for local advertising. For provisions relating to the method of determining whether a payment by a manufacturer is or is not attributable to an excluded local advertising

charge, see paragraph (b)(3) of § 53.101. In any case where the payment is determined to be attributable to such a charge, the date of the sale in connection with which the charge was made shall be determined on a first-in-first-out basis in respect of the vendee to whom the charge was billed by the manufacturer.

[T.D. ATF–308, 56 FR 303, Jan. 3, 1991, as amended by T.D. ATF–312, 56 FR 31083, July 9, 1991]

§ 53.101 Limitation on aggregate of exclusions and price readjustments.

(a) *In general.* The sum of the amount excluded from taxable price in respect of charges for local advertising, as provided in section 4216(e)(1) of the Code and § 53.100, plus the amount of the readjustments for which credits or refunds may be claimed in respect of local advertising, as provided in section 6416(b)(1) of the Code and § 53.175, is subject to an overall 5 percent limitation. This limitation applies to each manufacturer, as of the close of each calendar quarter, in respect of all articles taxable under the same section of chapter 32 of the Code which were sold by such manufacturer in such quarter (and the preceding quarter or quarters, if any, in the calendar year).

(b) *Computation of overall 5 percent limitation*—(1) *In general.* The limitation prescribed by section 4216(e)(2) of the Code (the "overall 5 percent limitation" referred to in paragraph (a) of this section) as to the total of the exclusions from price and readjustments of price which may be claimed for local advertising in respect of all articles taxable under the same section of Chapter 32 of the Code shall be computed as of the close of each calendar quarter of the calendar year. The overall 5 percent limitation is 5 percent of the difference between:

(i) The amount which would constitute the total taxable price (computed at the time of sale) of all articles taxable under the same section of chapter 32 of the Code sold by the manufacturer during the elapsed calendar quarters of the calendar year, if no part of any charge for local advertising were excludable in computing taxable price, and

(ii) The total of all amounts billed as separate charges for local advertising of such articles (whatever the amount of any single charge of the total of all charges).

(iii) In making the computations under paragraphs (b)(1) (i) and (ii) of this section, credits or refunds under section 6416(b) of the Code of tax paid on the sale of any such articles are to be disregarded and articles sold tax-free by the manufacturer are to be excluded. The amount by which the overall 5 percent limitation computed as of the close of a particular calendar quarter in respect of articles taxable under the same section of chapter 32 of the Code exceeds the sum of the charges for local advertising excluded in computing the taxable price and the amount of reimbursements for local advertising of such articles made during the elapsed calendar quarters of the calendar year, in respect of which credit or refund has been claimed, represents the unused portion of the overall 5 percent limitation. Such unused portion is the maximum amount of reimbursements for local advertising in respect of which credit or refund may be claimed at the close of the particular calendar quarter, subject to the applicable conditions and limitations governing the right to claim a credit or refund in respect of local advertising (see § 53.175). The unused portion of the overall 5 percent limitation as of the close of the fourth calendar quarter of a calendar year in respect of which credit or refund may not be claimed as of the close of such quarter must be disregarded in computing the overall 5 percent limitation for any subsequent calendar quarter. Moreover, the amount of any reimbursements for local advertising made by a manufacturer in a calendar year which is in excess of the amount of such reimbursements in respect of which credit or refund may be claimed, within the overall limitation, as of the close of the calendar year, may not subsequently serve as the basis for a credit or refund.

(2) *Alternative method of computation in certain cases.* If during the portion of the calendar year ending with the date as of which the overall 5 percent limitation is being computed the amount of the local advertising charge separately

billed by the manufacturer has not, in respect of any sale of any articles taxable under the same section of chapter 32 of the Code, exceeded the amount excludable pursuant to §53.100 in computing taxable price, the overall 5 percent limitation as of the close of a particular calendar quarter in respect of articles taxable under such section is 5 percent of the total taxable price (computed at the time of the sale) of all such articles sold taxpaid during the calendar year.

(3) *Allocation of amounts paid in reimbursement of expenditures for local advertising.* If a manufacturer makes contributions to a local advertising program in connection with which he makes excludable local advertising charges, it is necessary that reimbursements by the manufacturer for local advertising be attributed to the charges for local advertising, to the manufacturer's contributions, or allocated between them. Whether an amount paid by a manufacturer in reimbursement of expenses for local advertising is or is not a repayment of a local advertising charge which was excluded from taxable price under section 4216(e)(1) of the Code and §53.100, shall be determined on the basis of an allocation made under the agreement between the manufacturer and his vendee (or any subsequent vendee).

(c) *Examples.* The application of paragraphs (a) and (b) of this section may be illustrated by the following examples:

Example (1). During the first and second calendar quarters of the year, a manufacturer makes sales of articles taxable under section 4181 to his distributors. The total charges for such sales, exclusive of the tax, transportation charges, delivery charges, or other charges which are excludable, pursuant to section 4216(a) of the Code, in computing taxable price, are as follows:

First Quarter:	
Articles taxable under Section 4181	$100,000
Local advertising charges	3,000
Total Charges	103,000
Second Quarter:	
Articles taxable under Section 4181	$150,000
Local advertising charges	4,000
Total Charges	154,000

Assume further that the manufacturer contributes to the advertising plan and that the manufacturer pays $5,500 and $1,000 during the first and second calendar quarters of the year, respectively, to his distributors in reimbursement of expenses incurred by them for local advertising of the articles purchased from the manufacturer.

Computation as of close of first calendar quarter:	
1. Amount which would constitute total taxable price (computed at time of sale) if no part of any charge for local advertising were excludable in computing taxable price	$103,000
2. Amounts billed as separate charges for local advertising	−3,000
3. Difference	100,000
4. Overall 5 percent limitation (5 percent of item 3)	$5,000
5. Amount excluded in computing taxable price	−3,000
6. Unused portion of limitation	2,000
7. Allocation, pursuant to agreement, of $5,500 paid to distributors:	
Charges for local advertising	$3,000
Contributions by manufacturer	$2,500

Readjustment may be claimed in respect of that portion of the total amount repaid to the distributors which is allocated to the manufacturer's contribution ($2,500) to the extent that such portion does not exceed the unused portion of the overall 5 percent limitation ($2,000). Accordingly, as of the close of the first calendar quarter the manufacturer may claim credit or refund in respect of a readjustment of price in the amount of $2,000.

Computation as of close of second calendar quarter:	
1. Amount which would constitute total taxable price (computed at time of sale) if no part of any charge for local advertising were excludable in computing taxable price ($103,000+$154,000)	$257,000
2. Amounts billed as separate charges for local advertising ($3,000+$4,000)	−7,000
3. Difference	250,000
4. Overall 5 percent limitation (5 percent of item 3)	$12,500

5. Amount excluded in computing taxable price ($3,000+$4,000) plus readjustment claimed at end of first calendar quarter ($2,000)	−9,000
6. Unused portion of limitation	3,500
7. Allocation, pursuant to agreement, of $6,500 ($5,500+$1,000) paid to distributors:	
Charges for local advertising	$3,500
Contributions by manufacturer	$3,000

Although the total reimbursements for local advertising expenses attributable to contributions by the manufacturer ($3,000) does not exceed the unused portion of the overall 5 percent limitation ($3,500), the manufacturer, having taken, at the close of the first calendar quarter, a price readjustment in the amount of $2,000 in respect to his contributions, is entitled at the close of the second calendar quarter to claim credit or refund in respect of a price readjustment in the amount of $1,000 ($3,000−$2,000).

Example (2). During the first calendar quarter of the year, a manufacturer sold articles taxable under section 4181 to his distributors at a total charge of $106,000, exclusive of the tax, transportation charges, delivery charges, or other charges which are excludable, pursuant to section 4216(a) of the Code, in computing taxable price. This total charge of $106,000 was billed as follows:

Total Charge:	
Articles taxable under Section 4181	$100,000
Local advertising charges	6,000
Total charges	106,000

Assume further that the manufacturer contributes to the advertising plan and that the manufacturer pays $3,000 during the first calendar quarter of the year to his distributors in reimbursement of expenses incurred by them for local advertising of the articles purchased from the manufacturer.

Computation as of close of first calendar quarter:	
1. Amount which would constitute total taxable price (computed at time of sale) if no part of any charge for local advertising were excludable in computing taxable price	$106,000
2. Amounts billed as separate charges for local advertising	−6,000
d. Difference	100,000
4. Overall 5 percent limitation (5 percent of item 3)	5,000
5. Amount excluded in computing taxable price (see paragraph (c) of § 53.100	−5,000
6. Unused portion of limitation	0
7. Allocation, pursuant to agreement, of $3,000 paid to distributors:	....
Charges for local advertising	2,000
Contributions by manufacturer	1,000

Credit or refund may not be claimed in respect of that portion of the total amount repaid to the distributors ($3,000) which is allocated to the manufacturer's contribution ($1,000) since the amount excluded in computing taxable price is equal to the overall 5 percent limitation.

[T.D. ATF–308, 56 FR 303, Jan. 3, 1991, as amended by T.D. ATF–312, 56 FR 31084, July 9, 1991]

§ 53.102 No exclusion or readjustment for other advertising charges or reimbursements.

(a) *Exclusions from price.* No exclusion in computing the taxable price of any article sold by the manufacturer may be allowed in respect of any charge for advertising if, and to the extent that, such charge:

(1) Is for advertising which does not qualify as local advertising within the meaning of section 4216(e)(4) of the Code and paragraphs (a) and (b) of § 53.100, or

(2) Does not satisfy all of the conditions and limitations stated in section 4216(e)(1) of the Code and paragraph (c) of § 53.100.

(b) *Readjustments of price.* No credit or refund under section 6416(b)(1) of the Code may be allowed in respect of any amount which was included in the taxable price of an article sold by the manufacturer and which was later paid by him to his vendee in reimbursement of costs incurred for advertising, if, and to the extent that, the amount so paid:

(1) Is for advertising which does not qualify as local advertising within the meaning of section 4216(e)(4) of the Code and paragraph (b) of § 53.100, or

(2) Is not within the limitation provided in section 4216(e)(2) of the Code, as computed in accordance with § 53.101, as of the close of the calendar

quarter in which the amount is so paid over or as of the close of any subsequent calendar quarter in the same calendar year. See, however, §53.175, relating to redetermination of price readjustments in cases where local advertising charges excluded from taxable price in one calendar year become taxable as of May 1 of the following calendar year.

[T.D. ATF-308, 56 FR 303, Jan. 3, 1991, as amended by T.D. ATF-312, 56 FR 31084, July 9, 1991]

§53.103 Lease considered as sale.

For purposes of chapter 32 of the Code, the lease of an article by a manufacturer, producer, or importer shall be considered a sale of the article. The term *lease* means a contract or agreement, written or verbal, which gives the lessee an exclusive, continuous right to the possession or use of a particular article for a period of time. The term includes any renewal or extension of a lease or any subsequent lease of the article.

[T.D. ATF-308, 56 FR 303, Jan. 3, 1991, as amended by T.D. ATF-312, 56 FR 31084, July 9, 1991; T.D. 372, 61 FR 20724, May 8, 1996]

§53.104 Limitation on amount of tax applicable to certain leases.

(a) *Conditions for eligibility.* Section 4217(b) of the Code provides for a limitation on the amount of tax that shall apply to the lease, any renewal, or further lease, of an article which, if sold, would be subject to tax on the basis of sale price. Such limitation on the amount of the tax applies with respect to the lease of an article only if, at the time of making the lease, the lessor is engaged in the business of selling in arm's length transactions the same type and model of article. In case of a lease to which section 4217(b) of the Code does not apply, tax shall be computed and paid as provided in section 4216(c) of the Code and paragraph (a) of §53.98.

(b) *Lessor engaged in business of selling.* The lessor will be regarded as being engaged in the business of selling in arm's length transactions the same type and model of an article as the one being leased if it periodically and recurringly makes bona fide offers for sale of such articles in the regular course of operation of its business, which offers if accepted would constitute sales at arm's length. Whether the offers are bona fide shall be determined on the basis of the facts in each case, such as sales actually made, the nature of the advertising, sales literature, and other means used to effectuate sales. It is not necessary that the offers for sale be made to the same class of purchasers as those to whom the article is being leased.

(c) *Same type and model of article.* To qualify as the "same type and model of article", the article offered for sale must be an unused article essentially the same in size, design, and function as the article being leased. Slight differences in appearance or accessories will not render articles dissimilar which are identical in all other respects.

(d) *Basis for tax*—(1) *Tax payable until total tax in paid.* In case of a lease of an article to which section 4217(b) of the Code applies, tax shall be paid on each lease payment in an amount computed by applying to such lease payment a percentage equal to the rate of tax in effect on the date of the lease payment. Such tax payments shall continue to be made under such lease, or any subsequent lease of the article, until the cumulative total of the tax payments equals the total tax. Lease payments made thereafter with respect to that article shall not be subject to tax. For definition of the term "total tax," see paragraph (e) of this section.

(2) *Changes in tax rates.* If the rate of tax is increased or decreased during a lease period, the new rate shall apply to the lease payments made on and after the date of the change, but the amount of the total tax shall remain the same.

(e) *Total tax.* For purposes of this section, the term "total tax" means the amount of tax, computed at the rate in effect on the date of the first lease of the article to which section 4217(b) of the Code applies, which would be due on the constructive sale price of the article as determined under section 4216(b) of the Code and §53.95, as if the article had been sold by a manufacturer at retail on such date.

(f) *Sale of article before total tax becomes payable.* If the lessor sells the article before the total tax has become payable, the tax payable on the sale shall be the lesser of the following amounts:

(1) The difference between:

(i) The total tax, and

(ii) The aggregate tax applicable to lease payments already received; or

(2) A tax computed, at the rate in effect on the date of the sale, on the price for which the article is sold. For purposes of (f)(2) of this section, the provisions of section 4216(b) of the Code for determining a constructive sale price shall not apply if the sale is at arm's length. If the sale is not at arm's length, the tax referred to in (f)(2) of this section shall be computed on a constructive sale price as provided in § 53.95.

(g) *Sale of article after total tax has become payable.* If the lessor sells an article after the total tax has become payable, the tax imposed under chapter 32 of the Code shall not apply to such sale.

USE BY MANUFACTURER OR IMPORTER CONSIDERED SALE

§ 53.111 Tax on use by manufacturer, producer, or importer.

(a) *In general.* Section 4218 of the Code imposes tax in respect of certain uses of articles by the actual manufacturer, producer, or importer thereof. This section also applies in respect of the use of articles by any other person who, pursuant to a provision of chapter 32 of the Code, is considered to be, or is treated as, the manufacturer or producer of the articles. See, for example, section 4223 of the Code relating to articles purchased tax free for use in further manufacture.

(b) *Taxable articles in general*—(1) *Application of tax.* If the manufacturer, producer, or importer of an article taxable under chapter 32 of the Code uses the article for any purpose other than that indicated in paragraph (b) (3) of this section, he shall be liable for tax with respect to the use of such article in the same manner as if the article were sold by him.

(2) *Taxable use in manufacturer of nontaxable articles*—(i) *In general.* In the case of an article to which paragraph (b)(1) of this section applies, tax attaches when the manufacturer, producer, or importer of the articles uses it as material in the manufacture or production of, or as a component part of, another article which is not taxable under chapter 32 of the Code, regardless of the disposition made of such other article. (See paragraph (c) of § 53.115 for computation of tax on such use.)

(ii) *Types of use in manufacture of nontaxable articles.* Taxable use may consist of the incorporation of a taxable article into a nontaxable article. Taxable use may also result from the combining of a taxable article (or the components thereof) with a nontaxable article (or the components of a nontaxable article) resulting in a combination end article which itself is not taxable. Although the taxable article may not be a completely separable unit, within the contemplation of the law a taxable article has been produced and incorporated in the combination end article.

(3) *Nontaxable use in manufacturer of taxable articles.* The tax on the use of an article to which paragraph (b)(1) of this section has application shall not apply if the article is used by the manufacturer, producer, or importer thereof as material in the manufacturer or production of, or as a component part of, another article taxable under chapter 32 of the Code to be manfactured or produced by him. It is immaterial what disposition is made of such other article.

(c) *Use after lease.* If the manufacturer, producer, or importer of a taxable article leases such article and thereafter uses the article, he incurs liability for tax on such use as provided in these regulations to the same extent as if the article were sold after being leased. See section 4217 of the Code and the regulations thereunder in this subpart for application and computation of tax in case of leased articles.

(d) *Time of application of tax.* In the case of a taxable use of an article by the manufacturer, producer, or importer thereof, the tax attaches at the time such use begins. If tax applies by reason of the sale of an article by the manufacturer, producer, or importer thereof on or in connection with his sale of another article, the tax attaches at the time of the sale of such other article.

(e) *Exemptions because of other statutory provisions.* Tax does not apply on the use of an article by the manufacturer, producer, or importer thereof if under the applicable provisions of the Code the sale of the article for a similar use would not be subject to tax. Also, tax need not be paid with respect to the use of an article by the manufacturer, producer, or importer thereof if such use would qualify, under the provisions of section 6416(b) of the Code, for credit or refund of the tax paid.

[T.D. ATF–308, 56 FR 303, Jan. 3, 1991]

EDITORIAL NOTE: At 56 FR 31084, July 9, 1991, §53.111 was amended by removing the word "manufacturer" and adding the word "manufacture" in the heading of paragraph (a)(2), and removing the word "manufacturer" and adding the word "manufacture" in the first sentence of paragraph (a)(3), effective July 9, 1991; however, these sub-paragraph designations are not included in §53.111(a). The issuing agency will publish a correction in the FEDERAL REGISTER at a later date.

§53.112 Business or personal use of articles.

(a) *Business use.* Section 4218 of the Code applies to the use by a person, in the operation of any business in which he is engaged, of a taxable article which has been manufactured, produced, or imported by him or his agent.

(b) *Personal use.* The tax on use of a taxable article does not attach in cases where an individual incidentially manufacturers, produces, or imports a taxable article for his personal use or causes a taxable article to be manufactured, produced, or imported for his personal use.

§53.113 Events subsequent to taxable use of article.

Liability for tax incurred on the use of an article is not extinguished or reduced because of any subsequent sale or lease of the article even if such sale or lease would have been exempt if the article had been so sold or leased prior to use. If a manufacturer, producer, or importer of an article incurs liability for tax on his use thereof, and thereafter sells or leases the article in a transaction which otherwise would be subject to tax, liability for tax is not incurred on such sale or lease.

[T.D. ATF–308, 56 FR 303, Jan. 3, 1991, as amended by T.D. ATF–312, 56 FR 31084, July 9, 1991]

§53.114 Use in further manufacture.

For purposes of section 4218 and §53.111, an article is used as material in the manufacture or production of, or as a component part of, another article, if it is incorporated in, or is a part or accessory of, the other article. In addition, an article is considered to be used as material in the manufacturer of another article if it is partly or entirely consumed in testing such other article; for example, shells or cartridges used in testing new firearms. Similarly, if an article is partly or wholly consumed in quality testing a production run of like articles, such article is also considered to have been used as material in the manufacture of another article. However, if a taxable article that has been used tax free and only partly consumed in testing is later sold, or put to a taxable use by the manufacturer, tax attaches to such sale or use. An article that is consumed in the manufacturing process other than in testing, so that it is not a physical part of the manufactured article, is not used as material in the manufacture or production of or as a component part of, such other article.

[T.D. ATF–308, 56 FR 303, Jan. 3, 1991, as amended by T.D. ATF–312, 56 FR 31084, July 9, 1991]

§53.115 Computation of tax.

(a) *Tax based on price.* Tax liability incurred on the use of an article shall be computed on the price at which such or similar articles are sold in the ordinary course of trade by manufacturers, producers, or importers thereof and in the absence of special arrangements. For additional provisions applicable in computing the tax in the case of the use of an article by a manufacturer and producer who purchased the article free of tax under section 4221(a)(1) of the Code for use by him in further manufacture, see section 4223(b) of the Code and the regulations thereunder (§53.143).

(b) *Articles regularly sold by manufacturer.* If the manufacturer, producer, or importer of an article regularly sells such articles at wholesale in arm's length transactions, tax liability on his use of any such article shall be computed on his lowest established wholesale price for such articles in effect at the time of the taxable use. In establishing such price, there shall be included and excluded, as applicable, the charges and readjustments specified in sections 4216(a) and 6416(b)(1) of the Code, as in effect at the time tax liability on the use of the article is incurred, and the regulations thereunder contained in this subpart and subpart L (§§ 53.91–53.94 and 53.173–53.176). If the manufacturer, producer, or importer of an article does not regularly sell such articles at wholesale in arm's length transactions, a constructive price on which the use tax shall be computed will be determined by the appropriate TTB officer. This price will be established after considering the selling practices and price structures of manfacturers, producers, and importers of similar articles.

(c) *Articles governed by section 4218(a) used in manufacture of nontaxable combination articles.* If the manufacturer, producer, or importer of an article to which section 4218(a) of the Code applies does not regularly sell such article separately but uses it as material in the manufacture or production of, or as a component part of, a nontaxable combination article consisting of a taxable and nontaxable article, liability for tax on his use shall be computed on the constructive price of the taxable article at the time of use. To determine the constructive price of the taxable article in such case, the combination article is considered to be composed of:

(1) Parts used exclusively in the functioning of the taxable article in the combination;

(2) Parts used exclusively in the functioning of the nontaxable article in the combination, and

(3) Parts, called common parts, which serve a dual function in connection with the parts in both paragraphs (c) (1) and (2) of this section.

The ratio which the cost of the parts in paragraph (c)(1) of this section bears to the sum of the cost of such parts and the parts in paragraph (c)(2) of this section is applied to the lowest established wholesale price for which like combination articles are at the time of the taxable use being sold by the manufacturer or producer in the ordinary course of trade. The resulting amount is the constructive sale price for the taxable article on which tax is to be computed. The cost of the common parts is allocable to the parts in paragraphs (c) (1) and (2) of this section in the same ratio, and, therefore, need not be taken into account in the computation since the inclusion and allocation of the cost of such parts in the determination would not result in a different ratio. In determining the lowest establishment wholesale price for the combination article, there shall be included and excluded, as applicable, the charges and readjustments specified in sections 4216(a) and 6416(b)(1) of the Code, as in effect at the time tax liability on the use of the taxable article is incurred, and the regulations thereunder contained in this subpart and subpart L of this part (§§ 53.91–53.94 and §§ 53.173–53.176). The tax applicable to the use of the article for which a constructive sale price has been computed is not affected by any charges or readjustments of the price for which the nontaxable combination article is sold, whether by reason of the return or repossession of the nontaxable article or its covering or container, or by a bona fide discount, rebate, allowance, or other factor.

[T.D. ATF–308, 56 FR 303, Jan. 3, 1991, as amended by T.D. ATF–312, 56 FR 31084, July 9, 1991]

APPLICATION OF TAX IN CASE OF SALES BY OTHER THAN MANUFACTURER OR IMPORTER

§ 53.121 Sales of taxable articles by a person other than the manufacturer, producer, or importer.

(a) *General rule.* If the title to, or ownership of, an article taxable under chapter 32 of the Code is transferred from the manufacturer, producer, or importer thereof, and, under the law, no tax attaches to such transfer, the subsequent sale, lease, or use of such article by the transferee is subject to tax to the same extent and manner as if such transferee were the manufacturer, producer, or importer of the article. The following examples illustrate this rule:

(1) The surviving spouse, child or children, executors or administrators, or other legal representatives, as the case may be, of a deceased manufacturer, producer, or importer of taxable articles, incur liability for tax on all such articles sold by them.

(2) A receiver or trustee in bankruptcy who under a court order conducts or liquidates the business of a manufacturer, producer, or importer of taxable articles, incurs liability for tax on all taxable articles sold by him, regardless of whether the articles were manufactured, produced, or imported before or after he took charge of the business.

(3) An assignee for the benefit of creditors of a manufacturer, producer, or importer incurs liability for tax with respect to all taxable articles sold by him as such assignee.

(4) If one or more member of a partnership withdraw, or if new partners are admitted, the new partnership so constituted incurs liability for tax on all taxable articles sold by it regardless of when such articles were manufactured, produced, or imported.

(5) A person who acquires title to taxable articles as a result of default of the manufacturer, producer, or importer pursuant to an agreement under the terms of which the articles were pledged as collateral incurs liability for tax with respect to his sale of the articles so acquired.

(6) A person who succeeds to the business of a manufacturer, producer, or importer of taxable articles, such as:

(i) A corporation which results from a consolidation, merger, or reorganization;

(ii) A corporation which acquires the business of an individual or partnership; or

(iii) A stockholder in a corporation who, after its dissolution, continues the business;

incurs liability for the tax on all taxable articles sold by such person. However, where a manufacturer, producer, or importer sells only his assets, rather than ownership of his business, he incurs liability for tax on the sale of any taxable articles included in such assets.

(b) *Transfer of title to damaged articles.* If title to a damaged taxable article is transferred by the manufacturer, producer, or importer thereof to a carrier or insurance company in adjustment of a damage claim, such transfer is not considered a taxable sale of the article. If the article is usable, even though damaged, the carrier or insurance company incurs liability for tax on its sale, lease, or use of the article. Where the article has been damaged to the extent that its only value is as scrap, and it is not restored to usable condition, sale thereof by the carrier or insurance company is not subject to tax.

Subpart K—Exemptions, Registration, Etc.

§53.131 Tax-free sales; general rule.

(a) *In general.* Section 4221(a) of the Code sets forth the following exempt purposes for which an article subject to tax under chapter 32 of the Code may be sold tax-free by the manufacturer, producer, or importer:

(1) For use by the purchaser for further manufacture, or for resale by the purchaser to a second purchaser for use by such second purchaser in further manufacture,

(2) For export, or for resale by the purchaser to a second purchaser for export,

(3) For use by the purchaser as supplies for vessels or aircraft,

(4) To a State or local government for the exclusive use of a State or local government, and

(5) To a nonprofit educational organization for its exclusive use.

Section 4221(a) of the Code applies only in those cases where the exportation or use referred to is to occur before any other use, and where the seller, first purchaser, and second purchaser, as may be appropriate, have registered as required under section 4222 of the Code and paragraph (a) of §53.140. See paragraph (c) of this section for provisions relating to evidence required in support of tax-free sales. See §53.141 for exceptions to the requirement for registration. Where tax is paid on the sale of an article, but the article is used or resold for use for an exempt purpose, a claim for credit or refund may be filed in accordance with and to the extent provided in sections 6402(a) and 6416 of the Code, and the regulations thereunder (§§ 53.161 and 53.171–53.186).

(b) *Manufacturer relieved of liability in certain cases*—(1) *General rule.* Under the provisions of section 4221(c) of the Code, if an article subject to tax under Chapter 32 of the Code is sold free of tax by the manufacturer of the article for an exempt purpose referred to in section 4221(c) of the Code and paragraph (b)(2) of this section, the manufacturer shall be relieved of any tax liability under chapter 32 of the Code with respect to such sale if the manufacturer in good faith accepts a proper certification by the purchaser that the article or articles will be used by the purchaser in the stated exempt manner. See paragraph (b)(2) of this section for a list of the exempt purposes referred to in section 4221(c) of the Code.

(2) *Situations wherein section 4221(c) of the Code is applicable.* The following are situations wherein section 4221(c) of the Code is applicable with respect to sales made tax free on the assumption that one of the following sections of the Code provides exemption for such sales:

(i) Section 4221(a)(1) of the Code, to the extent that it relates to sales for further manufacture by a first purchaser (see § 53.132),

(ii) Section 4221(a)(3) of the Code, relating to supplies for vessels and aircraft (see § 53.134),

(iii) Section 4221(a)(4) of the Code, relating to sales to State or local governments (see § 53.135),

(iv) Section 4221(a)(5) of the Code, relating to sales to nonprofit educational organizations (see § 53.136).

(3) *Situations wherein section 4221(c) of the Code is not applicable.* The relief from liability for the payment of tax provided by section 4221(c) of the Code is not applicable with respect to sales made tax free on the assumption that one of the following sections of the Code provides exemption for such sales:

(i) Section 4221(a)(1) of the Code, to the extent that it relates to sales for resale to a second purchaser for use by the second purchaser in further manufacture (see § 53.132),

(ii) Section 4221(a)(2) of the Code, relating to sales for export (see § 53.133).

(4) *Duty of seller to ascertain validity of tax-free sale.* If the manufacturer at the time of its sale has reason to believe that the article sold by it is not intended for the exempt purpose indicated by the purchaser, or that the purchaser has failed to register as required, the manufacturer is not considered to have accepted certification from the purchaser in good faith, and is not relieved from liability under the provisions of section 4221(c) of the Code.

(5) *Information to be furnished to purchaser.* A manufacturer selling articles free of tax under this section shall indicate to the purchaser that:

(i) Certain articles normally subject to tax are being sold tax free, and

(ii) The purchaser is obtaining those articles tax free for an exempt purpose under an exemption certificate or its equivalent.

(6) The manufacturer may transmit this information by any convenient means, such as coding of sales invoices, provided that the information is presented with sufficient particularity so that the purchaser is informed that he has obtained the articles tax free and:

(i) The purchaser can compute and remit the tax due if an article sold tax free for further manufacture is diverted to a taxable use,

(ii) The manufacturer can remit the tax due with respect to an article purchased tax free for resale for use in further manufacture or for export if, within the 6-month period described in § 53.132(c) or § 53.133(c), the manufacturer does not receive proof that the article has been exported or resold for use in further manufacturer, or

(iii) The purchaser can notify the manufacturer if an article otherwise purchased tax free is diverted to a taxable use.

(c) *Evidence required in support of tax-free sales*—(1) *Purchasers required to be registered.* Every purchaser who is required to be registered (see § 53.140) shall furnish to the seller, as evidence in support of each tax-free sale made by the seller to such purchaser, the exempt purpose for which the article or articles are being purchased and the registration number of the purchaser.

Such information must be in writing and may be noted on the purchase order or other document furnished by the purchaser to the seller in connection with each sale.

(2) *Purchasers not required to be registered.* For the evidence which purchasers not required to register must furnish to the seller in support of each tax-free sale made by the seller to such purchasers, see paragraph (b) of §53.133 for sales or resales to a foreign purchaser for export, paragraph (d) of §53.134 for sales of supplies to vessels or aircraft, paragraph (c) of §53.135 for sales to State and local governments, and paragraph (c) of §53.141 for sales and purchases by the United States.

[T.D. ATF–308, 56 FR 303, Jan. 3, 1991, as amended by T.D. ATF–380, 61 FR 37005, July 16, 1996]

§53.132 Tax-free sale of articles to be used for, or resold for, further manufacture.

(a) *Further manufacture*—(1) *In general.* Under prescribed conditions, an article subject to tax under Chapter 32 of the Code may be sold tax free by the manufacturer, pursuant to section 4221(a)(1) of the Code, for use by the purchaser in further manufacture, or for resale by the purchaser to a second purchaser for use by the second purchaser in further manufacture. See section 4221(d) (6) of the Code and paragraph (b) of this section for the circumstances under which an article is considered to have been sold for use in further manufacture. See section 6416(b)(3) of the Code and §53.180 for the circumstances under which credit or refund is available when tax-paid articles are used in further manufacture.

(2) *Proof of resale for use in further manufacture.* See section 4221(b)(1) of the Code and paragraph (c) of this section for provisions under which the exemption provided in section 4221(a)(1) of the Code shall cease to apply in the case of an article sold by the manufacturer to a purchaser for resale to a second purchaser for use in further manufacture unless the manufacturer receives timely proof of resale for further manufacture.

(b) *Circumstances under which an article is considered to have been sold for use in further manufacture.* (1) For purposes of the exemption from the manufacturers excise tax provided by section 4221(a)(1) of the Code, an article shall be treated as sold for use in further manufacture if the article is sold for use by the purchaser as material in the manufacture or production of, or as a component part of, another article taxable under chapter 32 of the Code;

(2) An article is used as material in the manufacture or production of, or as a component of, another article if it is incorporated in, or is a part or accessory of, the other article when the other article is sold by the manufacturer. In addition, an article is considered to be used as material in the manufacture of another article if it is consumed in whole or in part in testing such other article; for example, shells or cartridges that are used by the manufacturer of firearms to test new firearms. However, an article that is consumed in the manufacturing process other than in testing, so that it is not a physical part of the manufactured article, is not considered to have been used as material in the manufacture of, or as a component part of, another article.

(c) *Proof of resale for further manufacture*—(1) *Cessation of exemption.* The exemption provided in section 4221(a)(1) of the Code and described in paragraph (a) of this section in respect of an article sold by the manufacturer to a purchaser for resale to a second purchaser for use by the second purchaser in further manufacture shall cease to apply on the first day following the close of the 6-month period which begins on the date of the sale of such article by the manufacturer, or the date of shipment of the article by the manufacturer, whichever is earlier, unless, within such 6-month period, the manufacturer receives proof, in the form prescribed by paragraph (c)(2) of this section, that the article was actually resold by the purchaser to a second purchaser for such use. If, on the first day following the close of the 6-month period, such proof has not been received, the manufacturer shall become liable for tax at that time at the rate in effect when the sale was made but otherwise in the same manner as if the article had been sold by it on such first day at a taxable price equivalent to that at which the article was actually sold. If the manufacturer later obtains such proof, it may file a claim for refund or credit of this tax. The payment of this tax by the manufacturer is not considered an overpayment by the subsequent manufacturer or producer for which the subsequent manufacturer or producer is entitled to a credit or refund under section 6416(b)(3) of the Code. See section 4221(d)(6) of the Code and paragraph (b) of this section for the circumstances under which an article is considered to have been sold for use in further manufacture.

(2) *Proof of resale*—(i) *Certificate of purchaser.* The proof of resale to be received by the manufacturer, as required under section 4221(b)(1) of the Code, may consist of either a copy of the invoice of the manufacturer's vendee directed to his purchaser which discloses the certificate of registry number held by each party or a statement described in this paragraph. In the case of an invoice of manufacturer's vendee, it must appear from such invoice (or by statement attached thereto) that the article was in fact resold for use in further manufacture. In lieu of such an invoice, proof of resale may consist of a statement, executed and signed by the manufacturer's vendee which includes the following:

(A) Date statement was executed.

(B) Name and address of manufacturer's vendee (if other than the person executing statement).

(C) Certificate of registry number held by vendee.

(D) Specify article(s) purchased tax-free, by whom purchased, certificate of registry number of second purchaser, date of purchase(s), whether articles were purchased as material in the manufacture or production of, or as a component part or parts of, an article or articles taxable under Chapter 32 of the Code.

(E) Statement that person executing statement or manufacturer's vendee possesses proof of tax-free resale of the article(s) in the form of purchase orders and sales invoices and identifying the person who will maintain custody of such proof for 3 years from the date of the statement and will make such proof available for inspection by TTB during such 3 year period.

(F) Statement that a previous statement has not been executed in respect of such certificate of resale and that the person signing the statement is aware that fraudulent use of the statement may subject the person signing the statement and all parties making fraudulent use of the statement to all applicable criminal penalties under the Code.

(G) Name, signature, and title of individual executing statement.

(ii) *Period covered.* Any statement executed and signed by the manufacturer's vendee, as provided in paragraph (c)(2)(i) of this section, may be executed with respect to any one or more articles purchased tax free from a manufacturer and resold for use in further manufacture within the 6-month period prescribed in section 4221(a)(1) of the Code and paragraph (c)(1) of this section. Such statement (or other prescribed proof of resale) must be retained for inspection by the appropriate TTB officer as provided in section 6001 of the Code.

(iii) *TTB I 5600.37.* A preprinted statement, TTB I 5600.37, Statement of Manufacturer's Vendee, which is available as provided in § 53.21(b), when completed, contains all necessary information for a properly executed statement. Extra copies of TTB I 5600.37 may be reproduced as needed.

[T.D. ATF–308, 56 FR 303, Jan. 3, 1991, as amended by T.D. ATF–380, 61 FR 37005, July 16, 1996]

§ 53.133 Tax-free sale of articles for export, or for resale by the purchaser to a second purchaser for export.

(a) *In general.* (1) An article subject to tax under chapter 32 of the Code may be sold tax free by the manufacturer, pursuant to section 4221(a)(2) of the Code and this section, for export, or for resale by the purchaser to a second purchaser for export. See § 53.11 for the meaning of the term "exportation". An article may be sold tax free by the manufacturer under the provisions of this section only if the person to whom the manufacturer sells the article intends either to export the article or to resell it to a person who intends to export it. An article may not be sold tax free under the provisions of this section by a manufacturer to a purchaser for resale to a second purchaser which does not intend to export the article itself but plans to resell it to a third purchaser for export. See section 6416(b)(2)(A) of the Code and §53.177 for the circumstances under which credit or refund of tax is available where tax-paid articles are exported from the United States.

(2) If an article, otherwise taxable under chapter 32 of the Code:

(i) Is sold tax free by the manufacturer pursuant to section 4221(a)(2) of the Code and this section, and

(ii) Is returned subsequently to the United States in an unused and undamaged condition,

then the importer is liable for the tax imposed by chapter 32 of the Code on the subsequent sale or use of the article in the United States. The provisions of this paragraph (a)(2) of this section may be illustrated by the following examples:

Example (1). Q, a U.S. manufacturer of shells and cartridges, previously sold shells and cartridges to R, a company in Canada. The sale was tax free under section 4221(a)(2). Prior to use, R sold the shells and cartridges to S, who imports the articles into the United States and sells them. The sale of the shells and cartridges subjects S to an excise tax liability under section 4181.

Example (2). X, a U.S. firearms manufacturer, sold a rifle to Y company in France. The sale was tax free under section 4221(a)(2). The rifle was sold by Y to W, an individual in the City of Nice, France. After initial use, W resold the rifle to X. X returned the rifle to the United States where it was resold. The resale of the rifle by X does not subject X to an excise tax liability under section 4181.

(b) *Sales or resales to a foreign purchaser for export.* In the case of sales or resales to a foreign purchaser for export, if the first or the second purchaser is located in a foreign country or possession of the United States, such purchaser is not required to register as provided in section 4222(a) of the Code and §53.140. To establish the right to sell articles tax free for export to a purchaser who is not registered and who is located in a foreign country or a possession of the United States, the manufacturer must obtain from such purchaser at the time title to the article passes or at the time of shipment, whichever is earlier, either:

(1) A written order or contract of sale showing that the manufacturer is to ship the article to a foreign destination; or

(2) Where delivery by the manufacturer is to be made within the United States, a statement from the purchaser showing:

(i) That the article is purchased either to fill existing or future orders for delivery to a foreign destination or for resale to another person engaged in the business of exporting who will export the article, and

(ii) That such article will be transported to its foreign destination in due course prior to use or further manufacture and prior to any resale except for export. See section 4221(b) of the Code and paragraphs (c) and (d) of this section for requirements as to timely proof of exportation and cessation of the exemption for export unless the evidence to show actual exportation has been received by the manufacturer.

(c) *Cessation of exemption.* The exemption provided in section 4221(a)(2) of the Code and paragraph (a) of this section for an article sold by the manufacturer for export or for resale by the purchaser to a second purchaser for export shall cease to apply on the first day following the close of the 6-month period which begins on the date of the sale of the article by the manufacturer, or the date of shipment of the article by the manufacturer, whichever is earlier, unless within the 6-month period the manufacturer receives proof, in the form prescribed by paragraph (d) of this section, that the article was actually exported. If, on the first day following the close of the 6-month period, the proof has not been received, the manufacturer shall become liable for tax at that time at the rate in effect when the sale was made but otherwise in the same manner as if the article had been sold by it on such first day at a taxable price equivalent to that at which the article was actually sold.

(d) *Proof of exportation.* (1) Exportation may be evidenced by:

(i) A copy of the export bill of lading issued by the delivering carrier,

(ii) A certificate by the agent or representative of the export carrier showing actual exportation of the article,

(iii) A certificate of landing signed by a customs officer of the foreign country to which the article is exported,

(iv) Where the foreign country has no customs administration, a statement of the foreign consignee showing receipt of the article, or

(v) Where a department or agency of the United States Government is unable to furnish any one of the foregoing four types of proof of exportation, a statement or certification on the department or agency stationery, executed by an authorized officer, that the listed or identified articles have, in fact, been exported.

(2) In any case where the manufacturer is not the exporter, the manufacturer must have in its possession a statement from the vendee to whom the manufacturer sold the article stating the following:

(i) Date statement was executed.

(ii) Name and address of manufacturer's vendee (if other than the person executing statement).

(iii) Certificate of registry number held by vendee.

(iv) Specify article(s) purchased tax-free, by whom purchased, and date of purchase.

(v) Statement that article(s) was either exported in due course by the vendee or was sold to another person who in due course exported the article(s).

(vi) Name and address of vendee who will maintain possession of the proof of exportation documents, description of the documents, and statement that vendee will maintain documents for 3 years and make them available to TTB for inspection.

(vii) Statement that a previous statement has not been executed in respect of the articles covered by this statement and that fraudulent use of this statement may subject person executing statement and all parties making fraudulent use of statement to all applicable criminal penalties under the Code.

(viii) Name, signature, title, and address of individual executing certificate.

(3) The statement executed and signed by the manufacturer's vendee, as provided in paragraph (d)(2) of this section, may be executed with respect to any one or more articles purchased tax free from a manufacturer and exported within the 6-month period prescribed in section 4221(b)(2) of the Code and paragraph (c) of this section. Such statement shall be kept for inspection by the appropriate TTB officer as provided in section 6001 of the Code.

(4) *TTB I 5600.36.* A preprinted statement, TTB I 5600.36, Statement of Manufacturer's Vendee, which is available as provided in §53.21(b), when completed, contains all necessary information for a properly executed statement. Extra copies of TTB I 5600.36 may be reproduced as needed.

[T.D. ATF–308, 56 FR 303, Jan. 3, 1991, as amended by T.D. ATF–344, 58 FR 40354, July 28, 1993; T.D. 372, 61 FR 20724, May 8, 1996; T.D. ATF–380, 61 FR 37006, July 16, 1996]

§53.134 Tax-free sale of articles for use by the purchaser as supplies for vessels or aircraft.

(a) *Supplies for vessels or aircraft*—(1) *In general.* An article subject to tax under chapter 32 of the Code may be sold tax free by the manufacturer, pursuant to section 4221(a)(3) of the Code and this section, for use by the purchaser as supplies for vessels or aircraft. See paragraph (b) of this section for the meaning of the term "supplies for vessels or aircraft." An article may be sold tax free under the provisions of this section only in those cases where the sale of an article by the manufacturer is made directly to the owner, officer, charterer, or authorized agent of a vessel or aircraft for use as supplies for the vessel or aircraft. No sale may be made tax free to a dealer for resale for use as supplies for vessels or aircraft, even though it is known at the time of sale by the manufacturer that the article will be so resold. See section 6416(b)(2)(B) of the Code and paragraph (c) of §53.178 for circumstances under which credit or refund of tax is available where tax-paid articles are used, or sold for use, as supplies for vessels or aircraft. An article may not be sold tax free under the provisions of this section by the manufacturer to passengers or members of the crew of a vessel or aircraft.

(2) *Civil aircraft of foreign registry.* In the case of any article sold by the manufacturer for use by the purchaser as

supplies for civil aircraft of foreign registry employed in foreign trade or in trade between the United States and any of its possessions, the provisions of this paragraph apply only if the reciprocity requirements of section 4221(e)(1) of the Code are met. See paragraph (c) of this section.

(b) *Meaning of terms*—(1) *Supplies for vessels or aircraft.* The term "supplies for vessels or aircraft" means fuel supplies, ships' stores, sea stores, or legitimate equipment on vessels of war of the United States or of any foreign nation, vessels employed in the fisheries or in the whaling business, or vessels actually engaged in foreign trade or trade between the Atlantic and Pacific ports of the United States or between the United States and any of its possessions.

(2) *Fuel supplies, ships' stores, and legitimate equipment.* The terms "fuel supplies", "ships' stores", and "legitimate equipment" include all articles, materials, supplies, and equipment necessary for the navigation, propulsion, and upkeep of vessels of war of the United States or of any foreign nation, vessels employed in the fisheries or in the whaling business, or vessels actually engaged in foreign trade or in trade between the Atlantic and Pacific ports of the United States or between the United States and any of its possessions, even though such vessels may make intermediate stops in the United States. The term does not include supplies for vessels engaged in trade:

(i) Between domestic ports in the Atlantic Ocean and the Gulf of Mexico,

(ii) Between domestic ports on the Pacific Ocean,

(iii) Between domestic ports on the Great Lakes, or

(iv) On the inland waterways of the United States.

(3) *Sea stores.* The term *sea stores* includes any article purchased for use or consumption by the passengers or crew, or both, of a vessel during its voyage.

(4) *Vessel.* The term *vessel* includes:

(i) Every description of watercraft or other contrivance used, or capable of being used, as a means of transportation on water,

(ii) Civil aircraft registered in the United States and employed in foreign trade or in trade between the United States and any of its possessions, and

(iii) Civil aircraft registered in a foreign country and employed in foreign trade or trade between the U.S. and its possessions.

(5) *Vessels of war of the United States or of any foreign nation.* The term *vessels of war of the United States or of any foreign nation* includes:

(i) Every description of watercraft or other contrivance used, or capable of being used, as a means of transportation on water and constituting equipment of the armed forces (including the U.S. Coast Guard and U.S. National Guard) of the United States or of a foreign nation, and

(ii) Aircraft owned by the United States or by any foreign nation and constituting equipment of the armed forces thereof.

(iii) For purposes of this section, vessels or aircraft owned by armed forces are not considered to be equipment of such armed forces while on lease or loan to an organization that is not part of the armed forces.

(6) *Vessels used in fisheries or whaling business.* The exemption provided by section 4221(a)(3) of the Code and paragraph (a) of this section in the case of articles sold for the prescribed use on vessels employed in the fisheries or whaling business is limited to articles sold by the manufacturer for such use on vessels while employed, and to the extent employed, exclusively in the fisheries or in the whaling business. For purposes of this section, vessels engaged in sport fishing are not considered to be employed in the fisheries business.

(7) *Civil aircraft.* The exemption provided by section 4221(a)(3) of the Code and paragraph (a) of this section relating to supplies for vessels or aircraft, with respect to civil aircraft, extends only to civil aircraft when employed in foreign trade, or in trade between the United States and any of its possessions. Sales of supplies to civil aircraft when engaged in trade between the Atlantic and the Pacific ports of the United States are not exempt from the tax imposed under chapter 32 of the Code. See section 4221(e)(1) of the Code and paragraph (c) of this section for requirement of reciprocal exemption in

the case of a civil aircraft registered in a foreign country.

(8) *Trade.* The term "trade" includes the transportation of persons or property for hire and the making of the necessary preparations for such transportation. The term "trade" also includes the transportation of property on a vessel or aircraft owned or chartered by the owner of the property in connection with the purchase, sale, or exchange of the property in a commercial business operation. However, a vessel owned or chartered by a company and used in the transportation of personnel or property of such company to or from its business properties located in a foreign country, or in a possession of the United States, is not engaged in "trade".

(c) *Reciprocity required in the case of civil aircraft.* The exemption provided by section 4221(a)(3) of the Code and paragraph (a) of this section with respect to the sales of supplies for civil aircraft registered in a foreign country is further limited in that the privilege of exemption may be granted only if the Secretary of Commerce advises the Secretary of the Treasury that the foreign country allows, or will allow, substantially the same reciprocal privileges. If a foreign country discontinues the allowance of such substantially reciprocal exemption, the exemption allowed by the United States will not apply after the Secretary of the Treasury is notified by the Secretary of Commerce of the discontinuance of the exemption allowed by the foreign country.

(d) *Evidence required to establish*—(1) *In general.* The exemption provided in section 4221(a)(3) of the Code and paragraph (a) of this section for articles sold for use by the purchaser as supplies for vessels or aircraft applies only:

(i) If both the manufacturer and purchaser are registered under the provisions of section 4222 of the Code, or

(ii) The purchaser or both the manufacturer and the purchaser are not registered but have satisfied the provisions of paragraph (d)(2) of this section.

See paragraph (c) of § 53.131 for the evidence required to establish exemption where the purchaser is registered pursuant to section 4222 of the Code and § 53.140.

(2) *Exemption certificates for use in support of tax-free sales of supplies for vessels and aircraft.* (i) In order to establish exemption from tax under section 4221(a)(3) of the Code in those instances where the purchaser or both the manufacturer and purchaser are not registered under section 4222 of the Code, the manufacturer must obtain (prior to or at the time of the sale) from the owner, charterer, or authorized agent of the vessel or aircraft and retain in the manufacturer's possession a properly executed exemption certificate in the form prescribed by paragraph (d)(2)(iii) of this section. If articles are sold tax-free for use as supplies for civil aircraft employed in foreign trade or in trade between the United States and any of its possessions, the exemption certificate must show the name of the country in which the aircraft is registered.

(ii) Where only occasional sales of articles are made to a purchaser for use as supplies for vessels or aircraft, a separate exemption certificate shall be furnished for each order. However, where sales are regularly or frequently made to a purchaser for such exempt use, a certificate covering all orders for a specified period not to exceed 12 calendar quarters will be acceptable. Such certificates and proper records of invoices, orders, etc., relative to tax-free sales must be kept for inspection by the appropriate TTB officer as provided in section 6001 of the Code.

(iii) *Acceptable form of exemption certificate.* A certificate of exemption to support tax-free sales under this section must include the following:

(A) Name of owner, charterer, or authorized agent.

(B) Name of company and vessel.

(C) List article(s) covered by the certificate or beginning and ending dates during which orders will be placed (not to exceed 12 calendar quarters).

(D) Statement that articles will be used only for fuel supplies, ships' stores, sea stores, or legitimate equipment on a vessel belonging to one of the class of vessels to which section 4221 of the Code applies. Identify class of vessel certificate covers (see paragraphs (a) and (b) of this section).

(E) If articles are purchased for use on civil aircraft engaged in foreign trade or trade between the United States and any of its possessions, state the country in which the aircraft is registered.

(F) Statement that it is understood that if any articles are used for any purpose other than as stated in the certificate, or are resold or otherwise disposed of, the person executing the certificate must notify the manufacturer.

(G) Statement that the certificate shall not be used to purchase tax-free articles for use as supplies, etc. on pleasure vessels or any type of aircraft except:

(*1*) Civil aircraft employed in foreign trade or trade between the United States and any of its possessions;

(*2*) Aircraft owned by the United States or any foreign country and constituting a part of the armed forces thereof.

(H) Statement that it is understood that any fraudulent use of the certificate may subject person executing certificate and all parties making fraudulent use of the certificate to all applicable criminal penalties under the Code.

(I) Statement that person executing certificate is prepared to establish by satisfactory evidence the purpose for which the article(s) was used.

(J) Date, name, signature, and address of person executing the certificate.

(iv) *TTB I 5600.34.* A preprinted certificate, TTB I 5600.34, Exemption Certificate, which is available as provided in §53.21(b), when completed, contains all necessary information for a properly executed certificate. Extra copies of TTB I 5600.34 may be reproduced as needed.

[T.D. ATF–308, 56 FR 303, Jan. 3, 1991, as amended by T.D. ATF–380, 61 FR 37006, July 16, 1996; T.D. TTB–44, 71 FR 16957, Apr. 4, 2006]

§53.135 Tax-free sale of articles to State and local governments for their exclusive use.

(a) *In general.* An article subject to tax under Chapter 32 of the Code may be sold tax free by the manufacturer, pursuant to section 4221(a)(4) of the code and this section, to a State or local government for the exclusive use of such State or local government. See paragraph (b) of this section for the meaning of the term "State or local government". An article may be sold tax free by the manufacturer under this paragraph only in those cases where the sale is made directly to a State or local government for its exclusive use. Accordingly, no sale may be made tax free to a dealer for resale to a State or local government for its exclusive use, even though it is known at the time of sale by the manufacturer that the article will be so resold. A sale of an article to a State or local government for resale is not considered to be a sale for the "exclusive use" of the State or local government, within the meaning of section 4221(a)(4) of the Code, and, therefore, such sales may not be made tax free. Such sales are not exempt regardless of whether the resales are made to government employees, or the fact that the article is an item of equipment the employee is required to possess in carrying out his duties. For example, pistols or revolvers may not be sold tax free to a State or local government for resale to its police officers. See section 6416(b)(2)(C) of the Code, and paragraph (d) of §53.178, for the circumstances under which credit or refund of tax is available where tax-paid articles are sold for the exclusive use of a State or local government.

(b) *State or local government.* The term *State or local government* includes any State, the District of Columbia, and any political subdivision of any of the foregoing. *See,* section 7871(a)(2)(B) of the Code and 26 CFR 305.7701–1 *et seq.*, which provide that an Indian tribal government shall be treated as a State for purposes of exemption from an excise tax imposed by chapter 32. Section 7871(b) of the Code provides that the exemption from tax applies only if the transaction involves the exercise of an essential governmental function of the Indian tribal government.

(c) *Evidence required in support of tax-free sales to State or local governments.* (1) In the case of a State or local government which is registered (see §53.141 for provisions under which a State or local government may register if it so desires), the provisions of paragraph (c) of § 53.131 have application as to the evidence required in support of tax-free sales. If a State or local government is not registered, the evidence required in support of a tax-free sale to the State or local government shall, except as provided in paragraph (c)(2) of this section, consist of a certificate, executed and signed by an officer or employee authorized by the State or local government to execute and sign the certificate. If it is impracticable to furnish a separate certificate for each order or contract because of frequency of purchases, a certificate covering all orders between given dates (such period not to exceed 12 calendar quarters) will be acceptable. The certificates and proper records of invoices, orders, etc., relative to tax-free sales must be retained by the manufacturer as provided in § 53.24(d). A certificate of exemption to support tax-free sales under this section must contain the following:

(i) Title of official executing certificate, branch of government, date executed, and statement that official is authorized to execute certificate.

(ii) List articles covered by the certificate or beginning and ending dates during which orders will be placed by the purchaser (period not to exceed 12 calendar quarters).

(iii) Name of manufacturer from which articles purchased.

(iv) Governmental unit purchasing articles.

(v) Statement that is understood that articles purchased under this certificate of exemption are limited to use exclusively by the purchasing governmental entity.

(vi) Statement that is understood that any fraudulent use of this certificate may subject the person executing the certificate and all parties making fraudulent use of the certificate to all applicable criminal penalties under the Code.

(vii) Name, address, and signature of person executing the certificate.

(2) A purchase order, provided that all of the information required by paragraph (c)(1) of this section is included therein, is acceptable in lieu of a separate exemption certificate.

(3) *TTB I 5600.35.* A preprinted certificate, TTB I 5600.35, Exemption Certificate, which is available as provided in § 53.21(b), when completed, contains all necessary information for a properly executed certificate. Extra copies of TTB I 5600.35 may be reproduced as needed.

(d) *Resale of articles purchased tax free by a State or local government.* If articles purchased tax free for the exclusive use of a State or local government (whether on the basis of a registration number or an exemption certificate) are, prior to use by the State or local government, resold under circumstances that do not amount to an exclusive use by the State or local government (such as pistols or revolvers that are resold by a police department to its police officers), the parties responsible in the State or local government are required to inform the manufacturer, producer, or importer from whom the articles were purchased that they were disposed of in a manner that did not amount to an exclusive use by the State or local government. A willful failure to supply the manufacturer, producer, or importer with the information required by this subparagraph will subject responsible parties to the penalties provided by section 7203 of the Code.

[T.D. ATF–308, 56 FR 303, Jan. 3, 1991, as amended by T.D. ATF–380, 61 FR 37006, July 16, 1996]

§ 53.136 Tax-free sales of articles to nonprofit educational organizations.

(a) *In general.* An article subject to tax under chapter 32 of the Code may be sold tax free by the manufacturer, pursuant to section 4221(a)(5) of the Code and this section, to a nonprofit educational organization for its exclusive use. See paragraph (b) of this section for the meaning of the term "nonprofit educational organization". An article may be sold tax free by the manufacturer under this paragraph only in those cases where the sale of an article by the manufacturer is made directly to a nonprofit educational organization for its exclusive use. Accordingly, no sale may be made tax free to a dealer for resale to a nonprofit educational organization for its exclusive use even though it is known at the time of sale by the manufacturer that the article will be so resold. See section 6416(b)(2)(D) of the Code, and paragraph (e) of §53.178, for the circumstances under which credit or refund of tax is available where tax-paid articles are sold for the exclusive use of a nonprofit educational organization.

(b) *Nonprofit educational organization.* The term "nonprofit educational organization" means an organization described in section 170(b)(1)(A)(ii) of the Code that is exempt from income tax under section 501(a) of the Code. Section 170(b)(1)(A)(ii) describes an "educational organization" as one that normally maintains a regular faculty and curriculum and normally has a regularly enrolled body of pupils or students in attendance at the place where its educational activities are regularly carried on. The term also includes a school operated as an activity of an organization described in section 501(c)(3) of the Code which is exempt from income tax under section 501(a) of the Code, provided the primary function of such school is the presentation of formal instruction and provided such school normally maintains a regular faculty and curriculum and normally has a regularly enrolled body of pupils or students in attendance at the place where its educational activities are regularly carried on.

(c) *Evidence required in support of tax-free sales to nonprofit educational organizations.* Every nonprofit educational organization purchasing tax free under section 4221(a)(5) of the Code must furnish the following information to the seller:

(1) The tax exempt purpose for which the article or articles are being purchased, and

(2) Its registration number. Such information must be in writing and may be noted on the purchase order or other document furnished by the purchaser to the seller in connection with each sale "except that a single notification containing the information described in this paragraph may cover all sales by the seller to the purchaser made during a designated period not to exceed 12 successive calendar quarters.". See paragraph (c) of §53.131 for the evidence required to establish exemption.

[T.D. ATF-308, 56 FR 303, Jan. 3, 1991, as amended by T.D. ATF-447, 66 FR 19088, Apr. 13, 2001]

§§53.137–53.139 [Reserved]

§53.140 Registration.

(a) *General rule.* Except as provided in §53.141, tax-free sales under section 4221 of the Code may be made only if the manufacturer, first purchaser, and second purchaser, as the case may be, have registered as required by this section. To secure a Certificate of Registry, the applicant must furnish the information required in paragraph (b) of this section.

(b) *Information to be submitted.* Except as provided in §53.141, any person who is eligible to sell or purchase articles free of a tax imposed by section 4181 of the Code and who has not registered with the Commissioner of the Internal Revenue Service prior to January 1, 1991 or with TTB in accordance with the provisions of this section shall, prior to making a tax-free sale or purchase, file TTB Form 5300.28, in duplicate, executed in accordance with the instructions contained on the reverse of TTB Form 5300.28. The person who receives an approved Certificate of Registry shall be considered to be registered for purposes of selling or purchasing articles tax free as provided in this section. In the case of a nonprofit educational organization, information shall be furnished showing that the organization is an educational organization described in section 170(b)(1)(A)(ii) of the Code that is exempt from income tax under section 501(a) of the Code, or is a school operated as an activity of an organization described in section 501(c)(3) that is exempt from income tax under section 501(a).

(c) *Evidence required in support of tax-free sales.* See §53.131(c)(1) for evidence required in support of tax-free sales to purchasers who are required to be registered.

(d) *Failure to register.* If either the seller or purchaser is not registered as required by this section of the regulations, tax-free sales may not be made, except as indicated in §53.141.

(e) *Cross references.* (1) For exceptions to the requirement for registration, see section 4222(b) of the Code and § 53.141.

(2) For revocation or suspension of registration, see § 53.142.

[T.D. ATF–308, 56 FR 303, Jan. 3, 1991, as amended by ATF–447, 66 FR 19088, Apr. 13, 2001]

§ 53.141 Exceptions to the requirement for registration.

(a) *State and local governments.* (1) A State or local government purchasing articles direct from the manufacturer for its exclusive use may, but is not required to, register as provided in § 53.140. To establish the right to sell articles tax free to a State or local government that is not registered, the manufacturer must obtain from an authorized official of the State or local government and retain in the manufacturer's possession either a properly executed exemption certificate, or a purchase order that contains the same information required to be furnished in an exemption certificate. See § 53.135(c) for the information necessary to substantiate a tax-free sale under such circumstances.

(2) Each State requesting registration will be assigned one Certificate of Registry. The registration number shown on this certificate may be used by all agencies, boards, and commissions of the State that are authorized by the State to make purchases for the exclusive use of the State. However, the registration number assigned to a State may not be used by any political subdivision of that State, such as a county or municipality. Each political subdivision of a State desiring to obtain a Certificate of Registry must obtain a separate registration number.

(b) *Sales or resales to foreign purchasers for export.* Persons whose principal place of business is not within the United States may, but are not required to, register in order to purchase articles tax free for export. To establish the right to sell articles tax free for export to a purchaser who is not registered and who is located in a foreign country or a possession of the United States, the manufacturer must obtain the evidence required by § 53.133(b).

(c) *United States.* The registration requirements of the regulations in this part do not apply to purchases and sales by the United States or any of its agencies or instrumentalities. The evidence required in support of such tax-free purchases and sales is a notation on the purchase order or other document furnished to the seller clearly indicating that the article or articles are being purchased tax free as authorized by chapter 32 of the Code.

(d) *Supplies for vessels and aircraft.* An article subject to an excise tax imposed by chapter 32 of the Code may be sold tax free by the manufacturer under the provisions of § 53.134 for use by the purchaser as supplies for a vessel or aircraft if both the manufacturer and the purchaser are registered under the provisions of § 53.140. The article also may be sold tax free for such use even though neither the manufacturer nor the purchaser is so registered if the provisions of paragraph (d) of § 53.134 are satisfied.

[T.D. ATF–308, 56 FR 303, Jan. 3, 1991, as amended by T.D. ATF–312, 56 FR 31084, July 9, 1991]

§ 53.142 Denial, revocation or suspension of registration.

(a) The appropriate TTB officer is authorized to deny, revoke or temporarily suspend, upon written notice, the registration of any person and the right of such person to sell or purchase articles tax free under section 4221 of the Code in any case in which he finds that:

(1) The registrant is not a bona fide manufacturer, or a purchaser reselling direct to manufacturers or exporters;

(2) The registrant is for some other reason not eligible under these regulations to retain a Certificate of Registry; or

(3) The registrant has used his registration to avoid payment of the tax imposed by section 4181 of the Code, or to postpone or interfere in any manner with the collection of such tax;

(4) Such denial, revocation, or suspension is necessary to protect the revenue; or

(5) The registrant failed to comply with the requirements of paragraph (c) of § 53.140, relating to the evidence required to support a tax-free sale.

(b) The denial, revocation, or suspension of registration is in addition to any other penalty that may apply under the law for any act or failure to act.

[T.D. ATF–308, 56 FR 303, Jan. 3, 1991, as amended by T.D. ATF–365, 60 FR 33671, June 28, 1995]

§53.143 Special rules relating to further manufacture.

(a) *Purchasing manufacturer to be treated as the manufacturer.* For purposes of Chapter 32 of the Code, a manufacturer or producer to whom an article is sold or resold tax free under section 4221(a)(1) of the Code for use by it in further manufacture shall be treated as the manufacturer or producer of such article. If a manufacturer who purchases an article tax free for further manufacture does not use the article for further manufacture, the sale of the article by it, or its use of the article other than in further manufacture, shall, for purposes of the taxes imposed by chapter 32 of the Code, be treated as a sale or use of the article by the manufacturer thereof. See paragraphs (b) and (c) of this section for determination of taxable sale price where an article purchased tax free for further manufacture is resold, or used other than in further manufacture.

(b) *Computation of tax.* Except as provided in paragraph (c) of this section, the tax liability referred to in paragraph (a) of this section shall be based on the price for which the article was sold by the purchasing manufacturer, or, where the manufacturer uses the article for a purpose other than that for which it was purchased, the tax shall be based on the price at which such or similar articles are sold, in the ordinary course of trade, by manufacturers, producers, or importers thereof. See section 4218(e) of the Code and §53.115.

(c) *Election.* (1) Instead of computing the tax as described under paragraph (b) of this section, the purchasing manufacturer who has incurred liability for tax on its sale or use of an article as provided by paragraph (a) of this section may compute the tax incurred under chapter 32 of the Code by using as the tax base either the price for which the article was sold to it by the first purchaser, if any, or the price for which such article was sold by the actual manufacturer, producer, or importer of such article. The purchasing manufacturer must have in its possession information upon which to substantiate such basis for tax. For purposes of this paragraph, the price for which the article was sold by the actual manufacturer or by the first purchaser shall be determined as provided in section 4216 of the Code and §§53.91–53.102. However, such price shall not be adjusted for any discount, rebate, allowance, return, or repossession of a container or covering, or otherwise.

(2) The election under this paragraph shall be in the form of a statement attached to the return reporting the tax applicable to the sale or use of the article which gave rise to such tax liability. Such election, once made, may not be revoked.

Subpart L—Refunds and Other Administrative Provisions of Special Application to Manufacturers Taxes

§53.151 Returns.

(a) *In general.* (1) Liability for tax imposed under chapter 32 of the Code shall be reported on TTB Form 5300.26, Federal Firearms and Ammunition Excise Tax Return. Except as provided in paragraphs (a)(2) and (b) of this section, a return on Form 5300.26 shall be filed for a period of one calendar quarter.

(2) *Return periods after September 30, 1992.* For return periods after September 30, 1992, every person required to make a return on TTB Form 5300.26 who does not incur any firearms and ammunition excise tax liability in a given calendar quarter shall not be required to file a return on TTB Form 5300.26 for that calendar quarter. Except as provided in paragraph (a)(5) of this section, every person required to make a return on TTB Form 5300.26 who does not incur any firearms and ammunition excise tax liability for the entire calendar year and who has not filed a final return in accordance with §53.152 shall file an annual return on TTB Form 5300.26.

(3) *Return periods prior to October 1, 1992.* For return periods prior to October 1, 1992, every person required to make a return on TTB Form 5300.26 shall make a return for each calendar quarter (whether or not liability was incurred for any tax reportable on the return for the return period) until the person has filed a final return in accordance with §53.152.

(4) *Forms, etc.* Each return required under the regulations in this part, together with any prescribed copies, records, or supporting data, shall be completed in accordance with the applicable forms, instructions, and regulations.

(5) *Special rule for one-time or occasional filings for return periods on or after July 1, 1995.* One-time or occasional filers are not required to file quarterly or annual returns pursuant to paragraph (a)(2) of this section if the person reporting tax does not engage in any activity with respect to which tax is reportable on the return in the course of a trade or business. Such persons shall file and pay tax for periods only when liability is incurred. See §53.159(b)(2), providing that a deposit of taxes is not required for a one-time or occasional filing.

(b) *Monthly and semimonthly returns*—(1) *Requirement.* If the appropriate TTB officer determines that any taxpayer who is required to deposit taxes under the provision of §§53.157 or 53.159 has failed to make deposits of those taxes, the taxpayer shall be required, if so notified in writing by the appropriate TTB officer, to file a monthly or semimonthly return on TTB Form 5300.26. Every person so notified by the appropriate TTB officer shall file a return for the calendar month or semimonthly period in which the notice is received and for each calendar month or semimonthly period thereafter until the person has filed a final return in accordance with §53.152 or is required to file returns on the basis of a different return period pursuant to notification as provided in paragraph (b)(2) of this section.

(2) *Change of requirement.* The appropriate TTB officer may require the taxpayer, by notice in writing, to file a quarterly or monthly return, if the taxpayer has been filing returns for a semimonthly period, or may require the taxpayer to file a quarterly or semimonthly return, if the taxpayer has been filing monthly returns.

(3) *Return for period change takes effect.* (i) If a taxpayer who has been filing quarterly returns receives notice to file a monthly or semimonthly return, or a taxpayer who has been filing monthly returns receives notice to file a semimonthly return, the first return required pursuant to the notice shall be filed for the month or semimonthly period in which the notice is received and all months or semimonthly periods which are not includable in an earlier period for which the taxpayer is required to file a return.

(ii) If a taxpayer who has been filing monthly or semimonthly returns receives notice to file a quarterly return, the last month or semimonthly period for which a return shall be filed is the last month or semimonthly period of the calendar quarter in which the notice is received.

(iii) If a taxpayer who has been filing semimonthly returns receives notice to file a monthly return, the last semimonthly period for which a return shall be made is the last semimonthly period of the month in which the notice is received.

[T.D. ATF–308, 56 FR 303, Jan. 3, 1991, as amended by T.D. ATF–330, 57 FR 40325, Sept. 3, 1992; T.D. ATF–365, 60 FR 33671, June 28, 1995; T.D. TTB–91, 76 FR 5481, Feb. 1, 2011]

§53.152 Final returns.

(a) *In general.* Any person who is required to make a return on TTB Form 5300.26 pursuant to §53.151 and who in any return period ceases operations in respect of which the person is required to make a return on the form, shall make the return for that return period as a final return. A return made as a final return shall be marked "Final Return" by the person filing the return. A taxpayer who has only temporarily ceased to incur liability for tax required to be reported on TTB Form 5300.26 because of temporary or seasonal suspension of business or for other reasons, shall not make a final return until such operations are permanently ceased.

(b) *Statement to accompany final return.* Each final return shall have attached a statement showing the address at which the records required by the regulations in this part will be kept, the name of the person keeping the records, and, if the business of the taxpayer has been sold or otherwise transferred to another person, the name and address of that person and the date on which the sale or transfer took place. If no sale or transfer occurred or if the taxpayer does not know the name of the person to whom the business was sold or transferred, that fact should be included in the statement.

[T.D. ATF–308, 56 FR 303, Jan. 3, 1991, as amended by T.D. ATF–330, 57 FR 40325, Sept. 3, 1992. Redesignated in part by T.D. ATF–365, 60 FR 33670, June 28, 1995]

§ 53.153 Time for filing returns.

(a) *Quarterly returns.* Each return required to be made under § 53.151(a) for a return period of one calendar quarter shall be filed on or before the last day of the first calendar month following the close of the period for which it is made. However, a return may be filed on or before the 10th day of the second calendar month following the close of the period if timely deposits under section 6302(c) of the Code and § 53.157 have been made in full payment of the taxes due for the period. For purposes of the preceding sentence, a deposit which is not required by regulations in respect of the return period may be made on or before the last day of the first calendar month following the close of the period.

(b) *Monthly, semimonthly and annual returns*—(1) *Monthly returns.* Each return required to be made under § 53.151(b) for a monthly period shall be filed not later than the 15th day of the month following the close of the period for which it is made.

(2) *Semimonthly returns.* Each return required to be made under § 53.151(b) for a semimonthly period shall be filed not later than the 10th day of the semimonthly period following the close of the period for which it is made.

(3) *Annual returns.* Each return filed under the provisions of § 53.151(a) for a return period of one calendar year shall be filed not later than the 31st day following the close of the calendar year.

(c) *Last day for filing.* If the due date falls on a Saturday, Sunday, or legal holiday, the return and remittance shall be due on the next succeeding day which is not a Saturday, Sunday, or legal holiday. For purposes of this section, "legal holiday" is defined by section 7503 of the Code and 26 CFR 301.7503(b).

(d) *Late filing.* The taxpayer is subject to a penalty for failure to file a return or to pay tax within the prescribed time as imposed by section 6651 of the Code, if the return and remittance are not filed before the close of business on the prescribed last day of filing. For additions to the tax in the case of failure to file a return within the prescribed time, see 27 CFR 70.96.

[T.D. ATF–308, 56 FR 303, Jan. 3, 1991, as amended by T.D. ATF–330, 57 FR 40325, Sept. 3, 1992]

§ 53.154 Manner of filing returns.

(a) Each return on TTB Form 5300.26 shall be filed with TTB, in accordance with the instructions on the form.

(b) When the taxpayer sends the return on TTB Form 5300.26 by U.S. Mail, the official postmark of the U.S. Postal Service stamped on the cover in which the return was mailed shall be considered the date of delivery of the return. When the postmark on the cover is illegible, the burden of proving when the postmark was made will be on the taxpayer. When the taxpayer sends the return with or without remittance by registered mail or by certified mail, the date of registry or the date of the postmark on the sender's receipt of certified mail, as the case may be, shall be treated as the date of delivery of the return and, if accompanied, of the remittance.

[T.D. ATF–308, 56 FR 303, Jan. 3, 1991, as amended by T.D. ATF–330, 57 FR 40325, Sept. 3, 1992]

§ 53.155 Extension of time for filing returns.

(a) *In general.* Ordinarily, no extension of time will be granted for filing any return statement or other document required with respect to the taxes impose by chapter 32, because the information required for the filing of those documents is under normal circumstances readily available. However, if because of temporary conditions beyond the taxpayer's control, a taxpayer believes an extension of time for filing is justified, the taxpayer may apply to the appropriate TTB officer for an extension. An extension of time for filing a return does not operate to extend the time for payment of the tax or any part of the tax unless so specified in the extension. For extensions of time for payment of the tax, see § 53.156.

(b) *Application for extension of time.* The application for an extension of time for filing the return shall be addressed to the appropriate TTB officer with whom the return is to be filed and must contain a full recital of the causes for the delay. It should be made on or before the due date of the return, and failure to do so many indicate negligence and constitute sufficient cause for denial. It should, where possible, be made sufficiently early to permit consideration of the matter and reply before what otherwise would be the due date of the return.

(c) *Filing the return.* If an extension of time for filing the return is granted, a return shall be filed before the expiration of the period of extension.

§ 53.156 Extension of time for paying tax shown on return.

(a) *In general.* (1) Ordinarily, no extensions of time will be granted for payment of any tax imposed by Chapter 32 of the Code, and shown or required to be shown on any return. However, if because of temporary conditions beyond the taxpayer's control a taxpayer believes an extension of time for payment is justified, the taxpayer may apply for an extension filing TTB Form 5600.38. The period of an extension shall not be in excess of 6 months from the date fixed for payment of the tax, except that if the taxpayer is abroad the period of the extension may be in excess of 6 months.

(2) The granting of an extension of time for filing a return does not operate to extend the time for the payment of the tax or any part of the tax unless so specified in the extension. See § 53.155.

(b) *Undue hardship required for extension.* An extension of the time for payment shall be granted only upon a satisfactory showing that payment on the due date of the amount with respect to which the extension is desired will result in an undue hardship. The extension will not be granted upon a general statement of hardship. The term "undue hardship" means more than an inconvenience to the taxpayer. It must appear that substantial financial loss, for example, loss due to the sale of property at a sacrifice price, will result to the taxpayer from making payment on the due date of the amount with respect to which the extension is desired. If a market exists, the sale of property at the current market price is not ordinarily considered as resulting in an undue hardship.

(c) *Application for extension.* An application for an extension of time for payment of the tax shown or required to be shown on any return shall be made on TTB Form 5600.38, Application for Extension of Time for Payment of Tax, and shall be accompanied by evidence showing the undue hardship that would result to the taxpayer if the extension were refused. The application shall also be accompanied by a statement of the assets and liabilities of the taxpayer and an itemized statement showing all receipts and disbursements for each of the 3 months immediately preceding the due date of the amount to which the application relates. The application, with supporting documents, must be filed on or before the date prescribed for payment of the amount with respect to which the extension is desired. The application will be examined, and within 30 days, if possible, will be denied, granted, or tentatively granted subject to certain conditions of which the taxpayer will be notified. If an additional extension is desired, the request for it must be made on or before the expiration of the period for which the prior extension is granted.

(d) *Payment pursuant to extension.* If an extension of time for payment is granted, the payment shall be made on or before the expiration of the period of the extension without the necessity of notice and demand. The granting of an extension of time for payment of the tax does not relieve the taxpayer from liability for the payment of interest on the tax during the period of the extension. See section 6601 of the Code and 26 CFR 301.6601–1.

[T.D. ATF–308, 56 FR 303, Jan. 3, 1991, as amended by T.D. ATF–312, 56 FR 31084, July 9, 1991; T.D. ATF–447, 66 FR 19088, Apr. 13, 2001]

§53.157 Deposit requirement for deposits made for calendar quarters prior to July 1, 1995.

NOTE: For deposit requirement for deposits made for calendar quarters beginning on or after July 1, 1995, see §53.159.

(a) *Monthly deposits.* Except as provided in paragraph (b) of this section, if for any calendar month (other than the last month of a calendar quarter) any person required to file a quarterly excise tax return on TTB Form 5300.26 has a total liability under this part of more than $100 for all excise taxes reportable on that form, the amount of liability for taxes shall be deposited by the person in accordance with the instructions on TTB Form 5300.27 on or before the last day of the month following the calendar month.

(b) *Semimonthly deposits.* (1) If any person required to file an excise tax return on TTB Form 5300.26 for any calendar quarter has a total liability under this part of more than $2,000 for all excise taxes reportable on that form for any calendar month in the preceding calendar quarter, the amount of that liability for taxes under this part for any semimonthly period (as defined in paragraph (d)(1) of this section) in the succeeding calendar quarter shall be deposited by the person in accordance with the instructions on TTB Form 5300.27 on or before the depositary date (as defined in paragraph (d)(2) of this section) applicable to the semimonthly period.

(2) A person will be considered to have complied with the requirements of paragraph (b)(1) of this section for a semimonthly period if—

(i)(A) The person's deposit for the semimonthly period is not less than 90 percent of the total amount of the excise taxes reportable by the person on TTB Form 5300.26 for the period, and

(B) If the semimonthly period occurs in a calendar month other than the last month in a calendar quarter, the person deposits any underpayment for the month by the 9th day of the second month following the calendar month; or

(ii)(A) The person's deposit for each semimonthly period in the calendar month is not less than 45 percent of the total amount of the excise taxes reportable by the person on TTB Form 5300.26 for the month, and

(B) If such month is other than the last month in a calendar quarter, the person deposits any underpayment for such month by the 9th day of the second month following the calendar month; or

(iii)(A) The person's deposit for each semimonthly period in the calendar month is not less than 50 percent of the total amount of the excise taxes reportable by the person on TTB Form 5300.26 for the second preceding calendar month, and

(B) If such month is other than the last month in a calendar quarter, the person deposits any underpayment for such month by the 9th day of the second month following the calendar month; or

(iv)(A) The requirements of paragraph (b)(2) (i)(A), (ii)(A), or (iii)(A) of this section are satisfied for the first semimonthly period of a calendar month after December 1990,

(B) If the person's deposit for the second semimonthly period of the calendar month is, when added to the deposit for the first semimonthly period, not less than 90 percent of the total amount of the excise taxes reportable by the person on TTB Form 5300.26 for the calendar month, and

(C) If the semimonthly periods occur in a calendar month other than the last month in a calendar quarter, the person deposits any underpayment for the month by the 9th day of the second month following the calendar month.

(3)(i) Paragraph (b)(2) (ii) and (iii) of this section shall not apply to any person who normally incurs in the first semimonthly period in each calendar month more than 75 percent of the person's total excise tax liability under this part for the month.

(ii) Persons who make their deposits in accordance with paragraph (b)(2) (ii), (iii), or (iv) of this section will find it unnecessary to keep their books and records on a semimonthly basis.

(c) *Deposit of certain excess undeposited amounts.* Notwithstanding paragraphs (a) and (b) of this section, if any person required to file an excise tax return on TTB Form 5300.26 for any calendar quarter beginning after December 31, 1990, has a total liability under this part for all excise taxes reportable on the form for the calendar quarter which exceeds by more than $100 the total amount of taxes deposited by the person pursuant to paragraph (a) or (b) of this section for the calendar quarter, the person shall, on or before the last day of the calendar month following the calendar quarter for which the return is required to be filed, deposit in accordance with the instructions on TTB Form 5300.27 the full amount by which the person's liability for all excise taxes reportable on the return for that calendar quarter exceeds the amount of excise taxes previously deposited by the person for that calendar quarter.

(d) *Definitions*—(1) *Semimonthly period.* The term *semimonthly period* means the first 15 days of a calendar month or the portion of a calendar month following the 15th day of that month.

(2) *Depositary date.* The term *depositary date* means, in the case of deposits for semimonthly periods beginning after December 31, 1990, the 9th day of the semimonthly period following the semimonthly period for which the taxes are reportable.

(3) *Lockbox financial institution.* The term *lockbox financial institution* means the financial institution designated as a depository for the payment of excise taxes on TTB Form 5300.27, Federal Firearms and Ammunition Excise Tax Deposit form.

(e) *Depositary forms and procedures*—(1) *In general.* Each remittance of amounts required to be deposited for periods beginning after December 31, 1990 shall be accompanied by an TTB Form 5300.27, Federal Firearms and Ammunition Excise Tax Deposit form, or TTB Form 5300.26, Federal Firearms and Ammunition Excise Tax Return, which shall be prepared in accordance with the applicable instructions. Taxpayers electing to remit deposits by EFT pursuant to § 53.158 shall prepare and submit TTB Form 5300.26 or TTB Form 5300.27 in accordance with the instructions on the form. The timeliness of the deposit will be determined by the date it is received (or is deemed received under section 7502(e) and 26 CFR 301.7502–1) by the lockbox financial institution, or the TTB officer designated on TTB Form 5300.27 or TTB Form 5300.26 accompanying the deposit, or when made by electronic fund transfer, the Treasury Account. Amounts deposited pursuant to this paragraph shall be considered to be paid on the last day prescribed for filing the return in respect of the tax (determined without regard to any extension of time for filing the returns), or at the time deposited, whichever is later.

(2) *Number of remittances.* A person required by this section to make deposits may make one or more remittances with respect to the amount required to be deposited. An amount of tax which is not otherwise required by this section to be deposited may, nevertheless, be deposited if the person liable for the tax so desires.

(3) *Information required.* Each person making deposits pursuant to this section shall report on the return for the period with respect to which the deposits are made information regarding the deposits in accordance with the instructions applicable to the return and pay (or deposits by the due date of the return) the balance, if any, of the taxes due for the period.

(4) *Procurement of prescribed forms.* Copies of the Federal Firearms and Ammunition Excise Tax Deposit form will be furnished, so far as possible, to persons required to make deposits under this section. Such a person will not be excused from making a deposit, however, by the fact that no form has been furnished. A person not supplied with the form is required to apply for it in ample time to make the required deposits within the time prescribed, supplying with the application the person's name, employer identification number, address, and the taxable period to which the deposits will relate. Copies of the Federal Firearms and Ammunition Excise Tax Deposit form are available as provided in § 53.21(b).

(f) *Nonapplication to certain taxes.* This section does not apply to taxes for:

(1) Any month or semimonthly period in which the taxpayer receives notice pursuant to §53.151(b) to file TTB Form 5300.26 or

(2) Any subsequent month or semimonthly period for which a return on TTB Form 5300.26 is required.

[T.D. ATF-308, 56 FR 303, Jan. 3, 1991, as amended by T.D. ATF-312, 56 FR 31084, July 9, 1991; T.D. ATF-330, 57 FR 40325, Sept. 3, 1992; T.D. ATF-365, 60 FR 33671, June 28, 1995; T.D. ATF-447, 66 FR 19088, Apr. 13, 2001; T.D. TTB-44, 71 FR 16958, Apr. 4, 2006]

§53.158 Payment of tax by electronic fund transfer.

(a) *In general.* For return periods after September 30, 1992, any taxpayer liable for firearms and ammunition excise taxes incurred under this part may elect to remit payments and deposits of the taxes (taxpayments) by electronic fund transfer (EFT). A taxpayer who elects to make remittance by EFT must use that method of remitting excise taxes on firearms and ammunition for a minimum of four consecutive calendar quarters. A taxpayer who makes remittance by EFT for a calendar quarter may not use any other method of remitting and ammunition excise taxes for that quarter.

(b) *Requirements.* (1) On or before the 10th day of the calendar quarter preceding the calendar quarter in which the taxpayer will begin remitting taxes by EFT, each taxpayer who elects to make remittances by EFT of firearms and ammunition excise taxes incurred under this part shall give written notice to the appropriate TTB officer, indicating that remittances will be paid by EFT. Taxpayers who gave written notification in a previous calendar quarter electing to make remittances of tax by EFT are not required to give additional written notifications to continue remitting tax by EFT for succeeding calendar quarters.

(2) For each deposit made or return filed in accordance with this subpart, the taxpayer shall direct the taxpayer's financial institution to make an EFT in the amount of the taxpayment to the Treasury Account as provided in paragraph (e) of this section. The request will be made to the financial institution early enough for the transfer of funds to be made to the Treasury Account no later than the close of business on the last day for making the deposit or filing the return as prescribed in §§53.157 or 53.159, and 53.153. The request will take into account any time limit established by the financial institution.

(3) Taxpayers who elect to discontinue making remittances by EFT of firearms and ammunition excise taxes may make such election at any time following four consecutive calendar quarters in which tax is remitted by EFT. Taxpayers electing to discontinue making remittances by EFT shall remit the tax with the next deposit or return as prescribed in §§53.157 or 53.159, and 53.151 for remittances not made by EFT and notify the appropriate TTB officer by attaching a written notification to the tax deposit form or return stating that remittance of firearms and ammunition excise taxes will no longer be made by EFT.

(c) *Remittance.* (1) Taxpayers who elect to make firearms and ammunition excise taxpayments by EFT shall file the deposit form and/or return with TTB in accordance with the applicable instructions on the forms.

(2) Remittances will be considered as made when the taxpayment by EFT is received by the Treasury Account when it is paid to a Federal Reserve Bank.

(3) When the taxpayer directs the financial institution to effect an electronic fund transfer message as required by paragraph (b)(2) of this section, the transfer data record furnished to the taxpayer through normal banking procedures will serve as the record of payment and will be retained as part of the required records.

(d) *Failure to make a taxpayment by EFT.* The taxpayer is subject to penalties imposed by 26 U.S.C. 6651 and 6656, as applicable, for failure to make a payment or deposit of tax by EFT on or before the close of business on the prescribed last day for making such payment or deposit.

(e) *Procedure.* Upon the notification required under paragraph (b)(1) of this section, the appropriate TTB officer will issue to the taxpayer an TTB Procedure entitled Payment of Tax by Electronic Fund Transfer. This publication outlines the procedure a taxpayer follows when preparing deposits, returns and EFT remittances in accordance with this subpart.

[T.D. ATF–330, 57 FR 40326, Sept. 3, 1992, as amended by T.D. ATF–365, 60 FR 33671, June 28, 1995; T.D. ATF–447, 66 FR 19088, Apr. 13, 2001]

§53.159 Deposit requirement for deposits made for calendar quarters beginning on or after July 1, 1995.

(a) *Definitions*—(1) *Definition of tax liability.* For purposes of this section, the term "tax liability" means the total tax liability for the specified period plus or minus any allowable adjustments made in accordance with the instructions applicable to the form on which the return is made.

(2) *Semimonthly period.* Except as provided in paragraph (c)(4)(ii) of this section, the term "semimonthly period" means the first 15 days of a calendar month or the remaining portion of a calendar month following the 15th day of that month.

(b) *In general*—(1) *Semimonthly deposits.* Except as provided in paragraphs (b)(2), (c)(2), and (j) of this section, any person required to file a quarterly excise tax return on TTB Form 5300.26 must make a deposit of tax for each semimonthly period as prescribed in paragraph (c) of this section.

(2) *One-time or occasional filings.* No deposit is required in the case of any taxes reportable on a one-time or occasional filing (as defined in §53.151(a)(5)).

(c) *Amount of deposit*—(1) *In general.* Except as provided in paragraphs (c)(2), (c)(3) and (c)(6) of this section, the deposit of tax for each semimonthly period must be equal to the amount of tax liability incurred during that semimonthly period. Except as provided in paragraph (c)(3) of this section, no deposit is required for any semimonthly period in which no tax liability is incurred.

(2) *De minimis exception.* Except as provided in paragraph (c)(3) of this section, any person who has a tax liability for the current calendar quarter of $2,000 or less is not required to make deposits for that quarter. However, semimonthly deposits of tax are required beginning with the semimonthly period in which unpaid tax liability exceeds $2,000 and for every semimonthly period thereafter in which tax liability is incurred. The first deposit for the current quarter shall be equal to the unpaid tax liability; thereafter, deposits shall be equal to the amount of tax liability incurred during that semimonthly period.

(3) *Amount of deposit; safe harbor rule based on look-back quarter liability; In general.* Except as provided in paragraph (c)(6) of this section, any person who made a return of tax on TTB Form 5300.26 reporting taxes for the second preceding calendar quarter (the "look-back quarter"), or who did not file a return for the look-back quarter because of the provisions of §53.151(a)(2), is considered to have complied with the requirement for deposit of taxes for the current calendar quarter if—

(i) The deposit of taxes for each semimonthly period in the current calendar quarter is an amount equal to not less than 1/6 (16.67 percent) of the total tax liability incurred for the look-back quarter;

(ii) Each deposit is made on time; and

(iii) The amount of any underpayment of taxes for the current calendar quarter is paid by the due date of the return.

(4) *Modification for third calendar quarter.* The safe harbor rule in paragraph (c)(3) of this section does not apply for the third calendar quarter unless—

(i) The deposit of taxes for the semimonthly period July 1–September 15 meets the requirements of paragraph (c)(3) of this section; and

(ii) Each deposit of taxes for the periods September 16–25 and September 26–30 is not less than 1/12th (8.34 percent) of the total tax liability incurred for the look-back quarter.

(5) *Modification for tax rate increase*—(i) *Application.* The safe harbor rule as prescribed in paragraph (c)(3) is modified for the first and second calendar quarters beginning on or after the effective date of an increase in the rate of any tax prescribed by 26 U.S.C. 4181 to which this part 53 applies.

(ii) *Modification.* The amount of deposit for calendar quarters referred to in paragraph (c)(3) of this section must be adjusted so that the deposit of taxes for each semimonthly period in the calendar quarter is not less than 1/6 (16.67 percent) of the tax liability the person would have had with respect to the tax for the look-back quarter if the increased rate of tax had been in effect for that look-back quarter.

(6) *First time filers.* Any person who did not file a return of tax on TTB Form 5300.26 for the first and second preceding calendar quarters because they were not engaged in any activity with respect to which tax is reportable on the return in the course of a trade or business, is considered to have complied with the requirement for deposit of taxes for the current calendar quarter if—

(i) The deposit of taxes for each semimonthly period in the calendar quarter is not less than 95 percent of the tax liability incurred with respect to those taxes during the semimonthly period;

(ii) Each deposit is made on time; and

(iii) The amount of any underpayment of taxes for the current calendar quarter is paid by the due date of the return.

(d) *Failure to comply with deposit requirements.* (1) If a person fails to make deposits as required under this part, the appropriate TTB officer may withdraw the person's right to use the safe harbor rule provided by paragraph (c)(3) of this section.

(2) *Cross reference.* The appropriate TTB officer may also require a taxpayer who fails to make deposits of tax to file a monthly or semimonthly return, see § 53.151(b)(1).

(e) *Time for making deposit.* Except for deposits for the period September 16–25, each deposit required to be made by this section shall be made not later than the 9th day of the semimonthly period following the close of the period for which it is made. The deposit for the period September 16–25 shall be made not later than September 28. The deposit for the period September 26–30, is due not later than October 9.

(f) *Last day for filing.* (1) Except as provided by paragraph (f)(2) of this section, if the due date of the deposit falls on a Saturday, Sunday, or legal holiday, the deposit and remittance shall be due on the next succeeding day which is not a Saturday, Sunday, or legal holiday. For purposes of this section, "legal holiday" is defined by section 7503 of the Code and 27 CFR 70.306(b) of this chapter.

(2) If the required due date of the deposit for the period September 16–25 falls on a Saturday, the deposit and remittance shall be due on the preceding day. If such required due date falls on a Sunday, the return and remittance shall be due on the following day.

(g) *Forms and procedures.* Each remittance of amounts required to be deposited shall be accompanied by Form 5300.27, Federal Firearms and Ammunition Excise Tax Deposit form, or Form 5300.26, Federal Firearms and Ammunition Excise Tax Return, which shall be prepared in accordance with the applicable instructions. Taxpayers electing to remit deposits by EFT pursuant to § 53.158 shall prepare and submit Form 5300.26 or Form 5300.27 in accordance with the instructions contained in Procedure 92–1, Publication 5000.11. The timeliness of the deposit will be determined by the date it is received by the lockbox financial institution, or the TTB officer designated on the form accompanying the deposit, or the Treasury Account, when made by EFT. In order for deposits of less than $20,000 made by U.S. Mail to be considered received timely, the date of mailing must be on or before the second day preceding the due date of the deposit as evidenced by the official postmark of the U.S. Postal Service stamped on the cover in which the deposit was mailed. When the postmark on the cover is illegible, the burden of proving when the postmark was made will be on the taxpayer. When the taxpayer sends the deposit by registered mail or by certified mail, the date of registry or the date of the postmark on the sender's receipt of certified mail, as the case may be, shall be treated as the date of delivery of the deposit. Any deposit of $20,000 or more must be received by the last day prescribed for making such deposit, regardless of when mailed. Amounts deposited pursuant to this paragraph shall be considered to be paid on the last day prescribed for filing the return in respect of the tax (determined without regard to any extension of time for filing the returns), or at the time deposited, whichever is later.

(h) *Number of remittances.* A person required by this section to make deposits shall make one deposit for a semimonthly period.

(i) *Procurement of prescribed forms.* Copies of the Federal Firearms and Ammunition Excise Tax Deposit form will be furnished, so far as possible, to persons required to make deposits under this section. Such a person will not be excused from making a deposit however, by the fact that no form has been furnished. A person not supplied with the form is required to obtain the form in ample time to make the required deposits within the time prescribed. Copies of the Federal Firearms and Ammunition Excise Tax Deposit form are available as provided in § 53.21(b).

(j) *Taxpayers required to file monthly or semimonthly returns.* This section does not apply to taxes for:

(1) Any month or semimonthly period in which the taxpayer receives notice pursuant to section 53.151(b) to file TTB Form 5300.26; or

(2) Any subsequent month or semimonthly period for which a return on TTB Form 5300.26 is required.

(3) Taxpayers required to file monthly returns shall make semimonthly deposits of 100 percent of the liability incurred during each semimonthly period by the 9th day of the month following the last day of the semimonthly period. Taxpayers required to file semimonthly returns shall pay any tax due for the semimonthly period with each return.

(k) *Examples.*

Example 1. One-time filing or occasional filing. (1) *Facts.* On October 18, 1995, A, an individual who lives in the United States purchases a custom made rifle outside the United States and imports it into the United States. A uses the rifle on October 20, 1995. A is liable for the firearms excise tax imposed by sections 4181 and 4218(a). Since A does not regularly sell rifles in arm's length transactions, a constructive sale price of $20,000 is determined (§ 53.115(b)). The amount of A's tax liability is $2200, 11 percent of the constructive sale price of the rifle. The liability is incurred during the fourth calendar quarter of 1995, the quarter during which the rifle is used (§ 53.111(d)). A did not import the rifle in the course of its trade or business and does not engage in any activities with respect to which tax is reportable on TTB Form 5300.26 in the course of a trade or business.

(2) *Filing requirement.* A must file a return on Form 5300.26 (§ 53.151(a)) for the fourth calendar quarter of 1995 reporting A's $2200 firearms excise tax liability. The Form 5300.26 is due by January 31, 1996, the last day of the first month following the calendar quarter (§ 53.153(a)). Because A did not import the firearm in the course of its trade or business and does not engage in any activities with respect to which tax is reportable in the course of a trade or business, the return is a one-time filing or occasional filing.

(3) *Payment requirement.* Because A's Form 5300.26 is a one-time filing, A is not required to make deposits of tax (§ 53.159(b)(2)). Instead, A pays the $2200 of tax with the return.

Example 2. Deposit requirement; based on look-back quarter liability. (1) *Facts.* B is a manufacturer of firearms. B sells 75 pistols which have a taxable sale price of $500 each during the second calendar quarter of 1996. B sold 50 of the pistols in the first semimonthly period of May, 1996, and the other 25 pistols in the second semimonthly period of April, 1996. B did not incur tax liability in any other semimonthly period in the second quarter. The amount of B's tax liability for the second calendar quarter is $3,750, 10 percent of the taxable sale price of the pistols. B filed Form 5300.26 for the second preceding calendar quarter, the look-back quarter, on January 31, 1996 reporting tax liability in the amount of $2,700.

(2) *Deposit requirement.* B is required to make deposits of tax for each semimonthly period in the calendar quarter because B has incurred more than $2,000 in liability for the current quarter. B may use the safe harbor rule based on look-back quarter liability to determine the amount of the required deposits (§ 53.159(c)(3)). Under this safe harbor rule, B's deposit for each semimonthly period must equal at least $450.00, 1/6 (16.67 percent) of the tax liability incurred for the look-back quarter. B's deposit must be timely and B must pay the amount of any underpayment by the due date of the return. Accordingly, B meets the deposit requirement if B makes the following deposits:

Semimonthly period	Deposit due by	Amount of deposit
April 1–15	April 24, 1996	$450.00
April 16–31	May 9, 1996	450.00
May 1–15	May 24, 1996	450.00
May 16–30	June 10, 1996	450.00
June 1–15	June 24, 1996	450.00
June 16–30	July 9, 1996	450.00

The deposit due on June 10, 1996, would ordinarily be due on June 9, 1996. However, because June 9, 1996 is a Sunday, under section 7503, B has an additional day to make the required deposit.

(3) *Filing requirement.* B must file a return on Form 5300.26 for the second calendar quarter of 1996 reporting B's $3750 tax liability (§ 53.151(a)). The form 5300.26 is due by July

31, 1996, the last day of the first month following the calendar quarter (§ 53.153(a)). B must also pay $1050.00, the underpayment amount by which the total tax liability for the second calendar quarter exceeds the total tax liability for the look-back quarter, by the due date of the return.

Example 3. Deposit amount; no liability in look-back quarter. (1) *Facts.* C, a manufacturer of ammunition, filed returns for the first, second and third quarters of 1995 reporting C's tax liability. During the fourth quarter of 1995, C did not make any taxable sales of shells or cartridges, thereby incurring no tax liability for that return period. C did not file Form 5300.26 for the fourth calendar quarter since no tax liability was incurred (§ 53.151(a)(2)). C made taxable sales in the second quarter of 1996 amounting to $25,500.00, incurring a tax liability of $2805.

(2) *Deposit requirement.* Ordinarily, C would be required to make deposits of tax for each semimonthly period in the calendar quarter because C's total liability for the current calendar quarter exceeds $2,000. However, since C incurred a tax liability of $0 in the second preceding calendar quarter (the look-back quarter) (§ 53.159(c)(3)), under the safe harbor rule, C is not required to make deposits of tax.

(3) *Filing requirement.* C is required to file a return on Form 5300.26 reporting C's $2805 ammunition excise tax liability. The form 5300.26 is due by July 31, 1996.

(4) *Payment requirement.* C must pay the $2805 tax with the return.

Example 4. Deposit requirement; First time Filer. (1) *Facts.* D, a manufacturer of firearms, began business on 2/16/96. D sold 300 shotguns which had a taxable sales price of $210 each during the first quarter of 1996. D sold 70 shotguns in the second semimonthly period of February, 1996, 130 shotguns in the first semimonthly period of March, 1996 and 100 shotguns in the second semimonthly period of March, 1996. The amount of D's tax liability for the first quarter of 1996 is $6,930, 11 percent of the taxable sale price of the shotguns.

(2) *Deposit requirement.* D is required to make a deposit of tax when D's tax liability exceeds $2,000 (§ 53.159(c)(2)). Therefore, D must make a deposit of tax beginning with the first semimonthly period in March, the semimonthly period in which D's unpaid tax liability exceeded $2,000. Because D, a first time filer, does not have an established look-back quarter, D's deposit of tax must be at least 95 percent of the incurred tax liability. D is required to make deposits of at least 95 percent of incurred tax liability for every semimonthly period in the quarter thereafter. D's deposits must be timely and any underpayment of tax must be paid by the due date of the return. Accordingly, D meets the deposit requirement if D makes the following deposits:

Semimonthly period	Deposit due by	Amount of deposit
Feb. 16–29	March 11, 1996	$0
March 1–15	March 25, 1996	4,389
March 16–31	April 9, 1996	2,194.50

The deposits due on March 11, 1996, and March 25, 1996, would ordinarily be due on March 9, 1996, and March 24, 1996, respectively. However, because March 9, 1996, is a Saturday, and March 24, 1996, is a Sunday, under section 7503, D has until March 11, 1996, to make the deposit due on March 9, 1996, and until March 25, 1996, to make the deposit due on March 24, 1996.

(3) *Filing requirement.* D must file a return on Form 5300.26 for the first calendar quarter of 1996 reporting D's $6,930 tax liability (§ 53.151(a)). The form 5300.26 is due by April 30, 1996, the last day of the first month following the calendar quarter (§ 53.153(a)). D must also pay $346.50, the amount by which the tax liability for the quarter was underpaid, by the due date of the return.

Example 5. Deposit amount; third calendar quarter. (1) *Facts.* E, a manufacturer of firearms, is a semimonthly depositor who makes deposits of tax using the safe harbor rule based on the look-back quarter to determine the amount of tax required to be deposited for the third calendar quarter of 1995. E incurred a tax liability amounting to $38,000 for the third quarter. E filed Form 5300.26 for the second preceding calendar quarter, the look-back quarter on May 1, 1995, reporting tax liability in the amount of $30,000.

(2) *Deposit requirement.* Because E has incurred more than $2,000 in liability and has chosen to make deposits of tax based on the look-back quarter, E is required to make deposits of tax equal to $5,000, 1/6 (16.67 percent) of the tax liability incurred in the look-back quarter, for each semimonthly period in the calendar quarter. However, because of the special rule which modifies the safe harbor rule for deposits of tax for the month of September (§ 53.159(c)(4)), E must make deposits equal to $2500.00 each, 1/12th (8.34 percent) of the tax liability incurred in the look-back quarter for the periods September 16–25 and September 26–30. E's deposits must be timely and E must pay the amount of any underpayment by the due date of the return. Accordingly, E meets the deposit requirement if E makes the following deposits:

Semimonthly period	Deposit due by	Amount of deposit
July 1–15	July 24, 1995	$5000.00
July 16–31	August 9, 1995	5000.00
Aug. 1–15	August 24, 1995	5000.00
Aug. 16–31	Sept. 11, 1995	5000.00
Sept. 1–15	Sept. 25, 1995	5000.00
Sept. 16–25	Sept. 28, 1995	2500.00
Sept. 26–30	October 9, 1995	2500.00

The deposits due on September 11, 1995, and September 25, 1995, would ordinarily be due on September 9, 1995, and September 24, 1995, respectively. However, because September 9, 1995, is a Saturday, and September 24, 1995, is a Sunday, under section 7503, D has until September 11, 1995, to make the deposit due on September 9, 1995, and until September 25, 1995, to make the deposit due on September 24, 1995.

(3) *Filing requirement.* E must file a return on Form 5300.26 for the third calendar quarter of 1995 reporting E's $38,000 tax liability (§ 53.153(a)). E must also pay $8,000, the underpayment amount by which the total tax liability for the third calendar quarter exceeds the total tax liability for the lookback quarter, by the due date of the return.

[T.D. ATF–365, 60 FR 33671, June 28, 1995, as amended by T.D. ATF–447, 66 FR 19089, Apr. 13, 2001; T.D. TTB–44, 71 FR 16958, Apr. 4, 2006]

§ 53.161 Authority to make credits or refunds.

For provisions relating to credits and refunds of certain taxes on sales and services see section 6416 of the Code and §§ 53.171–53.186. For regulations under section 6402 of the Code of general application in respect of credits or refunds, see 27 CFR 70.122, 70.123, and 70.124 (Procedure and Administration).

§ 53.162 Abatements.

For regulations under section 6404 of the Code of general application in respect of abatements of assessments to tax, see 27 CFR 70.125 (Procedure and Administration).

§§ 53.163–53.170 [Reserved]

§ 53.171 Claims for credit or refund of overpayments of manufacturers taxes.

Any claims for credit or refund of an overpayment of a tax imposed by chapter 32 of the Code shall be made in accordance with the applicable provisions of this subpart and the applicable provisions of 27 CFR 70.123 (Procedure and Administration). A claim on TTB Form 2635 (5620.8) is not required in the case of a claim for credit, but the amount of the credit shall be claimed by entering that amount as a credit on a return of tax under this subpart filed by the person making the claim. In this regard, see § 53.185.

§ 53.172 Credit or refund of manufacturers tax under chapter 32.

(a) *Overpayment not described in section 6416(b)(2) of the Code*—(1) *Claims included.* This paragraph applies only to claims for credit or refund of an overpayment of manufacturers tax imposed by Chapter 32. It does not apply, however, to a claim for credit or refund on any overpayment described in paragraph (b) of this section which arises by reason of the application of section 6416(b)(2) of the Code.

(2) *Supporting evidence required.* No credit or refund of any overpayment to which this paragraph (a) applies shall be allowed unless the person who paid the tax submits with the claim a written consent of the ultimate purchaser to the allowance of the credit or refund, or submits with the claim a statement, supported by sufficient available evidence, asserting that:

(i) The person has neither included the tax in the price of the article with respect to which it was imposed nor collected the amount of the tax from a vendee, and identifying the nature of the evidence available to establish these facts, or

(ii) The person has repaid the amount of the tax to the ultimate purchaser of the article.

(3) *Ultimate purchaser*—(i) *General rule.* The term "ultimate purchaser", as used in paragraph (a)(2) of this section, means the person who purchased the article for consumption, or for use in the manufacture of other articles and not for resale in the form in which purchased.

(ii) *Special rule under section 6416(a)(3)*—(A) *Conditions to be met.* If tax under chapter 32 of the Code is paid in respect of an article and the appropriate TTB officer determines that the article is not subject to tax under chapter 32, the term "ultimate purchaser", as used in paragraph (a)(2) of this section, includes any wholesaler, jobber, distributor, or retailer who, on the 15th day after the date of the determination holds for sale any such article with respect to which tax has been paid, if the claim for credit or refund of the overpayment in respect of the articles held for sale by wholesaler, jobber, distributor, or retailer is filed on or before the date on which the person who paid the tax is required to file a return for the period ending with the first calendar quarter which begins more than 60 days after the date of the determination by the appropriate TTB officer.

(B) *Supporting statement.* A claim for credit or refund of an overpayment of tax in respect of an article as to which a wholesaler, jobber, distributor, or retailer is the ultimate purchaser, as provided in this paragraph (a)(3)(ii), must be supported by a statement that the person filing the claim has a statement, by each wholesaler, jobber, distributor, or retailer whose articles are covered by the claim, showing total inventory, by model number and quantity, of all such articles purchased taxpaid and held for sale as of 12:01 a.m. of the 15th day after the date of the determination by the appropriate TTB officer that the article is not subject to tax under chapter 32 of the Code.

(C) *Inventory requirement.* The inventory shall not include any such article, title to which, or possession of which, has previously been transferred to any person for purposes of consumption unless the entire purchase price was repaid to the person or credited to the person's account and the sale was rescinded or any such article purchased by the wholesaler, jobber, distributor, or retailer as a component part of, or on or in connection with, another article. An article in transit at the first moment of the 15th day after the date of the determination is regarded as being held by the person to whom it was shipped, except that if title to the article does not pass until delivered to the person the article is deemed to be held by the shipper.

(b) *Overpayments described in section 6416(b)(2) of the Code*—(1) *Claims included.* This paragraph applies only to claims for credit or refund of amounts paid as tax under chapter 32 of the Code that are determined to be overpayments by reason of section 6416(b)(2) of the Code (relating to tax payments in respect of certain uses, sales, or resales of a taxable article).

(2) *Supporting evidence required.* No credit or refund of an overpayment to which this paragraph (b) applies shall be allowed unless the person who paid the tax submits with the claim a statement, supported by sufficient available evidence, asserting that:

(i) The person neither included the tax in the price of the article with respect to which it was imposed nor collected the amount of the tax from a vendee, and identifying the nature of the evidence available to establish these facts, or

(ii) The person repaid, or agreed to repay, the amount of the tax to the ultimate vendor of the article, or

(iii) The person has secured, and will submit upon request of the appropriate TTB officer, the written consent of the ultimate vendor to the allowance of the credit or refund.

(3) *Ultimate vendor—General rule.* The term *ultimate vendor,* as used in paragraph (b)(2) of this section, means the seller making the sale which gives rise to the overpayment or which last precedes the exportation or use which has given rise to the overpayment.

(c) *Overpayments not included.* This section does not apply to any overpayment determined under section 6416(b)(1) of the Code (relating to price readjustments), section 6416(b)(3)(A) of the Code (relating to certain cases in which refund or credit is allowable to the manufacturer who uses, in the further manufacture of a second article, a taxable article purchased by the manufacturer taxpaid), or section 6416(b)(5) of the Code (relating to the return to the seller of certain installment accounts which the seller had previously sold). In this regard, see §§53.173, 53.180, and 53.183.

[T.D. ATF–308, 56 FR 303, Jan. 3, 1991, as amended by T.D. ATF–312, 56 FR 31084, July 9, 1991]

§53.173 Price readjustments causing overpayments of manufacturers tax.

In the case of any payment of tax under chapter 32 of the Code that is determined to be an overpayment by reason of a price readjustment within the meaning of section 6416(b)(1) of the Code and §53.174 or §53.175, the person who paid the tax may file a claim for refund of the overpayment or may claim credit for the overpayment on any return of tax under this subpart which the person subsequently files. Price readjustments may not be anticipated. However, if the readjustment has actually been made before the return is filed for the period in which the sale was made, the tax to be reported in respect of the sale may, at the election of the taxpayer, be based either:

(a) On the price as so readjusted, or

(b) On the original sale price and a credit or refund claimed in respect of the price readjustment.

A price readjustment will be deemed to have been made at the time when the amount of the readjustment has been refunded to the vendor or the vendor has been informed that the vendor's account has been credited with the amount. No interest shall be paid on any credit or refund allowed under this section. For provisions relating to the evidence required in support of a claim for credit or refund, see 27 CFR 70.123 (Procedure and Administration), § 53.172(a)(2) and § 53.176. For provisions authorizing the taking of a credit in lieu of filing a claim for refund, see section 6416(d) of the Code and § 53.185.

[T.D. ATF–308, 56 FR 303, Jan. 3, 1991, as amended by T.D. ATF–312, 56 FR 31084, July 9, 1991]

§ 53.174 Determination of price readjustments.

(a) *In general*—(1) *Rules of usual application*—(i) *Amount treated as overpayment.* If the tax imposed by chapter 32 of the Code has been paid and thereafter the price of the article on which the tax was based is readjusted, that part of the tax which is proportionate to the part of the price which is repaid or credited to the purchaser is considered to be an overpayment. A readjustment of price to the purchaser may occur by reason of:

(A) The return of the article,

(B) The repossession of the article,

(C) The return or repossession of the covering or container of the article, or

(D) A bona fide discount, rebate, or allowance against the price at which the article was sold.

(ii) *Requirements of price readjustment.* A price readjustment will not be deemed to have been made unless the person who paid the tax either:

(A) Repays part or all of the purchase price in cash to the vendee,

(B) Credits the vendee's account for part or all of the purchase price, or

(C) Directly or indirectly reimburses a third party for part or all of the purchase price for the direct benefit of the vendee.

In addition, to be deemed a price readjustment, the payment or credit must be contractually or economically related to the taxable sale that the payment or credit purports to adjust. Thus, commissions or bonuses paid to a manufacturer's own agents or salesperson for selling the manufacturer's taxable products are not price readjustments for purposes of this section, since those commissions or bonuses are not paid or credited either to the manufacturer's vendee or to a third party for the vendee's benefit. On the other hand, a bonus paid by the manufacturer to a dealer's salesperson for negotiating the sale of a taxable article previously sold to the dealer by the manufacturer is considered to be a readjustment of the price on the original sale of the taxable article, regardless of whether the payment to the salesperson is made directly by the manufacturer or to the salesperson through the dealer. In such a case, the payment is related to the sale of a taxable article and is made for the benefit of the dealer because it is made to the dealer's salesperson to encourage the sale of a product owned by the dealer. Similarly, payments or credits made by a manufacturer to a vendee as reimbursement of interest expense incurred by the vendee in connection with a so-called "free flooring" arrangement for the purchase of taxable articles is a price readjustment, regardless of whether the payment or credit is made directly to the vendee or to the vendee's creditor on behalf of the vendee.

(iii) *Limitation on credit or refund.* The credit or refund allowable by reason of a price readjustment in respect of the sale of a taxable article may not exceed an amount which bears the same ratio to the total tax originally due and payable on the article as the amount of the tax-included readjustment bears to the original tax-included sale price of the article.

(2) *Rules of special application*—(i) *Constructive sale price.* If, in the case of a taxable sale, the tax imposed by chapter 32 of the Code is based on a constructive sale price determined

under any paragraph of section 4216(b) of the Code and §§53.94–53.97, as determined without reference to section 4218 of the Code, then any price readjustment made with respect to the sale may be taken into account under this section only to the extent that the price readjustment reduces the actual sale price of the article below the constructive sale price.

Examples: (A) A manufacturer sells a taxable article at retail for $110 tax included. Under section 4216(b)(1) of the Code the constructive sale price (tax included) of the article is determined to be $93. Thereafter, the manufacturer grants an allowance of $10 to the purchaser, which reduces the actual selling price (tax included) to $100. Since the readjustment price exceeds the amount of the constructive sale price, this readjustment is not recognized as a price readjustment under this section.

(B) Subsequently, the manufacturer extends to the purchaser an additional price allowance of $10, thereby reducing the actual sale price to $90. Since the actual sale price is now $3 less than the constructive sale price of $93, the manufacturer has overpaid by the amount of tax attributable to the $3. Assuming the tax rate involved is 10 percent, and the prices involved are tax-included, the overpayment of tax would be $0.27, determined as follows:

$$\frac{\text{tax rate}}{100+\text{tax rate}} \times \text{tax - included readjustment} = \text{tax overpayment } ((10/110)\times \$3 = \$0.27)$$

(ii) *Price determined under section 4223(b)(2) of the Code.* If a manufacturer (within the meaning of section 4223(a) of the Code) to whom an article is sold or resold free of tax in accordance with the provisions of section 4221(a)(1) of the Code for use in further manufacture diverts the article to a taxable use or sells it in a taxable sale, and pursuant to the provisions of section 4223(b)(2) of the Code computes the tax liability in respect of the use or sale on the price for which the article was sold to the manufacturer or on the price at which the article was sold by the actual manufacturer, a reduction of the price on which the tax was based does not result in an overpayment within the meaning of section 6416(b)(1) of the Code of this section. Moreover, if a manufacturer purchases an article tax free and computes the tax in respect of a subsequent sale of the article pursuant to the provisions of section 4223(b)(2) of the Code, an overpayment does not arise by reason of readjustment of the price for which the article was sold by the manufacturer except where the readjustment results from the return or repossession of the article by the manufacturer, and all of the purchase price is refunded by the manufacturer. See, however, paragraph (b)(4) of this section as to repurchased articles.

(b) *Return of an article*—(1) *Price readjustment.* If a taxable article is returned to the manufacturer who paid the tax imposed by Chapter 32 of the Code on the sale of the article, a price readjustment giving rise to an overpayment results:

(i) If the article is returned before use, and all of the purchase price is repaid to the vendee or credited to the vendee's account, or

(ii) If the article is returned under an express or implied warranty as to quality or service, and all or a part of the purchase price is repaid to the vendee or credited to the vendee's account, or

(iii) If title is still in the seller, as, for example, in the case of certain installment sales contracts, and all or a part of the purchase price is repaid to the vendee or credited to the vendee's account.

(2) *Return of purchase price.* For purposes of paragraph (b)(1) of this section, if all of the purchase price of an article has been returned to the vendee, except for an amount retained by the manufacturer pursuant to contract as reimbursement of expense incurred in connection with the sale (such as a handling or restocking charge), all of the purchase price is considered to have been returned to the vendee.

(3) *Taxability of subsequent sale or use.* If, under any of the conditions described in paragraph (b)(1) of this section, an article is returned to the manufacturer who paid the tax and all of the purchase price is returned to the vendee, the sale is considered to have been rescinded. Any subsequent sale or use of the article by the manufacturer will be considered to be an original sale or use of the article by the manufacturer which is subject to tax under Chapter 32 of the Code unless otherwise exempt. If under any such condition an article is returned to the manufacturer who paid the tax and only part of the purchase price is returned to the vendee, a subsequent sale of the article by the manufacturer will be subject to tax to the extent that the sale price exceeds the adjusted sale price of the first taxable sale.

(4) *Treatment of other transactions as repurchases.* Except as provided in paragraph (b)(1) of this section, a price readjustment will not result when a taxable article is returned to the manufacturer who paid the tax on the sale of the article, even though all or a part of the purchase price is repaid to the vendee or credited to the vendee's account, since such a transaction will be considered to be a repurchase of the article by the manufacturer.

(c) *Repossession of an article.* If a taxable article is repossessed by the manufacturer who paid the tax imposed by chapter 32 of the Code on the sale of the article, and all or a part of the purchase price is repaid to the vendee or credited to the vendee's account, a price readjustment giving rise to an overpayment will result. However, if the manufacturer later resells the repossessed article for a price in excess of the original adjusted sale price, the manufacturer will be liable for tax under chapter 32 of the Code to the extent that the resale price exceeds the original adjusted sale price.

(d) *Return or repossession of covering or container.* If the covering or container of a taxable article is returned to, or repossessed by the manufacturer who paid the tax imposed by chapter 32 of the Code on the sale of the article, and all or a portion of the purchase price is repaid to the vendee or credited to the vendee's account by reason of the return or repossession of the covering or container, a price adjustment giving rise to an overpayment will result. If a taxable article is considered to have been repurchased, as provided in paragraph (b)(4) of this section, and the covering or container accompanies the taxable article as part of the transaction, the covering or container will also be considered to have been repurchased.

(e) *Bona fide discounts, rebates, or allowances*—(1) *In general.* Except as provided in § 53.175 (relating to readjustments in respect of local advertising), the basic consideration in determining, for purposes of this section, whether a bona fide discount, rebate, or allowance has been made is whether the price actually by, or charged against, the purchaser has in fact been reduced by subsequent transactions between the parties. Generally, the price will be considered to have been readjusted by reason of a bona fide discount, rebate, or allowance, only if the manufacturer who made the taxable sale repays a part of the purchase price in cash to the vendee, or credits the vendee's account, or directly or indirectly reimburses a third party for part or all of the purchase price for the direct benefit of the vendee, in consideration of factors which, if taken into account at the time of the original transaction, would have resulted at that time in a lower sale price. For example, a price readjustment will be considered to have been made when a bona fide discount, rebate, or allowance is given in consideration of such factors as prompt payment, quantity buying over a specified period, the vendee's inventory of an article when new models are introduced, or a general price reduction affecting articles held in stock by the vendee as of a certain date. On the other hand, repayments made to the vendee do not effectuate price readjustments if given in consideration of circumstances under which the vendee has incurred, or is required to incur, an expense which, if treated as a separate item in the original transaction, would have been incudable in the price of the article for purposes of computing the tax.

Examples. The provisions of paragraph (e)(1) of this section may be illustrated by the following examples:

Example (1). B, a manufacturer of shotguns, bills its distributors in a specified amount per shotgun purchased by them. Thereafter, B issues to each distributor a credit memorandum in the amount of X dollars for each demonstration by the distributor of the shotguns at a sporting goods exhibition. The credit which B allows the distributor for demonstration of B's product does not effect a readjustment of price.

Example (2). C, a manufacturer of firearms, bills its dealers in a specified amount per firearm purchased by them. Thereafter, C remits to the dealer X dollars of the original sale price for each firearm sold by the dealer. An additional amount of Y dollars is paid to the dealer upon a showing by the dealer that the dealer has paid Y dollars to the salesperson who made the sale. In this case, the X dollars paid to the dealer by C constitutes a bona fide discount, rebate, or allowance since payment of such amount is in the nature of a price reduction. In addition, the Y dollars paid to the dealer in reimbursement for the amount paid by the dealer to the salesperson who made the sale, also constitutes a bona fide discount, rebate, or allowance.

(2) *Inability to collect price.* A charge-off of an amount outstanding in an open account, due to inability to collect, is not a bona fide discount, rebate, or allowance and does not, in and of itself, give rise to a price readjustment within the meaning of this section.

(3) *Loss or damage in transit.* If title to an article has passed to the vendee, the subsequent loss, damage, or destruction of the article while in the possession of a carrier for delivery to the vendee does not, in and of itself, affect the price at which the article was sold. However, if the article was sold under a contract providing that, if the article was lost, damaged, or destroyed in transit, title would revert to the vendor and the vendor would reimburse the vendee in full for the sale price, then the original sale is considered to have been rescinded. The vendor is entitled to credit or refund of the tax paid upon reimbursement of the full tax-included sale price to the vendee.

§53.175 Readjustment for local advertising charges.

(a) *In general.* If a manufacturer has paid the tax imposed by chapter 32 of the Code on the price of any article sold by the manufacturer and thereafter has repaid a portion of the price to the purchaser or any subsequent vendee in reimbursement of expenses for local advertising of the article or any other article sold by the manufacturer which is taxable at the same rate under the same section of chapter 32 of the Code, the reimbursement will be considered a price readjustment constituting an overpayment which the manufacturer may claim as a credit or refund. The amount of the reimbursement may not, however, exceed the limitation provided by section 4216(e)(2) of the Code and §53.101, determined as of the close of the calendar quarter in which the reimbursement is made or as of the close of any subsequent calendar quarter of the same calendar year in which it is made. The term "local advertising," as used in this section, has the same meaning as prescribed by section 4216(e)(4) of the Code and includes generally, advertising which is broadcast over a radio station or television station, or appears in a newspaper or magazine, or is displayed by means of an outdoor advertising sign or poster.

(b) *Local advertising charges excluded from taxable price in one year but repaid in following year*—(1) *Determination of price readjustments for year in which charge is repaid.* If the tax imposed by chapter 32 of the Code was paid with respect to local advertising charges that were excluded in computing the taxable price of an article sold in any calendar year but are not repaid to the manufacturer's purchaser or any subsequent vendee before May 1 of the following calendar year, the subsequent repayment of those charges by the manufacturer in reimbursement of expenses for local advertising will be considered a price readjustment constituting an overpayment which the manufacturer may claim as a credit or refund. The amount of the reimbursement may not, however, exceed the limitation provided by section 4216(e)(2) of the Code and §53.101, determined as of the close of the calendar quarter in which the reimbursement is made or as of the close of any subsequent calendar quarter of the same calendar year in which it is made.

(2) *Redetermination of price readjustments for year in which charge was made.* If the tax imposed by chapter 32 of the Code was paid with respect to local advertising charges that were excluded in computing the taxable price of an article sold in any calendar year but are not repaid to the manufacturer's purchaser or any subsequent vendor before May 1 of the following calendar year, the manufacturer may make a redetermination, in respect of the calendar year in which the charge was made, of the price readjustments constituting an overpayment which the manufacturer may claim as a credit or refund. This redetermination may be made by excluding the local advertising charges made in the calendar year that became taxable as of May 1 of the following calendar year.

§ 53.176 Supporting evidence required in case of price readjustments.

No credit or refund of an overpayment arising by reason of a price readjustment described in § 53.174 or § 53.175 shall be allowed unless the manufacturer who paid the tax submits a statement, supported by sufficient available evidence:

(a) Describing the circumstances which gave rise to the price readjustment,

(b) Identifying the article in respect of which the price readjustment was allowed,

(c) Showing the price at which the article was sold, the amount of tax paid in respect of the article, and the date on which the tax was paid,

(d) Giving the name and address of the purchaser to whom the article was sold, and

(e) Showing the amount repaid to the purchaser or credited to the purchaser's account.

§ 53.177 Certain exportations, uses, sales, or resales causing overpayments of tax.

In the case of any payment of tax under chapter 32 of the Code that is determined to be an overpayment by reason of certain exportations, uses, sales, or resales described in section 6416(b)(2) of the Code and § 53.178, the person who paid the tax may file a claim for refund of the overpayment or, in the case of overpayments under chapter 32 of the Code, may claim credit for the overpayment on any return of tax under this subpart which the person subsequently files. However, under the circumstances described in section 6416(c) of the Code and § 53.184, the overpayments under chapter 32 may be refunded to an exporter or shipper. No interest shall be paid on any credit or refund allowed under this section. For provisions relating to the evidence required in support of a claim for credit or refund under this section, see 27 CFR 70.123 (Procedure and Administration) and 53.179. For provisions authorizing the taking of a credit in lieu of filing a claim for refund, see section 6416(d) of the Code and § 53.185.

§ 53.178 Exportations, uses, sales, and resales included.

(a) *In general.* The payment of tax imposed by chapter 32 of the Code on the sale of any article, will be considered to be an overpayment by reason of any exportation, use, sale, or resale described in any one of paragraphs (b) to (e), inclusive, of this section. This section applies only in those cases where the exportation, use, sale, or resale (or any combination thereof) referred to in any one or more of these paragraphs occurs before any other use. If any article is sold or resold for a use described in any one of these paragraphs and is not in fact so used, the paragraph is treated in all respects as inapplicable.

(b) *Exportation of tax-paid articles.* A payment of tax under chapter 32 of the Code on the sale of any article will be considered to be an overpayment under section 6416(b)(2)(A) of the Code if the article is by any person exported to a foreign country or shipped to a possession of the United States. It is immaterial for purposes of this paragraph, whether the person who made the taxable sale had knowledge at the time of the sale that the article was being purchased for export to a foreign country or shipment to a possession of the United States. See § 53.184 for the circumstances under which a claim for refund by reason of the exportation of an article may be claimed by the exporter or shipper, rather than by the person who paid the tax. For definition of the term "possession of the United States", see §53.11.

(c) *Supplies for vessels or aircraft.* A payment of tax under chapter 32 of the Code on the sale of any article, will be considered to be an overpayment under section 6416(b)(2)(B) of the Code if the article is used by any person, or is sold by any person for use by the purchaser, as supplies for vessels or aircraft. The term "supplies for vessels or aircraft", as used in this paragraph, has the same meaning as when used in sections 4221(a)(3), 4221(d)(3), and 4221(e)(1) of the Code, and the regulations thereunder (§53.134(b)(1)).

(d) *Use by State or local government.* A payment of tax under chapter 32 of the Code on the sale of any article will be considered to be an overpayment under section 6416(b)(2)(C) of the Code if the article is sold by any person to a State, any political subdivision thereof, or the District of Columbia for the exclusive use of a State, any political subdivision thereof, or the District of Columbia. For provisions relating to tax-free sales to a State, any political subdivision thereof, or the District of Columbia, see section 4221(a)(4) of the Code and §53.131.

(e) *Use by nonprofit educational organization.* A payment of tax under chapter 32 of the Code on the sale of any article will be considered to be an overpayment under section 6416(b)(2)(D) of the Code if the article is sold by any person to a nonprofit educational organization for its exclusive use. The term "nonprofit educational organization", as used in this paragraph (e), has the same meaning as when used in section 4221 (a)(5) or (d)(5) of the Code, whichever applies, and the regulations under §53.136.

§53.179 Supporting evidence required in case of manufacturers tax involving exportations, uses, sales, or resales.

(a) *Evidence to be submitted by claimant.* No claim for credit or refund of an overpayment, within the meaning of section 6416(b)(2) of the Code and §53.178, of tax under chapter 32 of the Code shall be allowed unless the person who paid the tax submits with the claim the evidence required by §53.172(b)(2) and a statement, supported by sufficient available evidence:

(1) Showing the amount claimed in respect of each category of exportations, uses, sales, or resales on which the claim is based and which give rise to a right of credit or refund under section 6416(b)(2) of the Code and §53.177,

(2) Identifying the article, both as to nature and quantity, in respect of which credit or refund is claimed,

(3) Showing the amount of tax paid in respect of the article or articles and the dates of payment, and

(4) Indicating that the person claiming a credit or refund possesses evidence (as set forth in paragraph (b)(1) of this section) that the article has been exported, or has been used, sold, or resold in a manner or for a purpose which gives rise to an overpayment within the meaning of section 6416(b)(2) of the Code and §53.178.

(b) *Evidence required to be in possession of claimant*—(1) *Evidence required under paragraph (a)(4)*—(i) *In general.* The evidence required to be retained by the person who paid the tax, as provided in paragraph (a)(4) of this section, must, in the case of an article exported, consist of proof of exportation in the form prescribed in §53.133 or must, in the case of other articles sold tax-paid by that person, consist of a certificate, executed and signed by the ultimate purchaser of the article, in the form prescribed in paragraph (b)(1)(ii) of this section. However, if the article to which the claim relates has passed through a chain of sales from the person who paid the tax to the ultimate purchaser, the evidence required to be retained by the person who paid the tax may consist of a certificate, executed and signed by the ultimate vendor of the article, in the form provided in paragraph (b)(1)(iii) of this section, rather than the proof of exportation itself or the certificate of the ultimate purchaser.

(ii) *Certificate of ultimate purchaser.* (A) The certificate executed and signed by the ultimate purchaser of the article to which the claim relates must identify the article, both as to nature and quantity; show the address of the ultimate purchaser of the article, and the name and address of the ultimate vendor of the article; and describe the use actually made of the article in sufficient detail to establish that credit or refund is due, except that the use to be made of the article must be described in lieu of actual use if the claim is made by reason of the sale or resale of an article for a specified use which gives rise to the overpayment.

(B) If the certificate sets forth the use to be made of any article, rather than its actual use, it must show that the ultimate purchaser has agreed to notify the claimant if the article is not in fact used as specified in the certificate.

(C) The certificate must also contain a statement that the ultimate purchaser understands that the ultimate purchaser and any other party may, for fraudulent use of the certificate, be subject to all applicable criminal penalties under the Internal Revenue Code.

(D) A purchase order will be acceptable in lieu of a separate certificate of the ultimate purchaser if it contains all the information required by this paragraph.

(iii) *Certificate of ultimate vendor.* Any certificate executed and signed by an ultimate vendor as evidence to be retained by the person who paid the tax as provided in paragraph (a)(4) of this section may be executed with respect to any one or more overpayments by the person which arose under section 6416(b)(2) and § 53.178 by reason of exportations, uses, sales or resales, occurring within any period of not more than 12 consecutive calendar quarters, the beginning and ending dates of which are specified in the certificate. A certificate supporting a claim for credit or refund under this section shall contain the following:

(A) Name of ultimate vendor if other than person executing the certificate.

(B) Statement that article(s) was purchased by the ultimate vendor tax-paid and was thereafter exported, used, sold, or resold.

(C) Description of proof which supports exportation or certificate as to use executed by ultimate purchaser.

(D) Statement that ultimate vendor retains such proof for 3 years from the date of the statement and will, upon request, supply such proof at any time within such 3 year period to the taxpayer to establish that credit or refund is due in respect of the article.

(E) Statement that to the best knowledge and belief of the person executing the certificate, no statement in respect of the proof of exportation or certificate has previously been executed and that the person executing the certificate understands that any fraudulent use of the certificate may subject the person executing the certificate or any other party to all applicable criminal penalties under the Code.

(F) Name, title, address and signature of person executing certificate and date signed.

(G) Description of all articles covered by the certificate, with the corresponding vendor's invoice number, date of resale of article, quantity, whether articles were exported or used and the use made of article or to be made of article.

(iv) *TTB I 5600.33.* TTB I 5600.33, Statement of Ultimate Vendor, which is available as provided in § 53.21(b), when completed, contains all necessary information for a properly executed certificate. Additional copies may be reproduced as needed.

(2) *Repayment or consent of ultimate vendor.* If the person claiming credit or refund or an overpayment to which this section applies has repaid, or agreed to repay, the amount of the overpayment to the ultimate vendor or if the ultimate vendor consents to the allowance of the credit or refund, a statement to that effect, signed by the ultimate vendor, must be shown on, or made a part of, the supporting evidence required under this section to be retained by the person claiming the credit or refund. In this regard, see § 53.172(b)(2).

[T.D. ATF–308, 56 FR 303, Jan. 3, 1991, as amended by T.D. ATF–380, 61 FR 37007, July 16, 1996; T.D. TTB–44, 71 FR 16958, Apr. 4, 2006]

§ 53.180 Tax-paid articles used for further manufacture and causing overpayments of tax.

In the case of any payment of tax under chapter 32 of the Code that is determined to be an overpayment under section 6416(b)(3) of the Code and

§53.181 by reason of the sale of an article, directly or indirectly, by the manufacturer of the article to a subsequent manufacturer who uses the article in further manufacture of a second article or who sells the article with, or as a part of, the second article manufactured or produced by the subsequent manufacturer, the subsequent manufacturer may file claim for refund of the overpayment or may claim credit for the overpayment on any return of tax under this subpart subsequently filed. No interest shall be paid on any credit or refund allowed under this section. For provisions relating to the evidence required in support of a claim for credit or refund, see 27 CFR §70.123 (Procedure and Administration), 53.172 and 53.182. For provisions authorizing the taking of a credit in lieu of filing a claim for refund, see section 6416(d) of the Code and §53.185.

§53.181 Further manufacture included.

(a) *In general.* The payment of tax imposed by chapter 32 of the Code on the sale of any article by a manufacturer of the article will be considered to be an overpayment by reason of any use in further manufacture, or sale as part of a second manufactured article, described in paragraph (b) of this section. This section applies in those cases where the exportation, use, or sale (or any combination of those activities) referred to in this paragraph occurs before any other use.

(b) *Use of tax-paid articles in further manufacture described in section 6416(b)(3)(A) of the Code.* A payment of tax under chapter 32 of the Code on the sale of any article, directly or indirectly, by the manufacturer of the article to a subsequent manufacturer will be considered to be an overpayment under section 6416(b)(3)(A) of the Code if the article is used by the subsequent manufacturer as material in the manufacture or production of, or as a component part of, a second article manufactured or produced by the subsequent manufacturer which is taxable under chapter 32 of the Code. For this purpose it is immaterial whether the second article is sold or otherwise disposed of, or if sold, whether the sale is a taxable sale. Any article to which this paragraph applies which would have been used in the manufacture or production of a second article, except for the fact that it was broken or rendered useless in the process of manufacturing or producing the second article, will be considered to have been used as a component part of the second article.

[T.D. ATF–308, 56 FR 303, Jan. 3, 1991, as amended by T.D. ATF–312, 56 FR 31084, July 9, 1991]

§53.182 Supporting evidence required in case of tax-paid articles used for further manufacture.

(a) *Evidence to be submitted by claimant.* No claim for credit or refund of an overpayment, within the meaning of section 6416(b)(3) of the Code and §53.181 shall be allowed unless the subsequent manufacturer submits with the claim the evidence required by §53.132 and a statement, supported by sufficient available evidence:

(1) Showing the amount claimed in respect of each category of exportations, uses, or sales on which the claim is based and which give rise to a right of credit or refund under section 6416(b)(3) of the Code and §53.180,

(2) Showing the name and address of the manufacturer, producer, or importer of the article in respect of which credit or refund is claimed,

(3) Identifying the article, both as to nature and quantity, in respect of which credit or refund is claimed,

(4) Showing the amount of tax paid in respect of the article by the manufacturer or producer of the article and the date of payment.

(5) Indicating that the article was used by the claimant as material in the manufacture or production of, or as a component part of, a second article manufactured or produced by the manufacturer or was sold on or in connection with, or with the sale of, a second article manufactured or produced by the manufacturer, and

(6) Identifying the second article, both as to nature and quantity.

(b) *Evidence required to be in possession of claimant*—(1) *Certificate of ultimate purchaser of second article.* The certificate executed and signed by the ultimate purchaser of the second article must contain the same information as that required in §53.179(b)(1)(ii), except that the information must be furnished in respect of the second article, rather than the article to which the claim relates.

(2) *Certificate of ultimate vendor of second article.* Any certificate executed and signed by an ultimate vendor as evidence to be retained by the person claiming credit or refund must be executed in the same form and manner as that provided in § 53.179(b)(2)(iii).

(3) *Repayment or consent of ultimate vendor.* If the person claiming credit or refund of an overpayment to which this section applies has repaid, or agreed to repay, the amount of the overpayment to the ultimate vendor or if the ultimate vendor consents to the allowance of the credit or refund, a statement to that effect, signed by the ultimate vendor, must be shown on, or made a part of, the evidence required to be retained by the person claiming the credit or refund. In this regard, see § 53.172(b)(2).

[T.D. ATF–308, 56 FR 303, Jan. 3, 1991, as amended by T.D. ATF–312, 56 FR 31085, July 9, 1991]

§ 53.183 Return of installment accounts causing overpayments of tax.

(a) *In general.* In the case of any payment of tax under section 4216(d)(1) of the Code in respect of the sale of any installment account that is determined to be an overpayment under section 6416(b)(5) of the Code and paragraph (b) of this section upon return of the installment account, the person who paid the tax may file a claim for refund of the overpayment or may claim credit for the overpayment on any return of tax under this subpart which that person subsequently files. No interest shall be paid on any credit or refund allowed under this section. For provisions relating to the evidence required in support of a claim for credit or refund under this section, see 27 CFR 70.123 (Procedure and Administration) and paragraph (c) of this section. For provisions authorizing the taking of a credit in lieu of filing a claim for refund, see section 6416(d) of the Code and § 53.185.

(b) *Overpayment of tax allocable to repaid consideration.* The payment of tax imposed by section 4216(d)(1) of the Code on the sale of an installment account by the manufacturer will be considered to be an overpayment under section 6416(b)(5) of the Code to the extent of the tax allocable to any consideration repaid or credited to the purchaser of the installment account upon the return of the account to the manufacturer pursuant to the agreement under which the account originally was sold, if the readjustment of the consideration occurs pursuant to the provisions of the agreement. The tax allocable to the repaid or credited consideration is the amount which bears the same ratio to the total tax paid under section 4216(d)(1) of the Code with respect to the installment account as the amount of consideration repaid or credited to the purchaser bears to the total consideration for which the account was sold. This paragraph (b) does not apply where an installment account is originally sold pursuant to the order of, or subject to the approval of, a court of competent jurisdiction in a bankruptcy or insolvency proceeding.

(c) *Evidence to be submitted by claimant.* No claim for credit or refund of an overpayment, within the meaning of section 6416(b)(5) of the Code and paragraph (b) of this section, of tax under section 4216(d)(1) of the Code shall be allowed unless the person who paid the tax submits with the claim a statement, supported by sufficient available evidence, indicating:

(1) The name and address of the person to whom the installment account was sold,

(2) The amount of tax due under section 4216(d)(1) of the Code by reason of the sale of the installment account, the amount of the tax paid under section 4216(d)(1) with respect to the sale, and the date of payment,

(3) The amount for which the installment account was sold,

(4) The amount which was repaid or credited to the purchaser of the account by reason of the return of the account to the person claiming the credit or refund, and

(5)(i) The fact that the amount repaid or credited to the purchaser of the account was so repaid or credited pursuant to the agreement under which the account was sold, and

(ii) The fact that the account was returned to the manufacturer pursuant to that agreement.

§ 53.184 Refund to exporter or shipper.

(a) *In general.* Any payment of tax imposed by chapter 32 of the Code that is determined to be an overpayment within the meaning of section 6416(b)(2)(A) of the Code and §§ 53.178 and 53.179, by reason of the exportation of any article may be refunded to the exporter or shipper of the article pursuant to section 6416(c) of the Code, if:

(1) The exporter or shipper files a claim for refund of the overpayment, and

(2) The person who paid the tax waives the right to claim credit or refund of the tax.

No interest shall be paid on any refund allowed under this section. For provisions relating to the evidence required in support of a claim under this paragraph, see 27 CFR 70.123 (Procedure and Administration) and paragraph (b) of this section.

(b) *Supporting evidence required.* No claim for refund of any overpayment of tax to which this section applies shall be allowed unless the exporter or shipper submits with that claim proof of exportation in the form prescribed by § 53.133, and a statement, signed by the person who paid the tax, showing:

(1) That the person who paid the tax waives the right to claim credit or refund of the tax, and

(2) The amount of tax paid on the sale of the article and the date of payment.

§ 53.185 Credit on returns.

Any person entitled to claim refund of any overpayment of tax imposed by chapter 32 of the Code may, in lieu of claiming refund of the overpayment, claim credit for the overpayment on any return of tax under this subpart subsequently filed. Any such credit claimed on a return must be supported by the evidence prescribed in the applicable regulations in this subpart and 27 CFR 70.123 (Procedure and Administration).

§ 53.186 Accounting procedures for like articles.

(a) *Identification of manufacturer.* In applying section 6416 of the Code and the regulations thereunder, a person who has purchased like articles from various manufacturers may determine the particular manufacturer from whom that person purchased any one of those articles by a first-in, first-out (FIFO) method, by a last-in, first-out (LIFO) method, or by any other consistent method approved by the appropriate TTB officer. For the first year for which a person makes a determination under this section, the person may adopt any one of the following methods without securing prior approval by the appropriate TTB officer.

(1) FIFO method.

(2) LIFO method.

(3) Any method by which the actual manufacturer of the article is in fact identified.

(4) Any other method of determining the manufacturer of a particular article must be approved by the appropriate TTB officer before its adoption. After any method for identifying the manufacturer has been properly adopted, it may not be changed without first securing the consent of the appropriate TTB officer.

(b) *Determining amount of tax paid.* In applying section 6416 and §§ 53.171–53.186, if the identity of the manufacturer of any article has been determined by a person pursuant to a method prescribed in paragraph (a) of this section, that manufacturer of the article must determine the tax paid under Chapter 32 of the Code with respect to that article consistently with the method used in identifying the manufacturer.

§ 53.187 OMB control numbers.

(a) *Purpose.* This section collects and displays the control numbers assigned to collections of information in this part by the Office of Management and Budget (OMB) under the Paperwork Reduction Act of 1980. TTB intends that this section comply with the requirements of §§ 1320.12, 1320.13, and 1320.14 of 5 CFR part 1320 (OMB regulations implementing the Paperwork Reduction Act), for the display of control numbers assigned by OMB to collections of information in the regulations in this part.

(b) *Display*.

27 CFR part 53 section number	OMB control number(s)
§ 53.1	1545–0723
§ 53.3	1545–0685
§ 53.11	1545–0723
§ 53.92	1545–0023
§ 53.93	1545–0023
§ 53.99	1545–0023
§ 53.131	1545–0023
§ 53.132	1545–0023
§ 53.133	1545–0023
§ 53.134	1545–0023
§ 53.136	1545–0023
§ 53.140	1545–0023
§ 53.141	1545–0023
§ 53.142	1545–0023
§ 53.143	1545–0023
§ 53.151	1545–0023, 1545–0723
§ 53.152	1545–0723
§ 53.153	1545–0257, 1545–0723
§ 53.155	1545–0723
§ 53.157	1545–0257
§ 53.171	1545–0023, 1545–0723
§ 53.172	1545–0723
§ 53.173	1545–0723
§ 53.174	1545–0723
§ 53.175	1545–0723
§ 53.176	1545–0723
§ 53.177	1545–0723
§ 53.178	1545–0723
§ 53.179	1545–0723
§ 53.180	1545–0723
§ 53.181	1545–0723
§ 53.182	1545–0723
§ 53.183	1545–0723
§ 53.184	1545–0023, 1545–0723
§ 53.185	1545–0023, 1545–0723
§ 53.186	1545–0723

SUBCHAPTERS D–E [RESERVED]

SUBCHAPTER F—PROCEDURES AND PRACTICES

PART 70—PROCEDURE AND ADMINISTRATION

Subpart A—Scope

Subpart B—Definitions

Subpart C—Discovery of Liability and Enforcement of Laws

EXAMINATION AND INSPECTION

GENERAL POWERS AND DUTIES

Subpart D—Collection of Excise and Special (Occupational) Tax

COLLECTION—GENERAL PROVISIONS

RECEIPT OF PAYMENT

ASSESSMENT

NOTICE AND DEMAND

INTEREST

ADDITIONS TO THE TAX, ADDITIONAL AMOUNTS, AND ASSESSABLE PENALTIES

Additions to the Tax and Additional Amounts

Assessable Penalties

ABATEMENTS, CREDITS AND REFUNDS

Procedure in General

AUTHORITY: 5 U.S.C. 301 and 552; 26 U.S.C. 4181, 4182, 5123, 5203, 5207, 5275, 5367, 5415, 5504, 5555, 5684(a), 5741, 5761(b), 5802, 6020, 6021, 6064, 6102, 6155, 6159, 6201, 6203, 6204, 6301, 6303, 6311, 6313, 6314, 6321, 6323, 6325, 6326, 6331–6343, 6401–6404, 6407, 6416, 6423, 6501–6503, 6511, 6513, 6514, 6532, 6601, 6602, 6611, 6621, 6622, 6651, 6653, 6656–6658, 6665, 6671, 6672, 6701, 6723, 6801, 6862, 6863, 6901, 7011, 7101, 7102, 7121, 7122, 7207, 7209, 7214, 7304, 7401, 7403, 7406, 7423, 7424, 7425, 7426, 7429, 7430, 7432, 7502, 7503, 7505, 7506, 7513, 7601–7606, 7608–7610, 7622, 7623, 7653, 7805.

SOURCE: T.D. ATF–6, 38 FR 32445, Nov. 26, 1973, unless otherwise noted.

EDITORIAL NOTE: Nomenclature changes to part 70 appear by T.D. ATF–450, 66 FR 29022–29030, May 29, 2001.

Subpart A—Scope

§ 70.1 General.

(a) The regulations in Subparts C, D, and E of this part set forth the procedural and administrative rules of the Alcohol and Tobacco Tax and Trade Bureau for:

(1) The issuance and enforcement of summonses, examination of books of account and witnesses, administration of oaths, entry of premises for examination of taxable objects, granting of rewards for information, canvass for taxable objects and persons, and authority of TTB officers.

(2) The use of commercial banks for payment of excise taxes imposed by 26 U.S.C. Subtitles E and F.

(3) The preparing or executing of returns; deposits; payment on notice and demand; assessment; abatements, credits and refunds; limitations on assessment; limitations on credit or refund; periods of limitation in judicial proceedings; interest; additions to tax, additional amounts, and assessable penalties; enforced collection activities; authority for establishment, alteration, and distribution of stamps, marks, or labels; jeopardy assessment of alcohol, tobacco, and firearms taxes, registration of dealers in alcohol fit for beverage use, and registration of persons paying a special tax.

(4) Distilled spirits, wines, beer, tobacco products, cigarette papers and tubes, firearms, ammunition, and explosives.

(b) The regulations in Subpart F of this part relate to the limitations imposed by 26 U.S.C. 6423, on the refund or credit of tax paid or collected in respect to any article of a kind subject to a tax imposed by Part I, Subchapter A of Chapter 51, I.R.C., or by any corresponding provision of prior internal revenue laws.

(c) The regulations in Subpart G of this part implement 26 U.S.C. 5064, which permits payments to be made by the United States for amounts equal to the internal revenue taxes paid or determined and customs duties paid on distilled spirits, wines, and beer, previously withdrawn, that were lost, made unmarketable, or condemned by a duly authorized official as a result of disaster, vandalism, or malicious mischief. This subpart applies to disasters or other specified causes of loss, occurring on or after February 1, 1979. This subpart does not apply to distilled spirits, wines, and beer manufactured in Puerto Rico and brought into the United States.

[T.D. ATF–376, 61 FR 31031, June 19, 1996, as amended by T.D. TTB–44, 71 FR 16958, Apr. 4, 2006; T.D. TTB–79, 74 FR 37424, July 28, 2009; T.D. TTB–91, 76 FR 5481, Feb. 1, 2011]

§70.2 Forms prescribed.

(a) The appropriate TTB officer is authorized to prescribe all forms required by this part. All of the information called for in each form shall be furnished as indicated by the headings on the form and the instructions on or pertaining to the form. In addition, information called for in each form shall be furnished as required by this part. The form will be filed in accordance with the instructions for the form.

(b) Forms prescribed by this part are available for printing through the TTB Web site (*http://www.ttb.gov*) or by mailing a request to the Alcohol and Tobacco Tax and Trade Bureau, National Revenue Center, 550 Main Street, Room 1516, Cincinnati, OH 45202.

[T.D. ATF–376, 61 FR 31031, June 19, 1996, as amended by T.D. ATF–450, 66 FR 29022, May 29, 2001; T.D. TTB–44, 71 FR 16959, Apr. 4, 2006]

§70.3 Delegations of the Administrator.

Most of the regulatory authorities of the Administrator contained in this part are delegated to appropriate TTB officers. These TTB officers are specified in TTB Order 1135.70, Delegation of the Administrator's Authorities in 27 CFR Part 70, Procedure and Administration. You may obtain a copy of this order by accessing the TTB Web site (*http://www.ttb.gov*) or by mailing a request to the Alcohol and Tobacco Tax and Trade Bureau, National Revenue Center, 550 Main Street, Room 1516, Cincinnati, OH 45202.

[T.D. TTB–44, 71 FR 16959, Apr. 4, 2006]

Subpart B—Definitions

§70.11 Meaning of terms.

When used in this part and in forms prescribed under this part, where not otherwise distinctly expressed or manifestly incompatible with the intent thereof, terms shall have the meaning ascribed in this section. Words in the plural form shall include the singular, and vice versa, and words imparting the masculine gender shall include the feminine. The terms "includes" and "including" do not exclude things not enumerated which are in the same general class.

Administrator. The Administrator, Alcohol and Tobacco Tax and Trade Bureau, Department of the Treasury, Washington, DC.

Appropriate TTB officer. An officer or employee of the Alcohol and Tobacco Tax and Trade Bureau (TTB) authorized to perform any functions relating to the administration or enforcement of this part by TTB Order 1135.70, Delegation of the Administrator's Authorities in 27 CFR Part 70, Procedure and Administration.

Bureau. The Alcohol and Tobacco Tax and Trade Bureau, Department of the Treasury, Washington, DC.

CFR. The Code of Federal Regulations.

Commercial bank. A bank, whether or not a member of the Federal Reserve System, which has access to the Federal Reserve Communications System (FRCS) or Fedwire. The "FRCS" or "Fedwire" is a communications network that allows Federal Reserve System member banks to effect a transfer of funds for their customers (or other commercial banks) to the Treasury Account at the Federal Reserve Bank of New York.

Electronic fund transfer or EFT. Any transfer of funds effected by a taxpayer's commercial bank, either directly or through a correspondent banking relationship, via the Federal Reserve Communications System (FRCS) or Fedwire to the Treasury Account at the Federal Reserve Bank of New York.

Enforced collection. Collection of taxes when a taxpayer neglects or refuses to pay voluntarily. Includes such administrative measures as liens and levies.

IRC. IRC refers to the Internal Revenue Code of 1986, as amended (codified in 26 U.S.C.).

Levy. The taking of property by seizure and sale or by collection of money due to the debtor, such as wages.

Lien. A charge upon real or personal property for the satisfaction of some debt or performance of an obligation.

Person. An individual, a trust, estate, partnership, association or other unincorporated organization, fiduciary, company, or corporation, or the District of Columbia, a State, or a political subdivision thereof (including a city, county, or other municipality).

Provisions of 26 U.S.C. enforced and administered by the Bureau. Sections 4181 and 4182 of the IRC; subchapters F and G of chapter 32 of the IRC insofar as they relate to activities administered and enforced with respect to sections 4181 and 4182 of the IRC; chapters 51 and 52 of subtitle E of the IRC; and subtitle F of the IRC insofar as it relates to any of the foregoing.

Secretary. The Secretary of the Treasury or designated delegate.

Seizure. The act of taking possession of property to satisfy a tax liability or by virtue of an execution.

Treasury Account. The Department of the Treasury's General Account at the Federal Reserve Bank of New York.

U.S.C. The United States Code.

(Aug. 16, 1954, Ch. 736, 68A Stat. 775 (26 U.S.C. 6301); June 29, 1956, Ch. 462, 70 Stat. 391 (26 U.S.C. 6301))

[T.D. ATF–48, 43 FR 13535, Mar. 31, 1978; 44 FR 55841, Sept. 28,979, as amended by T.D. ATF–77, 46 FR 3002, Jan. 13, 1981; T.D. ATF–301, 55 FR 47608, Nov. 14, 1990; T.D. ATF–331, 57 FR 40327, Sept. 3, 1992; T.D. ATF–378, 61 FR 29955, June 13, 1996; T.D. ATF–450, 66 FR 29022, May 29, 2001; T.D. TTB–44, 71 FR 16959, Apr. 4, 2006; T.D. TTB–91, 76 FR 5481, Feb. 1, 2011]

Subpart C—Discovery of Liability and Enforcement of Laws

EXAMINATION AND INSPECTION

§ 70.21 Canvass for taxable persons and objects.

Each appropriate TTB officer shall, to the extent deemed practicable, cause officers or employees under the appropriate TTB officer's supervision and control to proceed, from time to time, and inquire after and concerning all persons therein who may be liable to pay any tax, imposed under provisions of 26 U.S.C. enforced and administered by the Bureau, and all persons owning or having the care and management of any objects with respect to which such tax is imposed.

[T.D. ATF–331, 57 FR 40327, Sept. 3, 1992, as amended by T.D. ATF–450, 66 FR 29023, May 29, 2001]

§ 70.22 Examination of books and witnesses.

(a) *In general.* For the purpose of ascertaining the correctness of any return, making a return where none has been made, determining the liability of any person for any tax (including any interest, additional amount, addition to the tax, or civil penalty) imposed under provisions of the IRC enforced and administered by the Bureau or the liability at law or in equity of any transferee or fiduciary of any person in respect of any such tax, or collecting any such liability, or inquiring into any offense connected with the administration or enforcement of the internal revenue laws that are administered and enforced by the Bureau, any appropriate TTB officer may examine any books, papers, records or other data which may be relevant or material to such inquiry; and take such testimony of the person concerned, under oath, as may be relevant to such inquiry.

(b) *Summonses.* For the purposes described in paragraph (a) of this section the appropriate TTB officers are authorized to summon the person liable for tax or required to perform the act, or any officer or employee of such person, or any person having possession, custody, or care of books of accounts containing entries relating to the business of the person liable for tax or required to perform the act, or any person deemed proper, to appear before a designated officer or employee of the Bureau at a time and place named in the summons and to produce such books, papers, records, or other data, and to give such testimony, under oath, as may be relevant or material to such inquiry; and take such testimony of the person concerned, under oath, as may be relevant or material to such inquiry. Such TTB officer may designate an appropriate TTB officer as the individual before whom a person summoned pursuant to 26 U.S.C. 7602 shall appear. Any such officer, when so designated in a summons, is authorized to take testimony under oath of the person summoned and to receive and examine books, papers, records, or other data produced in compliance with the summons. The authority to issue a summons may not be redelegated. See §70.302 of this part for rules concerning payments to certain persons who are summoned to give information to the Bureau under 26 U.S.C. 7602 and this section.

(Aug. 16, 1954, Chapter 736, 68A Stat. 901; (26 U.S.C. 7602))

[T.D. ATF–6, 38 FR 32445, Nov. 26, 1973, as amended by T.D. ATF–42, 42 FR 8367, Feb. 10, 1977; T.D. ATF–301, 55 FR 47608, Nov. 14, 1990; T.D. ATF–331, 57 FR 40328, Sept. 3, 1992; T.D. ATF–450, 66 FR 29023, May 29, 2001; T.D. TTB–91, 76 FR 5481, Feb. 1, 2011]

§ 70.23 Service of summonses.

(a) *In general.* A summons issued under 26 U.S.C. 7602 shall be served by an attested copy delivered in hand to the person to whom it is directed, or left at his last and usual place of abode. The certificate of service signed by the person serving the summons shall be evidence of the facts it states on the hearing of an application for the enforcement of the summons. When the summons requires the production of books, papers, records, or other data, it shall be sufficient if such books, papers, records, or other data are described with reasonable certainty.

(b) *Persons who may serve summonses.* Any appropriate TTB officer may serve a summons issued under 26 U.S.C. 7602.

(68A Stat. 902, as amended (26 U.S.C. 7603); 26 U.S.C. 7805 (68A Stat. 917), 27 U.S.C. 205 (49 Stat. 981 as amended), 18 U.S.C. 926 (82 Stat. 959), and sec. 38, Arms Export Control Act (22 U.S.C. 2778, 90 Stat. 744), 27 U.S.C. 205, 22 U.S.C. 2778, 26 U.S.C. 7602, and 5 U.S.C. 301)

[T.D. ATF–6, 38 FR 32445, Nov. 26, 1973, as amended by T.D. ATF–48, 43 FR 13531, Mar. 31, 1978; T.D. ATF–201, 50 FR 12533, Mar. 29, 1985; T.D. ATF–249, 52 FR 5961, Feb. 27, 1987; T.D. ATF–301, 55 FR 47608, Nov. 14, 1990; T.D. ATF–450, 66 FR 29023, May 29, 2001]

§ 70.24 Enforcement of summonses.

(a) *In general.* Whenever any person summoned under 26 U.S.C. 7602 neglects or refuses to obey such summons, or to produce books, papers, records, or other data, or to give testimony, as required, application may be made to the judge of the district court or to a U.S. magistrate for the district within which the person so summoned resides or is found for an attachment against him as for a contempt.

(b) *Persons who may apply for an attachment.* Appropriate TTB officers are authorized to apply for an attachment as provided in paragraph (a) of this section. The authority to apply for an attachment for the enforcement of a summons may not be redelegated.

(68A Stat. 902, as amended (26 U.S.C. 7604))

[T.D. ATF–6, 38 FR 32445, Nov. 26, 1973; 38 FR 33767, Dec. 7, 1973, as amended by T.D. ATF–450, 66 FR 29023, May 29, 2001]

§ 70.25 Special procedures for third-party summonses.

(a) When the Bureau summons the records of persons defined by 26 U.S.C. 7609(a)(3) as "third-party recordkeepers", the person about whom information is being gathered must be notified in advance, except when:

(1) The summons is served on the person about whom information is being gathered, or any officer or employee of such person, or

(2) The summons is served to determine whether or not records of the business transactions or affairs of an identified person have been made or kept, or

(3) The summons does not identify the person with respect to whose liability the summons is issued (a "John Doe" summons issued under the provisions of 26 U.S.C. 7609(f)), or

(4) The appropriate TTB officer petitions, and the court determines, on the basis of the facts and circumstances alleged, that there is reasonable cause to believe the giving of notice may lead to attempts to conceal, destroy, or alter records relevant to the examination, to prevent the communication of information from other persons through intimidation, bribery, or collusion, or to flee to avoid prosecution, testifying or production of records.

(b) Within 3 days of the day on which the summons was served, the notice required by paragraph (a) of this section shall be served upon the person entitled to notice, or mailed by certified or registered mail to the last known address of such person, or, in the absence of a last known address, left with the person summoned. No examination of any records required to be produced under a summons as to which notice is required under paragraph (a) of this section may be made:

(1) Before the close of the 23rd day after the day notice with respect to the summons is given in the manner provided in this paragraph, or

(2) Where a proceeding under paragraph (c) of this section was begun within the 20-day period referred to in that paragraph and the requirements of paragraph (c) of this section have been met, expect in accordance with an order of the court having jurisdiction of such proceeding or with the consent of the person beginning the proceeding to quash.

(c) If the person about whom information is being gathered has been given notice, that person has the right to institute, until and including the 20th day following the day such notice was served on or mailed, by certified or registered mail, to such notified person, a proceeding to quash the summons. During the time the validity of the summons is being litigated, the statutes of limitation are suspended under 26 U.S.C. 7609(e). Title 26 U.S.C. 7609 does not restrict the authority under 26 U.S.C. 7602 (or under any other provision of law) to examine records and witnesses without serving a summons and without giving notice of an examination.

(26 U.S.C. 7609)

[T.D. ATF–301, 55 FR 47608, Nov. 14, 1990]

§ 70.26 Third-party recordkeepers.

(a) *Definitions*—(1) *Accountant.* A person is an "accountant" under 26 U.S.C. 7609(a)(3)(F) for purposes of determining whether that person is a third-party recordkeeper if the person is registered, licensed, or certified under State law as an accountant.

(2) *Attorney.* A person is an "attorney" under 26 U.S.C. 7609(a)(3)(E) for purposes of determining whether that person is a third-party recordkeeper if the person is admitted to the bar of a State or the District of Columbia.

(3) *Credit cards*—(i) *Person extending credit through credit cards.* The term "person extending credit through credit cards or similar devices" under 26 U.S.C. 7609(a)(3)(C) generally includes any person who issues a credit card. It does not include a seller of goods or services that honors credit cards issued by other parties but does not extend credit on the basis of credit cards or similar devices issued by itself.

(ii) [Reserved]

(iii) *Similar devices to credit cards.* An object is a "similar device" to a credit card under 26 U.S.C. 7609(a)(3)(C) only if it is physical in nature, such as a coupon book, a charge plate, or a letter of credit. Thus, a person who extends credit by requiring credit customers to sign sales slips without requiring use of physical objects issued by that person is not a third-party recordkeeper under 26 U.S.C. 7609(a)(3)(C).

(b) *When third-party recordkeeper status arises.* A person is a "third-party recordkeeper" with respect to a given set of records only if the person made or kept the records in the person's capacity as a third-party recordkeeper. Thus, for instance, an accountant is not a third-party recordkeeper (by reason of being an accountant) with respect to the accountant's records of a sale of property by the accountant to another person. Similarly, a credit card issuer is not a third-party recordkeeper (by reason of being a person extending credit through the use of credit cards or similar devices) with respect to:

(1) Records relating to noncredit card transactions, such as a cash sale by the issuer to a holder of the issuer's credit card; or

(2) Records relating to transactions involving the use of another issuer's credit card.

(c) *Duty of third-party recordkeeper*—(1) *In General.* Upon receipt of a summons, the third-party recordkeeper ("recordkeeper") must begin to assemble the summoned records. The recordkeeper must be prepared to produce the summoned records on the date which the summons states the records are to be examined regardless of the institution or anticipated institution of a proceeding to quash or the recordkeeper's intervention (as allowed under 26 U.S.C. 7609(a)(3)(C)) into a proceeding to quash.

(2) *Disclosing recordkeepers not liable*—(i) *In general.* A recordkeeper, or an agent or employee thereof, who makes a disclosure of records as required by this section, in good faith reliance on the "Certificate of the Secretary" (as defined in paragraph (c)(2)(ii) of this section) or an order of a court requiring production of records, will not be liable for such disclosure to any customer, or to any party with respect to whose tax liability the summons was issued, or to any other person.

(ii) *Certificate of the Secretary.* The appropriate TTB officer may issue to the recordkeeper a "Certificate of the Secretary" stating both:

(A) That the 20-day period, within which a notified person may institute a proceeding to quash the summons has expired; and

(B) That no proceeding has been properly instituted within that period.

The appropriate TTB officer may also issue a "Certificate of the Secretary" to the recordkeeper if the taxpayer, with respect to whose tax liability the summons was issued, expressly consents to the examination of the records summoned.

(3) *Reimbursement of costs.* Recordkeepers may be entitled to reimbursement of their costs of assembling and preparing to produce summoned records, to the extent allowed by 26 U.S.C. 7610, even if the summons ultimately is not enforced.

(26 U.S.C. 7609)

[T.D. ATF–301, 55 FR 47608, Nov. 14, 1990]

§ 70.27 Right to intervene; right to institute a proceeding to quash.

(a) *Notified person.* Under 26 U.S.C. 7609(a), the Bureau must give a notice of summons to any person, other than the person summoned, who is identified in the description of the books and records contained in the summons in order that such person may contest the right of the Bureau to examine the summoned records by instituting a proceeding to quash the summons. Thus, if the Bureau issues a summons to a bank requesting checking account records of more than one person all of whom are identified in the description of the records contained in the summons, then all such persons are notified persons entitled to notice under 26 U.S.C. 7609(a). Therefore, if the Bureau requests the records of a joint bank account of A and B, both of whom are named in the summons, then both A and B are notified persons entitled to notice under 26 U.S.C. 7609(a).

(b) *Right to institute a proceeding to quash*—(1) *In general.* Title 26 U.S.C. 7609(b) grants a notified person the right to institute a proceeding to quash the summons in the United States district court for the district within which the person summoned resides or is found. Jurisdiction of the court is based on 26 U.S.C. 7609(b). The act of filing a petition in district court does not in and of itself institute a proceeding to quash under 26 U.S.C. 7609(b)(2). Rather, the filing of the petition must be coupled with notice as required by 26 U.S.C. 7609(b)(2)(B).

(2) *Elements of institution of a proceeding to quash.* In order to institute a proceeding to quash a summons, the notified person (or the notified person's agent, nominee, or other person acting under the direction or control of the notified person) must, not later than the 20th day following the day the notice of the summons was served on or mailed to such notified person:

(i) File a petition to quash in the name of the notified person in a district court having jurisdiction.

(ii) Notify the Bureau by sending a copy of that petition by registered or certified mail to the Bureau employee and office designated to receive the copy in the notice of summons that was given to the notified person, and

(iii) Notify the recordkeeper by sending to that recordkeeper by registered or certified mail a copy of the petition.

Failure to give timely notice to either the summoned party or the Bureau in the manner described in this paragraph means that the notified person has failed to institute a proceeding to quash and the district court has no jurisdiction to hear the proceeding. Thus, for example, if the notified person mails a copy of the petition to the summoned person but not to the designated Bureau employee and office, the notified person has failed to institute a proceeding to quash. Similarly, if the notified person mails a copy of such petition to the summoned person, but instead of sending a copy of the petition by registered or certified mail to the designated employee and office, the notified person gives the designated employee and office the petition by some other means, the notified person has failed to institute a proceeding to quash.

(3) *Failure to institute a proceeding to quash.* If the notified person fails to institute a proceeding to quash within 20 days following the day the notice was served on or mailed to such notified person, the Bureau may examine the summoned records following the 23rd day after notice of the summons was served on or mailed to the notified person (see 26 U.S.C. 7609(d)(1)).

(c) *Presumption no notice has been mailed.* Title 26 U.S.C. 7609(b)(2)(B) permits a notified person to institute a proceeding to quash by filing a petition in district court and notifying both the Bureau and the summoned person. Unless the notified person has notified both the Bureau and the summoned person in the appropriate manner, the notified person has failed to institute a proceeding to quash. If the copy of the petition has not been delivered to the summoned person or the person and office designated to receive the notice on behalf of the Bureau within 3 days from the close of the 20-day period allowed to institute a proceeding to quash, it is presumed that the notification has not been timely mailed.

(26 U.S.C. 7609)

[T.D. ATF–301, 55 FR 47609, Nov. 14, 1990]

§ 70.28 Summonses excepted from 26 U.S.C. 7609 procedures.

(a) *In aid of the collection of certain liabilities*—(1) *In general.* Title 26 U.S.C. 7609(c)(2)(B) contains an exception to the general notice requirement when a summons is issued to a third-party recordkeeper. That section excepts summonses issued in aid of the collection of the liability of any person against whom an assessment has been made or judgment rendered or the liability at law or in equity of any transferee of such a person.

(2) *Examples.* Examples of summonses referred to in paragraph (a)(1) of this section are:

(i) Summonses issued to determine the amount held in a bank in the name of a person against whom an assessment has been made or judgment rendered;

(ii) Summonses issued to enforce transferee liability for a tax which has been assessed.

(b) *Numbered account (or similar arrangement).* Under 26 U.S.C. 7609(c)(2), a summons issued solely to determine the identity of a person having a numbered account (or similar arrangement) with a bank or other institution is excepted from the requirements of 26 U.S.C. 7609. A "numbered account (or similar arrangement)" under 26 U.S.C. 7609(c)(2) is an account through which a person may authorize transactions solely through the use of a number, symbol, code name, or other device not involving the disclosure of the person's identity. A "person having a numbered account (or similar arrangement)" includes the person who opened the account and any person authorized to use the account or to receive records or statements concerning it.

(26 U.S.C. 7609)

[T.D. ATF–301, 55 FR 47610, Nov. 14, 1990]

§ 70.29 Suspension of statutes of limitations.

(a) *Suspension while a proceeding under 26 U.S.C. 7609(b) is pending.* Under

26 U.S.C. 7609(e)(1), the statutes of limitations of 26 U.S.C. 6501 and 6531 are suspended if a notified person with respect to whose liability a summons is issued, or the notified person's agent, nominee, or other person acting under the direction or control of the notified person, takes any action as provided in 26 U.S.C. 7609(b).

(1) *Agent, nominee, etc.* A person is a notified person's agent, nominee, or other person acting under the direction or control of a notified person for purposes of 26 U.S.C. 7609(e) if the person with respect to whose liability the summons is issued has the ability in fact or at law to cause the agent, etc., to take the actions permitted under 26 U.S.C. 7609(b). Thus, in the case of a corporation, direction or control by the notified person may exist even though less than 50 percent of the voting power of the corporation is held by the notified person.

(2) *Period during which a proceeding, etc., is pending.* Under 26 U.S.C. 7609(e), the statute of limitations shall be suspended for the period during which a proceeding and any appeals regarding the enforcement of such summons is pending. This period begins on the date the petition to quash the summons is filed in district court. The period continues until all appeals are disposed of, or until the expiration of the period in which an appeal may be taken or a request for a rehearing may be made. Full compliance, partial compliance, and noncompliance have no effect on the suspension provisions. The periods of limitations which are suspended under 26 U.S.C. 7609(e) are those which apply to the taxable periods to which the summons relates.

(3) *Taking of action as provided in 26 U.S.C. 7609(b).* Title 26 U.S.C. 7609(b) allows intervention by a notified person as a matter of right upon compliance with the Federal Rules of Civil Procedure. The phrase "takes any action as provided in subsection (b)", found in 26 U.S.C. 7609(e), includes any intervention whether or not 26 U.S.C. 7609(b) is specifically mentioned in the order of the court allowing intervention. The phrase also includes the fulfilling of only part of the requirements of 26 U.S.C. 7609(b)(2), relating to the right of a person to institute a proceeding to quash. Thus, for instance, if a notified person notifies a person who has been summoned by sending a copy of the petition by registered or certified mail but does not mail a copy of that notice to the appropriate person and office under 26 U.S.C. 7609(b)(2)(B), the notified person has taken an action under 26 U.S.C. 7609(e).

(b) *Suspension after 6 months of service of summons.* In the absence of the resolution of the third-party recordkeeper's response to the summons described in 26 U.S.C. 7609(c) or the summoned party's response to a summons described in 26 U.S.C. 7609(f) the running of any period of limitations under 26 U.S.C. 6501 or under 26 U.S.C. 6531 with respect to any person with respect to whose liability the summons is issued (other than a person taking action as provided in 26 U.S.C. 7609(b)) shall be suspended for the period:

(1) Beginning on the date which is 6 months after the service of such summons, and

(2) Ending with the final resolution of such response.

(26 U.S.C. 7609)

[T.D. ATF–301, 55 FR 47610, Nov. 14, 1990]

§ 70.30 Time and place of examination.

(a) *Time and place.* The time and place of examination pursuant to the provisions of 26 U.S.C. 7602 must be such time and place as may be fixed by an appropriate TTB officer and as are reasonable under the circumstances. The date fixed for appearance shall not be less than 10 days from the date of the summons.

(b) *Restrictions on examination of taxpayer.* No taxpayer is to be subjected to unnecessary examination or investigations, and only one inspection of a taxpayer's books of account shall be made for each taxable year unless the taxpayer requests otherwise or unless an authorized internal revenue or an appropriate TTB officer, after investigation, notifies the taxpayer in writing that an additional inspection is necessary.

(68A Stat. 902, as amended (26 U.S.C. 7605))

[T.D. ATF–450, 66 FR 29023, May 29, 2001]

§ 70.31 Entry of premises for examination of taxable objects.

(a) *General.* An appropriate TTB officer may, in the performance of his or her duty, enter in the daytime any building or place where any articles or objects subject to tax are made, produced, or kept, so far as it may be necessary for the purpose of examining said articles or objects and also enter at night any such building or place, while open, for a similar purpose.

(b) *Distilled spirits plants.* Any appropriate TTB officer may, at all times, as well by night as by day, enter any plant or any other premises where distilled spirits are produced or rectified, or structure or place used in connection therewith for storage or other purposes; to make examination of the materials, equipment and facilities thereon; and make such gauges and inventories as such officer deems necessary. Whenever any appropriate TTB officer, having demanded admittance, and having declared his or her name and office, is not admitted to such premises by the proprietor or other person having charge thereof, such officer may at all times, use such force as is necessary for such officer to gain entry to such premises.

(c) *Authority to break up grounds.* An appropriate TTB officer, and any person acting in his or her aid, may break up the ground on any part of a distilled spirits plant, or any other premises where spirits are produced or rectified, or any ground adjoining or near to such plant or premises, or any wall or partition thereof, or belonging thereto, or other place, to search for any pipe, cock, private conveyance, or utensil; and, upon finding any such pipe or conveyance leading therefrom or thereto, to break up any ground, house, wall, or other place through or into which such pipe or other conveyance leads, and to break or cut away such pipe or other conveyance, and turn any cock, or to determine whether such pipe or other conveyance conveys or conceals any spirits, mash, wort, or beer, or other liquor, from the sight or view of the appropriate TTB officer, so as to prevent or hinder such officer from taking a true account thereof.

(68A Stat. 903, 72 Stat. 1357 (26 U.S.C. 7606, 5203))

[T.D. ATF–450, 66 FR 29023, May 29, 2001]

§ 70.32 Examination of records and objects.

Any appropriate TTB officer may enter, during business hours, the premises of any regulated establishment for the purpose of inspecting and examining any records, articles, or other objects required to be kept by such establishment under 18 U.S.C. chapter 40 or 44, or provisions of 26 U.S.C. enforced and administered by the Bureau, or regulations issued pursuant thereto.

(68A Stat. 715, as amended, 903, 72 Stat. 1348, 1361, 1373, 1381, 1390, 1391, 1395, 82 Stat. 231, as amended, 84 Stat. 955; (26 U.S.C. 5741, 7606, 5146, 5207, 5275, 5367, 5415, 5504, 5555, 18 U.S.C. 923, 843))

[T.D. ATF–331, 57 FR 40328, Sept. 3, 1992, as amended by T.D. ATF–450, 66 FR 29023, May 29, 2001]

§ 70.33 Authority of enforcement officers of the Bureau.

Appropriate TTB officers may perform the following functions:

(a) Carry firearms;

(b) Execute and serve search warrants and arrest warrants, and serve subpoenas and summonses issued under authority of the United States;

(c) In respect to the performance of such duty, make arrests without warrant for any offense against the United States committed in his presence, or for any felony cognizable under the laws of the United States if he has reasonable grounds to believe that the person to be arrested has committed, or is committing, such felony; and

(d) In respect to the performance of such duty, make seizures of property subject to forfeiture to the United States.

(53 Stat. 1291, 62 Stat. 840, 68 Stat. 848, as amended, 72 Stat. 1429, as amended, 82 Stat. 233, as amended, 84 Stat. 956 (49 U.S.C. 782, 18 U.S.C. 3615, 22 U.S.C. 1934, 26 U.S.C. 7608, 18 U.S.C. 924, 844); 26 U.S.C. 7805 (68A Stat. 917), 27 U.S.C. 205 (49 Stat. 981 as amended), 18 U.S.C. 926 (82 Stat. 959), and sec. 38, Arms Export Control Act (22 U.S.C. 2778, 90 Stat. 744))

[T.D. ATF–6, 38 FR 32445, Nov. 26, 1973, as amended by T.D. ATF–48, 43 FR 13531, Mar. 31, 1978. Redesignated by T.D. ATF–301, 55 FR 47606, Nov. 14, 1990; T.D. ATF–450, 66 FR 29023, May 29, 2001]

§ 70.34 Listing by appropriate TTB officers of taxable objects owned by nonresidents.

Whenever there are any articles in any internal revenue district subject to tax, which are not owned or possessed by, or under the care or control of, any person within such district, and of which no list has been transmitted to the appropriate TTB officer, as required by law or by regulations prescribed pursuant to law, an appropriate TTB officer shall enter the premises where such articles are situated, make such inspection of the articles as may be necessary, and make lists of the same according to the forms prescribed. Such lists, being subscribed by the appropriate TTB officer, are sufficient lists of such articles for all purposes.

[T.D. ATF–450, 66 FR 29023, May 29, 2001]

GENERAL POWERS AND DUTIES

§ 70.40 Authority to administer oaths and certify.

Appropriate TTB officers are authorized to administer such oaths or affirmations and to certify to such papers as may be necessary under the tax laws administered by the Bureau, the Federal Alcohol Administration Act, or regulations issued thereunder, except that the authority to certify must not be construed as applying to those papers or documents the certification of which is authorized by separate order or directive.

(68A Stat. 904 (26 U.S.C. 7622))

[T.D. ATF–450, 66 FR 29023, May 29, 2001]

§ 70.41 Rewards for information relating to violations of tax laws administered by the Bureau.

(a) *In general.* An appropriate TTB officer may approve such reward as he or she deems suitable for information that leads to the detection and punishment of any person guilty of violating any tax law administered by the Bureau or conniving at the same. The rewards provided for by 26 U.S.C. 7623 are limited in their aggregate to the sum appropriated therefor and shall be paid only in cases not otherwise provided for by law.

(b) *Eligibility to file claim for reward*—(1) *In general.* Any person, other than certain present or former federal employees (see paragraph (b)(2) of this section), who submits, in the manner set forth in paragraph (d) of this section, information relating to the violation of tax laws administered and enforced by the Bureau, is eligible to file a claim for reward under 26 U.S.C. 7623.

(2) *Federal employees.* No person who was an officer or employee of the Department of the Treasury at the time he came into possession of information relating to violations of tax laws administered by the Bureau, or at the time he divulged such information, shall be eligible for reward under 26 U.S.C. 7623 and this section. Any other federal employee, or former federal employee, is eligible to file a claim for reward if the information submitted came to his knowledge other than in the course of his official duties.

(3) *Deceased informants.* A claim for reward may be filed by an executor, administrator, or other legal representative on behalf of a deceased informant if, prior to his death, the informant was eligible to file a claim for such reward under 26 U.S.C. 7623 and this section. Certified copies of the letters testamentary, letters of administration, or other similar evidence must be annexed to such a claim for reward on behalf of a deceased informant in order to show the authority of the legal representative to file the claim for reward.

(c) *Amount and payment of reward.* All relevant factors, including the value of the information furnished in relation to the facts developed by the investigation of the violation, must be taken into account in determining whether a reward must be paid, and, if so, the amount thereof. The amount of a reward shall represent what the appropriate TTB officer deems to be adequate compensation in the particular case, normally not to exceed 10 percent of the additional taxes, penalties, and fines which are recovered as a result of the information. No reward, however, shall be paid with respect to any additional interest that may be collected. Payment of a reward will be made as promptly as the circumstances of the case permit, but generally not until the taxes, penalties, or fines involved have been collected. However, the informant may waive any claim for reward with respect to an uncollected portion of the taxes, penalties, or fines involved, in which case the claim may be immediately processed. No person is authorized under these regulations to make any offer, or promise, or otherwise to bind the appropriate TTB officer with respect to the payment of any reward or the amount thereof.

(d) *Submission of information.* Persons desiring to claim rewards under the provisions of 26 U.S.C. 7623 and this section may submit information relating to violations of tax laws administered by the Bureau to an appropriate TTB officer. If the information is submitted in person, either orally or in writing, the name and official title of the person to whom it is submitted and the date on which it is submitted must be included in the formal claim for reward.

(e) *Anonymity.* No unauthorized person shall be advised of the identity of an informant.

(f) *Filing claim for reward.* An informant who intends to claim a reward under 26 U.S.C. 7623 should notify the person to whom he submits his information of such intention, and must file a formal claim, signed with his true name, as soon after submission of the information as practicable. If other than the informant's true name was used in furnishing the information, the claimant must include with his claim satisfactory proof of his identity as that of the informant. Claim for reward under the provisions of 26 U.S.C. 7623 must be made on TTB Form 3200.13. TTB Form 3200.13 should be obtained from the office where the information is filed.

(68A Stat. 904 (26 U.S.C. 7623); 26 U.S.C. 7805 (68A Stat. 917), 27 U.S.C. 205 (49 Stat. 981 as amended), 18 U.S.C. 926 (82 Stat. 959), and sec. 38, Arms Export Control Act (22 U.S.C. 2778, 90 Stat. 744))

[T.D. ATF–6, 38 FR 32445, Nov. 26, 1973, as amended by T.D. ATF–48, 43 FR 13531, Mar. 31, 1978; 44 FR 55841, Sept. 28, 1979. Redesignated by T.D. ATF–301, 55 FR 47606, Nov. 14, 1990; T.D. ATF–312, 56 FR 31085, July 9, 1991; T.D. ATF–450, 66 FR 29024, May 29, 2001]

§ 70.42 Returns prepared or executed by appropriate TTB officers.

(a) *Preparation of returns*—(1) *General.* If any person, required by provisions of 26 U.S.C. enforced and administered by the Bureau or by the regulations prescribed thereunder to make a return, fails to make such return, it may be prepared by an appropriate TTB officer provided the person required to make the return consents to disclose all information necessary for the preparation of such return. The return upon being signed by the person required to make it must be received by the appropriate TTB officer, as the return of such person.

(2) *Responsibility of person for whom return is prepared.* A person for whom a return is prepared in accordance with paragraph (a)(1) of this section shall for all legal purposes remain responsible for the correctness of the return to the same extent as if the return had been prepared by such person.

(b) *Execution of returns*—(1) *General.* If any person, required by provisions of 26 U.S.C. enforced and administered by the Bureau or by the regulations prescribed thereunder to make a return, fails to make a return at the time prescribed therefor, or makes, willfully or otherwise, a false or fraudulent return, the appropriate TTB officer must make such return from such officer's own knowledge and from such information as the officer can obtain through testimony or otherwise.

(2) *Status of returns.* Any return made in accordance with paragraph (b)(1) of this section and subscribed by the appropriate TTB officer is prima facie good and sufficient for all legal purposes.

(c) *Cross references.* (1) For provisions that the return executed by an appropriate TTB officer will not start the running of the period of limitations on assessment and collection, see 26 U.S.C. 6501(b)(3) and §70.222(b) of this part.

(2) For additions to the tax and additional amounts for failure to file returns, see section 6651 of the Internal Revenue Code.

(3) For additions to the tax for failure to pay tax, see sections 5684, 5761, and 6653 of the Internal Revenue Code.

(4) For failure to make deposit of taxes or overstatement of deposit claims, see section 6656 of the Internal Revenue Code.

(5) For an additional penalty for tendering a bad check or money order, see section 6657 of the Internal Revenue Code.

(6) For certain failures to pay tax with respect to cases pending under Title 11 of the United States Code, see section 6658 of the Internal Revenue Code.

(7) For failure to supply identifying numbers, see section 6676 of the Internal Revenue Code.

(8) For penalties for aiding and abetting understatement of tax liability, see section 6701 of the Internal Revenue Code.

(9) For criminal penalties for willful failure to make returns, see sections 7201, 7202, and 7203 of the Internal Revenue Code.

(10) For criminal penalties for willfully making false or fraudulent returns, see sections 7206 and 7207 of the Internal Revenue Code.

(11) For authority to examine books and witnesses, see section 7602 of the Internal Revenue Code and §70.22.

(26 U.S.C. 6020)

[T.D. ATF–251, 52 FR 19314, May 22, 1987. Redesignated and amended by T.D. ATF–301, 55 FR 47606, 47610, Nov. 14, 1990; T.D. ATF–450, 66 FR 29024, May 29, 2001]

Subpart D—Collection of Excise and Special (Occupational) Tax

COLLECTION—GENERAL PROVISIONS

§70.51 Collection authority.

The taxes imposed by provisions of 26 U.S.C. enforced and administered by the Bureau must be collected by appropriate TTB officers.

(26 U.S.C. 6301)

[T.D. ATF–450, 66 FR 29024, May 29, 2001]

§70.52 Signature presumed authentic.

An individual's name signed to a return, statement, or other document shall be prima facie evidence for all purposes that the return, statement or other document was actually signed by that individual.

(26 U.S.C. 6064)

[T.D. ATF–301, 55 FR 47611, Nov. 14, 1990]

RECEIPT OF PAYMENT

§70.61 Payment by check or money order.

(a) *Authority to Receive*—(1) *General.* (i) The appropriate TTB officer may accept checks drawn on any bank or trust company incorporated under the laws of the United States or under the laws of any State, Territory, or possession of the United States, or money orders in payment for internal revenue taxes, provided such checks or money orders are collectible in U.S. currency at par, and subject to the further provisions contained in this section. The appropriate TTB officer may accept such checks or money orders in payment for internal revenue stamps (authorized under Subtitle E of the Internal Revenue Code or any provision of Subtitle F which relates to Subtitle E) to the extent and under the conditions prescribed in paragraph (a)(2) of this section. A check or money order in payment for internal revenue taxes or internal revenue stamps should be made payable to the Alcohol and Tobacco Tax and Trade Bureau. A check or money order is payable at par only if the full amount thereof is payable without any deduction for exchange or other charges. As used in this section, the term "money order" means:

(A) U.S. postal, bank, express, or telegraph money order; and

(B) Money order issued by a domestic building and loan association (as defined in section 7701(a)(19) of the Internal Revenue Code) or by a similar association incorporated under the laws of a possession of the United States;

(C) A money order issued by such other organization as the appropriate TTB officer may designate; and

(D) A money order described in paragraph (a)(1)(ii) of this section in cases therein described. However, the appropriate TTB officers may refuse to accept any personal check whenever there is good reason to believe that such check will not be honored upon presentment.

(ii) An American citizen residing in a country with which the United States maintains direct exchange of money orders on a domestic basis may pay his/her tax by postal money order of such country. For a list of such countries, see section 171.27 of the Postal Manual of the United States.

(iii) If one check or money order is remitted to cover two or more persons' taxes, the remittance should be accompanied by a letter of transmittal clearly identifying—

(A) Each person whose tax is to be paid by the remittance;

(B) The amount of the payment on account of each such person; and

(C) The kind of tax paid.

(2) *Payment for internal revenue stamps—In general.* The appropriate TTB officer may accept checks and money orders described in paragraph (a)(1) of this section, in payment for internal revenue stamps authorized under Subtitle E of the Internal Revenue Code or under any provision of Subtitle F which relates to Subtitle E. However, the appropriate TTB officer may refuse to accept any personal check whenever there is good reason to believe that the check will not be honored upon presentment.

(3) *Payment of tax on distilled spirits, wine, beer, tobacco products, pistols, revolvers, firearms (other than pistols and revolvers), shells and cartridges; proprietor in default.* Where a check or money order tendered in payment for taxes on distilled spirits, wine or beer products (imposed under Chapter 51 of the Internal Revenue Code), or tobacco products (imposed under chapter 52 of the Internal Revenue Code), or pistols, revolvers, firearms (other than pistols and revolvers), shells and cartridges (imposed under chapter 32 of the Internal Revenue Code) is not paid on presentment, or where a taxpayer is otherwise in default in payment of such taxes, any remittance for such taxes made during the period of such default, and until the appropriate TTB officers finds that the revenue will not be jeopardized by the acceptance of personal checks, shall be in cash, or shall be in the form of a certified, cashier's, or treasurer's check, drawn on any bank or trust company incorporated under the laws of the United States, or under the laws of any State or possession of the United States, or a money order as described in paragraph (a)(1) of this section.

(b) *Checks or money orders not paid*—(1) *Ultimate liability.* The person who tenders any check (whether certified or uncertified, cashier's, treasurer's, or other form of check) or money order in payment for taxes is not released from liability until the check or money order is paid; and, if the check or money order is not duly paid, the person shall also be liable for all legal penalties and additions, to the same extent as if such check or money order had not been tendered. For the penalty in case a check or money order is not duly paid, see section 6657 of the Internal Revenue Code. For assessment of the amount of a check or money order not duly paid see section 6201(a)(2)(B) of the Internal Revenue Code.

(2) *Liability of banks and others.* If any certified, treasurer's, or cashier's check (or other guaranteed draft) or money order is not duly paid, the United States shall have a lien for the amount of such check upon all assets of the bank or trust company on which drawn or for the amount of such money order upon the assets of the issuer thereof. The unpaid amount shall be paid out of such assets in preference to any other claims against such bank or issuer except the necessary costs and expenses of administration and the reimbursement of the United States for the amount expended in the redemption of the circulating notes of such bank. In addition, the Government has

the right to exact payment from the person required to make the payment.

(26 U.S.C. 6311)

[T.D. ATF–251, 52 FR 19314, May 22, 1987. Redesignated by T.D. ATF–301, 55 FR 47606, Nov. 14, 1990; T.D. ATF–331, 57 FR 40328, Sept. 3, 1992; T.D. ATF–353, 59 FR 2522, Jan. 18, 1994]

§ 70.62 Fractional parts of a cent.

In the payment of any tax, a fractional part of a cent shall be disregarded unless it amounts to one-half cent or more, in which case it shall be increased to one cent. Fractional parts of a cent shall not be disregarded in the computation of taxes.

(26 U.S.C. 6313)

[T.D. ATF–251, 52 FR 19314, May 22, 1987. Redesignated by T.D. ATF–301, 55 FR 47606, Nov. 14, 1990]

§ 70.63 Computations on returns or other documents.

(a) *Amounts shown on forms.* To the extent permitted by any TTB form or instructions prescribed for use with respect to any TTB return, declaration, statement, or other document, or supporting schedules, any amount required to be reported in such form may be entered at the nearest whole dollar amount. The extent to which, and the conditions under which, such whole dollar amounts may be entered on any form will be set forth in the instructions issued with respect to such form. For the purpose of the computation to the nearest dollar, a fractional part of a dollar shall be disregarded unless it amounts to one-half dollar or more, in which case the amount (determined without regard to the fractional part of a dollar) shall be increased by $1. The following illustrates the application of this paragraph:

Exact amount	To be reported as
$18.49	$18
$18.50	19
$18.51	19

(b) *Election not to use whole dollar amounts*—(1) *Method of election.* Where any TTB form, or the instructions issued with respect to such form, provide that whole dollar amounts shall be reported, any person making a return, declaration, statement, or other document on such form may elect not to use whole dollar amounts by reporting thereon all amounts in full, including cents.

(2) *Time of election.* The election not to use whole dollar amounts must be made at the time of filing the return, declaration, statement, or other document. Such election may not be revoked after the time prescribed for filing such return, declaration, statement, or other document, including extensions of time granted for such filing. Such election may be made on any return, declaration, statement, or other document which is filed after the time prescribed for filing (including extensions of time), and such an election is irrevocable.

(3) *Effect of election.* The taxpayer's election shall be binding only on the return, declaration, statement, or other document filed for a taxable year or period, and a new election may be made on the return, declaration, statement, or other document filed for a subsequent taxable year or period.

(4) *Fractional part of a cent.* For treatment of the fractional part of a cent in the payment of taxes, see 26 U.S.C. 6313 and § 70.62 of this part.

(c) *Inapplicability to computation of amount.* The provisions of paragraph (a) of this section apply only to amounts required to be reported on a return, declaration, statement, or other document. They do not apply to items which must be taken into account in making the computations necessary to determine such amounts. For example, each item of liability must be taken into account at its exact amount, including cents, in computing the amount of total liability required to be reported on a tax return or supporting schedule. It is the amount of total liability, so computed, which is to be reported at the nearest whole dollar on the return or supporting schedule.

(26 U.S.C. 6102)

[T.D. ATF–301, 55 FR 47611, Nov. 14, 1990]

§ 70.64 Receipt for taxes.

The appropriate TTB officer must, upon request, issue a receipt for each tax payment made (other than a payment for stamps sold or delivered). In addition, an appropriate TTB officer or employee must issue a receipt for each payment of 1 dollar or more made in cash, whether or not requested. In the case of payments made by check, the canceled check is usually a sufficient receipt. No receipt shall be issued in lieu of a stamp representing a tax, whether the payment is in cash or otherwise.

(26 U.S.C. 6314)

[T.D. ATF–301, 55 FR 47611, Nov. 14, 1990, as amended by T.D. ATF–450, 66 FR 29024, May 29, 2001]

§ 70.65 Use of commercial banks.

For provisions relating to the use of commercial banks and electronic fund transfer of taxpayment to the Treasury Account, see the regulations relating to the particular tax.

(Aug. 16, 1954, ch. 736, 68A Stat. 775 (26 U.S.C. 6301); June 29, 1956, ch. 462, 70 Stat. 391 (26 U.S.C. 6301))

[T.D. ATF–77, 46 FR 3002, Jan. 13, 1981. Redesignated by T.D. ATF–301, 55 FR 47606, Nov. 14, 1990]

ASSESSMENT

§ 70.71 Assessment authority.

The appropriate TTB officers are authorized and required to make all inquiries necessary to the determination and assessment of all taxes imposed under the provisions of 26 U.S.C. enforced and administered by the Bureau. The appropriate TTB officers are further authorized and required to make the determinations and the assessments of such taxes. The term "taxes" includes interest, additional amounts, additions to the taxes, and assessable penalties. The authority of the appropriate TTB officers to make assessment includes the following:

(a) *Taxes shown on return.* The appropriate TTB officer shall assess all taxes determined by the taxpayer or by the appropriate TTB officer and disclosed on a return or list.

(b) *Unpaid taxes payable by stamp.* (1) If without use of the proper stamp:

(i) Any article upon which a tax is required to be paid by means of a stamp is sold or removed for sale or use by the manufacturer thereof, or

(ii) Any transaction or act upon which a tax is required to be paid by means of a stamp occurs, the appropriate TTB officer, upon such information as can be obtained, must estimate the amount of the tax which has not been paid and the appropriate TTB officer must make assessment therefor upon the person the appropriate TTB officer determines to be liable for the tax. However, the appropriate TTB officer may not assess any tax which is payable by stamp unless the taxpayer fails to pay such tax at the time and in the manner provided by law or regulations.

(2) If a taxpayer gives a check or money order as a payment for stamps but the check or money order is not paid upon presentment, then the appropriate TTB officer shall assess the amount of the check or money order against the taxpayer as if it were a tax due at the time the check or money order was received by appropriate TTB officer.

(26 U.S.C. 6201)

[T.D. ATF–301, 55 FR 47611, Nov. 14, 1990]

§ 70.72 Method of assessment.

The assessment shall be made by an appropriate TTB officer signing the summary record of assessment. The summary record, through supporting records, shall provide identification of the taxpayer, the character of the liability assessed, the taxable period, if applicable, and the amount of the assessment. The amount of the assessment shall, in the case of tax shown on a return by the taxpayer, be the amount so shown, and in all other cases the amount of the assessment shall be the amount shown on the supporting list or record. The date of the assessment is the date the summary record is signed by an appropriate TTB officer. If the taxpayer requests a copy of the record of assessment, the taxpayer shall be furnished a copy of the pertinent parts of the assessment which set forth the name of the taxpayer, the date of assessment, the character of the liability assessed, the taxable period, if applicable, and the amounts assessed.

(26 U.S.C. 6203)

[T.D. ATF–251, 52 FR 19314, May 22, 1987. Redesignated and amended by T.D. ATF–301, 55 FR 47606, 47612, Nov. 14, 1990; T.D. ATF–450, 66 FR 29025, May 29, 2001]

§ 70.73 Supplemental assessments.

If any assessment is incomplete or incorrect in any material respect, the appropriate TTB officer, subject to the applicable period of limitation, may make a supplemental assessment for the purpose of correcting or completing the original assessment.

(26 U.S.C. 6204)

[T.D. ATF–301, 55 FR 47612, Nov. 14, 1990]

§ 70.74 Request for prompt assessment.

(a) Except as otherwise provided in § 70.223 of this part, any tax for which a return is required and for which:

(1) A decedent or an estate of a decedent may be liable, or

(2) A corporation which is contemplating dissolution, is in the process of dissolution, or has been dissolved, may be liable, shall be assessed, or a proceeding in court without assessment for the collection of such tax shall be begun, within 18 months after the receipt of a written request for prompt assessment thereof.

(b) The executor, administrator, or other fiduciary representing the estate of the decedent, or the corporation, or the fiduciary representing the dissolved corporation, as the case may be, shall, after the return in question has been filed, file the request for prompt assessment in writing with the appropriate TTB officer. The request, in order to be effective, must be transmitted separately from any other document, must set forth the classes of tax and the taxable periods for which the prompt assessment is requested, and must clearly indicate that it is a request for prompt assessment under the provisions of 26 U.S.C. 6501(d). The effect of such a request is to limit the time in which an assessment of tax may be made, or a proceeding in court without assessment for collection of tax may be begun, to a period of 18 months from the date the request is filed with the appropriate TTB officer. The request does not extend the time within which an assessment may be made, or a proceeding in court without assessment shall be begun, after the expiration of 3 years from the date the return was filed. This special period of limitations will not apply to any return filed after a request for prompt assessment has been made unless an additional request is filed in the manner provided herein.

(c) In the case of a corporation the 18-month period shall not apply unless:

(1) The written request notifies the appropriate TTB officer that the corporation contemplates dissolution at or before the expirationof such 18-month period; the dissolution is in good faith begun before the expiration of such 18-month period; and the dissolution so begun is completed either before or after the expiration of such 18-month period; or

(2) The written request notifies the appropriate TTB officer that a dissolution has in good faith begun, and the dissolution is completed either before or after the expiration of such 18-month period; or

(3) A dissolution has been completed at the time the written request is made.

(26 U.S.C. 6501(d))

[T.D. ATF–301, 55 FR 47612, Nov. 14, 1990, as amended by T.D. ATF–353, 59 FR 2522, Jan. 18, 1994]

§ 70.75 Jeopardy assessment of alcohol, tobacco, and firearms taxes.

(a) If the appropriate TTB officer believes that the collection of any tax imposed under provisions of 26 U.S.C. enforced and administered by the Bureau will be jeopardized by delay, the appropriate TTB officer must, whether or not the time otherwise prescribed by law for filing the return or paying such tax has expired, immediately assess such tax, together with all interest, additional amounts and additions to the tax provided by law. An appropriate TTB officer will make an assessment under this section if collection is determined to be in jeopardy because at least one of the following conditions exists.

(1) The taxpayer is or appears to be designing quickly to depart from the

United States or to conceal himself or herself.

(2) The taxpayer is or appears to be designing quickly to place the taxpayer's property beyond the reach of the Government either by removing it from the United States, by concealing it, or by dissipating it, or by transferring it to other persons.

(3) The taxpayer's financial solvency is or appears to be threatened.

(b) The tax, interest, additional amounts, and additions to the tax will, upon assessment, become immediately due and payable, and the appropriate TTB officer shall, without delay, issue a notice and demand for payment thereof in full.

(c) See 26 U.S.C. 7429 with respect to requesting the appropriate TTB officer to review the making of the jeopardy assessment.

(d) For provisions relating to stay of collection of jeopardy assessments, see § 70.76 of this part.

(26 U.S.C. 6862 and 6863)

[T.D. ATF–301, 55 FR 47612, Nov. 14, 1990, as amended by T.D. ATF–450, 66 FR 29025, May 29, 2001]

§ 70.76 Stay of collection of jeopardy assessment; bond to stay collection.

(a) The collection of taxes assessed under 26 U.S.C. 6862 (referred to as a "jeopardy assessment" for purposes of this section) of any tax may be stayed by filing with the appropriate TTB officer a bond on the form to be furnished by TTB upon request.

(b) The bond may be filed:

(1) At any time before the time collection by levy is authorized under 26 U.S.C. 6331(a), or

(2) After collection by levy is authorized and before levy is made on any property or rights to property, or

(3) In the discretion of the appropriate TTB officer, after any such levy has been made and before the expiration of the period of limitations on collection.

(c) The bond must be in an amount equal to the portion (including interest thereon to the date of payment as calculated by the appropriate TTB officer) of the jeopardy assessment collection of which is sought to be stayed. See 26 U.S.C. 7101 and § 70.281, relating to the form of bond and the sureties thereon. The bond shall be conditioned upon the payment of the amount (together with interest thereon), for which the collection is stayed, at the time at which, but for the making of the jeopardy assessment, such amount would be due.

(d) Upon the filing of a bond in accordance with this section, the collection of so much of the assessment as is covered by the bond will be stayed. The taxpayer may at any time waive the stay of collection of the whole or of any part of the amount covered by the bond. If as a result of such waiver any part of the amount covered by the bond is paid, or if any portion of the jeopardy assessment is abated by the appropriate TTB officer, then the bond shall (at the request of the taxpayer) be proportionately reduced.

(26 U.S.C. 6863)

[T.D. ATF–301, 55 FR 47613, Nov. 14, 1990]

§ 70.77 Collection of jeopardy assessment; stay of sale of seized property pending court decision.

(a) *General rule.* In the case of an assessment under 26 U.S.C. 6862, and property seized for the collection of such assessment shall not (except as provided in paragraph (b) of this section) be sold until the latest of the following occurs:

(1) The period provided in 26 U.S.C. 7429(a)(2) to request the appropriate TTB officer to review the action taken expires.

(2) The period provided in 26 U.S.C. 7429(b)(1) to file an action in U.S. District Court expires if a request for redetermination is made to the appropriate TTB officer.

(3) The U.S. District Court judgment in such action becomes final, if a civil action is begun in accordance with 26 U.S.C. 7429(b).

(b) *Exceptions.* Notwithstanding the provisions of paragraph (a) of this section, any property seized may be sold:

(1) If the taxpayer files with the appropriate TTB officer a written consent to the sale, or

(2) If the appropriate TTB officer determines that the expenses of conservation and maintenance of the property will greatly reduce the net proceeds from the sale of such property, or

(3) If the property is of a type to which 26 U.S.C. 6336 (relating to sale of perishable goods) is applicable.

(26 U.S.C. 6863)

[T.D. ATF-301, 55 FR 47613, Nov. 14, 1990, as amended by T.D. ATF-353, 59 FR 2522, Jan. 18, 1994]

NOTICE AND DEMAND

§70.81 Notice and demand for tax.

(a) *General rule.* Where it is not otherwise provided by provisions of 26 U.S.C. enforced and administered by the Bureau, the appropriate TTB officer shall, after the making of an assessment of a tax pursuant to §70.71 of this part, give notice to each person liable for the unpaid tax, stating the basis for the tax due, the amount of tax, interest, additional amounts, additions to the tax and assessable penalties, and demanding payment thereof. Such notice shall be given as soon as possible and within 60 days. However, the failure to give notice within 60 days does not invalidate the notice. Such notice shall be left at the dwelling or usual place of business of such person, or shall be sent by mail to such person's last known address.

(b) *Assessment prior to last date for payment.* If any tax is assessed prior to the last date prescribed for payment of such tax, demand that such tax be paid will not be made before such last date, except where it is believed collection would be jeopardized by delay.

(26 U.S.C. 6303 and 7521)

[T.D. ATF-301, 55 FR 47613, Nov. 14, 1990]

§70.82 Payment on notice and demand.

Upon receipt of notice and demand from the appropriate TTB officer, there shall be paid at the place and time stated in such notice the amount of any tax (including any interest, additional amounts, additions to the tax, and assessable penalties) stated in such notice and demand.

(26 U.S.C. 6155)

[T.D. ATF-301, 55 FR 47613, Nov. 14, 1990]

INTEREST

§70.90 Interest on underpayments.

(a) *General rule.* Interest at the underpayment rate referred to in §70.93 of this part shall be paid on any unpaid amount of tax from the last date prescribed for payment of the tax (determined without regard to any extension of time for payment) to the date on which payment is received.

(b) *Interest on penalties, additional amounts, or additions to the tax*—(1) *General.* Interest shall be imposed on any assessable penalty, additional amount, or addition to the tax (other than an addition to tax imposed under section 6651(a)(1) of the Internal Revenue Code) only if such assessable penalty, additional amount, or addition to the tax is not paid within 10 days from the date of notice and demand therefor, and in such case interest shall be imposed only for the period from the date of the notice and demand to the date of payment.

(2) *Interest on certain additions to tax.* Interest shall be imposed under this section on any addition to tax imposed by section 6651(a)(1) of the Internal Revenue Code for the period which (i) begins on the date on which the return of the tax with respect to which such addition to tax is imposed is required to be filed (including any extensions), and (ii) ends on the date of payment of such addition to tax.

(c) *Payments made within 10 days after notice and demand.* If notice and demand is made for payment of any amount, and if such amount is paid within 10 days after the date of such notice and demand, interest under this section on the amount so paid shall not be imposed for the period after the date of such notice and demand.

(d) *Satisfaction by credits.* If any portion of a tax is satisfied by credit of an overpayment, then no interest shall be imposed under section 6601 of the Internal Revenue Code on the portion of the tax so satisfied for any period during which, if the credit had not been made, interest would have been allowable with respect to such overpayment.

(e) *Last date prescribed for payment.* (1) In determining the last date prescribed for payment, any extension of time granted for payment of tax shall be disregarded. The granting of an extension of time for the payment of tax does not relieve the taxpayer from liability for the payment of interest thereon during the period of the extension. Thus, except as provided in paragraph (d) of this section, interest at the underpayment rate referred to in § 70.93 of this part is payable on any unpaid portion of the tax for the period during which such portion remains unpaid by reason of an extension of time for the payment thereof.

(2) In the case of taxes payable by stamp and in all other cases where the last date for payment of the tax is not otherwise prescribed, such last date for the purpose of the interest computation shall be deemed to be the date on which the liability for the tax arose. However, such last date shall in no event be later than the date of issuance of a notice and demand for the tax.

(26 U.S.C. 6601)

[T.D. ATF–251, 52 FR 19314, May 22, 1987, as amended by T.D. ATF–301, 55 FR 47613, Nov. 14, 1990]

§ 70.91 Interest on erroneous refund recoverable by suit.

Any portion of an internal revenue tax (or any interest, assessable penalty, additional amount, or addition to tax) which has been erroneously refunded, and which is recoverable by a civil action pursuant to 26 U.S.C. 7405, shall bear interest at the underpayment rate referred to in § 70.93 of this part.

(26 U.S.C. 6602)

[T.D. ATF–301, 55 FR 47614, Nov. 14, 1990]

§ 70.92 Interest on overpayments.

(a) *General rule.* Except as otherwise provided, interest shall be allowed on any overpayment of any tax at the overpayment rate referred to in § 70.93 of this part from the date of overpayment of the tax.

(b) *Date of overpayment.* Except as provided in section 6401(a) of the Internal Revenue Code, relating to assessment and collection after the expiration of the applicable period of limitation, there can be no overpayment of tax until the entire tax liability has been satisfied. Therefore, the dates of overpayment of any tax are the date of payment of the first amount which (when added to previous payments) is in excess of the tax liability (including any interest, addition to the tax, or additional amount) and the dates of payment of all amounts subsequently paid with respect to such tax liability.

(c) *Period for which interest is allowable in case of refunds.* If an overpayment of tax is refunded, interest shall be allowed from the date of the overpayment to a date determined by the appropriate TTB officer which shall not be more than 30 days prior to the date of the refund check. The acceptance of a refund check shall not deprive the taxpayer of the right to make a claim for any additional overpayment and interest thereon, provided the claim is made within the applicable period of limitation. However, if a taxpayer does not accept a refund check, no additional interest on the amount of the overpayment included in such check shall be allowed.

(d) *Period for which interest allowable in case of credits*—(1) *General rule.* If an overpayment of tax is credited, interest shall be allowed from the date of overpayment to the due date (as determined under paragraph (d)(2) of this section of the amount against which such overpayment is credited.

(2) *Determination of due date*—(i) *General.* The term *due date*, as used in this section, means the last day fixed by law or regulations for the payment of the tax (determined without regard to any extension of time), and not the date on which the appropriate TTB officer makes demand for the payment of the tax. Therefore, the due date of the tax is the date fixed for the payment of the tax;

(ii) *Tax not due yet.* If a taxpayer agrees to the crediting of an overpayment against tax and the schedule of allowance is signed prior to the date on which such tax would otherwise become due, then the due date of such tax shall be the date on which such schedule is signed;

(iii) *Interest.* In the case of a credit against interest that accrues for any period ending prior to January 1, 1983, the due date is the earlier of the date of assessment of such interest or December 31, 1982. In the case of a credit against interest that accrues from any period beginning on or after December 31, 1982, such interest is due as it economically accrues on a daily basis, rather than when it is assessed.

(iv) *Additional amount, addition to the tax, or assessable penalty.* In the case of a credit against an additional amount, addition to the tax, or assessable penalty, the due date is the earlier of the date of assessment or the date from which such amount would bear interest if not satisfied by payment or credit.

(26 U.S.C. 6611)

[T.D. ATF-251, 52 FR 19314, May 22, 1987, as amended by T.D. ATF-301, 55 FR 47614, Nov. 14, 1990; T.D. ATF-358, 59 FR 29367, June 7, 1994]

§ 70.93 Interest rate.

(a) *In general.* The interest rate established under 26 U.S.C. 6621(a)(2) shall be:

(1) On amounts outstanding before July 1, 1975, 6 percent per annum.

(2) On amounts outstanding:

After	And before	Rate per annum (percent)
June 30, 1975	Feb. 1, 1976	9
Jan. 31, 1976	Feb. 1, 1978	7
Jan. 31, 1978	Feb. 1, 1980	6
Jan. 31, 1980	Feb. 1, 1982	12
Jan. 31, 1982	Jan. 1, 1983	20

(3) On amounts outstanding after December 31, 1982, the adjusted rates for overpayment and underpayment established by the Commissioner of Internal Revenue under 26 U.S.C. 6621. These adjusted rates shall be published by the Commissioner in a Revenue Ruling. See § 70.94 of this part for application of daily compounding in determining interest accruing after December 31, 1982. Because interest accruing after December 31, 1982, accrues at the prescribed rate per annum compounded daily, the effective annual percentage rate of interest will exceed the prescribed rate of interest.

(b) *Applicability of interest rates*—(1) *Computation.* Interest and additions to tax on any amount outstanding on a specific day shall be computed at the annual rate applicable on such day.

(2) *Additions to tax.* Additions to tax under any section of the Internal Revenue Code that refers to the annual rate established under 26 U.S.C. 6621, shall be computed at the same rate per annum as the interest rate set forth under paragraph (a) of this section.

(3) *Interest.* Interest provided for under any section of the Internal Revenue Code that refers to the annual rate established under this section, including 26 U.S.C. 6332(d)(1), 6343(c), 6601(a), 6602, 6611(a), 7426(g), and 28 U.S.C. 1961(c)(1) or 2411, shall be computed at the rate per annum set forth under paragraph (a) of this section.

[T.D. ATF-301, 55 FR 47614, Nov. 14, 1990]

§ 70.94 Interest compounded daily.

(a) *General rule.* Effective for interest accruing after December 31, 1982, in computing the amount of any interest required to be paid under any provision of 26 U.S.C. or under 28 U.S.C. 1961(c)(1) or 2411, by the appropriate TTB officer or by the taxpayer, or in computing any other amount determined by reference to such amount of interest, or by reference to the interest rate established under 26 U.S.C. 6621, such interest or such other amount shall be compounded daily by dividing such rate of interest by 365 (366 in a leap year) and compounding such daily interest rate each day.

(b) *Applicability to unpaid amounts on December 31, 1982.* The unpaid interest (or other amount) that shall be compounded daily includes the interest (or other amount) accrued but unpaid on December 31, 1982.

(26 U.S.C. 6622)

[T.D. ATF-301, 55 FR 47614, Nov. 14, 1990]

ADDITIONS TO THE TAX, ADDITIONAL AMOUNTS, AND ASSESSABLE PENALTIES

Additions to the Tax and Additional Amounts

§ 70.95 Scope.

For purposes of the administration of excise taxes by the Alcohol and Tobacco Tax and Trade Bureau in accordance with Title 26 of the United States Code, the penalties prescribed in §§ 70.96 through 70.107 shall apply.

[T.D. ATF-251, 52 FR 19314, May 22, 1987, as amended by T.D. ATF-301, 55 FR 47614, Nov. 14, 1990]

§ 70.96 Failure to file tax return or to pay tax.

(a) *Addition to the tax*—(1) *Failure to file tax return.* In the case of failure to file a return required under authority of:

(i) Title 26 U.S.C. 61, relating to returns and records;

(ii) Title 26 U.S.C. 51, relating to distilled spirits, wines and beer;

(iii) Title 26 U.S.C. 52, relating to tobacco products, and cigarette papers and tubes; or

(iv) Title 26 U.S.C. 53, relating to machine guns, destructive devices, and certain other firearms; and the regulations thereunder, on or before the date prescribed for filing (determined with regard to any extension of time for such filing), there shall be added to the tax required to be shown on the return the amount specified below unless the failure to file the return within the prescribed time is shown to the satisfaction of the appropriate TTB officer to be due to reasonable cause and not to willful neglect. The amount to be added to the tax is 5 percent therof if the failure is not for more than one month, with an additional 5 percent for each additional month or fraction thereof during which the failure continues, but not to exceed 25 percent in the aggregate. The amount of any addition under paragraph (a)(1) of this section shall be reduced by the amount of the addition under paragraph (a)(2) of this section for any month to which an addition to tax applies under both paragraphs (a)(1) and (a)(2) of this section.

(2) *Failure to pay tax shown on return.* In case of failure to pay the amount shown as tax on any return required to be filed after December 31, 1969 (without regard to any extension of time for filing thereof), specified in paragraph (a)(1) of this section, on or before the date prescribed for payment of such tax (determined with regard to any extension of time for payment), there shall be added to the tax shown on the return the amount specified below unless the failure to pay the tax within the prescribed time is shown to the satisfaction of the appropriate TTB officer to be due to reasonable cause and not to willful neglect. The amount to be added to the tax is 0.5 percent of the amount of tax shown on the return if the failure is for not more than 1 month, with an additional 0.5 percent for each additional month or fraction thereof during which the failure continues, but not to exceed 25 percent in the aggregate.

(3) *Failure to pay tax not shown on return.* In case of failure to pay any amount in respect of any tax required to be shown on a return specified in paragraph (a)(1) of this section, which is not so shown (including an assessment made pursuant to 26 U.S.C. 6213(b)) within 10 days from the date of the notice and demand therefor, there shall be added to the amount shown in the notice and demand the amount specified below unless the failure to pay the tax within the prescribed time is shown to the satisfaction of the appropriate TTB officer to be due to reasonable cause and not to willful neglect. The amount to be added to the tax is 0.5 percent of the amount stated in the notice and demand if the failure is for not more than one month, with an additional 0.5 percent for each additional month or fraction thereof during which the failure continues, but not to exceed 25 percent in the aggregate. The maximum amount of the addition permitted under this subparagraph shall be reduced by the amount of the addition under paragraph (a)(1) of this section, which is attributable to the tax for which the notice and demand is made and which is not paid within 10 days from the date of notice and demand. The preceding sentence applies to amounts assessed on or before December 31, 1986.

(4) *Increases in penalties in certain cases.* For increases in penalties for failure to file a return or pay tax in certain cases, see 26 U.S.C. 6651(d) or (f).

(b) *Month defined.* (1) If the date prescribed for filing the return or paying tax is the last day of a calendar month, each succeeding calendar month or fraction thereof during which the failure to file or pay tax continues shall constitute a month for purposes of section 6651.

(2) If the date prescribed for filing the return or paying tax is a date other than the last day of a calendar month, the period which terminates with the

date numerically corresponding thereto in the succeeding calendar month and each such successive period shall constitute a month for purposes of section 6651. If, in the month of February, there is no date corresponding to the date prescribed for filing the return or paying tax, the period from such date in January through the last day of February shall constitute a month for purposes of section 6651. Thus, if a return is due on January 30, the first month shall end on February 28 (or 29 if a leap year), and the succeeding months shall end on March 30, April 30, etc.

(3) If a return is not timely filed or tax is not timely paid, the fact that the date prescribed for filing the return or paying tax, or the corresponding date in any succeeding calendar month, falls on a Saturday, Sunday, or legal holiday is immaterial in determining the number of months for which the addition to the tax under section 6651 applies.

(c) *Showing of reasonable cause.* A taxpayer who wishes to avoid the addition to the tax for failure to file a tax return or pay tax must make an affirmative showing of all facts alleged as a reasonable cause for the taxpayers failure to file such return or pay such tax on time in the form of a written statement containing a declaration that it is made under penalties of perjury. Such statement should be filed with the appropriate TTB officer. In addition, where special tax returns are delivered to an appropriate TTB officer, such statement may be delivered with the return. If the appropriate TTB officer determines that the delinquency was due to a reasonable cause and not to willful neglect, the addition to the tax will not be assessed. If the taxpayer exercised ordinary business care and prudence and was nevertheless unable to file the return within the prescribed time, then the delay is due to a reasonable cause. A failure to pay will be considered to be due to reasonable cause to the extent that the taxpayer has made a satisfactory showing that the taxpayer exercised ordinary business care and prudence in providing for payment of the tax liability and was nevertheless either unable to pay the tax or would suffer an undue hardship (as described in 26 CFR 1.6161–1(b)) if paid on the due date. In determining whether the taxpayer was unable to pay the tax in spite of the exercise of ordinary business care and prudence in providing for payment of a tax liability, consideration will be given to all the facts and circumstances of the taxpayer's financial situation, including the amount and nature of the taxpayer's expenditures in light of the income (or other amounts) the taxpayer could, at the time of such expenditures, reasonably expect to receive prior to the date prescribed for the payment of the tax. Thus, for example, a taxpayer who incurs lavish or extravagant living expenses in an amount such that the remainder of assets and anticipated income will be insufficient to pay the tax, has not exercised ordinary business care and prudence in providing for the payment of a tax liability. Further, a taxpayer who invests funds in speculative or illiquid assets has not exercised ordinary business care and prudence in providing for the payment of a tax liability unless, at the time of the investment, the remainder of the taxpayer's assets and estimated income will be sufficient to pay the tax or it can be reasonably foreseen that the speculative or illiquid investment made by the taxpayer can be utilized (by sale or as security for a loan) to realize sufficient funds to satisfy the tax liability. A taxpayer will be considered to have exercised ordinary business care and prudence if such taxpayer made reasonable efforts to conserve sufficient assets in marketable form to satisfy a tax liability and nevertheless was unable to pay all or a portion of the tax when it became due.

(d) *Penalty imposed on net amount due*—(1) *Credits against the tax.* The amount of tax required to be shown on the return for purposes of section 6651(a)(1) and the amount shown as tax on the return for purposes of section 6651(a)(2) shall be reduced by the amount of any part of the tax which is paid on or before the date prescribed for payment of the tax and by the amount of any credit against the tax which may be claimed on the return.

(2) *Partial payments.* (i) The amount of tax required to be shown on the return for purposes of section 6651(a)(2) of the Internal Revenue Code shall, for

the purpose of computing the addition for any month, be reduced by the amount of any part of the tax which is paid after the date prescribed for payment and on or before the first day of such month, and

(ii) The amount of tax stated in the notice and demand for purposes of section 6651(a)(3) of the Internal Revenue Code shall, for the purpose of computing the addition for any month, be reduced by the amount of any part of the tax which is paid before the first day of such month.

(e) *No addition to tax if fraud penalty assessed.* No addition to the tax under section 6651 of the Internal Revenue Code shall be assessed with respect to an underpayment of tax if an addition to the tax for fraud is assessed with respect to the same underpayment under section 6653(b). See section 6653(d) of the Internal Revenue Code.

(26 U.S.C. 6651)

[T.D. ATF–251, 52 FR 19314, May 22, 1987, as amended by T.D ATF–301, 55 FR 47614, Nov. 14, 1990; T.D. ATF–353, 59 FR 2522, Jan. 18, 1994; T.D. ATF–450, 66 FR 29025, May 29, 2001; T.D. TTB–79, 74 FR 37424, July 28, 2009]

§ 70.97 Failure to pay tax.

(a) *Negligence*—(1) *General.* If any part of any underpayment (as defined in paragraph (d) of this section) is due to negligence or disregard of rules or regulations, there shall be added to the tax an amount equal to the sum of 5 percent of the underpayment, and an amount equal to 50 percent of the interest payable under section 6601 of the Internal Revenue Code with respect to the portion of such underpayment which is attributable to negligence for the period beginning on the last date prescribed by law for payment of such underpayment (determined without regard to any extension) and ending on the date of the assessment of the tax (or if earlier, the date or the payment of the tax).

(2) Underpayment taken into account reduced by a portion attributable to fraud. There shall not be taken into account under paragraph (a) of this section any portion of an underpayment attributable to fraud with respect to which a penalty is imposed under paragraph (b) of this section.

(3) *Negligence.* For purposes of paragraph (a) of this section, the term "negligence" includes any failure to make a reasonable attempt to comply with the provisions of the Internal Revenue Code, and the term "disregard" includes any careless, reckless, or intentional disregard.

(4) The provisions of paragraph (a) apply to returns the due date for which (determined without regard to extensions) is after December 31, 1986.

(b) *Fraud*—(1) *General.* If any part of any underpayment (as defined in paragraph (d) of this section) of tax required to be shown on a return is due to fraud, there shall be added to the tax an amount equal to 50 percent of the portion of the underpayment which is attributable to fraud and an amount equal to 50 percent of the interest payable under section 6601 of the Internal Revenue Code with respect to such portion for the period beginning on the last day prescribed by law for payment of such underpayment (determined without regard to any extension) and ending on the date of the assessment of the tax or, if earlier, the date of the payment of the tax.

(2) The provisions of paragraph (b) of this section, apply to returns the due date for which (determined without regard to extensions) is on or before December 31, 1986.

(c) *Fraud*—(1) *General.* If any part of any underpayment (as defined in paragraph (d) of this section) of tax required to be shown on a return is due to fraud, there shall be added to the tax an amount equal to the sum of 75 percent of the portion of the underpayment which is attributable to fraud and an amount equal to 50 percent of the interest payable under section 6601 of the Internal Revenue Code with respect to such portion for the period beginning on the last day prescribed by law for payment of such underpayment (determined without regard to any extension) and ending on the date of the assessment of the tax or, if earlier, the date of the payment of the tax.

(2) Determination of portion attributable to fraud. If the appropriate TTB officer establishes that any portion of an underpayment is attributable to fraud, the entire underpayment shall

be treated as attributable to fraud, except with respect to any portion of the underpayment which the taxpayer establishes is not attributable to fraud.

(3) The provisions of this paragraph (c) apply to returns the due date for which (determined without regard to extensions) is after December 31, 1986.

(d) *Definition of underpayment.* For purposes of this section, the term *underpayment* means the amount by which such tax imposed by the Internal Revenue Code exceeds the excess of—

(1) The sum of,

(i) The amount shown as the tax by the taxpayer upon the taxpayers return (determined without regard to any credit for an overpayment for any prior period, and without regard to any adjustment under authority of sections 6205(a) and 6413(a) of the Internal Revenue Code), if a return was made by the taxpayer within the time prescribed for filing such return (determined with regard to any extension of time for such filing) and an amount was shown as the tax by the taxpayer thereon, plus;

(ii) Any amount, not shown on the return, paid in respect of such tax, over—

(2) *The amount of rebates made.* For purposes of paragraph (d) of this section, the term *rebate* means so much of an abatement, credit, refund, or other repayment, as was made on the ground that the tax imposed was less than the excess of the amount specified in paragraph (d)(1) of this section over the rebates previously made.

(e) *No delinquency penalty if fraud assessed.* If any penalty is assessed under paragraph (b) or (c) of this section (relating to fraud) for an underpayment of tax which is required to be shown on a return, no penalty under section 6651 of the Internal Revenue Code (relating to failure to file such return or pay tax) shall be assessed with respect to the portion of the underpayment which is attributable to fraud.

(f) *Failure to pay stamp tax.* Any person who willfully fails to pay any tax which is payable by stamp or willfully attempts in any manner to evade or defeat any such tax or payment thereof, shall, in addition to other penalties provided by law, be liable to a penalty of 50 percent of the total amount of the underpayment of the tax.

(g) *Additional penalty.* For additional penalty for failure to pay certain liquor and tobacco taxes, see 27 CFR 70.102.

(26 U.S.C. 6653)

[T.D. ATF–6, 38 FR 32445, Nov. 26, 1973, as amended by T.D. ATF–353, 59 FR 2522, Jan. 18, 1994]

§ 70.98 Penalty for underpayment of deposits.

(a) *General rule.* If any person is required by the provisions of 26 U.S.C. enforced and administered by the Bureau or regulations prescribed thereunder to deposit any tax in a government depository that is authorized under 26 U.S.C. 6302(c) to receive the deposit, and fails to deposit the tax within the time prescribed therefor, a penalty shall be imposed on such person unless the failure is shown to be due to reasonable cause and not due to willful neglect. The penalty shall be:

(1) For penalties assessed before October 22, 1986, 5 percent of the amount of the underpayment without regard to the period during which the underpayment continues.

(2) For penalties assessed after October 21, 1986, on deposits of taxes required to be made before January 1, 1990, 10 percent of the amount of the underpayment without regard to the period during which the underpayment continues.

(3) For deposits of taxes required to be made after December 31, 1989.

(i) 2 percent of the amount of the underpayment if the failure is for not more than 5 days,

(ii) 5 percent of the amount of the underpayment if the failure is for more than 5 days but not more than 15 days,

(iii) 10 percent of the amount of the underpayment if the failure is for more than 15 days,

(iv) 15 percent of the amount of the underpayment if the tax is not deposited before the earlier of:

(A) The day 10 days after the date of the first delinquency notice to the taxpayer under section 6303, or

(B) The day on which notice and demand for immediate payment is given under 26 U.S.C. 6862 or the last sentence of 26 U.S.C. 6331(a).

For purposes of this section, the term "underpayment" means the amount of tax required to be deposited less the amount, if any, that was deposited on or before the date prescribed therefor. Section 7502(e) of the Internal Revenue Code applies in determining the date a deposit is made.

(b) *Assertion of reasonable cause.* To show that the underpayment was due to reasonable cause and not due to willful neglect, a taxpayer must make an affirmative showing of all facts alleged as a reasonable cause in a written statement containing a declaration that it is made under the penalties of perjury. The statement must be filed with the appropriate TTB officer. If the appropriate TTB officer determines that the underpayment was due to reasonable cause and not due to willful neglect, the penalty will not be imposed.

(26 U.S.C. 6656)

[T.D. ATF–251, 52 FR 19314, May 22, 1987, as amended by T.D. ATF–301, 55 FR 47615, Nov. 14, 1990; T.D. ATF–353, 59 FR 2523, Jan. 18, 1994]

§ 70.100 Penalty for fraudulently claiming drawback.

Whenever any person fraudulently claims or seeks to obtain an allowance of drawback on goods, wares, or merchandise on which no internal revenue tax shall have been paid, or fraudulently claims any greater allowance of drawback than the tax actually paid, that person shall forfeit triple the amount wrongfully or fraudulently claimed or sought to be obtained, or the sum of $500, at the election of the appropriate TTB officer.

(26 U.S.C. 7304)

[T.D. ATF–301, 55 FR 47615, Nov. 14, 1990]

§ 70.101 Bad checks.

If any check or money order in payment of any amount receivable under Title 26 of the United States Code is not duly paid, in addition to any other penalties provided by law, there shall be paid as a penalty by the person who tendered such check, upon notice and demand, in the same manner as tax, an amount equal to 1 percent of the amount of such check, except that if the amount of such check is less than $500, the penalty under this section shall be $5 or the amount of such check, whichever is the lesser. This section shall not apply if the person establishes to the satisfaction of the appropriate TTB officer that such check was tendered in good faith and that such person had reasonable cause to believe that such check would be duly paid.

(26 U.S.C. 6657)

[T.D. ATF–251, 52 FR 19314, May 22, 1987. Redesignated and amended by T.D. ATF–301, 55 FR 47606, 47615, Nov. 14, 1990]

§ 70.102 Coordination with title 11.

(a) *Certain failures to pay tax.* No addition to the tax shall be made under section 6651 of the Internal Revenue Code for failure to make timely payment of tax with respect to a period during which a case is pending under Title 11 of the United States Code—

(1) If such tax was incurred by the estate and the failure occurred pursuant to an order of the court finding probable insufficiency of funds of the estate to pay administrative expenses, or

(2) If such tax was incurred by the debtor before the earlier of the order for relief or (in the involuntary case) the appointment of a trustee and

(i) The petition was filed before the due date prescribed by law (including extensions) for filing a return of such tax, or

(ii) The date for making the addition to the tax occurs on or after the day on which the petition was filed.

(b) *Exception for collected taxes.* Paragraph (a) of this section shall not apply to any liability for an addition to the tax which arises from the failure to pay or deposit a tax withheld or collected from others and required to be paid to the United States.

(26 U.S.C. 6658)

[T.D. ATF–251, 52 FR 19314, May 22, 1987. Redesignated by T.D. ATF–301, 55 FR 47606, Nov. 14, 1990]

§ 70.103 Failure to pay tax.

Whoever fails to pay any tax imposed by Part I of Subchapter A of Chapter 51 of the Internal Revenue Code (liquor taxes) or by Chapter 52 (tobacco taxes) at the time prescribed shall, in addition to any other penalty provided in the Internal Revenue Code, be liable to a penalty of 5 percent of the tax due but unpaid. For additional penalties for failure to pay tax, see 27 CFR 70.97.

(26 U.S.C. 5684(a) and 5761(b))

[T.D. ATF–251, 52 FR 19314, May 22, 1987. Redesignated by T.D. ATF–301, 55 FR 47606, Nov. 14, 1990]

Assessable Penalties

§70.111 Rules for application of assessable penalties.

(a) *Penalty assessed as tax.* The penalties and liabilities provided by Subchapter B, Chapter 68, of the Internal Revenue Code shall be assessed and collected in the same manner as taxes. Except as otherwise provided, any reference in the Internal Revenue Code to "tax" imposed thereunder shall also be deemed to refer to the penalties and liabilities provided by Subchapter B of Chapter 68.

(b) *Person defined.* For purposes of Subchapter B of Chapter 68 of the Internal Revenue Code, the term "person" includes an officer or employee of a corporation, or a member or employee of a partnership, who as such officer, employee, or member is under a duty to perform the act in respect of which the violation occurs.

(26 U.S.C. 6671)

[T.D. ATF–251, 52 FR 19314, May 22, 1987. Redesignated by T.D. ATF–301, 55 FR 47606, Nov. 14, 1990]

§70.112 Failure to collect and pay over tax, or attempt to evade or defeat tax.

Any person required to collect, truthfully account for, and pay over any tax imposed by the Internal Revenue Code who willfully fails to collect such tax, or truthfully account for and pay over such tax, or willfully attempts in any manner to evade or defeat any such tax or the payment thereof, shall, in addition to other penalties, be liable to a penalty equal to the total amount of the tax evaded, or not collected, or not accounted for and paid over. The penalty imposed by section 6672 of the Internal Revenue Code applies only to the collection, accounting for, or payment over of taxes imposed on a person other than the person who is required to collect, account for, and pay over such taxes. No penalty under section 6653 of the Internal Revenue Code, relating to failure to pay tax, shall be imposed for any offense to which this section is applicable.

(26 U.S.C. 6672)

[T.D. ATF–251, 52 FR 19314, May 22, 1987. Redesignated by T.D. ATF–301, 55 FR 47606, Nov. 14, 1990]

§70.113 Penalty for failure to supply taxpayer identification number.

(a) *In general.* Except as provided in paragraph (b) of this section, any person who is required by the regulations under section 6109 of the Internal Revenue Code to include the taxpayer identification number in any return, statement, or other document, fails to comply with such requirement at the time prescribed by such regulations, such person shall pay a penalty of $50 for each such failure, except that the total amount imposed on such person for all such failures during any calendar year shall not exceed $100,000. For returns having a due date (determined without regard to extensions) after December 31, 1986, the total amount imposed on such person for all such failures during any calendar year shall not exceed $100,000. Such penalty shall be paid in the same manner as tax upon the issuance of a notice and demand therefor.

(b) *Reasonable cause.* If any person who is required by the regulations under section 6109 of the Internal Revenue Code to supply a taxpayer identification number fails to comply with such requirement at the time prescribed by such regulations, but establishes to the satisfaction of the appropriate TTB officer that such failure was due to reasonable cause, the penalty set forth in paragraph (a) of this section shall not apply.

(c) *Persons required to supply taxpayer identification numbers.* For regulations under section 6109 of the Internal Revenue Code relating to persons required to supply an identifying number, see the regulations relating to the particular tax.

(26 U.S.C. 6723)

[T.D. ATF–251, 52 FR 19314, May 22, 1987. Redesignated and amended by T.D. ATF–301, 55 FR 47606, 47615, Nov. 14, 1990]

§ 70.114 Penalties for aiding and abetting understatement of tax liability.

(a) *Imposition of penalty.* Any person—

(1) Who aids or assists in, procures, or advises with respect to, the preparation or presentation of any portion of a return, affidavit, claim, or other document in connection with any matter arising under the internal revenue laws,

(2) Who knows that such portion will be used in connection with any material matter arising under the internal revenue laws, and

(3) Who knows that such portion (if so used) will result in an understatement of the liability for tax of another person, shall pay a penalty with respect to each such document in the amount determined under paragraph (b).

(b) *Amount of penalty*—(1) *General.* Except as provided in paragraph (b)(2) of this section, the amount of the penalty imposed by paragraph (a) of this section shall be $1,000.

(2) *Corporations.* If the return, affidavit, claim, or other document relates to the tax liability of a corporation, the amount of the penalty imposed by paragraph (a) of this section shall be $10,000.

(3) *Only one penalty per person per period.* If any person is subject to a penalty under paragraph (a) of this section with respect to any document relating to any taxpayer for any taxable period (or where there is no taxable period, any taxable event), such person shall not be subject to a penalty under paragraph (a) of this section with respect to any other document relating to such taxpayer for such taxable period (or event).

(c) *Activities of subordinates*—(1) *General.* For purpose of paragraph (a) of this section, the term "procures" includes,

(i) Ordering (or otherwise causing) a subordinate to do an act, and

(ii) Knowing of, and not attempting to prevent, participation by a subordinate in an act.

(2) For purposes of paragraph (c)(1) of this section, the term "subordinate" means any other person (whether or not a director, officer, employee, or agent of the taxpayer involved) over whose activities the person has direction, supervision, or control.

(d) *Taxpayer not required to have knowledge.* Paragraph (a) shall apply whether or not the understatement is with the knowledge or consent of the persons authorized or required to present the return, affidavit, claim, or other document.

(e) *Certain actions not treated as aid or assistance.* For purposes of paragraph (a)(1) of this section, a person furnishing typing, reproducing, or other mechanical assistance with respect to a document shall not be treated as having aided or assisted in the preparation of such document by reason of such assistance.

(f) *Penalty in addition to other penalties.* The penalty imposed by this section shall be in addition to any other penalty provided by law.

(26 U.S.C. 6701)

[T.D. ATF–251, 52 FR 19314, May 22, 1987. Redesignated by T.D. ATF–301, 55 FR 47606, Nov. 14, 1990]

ABATEMENTS, CREDITS AND REFUNDS

Procedure in General

§ 70.121 Amounts treated as overpayments.

(a) The term *overpayment* includes any payment of any internal revenue tax which is assessed or collected after the expiration of the period of limitation applicable thereto.

(b) An amount paid as tax shall not be considered not to constitute an overpayment solely by reason of the fact that there was no tax liability in respect of which such amount was paid.

(26 U.S.C. 6401)

[T.D. ATF–251, 52 FR 19314, May 22, 1987. Redesignated by T.D. ATF–301, 55 FR 47606, Nov. 14, 1990]

§ 70.122 Authority to make credits or refunds.

The appropriate TTB officer, within the applicable period of limitations, may credit any overpayment of tax, including interest thereon, against any outstanding liability for any tax (or for any interest, additional amount, addition to the tax, or assessable penalty) owed by the person making the overpayment and the balance, if any, shall be refunded, subject to 26 U.S.C. 6402 (c) and (d) and the regulations thereunder, to such person by the appropriate TTB officer.

(26 U.S.C. 6402)

[T.D. ATF-301, 55 FR 47615, Nov. 14, 1990]

§ 70.123 Claims for credit or refund.

(a) *Requirement that claim be filed.* (1) Credits or refunds of overpayments may not be allowed or made after the expiration of the statutory period of limitation properly applicable unless, before the expiration of such period, a claim therefor has been filed by the taxpayer. Furthermore, under section 7422 of the Internal Revenue Code, a civil action for refund may not be instituted unless a claim has been filed within the properly applicable period of limitation.

(2) All claims relating to provisions of 26 U.S.C. enforced and administered by the Bureau, together with appropriate supporting evidence, shall be filed with the appropriate TTB officer. As to interest in the case of credits or refunds, see section 6611 of the Internal Revenue Code. See section 7502 for provisions treating timely mailing as timely filing and section 7503 for time for filing claim when the last day falls on a Saturday, Sunday, or legal holiday.

(b) *Grounds set forth in claim.* (1) No refund or credit will be allowed after the expiration of the statutory period of limitation applicable to the filing of a claim therefor except upon one or more of the grounds set forth in a claim filed before the expiration of such period. The claim must set forth in detail each ground upon which credit or refund is claimed and facts sufficient to apprise the appropriate TTB officer of the exact basis thereof. The statement of the grounds and facts must be verified by a written declaration that it is made under the penalties of perjury. A claim which does not comply with this paragraph will not be considered for any purpose as a claim for the refund or credit.

(2) The appropriate TTB officers do not have authority to refund on equitable grounds penalties or other amounts legally collected.

(c) *Form for filing claim.* All claims by taxpayers for the refunding of taxes, interest, penalties, and additions to tax shall be made on Form 2635 (5620.8).

(d) *Proof of representative capacity.* If a return is filed by an individual and, after the individuals death, a refund claim is filed by a legal representative, certified copies of the letters testamentary, letters of administration, or other similar evidence must be annexed to the claim, to show the authority of the legal representative to file the claim. If an executor, administrator, guardian, trustee, receiver, or other fiduciary files a return and thereafter a refund claim is filed by the same fiduciary, documentary evidence to establish the legal authority of the fiduciary need not accompany the claim, provided a statement is made in the claim showing that the return was filed by the fiduciary and that the latter is still acting. In such cases, if a refund is to be paid, letters testamentary, letters of administration, or other evidence may be required, but should be submitted only upon the receipt of a specific request therefor. If a claim is filed by a fiduciary other than the one by whom the return was filed, the necessary documentary evidence should accompany the claim. A claim may be executed by an agent of the person assessed, but in such case a power of attorney must accompany the claim.

(e) *Mailing of refund check.* (1) Checks in payment of claims allowed will be drawn in the names of the persons entitled to the money and, except as provided in paragraph (e)(2) of this section, the checks may be sent direct to the claimant or to such person in care of an attorney or agent who has filed a power of attorney specifically authorizing the attorney or agent to receive such checks.

(2) Checks in payment of claims which have either been reduced to judgment or settled in the course or as a result of litigation will be drawn in the name of the person or persons entitled to the money and will be sent to the Assistant Attorney General, Tax Division, Department of Justice, for delivery to the taxpayer or the counsel of record in the court proceeding.

(3) For restrictions on the assignment of claims, see 31 U.S.C. 3727.

(Approved by the Office of Management and Budget under control number 1512–0141)

(26 U.S.C. 6402)

[T.D. ATF–251, 52 FR 19314, May 22, 1987. Redesignated and amended by T.D. ATF–301, 55 FR 47606, 47615, Nov. 14, 1990; T.D. ATF–450, 66 FR 29025, May 29, 2001]

§ 70.124 Payments in excess of amounts shown on return.

In certain cases, the taxpayer's payments in respect of a tax liability, made before the filing of the taxpayer's return, may exceed the amount of tax shown on the return. In any case in which the appropriate TTB officer determines that the payments by the taxpayer (made within the period prescribed for payment and before the filing of the return) are in excess of the amount of tax shown on the return, the appropriate TTB officer may make credit or refund of such overpayment without awaiting examination of the completed return and without awaiting filing of a claim for refund. However, the provisions of § 70.123 of this part are applicable to such overpayment, and taxpayers should submit claims for refund to protect themselves in the event the appropriate TTB officer fails to make such determination and credit or refund.

(Approved by the Office of Management and Budget under control number 1512–0141)

(26 U.S.C. 6402)

[T.D. ATF–301, 55 FR 47616, Nov. 14, 1990]

§ 70.125 Abatements.

(a) The appropriate TTB officer may abate the unpaid portion of any assessment or liability, if the assessment is in excess of the correct tax liability, if the assessment is made subsequent to the expiration of the period of limitation applicable thereto, or if the assessment has been erroneously or illegally made.

(b) If more than the correct amount of tax, interest, additional amount, addition to the tax, or assessable penalty is assessed but not paid to TTB, the person against whom the assessment is made may file a claim for abatement of such overassessment. Each claim for abatement under this section shall be made on Form 2635 (5020.8), Claim—Alcohol, Tobacco and Firearms Taxes, in accordance with the instructions on the form. All such claims must be filed with the appropriate TTB officer who made demand for the amount assessed.

(c) The appropriate TTB officer may issue uniform instructions to abate amounts the collection of which is not warranted because of the administration and collection costs.

(Approved by the Office of Management and Budget under control number 1512–0141)

(26 U.S.C. 6404)

[T.D. ATF–301, 55 FR 47616, Nov. 14, 1990, as amended by T.D. ATF–450, 66 FR 29025, May 29, 2001]

§ 70.126 Date of allowance of refund or credit.

The date on which the appropriate TTB officer, first certifies the allowance of an overassessment in respect of any internal revenue tax imposed by the provisions of 26 U.S.C. enforced and administered by the Bureau shall be considered as the date of allowance of refund or credit in respect of such tax.

(26 U.S.C. 6407)

[T.D. ATF–301, 55 FR 47616, Nov. 14, 1990, as amended by T.D. ATF–450, 66 FR 29025, May 29, 2001]

§ 70.127 Overpayment of installment.

If any installment of tax is overpaid, the overpayment shall first be applied against any outstanding installments of such tax. If the overpayment exceeds the correct amount of tax due, the overpayment shall be credited or refunded as provided in §§ 70.122 to 70.124 of this part, inclusive.

(26 U.S.C. 6403)

[T.D. ATF–301, 55 FR 47616, Nov. 14, 1990]

RULE OF SPECIAL APPLICATION

§ 70.131 Conditions to allowance.

(a) For regulations under section 6416 of the Internal Revenue Code, see part 53 of this chapter, relating to manufacturers excise taxes on firearms and ammunition.

(b) For regulations under section 6423 of the Internal Revenue Code, see part 29 of this chapter, relating to distilled spirits, wine, and beer; and part 46 of this chapter, relating to tobacco products, and cigarette papers and tubes.

(26 U.S.C. 6416 and 6423)

[T.D. ATF-331, 57 FR 40328, Sept. 3, 1992, as amended by T.D. ATF-457, 66 FR 32219, June 14, 2001; T.D. ATF-462, 66 FR 42737, Aug. 15, 2001]

LIEN FOR TAXES

SOURCE: Sections 70.141 through 70.151 added by T.D. ATF-301, 55 FR 47616, Nov. 14, 1990, unless otherwise noted.

§ 70.141 Lien for taxes.

If any person liable to pay any tax under provisions of 26 U.S.C. enforced and administered by the Bureau neglects or refuses to pay the same after demand, the amount (including any interest, additional amount, addition to tax, or assessable penalty, together with any costs that may accrue in addition thereto) shall be a lien in favor of the United States upon all property and rights to property, whether real or personal, tangible or intangible, belonging to such person. The lien attaches to all property and rights to property belonging to such person at any time during the period of the lien, including any property or rights to property acquired by such person after the lien arises. Solely for purposes of this section and §§ 70.161 and 70.162 of this part, any interest in restricted land held in trust by the United States for an individual noncompetent Indian (and not for a tribe) shall not be deemed to be property, or a right to property, belonging to such Indian.

(26 U.S.C. 6321)

§ 70.142 Scope of definitions.

Except as otherwise provided by § 70.143 of this part, the definitions provided by §§ 70.143 apply for purposes of § 70.142 through 70.149 and §§ 70.231 through 70.234 of this part.

§ 70.143 Definitions.

(a) *Security interest*—(1) *In general.* The term *security interest* means any interest in property acquired by contract for the purpose of securing payment or performance of an obligation or indemnifying against loss or liability. A security interest exists ay any time:

(i) If, at such time, the property is in existence and the interest has become protected under local law against a subsequent judgment lien (as provided in paragraph (a)(2) of this section) arising out of an unsecured obligation; and

(ii) To the extent that, at such time, the holder has parted with money or money's worth (as defined in paragraph (a)(3) of this section). For purposes of paragraph (a)(1) of this section, a contract right (as defined in § 70.232(c)(2)(i) of this part) is in existence when the contract is made. An account receivable (as defined in § 70.232(c)(2)(ii) of this part) is in existence when, and to the extent, a right to payment is earned by performance. A security interest must be in existence, within the meaning of paragraph (a) of this section, at the time as of which its priority against a tax lien is determined. For example, to be afforded priority under the provisions of § 70.145(a) of this part, a security interest must be in existence within the meaning of paragraph (a) of this section before a notice of lien is filed.

(2) *Protection against a subsequent judgment lien.* For purposes of paragraph (a) of this section, a security interest is deemed to be protected against a subsequent judgment lien on:

(i) The date on which all actions required under local law to establish the priority of a security interest against a judgment lien have been taken, or

(ii) If later, the date on which all required actions are deemed effective, under local law, to establish the priority of the security interest against a judgment lien.

For purposes of paragraph (a)(2) of this section, the dates described in paragraphs (a)(2) (i) and (ii) of this section shall be determined without regard to any rule or principle of local law which permits the relation back or the making of any requisite action retroactive to a date earlier than the date on which the action is actually performed. For purposes of paragraph (a) of this section, a judgment lien is a lien held by a judgment lien creditor as defined in paragraph (g) of this section.

(3) *Money or money's worth.* For purposes of paragraph (a) of this section,

the term "money or money's worth" includes money, a security (as defined in paragraph (d) of this section), tangible or intangible property, services, and other consideration reducible to a money value. Money or money's worth also includes any consideration which otherwise would constitute money or money's worth under the preceding sentence which was parted with before the security interest would otherwise exist if, under local law, past consideration is sufficient to support an agreement giving rise to a security interest. A relinquishing or promised relinquishment of dower, curtesy, or of a statutory estate created in lieu of dower or curtesy, or of other marital rights is not a consideration in money or money's worth. Nor is love and affection, promise of marriage, or any other consideration not reducible to a money value a consideration in money or money's worth.

(4) *Holder of a security interest.* For purposes of paragraph (a) of this section, the holder of a security interest is the person in whose favor there is a security interest. For provisions relating to the treatment of a purchaser of commercial financing security as a holder of a security interest, see § 70.232(e) of this part.

(b) *Mechanic's lienor.* The term *mechanic's lienor* means any person who under local law has a lien on real property (or on the proceeds of a contract relating to real property) for services, labor, or materials furnished in connection with the construction or improvement (including demolition) of the property. A mechanic's lienor is treated as having a lien on the later of:

(1) The date on which the mechanic's lien first becomes valid under local law against subsequent purchasers of the real property without actual notice, or

(2) The date on which the mechanic's lienor begins to furnish the services, labor, or materials.

(c) *Motor vehicle.* (1) The term *motor vehicle* means a self-propelled vehicle which is registered for highway use under the laws of any State, the District of Columbia, or a foreign country.

(2) A motor vehicle is "registered for highway use" at the time of a sale if immediately prior to the sale it is so registered under the laws of any State, the District of Columbia, or a foreign country. Where immediately prior to the sale of a motor vehicle by a dealer, the dealer is permitted under local law to operate it under a dealer's tag, license, or permit issued to the dealer, the motor vehicle is considered to be registered for highway use in the name of the dealer at the time of the sale.

(d) *Security.* The term *security* means any bond, debenture, note, or certificate or other evidence of indebtedness, issued by a corporation or a government or political subdivision thereof, with interest coupons or in registered form, share of stock, voting trust certificate, or any certificate of interest or participation in, certificate of deposit or receipt for, temporary or interim certificate for, or warrant or right to subscribe to or purchase, any of the foregoing; negotiable instrument; or money.

(e) *Tax lien filing.* The term *tax lien filing* means the filing of notice of the lien imposed by 26 U.S.C. 6321 in accordance with § 70.148 of this part.

(f) *Purchaser*—(1) *In general.* The term *purchaser* means a person who, for adequate and full consideration in money or money's worth (as defined in paragraph (f)(3) of this section), acquires an interest (other than a lien or security interest) in property which is valid under local law against subsequent purchasers without actual notice.

(2) *Interest in property.* For purposes of paragraph (f) of this section, each of the following interests is treated as an interest in property, if it is not a lien or security interest:

(i) A lease of property,

(ii) A written executory contract to purchase or lease property,

(iii) An option to purchase or lease property and any interest therein, or

(iv) An option to renew or extend a lease of property.

(3) *Adequate and full consideration in money or money's worth.* For purposes of paragraph (f) of this section, the term "adequate and full consideration in money or money's worth" means a consideration in money or money's worth having a reasonable relationship to the true value of the interest in property acquired. See paragraph (a)(3) of this section for definition of the term "money or money's worth." Adequate

and full consideration in money or money's worth may include the consideration in a bona fide bargain purchase. The term also includes the consideration in a transaction in which the purchaser has not completed performance of an obligation, such as the consideration in an installment purchase contract where the purchaser has not completed the installment payments.

(g) *Judgment lien creditor.* The term *judgment lien creditor* means a person who has obtained a valid judgment, in a court of record and of competent jurisdiction, for the recovery of specifically designated property or for a certain sum of money. In the case of a judgment for the recovery of a certain sum of money, a judgment lien creditor is a person who has perfected a lien under the judgment on the property involved. A judgment lien is not perfected until the identity of the lienor, the property subject to the lien, and the amount of the lien are established. Accordingly, a judgment lien does not include an attachment or garnishment lien until the lien has ripened into judgment, even though under local law the lien of the judgment relates back to an earlier date. If recording or docketing is necessary under local law before a judgment becomes effective against third parties acquiring liens on real property, a judgment lien under such local law is not perfected with respect to real property until the time of such recordation or docketing. If, under local law, levy or seizure is necessary before a judgment lien becomes effective against third parties acquiring liens on personal property, then a judgment lien under such local law is not perfected until levy or seizure of the personal property involved. The term "judgment" does not include the determination of a quasi-judicial body or of an individual acting in a quasi-judicial capacity such as the action of State taxing authorities.

(26 U.S.C. 6323)

§ 70.144 Special rules.

(a) *Actual notice or knowledge.* For purposes of 26 U.S.C. 6321 through 6327, an organization is deemed, in any transaction, to have actual notice or knowledge of any fact from the time the fact is brought to the attention of the individual conducting the transaction, and in any event from the time the fact would have been brought to the individual's attention if the organization had exercised due diligence. An organization exercises due diligence if it maintains reasonable routines for communicating significant information to the person conducting the transaction and there is reasonable compliance with the routines. Due diligence does not require an individual acting for the organization to communicate information unless such communication is part of the individual's regular duties or unless the individual has reason to know of the transaction and that the transaction would be materially affected by the information.

(b) *Subrogation:* Where, under local law, one person is subrogated to the rights of another with respect to a lien or interest, such person shall be subrogated to such rights for purposes of any lien imposed by 26 U.S.C. 6321 or 6324. Thus, if a tax lien imposed by 26 U.S.C. 6321 or 6324 is not valid with respect to a particular interest as against the holder of that interest, then the tax lien also is not valid with respect to that interest as against any person who, under local law, is a successor in interest to the holder of that interest.

(c) *Disclosure of amount of outstanding lien.* If a notice of lien has been filed (see § 70.148 of this part), the amount of the outstanding obligation secured by the lien is authorized to be disclosed as a matter of public record on TTB Form 5651.2 "Notice of Federal Tax Lien Under Internal Revenue Laws." The amount of the outstanding obligation secured by the lien remaining unpaid at the time of an inquiry is authorized to be disclosed to any person who has a proper interest in determining this amount. Any person who has a right in the property or intends to obtain a right in the property by purchase or otherwise will, upon presentation of satisfactory evidence, be considered to have a proper interest. Any person desiring this information may make a request to the office of the Bureau named on the notice of lien with respect to which the request is made. The request should clearly describe the property subject to the lien, identify the applicable lien, and give the reasons for requesting the information.

(26 U.S.C. 6323)

§ 70.145 Purchasers, holders of security interests, mechanic's lienors, and judgment lien creditors.

(a) *Invalidity of lien without notice.* The lien imposed by 26 U.S.C. 6321 is not valid against any purchaser (as defined in § 70.143(f) of this part), holder of a security interest (as defined in § 70.143(a) of this part), mechanic's lienor (as defined in § 70.143(b) of this part), or judgment lien creditor (as defined in § 70.143(g) of this part) until a notice of lien is filed in accordance with § 70.148 of this part. Except as provided by 26 U.S.C. 6323, if a person becomes a purchaser, holder of a security interest, mechanic's lienor, or judgment lien creditor after a notice of lien is filed in accordance with § 70.148 of this part, the interest acquired by such person is subject to the lien imposed by 26 U.S.C. 6321.

(b) *Cross references.* For provisions relating to the protection afforded a security interest arising after tax lien filing, which interest is covered by a commercial transactions financing agreement, real property construction or improvement financing agreement, or an obligatory disbursement agreement, see §§ 70.232, 70.233, and 70.234 of this part, respectively. For provisions relating to the protection afforded to a security interest coming into existence by virtue of disbursements, made before the 46th day after the date of tax lien filing, see § 70.146 of this part. For provisions relating to priority afforded to interest and certain other expenses with respect to a lien or security interest having priority over the lien imposed by 26 U.S.C. 6321, see § 70.147 of this part. For provisions relating to certain other interests arising after tax lien filing, see § 70.231 of this part.

(26 U.S.C. 6323)

§ 70.146 45-day period for making disbursements.

Even though a notice of a lien imposed by 26 U.S.C. 6321 is filed in accordance with § 70.149 of this part, the lien is not valid with respect to a security interest which comes into existence, after tax lien filing, by reason of disbursements made before the 46th day after the date of tax lien filing, or if earlier, before the person making the disbursements has actual notice or knowledge of the tax lien filing, but only if the security interest is:

(a) In property which is subject, at the time of tax lien filing, to the lien imposed by 26 U.S.C. 6321 and which is covered by the terms of a written agreement entered into before tax lien filing, and

(b) Protected under local law against a judgment lien arising, as of the time of tax lien filing, out of an unsecured obligation.

For purposes of paragraph (a) of this section, a contract right (as defined in § 70.232(c)(2)(i) of this part) is subject, at the time of tax lien filing, to the lien imposed by 26 U.S.C. 6321 if the contract has been made by such time. An account receivable (as defined in § 70.232(c)(2)(ii) of this part) is subject, at the time of tax lien filing, to the lien imposed by 26 U.S.C. 6321 if, and to the extent, a right to payment has been earned by performance at such time. For purposes of paragraph (b) of this section, a judgment lien is a lien held by a judgment lien creditor as defined in § 70.143(g) of this part. For purposes of this section, it is immaterial that the written agreement provides that the disbursements are to be made at the option of the person making the disbursements. See § 70.143 (a) and (e) of this part for definitions of the terms "security interest" and "tax lien filing," respectively. See § 70.144(a) of this part for certain circumstances under which a person is deemed to have actual notice or knowledge of a fact.

(26 U.S.C. 6323)

§ 70.147 Priority of interest and expenses.

(a) *In general.* If the lien imposed by 26 U.S.C. 6321 is not valid as against another lien or security interest, the priority of the other lien or security interest also extends to each of the following items to the extent that under local law the item has the same priority as the lien or security interest to which it relates:

(1) Any interest or carrying charges (including finance, service, and similar charges) upon the obligation secured,

(2) The reasonable charges and expenses of an indenture trustee (including, for example, the trustee under a deed of trust) or agent holding the security interest for the benefit of the holder of the security interest,

(3) The reasonable expenses, including reasonable compensation for attorneys, actually incurred in collecting or enforcing the obligation secured,

(4) The reasonable costs of insuring, preserving, or repairing the property to which the lien or security interest relates,

(5) The reasonable costs of insuring payment of the obligation secured (including amounts paid by the holder of the security interest for mortgage insurance, such as that issued by the Federal Housing Administration), and

(6) Amounts paid to satisfy any lien on the property to which the lien or security interest relates, but only if the lien so satisfied is entitled to priority over the lien imposed by 26 U.S.C. 6321.

(b) *Collection expenses.* The reasonable expenses described in paragraph (a)(3) of this section include expenditures incurred by the protected holder of the lien or security interest to establish the priority of the holder's interest or to collect, by foreclosure or otherwise, the amount due the holder from the property subject to the protected holder's lien. Accordingly, the amount of the encumbrance which is protected is increased by the amounts so expended by the holder of the security interest.

(c) *Costs of insuring, preserving, etc.* The reasonable costs of insuring, preserving, or repairing described in paragraph (a)(4) of this section include expenditures by the holder of a security interest for fire and casualty insurance on the property subject to the security interest and amounts paid by the holder of the lien or security interest to repair the property. Such reasonable costs also include the amounts paid by the holder of the lien or security interest in a leasehold to the lessor of the leasehold to preserve the leasehold subject to the lien or security interest. Accordingly, the amount of the lien or security interest which is protected is increased by the amounts so expended by the holder of the lien or security interest.

(d) *Satisfaction of liens.* The amounts described in paragraph (a)(6) of this section include expenditures incurred by the protected holder of a lien or security interest to discharge a statutory lien for State sales taxes on the property subject to the lien or security interest if both the lien or security interest and the sales tax lien have priority over a Federal tax lien. Accordingly, the amount of the lien or security interest is increased by the amounts so expended by the holder of the lien or security interest even though under local law the holder of the lien or security interest is not subrogated to the rights of the holder of the State sales tax lien. However, if the holder of the lien or security interest is subrogated, within the meaning of § 70.144(b) of this part, to the rights of the holder of the sales tax lien, the holder of the lien or security interest will also be entitled to any additional protection afforded by 26 U.S.C. 6323(i)(2)

(26 U.S.C. 6323).

§ 70.148 Place for filing notice; form.

(a) *Place for filing.* The notice of lien referred to in § 70.145 of this part shall be filed as follows:

(1) *Under State laws*—(i) *Real property.* In the case of real property, notice shall be filed in one office within the State (or the county or other governmental subdivision), as designated by the laws of the State, in which the property subject to the lien is deemed situated under the provisions of paragraph (b)(1) of this section.

(ii) *Personal property.* In the case of personal property, whether tangible or intangible, the notice shall be filed in one office within the State (or the county or other governmental subdivision), as designated by the laws of the State, in which the property subject to the lien is deemed situated under the provision of paragraph (b)(2) of this section, except that State law merely conforming to or reenacting Federal law establishing a national filing system does not constitute a second office for filing as designated by the laws of such State.

(2) *With the clerk of the United States district court.* Whenever a State has not

by law designated one office which meets the requirements of paragraph (a)(1) (i) or (ii) of this section, the notice shall be filed in the office of the clerk of the U.S. district court for the judicial district in which the property subject to the lien is deemed situated under the provisions of paragraph (b) of this section. For example, a State has not by law designated one office meeting the requirements of paragraph (a)(1)(i) of this section, if more than one office is designated within the State, county, or other governmental subdivision for filing notices with respect to all property located in such State, county or other governmental subdivision. A State has not by law designated one office meeting the requirements of paragraph (a)(1)(ii) of this section, if more than one office is designated in the State, county, or other governmental subdivision for filing notices with respect to all of the personal property of a particular taxpayer.

(3) *With the Recorder of Deeds of the District of Columbia.* If the property subject to the lien imposed by 26 U.S.C. 6321 is deemed situated, under the provision of paragraph (b) of this section, in the District of Columbia, the notice shall be filed in the office of the Recorder of Deeds of the District of Columbia.

(b) *Situs of property subject to lien.* For purposes of paragraph (a) of this section, property is deemed situated as follows:

(1) *Real property.* Real property is deemed situated at its physical location.

(2) *Personal property.* Personal property, whether tangible or intangible, is deemed situated at the residence of the taxpayer at the time the notice of lien is filed.

For purposes of paragraph (b)(2) of this section, the residence of a corporation or partnership is deemed to be the place at which the principal executive office of the business is located, and the residence of a taxpayer whose residence is not within the United States is deemed to be in the District of Columbia.

(c) *Form*—(1) *In general.* The notice referred to in § 70.145 of this part shall be filed on TTB Form 5651.2, "Notice of Federal Tax Lien under Internal Revenue Laws". Such notice is valid notwithstanding any other provision of law regarding the form or content of a notice of lien. For example, omission from the notice of lien of a description of the property subject to the lien does not affect the validity thereof even though State law may require that the notices contain a description of the property subject to the lien.

(2) *TTB Form 5651.2 defined.* The term "TTB Form 5651.2" generally means a paper form. However, if a State in which a notice referred to in § 70.145 of this part is filed permits a notice of Federal tax lien to be filed by the use of an electronic or magnetic medium the term "TTB Form 5651.2" includes a TTB Form 5651.2 filed by the use of any electronic or magnetic medium permitted by that State. A TTB Form 5651.2 must identify the taxpayer, the tax liability giving rise to the lien, and the date the assessment arose regardless of the method used to file the notice of Federal tax lien.

(26 U.S.C. 6323)

[T.D. ATF–301, 55 FR 47616, Nov. 14, 1990, as amended by T.D. TTB–91, 76 FR 5481, Feb. 1, 2011]

§ 70.149 Refiling of notice of tax lien.

(a) *In general*—(1) *Requirement to refile.* In order to continue the effect of a notice of lien, the notice must be refiled in the place described in paragraph (b) of this section during the required refiling period (described in paragraph (c) of this section). In the event that two or more notices of lien are filed with respect to a particular tax assessment, the failure to comply with the provision of paragraphs (b)(1) (i) and (c) of this section in respect of one of the notices of lien does not affect the effectiveness of the refiling of any other notice of lien. Except for the filing of a notice of lien required by paragraph (b)(1)(ii) of this section (relating to a change of residence), the validity of any refiling of a notice of lien is not affected by the refiling or nonrefiling of any other notice of lien.

(2) *Effect of refiling.* A timely refiled notice of lien is effective as of the date on which the notice of lien to which it relates was effective.

(3) *Effect of failure to refile.* Except as provided below, if the appropriate TTB officer fails to refile a notice of lien in the manner described in paragraphs (b) and (c) of this section, the notice of lien is not effective, after the expiration of the required refiling period, as against any person without regard to when the interest of the person in the property subject to the lien was acquired. However, the failure of the appropriate TTB officer to refile a notice of lien during the required refiling period will not, following the expiration of the refiling period, affect the effectiveness of the notice with respect to:

(i) Property which is the subject matter of a suit, to which the United States is a party, commenced prior to the expiration of the required refiling period, or

(ii) Property which has been levied upon by the United States prior to the expiration of the refiling period. However, if a suit or levy referred to in the preceding sentence is dismissed or released, respectively, and property is subject to the lien at such time, a notice of lien with respect to the property is not effective after the suit or levy is dismissed or released unless refiled during the required refiling period. Failure to refile a notice of lien does not affect the existence of the lien.

(4) *Filing of new notice.* If a notice of lien is not refiled, and if the lien remains in existence, the Bureau may nevertheless file a new lien either on the prescribed form for the filing of a notice of lien or on the form prescribed for refiling a notice of lien. This new filing must meet the requirements of 26 U.S.C. 6323(f) and §70.148 of this part and is effective from the date on which such filing is made.

(b) *Place for refiling notice of lien*—(1) *In general.* A notice of lien refiled during the required refiling period (described in paragraph (c) of this section) shall be effective only:

(i) If the notice of lien is refiled in the office in which the prior notice of lien (including a refiled notice) was filed under the provisions of 26 U.S.C. 6323; and

(ii) In any case in which 90 days or more prior to the date the refiling of the notice of lien under paragraph (a)(1)(i) of this section is completed, the Bureau receives written information (in the manner described in paragraph (b)(2) of this section) concerning a change in the taxpayer's residence, if a notice of such lien is also filed in accordance with 26 U.S.C. 6323(f)(1)(A)(ii) in the State in which such new residence is located (or, if such new residence is located in the District of Columbia or outside the United States, in the District of Columbia).

A notice of lien is considered as refiled in the office in which the prior notice or refiled notice was filed under the provisions of 26 U.S.C. 6323 if it is refiled in the office which, pursuant to a change in the applicable local law, assumed the functions of the office in which the prior notice or refiled notice was filed. If on or before the 90th day referred to in paragraph (b)(1)(ii) of this section, more than one written notice is received concerning a change in the taxpayer's residence, a notice of lien is required by this subdivision to be filed only with respect to the residence shown on the written notice received on the most recent date. Paragraph (b)(1)(ii) of this section is applicable regardless of whether the taxpayer resides at the new residence on the date the refiling of notice of lien under paragraph (b)(1)(i) of this section is completed.

(2) *Notice of change of taxpayer's residence*—(i) *In general.* For purposes of this section, a notice of change of a taxpayer's residence will be effective only if it:

(A) Is received, in writing, from the taxpayer or the taxpayer's representative by the appropriate TTB officer who filed the original notice of lien.

(B) Relates to an unpaid tax liability of the taxpayer, and

(C) States the taxpayer's name and the address of the taxpayer's new residence.

Although it is not necessary that a written notice contain the taxpayer's identifying number authorized by section 6109, it is preferable that it include such number. A return or amended return filed by the taxpayer with the Bureau which on its face indicates that there is a change in the taxpayer's address and correctly states the taxpayer's name, the address of the taxpayer's new residence, and the taxpayer's identifying number required by 26 U.S.C. 6109 is sufficient notice under this paragraph.

(ii) *Other rules applicable.* Except as provided in paragraph (b)(2)(i) of this section, no communication (either written or oral) to the Bureau will be considered effective as notice of a change of a taxpayer's residence under this section, whether or not the Bureau has actual notice or knowledge of the taxpayer's new residence. For the purpose of determining the date on which a notice of change of a taxpayer's residence is received under this section, the notice shall be treated as received on the date it is actually received by the Bureau without reference to the provisions of 26 U.S.C. 7502.

(c) *Required refiling period.* For the purpose of this section, the term "required refiling period" means:

(1) The 1-year period ending 30 days after the expiration of 6 years after the date of the assessment of the tax, and

(2) The 1-year period ending with the expiration of 6 years after the close of the preceding required refiling period for such notice of lien.

(26 U.S.C. 6323)

§ 70.150 Release of lien or discharge of property.

(a) *Release of lien.* An appropriate TTB officer is charged with releasing liens or discharging property from liens. The appropriate TTB officer must issue a certificate of release of a lien imposed with respect to any tax imposed by a provision of 26 U.S.C. enforced and administered by the Bureau, not later than 30 days after the day on which either:

(1) The appropriate TTB officer finds that the entire liability for the tax has been satisfied or has become unenforceable as a matter of law (and not merely uncollectible or unenforceable as a matter of fact). Tax liabilities frequently are unenforceable in fact for the time being, due to the temporary nonpossession by the taxpayer of discoverable property or property rights. In all cases the liability for the payment of the tax continues until satisfaction of the tax in full or until the expiration of the statutory period for collection, including such extension of the period for collection as may be agreed upon in writing by the taxpayer and the appropriate TTB officer.

(2) The appropriate TTB officer is furnished and accepts a bond that is conditioned upon the payment of the amount assessed (together with all interest in respect thereof and any expenses to which the Government has been put in the matter), within the time agreed upon in the bond, but not later than 6 months before the expiration of the statutory period for collection, including any period for collection agreed upon in writing by the appropriate TTB officer and the taxpayer. For provisions relating to bonds, see 26 U.S.C. 7101 and 7102 and §§ 70.281 and 70.282 of this part.

(b) *Discharge of specific property from the lien*—(1) *Property double the amount of the liability.* The appropriate TTB officer may, in that officer's discretion, issue a certificate of discharge of any part of the property subject to a lien imposed under 26 U.S.C. 64 if the Bureau determines that the fair market value of that part of the property remaining subject to the lien is at least double the sum of the amount of the unsatisfied liability secured by the lien and of the amount of all other liens upon the property which have priority over the lien. In general, fair market value is that amount which one ready and willing but not compelled to buy would pay to another ready and willing but not compelled to sell the property.

(2) *Part payment; interest of United States valueless*—(i) *Part payment.* The appropriate TTB officer may, in that officer's discretion, issue a certificate of discharge of any part of the property subject to a lien imposed under 26 U.S.C. 64 if there is paid over to the Bureau in partial satisfaction of the liability secured by the lien an amount determined by the Bureau to be not less than the value of the interest of the United States in the property to be so discharged. In determining the amount to be paid, the appropriate TTB officer will take into consideration all the facts and circumstances of the case, including the expenses to which the Government has been put in

the matter. In no case shall the amount to be paid be less than the value of the interest of the United States in the property with respect to which the certificate of discharge is to be issued.

(ii) *Interest of the United States valueless.* The appropriate TTB officer may, in that official's discretion, issue a certificate of discharge of any part of the property subject to the lien if the Bureau determines that the interest of the United States in the property to be so discharged has no value.

(iii) *Valuation of interest of United States.* For purposes of this paragraph (b)(2), in determining the value of the interest of the United States in the property, or any part thereof, with respect to which the certificate of discharge is to be issued, the appropriate TTB officer shall give consideration to the value of the property and the amount of all liens and encumbrances thereon having priority over the Federal tax lien. In determining the value of the property, the appropriate TTB officer may, in that official's discretion, give consideration to the forced sale value of the property in appropriate cases.

(3) *Discharge of property by substitution of proceeds of sale.* The appropriate TTB officer may, in that officer's discretion, issue a certificate of discharge of any part of the property subject to a lien imposed under 26 U.S.C. 64 if such part of the property is sold and, pursuant to a written agreement with the appropriate TTB officer, the proceeds of the sale are held, as a fund subject to the liens and claims of the United States, in the same manner and with the same priority as the lien or claim had with respect to the discharged property. This subparagraph does not apply unless the sale divests the taxpayer of all right, title, and interest in the property sought to be discharged. Any reasonable and necessary expenses incurred in connection with the sale of the property and the administration of the sale proceeds shall be paid by the applicant or from the proceeds of the sale before satisfaction of any lien or claim of the United States.

(4) *Application for certificate of discharge.* Any person desiring a certificate of discharge under this paragraph shall submit an application in writing to the appropriate TTB officer. The application shall contain such information as the appropriate TTB officer may require.

(c) *Subordination of lien*—(1) *By payment of the amount subordinated.* The appropriate TTB officer may, in that officer's discretion, issue a certificate of subordination of a lien imposed under 26 U.S.C. 64 upon any part of the property subject to the lien if there is paid over to the appropriate TTB officer an amount equal to the amount of the lien or interest to which the certificate subordinates the lien of the United States. For this purpose, the tax lien may be subordinated to another lien or interest on a dollar-for-dollar basis. For example, if a notice of a Federal tax lien is filed and a delinquent taxpayer secures a mortgage loan on a part of the property subject to the tax lien and pays over the proceeds of the loan to the appropriate TTB officer after an application for a certificate of subordination is approved, the appropriate TTB officer will issue a certificate of subordination. This certificate will have the effect of subordinating the tax lien to the mortgage.

(2) *To facilitate tax collection.* The appropriate TTB officer may, in that officer's discretion, issue a certificate of subordination of a lien imposed under 26 U.S.C. 64 upon any part of the property subject to the lien if the appropriate TTB officer believes that the subordination of the lien will ultimately result in an increase in the amount realized by the United States from the property subject to lien and will facilitate the ultimate collection of the tax liability.

(3) *Application for certificate of subordination.* Any person desiring a certificate of subordination under this paragraph shall submit an application therefor in writing to the appropriate TTB officer. The application shall contain such information as the appropriate TTB officer may require.

(d) *Nonattachment of lien.* If the appropriate TTB officer determines that, because of confusion of names or otherwise, any person (other than the person against whom the tax was assessed) is or may be injured by the appearance that a notice of lien filed in accordance with § 70.148 of this part refers to such person, the appropriate TTB officer may issue a certificate of nonattachment. Such certificate shall state that the lien, notice of which has been filed, does not attach to the property of such person. Any person desiring a certificate of nonattachment under this paragraph shall submit an application therefor in writing to the appropriate TTB officer. The application shall contain such information as the appropriate TTB officer may require.

(e) *Effect of certificate*—(1) *Conclusiveness.* Except as provided in paragraphs (e) (2) and (3) of this section, if a certificate is issued under 26 U.S.C. 6325 by the appropriate TTB officer and the certificate is filed in the same office as the notice of lien to which it relates (if the notice of lien has been filed), the certificate shall have the following effect:

(i) In the case of a certificate of release issued under paragraph (a) of this section, the certificate shall be conclusive that the tax lien referred to in the certificate is extinguished;

(ii) In the case of a certificate of discharge issued under paragraph (b) of this section, the certificate shall be conclusive that the property covered by the certificate is discharged from the tax lien;

(iii) In the case of a certificate of subordination issued under paragraph (c) of this section, the certificate shall be conclusive that the lien or interest to which the Federal tax lien is subordinated is superior to the tax lien; and

(iv) In the case of a certificate of nonattachment issued under paragraph (d) of this section, the certificate shall be conclusive that the lien of the United States does not attach to the property of the person referred to in the certificate.

(2) *Revocation of certificate of release or nonattachment*—(i) *In general.* If the appropriate TTB officer determines that either:

(A) A certificate of release or a certificate of nonattachment of the general tax lien imposed by 26 U.S.C. 6321 was issued erroneously or improvidently, or

(B) A certificate of release of such lien was issued in connection with a compromise agreement under 26 U.S.C. 7122 which has been breached,and if the period of limitation on collection after assessment of the tax liability has not expired, the appropriate TTB officer may revoke the certificate and reinstate the tax lien.

(ii) *Method of revocation and reinstatement.* The revocation and reinstatement described in paragraph (e)(2)(i) of this section is accomplished by:

(A) Mailing notice of the revocation to the taxpayer at the taxpayer's last known address, and

(B) Filing notice of the revocation of the certificate in the same office in which the notice of lien to which it relates was filed (if the notice of lien has been filed).

(iii) *Effect of reinstatement*—(A) *Effective date.* A tax lien reinstated in accordance with the provisions of this paragraph (e)(2) is effective on and after the date the notice of revocation is mailed to the taxpayer in accordance with the provisions of paragraph (e)(2)(ii)(A) of this section, but the reinstated lien is not effective before the filing of notice of revocation, in accordance with the provisions of paragraph (e)(2)(ii)(B) of this section, if the filing is required by reason of the fact that a notice of the lien had been filed.

(B) *Treatment of reinstated lien.* As of the effective date of reinstatement, a reinstated lien has the same force and effect as a general tax lien imposed by 26 U.S.C. 6321 which arises upon assessment of a tax liability. The reinstated lien continues in existence until the liability is satisfied or until the expiration of the period of limitation on collection after assessment of the tax liability to which it relates. The reinstatement of the lien does not retroactively reinstate a previously filed notice of lien. The reinstated lien is not valid against any holder of a lien or interest described in § 70.145 of this part until notice of the reinstated lien has been filed in accordance with the provisions of § 70.148 of this part subsequent to or concurrent with the time the reinstated lien became effective.

(3) *Certificates void under certain conditions.* Notwithstanding any other provisions of 26 U.S.C. subtitle F, any lien for Federal taxes attaches to any property with respect to which a certificate

of discharge has been issued if the person liable for the tax reacquires the property after the certificate has been issued. Thus, if property subject to a Federal tax lien is discharged therefrom and is later reacquired by the delinquent taxpayer at a time when the lien is still in existence, the tax lien attaches to the reacquired property and is enforceable against it as in the case of after-acquired property generally.

(f) *Filing of certificates and notices.* If a certificate or notice described in this section may not be filed in the office designated by State law in which the notice of lien imposed by 26 U.S.C. 6321 (to which the certificate or notice relates) is filed, the certificate or notice is effective if filed in the office of the clerk of the United States district court for the judicial district in which the State office where the notice of lien is filed is situated.

(26 U.S.C. 6325)

[T.D. ATF-301, 55 FR 47616, Nov. 14, 1990, as amended by T.D. ATF-450, 66 FR 29025, May 29, 2001]

§70.151 Administrative appeal of the erroneous filing of notice of Federal tax lien.

(a) *In general.* Any person may appeal to the officer who filed the Federal tax lien on the property or rights to property of such person for a release of lien alleging an error in the filing of notice of lien. Such appeal may be used only for the purpose of correcting the erroneous filing of a notice of lien, not to challenge the underlying tax liability that led to the imposition of a lien.

(b) *Certificate of Release.* If the officer who filed the lien determines that the filing of the notice of any lien was erroneous that officer shall expeditiously, and to the extent practicable, within 14 days after such determination, issue a certificate of release of lien. The certificate of release of such lien shall include a statement that the filing of notice of lien was erroneous.

(c) *Appeal alleging an error in the filing of notice of lien.* For purposes of paragraph (a) of this section, an appeal of the filing of notice of Federal tax lien must be based on any one of the following allegations:

(1) The tax liability that gave rise to the lien, plus any interest and additions to tax associated with said liability, was satisfied prior to the filing of notice of lien;

(2) The tax liability that gave rise to the lien was assessed in violation of title 11 of the United States Code (the Bankruptcy Code); or

(3) The statutory period for collection of the tax liability that gave rise to the lien expired prior to the filing of notice of Federal tax lien.

(d) *Notice of Federal tax lien that lists multiple liabilities.* When a notice of Federal tax lien lists multiple liabilities, a person may appeal the filing of notice of lien with respect to one or more of the liabilities listed in the notice, if the notice was erroneously filed with respect to such liabilities. If a notice of Federal tax lien was erroneously filed with respect to one or more liabilities listed in the notice, the officer who filed the Federal tax lien shall issue a certificate of release with respect to such liabilities.

(e) *Procedures for appeal*—(1) *Manner.* An appeal of the filing of notice of Federal tax lien shall be made in writing to the officer who filed the lien.

(2) *Form.* The appeal shall include the following information and documents:

(i) Name, current address, and taxpayer identification number of the person appealing the filing of notice of Federal tax lien;

(ii) A copy of the notice of Federal tax lien affecting the property, if available; and

(iii) The grounds upon which the filing of notice of Federal tax lien is being appealed.

(A) If the ground upon which the filing of notice is being appealed is that the tax liability in question was satisfied prior to the filing, proof of full payment as defined in paragraph (f) of this section must be provided.

(B) If the ground upon which the filing of notice is being appealed is that the tax liability that gave rise to the lien was assessed in violation of title 11 of the United States Code (the Bankruptcy Code), the appealing party must provide the identity of the court, the district in which the bankruptcy petition was filed, a docket number and the date of filing of the bankruptcy petition.

(3) *Time.* An administrative appeal of the erroneous filing of notice of Federal tax lien shall be made within 1 year after the taxpayer becomes aware of the erroneously filed tax lien.

(f) *Proof of full payment.* As used in paragraph (e)(2)(iii)(A) of this section, the term "proof of full payment" means:

(1) An Alcohol and Tobacco Tax and Trade Bureau, receipt reflecting full payment of the tax liability in question prior to the date the Federal tax lien was filed;

(2) A cancelled check payable to the Alcohol and Tobacco Tax and Trade Bureau in an amount which was sufficient to satisfy the tax liability for which release is being sought; or

(3) Any other manner of proof acceptable to the officer who filed the lien.

(g) *Exception.* Whenever necessary to protect the interests of the government, an appropriate TTB officer other than the officer who filed the lien, may receive and act on an administrative appeal of a lien in accordance with this section.

(h) *Exclusive remedy.* The appeal established by section 6326 of the Internal Revenue Code and by this section shall be the exclusive administrative remedy with respect to the erroneous filing of a notice of Federal tax lien.

[T.D. ATF–316, 56 FR 55079, Oct. 24, 1991]

SEIZURE OF PROPERTY FOR COLLECTION OF TAXES

§ 70.161 Levy and distraint.

(a) *Authority to levy*—(1) *In general.* If any person liable to pay any tax neglects or refuses to pay the tax within 10 days after notice and demand, the appropriate TTB officer who initiated the assessment may proceed to collect the tax by levy, provided the taxpayer has been furnished the notice described in § 70.162(a) of this part. The appropriate TTB officer may levy upon any property, or rights to property, whether real or personal, tangible or intangible, belonging to the taxpayer. The appropriate TTB officer may also levy upon property with respect to which there is a lien provided by 26 U.S.C. 6321 for the payment of the tax. For exemption of certain property from levy, see 26 U.S.C. 6334 and §§ 70.241 through 70.245 of this part. For exemption of certain property from levy, see 26 U.S.C. 6334 and §§ 70.241 through 70.245 of this part. As used in 26 U.S.C. 6331 and this section, the term "tax" includes any interest, additional amount, addition to tax, or assessable penalty, together with costs and expenses. Property subject to a Federal tax lien which has been sold or otherwise transferred by the taxpayer may be seized while in the hands of the transferee or any subsequent transferee. However, see 26 U.S.C. 6323(i)(2) and § 70.144 of this part concerning the subrogation rights of certain transferees. Levy may be made by serving a Notice of Levy on any person in possession of, or obligated with respect to, property or rights to property subject to levy, including receivables, bank accounts, evidences of debt, securities, and salaries, wages, commissions, or other compensation. Except as provided in § 70.162(c) of this part with regard to a levy on salary or wages, a levy extends only to property possessed and obligations which exist at the time of the levy. Obligations exist when the liability of the obligor is fixed and determinable although the right to receive payment thereof may be deferred until a later date. For example, if on the first day of the month a delinquent taxpayer sold personal property subject to an agreement that the buyer remit the purchase price on the last day of the month, a levy made on the buyer on the 10th day of the month would reach the amount due on the sale, although the buyer need not satisfy the levy by paying over the amount to the appropriate TTB officer until the last day of the month. Similarly, a levy only reaches property in the possession of the person levied upon at the time the levy is made. For example, a levy made on a bank with respect to the account of a delinquent taxpayer is satisfied if the bank surrenders the amount of the taxpayer's balance at the time the levy is made, including interest thereon to the date of surrender. The levy has no effect upon any subsequent deposit made in the bank by the taxpayer. Subsequent deposits may be reached only by a subsequent levy on the bank.

(2) *Jeopardy cases.* If the appropriate TTB officer finds that the collection of any tax is in jeopardy, that officer may make notice and demand for immediate payment of such tax and, upon failure or refusal to pay such tax, collection thereof by levy shall be lawful without regard to the 10-day period provided in 26 U.S.C. 6331(a) or the 30-day period provided in 26 U.S.C. 6331(d).

(3) *Bankruptcy or receivership cases.* During a bankruptcy proceeding or a receivership proceeding in either a Federal or a State court, the assets of the taxpayer are in general under the control of the court in which such proceeding is pending. Taxes cannot be collected by levy upon assets in the custody of a court, whether or not such custody is incident to a bankruptcy or receivership proceeding, except where the proceeding has progressed to such a point that the levy would not interfere with the work of the court or where the court grants permission to levy. Any assets which under applicable provisions of law are not under the control of the court may be levied upon, for example, property exempt from court custody under State law or the bankrupt's earnings and property acquired after the date of bankruptcy. However, levy upon such property is not mandatory and the Government may rely upon payment of taxes in the proceeding.

(4) *Certain types of compensation*—(i) *Federal employees.* Levy may be made upon the salary or wages of any officer or employee (including members of the Armed Forces), or elected or appointed official, of the United States, the District of Columbia, or any agency or instrumentality of either, by serving a notice of levy on the employer of the delinquent taxpayer. As used in this paragraph, the term "employer" means:

(A) The officer or employee of the United States, the District of Columbia, or of the agency or instrumentality of the United States or the District of Columbia, who has control of the payment of the wages, or

(B) Any other officer or employee designated by the head of the branch, department, or agency, or instrumentality of the United States or of the District of Columbia as the party upon whom service of the notice of levy may be made.

If the head of such branch, department, agency or instrumentality designates an officer or employee other than one who has control of the payment of the wages, as the party upon whom service of the notice of levy may be made, such head shall promptly notify the appropriate TTB officer of the name and address of each officer or employee so designated and the scope or extent of the authority of such designee.

(ii) *State and municipal employees.* Salaries, wages, or other compensation of any officer, employee, or elected or appointed official of a State or Territory, or of any agency, instrumentality, or political subdivision thereof, are also subject to levy to enforce collection of any Federal tax.

(iii) *Seamen.* Notwithstanding the provisions of section 12 of the Seamen's Act of 1915 (46 U.S.C. 601), wages of seamen, apprentice seamen, or fishermen employed on fishing vessels are subject to levy. See 26 U.S.C. 6334(c).

(5) *Noncompetent Indians.* Solely for purposes of 26 U.S.C. 6321 and 6331, any interest in restricted land held in trust by the United States for an individual noncompetent Indian (and not for a tribe) shall not be deemed to be property, or a right to property, belonging to such Indian.

(b) *Successive seizures.* Whenever any property or rights to property upon which a levy has been made are not sufficient to satisfy the claim of the United States for which the levy is made, the appropriate TTB officer may thereafter, and as often as may be necessary, proceed to levy in like manner upon any other property or rights to property subject to levy of the person against whom such claim exists or on which there is a lien imposed by 26 U.S.C. 6321 (or the corresponding provision of prior law) for the payment of such claim until the amount due from such person, together with all costs and expenses, is fully paid.

(c) *Service of notice of levy by mail.* A notice of levy may be served by mailing the notice to the person upon whom the service of a notice of levy is authorized under paragraph (a)(1) of this section. In such a case the date and time the notice is delivered to the person to be served is the date and time the levy is made. If the notice is sent by certified or registered mail, return receipt requested, the date of delivery on the receipt is treated as the date the levy is made. If, after receipt of a notice of levy, an officer or other person authorized to act on behalf of the person served signs and notes the date and time of receipt on the notice of levy, the date and time so noted will be presumed to be, in the absence of proof to the contrary, the date and time of delivery. Any person may upon written notice to the appropriate TTB officer, have all notices of levy by mail sent to one designated ofice. After such a notice is received by the appropriate TTB officer, notices of levy by mail will sent to the designated office until a written notice withdrawing the request or a written notice designating a difference office is received by the appropriate TTB officer.

(26 U.S.C. 6331 and 6332)

[T.D. ATF–6, 38 FR 32445, Nov. 26, 1973,as amended by T.D. ATF–450, 66 FR 29026, May 29, 2001]

§ 70.162 Levy and distraint on salary and wages.

(a) *Notice of intent to levy.* Levy may be made for any unpaid tax only after the appropriate TTB officer has notified the taxpayer in writing of the intent to levy. The notice must be given in person, left at the dwelling or usual place of business of the taxpayer, or be sent by certified or registered mail to the taxpayer's last known address, no less than 30 days before the day of levy. The notice of intent to levy is in addition to, and may be given at the same time as, the notice and demand described in § 70.161 of this part.

(b) *Jeopardy.* Paragraph (a) of this section does not apply to a levy if the appropriate TTB officer has made a finding under § 70.161(a)(2) of this part that the collection of tax is in jeopardy.

(c) *Continuing effect of levy on salary or wages.* A levy on salary or wages is continuous from the time of the levy until the liability out of which the levy arose is released under 26 U.S.C. 6343 and § 70.167 of this part. For this purpose, the term "salary or wages"includes compensation for services paid in the form of fees, commissions, bonuses, and similar items. The levy attaches to both salary or wages earned but not yet paid at the time of the levy, and salary or wages earned and becoming payable (or paid in the form of an advance) subsequent to the date of the levy, until the levy is released pursuant to paragraph (d) of this section. In general, salaries or wages that are the subject of a continuing levy, if not exempt from levy under 26 U.S.C. 6334(a) (8) or (9), become payable to the officer who made the levy as the payor would otherwise be obligated to pay over the money to the taxpayer. For example, if the wage earner is paid on the Wednesday following the close of each workweek, a levy made upon the taxpayer's employer on any Monday would reach both the wages due for the prior workweek and the wages for succeeding workweeks as such wages become payable. In such a case the levy would be satisfied if the employer, on the first Wednesday after the levy and on each Wednesday thereafter, pays over to the officer who made the levy wages which would otherwise be paid to the employee on such Wednesday, until the employer receives a notice of release from levy described in paragraph (d) of this section. See, however, § 70.245(d) of this part for rules which permit a delayed payment to the officer who made the levy in certain cases where amounts payable to the taxpayer are exempt from levy under 26 U.S.C. 6334 (a)(9) and (d).

(d) *Release and notice of release from levy.* The officer who made the levy will promptly release a continuing levy on salary or wages when the conditions of 26 U.S.C. 6343 are met. The officer who made the levy will also promptly notify the person upon whom the levy was made that it has been released.

(26 U.S.C. 6331)

§ 70.163 Surrender of property subject to levy.

(a) *Requirement*—(1) *In general.* Except as otherwise provided in 26 U.S.C. 6332, relating to levy in the case of banks or life insurance and endowment contracts, any person in possession of (or obligated with respect to) property or rights to property subject to levy and upon which a levy has been made shall, upon demand of the officer who made the levy, surrender the property or rights (or discharge the obligation) to the officer who made the levy, except that part of the property or rights (or obligation) which, at the time of the demand, is actually or constructively under the jurisdiction of a court because of an attachment or execution under any judicial process.

(2) *Property held by banks.* (i) Any bank shall surrender any deposits (including interest thereon) in such bank only after 21 days after service of levy.

(ii) Notwithstanding paragraph (a)(1) of this section, if a levy has been made upon property or rights to property subject to levy which a bank engaged in the banking business in the United States or a possession of the United States is in possession of (or obligated with respect to), an appropriate TTB officer shall not enforce the levy with respect to any deposits held in an office of the bank outside the United States or a possession of the United States, unless the notice of levy specifies that such officer intends to reach such deposits. The notice of levy must not specify that such officer intends to reach such deposits unless that officer making such levy believes:

(A) That the taxpayer is within the jurisdiction of a U.S. court at the time the levy is made and that the bank is in possession of (or obligated with respect to) deposits of the taxpayer in an office of the bank outside the United States or a possession of the United States; or

(B) That the taxpayer is not within the jurisdiction of a U.S. court a the time the levy is made, that the bank is in possession of (or obligated with respect to) deposits of the taxpayer in an office outside the United States or a possession of the United States, and that such deposits consist, in whole or in part, of funds transferred from the United States or a possession of the United States in order to hinder or delay the collection of a tax imposed by provisions of 26 U.S.C. enforced and administered by the Bureau.

(b) *Enforcement of levy*—(1) *Extent of personal liability.* Any person who, upon demand of the appropriate TTB officer, fails or refuses to surrender any property or right to property subject to levy is liable in his/her own person and estate in a sum equal to the value of the property or rights not so surrendered, together with costs and interests. The liability, however, may not exceed the amount of the taxes for the collection of which the levy was made. Interest is to be computed at the annual rate referred to in regulations under 26 U.S.C. 6221 from the date of the levy, or, in the case of a continuing levy on salary or wages (see 26 U.S.C. 6331(e)), from the date the person would otherwise have been obligated to pay over the wages or salary to the taxpayer. Any amount recovered, other than cost, will be credited against the tax liability for the collection of which the levy was made.

(2) *Penalty for violation.* In addition to the personal liability described in paragraph (b)(1) of this section, any person who is required to surrender property or rights to property and who fails or refuses to surrender them without reasonable cause is liable for a penalty equal to 50 percent of the amount recoverable under 26 U.S.C. 6332(d)(2). No part of the penalty described in this subparagraph shall be credited against the tax liability for the collection of which the levy was made. The penalty described in this subparagraph is not applicable in cases where a bona fide dispute exists concerning the amount of the property to be surrendered pursuant to a levy or concerning the legal effectiveness of the levy. However, if a court in a later enforcement suit sustains the levy, then reasonable cause would usually not exist to refuse to honor a later levy made under similar circumstances.

(c) *Effect of honoring levy.* Any person in possession of, or obligated with respect to, property or rights to property subject to levy and upon which a levy has been made who, upon demand by the appropriate TTB officer, surrenders the property or rights to property, or discharges the obligation, to that officer, or who pays a liability described in paragraph (b)(1) of this section, is discharged from any obligation or liability to the delinquent taxpayer with respect to the property or rights to property arising from the surrender or payment. If an insuring organization satisfies a levy with respect to a life insurance or endowment contract in accordance with § 70.164 of this part, the insuring organization is discharged from any obligation or liability to any beneficiaries of the contract arising from the surrender or payment. Also, it is discharged from any obligation or liability to the insured or other owner. Any person who mistakenly surrenders to the United States property or rights to property not properly subject to levy is not relieved from liability to a third party who owns the property. The owners of mistakenly surrendered property may, however, secure from the United States the administrative relief provided for in 26 U.S.C. 6343(b) or may bring suit to recover the property under 26 U.S.C. 7426.

(d) *Person defined.* In addition to the definition given in § 70.11 of this part, the term "person," as used in 26 U.S.C.A 6332(a) and this section, includes an officer or employee of a corporation or a member or employee of a partnership, who is under a duty to surrender the property or rights to property or to discharge the obligation. In the case of a levy upon the salary or wages of an officer, employee, or elected or appointed official of the United States, the District of Columbia, or any agency or instrumentality of either, the term "person" includes the officer or employee of the United States, of the District of Columbia, or of such agency or instrumentality who is under a duty to discharge the obligation. As to the officer or employee who is under such duty, see § 70.161(a)(4)(i) of this part.

(26 U.S.C. 6332)

[T.D. ATF–6, 38 FR 32445, Nov. 26, 1973, as amended by T.D. ATF–450, 66 FR 29026, May 29, 2001]

§ 70.164 Surrender of property subject to levy in the case of life insurance and endowment contracts.

(a) *In general.* This section provides special rules relating to the surrender of property subject to levy in the case of life insurance and endowment contracts. The provisions of § 70.163 of this part which relate generally to the surrender of property subject to levy apply, to the extent not inconsistent with the special rules set forth in this section, to a levy in the case of life insurance and endowment contracts.

(b) *Effect of service of notice of levy*—(1) *In general.* A notice of levy served by an appropriate TTB officer on an insuring organization with respect to a life insurance or endowment contract issued by the organization shall constitute:

(i) A demand by the officer who made the levy for the payment of the cash loan value of the contract adjusted in accordance with paragraph (c) of this section, and

(ii) The exercise of the right of the person against whom the tax is assessed to the advance of such cash loan value.

It is unnecessary for the official who made the levy to surrender the contract document to the insuring organization upon which the levy is made. However, the notice of levy will include a certification by the official who made the levy that a copy of the notice of levy has been mailed to the person against whom the tax is assessed at that person's last known address. At the time of service of the notice of levy, the levy is effective with respect to the cash loan value of the insurance contract, subject to the condition that if the levy is not satisfied or released before the 90th day after the date of service, the levy can be satisfied only by payment of the amount described in paragraph (c) of this section. Other than satisfaction or release of the levy, no event during the 90-day period subsequent to the date of service of the notice of levy shall release the cash loan value from the effect of the levy. For example, the termination of the policy by the taxpayer or by the death of the insured during such 90-day period shall not release the levy. For the rules relating to the time when the insuring organization is to pay over the required amount, see paragraph (c) of this section.

(2) *Notification of amount subject to levy*—(i) *Full payment before the 90th*

day. In the event that the unpaid liability to which the levy relates is satisfied at any time during the 90-day period subsequent to the date of service of the notice of levy, the officer who filed the notice of levy will promptly give the insuring organization written notification that the levy is released.

(ii) *Notification after the 90th day*. In the event that notification is not given under paragraph (b)(2)(i) of this section, the officer who filed the notice of levy will, promptly following the 90th day after service of the notice of levy, give the insuring organization written notification of the current status of all accounts listed on the notice of levy, and of the total payments received since service of the notice of levy. This notification will be given to the insuring organization whether or not there has been any change in the status of the accounts.

(c) *Satisfaction of levy*. The levy described in paragraph (b) of this section with respect to a life insurance or endowment contract shall be deemed to be satisfied if the insuring organization pays over to the officer who made the levy the amount which the person against whom the tax is assessed could have had advanced by the organization on the 90th day after service of the notice of levy on the organization. However, this amount is increased by the amount of any advance (including contractual interest thereon), generally called a policy loan, made to the person on or after the date the orginzation has actual notice or knowledge, within the meaning of 26 U.S.C. 6323(i)(1), of the existence of the tax lien with respect to which the levy is made. The insuring organization may, nevertheless, make an advance (including contractual interest thereon), generally called an automatic premium loan, made automatically to maintain the contract in force under an agreement entered into before the organization has such actual notice or knowledge. In any event, the amount paid to the appropriate TTB officer by the insuring organization is not to exceed the amount of the unpaid liability shown on the notification described in paragraph (b)(2) of this section. The amount determined in accordance with the provisions of this section, subject to the levy, shall be paid to the appropriate TTB officer by the insuring organization promptly after receipt of the notification described in paragraph (b)(2) of this section. The satisfaction of a levy with respect to a life insurance or endowment contract will not discharge the contract from the tax lien. However, see 26 U.S.C. 6323(b)(9)(C) and §70.231(i) of this part concerning the liability of an insurance company after satisfaction of a levy with respect to a life insurance or endowment contract. If the person against whom the tax is assessed so directs, the insuring organization, on a date before the 90th day after service of the notice of levy, may satisfy the levy by paying over an amount computed in accordance with the provisions of this subparagraph substituting such date for the 90th day. In the event of termination of the policy by the taxpayer or by the death of the insured on a date before the 90th day after service of the notice of levy, the amount to be paid over to the appropriate TTB officer by the insuring organization in satisfaction of the levy shall be an amount computed in accordance with the provisions of this subparagraph substituting the date of termination of the policy or the date of death for the 90th day.

(d) *Other enforcement proceedings*. The satisfaction of the levy described in paragraph (b) of this section by an insuring organization shall be without prejudice to any civil action for the enforcement of any Federal tax lien with respect to a life insurance or endowment contract. Thus, this levy procedure is not the exclusive means of subjecting the life insurance and endowment contracts of the person against whom a tax is assessed to the collection of the person's unpaid assessment. The United States may choose to foreclose the tax lien in any case where it is appropriate, as, for example, to reach the cash surrender value (as distinguished from cash loan value) of a life insurance or endowment contract.

(e) *Cross references*. (1) For provisions relating to priority of certain advances with respect to a life insurance or endowment contract after satisfaction of a levy pursuant to 26 U.S.C. 6332(b), see 26 U.S.C. 6323(b)(9) and §70.231(i) of this part.

(2) For provisions relating to the issuance of a certificate of discharge of a life insurance or endowment contract subject to a tax lien, see 26 U.S.C. 6325(b) and § 70.150(b) of this part.

(26 U.S.C. 6332)

§ 70.165 Production of books.

If a levy has been made or is about to be made on any property or rights to property, any person, having custody or control of any books or records containing evidence or statements relating to the property or rights to property subject to levy, shall, upon demand of the appropriate TTB officer who has made or is about to make the levy, exhibit such books or records to such officer.

(26 U.S.C. 6333)

§ 70.167 Authority to release levy and return property.

(a) *Release of levy*—(1) *Authority*. An appropriate TTB officer may release the levy upon all or part of the property or rights to property levied upon as provided in paragraphs (a)(2), (3) and (4) of this section. A levy may be released under paragraph (a)(3) of this section only if the delinquent taxpayer complies with such of the conditions thereunder as an appropriate TTB officer may require and if the appropriate TTB officer determines that such action will facilitate the collection of the liability.

(2) *Conditions for mandatory release*. (i) An appropriate TTB officer shall release the levy as authorized under paragraph (a)(1) of this section, if any of the following conditions exist:

(A) The liability for which such levy was made is satisfied or becomes unenforceable by reason of lapse of time,

(B) Release of such levy will facilitate the collection of such liability,

(C) The taxpayer has entered into an agreement under 26 U.S.C. 6159 to satisfy such liability by means of installment payments, unless such agreement provides otherwise (an appropriate TTB officer is not required to release the levy in this case if release of such levy would jeopardize the secured creditor status of the United States).

(D) An appropriate TTB officer has determined that such levy is creating an economic hardship due to the financial condition of the taxpayer, or

(E) The fair market value of the property exceeds such liability and release of the levy on a part of such property could be made without hindering the collection of such liability.

(ii) In the case of any tangible personal property essential in carrying on the trade or business of the taxpayer, the appropriate TTB officer shall provide for an expedited determination under paragraph (a)(2)(i) if levy on such tangible personal property would prevent the taxpayer from carrying on such trade or business.

(3) *Conditions for discretionary release*. An appropriate TTB officer may release the levy as authorized under paragraph (a)(1) of this section, if:

(i) *Escrow arrangement*. The delinquent taxpayer offers a satisfactory arrangement, which is accepted by an appropriate TTB officer, for placing property in escrow to secure the payment of the liability (including the expenses of levy) which is the basis of the levy.

(ii) *Bond*. The delinquent taxpayer delivers an acceptable bond to an appropriate TTB officer conditioned upon the payment of the liability (including the expenses of levy) which is the basis of the levy. Such bond shall be in the form provided in 26 U.S.C. 7101 and § 70.281 of this part.

(iii) *Payment of amount of U.S. interest in the property*. There is paid to an appropriate TTB officer an amount determined by TTB to be equal to the interest of the United States in the seized property or the part of the seized property to be released.

(iv) *Assignment of salaries and wages*. The delinquent taxpayer executes an agreement directing the taxpayer's employer to pay to an appropriate TTB officer amounts deducted from the employee's wages on a regular, continuing, or periodic basis, in such manner and in such amount as is agreed upon with an appropriate TTB officer, until the full amount of the liability is satisfied, and such agreement is accepted by the employer.

(v) *Extension of statute of limitations*. The delinquent taxpayer executes an agreement to extend the statute of limitations in accordance with 26 U.S.C. 6502(a)(2) and § 70.224 of this part.

(4) Release where value of interest of United States is insufficient to meet expenses of sale. An appropriate TTB officer may release the levy as authorized under paragraph (a)(1) of this section if that officer determines that the value of the interest of the United States in the seized property, or in the part of the seized property to be released is insufficient to cover the expenses of the sale of such property.

(b) *Return of property*—(1) *General rule.* If an appropriate TTB officer determines that property has been wrongfully levied upon, the appropriate TTB officer may return:

(i) The specific property levied upon,

(ii) An amount of money equal to the amount of money levied upon (together with interest thereon at the overpayment rate from the date TTB receives the money to a date not more than 30 days before the date of return), or

(iii) An amount of money equal to the amount of money received by the United States from a sale of the property (together with interest thereon at the overpayment rate from the date of the sale of the property to a date not more than 30 days before the date of return).

If the United States is in possession of specific property, the property may be returned at any time. An amount equal to the amount of money levied upon or received from a sale of the property may be returned at any time before the expiration of 9 months from the date of the levy. When a request described in paragraph (b)(2) of this section is filed for the return of property before the expiration of 9 months from the date of levy, an amount of money may be returned after a reasonable period of time subsequent to the expiration of the 9-month period if necessary for the investigation and processing of such request. In cases where money is specifically identifiable, as in the case of a coin collection which may be worth substantially more than its face value, the money will be treated as specific property and, whenever possible, this specific property will be returned. For purposes of paragraph (b)(1)(iii) of this section, if property is declared purchased by the United States at a sale pursuant to 26 U.S.C. 6335(e), the United States is treated as having received an amount of money equal to the minimum price determined by the appropriate TTB officer before the sale or, if larger, the amount received by the United States from the resale of the property.

(2) *Request for return of property.* A written request for the return of property wrongfully levied upon shall be addressed to the officer who authorized the levy. The written request shall contain the following information:

(i) The name and address of the person submitting the request,

(ii) A detailed description of the property levied upon,

(iii) A description of the claimant's basis for claiming an interest in the property levied upon, and

(iv) The name and address of the taxpayer, the originating TTB office, and the date of lien or levy as shown on the Notice of Tax Lien, Notice of Levy, or, in lieu thereof, a statement of the reasons why such information cannot be furnished.

(3) *Inadequate request.* A request shall not be considered adequate unless it is a written request containing the information required by paragraph (b)(2) of this section. However, unless a notification is mailed by the officer who received the request to the claimant within 30 days of receipt of the request to inform the claimant of the inadequacies, any written request shall be considered adequate. If the officer who received the request timely notifies the claimant of the inadequacies of the request, the claimant shall have 30 days from the receipt of the notification of inadequacy to supply in writing any omitted information. Where the omitted information is so supplied within the 30-day period, the request shall be considered to be adequate from the time the original request was made for purposes of determining the applicable period of limitation upon suit under 26 U.S.C. 6532(c).

(26 U.S.C. 6343)

[T.D. ATF-6, 38 FR 32445, Nov. 26, 1973, as amended by T.D. ATF-450, 66 FR 29026, May 29, 2001]

§ 70.168 Redemption of property.

(a) *Before sale.* Any person whose property has been levied upon shall have the right to pay the amount due, together with costs and expenses of the proceeding, if any, to the appropriate TTB officer at any time prior to the sale of the property. Upon such payment the appropriate TTB officer shall restore such property to the owner and all further proceedings in connection with the levy on such property shall cease from the time of such payment.

(b) *Redemption of real estate after sale*—(1) *Period.* The owner of any real estate sold as provided in 26 U.S.C. 6335, the owner's heirs, executors, or administrators, or any person having any interest therein, or a lien thereon, or any person in their behalf, shall be permitted to redeem the property sold, or any particular tract of such property, at any time within 180 days after the sale thereof.

(2) *Price.* Such property or tract of property may be redeemed upon payment to the purchaser, or in case the purchaser cannot be found in the county in which the property to be redeemed is situated, then to the appropriate TTB officer, for the use of the purchaser, the purchaser's heirs, or assigns, the amount paid by such purchaser and interest thereon at the rate of 20 percent per annum. In case real and personal property (or several tracts of real property) are purchased in the aggregate, the redemption price of the real property (or of each of the several tracts) shall be determined on the basis of the ratio, as of the time of sale, of the value of the real property (or tract) to the value of the total property purchased. For this purpose the minimum price or the highest bid price, whichever is higher, offered for the property separately or in groups shall be treated as the value.

(c) *Record.* When any real property is redeemed, the appropriate TTB officer must cause entry of the fact to be made upon the record of sale kept in accordance with 26 U.S.C. 6340 and § 70.187 of this part, and such entry is evidence of such redemption. The party who redeems the property must notify the appropriate TTB officer of the date of such redemption and of the transfer of the certificate of sale, the amount of the redemption price, and the name of the party to whom such redemption price was paid.

(26 U.S.C. 6337)

[T.D. ATF–6, 38 FR 32445, Nov. 26, 1973, as amended by T.D. ATF–450, 66 FR 29026, May 29, 2001]

§ 70.169 Expense of levy and sale.

The appropriate TTB officer shall determine the expenses to be allowed in all cases of levy and sale. Such expenses shall include the expenses of protection and preservation of the property during the period subsequent to the levy, as well as the actual expenses incurred in connection with the sale thereof. In case real and personal property (or several tracts of real property) are sold in the aggregate, the appropriate TTB officer shall properly apportion the expenses to the real property (or to each tract).

(26 U.S.C. 6341)

§ 70.170 Application of proceeds of levy.

(a) *Collection of liability.* Any money realized by proceedings under 26 U.S.C. 6331 through 6344, or by sale of property redeemed by the United States (if the interest of the United States in the property was a lien arising under the provisions of 26 U.S.C. enforced and administered by the Bureau), is applied in the manner specified in paragraphs (a)(1), (2), and (3) of this section. Money realized by proceedings under 26 U.S.C. 6331 through 6344, includes money realized by seizure, by sale of seized property, or by surrender under 26 U.S.C. 6332 except money realized by the imposition of a 50 percent penalty pursuant to 26 U.S.C. 6332(d)(2)).

(1) *Expense of levy and sale.* First, against the expenses of the proceedings or sale, including expenses allowable under 26 U.S.C. 6341 and amounts paid by the United States to redeem property.

(2) *Specific tax liability on seized property.* If the property seized and sold is subject to a tax imposed by any provision of 26 U.S.C. which has not been paid, the amount remaining after applying paragraph (a)(1) of this section, shall then be applied against such tax

liability (and, if such tax was not previously assessed, it shall then be assessed):

(3) *Liability of delinquent taxpayer.* The amount, if any, remaining after applying paragraphs (a)(1) and (2) of this section, shall then be applied against the liability in respect of which the levy was made or the sale of redeemed property was conducted.

(b) *Surplus proceeds.* Any surplus proceeds remaining after the application of paragraph (a) of this section shall, upon application and satisfactory proof in support thereof, be credited or refunded by the appropriate TTB officer to the person or persons legally entitled thereto. The delinquent taxpayer is the person entitled to the surplus proceeds unless another person establishes a superior claim thereto.

(26 U.S.C. 6342)

DISPOSITION OF PROPERTY

SOURCE: Sections 70.181 through 70.188 added by T.D. ATF–301, 55 FR 47627, Nov. 14, 1990, unless otherwise noted.

§70.181 Disposition of seized property.

(a) *Notice of seizure.* As soon as practicable after seizure of property, the appropriate TTB officer seizing the property shall give notice in writing to the owner of the property (or, in the case of personal property, to the possessor thereof). The written notice shall be delivered to the owner (or to the possessor, in the case of personal property) or left at the owner's usual place of abode or business, if located within the TTB region where the seizure is made. If the owner cannot be readily located, or has no dwelling or place of business within such region, the notice may be mailed to the owner's last known address. Such notice shall specify the sum demanded and shall contain, in the case of personal property, a list sufficient to identify the property seized and, in the case of real property, a description with reasonable certainty of the property seized.

(b) *Notice of sale.* (1) As soon as practicable after seizure of the property, the appropriate TTB officer shall give notice of sale in writing to the owner. Such notice shall be delivered to the owner or left at the owner's usual place of abode or business if located. If the owner cannot be readily located, or has no dwelling or place of business, the notice may be mailed to the owner's last known address. The notice shall specify the property to be sold, and the time, place, manner, and conditions of the sale thereof, and shall expressly state that only the right, title, and interest of the delinquent taxpayer in and to such property is to be offered for sale. The notice shall also be published in some newspaper published in the county wherein the seizure is made or in a newspaper generally circulated in that county. For example, if a newspaper of general circulation in a county but not published in that county will reach more potential bidders for the property to be sold than a newspaper published within the county, or if there is a newspaper of general circulation within the county but no newspaper published within the county, the appropriate TTB officer may cause public notice of the sale to be given in the newspaper of general circulation within the county. If there is no newspaper published or generally circulated in the county, the notice shall be posted at the post office nearest the place where the seizure is made, and in not less than two other public places.

(2) The appropriate TTB officer may use other methods of giving notice of sale and of advertising seized property in addition to those referred to in paragraph (b)(1) of this section, when the appropriate TTB officer believes that the nature of the property to be sold is such that a wider or more specialized advertising coverage will enhance the possibility of obtaining a higher price for the property.

(3) Whenever levy is made without regard to the 10-day period provided in 26 U.S.C. 6331(a) (relating to cases in which collection is in jeopardy), a public notice of sale of the property seized shall not be made within such 10-day period unless 26 U.S.C. 6336 (relating to perishable goods) is applicable.

(c) *Time, place, manner, and conditions of sale.* The time, place, manner, and conditions of sale of property seized by levy shall be as follows:

(1) *Time and place of sale*—(i) *In general.* The time of sale shall not be less than 10 days nor more than 40 days from the time of giving public notice under 26 U.S.C. 6335(b) (see paragraph (b) of this section). The place of sale shall be within the county in which the property is seized, except that if it appears to the appropriate TTB officer under whose supervision the seizure was made that substantially higher bids may be obtained for the property if the sale is held at a place outside such county, the appropriate TTB officer may order that the sale be held in such other place. The sale shall be held at the time and place stated in the notice of sale.

(ii) *Right to request sale of seized property within 60 days.* The owner of any property seized by levy may request that the appropriate TTB officer sell such property within 60 days after such request (or within such longer period as may be specified by the owner). The appropriate TTB officer shall comply with such request unless it is determined (and the owner is notified within such period) that such compliance would not be in the best interests of the United States.

(2) *Adjournment of sale.* When it appears to the appropriate TTB officer that an adjournment of the sale will best serve the interest of the United States or that of the taxpayer, the appropriate TTB officer may adjourn the sale from time to time, but the date of the sale shall not be later than one month after the date fixed in the original notice of sale.

(3) *Minimum price.* (i) Before the sale of property seized by levy, the appropriate TTB officer shall determine:

(A) A minimum price, taking into account the expenses of levy and sale, for which the property shall be sold, and

(B) Whether the purchase of such property by the United States at such minimum price would be in the best interest of the United States.

If, at the sale, one or more persons offer to purchase such property for not less than the amount of the minimum price, the property shall be declared to be sold to the highest bidder. If no person offers for such property at the sale the amount of the minimum price and the appropriate TTB officer has determined that the purchase of such property by the United States would be in the best interest of the United States, the property shall be declared to be sold to the United States at such minimum price. If, at the sale, the property is not declared sold to the highest bidder or the United States, the property shall be released to the owner thereof and the expense of the levy and sale shall be added to the amount of tax for the collection of which the levy was made. Any property released to the owner under these circumstances shall remain subject to any lien imposed by 26 U.S.C. chapter 64, subchapter C.

(ii) The appropriate TTB officer conducting the sale shall either announce the minimum price before the sale begins or defer announcement of the minimum price until after the receipt of the highest bid, and, if the highest bid is greater than the minimum price, no announcement of the minimum price shall be made.

(4) *Offering of property*—(i) *Sale of indivisible property.* If any property levied upon is not divisible, so as to enable the appropriate TTB officer by sale of a part thereof to raise the whole amount of the tax and expenses of levy and sale, the whole of such property shall be sold. For application of surplus proceeds of sale, see 26 U.S.C. 6342(b).

(ii) *Separately, in groups, or in the aggregate.* The seized property may be offered for sale:

(A) As separate items, or

(B) As groups of items, or

(C) In the aggregate, or

(D) Both as separate items (or in groups) and in the aggregate. In such cases, the property shall be sold under the method which produces the highest aggregate amount.

The appropriate TTB officer shall select whichever of the foregoing methods of offering the property for sale as is most feasible under all the facts and circumstances of the case, except that if the property to be sold includes both real and personal property, only the personal property may be grouped for the purpose of offering such property for sale. However, real and personal property may be offered for sale in the aggregate, provided the real property, as separate items, and the personal as a group, or as groups, or as separate items, are first offered separately.

(iii) *Condition of title and of property.* Only the right, title, and interest of the delinquent taxpayer in and to the property seized shall be offered for sale, and such interest shall be offered subject to any prior outstanding mortgages, encumbrances, or other liens in favor of third parties which are valid as against the delinquent taxpayer and are superior to the lien of the United States. All seized property shall be offered for sale "as is" and "where is" and without recourse against the United States. No guaranty or warranty, express or implied, shall be made by the appropriate TTB officer offering the property for sale, as to the validity of the title, quality, quantity, weight, size, or condition of any of the property, or its fitness for any use or purpose. No claim shall be considered for allowance or adjustment or for rescission of the sale based upon failure of the property to conform with any representation, express or implied.

(iv) *Terms of payment.* The property shall be offered for sale upon whichever of the following terms is fixed by the appropriate TTB officer in the public notice of sale:

(A) Payment in full upon acceptance of the highest bid, without regard to the amount of such bid, or

(B) If the aggregate price of all property purchased by a successful bidder at the sale is more than $200, an initial payment of $200 or 20 percent of the purchase price, whichever is the greater, and payment of the balance (including all costs incurred for the protection or preservation of the property subsequent to the sale and prior to final payment) within a specified period, not to exceed 1 month from the date of the sale.

(5) *Method of sale.* The appropriate TTB officer shall sell the property either:

(i) At public auction, at which open competitive bids shall be received, or

(ii) At public sale under sealed bids. The following rules, in addition to the other rules provided in this paragraph, shall be applicable to public sale under sealed bids:

(A) *Invitation to bidders.* Bids shall be solicited through a public notice of sale.

(B) *Form for use by bidders.* A bid shall be submitted on a form which will be furnished by the appropriate TTB officer upon request. The form shall be completed in accordance with the instructions thereon.

(C) *Remittance with bid.* If the total bid is $200 or less, the full amount of the bid shall be submitted therewith. If the total bid is more than $200, 20 percent of such bid or $200, whichever is greater, shall be submitted therewith. (In the case of alternative bids submitted by the same bidder for items of property offered separately, or groups, or in the aggregate, the bidder shall remit the full amount of the highest alternative bid submitted, if the bid is $200 or less. If the highest alternative bid submitted is more than $200, the bidder shall remit 20 percent of the highest alternative bid or $200, whichever is greater.) Such remittance shall be by a certified, cashier's, or treasurer's check drawn on any bank or trust company incorporated under the laws of the United States or under the laws of any State, Territory, or possession of the United States, or by a U.S. postal, bank, express, or telegraph money order.

(D) *Time for receiving and opening bids.* Each bid shall be submitted in a securely sealed envelope. The bidder shall indicate in the upper left hand corner of the envelope the bidder's name and address and the time and place of sale as announced in the public notice of sale. A bid will not be considered unless it is received by the officer conducting the sale prior to the opening of the bids. The bids will be opened at the time and place stated in the notice or sale, or at the time fixed in the announcement of the adjournment of the sale.

(E) *Consideration of bids.* The public notice of sale shall specify whether the property is to be sold separately, by groups, or in the aggregate or by a combination of these methods, as provided in paragraph (c)(4)(ii) of this section. If the notice specifies an alternative method, bidders may submit bids under one or more of the alternatives. In case of error in the extension of prices in any bid, the unit price will govern. The officer conducting the sale shall have the right to waive any technical defects in a bid. In the event two or more highest bids are equal in amount, the officer conducting the sale shall determine the successful bidder by drawing lots. After the opening, examination, and consideration of all bids, the officer conducting the sale shall announce the amount of the highest bid or bids and the name of the successful bidder or bidders. Any remittance submitted in connection with an unsuccessful bid shall be returned at the conclusion of the sale.

(F) *Withdrawal of bids.* A bid may be withdrawn on written or telegraphic request received from the bidder prior to the time fixed for opening the bids. A technical defect in a bid confers no right on the bidder for the withdrawal of his bid after it has been opened.

(6) *Payment of bid price.* All payments for property sold under this section shall be made by cash or by a certified, cashier's, or treasurer's check drawn on any bank or trust company incorporated under the laws of the United States, or under the laws of any State, Territory, or possession of the United States, or by a U.S. postal, bank, express, or telegraph money order. If payment in full is required upon acceptance of the highest bid, the payment shall be made at such time. If deferred payment is permitted, the initial payment shall be made upon acceptance of the bid, and the balance shall be paid on or before the date fixed for payment thereof. Any remittance submitted with a successful sealed bid shall be applied toward the purchase price.

(7) *Delivery and removal of personal property.* Responsibility of the United States for the protection or preservation of seized personal property shall cease immediately upon acceptance of the highest bid. The risk of loss is on the purchaser of personal property upon acceptance of his bid. Possession of any personal property shall not be delivered to the purchaser until the purchase price has been paid in full. If payment of part of the purchase price for personal property is deferred, the United States will retain possession of such property as security for the payment of the balance of the purchase price and, as agent for the purchaser, will cause the property to be cared for until the purchase price has been paid in full or the sale is declared null and void for failure to make full payment of the purchase price. In such case, all charges and expenses incurred in caring for the property after the acceptance of the bid shall be borne by the purchaser.

(8) *Default in payment.* If payment in full is required upon acceptance of the bid and is not then and there paid, the officer conducting the sale shall forthwith proceed again to sell the property in the manner provided in 26 U.S.C. 6335(e) and this section. If the conditions of the sale permit part of the payment to be deferred, and if such part is not paid within the prescribed period, suit may be instituted against the purchaser for the purchase price or such part thereof as has not been paid, together with interest at the rate of 6 percent per annum from the date of the sale; or, in the discretion of the appropriate TTB officer, the sale may be declared by the appropriate TTB officer to be null and void for failure to make full payment of the purchase price and the property may again be advertised and sold as provided in 26 U.S.C. 6335(b), (c), and (e) and this section. In the event of such readvertisement and sale, any new purchaser shall receive such property or rights to property free and clear of any claim or right of the former defaulting purchaser, of any nature whatsoever, and the amount paid upon the bid price by such defaulting purchaser shall be forfeited to the United States.

(26 U.S.C. 6335)

[T.D. ATF–301, 55 FR 47627, Nov. 14, 1990, as amended by T.D. ATF–450, 66 FR 29025, May 29, 2001]

§ 70.182 Disposition of personal property acquired by the United States.

(a) *Sale*—(1) *In general.* Any personal property (except bonds, notes, checks, and other securities) acquired by the United States in payment of or as security for debts arising under the internal revenue laws may be sold by the appropriate TTB officer who acquired such property for the United States.

United States saving bonds shall not be sold by the appropriate TTB officer, but shall be transferred to the appropriate office of the Treasury Department for redemption. Other bonds, notes, checks, and other securities shall be disposed of in accordance with instructions issued by the appropriate TTB officer.

(2) *Time, place, manner and terms of sale.* The time, place, manner and terms of sale of personal property acquired for the United States shall be as follows:

(i) *Time, notice, and place of sale.* The property may be sold at any time after it has been acquired by the United States. A public notice of sale shall be posted at the post office nearest the place of sale and in at least two other public places. The notice shall specify the property to be sold and the time, place, manner, and conditions of sale. In addition, the appropriate TTB officer may use such other methods of advertising as such officer believes will result in obtaining the highest price for the property. Generally, the place of sale will be within the area where the property was originally acquired by the United States. However, if the appropriate TTB officer believes that a substantially higher price may be obtained, the sale may be held outside such area.

(ii) *Rejection of bids and adjournment of sale.* The officer conducting the sale reserves the right to reject any and all bids and withdraw the property from the sale. When it appears to the officer conducting the sale that an adjournment of the sale will best serve the interest of the United States, that officer may order the sale adjourned from time to time. If the sale is adjourned for more than 30 days in the aggregate, public notice of the sale must again be given in accordance with paragraph (a)(2)(i) of this section.

(iii) *Liquidated damages.* The notice shall state whether, in the case of default in payment of the bid price, any amount deposited with the United States will be retained as liquidated damages. In case liquidated damages are provided, the amount thereof shall not exceed $200.

(3) *Agreement to bid.* The appropriate TTB officer may, before giving notice of sale, solicit offers from prospective bidders and enter into agreements with such persons that they will bid at least a specified amount in case the property is offered for sale. In such cases, the appropriate TTB officer may also require such persons to make deposits to secure the performance of their agreements. Any such deposit, but not more than $200, shall be retained as liquidated damages in case such person fails to bid the specified amount and the property is not sold for as much as the amount specified in such agreement.

(4) *Terms of payment.* The property shall be offered for sale upon whichever of the following terms is fixed by the appropriate TTB officer in the public notice of sale:

(i) Payment in full upon acceptance of the highest bid, without regard to the amount of such bid, or

(ii) If the aggregate price of all property purchased by a successful bidder at the sale is more than $200, an initial payment of $200 or 20 percent of the purchase price, whichever is the greater, and payment of the balance (including all costs incurred for the protection or preservation of the property subsequent to the sale and prior to final payment) within a specified period, not to exceed one month from the date of the sale.

(5) *Method of sale.* The property may be sold either:

(i) At public auction, at which open competitive bids shall be received, or

(ii) At public sale under sealed bids.

(6) *Sales under sealed bids.* The following rules, in addition to the other rules provided in this paragraph, shall be applicable to public sales under sealed bids.

(i) *Invitation to bidders.* Bids shall be solicited through a public notice of sale.

(ii) *Form for use by bidders.* A bid shall be submitted on a form which will be furnished by the appropriate TTB officer upon request. The form shall be completed in accordance with the instructions thereon.

(iii) *Remittance with bid.* If the total bid is $200 or less, the full amount of the bid shall be submitted therewith. If the total bid is more than $200, 20 percent of such bid or $200, whichever is greater, shall be submitted therewith. Such remittance shall be by a certified, cashier's, or treasurer's check drawn on any bank or trust company incorporated under the laws of the United States or under the laws of any State, Territory, or possession of the United States, or by a U.S. postal, bank, express, or telegraph money order.

(iv) *Time for receiving and opening bids.* Each bid shall be submitted in a securely sealed envelope. The bidder shall indicate in the upper left hand corner of the envelope the bidder's name and address and the time and place of sale as announced in the public notice of sale. A bid will not be considered unless it is received by the officer conducting the sale prior to the opening of the bids. The bids will be opened at the time and place stated in the notice of sale, or at the time fixed in the announcement of the adjournment of the sale.

(v) *Consideration of bids.* The officer conducting the sale shall have the right to waive any technical defects in a bid. After the opening, examination, and consideration of all bids, the officer conducting the sale shall announce the amount of the highest bid or bids and the name of the successful bidder or bidders, unless in the opinion of the officer a higher price can be obtained for the property than has been bid. In the event the highest bids are equal in amount (and unless in the opinion of the officer conducting the sale a higher price can be obtained for the property than has been bid), the officer shall determine the successful bidder by drawing lots. Any remittance submitted in connection with an unsuccessful bid shall be returned to the bidder at the conclusion of the sale.

(vi) *Withdrawal of bids.* A bid may be withdrawn on written or telegraphic request received from the bidder prior to the time fixed for opening the bids. A technical defect in a bid confers no right on the bidder for the withdrawal of the bid after it has been opened.

(7) *Payment of bid price.* All payments for property sold pursuant to this section shall be made by cash or by a certified, cashier's or treasurer's check drawn on any bank or trust company incorporated under the laws of the United States or under the laws of any State, Territory, or possession of the United States, or by a U.S. postal, bank, express, or telegraph money order. If payment in full is required upon acceptance of the highest bid, the payment shall be made at such time. If payment in full is not made at such time, the officer conducting the sale may forthwith proceed again to sell the property in the manner provided in paragraph (a)(5) of this section. If deferred payment is permitted, the initial payment shall be made upon acceptance of the bid, and the balance shall be paid on or before the date fixed for payment thereof. Any remittance submitted with a successful sealed bid shall be applied toward the purchase price.

(8) *Delivery and removal of personal property.* The risk of loss is on the purchaser of the property upon acceptance of the purchaser's bid. Possession of any property shall not be delivered to the purchaser until the purchase price has been paid in full. If payment of part of the purchase price for the property is deferred, the United States will retain possession of such property as security for the payment of the balance of the purchase price and, as agent for the purchaser, will cause the property to be cared for until the purchase price has been paid is full or the sale in declared null and void for failure to make full payment of the purchase price. In such case, all charges and expenses incurred in caring for the property after acceptance of the bid shall be borne by the purchaser.

(9) *Certificate of sale.* The officer conducting the sale shall issue a certificate of sale to the purchaser upon payment in full of the purchase price.

(b) *Accounting.* In case of the resale of such property, the proceeds of the sale shall be paid into the Treasury as internal revenue collections and there shall be rendered by the appropriate TTB officer a distinct account of all charges incurred in such sale. For additional accounting rules, see 26 U.S.C. 7809.

(26 U.S.C. 7505)

[T.D. ATF–301, 55 FR 47627, Nov. 14, 1990, as amended by T.D. ATF–450, 66 FR 29027, May 29, 2001]

§ 70.183 Administration and disposition of real estate acquired by the United States.

(a) *Persons charged with.* The appropriate TTB officer shall have charge of all real estate which has been or shall be assigned, set off, or otherwise conveyed by purchase or otherwise to the United States in payment of debts or penalties arising under provisions of 26 U.S.C. enforced and administered by the Bureau or which has been or shall be vested in the United States by mortgage, or other security for payment of such debts, or which has been redeemed by the United States, or which has been or shall be acquired by the United States for payment of or as security for debts arising under provisions of 26 U.S.C. enforced and administered by the Bureau, and of all trusts created for the use of the United States in payment of such debts due the United States.

(b) *Sale.* The appropriate TTB officer may sell any real estate owned or held by the United States as aforesaid, subject to the following rules:

(1) *Property purchased at sale under levy.* If the property was acquired as a result of being declared purchased for the United States at a sale under 26 U.S.C. 6335, relating to sale of seized property, the property shall not be sold until after the expiration of 180 days after such sale under levy.

(2) *Notice of sale.* A notice of sale shall be published in some newspaper published or generally circulated within the county where the property is situated, or a notice shall be posted at the post office nearest the place where the property is situated and in at least two other public places. The notice shall specify the property to be sold and the time, place, manner and conditions of sale. In addition, the appropriate TTB officer may use other methods of advertising and of giving notice of the sale if the appropriate TTB officer believes such methods will enhance the possibility of obtaining a higher price for the property.

(3) *Time and place of sale.* The time of the sale shall be not less than 20 days from the date of giving public notice of sale under paragraph (b)(2) of this section. The place of sale shall be within the county where the property is situated. However, if the appropriate TTB officer believes a substantially better price may be obtained, the sale may be held outside such county.

(4) *Rejection of bids and adjournment of sale.* The officer conducting the sale reserves the right to reject any and all bids and withdraw the property from the sale. When it appears to the officer conducting the sale that an adjournment of the sale will best serve the interest of the United States, that officer may order the sale adjourned from time to time. If the sale is adjourned for more than 30 days in the aggregate, public notice of the sale must be given again in accordance with paragraph (b)(2) of this section.

(5) *Liquidated damages.* The notice shall state whether, in the cae of default in payment of the bid price, any amount deposited with the United States will be retained as liquidated damages. In case liquidated damages are provided, the amount thereof shall not exceed $200.

(6) *Agreement to bid.* The appropriate TTB officer may, before giving notice of sale, solicit offers from prospective bidders and enter into agreements with such persons that they will bid at least a specified amount in case the property is offered for sale. In such cases, the appropriate TTB officer may also require such persons to make deposits to secure the performance of their agreements. Any such deposit, but not more than $200, shall be retained as liquidated damages in case such person fails to bid the specified amount and the property is not sold for as much as the amount specified in such agreement.

(7) *Terms.* The property shall be offered for sale upon whichever of the following terms is fixed by the appropriate TTB officer in the public notice of sale:

(i) Payments in full upon acceptance of the highest bid, or

(ii) If the price of the property purchased by a successful bidder at the sale is more than $200, an initial payment of $200 or 20 percent of the purchase price, whichever is the greater, and payment of the balance within a specified period, not to exceed one month from the date of the sale.

(8) *Method of sale.* The property may be sold either:

(i) At public auction, at which open competitive bids shall be received, or

(ii) At public sale under sealed bids.

(9) *Sales under sealed bids.* The following rules, in addition to the other rules provided in this paragraph (b), shall be applicable to public sales under sealed bids.

(i) *Invitation to bidders.* Bids shall be solicited through a public notice of sale.

(ii) *Form for use by bidders.* A bid shall be submitted on a form which will be furnished by the appropriate TTB officer upon request. The form shall be completed in accordance with the instructions thereon.

(iii) *Remittance with bid.* If the total bid is $200 or less, the full amount of the bid shall be submitted therewith. If the total bid is more than $200, 20 percent of such bid or $200, whichever is greater, shall be submitted therewith. Such remittance shall be by a certified, cashier's, or treasurer's check drawn on any bank or trust company incorporated under the laws of the United States or under the laws of any State, Territory, or possession of the United States, or by a U.S. postal, bank, express, or telegraph money order.

(iv) *Time for receiving and opening bids.* Each bid shall be submitted in a securely sealed envelope. The bidder shall indicate in the upper left hand corner of the envelope the bidder's name and address and the time and place of sale as announced in the public notice of sale. A bid shall not be considered unless it is received by the officer conducting the sale prior to the opening of the bids. The bids will be opened at the time and place stated in the notice of sale, or at the time fixed in the announcement of the adjournment of the sale.

(v) *Consideration of bids.* The officer conducting the sale shall have the right to waive any technical defects in a bid. After the opening, examination, and consideration of all bids, the officer conducting the sale shall announce the amount of the highest bid or bids and the name of the successful bidder or bidders, unless in the opinion of the officer a higher price can be obtained for the property than has been bid. In the event the highest bids are equal in amount (and unless in the opinion of the officer conducting the sale a higher price can be obtained for the property than has been bid), the officer shall determine the successful bidder by drawing lots. Any remittance submitted in connection with an unsuccessful bid shall be returned to the bidder at the conclusion of the sale.

(vi) *Withdrawal of bid.* A bid may be withdrawn on written or telegraphic request received from the bidder prior to the time fixed for opening the bids. A technical defect in a bid confers no right on the bidder for the withdrawal of the bid after it has been opened.

(10) *Payment of bid price.* All payments for property sold pursuant to this section shall be made by cash or by a certified cashier's or treasurer's check drawn on any bank or trust company incorporated under the laws of the United States or under the laws of any State, Territory, or possession of the United States, or by a U.S. postal, bank, express, or telegraph money order. If payment in full is required upon acceptance of the highest bid, the payment shall be made at such time. If payment in full is not made at such time, the officer conducting the sale may forthwith proceed again to sell the property in the manner provided in paragraph (b)(8) of this section. If deferred payment is permitted, the initial payment shall be made upon acceptance of the bid, and the balance shall be paid on or before the date fixed for payment thereof. Any remittance submitted with a successful sealed bid shall be applied toward the purchase price.

(11) *Deed.* Upon payment in full of the purchase price, the appropriate TTB officer shall execute a quitclaim deed to the purchaser.

(c) *Lease.* Until real estate is sold, the appropriate TTB officer may lease such property.

(d) *Release to debtor.* In cases where real estate has or may become the property of the United States by conveyance or otherwise, in payment of or as security for a debt arising under the laws relating to internal revenue, and such debt shall have been paid, together with the interest thereon (at the rate of 1 percent per month), to the

United States within 2 years from the date of the acquisition of such real estate, the appropriate TTB officer may release by deed or otherwise convey such real estate to the debtor from whom it was taken, or to the debtor's heirs or other legal representatives. If property is declared purchased by the United States under 26 U.S.C. 6335, then, for the purpose of this paragraph, the date of such declaration shall be deemed to be the date of acquisition of such real estate.

(e) *Accounting*. The appropriate TTB officer shall, in accordance with 26 U.S.C. 7809, account for the proceeds of all sales or leases of the property and all expenses connected with the maintenance, sale, or lease of the property.

(f) *Authority of appropriate TTB officer*. Notwithstanding the other paragraphs of this section, the appropriate TTB officer may, when such officer deems it advisable, take charge of, and assume responsibility for, any real estate to which this section is applicable. In such case, such officer will notify in writing the appropriate TTB officer from whom he or she is taking charge and assuming responsibility. Also, in any case where a single parcel of real estate is situated in an area in which more than one officer has jurisdiction, the appropriate TTB officer may designate in writing one officer who is to be in charge of, and responsible for, the entire property.

(26 U.S.C. 7506)

[T.D. ATF-301, 55 FR 47627, Nov. 14, 1990, as amended by T.D. ATF-450, 66 FR 29027, May 29, 2001]

§70.184 Disposition of perishable goods.

(a) *Appraisal of certain seized property*. If the appropriate TTB officer determines that any property seized by levy is liable to perish or become greatly reduced in price or value by keeping, or that such property cannot be kept without great expense, the appropriate TTB officer shall appraise the value of such property and return it to the owner if the owner complies with the conditions prescribed in paragraph (b) of this section or, if the owner does not comply with such conditions, dispose of the property in accordance with paragraph (c) of this section.

(b) *Return to owner*. If the owner of the property can be readily found, the appropriate TTB officer shall give the owner written notice of the appropriate TTB officer's determination of the appraised value of the property. However, if the appropriate TTB officer determines that the circumstances require immediate action, the appropriate TTB officer may give the owner an oral notice of the determination of the appraised value of the property, which notice shall be confirmed in writing prior to sale. The property shall be returned to the owner if, within the time specified in the notice, the owner:

(1) Pays to the appropriate TTB officer an amount equal to the appraised value, or

(2) Gives an acceptable bond as prescribed by 26 U.S.C. 7101 and §70.281 of this part. Such bond shall be in an amount not less than the appraised value of the property and shall be conditioned upon the payment of such amount at such time as the appropriate TTB officer determines to be appropriate in the circumstances.

(c) *Immediate sale*. If the owner does not pay the amount of the appraised value of the seized property within the time specified in the notice, or furnish bond as provided in paragraph (b) of this section within such time, the appropriate TTB officer shall as soon as practicable make public sale of the property in accordance with the following terms and conditions:

(1) *Notice of sale*. If the owner can readily be found, a notice shall be given to the owner. A notice of sale also shall be posted in two public places in the county which the property is to be sold. The notice shall specify the time and place of sale, the property to be sold, and the manner and conditions of sale. The appropriate TTB officer may give such other notice and in such other manner as the appropriate TTB officer deems advisable under the circumstances.

(2) *Sale*. The property shall be sold at public auction to the higher bidder.

(3) *Terms*. The purchase price shall be paid in full upon acceptance of the highest bid. The payment shall be made by cash, or by a certified, cashier's or treasurer's check drawn on any bank or trust company incorporated

under the laws of the United States or under the laws of any State, Territory, or possession of the United States, or by a U.S. postal, bank, express, or telegraph money order.

(26 U.S.C. 6336)

§ 70.185 Certificate of sale; deed of real property.

(a) *Certificate of sale.* In the case of property sold as provided in 26 U.S.C. 6335 (relating to sale of seized property), the appropriate TTB officer shall give to the puchaser's a certificate of sale upon payment in full of the purchase price. A certificate of sale of real property shall set forth the real property purchased, for whose taxes the same was sold, the name of the purchaser, and the price paid therefor.

(b) *Deed to real property.* In case of any real property sold as provided in 26 U.S.C. 6335 and not redeemed in the manner and within the time prescribed in 26 U.S.C. 6337, the appropriate TTB officer shall execute (in accordance with the laws of the State in which the real property is situated pertaining to sales of real property under execution) to the purchaser of such real property at the sale or his assigns, upon surrender of the certificate of sale, a deed of the real property so purchased, reciting the facts set forth in the certificate.

(c) *Deed to real property purchased by the United States.* If real property is declared purchased by the United States at a sale pursuant to 26 U.S.C. 6335, the appropriate TTB officer shall at the proper time execute a deed therefor and shall, without delay, cause the deed to be duly recorded in the proper registry of deeds.

(26 U.S.C. 6338)

§ 70.186 Legal effect of certificate of sale of personal property and deed of real property.

(a) *Certificate of sale of property other than real property.* In all cases of sale pursuant to 26 U.S.C. 6335 of property (other than real property), the certificate of such sale.

(1) *As evidence.* Shall be prima facie evidence of the right of the officer to make such sale, and conclusive evidence of the regularity of the officer's proceedings in making the sale; and

(2) *As conveyance.* Shall transfer to the purchaser all right, title, and interest of the party delinquent in and to the property sold; and

(3) *As authority for transfer of corporate stock.* If such property consists of corporate stocks, shall be notice, when received, to any corporation, company, or association of such transfer, and shall be authority to such corporation, company, or association to record the transfer on its books and records in the same manner as if the stocks were transferred or assigned by the party holding the stock certificate, in lieu of any original or prior certificate, which shall be void, whether canceled or not; and

(4) *As receipts.* If the subject of sale is securities or other evidence of debt, shall be a good and valid receipt to the person holding the certificate of sale as against any person holding or claiming to hold possession of such securities or other evidences of debt; and

(5) *As authority for transfer of title to motor vehicle.* If such property consists of a motor vehicle, shall be notice, when received, to any public officer charged with the registration of title to motor vehicles, of such tranfer and shall be authority to such officer to record the transfer on his books and records in the same manner as if the certificate of title to such motor vehicle were transferred or assigned by the party holding the certificate of title, in lieu of any original or prior certificate, which shall be null and void, whether canceled or not.

(b) *Deed to real property.* In the case of the sale of real property pursuant to 26 U.S.C. 6335:

(1) *Deed as evidence.* The deed of sale given pursuant to 26 U.S.C. 6338 shall be prima facie evidence of the facts therein stated; and

(2) *Deed as conveyance of title.* If the proceedings of the appropriate TTB officer as set forth have been substantially in accordance with the provisions of law, such deed shall be considered and operate as a conveyance of all the right, title, and interest the party delinquent had in and to the real property thus sold at the time the lien of the United States attached thereto.

(c) *Effect of junior encumbrances.* A certificate of sale of personal property given or a deed to real property executed pursuant to 26 U.S.C. 6338 discharges the property from all liens, encumbrances, and titles over which the lien of the United States, with respect to which the levy was made, has priority. For example, a mortgage on real property executed after a notice of a Federal tax lien has been filed is extinguished when the appropriate TTB officer executes a deed to the real property to a purhcaser thereof at a sale pursuant to 26 U.S.C. 6335 following the seizure of the property by the United States. The proceeds of such a sale are distributed in accordance with priority of the liens, encumbrances, or titles. *See* 26 U.S.C. 6342(b) and 7426(a)(2) and §§ 70.170 and 70.207(a)(2) of this part with respect to surplus proceeds.

(26 U.S.C. 6339)

§ 70.187 Records of sale.

(a) *Requirement.* Each appropriate TTB officer shall make a record of all sales under 26 U.S.C. 6335 of real property situated within his or her jurisdiction and of redemptions of such property. The records shall set forth the tax for which any such sale was made, the dates of seizures and sale, the name of the party assessed and all proceedings in making such sale, the amount of expenses, the names of the purchasers, and the date of the deed. In the case of redemption of the property, the records shall additionally set forth the date of such redemption and of the transfer of the certificate of sale, the amount of the redemption price, and the name of the party to whom such redemption price was paid. The orginal record shall be retained by the appropriate TTB officer.

(b) *Copy as evidence.* A copy of such record, or any part thereof, certified by the appropriate TTB officer shall be evidence in any court of the truth of the facts therein stated.

(26 U.S.C. 6340)

[T.D. ATF–301, 55 FR 47627, Nov. 14, 1990, as amended by T.D. ATF–450, 66 FR 29027, May 29, 2001]

§ 70.188 Expense of levy and sale.

The appropriate TTB officer shall determine the expenses to be allowed in all cases of levy and sale. Such expenses shall include the expenses of protection and preservation of the property during the period subsequent to the levy, as well as the actual expenses incurred in connection with the sale thereof. In case real and personal property (or several tracts of real property) are sold in the aggregate, the appropriate TTB officer shall properly apportion the expenses to the real property (or to each tract).

(26 U.S.C. 6341)

JUDICIAL PROCEEDINGS

Civil Action by the United States

SOURCE: Sections 70.191 through 70.193 added by T.D. ATF–301, 55 FR 47633, Nov. 14, 1990.

§ 70.191 Authorization.

(a) *In general.* A civil action for the collection or recovery of taxes, or of any fine, penalty, or forfeiture (with respect to the provisions of 26 U.S.C. enforced and administered by the Bureau) will be commenced when the appropriate TTB officer, directs that the action be commenced.

(b) *Property held by banks.* The appropriate TTB officer shall not authorize or sanction any civil action for the collection or recovery of taxes, or of any fine, penalty, or forfeiture, from any deposits held in a foreign office of a bank engaged in the banking business in the United States or a possession of the United States unless the appropriate TTB officer believes:

(1) That the taxpayer is within the jurisdiction of a U.S. court at the time the civil action is authorized or sanctioned and that the bank is in possession of (or obligated with respect to) deposits of the taxpayer in an office of the bank outside the United States or a possession of the United States; or

(2) That the taxpayer is not within the jurisdiction of a U.S. court at the time the civil action is authorized or sanctioned, that the bank is in possession of (or obligated with respect to) deposits of the taxpayer in an office of the bank outside the United States or

a possession of the United States, and that such deposits consist, in whole or in part, of funds transferred from the United States or a possession of the United States in order to hinder or delay the collection of a tax imposed by the provisions of 26 U.S.C. enforced and administered by the Bureau.

(26 U.S.C. 7401)

[T.D. ATF–301, 55 FR 47633, Nov. 14, 1990, as amended by 66 FR 29027, May 29, 2001]

§ 70.192 Action to enforce lien or to subject property to payment of tax.

(a) *Civil actions.* In any case where there has been a refusal or neglect to pay any tax (with respect to the provisions of 26 U.S.C. enforced and administered by the Bureau) or to discharge any liability in respect thereof, whether or not levy has been made, the Attorney General or designated delegate at the request of the appropriate TTB officer, may direct a civil action to be filed in any court of the United States to enforce the lien of the United States under the Internal Revenue Code with respect to such tax or liability or to subject any property, of whatever nature, of the delinquent, or in which the delinquent has any right, title or interest, to the payment of such tax or liability. In any such proceeding, at the instance of the United States, the court may appoint a receiver to enforce the lien, or, upon certification by the appropriate TTB officer during the pendency of such proceedings that it is in the public interest, may appoint a receiver with all the powers of a receiver in equity.

(b) *Bid by the United States.* If property is sold to satisfy a first lien held by the United States, the United States may bid at the sale a sum which does not exceed the amount of its lien and the expenses of the sale. See also 31 U.S.C. 3715.

(26 U.S.C. 7403)

[T.D. ATF–301, 55 FR 47633, Nov. 14, 1990, as amended by 66 FR 29027, May 29, 2001]

§ 70.193 Disposition of judgments and moneys recovered.

All judgments and moneys recovered or received for taxes, costs, forfeitures, and penalties (with respect to the provisions of 26 U.S.C. enforced and administered by the Bureau) shall be paid to the Bureau as collections of taxes imposed under the provisions of 26 U.S.C. enforced and administered by the Bureau.

(26 U.S.C. 7406)

Proceedings by Taxpayers and Third Parties

SOURCE: Sections 70.202 through 70.213 added by T.D. ATF–301, 55 FR 47634, Nov. 14, 1990, unless otherwise noted.

§ 70.202 Intervention.

If the United States is not a party to a civil action or suit, the United States may intervene in such action or suit to assert any lien arising under provisions of 26 U.S.C. enforced and administered by the Bureau on the property which is the subject of such action or suit. The provisions of 28 U.S.C. 2410 (except subsection (b)) and of 28 U.S.C. 1444 shall apply in any case in which the United States intervenes as if the United States had originally been named a defendant in such action or suit. If the application of the United States to intervene is denied, the adjudication in such civil action or suit shall have no effect upon such lien.

(26 U.S.C. 7424)

§ 70.203 Discharge of liens; scope and application; judicial proceedings.

(a) *In general.* A tax lien of the United States, or a title derived from the enforcement of a tax lien of the United States, may be discharged or divested under local law only in the manner prescribed in 28 U.S.C. 2410 or in the manner prescribed in 26 U.S.C. 7425. Title 26 U.S.C. 7425(a) contains provisions relating to the discharge of a lien when the United States is not joined as a party in the judicial proceedings described in subsection (a) of 28 U.S.C. 2410. These judicial proceedings are plenary in nature and proceed on formal pleadings. Title 26 U.S.C. 7425(b) contains provisions relating to the discharge of a lien or a title derived from the enforcement of a lien in the event of a nonjudicial sale with respect to the property involved. Title 26 U.S.C. 7425(c) contains special rules relating to the notice of sale requirements contained in 26 U.S.C. 7425(b).

(b) *Judicial proceedings*—(1) *In general.* Title 26 U.S.C. 7425(a) provides rules, where the United States is not joined as a party, to determine the effect of a judgment in any civil action or suit described in subsection (a) of 28 U.S.C. 2410 (relating to joinder of the United States in certain proceedings), or a judicial sale pursuant to such a judgment, with respect to property on which the United States has or claims a lien under the provisions of 26 U.S.C. If the United States is improperly named as a party to a judicial proceeding, the effect is the same as if the United States were not joined.

(2) *Notice of lien filed when the proceeding is commenced.* Where the United States is not properly joined as a party in the court proceeding and a notice of lien has been filed in accordance with 26 U.S.C. 6323(f) or (g) in the place provided by law for such filing at the time the action or suit is commenced, a judgment or judicial sale pursuant to such a judgment shall be made subject to and without disturbing the lien of the United States.

(3) *Notice of lien not filed when the proceeding is commenced.* Where the United States is not joined as a party in the court proceeding and either a notice of lien has not been filed in accordance with 26 U.S.C. 6323(f) or (g) in the palce provided by law for such filing at the time the action or suit is commenced, or the law makes no provision for that filing, a judgment or judicial sale pursuant to such a judgment shall have the same effect with respect to the discharge or divestment of the lien of the United States as may be provided with respect to these matters by the local law of the place where the property is situated.

(4) *Proceeds of a judicial sale.* If a judicial sale of property pursuant to a judgment in any civil action or suit to which the United States is not a party discharges a lien of the United States arising under the provisions of 26 U.S.C., the United States may claim the proceeds of the sale (exclusive of costs) prior to the time that distribution of the proceeds is ordered. The claim of the United States in such a case is treated as having the same priority with respect to the proceeds as the lien had with respect to the property which was discharged from the lien by the judicial sale.

(26 U.S.C. 7425(a))

§ 70.204 Discharge of liens; nonjudicial sales.

(a) *In general.* Title 26 U.S.C. 7425(b) contains provisions with respect to the effect on the interest of the United States in property in which the United States has or claims a lien, or a title derived from the enforcement of a lien, of a sale made pursuant to:

(1) An instrument creating a lien on the property sold.

(2) A confession of judgment on the obligation secured by an instrument creating a lien on the property sold, or

(3) A statutory lien on the property sold.

For purposes of this section, such a sale is referred to as a "nonjudicial sale." The term "nonjudicial sale" includes, but is not limited to, the divestment of the taxpayer's interest in property which occurs by operation of law, by public or private sale, by forfeiture, or by termination under provisions contained in a contract for a deed or a conditional sales contract. Under 26 U.S.C. 7425(b)(1), if a notice of lien is filed in accordance with 26 U.S.C. 6323(f) or (g), or the title derived from the enforcement of a lien is recorded as provided by local law, more than 30 days before the date of sale and the appropriate TTB officer is not given notice of the sale (in the manner prescribed in § 70.205 of this part), the sale shall be made subject to and without disturbing the lien or title of the United States. Under 26 U.S.C. 7425(b)(2)(C), in any case in which notice of the sale is given to the appropriate TTB officer not less than 25 days prior to the date of sale (in the manner prescribed in 26 U.S.C. 7425(c)(1)), the sale shall have the same effect with respect to the discharge or divestment of the lien or title as may be provided by local law with respect to other junior liens or other titles derived from the enforcement of junior liens. A nonjudicial sale pursuant to a lien which is junior to a tax lien does not divest the tax lien, even though notice of the nonjudicial sale is given to the appropriate TTB officer. However, under the provisions of 26 U.S.C. 6325(b) and § 70.150 of this part, designated officers may discharge the property from a tax lien, including a tax lien which is senior to another lien upon the property.

(b) *Date of sale.* In the case of a nonjudicial sale subject to the provisions of 26 U.S.C. 7425(b), in order to compute any period of time determined with reference to the date of sale, the date of sale shall be determined in accordance with the following rules:

(1) In the case of divestment of junior liens on property resulting directly from a public sale, the date of sale is deemed to be the date the public sale is held, regardless of the date under local law on which junior liens on the property are divested or the title to the property is transferred.

(2) In the case of divestment of junior liens on property resulting directly from a private sale, the date of sale is deemed to be the date title to the property is transferred, regardless of the date junior liens on the property are divested under local law, and

(3) In the case of divestment of junior liens on property not resulting directly from a public or private sale, the date of sale is deemed to be the date on which junior liens on the property are divested under local law. For provisions relating to the right of redemption of the United States, see 26 U.S.C. 7425(d) and § 70.206 of this part.

(26 U.S.C. 7425(b))

§ 70.205 Discharge of liens; special rules.

(a) *Notice of sale requirements*—(1) *In general.* Except in the case of the sale of perishable goods described in paragraph (c) of this section, a notice (as described in paragraph (d) of this section) of a nonjudicial sale shall be given, in writing by registered or certified mail or by personal service, not less than 25 days prior to the date of sale (determined under the provisions of § 70.204(b) of this part), to the appropriate TTB officer. The provisions of 26 U.S.C. 7502 (relating to timely mailing treated as timely filing) and 7503 (relating to time for performance of acts where the last day falls on Saturday, Sunday, or legal holiday) apply in the case of notices required to be made under this paragraph.

(2) *Postponement of scheduled sale*—(i) *Where notice of sale is given.* In the event that notice of a sale is given in accordance with paragraph (a)(1) of this section, with respect to a scheduled sale which is postponed to a later time or date, the seller of the property is required to give notice of the postponement to the appropriate TTB officer, in the same manner as is required under local law with respect to other secured creditors. For example, assume that in State M local law requires that in the event of a postponement of a scheduled forclosure sale of real property, an oral announcement of the postponement at the place and time of the scheduled sale constitutes sufficient notice to secured creditors of the postponement. Accordingly, if at the place and time of a scheduled sale in State M an oral announcement of the postponement is made, the Bureau is considered to have notice of the postponement for the purpose of this paragraph (a)(2).

(ii) *Where noitce of sale is not given.* In the event that:

(A) Notice of a nonjudicial sale would not be required under paragraph (a)(1) of this section, if the sale were held on the originally scheduled date,

(B) Because of a postponement of the scheduled sale, more than 30 days elapse between the originally scheduled date of the sale and the date of the sale, and

(C) A notice of lien with respect to the property to be sold is filed more than 30 days before the date of the sale, notice of the sale is required to be given to the appropriate TTB officer in accordance with the provisions of paragraph (a)(1) of this section. In any case in which notice of sale is required to be given with respect to a scheduled sale, and notice of the sale is not given, any postponement of the scheduled sale does not affect the rights of the United States under 26 U.S.C. 7425(b).

(b) *Consent to sale*—(1) *In general.* Notwithstanding the notice of sale provisions of paragraph (a) of this section a nonjudicial sale of property shall discharge or divest the property of the lien or title of the United States if the appropriate TTB officer consents to the sale of the property free of the lien or title. Pursuant to 26 U.S.C. 7425(c)(2), where adequate protection is afforded the lien or title of the United States, the appropriate TTB officer may, in that officer's discretion, consent with respect to the sale of property in appropriate cases. Such consent shall be effective only if given in writing and shall be subject to such limitations and conditions as the appropriate TTB officer may require. However, the appropriate TTB officer may not consent to a sale of property under this section after the date of sale, as determined under §70.204(b) of this part. For provisions relating to releasing a lien or discharging property subject to a tax lien, *see* 26 U.S.C. 6325 and §70.150 of this part.

(2) *Application for consent.* Any person desiring the appropriate TTB officer's consent to sell property free of a tax lien or a title derived from the enforcement of a tax lien of the United States in the property shall submit to the appropriate TTB officer a written application, in triplicate, declaring that it is made under penalties of perjury, and requesting that such consent be given. The application shall contain the information required in the case of a noitice of sale, as set forth in paragraph (d)(1) of this section, and, in addition, shall contain a statement of the reasons why the consent is desired.

(c) *Sale of perishable goods*—(1) *In general.* A notice (as described in paragraph (d) of this section) of a nonjudicial sale of perishable goods (as defined in paragraph (c)(2) of this section) shall be given in writing, by registered or certified mail or delivered by personal service, at any time before the sale, to the appropriate TTB officer. If a notice of a nonjudicial sale is timely given in the manner described in this paragraph the nonjudicial sale shall discharge or divest the tax lien, or a title derived from the enforcement of a tax lien, of the United States in the property. The provisions of 26 U.S.C. 7502 (relating to timely mailing treated as timely filing) and 7503 (relating to time for performance of acts where the last days falls on Saturday, Sunday, or a legal holiday) apply in the case of notices required to be made under this paragraph. The seller of the perishable goods shall hold the proceeds (exclusive of costs) of the sale as a fund, for not less than 30 days after the date of the sale, subject to the liens and claims of the United States, in the same manner and with the same priority as the liens and claims of the United States had with respect to the property sold. If the seller fails to hold the proceeds of the sale in accordance with the provisions of this paragraph and if the appropriate TTB officer asserts a claim to the proceeds within 30 days after the date of sale, the seller shall be personally liable to the United States for an amount equal to the value of the interest of the United States in the fund. However, even if the proceeds of the sale are not so held by the seller, but all the other provisions of this paragraph are satisfied, the buyer of the property at the sale takes the property free of the liens and claims of the United States. In the event of a postponement of the scheduled sale of perishable goods, the seller is not required to notify the appropriate TTB officer of the postponement. For provisions relating to releasing a lien or discharging property subject to a tax lien, see 26 U.S.C. 6325 and §70.150 of this part.

(2) *Definition of perishable goods.* For the purpose of this paragraph, the term "perishable goods" means any tangible personal property which, in the reasonable view of the person selling the property, is liable to perish or become greatly reduced in price or value by keeping, or cannot be kept without great expense.

(d) *Forfeiture of land sales contract.* For purposes of paragraph (a) of this section, a nonjudicial sale of property includes any forfeiture of a land sales contract.

(e) *Content of notice of sale*—(1) *In general.* With respect to a noitice of sale described in paragraph (a) or (c) of this section, the notice will be considered adequate if it contains the information described in paragraph (d)(1) (i), (ii), (iii), and (iv) of this section.

(i) The name and address of the person submitting the notice of sale;

(ii) A copy of each Notice of Federal Tax Lien (TTB Form 5651.2) affecting the property to be sold, or the following information as shown on each such Notice of Federal Tax Lien:

(A) The initiating office named thereon,

(B) The name and address of the taxpayer, and

(C) The date and place of filing of the notice;

(iii) With respect to the property to be sold the following information:

(A) A detailed description, including location of the property affected by the notice (in the case of real property, the street address, city, and State and the legal description contained in the title or deed to the property and, if available, a copy of the abstract of title),

(B) The date, time, place, and terms of proposed sale of the property, and

(C) In case of a sale of perishable property described in paragraph (c) of this section, a statement of the reasons why the property is believed to be perishable; and

(iv) The approximate amount of the principal obligation, including interest, secured by the lien sought to be enforced and a description of the other expenses (such as legal expenses, selling costs, etc.) which may be charged against the sale proceeds.

(2) *Inadequate notice.* Except as otherwise provided in this subparagraph, a notice of sale described in paragraph (a) of this section which does not contain the information described in paragraph (d)(1) of this section shall be considered inadequate by the appropriate TTB officer. If the appropriate TTB officer determines that the notice is inadequate, that officer will give written notification of the items of information which are inadequate to the person who submitted the notice. A notice of sale which does not contain the name and address of the person submitting such notice shall be considered to be inadequate for all purposes without notification of any specific inadequacy. In any case where a notice of sale, does not contain the information required under paragraph (d)(1)(ii) of this section with respect to a Notice of Federal Tax Lien, the appropriate TTB officer may give written notification of such omission without specification of any other inadequacy and such notice of sale shall be considered inadequate for all purposes. In the event the appropriate TTB officer gives notification that the notice of sale is inadequate, a notice complying with the provisions of this section (including the requirement that the notice be given not less than 25 days prior to the sale in the case of a notice described in paragraph (a) of this section) must be given. However, in accordance with the provisions of paragraph (b)(1) of this section, in such a case the appropriate TTB officer may, in that officer's discretion, consent to the sale of the property free of the lien or title of the United States even though notice of the sale is given less than 25 days prior to the sale. In any case where the person who submitted a timely notice which indicates the person's name and address does not receive, more than 5 days prior to the date of the sale, written notification from the appropriate TTB officer that the notice is inadequate, the notice shall be considered adequate for purposes of this section.

(3) *Acknowledgment of notice.* If a notice of sale described in paragraph (a) or (c) of this section is submitted in duplicate to the appropriate TTB officer with a written request that receipt of the notice be acknowledged and returned to the person giving the notice, this request will be honored by the appropriate TTB officer. The acknowledgment by the appropriate TTB officer will indicate the date and time of the receipt of the notice.

(4) *Disclosure of adequacy of notice.* The appropriate TTB officer is authorized to disclose, to any person who has a proper interest, whether an adequate notice of sale was given under paragraph (d)(1) of tis section insofar as disclosure is authorized under 26 U.S.C. 6103. Any person desiring this information should submit to the appropriate TTB officer a written request which clearly describes the property sold or to be sold, identifies the applicable notice of lien, gives the reasons for requesting the information, and states the name and address of the person making the request.

(26 U.S.C. 7425(c))

[T.D. ATF–301, 55 FR 47634, Nov. 14, 1990, as amended by T.D. ATF–450, 66 FR 29027, May 29, 2001]

§ 70.206 Discharge of liens; redemption by United States.

(a) *Right to redeem*—(1) *In general.* In the case of a nonjudicial sale of real property to satisfy a lien prior to the tax lien or a title derived from the enforcement of a tax lien, the appropriate TTB officer may redeem the property within the redemption period (as described in paragraph (a)(2) of this section). The right of redemption of the United States exists under 26 U.S.C. 7425(d) even though a consent to the sale has been made under 26 U.S.C. 7425(c)(2) and § 70.205(b) of this part. For purposes of this section, the term "nonjudicial sale" shall have the same meaning as used in § 70.204(a) of this part.

(2) *Redemption period.* For purposes of this section, the redemption period shall be:

(i) The period beginning with the date of the sale (as determined under § 70.204(b)) and ending with the 120th day after such date, or

(ii) The period for redemption of real property allowable with respect to other secured creditors, under the local law of the place where the real property is located, whichever expires later.

Which ever period is applicable, 26 U.S.C. 7425 and this section shall govern the amount to be paid and the procedure to be followed.

(3) *Limitations.* In the event a sale does not ultimately discharge the property from tax lien (whether by reason of local law or the provisions of 26 U.S.C. 7425(b)), the provisions of this section do not apply because the tax lien will continue to attach to the property after the sale. In a case in which the Bureau is not entitled to a notice of sale under 26 U.S.C. 7425(b) and § 70.205 of this part, the United States does not have a right of redemption under 26 U.S.C. 7425(d). However, in such a case, if a tax lien has attached to the property at the time of sale, the United States has the same right of redemption, if any, which is afforded similar creditors under the local law of the place in which the property is situated.

(b) *Amount to be paid*—(1) *In general.* In any case in which an appropriate TTB officer exercises the right to redeem real property under 26 U.S.C. 7425(d), the amount to be paid is the sum of the following amounts:

(i) The actual amount paid for the property (as determined under paragraph (b)(2) of this section) being redeemed (which, in the case of a purchaser who is the holder of the lien being foreclosed, shall include the amount of the obligation secured by such lien to the extent legally satisfied by reason of the sale);

(ii) Interest on the amount paid (described in paragraph (b)(1)(i) of this section) at the sale by the purchaser of the real property computed at the rate of 6 percent per annum for the period from the date of the sale (as determined under § 70.204(b) of this part) to the date of redemption;

(iii) The amount, if any, equal to the excess of the expenses necessarily incurred to maintain such property (as determined under paragraph (b)(3) of this section) by the purchaser (and the purchaser's successor in interest, if any) over the income from such property realized by the purchaser (and the purchaser's successor in interest, if any) plus a reasonable rental value of such property (to the extent the property is used by or with the consent of the purchaser or the purchaser's successor in interest or is rented at less than its reasonable rental value); and

(iv) The amounts, if any, of a payment made by the purchaser or the purchaser's successor in interest after the foreclosure sale to a holder of a senior lien (to the extent provided under paragraph (b)(4) of this section).

(2) *Actual amount paid.* (i) The actual amount paid for property by a purchaser, other than holder of the lien being foreclosed, is the amount paid by the purchaser at the sale. For purposes of this paragraph, the amount paid by the purchaser at the sale includes deferred payments upon the bid price. The actual amount paid does not include costs and expenses incurred prior to the foreclosure sale by the purchaser except to the extent such expenses are included in the amount bid and paid for the property. For example, the actual amount paid does not normally include the expenses of the purchaser such as title searches, professional fees, or interest on debt incurred to obtain funds to purchase the property.

(ii) In the case of a purchaser who is the holder of the lien being foreclosed, the actual amount paid is the sum of:

(A) The amount of the obligation secured by such lien to the extent legally satisfied by reason of the sale and

(B) Any additional amount bid and paid at the sale.

For purposes of this section, a purchaser who acquires title as a result of a nonjudicial foreclosure sale is treated as the holder of the lien being foreclosed if a lien (or any interest reserved, created, or conveyed as security for the payment of a debt or fulfillment of other obligation) held by the purchaser is partially or fully satisfied by reason of the foreclosure sale. For example, a person whose title is derived from a tax deed issued under local law shall be treated as a purchaser who is the holder of the lien foreclosed in a case where a tax certificate, evidencing a lien on the property arising from the payment of property taxes, ripens into title. The amount paid by a purchaser at the sale includes deferred payments upon any portion of the bid price which is in excess of the amount of the lien being foreclosed. The actual amount paid does not include costs and expenses incurred prior to the foreclosure sale by the purchaser except to the extent such expenses are included in the amount of the lien being foreclosed which is legally satisfied by reason of the sale or in the amount bid and paid at the sale. Where the lien being foreclosed attaches to other property not subject to the foreclosure sale, the amount legally satisfied by reason of the sale does not include the amount of such lien that attaches to the other property. However, for purposes of the preceding sentences, the amount of the lien that attaches to the other property shall be considered to be equal to the amount by which the value of the other property exceeds the amount of any other senior lien on that property. Where, after the sale, the holder of the lien being foreclosed has the right to the unpaid balance of the amount due the holder, the amount legally satisfied by reason of the sale does not include the amount of such lien to the extent a deficiency judgment may be obtained therefor. However, for purposes of the preceding sentence, an amount, with respect to which the holder of the lien being foreclosed would otherwise have a right to a deficiency judgment, shall be considered to be legally satisfied by reason of the foreclosure sale to the extent that the holder has waived the holder's right to a deficiency judgment prior to the foreclosure sale. For this purpose, the waiver must be in writing and legally binding upon the foreclosing lienholder as of the time the sale is concluded. If, prior to the foreclosure, payments have been made by the foreclosing lienholder to a holder of a superior lien, the payments are included in the actual amount paid to the extent they give rise to an interest which is legally satisfied by reason of the foreclosure sale.

(3) *Excess expenses incurred by purchaser.* (i) Expenses necessarily incurred in connection with the property after the foreclosure sale and before redemption by the United States are taken into account in determining if there are excess expenses payable under paragraph (b)(1)(iii) of this section. Expenses incurred by the purchaser prior to the foreclosure sale are not considered under paragraph (b)(3) of this section. (See paragraph (b)(2)(ii) of this section for circumstances under which such expenses may be included in the amount to be paid.) Expenses necessarily incurred in connection with the property include, for example, rental agent commissions, repair and maintenance expenses, utilities expenses, legal fees incurred after the foreclosure sale and prior to redemption in defending the title acquired through the foreclosure sale, and a proportionate amount of casualty insurance premiums and ad valorem taxes. Improvements made to the property are not considered as an expense unless the amounts incurred for such improvements are necessarily incurred to maintain the property.

(ii) At any time prior to the expiration of the redemption period applicable under paragraph (a)(2) of this section, the appropriate TTB officer may, by certified or registered mail or hand delivery, request a written itemized statement of the amount claimed by the purchaser or the purchaser's successor in interest to be payable under paragraph (b)(1)(iii) of this section. Unless the purchaser or the purchaser's successor in interest furnishes the written itemized statement within 15 days after the request is made by the appropriate TTB officer, it shall be presumed that no amount is payable for expenses in excess of income and the Bureau shall tender only the amount otherwise payable under paragraph (b)(1) of this section. If a purchaser or the purchaser's successor in interest has failed to furnish the written itemized statement within 15 days after the request therefor is made by the appropriate TTB officer, or there is a disagreement as to the amount properly payable under paragraph (b)(1)(iii) of this section, a payment for excess expenses shall be made after the redemption within a reasonable time following the verification by the appropriate TTB officer of a written itemized statement submitted by the purchaser or the purchaser's successor in interest or the resolution of the disagreement as to the amount properly payable for excess expenses.

(4) *Payments made by purchaser or the purchaser's successor in interest to a senior lienor.* (i) The amount to be paid upon a redemption by the United States shall include the amount of a payment made by the purchaser or the purchaser's successor in interest to a holder of a senior lien to the extent a request for the reimbursement thereof (made in accordance with paragraph (b)(4)(ii) of this section) is approved as provided under paragraph (b)(4)(iii) of this section. This paragraph applies only to a payment made after the foreclosure sale and before the redemption to a holder of a lien that was, immediately prior to the foreclosure sale, superior to the lien foreclosed. A payment of principal or interest to a senior lienor shall be taken into account. Generally, the portion, if any, of a payment which is to be held in escrow for the payment of an expense, such as hazard insurance or real property taxes, is not considered under this paragraph. However, a payment by the escrow agent of a real property tax or special assessment lien, which was senior to the lien foreclosed, shall be considered to be a payment made by the purchaser or the purchaser's successor in interest for purposes of this paragraph. With respect to real property taxes assessed after the foreclosure sale, see paragraph (b)(3)(i) of this section, relating to excess expenses incurred by the purchaser.

(ii) Before the expiration of the redemption period applicable under paragraph (a)(2) of this section, the appropriate TTB officer shall, in any case where a redemption is contemplated, send notice to the purchaser (or the purchaser's successor in interest of record) by certified or registered mail or hand delivery of the right under paragraph (b)(4) of this section to request reimbursement (payable in the event the right to redeem under 26 U.S.C. 7425(d) is exercised) for a payment made to a senior lienor. No later than 15 days after the notice from the appropriate TTB officer is sent, the request for reimbursement shall be mailed or delivered to the office specified in such notice and shall consist of:

(A) A written itemized statement, signed by the claimant, of the amount claimed with respect to a payment made to a senior lienor, together with the supporting evidence requested in the notice from the appropriate TTB officer, and

(B) A waiver or other document that will be effective upon redemption by the United States to discharge the property from, or transfer to the United States, any interest in or lien on the property that may arise under local law with respect to the payment made to a senior lienor.

Upon a showing of reasonable cause, an appropriate TTB officer may, in that official's discretion and at any time before the expiration of the applicable period for redemption, grant an extension for a reasonable period of time to submit, amend, or supplement a request for reimbursement. Unless a request for reimbursement is timely submitted (determined with regard to any extension of time granted), no amount shall be payable to the purchaser or the purchaser's successor in interest on account of a payment made to a senior lienor if the right to redeem under 26 U.S.C. 7425(d) is exercised. A waiver or other document submitted pursuant to paragraph (b)(4)(ii) of this section shall be treated as effective only to the extent of the amount included in the redemption price under this paragraph. If the right to redeem is not exercised or a request for reimbursement is withdrawn, the appropriate TTB officer shall, by certified or registered mail or hand delivery, return to the purchaser or the purchaser's successor any waiver or other document submitted pursuant to paragraph (b)(4)(ii) of this section as soon as is practicable.

(iii) A request for reimbursement submitted in accordance with paragraph (b)(4)(ii) of this section shall be considered to be approved for the total amount claimed by the purchaser, and payable in the event the right to redeem is exercised, unless the appropriate TTB officer sends notice to the claimant, by certified or registered mail or hand delivery, of the denial of the amount claimed within 30 days after receipt of the request of 15 days before expiration of the applicable period for redemption, whichever is later. The notification of denial shall state the grounds for denial. If such notice of denial is given, the request for reimbursement for a payment made to a senior lienor shall be treated as having been withdrawn by the purchaser or the purchaser's successor and the Bureau shall tender only the amount otherwise payable under paragraph (b)(1) of this section. If a request for reimbursement is treated as having been withdrawn under the preceding sentence, payment for amounts described in paragraph (b)(4) of this section may, in the discretion of the appropriate TTB officer, be made after the redemption upon the resolution of the disagreement as to the amount properly payable under paragraph (b)(1)(iv) of this section.

(c) *Certificate of redemption*—(1) *In general.* If an appropriate TTB officer exercises the right of redemption of the United States described in paragraph (a) of this section, the appropriate TTB officer shall apply to the officer designated by local law, if any, for the documents necessary to evidence the fact of redemption and to record title to the redeemed property in the name of the United States. If no such officer has been designated by local law, or if the officer designated by local law fails to issue the necessary documents, the appropriate TTB officer is authorized to issue a certificate of redemption for the property redeemed by the United States.

(2) *Filing.* The appropriate TTB officer shall, without delay, cause either the documents issued by the local officer or the certificate of redemption executed by the appropriate TTB officer to be filed with the local office where certificates of redemption are generally filed. If a certificate of redemption is issued by the appropriate TTB officer and if the State in which the real property redeemed by the United States is situated has no office with which certificates of redemption may be filed, the appropriate TTB officer shall file the certificate of redemption in the office of the clerk of the United States district court for the judicial district in which the redeemed property is situated.

(3) *Effect of certificate of redemption.* A certificate of redemption executed pursuant to paragraph (c)(1) of this section, shall constitute prima facie evidence of the regularity of the redemption. When a certificate of redemption is recorded, it shall transfer to the United States all the rights, title, and interest in and to the redeemed property acquired by the person, from whom the appropriate TTB officer redeemed the property, by virtue of the sale of the property. Therefore, if under local law the purchaser takes title free of liens junior to the lien of the foreclosing lienholder, the United States takes the title free of such junior liens upon redemption of the property. If a certificate of redemption has been erroneously prepared and filed because the redemption was not effective, the appropriate TTB officer shall issue a document revoking such certificate of redemption and such document shall be conclusively binding upon the United States against a purchaser of the property or a holder of a lien upon the property.

(4) Application for release of right of redemption. Upon application of a party with a proper interest in the real property sold in a nonjudicial sale described in 26 U.S.C. 7425(b) and § 70.204 of this part, which real property is subject to the right of redemption of the United States described in this section, the appropriate TTB officer may, in that officer's discretion, release the

right of redemption with respect to the property. The application for the release must be submitted in writing to an appropriate TTB officer and must contain such information as the appropriate TTB officer may require. If the appropriate TTB officer determines that the right of redemption of the United States is without value, no amount shall be required to be paid with respect to the release of the right of redemption.

(26 U.S.C. 7425(d))

[T.D. ATF–301, 55 FR 47634, Nov. 14, 1990, as amended by T.D. ATF–450, 66 FR 29027, May 29, 2001]

§ 70.207 Civil actions by persons other than taxpayers.

(a) *Actions permitted*—(1) *Wrongful levy.* If a levy has been made on property, or property has been sold pursuant to a levy, any person (other than the person against whom is assessed the tax out of which such levy arose) may bring a civil action against the United States in a district court of the United States based upon such person's claim:

(i) That the person has an interest in, or a lien on, such property which is senior to the interest of the United States; and

(ii) That such property was wrongfully levied upon.

No action is permitted under 26 U.S.C. 7426(a)(1) unless there has been a levy upon the property claimed.

(2) *Surplus proceeds.* If property has been sold pursuant to levy, any person (other than the person against whom is assessed the tax out of which such levy arose) may bring a civil action against the United States in a district court of the United States based upon the claim that the person:

(i) Has an interest in or lien on such property junior to that of the United States; and

(ii) Is entitled to the surplus proceeds of such sale.

(3) *Substituted sale proceeds.* Any person who claims to be legally entitled to all or any part of the amount which is held as a fund from the sale of property pursuant to an agreement described in 26 U.S.C. 6325(b)(3) may bring a civil action against the United States in a district court of the United States to obtain the relief provided by 26 U.S.C. 7426(b)(4). It is not necessary that the claimant be a party to the agreement which provides for the substitution of the sale proceeds for the property subject to the lien.

(b) *Adjudication*—(1) *Wrongful levy.* If the court determines that property has been wrongfully levied upon, the court may:

(i) Grant an injunction to prohibit the enforcement of such levy or to prohibit a sale of such property if such sale would irreparably injure rights in the property which are superior to the rights of the United States in such property; or

(ii) Order the return of specific property if the United States is in possession of such property; or

(iii) Grant a judgment for the amount of money levied upon, with interest thereon at the overpayment rate established under 26 U.S.C. 6621 from the date that the officer who made the levy receives the money wrongfully levied upon to the date of payment of such judgment, or

(iv) Grant a judgment for an amount not exceeding the amount received by the United States from the sale of such property (which, in the case of property declared purchased by the United States at a sale, shall be the greater of the minimum amount determined pursuant to 26 U.S.C. 6335(e) or the amount received by the United States from the resale of such property), or the fair market value of such property immediately before the levy, with interest thereon at the overpayment rate established under 26 U.S.C. 6621 from the date of the sale of the property to the date of payment of such judgment.

For purposes of paragraph (b)(1) of this section, a levy is wrongful against a person (other than the taxpayer against whom the assessment giving rise to the levy is made), if the levy is upon property exempt from levy under 26 U.S.C. 6334, or the levy is upon property in which the taxpayer had no interest at the time the lien arose or thereafter, or the levy is upon property with respect to which such person is a purchaser against whom the lien is invalid under 26 U.S.C. 6323 or 6324(a)(2) or (b), or the levy or sale pursuant to levy will or does effectively destroy or otherwise irreparably injure such person's interest in the property which is senior to the Federal tax lien. A levy may be wrongful against a holder of a senior lien upon the taxpayer's property under certain circumstances although legal rights to enforce the holder's interest survive the levy procedure. For example, the levy may be wrongful against such a person if the property is an obligation which is collected pursuant to the levy rather than sold and nothing thereafter remains for the senior lienholder, or the property levied upon is of such a nature that when it is sold at a public sale the property subject to the senior lien is not available for the senior lienholder as a realistic source for the enforcement of the holder's interest. Some of the factors which should be taken into account in determining whether property remains or will remain a realistic source from which the senior lienholder may realize collection are: The nature of the property, the number of purchasers, the value of each unit sold or to be sold, whether, as a direct result of the distraint sale, the costs of realizing collection from the security have or will be so substantially increased as to render the security substantially valueless as a source of collection, and whether the property subject to the distraint sale constitutes substantially all of the property available as security for the payment of the indebtedness to the senior lienholder.

(2) *Surplus proceeds.* If the court determines that the interest or lien of any party to an action under 26 U.S.C. 7426 was transferred to the proceeds of a sale of the property, the court may grant a judgment in an amount equal to all or any part of the amount of the surplus proceeds of such sale. The term "surplus proceeds" means property remaining after application of the provisions of 26 U.S.C. 6342(a).

(3) *Substituted sale proceeds.* If the court determines that a party has an interest in or lien on the amount held as a fund pursuant to an agreement described in 26 U.S.C. 6325(b)(3), the court may grant a judgment in an amount equal to all or any part of the amount of such fund.

(26 U.S.C. 7426)

§ 70.208 Review of jeopardy assessment or jeopardy levy procedures; information to taxpayer.

Not later than 5 days after the day on which an assessment is made under 26 U.S.C. 6862 or when a levy is made less than 30 days after the notice and demand described in 26 U.S.C 6331(a), the officer who authorized the assessment or levy shall provide the taxpayer a written statement setting forth the information upon which that official relies in authorizing such assessment or levy.

(26 U.S.C. 7429(a)(1))

§ 70.209 Review of jeopardy assessment or levy procedures; administrative review.

(a) *Request for administrative review.* Any request for the review of a jeopardy assessment or levy provided for by 26 U.S.C. 7429(a)(2) shall be filed with the officer who authorized the assessment or levy, within 30 days after the statement described in § 70.208 of this part is given to the taxpayer. However, if no statement is given within the 5-day period described in § 70.208, any request for review of the jeopardy assessment shall be filed within 35 days after the date the assessment is made. Such request shall be in writing, shall state fully the reasons for the request, and shall be supported by such evidence as will enable the reviewing officer to make the redetermination described in 26 U.S.C. 7429(a)(3).

(b) *Administrative review.* In determining whether the assessment or levy is reasonable and the amount assessed appropriate, the reviewing officer shall take into account not only information available at the time the assessment is made but also information which subsequenbtly becomes available.

(26 U.S.C. 7429(a)(2))

§ 70.210 Review of jeopardy assessment or levy procedures; judicial action.

(a) *Time for bringing judicial action.* An action for judicial review described in 26 U.S.C. 7429(b) may be instituted by the taxpayer during the period beginning on the earlier of:

(1) The date of the reviewing officer notifies the taxpayer of the determination described in 26 U.S.C. 7429(a)(3); or

(2) The 16th day after the request described in 26 U.S.C. 7429(a)(2) was made by the taxpayer; and ending on the 90th day thereafter.

(b) Extension of the period for judicial review. The U.S. Government may not seek an extension of the 20-day period described in 26 U.S.C. 7429(b)(2), but it may join with the taxpayer in seeking such an extension.

(26 U.S.C. 7429)

§ 70.213 Repayments to officers or employees.

The appropriate TTB officer is authorized to repay to any officer or employee of the Bureau the full amount of such sums of money as may be recovered against such officer or employee in any court for any taxes imposed under provisions of 26 U.S.C. enforced and administered by the Bureau collected by such officer or employee with the cost and expense of suit, and all damages and costs recovered against any officer or employee of the Bureau in any suit brought against such officer or employee by reason of anything done in the official performance of duties under the provisions of 26 U.S.C. enforced and administered by the Bureau.

(26 U.S.C. 7423)

LIMITATIONS

Limitations on Assessment and Collection

§ 70.221 Period of limitations upon assessment.

(a) The amount of any tax imposed by the Internal Revenue Code (other than a tax collected by means of stamps) shall be assessed within 3 years after the return was filed. For rules applicable in cases where the return is filed prior to the due date thereof, see section 6501(b) of the Internal Revenue Code. In the case of taxes payable by stamps, assessment shall be made at any time after the tax becomes due and before the expiration of 3 years after the date on which any part of the tax was paid. For exceptions and additional rules, see subsections (b) and (c) of section 6501 of the Internal Revenue Code.

(b) No proceeding in court without assessment for the collection of any tax shall be begun after the expiration of the applicable period for the assessment of such tax.

(26 U.S.C. 6501)

[T.D. ATF–251, 52 FR 19314, May 22, 1987. Redesignated by T.D. ATF–301, 55 FR 47606, Nov. 14, 1990]

§ 70.222 Time return deemed filed for purposes of determining limitations.

(a) *Early Return.* Any return filed prior to the last day prescribed by law or regulations for the filing thereof (determined without regard to any extension of time for filing) shall be considered as filed on such last day.

(b) *Returns executed by appropriate TTB officers.* The execution of a return by an appropriate TTB officer under the authority of section 6020(b) of the Internal Revenue Code does not start the running of the statutory period of limitations on assessment and collection.

(26 U.S.C. 6501)

[T.D. ATF–251, 52 FR 19314, May 22, 1987. Redesignated by T.D. ATF–301, 55 FR 47606, Nov. 14, 1990; T.D. ATF–450, 66 FR 29028, May 29, 2001]

§ 70.223 Exceptions to general period of limitations on assessment and collection.

(a) *False return.* In the case of a false or fraudulent return with intent to evade any tax, the tax may be assessed, or a proceeding in court for the collection of such tax may be begun without assessment, at any time after such false or fraudulent return is filed.

(b) *Willful attempt to evade tax.* In the case of a willful attempt in any manner to defeat or evade any tax imposed by provisions of 26 U.S.C. enforced and administered by the Bureau, the tax may be assessed, or a proceeding in court for the collection of such tax may be begun without assessment, at any time.

(c) *No return.* In the case of a failure to file a return, the tax may be assessed, or a proceeding in court for the collection of such tax may be begun without assessment, at any time after the date prescribed for filing the return.

(d) *Extension by agreement.* The time prescribed by 26 U.S.C. 6501 for the assessment of any tax imposed by provisions of 26 U.S.C. enforced and administered by the Bureau may, prior to the expiration of such time, be extended for any period of time agreed upon in writing by the taxpayer and the appropriate TTB officer. The extension shall become effective when the agreement has been executed by both parties. The period agreed upon may be extended by subsequent agreements in writing made before the expiration of the period previously agreed upon.

(26 U.S.C. 6501)

[T.D. ATF–251, 52 FR 19314, May 22, 1987. Redesignated and amended by T.D. ATF–301, 55 FR 47606, 47641, Nov. 14, 1990; T.D. ATF–331, 57 FR 40328, Sept. 3, 1992]

§ 70.224 Collection after assessment.

(a) *Length of period*—(1) *General rule.* In any case in which a tax has been assessed within the statutory period of limitation properly applicable thereto, a proceeding in court to collect such tax may be begun, or levy for the collection of such tax may be made, within 10 years after the assessment thereof.

(2) *Extension by agreement.* (i) The 10-year period of limitation on collection after assessment of any tax may, prior to the expiration thereof, be extended for any period of time agreed upon in writing by the taxpayer and the appropriate TTB officer. Whenever necessary to protect the revenue, such officer may also execute a written agreement with the taxpayer to extend the period of limitation. The extension becomes effective upon execution of the agreement by both the taxpayer and such officer.

(ii) The period of limitation on collection after assessment of any tax (including any extension of such period) may be extended after the expiration thereof if there has been a levy on any part of the taxpayer's property prior to such expiration and if the extension is agreed upon in writing prior to a release of the levy under the provisions of 26 U.S.C. 6343. An extension under this paragraph has the same effect as an agreement made prior to the expiration of the period of limitation on collection after assessment, and during the period of the extension collection may be enforced as to all property or rights to property owned by the taxpayer whether or not seized under the levy which was released.

(iii) Any period agreed upon under the provisions of paragraph (a)(1) of this section may be extended by subsequent agreements in writing made before the expiration of the period previously agreed upon.

(3) If a timely proceeding in court for the collection of a tax is commenced, the period during which such tax may be collected by levy shall be extended and shall not expire until the liability for the tax (or a judgment against the taxpayer arising from such liability) is satisfied or becomes unenforceable.

(b) *Date when levy is considered made.* The date on which a levy on property or rights to property is made is the date on which the notice of seizure provided in 26 U.S.C. 6335(a) is given.

(26 U.S.C. 6502)

[T.D. ATF–301, 55 FR 47641, Nov. 14, 1990, as amended by T.D. ATF–450, 66 FR 29028, May 29, 2001]

§ 70.225 Suspension of running of period of limitation; assets of taxpayer in control or custody of court.

Where all or substantially all of the assets of a taxpayer are in the control or custody of the court in any proceeding before any court of the United States, or any State of the United States, or the District of Columbia, the period of limitations on collection after assessment prescribed in 26 U.S.C. 6502 is suspended with respect to the outstanding amount due on the assessment for the period such assets are in the control or custody of the court, and for 6 months thereafter.

(26 U.S.C. 6503)

[T.D. ATF–301, 55 FR 47642, Nov. 14, 1990]

§ 70.226 Suspension of running of period of limitation; taxpayer outside of United States.

The running of the period of limitations on collection after assessment prescribed in 26 U.S.C. 6502 (relating to collection after assessment) is suspended for the period during which the taxpayer is absent from the United States if such period is a continuous period of absence from the United States extending for 6 months or more. In a case where the running of the period of limitations has been suspended under the first sentence of this paragraph and at the time of the taxpayer's return to the United States the period of limitations would expire before the expiration of 6 months from the date of the taxpayer's return, the period of limitations shall not expire until after 6 months from the date of the taxpayer's return. The taxpayer will be deemed to be absent from the United States for purposes of this section if the taxpayer is generally and substantially absent from the United States, even though the taxpayer makes casual temporary visits during the period.

(26 U.S.C. 6503)

[T.D. ATF–301, 55 FR 47642, Nov. 14, 1990]

§70.227 Suspension of running of period of limitation; wrongful seizure of property of third party.

The running of the period of limitations on collection after assessment prescribed in 26 U.S.C. 6502 (relating to collection after assessment) shall be suspended for a period equal to a period beginning on the date property (including money) is wrongfully seized or received by an appropriate TTB officer and ending on the date 30 days after the date on which the appropriate TTB officer returns the property pursuant to 26 U.S.C. 6343(b) (relating to authority to return property) or the date 30 days after the date on which a judgment secured pursuant to 26 U.S.C. 7426 (relating to civil actions by persons other than taxpayers) with respect to such property becomes final. The running of the period of limitations on collection after assessment shall be suspended under this section only with respect to the amount of such assessment which is equal to the amount of money or the value of specific property returned.

(26 U.S.C. 6503)

[T.D. ATF–301, 55 FR 47642, Nov. 14, 1990, as amended by T.D. ATF–450, 66 FR 29028, May 29, 2001]

Limitations on Liens

SOURCE: Sections 70.231 through 70.234 added by T.D. ATF–301, 55 FR 47642, Nov. 14, 1990, unless otherwise noted.

§70.231 Protection for certain interests even though notice filed.

(a) *Securities.* Even though a notice of a lien imposed by 26 U.S.C. 6321 is filed in accordance with §70.148 of this part, the lien is not valid with respect to a security (as defined in §70.143(d) of this part) against:

(1) A purchaser (as defined in §70.143(f) of this part) of the security who at the time of purchase did not have actual notice or knowledge (as defined in §70.144(a) of this part) of the existence of the lien;

(2) A holder of a security interest (as defined in §70.143(a) of this part) in the security who did not have actual notice or knowledge (as defined in §70.144(a) of this part) of the existence of the lien at the time the security interest came into existence or at the time such security interest was acquired from a previous holder for a consideration in money or money's worth (as defined in §70.143(a) of this part); or

(3) A transferee of an interest protected under paragraph (a) (1) or (2) of this section to the same extent the lien is invalid against the transferor to the transferee. For purposes of this paragraph, no person can improve that person's position with respect to the lien by reacquiring the interest from an intervening purchaser or holder of a security interest against whom the lien is invalid.

(b) *Motor vehicles*—(1) *In general.* Even though a notice of a lien imposed by 26 U.S.C. 6321 is filed in accordance with §70.148 of this part, the lien is not valid against a purchaser (as defined in §70.143(f) of this part) of a motor vehicle (as defined in §70.143(c) of this part) if:

(i) At the time of purchase, the purchaser did not have actual notice or knowledge (as defined in §70.144(a) of this part) of the existence of the lien, and

(ii) Before the purchaser obtains such notice or knowledge, the purchaser has acquired actual possession of the motor vehicle and has not thereafter relinquished actual possession to the seller or seller's agent.

(2) *Cross reference.* For provisions relating to additional circumstances in which the lien imposed by 26 U.S.C. 6321 may not be valid against the purchaser of tangible personal property (including a motor vehicle) purchased at retail, see paragraph (c) of this section.

(c) *Personal property purchased at retail*—(1) *In general.* Even though a notice of a lien imposed by 26 U.S.C. 6321 is filed (with respect to any tax imposed under the provisions of 26 U.S.C. enforced and administered by the Bureau) in accordance with § 70.148 of this part, the lien is not valid against a purchaser (as defined in § 70.143(f) of this part) of tangible personal property purchased at a retail sale (as defined in paragraph (c)(2) of this section) unless at the time of purchase the purchaser intends the purchase to (or knows that the purchase will) hinder, evade, or defeat the collection of any tax imposed by the provisions of 26 U.S.C. enforced and administered by the Bureau.

(2) *Definition of retail sale.* For purposes of paragraph (c) of this section, the term "retail sale" means a sale, made in the ordinary course of the seller's trade or business, of tangible personal property of which the seller is the owner. Such term includes a sale in customary retail quantities by a seller who is going out of business, but does not include a bulk sale or an auction sale in which goods are offered in quantities substantially greater than are customary in the ordinary course of the seller's trade or business or an auction sale of goods the owner of which is not in the business of selling such goods.

(d) *Personal property purchased in casual sale*—(1) *In general.* Even though a notice of a lien imposed by 26 U.S.C. 6321 is filed in accordance with § 70.148 of this part, the lien is not valid against a purchaser (as defined in § 70.143(f) of this part) of household goods, personal effects, or other tangible personal property of a type described in § 70.241 of this part (which includes wearing apparel, school books, fuel, provisions, furniture, arms for personal use, livestock, and poultry (whether or not the seller is the head of a family); and books and tools of a trade, business, or profession (whether or not the trade, business, or profession of the seller)), purchased, other than for resale, in a casual sale for less than $250 (excluding interest and expenses described in § 70.147 of this part). For purposes of this paragraph, a casual sale is a sale not made in the ordinary course of the seller's trade or business.

(2) *Limitation.* This paragraph applies only if the purchaser does not have actual notice or knowledge (as defined in § 70.144(a) of this part):

(i) Of the existence of the tax lien, or

(ii) That the sale is one of a series of sales.

For purposes of paragraph (d)(2)(ii) of this section, a sale is one of a series of sales if the seller plans to dispose of, in separate transactions, substantially all of the seller's household goods, personal effects, and other tangible personal property described in § 70.241 of this part.

(e) *Personal property subject to possessory liens.* Even though a notice of a lien imposed by 26 U.S.C. 6321 is filed in accordance with § 70.148 of this part, the lien is not valid against a holder of a lien on tangible personal property which under local law secures the reasonable price of the repair or improvement of the property if the property is, and has been, continuously in the possession of the holder of the lien from the time the possessory lien arose. For example, if local law gives an automobile mechanic the right to retain possession of an automobile the mechanic has repaired as security for payment of the repair bill and the mechanic retains continuous possession of the automobile until such lien is satisfied, a tax lien filed in accordance with 26 U.S.C 6323(f)(1) which has attached to the automobile will not be valid to the extent of the reasonable price of the repairs. It is immaterial that the notice of tax lien was filed before the mechanic undertook the work or that the mechanic knew of the lien before undertaking the work.

(f) *Real property tax and special assessment liens.* Even though a notice of a lien imposed by 26 U.S.C. 6321 is filed in accordance with § 70.148 of this part, the lien is not valid against the holder of another lien upon the real property (regardless of when such other lien arises), if such other lien is entitled under local law to priority over security interests in real property which are prior in time and if such other lien on real property secures payment of:

(1) A tax of general application levied by any taxing authority based upon the value of the property, or

(2) A special assessment imposed directly upon the property by any taxing authority, if the assessment is imposed for the purpose of defraying the cost of any public improvement; or

(3) Charges for utilities or public services furnished to the property by the United States, a State or political subdivision thereof, or an instrumentality of any one or more of the foregoing.

(g) *Residential property subject to a mechanic's lien for certain repairs and improvements.* Even though a notice of lien imposed by 26 U.S.C. 6321 is filed in accordance with § 70.148 of this part, the lien is not valid against a mechanic's lienor (as defined in § 70.143(b) of this part) who holds a lien for the repair or improvement of a personal residence if:

(1) The residence is occupied by the owner and contains no more than four dwelling units, and

(2) The contract price on the prime contract with the owner for the repair or improvement (excluding interest and expenses described in § 70.147 of this part) is not more than $1,000. For purposes of this paragraph, the amounts of subcontracts under the prime contract with the owner are not to be taken into consideration for purposes of computing the $1,000 prime contract price. It is immaterial that the notice of tax lien was filed before the contractor undertakes the work or that the contractor knew of the lien before undertaking the work.

(h) *Attorney's liens*—(1) *In general.* Even though notice of a lien imposed by 26 U.S.C. 6321 is filed in accordance with § 70.148 of this part, the lien is not valid against an attorney who, under local law, holds a lien upon, or a contract enforceable against, a judgment or other amount in settlement of a claim or of a cause of action. The priority afforded an attorney's lien under this paragraph shall not exceed the amount of the attorney's reasonable compensation for obtaining the judgment or procuring the settlement. For purposes of this paragraph, reasonable compensation means the amount customarily allowed under local law for an attorney's service for litigating or settling a similar case or administrative claim. However, reasonable compensation shall be determined on the basis of the facts and circumstances of each individual case. It is immaterial that the notice of tax lien is filed before the attorney undertakes the work or that the attorney knows of the tax lien before undertaking the work. This paragraph does not apply to an attorney's lien which may arise from the defense of a claim or cause of action against a taxpayer except to the extent such lien is held upon a judgment or other amount arising from the adjudication or settlement of a counterclaim in favor of the taxpayer. In case of suits against the taxpayer, see § 70.150(d)(2) of this part for rules relating to the subordination of the tax lien to facilitate tax collection.

(2) *Claim or cause of action against the United States.* Paragraph (h)(1) of this section does not apply to an attorney's lien with respect to:

(i) Any judgment or other fund resulting from the successful litigation or settlement of an administrative claim or cause of action against the United States to the extent that the United States, under any legal or equitable right, offsets its liability under the judgment or settlement against any liability of the taxpayer to the United States, or

(ii) Any amount credited against any liability of the taxpayer in accordance with 26 U.S.C. 6402.

(i) *Certain insurance contracts.* Even though a notice of a lien imposed by 26 U.S.C. 6321 (with respect to any tax imposed under the provisions of 26 U.S.C. enforced and administered by the Bureau) is filed in accordance with § 70.148 of this part, the lien is not valid with respect to a life insurance, endowment, or annuity contract, against an organization which is the insurer under the contract, at any time:

(1) Before the insuring organization has actual notice or knowledge (as defined in § 70.144(a) of this part) of the existence of the tax lien.

(2) After the insuring organization has actual notice or knowledge of the lien (as defined in § 70.144(a) of this part) with respect to advances (including contractual interest thereon as provided in § 70.147(a) of this part) required to be made automatically to maintain the contract in force under an agreement entered into before the insuring organization had such actual notice or knowledge, or

(3) After the satisfaction of a levy pursuant to 26 U.S.C. 6332(b), unless and until the appropriate TTB officer delivers to the insuring organization a notice (for example, another notice of levy, a letter, *etc.*), executed after the date of such satisfaction, that the lien exists.

Delivery of the notice described in paragraph (i)(3) of this section may be made by any means, including regular mail, and delivery of the notice shall be effective only from the time of actual receipt of the notification by the insuring organization. The provisions of this paragraph are applicable to matured as well as unmatured insurance contracts.

(j) *Passbook loans*—(1) *In general.* Even though a notice of a lien imposed by 26 U.S.C. 6321 is filed in accordance with § 70.148 of this part, the lien is not valid against an institution described in 26 U.S.C. 581 or 591 to the extent of any loan made by the institution which is secured by a savings deposit, share, or other account evidenced by a passbook (as defined in paragraph (j)(2) of this section) if the institution has been continuously in possession of the passbook from the time the loan is made. This paragraph applies only to a loan made without actual notice or knowledge (as defined in § 70.144(a) of this part) of the existence of the lien. Even though an original passbook loan is made without actual notice or knowledge of the existence of the lien, this paragraph does not apply to any additional loan made after knowledge of the lien is acquired by the institution even if it continues to retain the passbook from the time the original passbook loan is made.

(2) *Definition of passbook.* For purposes of paragraph (j) of this section, the term "passbook" includes:

(i) Any tangible evidence of a savings deposit, share, or other account which, when in the possession of the bank or other savings institution, will prevent a withdrawal from the account to the extent of the loan balance, and

(ii) Any procedure or system, such as an automatic data processing system, the use of which by the bank or other savings institution will prevent a withdrawal from the account to the extent of the loan balance.

(26 U.S.C. 6323)

§ 70.232 Protection for commercial transactions financing agreements.

(a) *In general.* Even though a notice of a lien imposed by 26 U.S.C. 6321 is filed in accordance with § 70.148 of this part, the lien is not valid with respect to a security interest which:

(1) Comes into existence after the tax lien filing.

(2) Is in qualified property covered by the terms of a commercial transactions financing agreement entered into before the tax lien filing, and

(3) Is protected under local law against a judgment lien arising, as of the time of the tax lien filing, out of an unsecured obligation.

See § 70.143 (a) and (e) of this part for definitions of the terms "security interest" and "tax lien filing," respectively. For purposes of this section, a judgment lien is a lien held by a judgment lien creditor as defined in § 70.143(g) of this part.

(b) *Commercial transactions financing agreement.* For purposes of this section, the term "commercial transactions financing agreement" means a written agreement entered into by a person in the course of such person's trade or business:

(1) To make loans to the taxpayer (whether or not at the option of the person agreeing to make such loans) to be secured by commercial financing security acquired by the taxpayer in the ordinary course of the taxpayer's trade or business, or

(2) To purchase commercial financing security, other than inventory, acquired by the taxpayer in the ordinary

course of the taxpayer's trade or business.

Such an agreement qualifies as a commercial transactions financing agreement only with respect to loans or purchases made under the agreement before the 46th day after the date of tax lien filing or the time when the lender or purchaser has actual notice or knowledge (as defined in § 70.144(a) of this part) of the tax lien filing, if earlier. For purposes of this paragraph, a loan or purchase is considered to have been made in the course of the lender's or purchaser's trade or business if such person is in the business of financing commercial transactions (such as a bank or commercial factor) or if the agreement is incidental to the conduct of such person's trade or business. For example, if a manufacturer finances the accounts receivable of one of its customers, the manufacturer is considered to engage in such financing in the course of its trade or business. The extent of the priority of the lender or purchaser over the tax lien is the amount of the disbursement made before the 46th day after the date the notice of tax lien is filed, or made before the day (before such 46th day) on which the lender or purchaser has actual notice or knowledge of the filing of the notice of the tax lien.

(c) *Commercial financing security*—(1) *In general.* The term "commercial financing security" means:

(i) Paper of a kind ordinarily arising in commercial transactions,

(ii) Accounts receivable (as defined in paragraph (c)(2) of this section),

(iii) Mortgages on real property, and

(iv) Inventory.

For purposes of this subparagraph, the term "paper of a kind ordinarily arising in commercial transactions" in general includes any written document customarily used in commercial transactions. For example, such written documents include paper giving contract rights (as defined in paragraph (c)(2) of this section), chattel paper, documents of title to personal property, and negotiable instruments or securities. The term "commercial financing security" does not include general intangibles such as patents or copyrights. A mortgage on real estate (including a deed of trust, contract for sale, and similar instrument) may be commercial financing security if the taxpayer has an interest in the mortgage as a mortgagee or assignee. The term "commercial financing security" does not include a mortgage when the taxpayer is the mortgagor of realty owned by the taxpayer. For purposes of this subparagraph, the term "inventory" includes raw materials and goods in process as well as property held by the taxpayer primarily for sale to customers in the ordinary course of the taxpayer's trade or business.

(2) *Definitions.* For purposes of §§ 70.143 and 70.146 of this part, and this section:

(i) A contract right is any right to payment under a contract not yet earned by performance and not evidenced by an instrument or chattel paper, and

(ii) An account receivable is any right to payment for goods sold or leased or for services rendered which is not evidenced by an instrument or chattel paper.

(d) *Qualified property.* For purposes of paragraph (a) of this section, qualified property consists solely of commercial financing security acquired by the taxpayer-debtor before the 46th day after the date of tax lien filing. Commercial financing security acquired before such day may be qualified property even though it is acquired by the taxpayer after the lender received actual notice or knowledge of the filing of the tax lien. For example, although the receipt of actual notice or knowledge of the filing of the notice of the tax lien has the effect of ending the period within which protected disbursements may be made to the taxpayer, property which is acquired by the taxpayer after the lender receives actual notice or knowledge of such filing and before such 46th day, which otherwise qualifies as commercial financing security, becomes commercial financing security to which the priority of the lender extends for loans made before the lender received the actual notice or knowledge. An account receivable (as defined in paragraph (c)(2)(ii) of this section) is acquired by a taxpayer at the time, and to the extent, a right to payment is earned by performance. Chattel paper, documents of title, negotiable instruments, securities, and mortgages on real estate are acquired by a taxpayer when the taxpayer obtains rights in the paper or mortgage. Inventory is acquired by the taxpayer when title passes to the taxpayer. A contract right (as defined in paragraph (c)(2)(i) of this section) is acquired by a taxpayer when the contract is made. Indentifiable proceeds, which arise from the collection or disposition of qualified property by the taxpayer, are considered to be acquired at the time such qualified property is acquired if the secured party has a continuously perfected security interest in the proceeds under local law. The term "proceeds" includes whatever is received when collateral is sold, exchanged, or collected. For purposes of this paragraph, the term "identifiable proceeds" does not include money, checks and the like which have been commingled with other cash proceeds. Property acquired by the taxpayer after the 45th day following tax lien filing, by the expenditure of proceeds, is not qualified property.

(e) *Purchaser treated as acquiring security interest.* A person who purchases commercial financing security, other than inventory, pursuant to a commercial transactions financing agreement is treated, for purposes of this section, as having acquired a security interest in the commercial financing security. In the case of a bona fide purchase at a discount, a purchaser of commercial financing security who satisfies the requirements of this section has priority over the tax lien to the full extent of the security.

(26 U.S.C. 6323)

§ 70.233 Protection for real property construction or improvement financing agreements.

(a) *In general.* Even though a notice of a lien imposed by 26 U.S.C. 6321 is filed in accordance with § 70.148 of this part, the lien is not valid with respect to a security interest which:

(1) Comes into existence after the tax lien filing,

(2) Is on qualified property covered by the terms of a real property construction or improvement financing agreement entered into before the tax lien filing, and

(3) Is protected under local law against a judgment lien arising, as of the time of tax lien filing, out of an unsecured obligation.

For purposes of this section, it is immaterial that the holder of the security interest had actual notice or knowledge of the lien at the time disbursements are made pursuant to such an agreement. See § 70.143 (a) and (e) of this part for general definitions of the terms "security interest" and "tax lien filing." For purposes of this section, a judgment lien is a lien held by a judgment lien creditor as defined in § 70.143(g) of this part.

(b) *Real property construction or improvement financing agreement.* For purposes of this section, the term "real property construction or improvement financing agreement" means any written agreement to make cash disbursements (whether or not at the option of the party agreeing to make such disbursements):

(1) To finance the construction, improvement, or demolition of real property if the agreement provides for a security interest in the real property with respect to which the construction, improvement, or demolition has been or is to be made;

(2) To finance a contract to construct or improve, or demolish real property if the agreement provides for a security interest in the proceeds of the contract; or

(3) To finance the raising or harvesting of a farm crop or the raising of livestock or other animals if the agreement provides for a security interest in any property subject to the lien imposed by 26 U.S.C. 6321 at the time of tax lien filing, in the crop raised or harvested, or in the livestock or other animals raised.

For purposes of paragraphs (b) (1) and (2) of this section, construction or improvement may include demolition. For purposes of any agreement described in paragraph (b)(3) of this section, the furnishing of goods and services is treated as the disbursement of cash.

(c) *Qualified property.* For purposes of this section, the term "qualified property" includes only:

(1) In the case of an agreement described in paragraph (b)(1) of this section, the real property with respect to which the construction or improvement has been or is to be made;

(2) In the case of an agreement described in paragraph (b)(2) of this section, the proceeds of the contract to construct or improve real property; or

(3) In the case of an agreement described in paragraph (b)(3) of this section, property subject to the lien imposed by 26 U.S.C. 6321 at the time of tax lien filing, the farm crop raised or harvested, or the livestock or other animals raised.

(26 U.S.C. 6323)

§ 70.234 Protection for obligatory disbursement agreements.

(a) *In general.* Even though a notice of a lien imposed by 26 U.S.C. 6321 is filed in accordance with § 70.148 of this part, the lien is not valid with respect to security interest which:

(1) Comes into existence after the tax lien filing,

(2) Is in qualified property covered by the terms of an obligatory disbursement agreement entered into before the tax lien filing, and

(3) Is protected under local law against a judgment lien arising, as of the time of tax lien filing, out of an unsecured obligation.

See § 70.143 (a) and (e) of this part for definitions of the terms "security interest" and "tax lien filing." For purposes of this section, a judgment lien creditor as defined in § 70.143(g) of this part.

(b) *Obligatory disbursement agreement.* For purposes of this section, the term "obligatory disbursement agreement" means a written agreement, entered into by a person in the course of the person's trade or business, to make disbursements. An agreement is treated as an obligatory disbursement agreement only with respect to disbursements which are required to be made by reason of the intervention of the rights of a person other than the taxpayer. The obligation to pay must be conditioned upon an event beyond the control of the obligor. For example, the provisions of this section are applicable where an issuing bank obligates itself to honor drafts or other demands for payment on a letter of credit and a bank, in good faith, relies upon that letter of credit in making advances. The provisions of this section are also applicable, for example, where a bonding company obligates itself to make payments to indemnify against loss or liability and, under the terms of the bond, makes a payment with respect to a loss. The priority described in this section is not applicable, for example, in the case of an accommodation endorsement by an endorser who assumes the obligation other than in the course of the endorser's trade or business.

(c) *Qualified property.* Except as provided under paragraph (d) of this section, the term "qualified property," for purposes of this section, means property subject to the lien imposed by 26 U.S.C. 6321 at the time of tax lien filing and, to the extent that the acquisition is directly traceable to the obligatory disbursement, property acquired by the taxpayer after tax lien filing.

(d) *Special rule for surety agreements.* Where the obligatory disbursement agreement is an agreement insuring the performance of a contract of the taxpayer and another person, the term "qualified property" shall be treated as also including:

(1) The proceeds of the contract the performance of which was insured, and

(2) If the contract the performance of which was insured is a contract to construct or improve real property, to produce goods, or to furnish services, any tangible personal property used by the taxpayer in the performance of the insured contract.

For example, a surety company which holds a security interest, arising from cash disbursements made after tax lien filing under a payment or performance bond on a real estate construction project, has priority over the tax lien with respect to the proceeds of the construction contract and, in addition, with respect to any tangible personal property used by the taxpayer in the construction project if its security interest in the tangible personal property is protected under local law against a judgment lien arising, as of the time the tax lien was filed, out of an unsecured obligation.

(26 U.S.C. 6323)

Limitations on Levies

SOURCE: Sections 70.241 through 70.245 added by T.D. ATF–301, 55 FR 47646, Nov. 14, 1990, unless otherwise noted.

§ 70.241 Property exempt from levy.

(a) *Enumeration.* There shall be exempt from levy:

(1) *Wearing apparel and school books.* Such items of wearing apparel and such school books as are necessary for the taxpayer or for members of the taxpayer's family. Expensive items of wearing apparel, such as furs, which are luxuries and are not necessary for the taxpayer or for members of the taxpayer's family, are not exempt from levy.

(2) *Fuel, provisions, furniture, and personal effects.* If the taxpayer is the head of a family, so much of the fuel, provisions, furniture, and personal effects in the taxpayer's household, and of the arms for personal use, livestock, and poultry of the taxpayer, as does not exceed $1,650 in value. For purposes of this provision, an individual who is the only remaining member of a family and who lives alone is not the head of a family.

(3) *Books and tools of a trade, business or profession.* So many of the books and tools necessary for the trade, business, or profession of an individual taxpayer as do not exceed in the aggregate $1,100 in value.

(4) *Unemployment benefits.* Any amount payable to an individual with respect to that individual's unemployment (including any portion thereof payable with respect to dependents) under an unemployment compensation law of the United States, of any State, or of the District of Columbia or of the Commonwealth of Puerto Rico.

(5) *Undelivered mail.* Mail, addressed to any person, which has not been delivered to the addressee.

(6) *Certain annuity and pension payments.* Annuity or pension payments under the Railroad Retirement Act (45 U.S.C. chapter 9), benefits under the Railroad Unemployment Insurance Act (45 U.S.C. chapter 11), special pension payments received by a person whose name has been entered on the Army, Navy, Air Force, and Coast Guard Medal of Honor roll (38 U.S.C. 562), and annuities based on retired or retainer pay under 10 U.S.C. chapter 73.

(7) *Workmen's compensation.* Any amount payable to an individual as workmen's compensation (including any portion thereof payable with respect to dependents) under a workmen's compensation law of the United States, any State, the District of Columbia, or the Commonwealth of Puerto Rico.

(8) *Judgments for support of minor children.* If the taxpayer is required under any type of order or decree (including an interlocutory decree or a decree of support pendente lite) of a court of competent jurisdiction, entered prior to the day of levy, to contribute to the support of such taxpayer's minor children, so much of the taxpayer's salary, wages, or other income as is necessary to comply with such order or decree. The taxpayer must establish the amount necessary to comply with the order or decree. The appropriate TTB officer is not required to release a levy until such time as that officer is satisfied that the amount to be released from levy will actually be applied in satisfaction of the support obligation. The appropriate TTB officer may make arrangements with a delinquent taxpayer to establish a specific amount of such taxpayer's salary, wage, or other income for each pay period which shall be exempt from levy. Any request for such an arrangement shall be directed to the appropriate TTB officer. Where the taxpayer has more than one source of income sufficient to satisfy the support obligation imposed by the order or decree, the amount exempt from levy may at the discretion of the appropriate TTB officer be allocated entirely to one salary, wage, or source of other income or be apportioned between the several salaries, wages, or other sources of income.

(9) *Minimum exemption for wages, salary, and other income.* Amounts payable to or received by the taxpayer as wages or salary for personal services, or as other income, to the extent provided in §§ 70.242 through 70.245 of this part.

(10) *Certain service-connected disability payments.* Any amount payable to an individual as a service-connected (within the meaning of 38 U.S.C. 101(16)) disability benefit under:

(i) 38 U.S.C. chapter 11, subchapter II, III, IV, V, or VI, or

(ii) 38 U.S.C. chapter 13, 21, 23, 31, 32, 34, 35, 37, or 39 shall be exempt from levy.

(11) *Certain public assistance payments.* Any amount payable to an individual as a recipient of public assistance under:

(i) Title 42 U.S.C. subchapter IV (relating to aid to families with dependent children) or 42 U.S.C. subchapter XVI (relating to supplemental security income for the aged, blind, and disabled), or

(ii) State or local government public assistance or public welfare programs for which eligibility is determined by a needs or income test shall be exempt from levy.

(12) *Assistance under job training partnership act.* Any amount payable to a participant under the Job Training Partnership Act (29 U.S.C. 1501 *et seq.*) from funds appropriated pursuant to such Act shall be exempt from levy.

(13) *Principal residence exempt in absence of certain approval or jeopardy.* Except to the extent provided in § 70.166 of this part, the principal residence of the taxpayer (within the meaning of 26 U.S.C. 1034) is exempt from levy.

(b) *Appraisal.* The TTB officer seizing property of the type described in 26 U.S.C. 6334(a) shall appraise and set aside to the owner the amount of such property declared to be exempt. If the taxpayer objects at the time of the seizure to the valuation fixed by the officer making the seizure, such officer shall summon three disinterested individuals who shall make the valuation.

(c) *Other property.* No other property or rights to property are exempt from levy except the property specifically exempted by 26 U.S.C. 6334(a). No provisions of a State law may exempt property or rights to property from levy for the collection of any Federal tax. Thus, property exempt from execution under State personal or homestead exemption laws is, nevertheless, subject to levy by the United States for collection of its taxes.

(26 U.S.C. 6334)

§ 70.242 Wages, salary and other income.

(a) *In general.* Under 26 U.S.C. 6334(a)(9) and (d) certain amounts payable to or received by a taxpayer as wages, salary or other income are exempt from levy. This section described the income of a taxpayer that is eligible for the exemption from levy (paragraph (b) of this section) and how exempt amounts are to be paid to the taxpayer (paragraph (c) of this section). Section 70.243 of this part describes the sum which will be exempt from levy for each of the taxpayer's payroll periods. Payroll periods are described in § 70.244 of this part. Amounts exempt from levy are determined in part by the number of persons claimed by the taxpayer as dependents. Section 70.245 of this part describes the manner in which the taxpayer is to claim any dependent exemptions and the manner in which the employer is to compute the exempt amount and pay the balance to the appropriate TTB officer.

(b) *Eligible taxpayer income.* Only wages, salary or other income payable to the taxpayer after the levy is made on the payor may be exempt from levy under 26 U.S.C. 6334 (a)(9). No amount of wages, salary or other income which is paid to the taxpayer before levy is made on the payor will be so exempt from levy.

(c) *Payment of exempt amounts to taxpayer*—(1) *From wages, salary or other income not subject to levy.* In the case of a taxpayer who has more than one source of wages, salary or other income, the appropriate TTB officer may elect to levy on only one or more such source while leaving other sources of salary or other income free from levy. If those wages, salary or other income which the appropriate TTB officer leaves free from levy equal or exceed the amount to which the taxpayer is entitled as an exemption from levy under 26 U.S.C. 6334(a)(9) and (d) and § 70.243 of this part (and ar not otherwise exempt), then no amount of the taxpayer's wages, salary or other income on which the appropriate TTB officer elects to levy is exempt from levy. The appropriate TTB officer shall notify the employer or other person subject to levy that no amount of the taxpayer's wages, salary or other income is exempt from levy.

(2) *From wages, salary or other income subject to levy.* If the taxpayer's income upon which the appropriate TTB officer does not levy is less than that amount to which the taxpayer is entitled as an exemption, then an amount determined pursuant to § 70.243 of this part is to be paid to the taxpayer from those wages, salary or other income which are subject to levy. The appropriate TTB officer will designate those wages, salary or other income subject to levy from which such amount will be paid to the taxpayer. The appropriate TTB officer will generally make this designation by delivering to the employer, or other person levied upon, the form upon which the taxpayer is to claim any dependent exemption. The form will acompany the notice of levy. The person receiving the form from the appropriate TTB officer must promptly deliver it to the taxpayer. In the case of some employers having a large number of employees, however, the appropriate TTB officer will send the form upon which an employee is to claim any dependent exemption diretly to the employee. In such a case, the notice of levy will indicate that the form for claiming dependent exemptions has been sent to the taxpayer. If a notice of levy is not accompanied by the form for claiming dependent exemptions and does not indicate that the form was sent directly to the taxpayer, then the person levied upon must make payment to the appropriate TTB officer without regard to amounts prescribed by § 70.243 of this part as exempt from levy. If a notice of levy is accompanied by the form for claiming dependent exemptions or indicates that the form was sent directly to the taxpayer, then the person levied upon is to pay over to the taxpayer, amounts determined to be exempt from levy pursuant to § 70.243 and § 70.245 (b) and (c) of this part (relating to the requirement that the taxpayer submit a claim for any dependent exemption). Amounts not exempt from levy are to be paid to the appropriate TTB officer in accordance with the terms of the levy.

(26 U.S.C. 6334)

§ 70.243 Exempt amount.

Amount payable to the taxpayer as wages, salary, or other income for each payroll period described in § 70.244 of this part are exempt from levy as follows:

(a) If the payroll period is weekly, an amount equal to:

(1) The sum of:

(i) The standard deduction, and

(ii) The aggregate amount of the deductions for personal exemption allowed the taxpayer under 26 U.S.C. 151 in the taxable year in which such levy occurs, divided by

(2) 52.

(b) If the payroll period is not weekly, the amount exempt from levy shall be an amount which as nearly as possible will result in the same total exemption from levy for such individual over a period of time as such individual would have under paragraph (a) of this section if (during such period of time) the individual were paid or received such wages, salary or other income on a regular weekly basis.

(26 U.S.C. 6334)

§ 70.244 Payroll period.

For purpose of determining the amount of wages, salary or other income exempt from levy under 26 U.S.C. 6334(a)(9):

(a) *Regularly used calendar periods.* In the case of wages, salary or other income paid to the taxpayer on the basis of an established calendar period regularly used by the employer or other person levied upon for payroll or payment purpose (e.g., daily, weekly, biweekly, semimonthly, or monthly), that period is the taxpayer's payroll period.

(b) *Amounts paid on recurrent but irregular basis.* In the case of wages, salary, or other income paid to the taxpayer on a recurrent but irregular basis, the first day of the taxpayer's payroll period is that day following the day upon which the wages, salary, or other income were last paid to the taxpayer. The last day of the payroll period is that day upon which the current payment becomes payable to him or her. However, in any case in which:

(1) Amounts are paid to the taxpayer on a recurrent but irregular basis, and

(2) the last payment was paid to the taxpayer more than 60 days before the current payment becomes payable, the current payment will be deemed a one-

time payment (*see* paragraph (c) of this section).

(c) *Nonrecurrent payments.* In the case of wages, salary or other income paid to the taxpayer on a one-time basis, the taxpayer's payroll period is deemed to be weekly (*i.e.*, the 1-week period ending on the day of payment).

(26 U.S.C. 6334)

§70.245 Computation of exempt amount and payment of amounts not exempt from levy to the appropriate TTB officer.

(a) *General.* Unless advised by the appropriate TTB officer that no part of the money due to the taxpayer is exempt from levy, the employer or other person levied upon will compute the exempt amount, using the formula in §70.243 of this part and the taxpayer's statement of exemptions and filing status described in paragraph (b) of this section.

(b) *Statement of exemptions and filing status.* Unless the taxpayer submits a statement of exemptions and filing status to the employer or other person levied upon, the exempt amount will be applied as if the taxpayer were a married individual filing a separate return with only 1 personal exemption. A statement of exemptions and filing status shall be made by either:

(1) Completion of the form provided for this purpose by the Bureau, or

(2) A written statement that:

(i) Gives the taxpayer's filing status for income tax purposes,

(ii) Shows any additional standard deduction if the taxpayer or the taxpayer's spouse is at least 65 and/or blind,

(iii) Identified by name and by relationship to the taxpayer each person for whom a dependent exemption is claimed,

(iv) Is signed by the taxpayer, and

(v) Contains a declaration that it is made under the penalties of perjury.

(c) *Time for submission of statement.* The taxpayer must submit the statement of exemptions and filing status to the employer or other person levied upon no later than the later of:

(1) The third day before the last day of the payroll period for which the exemption is claimed (that is, the third day before payday), or

(2) If the appropriate TTB officer delivers the forms for the statement of exemption and filing status to the employer or other person levied upon (see §70.242(c)(2) of this part), the second day after the date the taxpayer receives the form.

For purposes of paragraphs (c) (1) and (2) of this section, the term "day" does not include Saturdays, Sunday or a legal holiday within the meaning of 26 U.S.C. 7503. Failure on the part of the taxpayer to submit a timely statement of exemptions and filing status will result in the computation of the exempt amount as if the taxpayer were a married individual filing a separate return with only 1 personal exemption for the applicable pay period, except that the employer or other person levied upon may accept a statement of exemptions and filing status not timely submitted in accordance with this paragraph, and may prepare a disbursement to the taxpayer based upon the information properly verified therein, if payment to the appropriate TTB officer in accordance with the levy is not thereby delayed.

(d) *Payment of amounts not exempt form levy to the appropriate TTB officer*—(1) *In General.* Wages, Salary, or other income the subject of a levy are payable to the appropriate TTB officer on the date the payor is otherwise obligated to pay the taxpayer (*see* §70.242(c) of this part).

(2) *Delayed payment in certain cases.* If, however, as described in paragraph (c)(2) of this section, the taxpayer may submit a statement of exemptions and filing status after the third day before payday, amounts payable to the taxpayer on that payday, to the extent not exempt from levy, are payable to the appropriate TTB officer on the third day following the date on which the taxpayer may timely submit the statement of exemptions and filing status under paragraph (c)(2) of this section. For purposes of this rule, the term "day" does not include Saturday, Sunday or a legal holiday within the meaning of 26 U.S.C. 7503.

(26 U.S.C. 6334)

Periods of Limitation in Judicial Proceedings

§ 70.251 Periods of limitation on suits by taxpayers.

(a) No suit or proceeding under section 7422(a) of the Internal Revenue Code for the recovery of any internal revenue tax, penalty, or other sum shall be begun until whichever of the following first occurs:

(1) The expiration of 6 months from the date of the filing of the claim for credit or refund, or

(2) A decision is rendered on such claim prior to the expiration of 6 months after the filing thereof. Except as provided in paragraph (b) of this section, no suit or proceeding for the recovery of any tax, penalty, or other sum imposed under the provision of 26 U.S.C. enforced and administered by the Bureau may be brought after the expiration of 2 years from the date of mailing, by either registered or certified mail, by an appropriate TTB officer, to a taxpayer of a statutory notice of disallowance of the part of the claim to which the suit or proceeding relates.

(b) The 2-year period described in paragraph (a) of this section may be extended if an agreement to extend the running of the period of limitations is executed. The agreement must be signed by the taxpayer or by an attorney, agent, trustee, or other fiduciary on behalf of the taxpayer. If the agreement is signed by a person other than the taxpayer, it shall be accompanied by an authenticated copy of the power of attorney or other legal evidence of the authority of such person to act on behalf of the taxpayer. If the taxpayer is a corporation, the agreement should be signed with the corporate name followed by the signature of a duly authorized officer of the corporation. The agreement will not be effective until signed by an appropriate officer.

(c) The taxpayer may sign a waiver of the requirement that the taxpayer be mailed a notice of disallowance. Such waiver is irrevocable and will commence the running of the 2-year period described in paragraph (a) of this section on the date the waiver is filed. The waiver shall set forth:

(1) The type of tax and the taxable period covered by the taxpayer's claim for refund;

(2) The amount of the claim;

(3) The amount of the claim disallowed;

(4) A statement that the taxpayer agrees the filing of the waiver will commence the running of the 2-year period provided for in section 6532(a)(1) as if a notice of disallowance had been sent the taxpayer by either registered or certified mail.

The filing of such a waiver prior to the expiration of 6 monthes from the date the claim was filed does not permit the filing of a suit for refund prior to the time specified in section 6532(a)(1) and paragraph (a) of this section.

(d) Any consideration, reconsideration, or other action with respect to a claim after the mailing, by either registered or certified mail, of a notice of disallowance or after the execution of a waiver referred to in paragraph (c) of this section, shall not extend the period for bringing suit or other proceeding under section 7422(a) of the Internal Revenue Code.

(26 U.S.C. 6532)

[T.D. ATF–251, 52 FR 19314, May 22, 1987. Redesignated and amended by T.D. ATF–301, 55 FR 47606, 47648, Nov. 14, 1990]

§ 70.252 Periods of limitation on suits by the United States.

The United States may not recover any erroneous refund by civil action under section 7405 of the Internal Revenue Code unless such action is begun within 2 years after the making of such refund. However, if any part of the refund was induced by fraud or misrepresentation of a material fact, the action to recover the erroneous refund may be brought at any time within 5 years from the date the refund was made.

(26 U.S.C. 6532)

[T.D. ATF–251, 52 FR 19314, May 22, 1987. Redesignated by T.D. ATF–301, 55 FR 47606, Nov. 14, 1990]

§ 70.253 Periods of limitation on suits by persons other than taxpayers.

(a) *General rule.* No suit or proceeding, except as otherwise provided in 26 U.S.C. 6532(c)(2) and paragraph (b) of this section, under 26 U.S.C. 7426 and

§ 70.207 of this part relating to civil actions by persons other than taxpayers, shall be begun after the expiration of 9 months from the date of levy or agreement under 26 U.S.C. 6325(b)(3) giving rise to such action.

(b) *Period when claim is filed.* The 9-month period described in 26 U.S.C. 6532(c)(1) and paragraph (a) of this section shall be extended to the shorter of

(1) 12 months from the date of filing by a third party of a written request under § 70.167(b)(2) of this part for the return of property wrongfully levied upon, or

(2) 6 months from the date of mailing by registered or certified mail by the appropriate TTB officer to the party claimant of a notice of disallowance of the part of the request to which the action relates. A request which, under § 70.167(b)(3) of this part, is not considered adequate does not extend the 9-month period described in paragraph (a) of this section.

(26 U.S.C. 6532)

[T.D. ATF-301, 55 FR 47648, Nov. 14, 1990, as amended by T.D. ATF-450, 66 FR 29028, May 29, 2001]

Limitations on Credit or Refund

§ 70.261 Period of limitation on filing claim.

(a) In the case of any tax (other than a tax payable by stamp):

(1) If a return is filed, a claim for credit or refund of an overpayment must be filed by the taxpayer within 3 years from the time the return was filed or within 2 years from the time the tax was paid, whichever of such periods expires the later.

(2) If no return is filed, the claim for credit or refund of an overpayment must be filed by the taxpayer within 2 years from the time the tax was paid.

(b) In the case of any tax payable by means of a stamp, a claim for credit or refund of an overpayment of such tax must be filed by the taxpayer within 3 years from the time the tax was paid. For provisions relating to redemption of unused stamps, see section 6805 of the Internal Revenue Code.

(c) For limitations on allowance of credit or refund, special rules, and exceptions, see subsections (b) and (c) of section 6511 of the Internal Revenue Code. For rules as to time return is deemed filed and tax considered paid, see section 6513 of the Internal Revenue Code.

(26 U.S.C. 6511)

[T.D. ATF-251, 52 FR 19314, May 22, 1987. Redesignated by T.D. ATF-301, 55 FR 47606, Nov. 14, 1990]

§ 70.262 Limitations on allowance of credits and refunds.

(a) *Effect of filing claim.* Unless a claim for credit or refund of an overpayment is filed within the period of limitation prescribed in section 6511(a), no credit or refund shall be allowed or made after the expiration of such period.

(b) *Limit on amount to be credited or refunded.* In the case of any tax (other than a tax payable by stamp):

(1) If a return was filed, and a claim is filed within 3 years from the time the return was filed, the amount of the credit or refund shall not exceed the portion of the tax paid within the period, immediately preceding the filing of the claim, equal to 3 years plus the period of any extension of time for filing the return.

(2) If a return was filed, and a claim is filed after the 3 year period described in paragraph (b)(1) of this section, but within 2 years from the time the tax was paid, the amount of the credit or refund shall not exceed the portion of the tax paid within the 2 years immediately preceding the filing of the claim.

(3) If no return was filed, but a claim is filed, the amount of the credit or refund shall not exceed the portion of the tax paid within the 2 years immediately preceding the filing of the claim.

(4) If no claim is filed, the amount of the credit or refund allowed or made shall not exceed the amount that would have been allowable under the preceding subparagraphs if a claim had been filed on the date the credit or refund is allowed.

(c) *In the case of a tax payable by stamp.* (1) If a claim is filed, the amount of the credit or refund shall not exceed the portion of the tax paid within the 3 years immediately preceding the filing of the claim.

(2) If no claim is filed, the amount of the credit or refund allowed or made shall not exceed the portion of the tax paid within the 3 years immediately preceding the allowance of the credit or refund. For provisions relating to redemption of unused stamps, see section 6805 of the Internal Revenue Code.

(26 U.S.C. 6511)

[T.D. ATF–251, 52 FR 19314, May 22, 1987. Redesignated and amended by T.D. ATF–301, 55 FR 47606, 47648, Nov. 14, 1990; T.D. ATF–450, 66 FR 29028, May 29, 2001]

§ 70.263 Special rules applicable in case of extension of time by agreement.

(a) *Scope.* If, within the period prescribed in section 6511(a) of the Internal Revenue Code for the filing of a claim for credit or refund, an agreement extending the period for assessment of a tax has been made in accordance with the provisions of section 6501(c)(4) of the Internal Revenue Code, the special rules provided in this section become applicable. This section shall not apply to any claim filed, or credit or refund allowed if no claim is filed, either (1) prior to the execution of an agreement extending the period in which assessment may be made, or (2) more than 6 months after the expiration of the period within which an assessment may be made pursuant to the agreement or any extension thereof.

(b) *Period in which claim may be filed.* Claim for credit or refund of an overpayment may be filed, or credit or refund may be allowed if no claim is filed, at any time within which an assessment may be made pursuant to an agreement, or any extension thereof, under section 6501(c)(4), and for 6 months thereafter.

(c) *Limit on amount to be credited or refunded.* (1) If a claim is filed within the time prescribed in paragraph (b) of this section, the amount of the credit or refund allowed or made shall not exceed the portion of the tax paid after the execution of the agreement and before the filing of the claim, plus the amount that could have been properly credited or refunded under the provisions of section 6511(b)(2) if a claim had been filed on the date of the execution of the agreement.

(2) If no claim is filed, the amount of credit or refund allowed or made within the time prescribed in paragraph (b) of this section shall not exceed the portion of the tax paid after the execution of the agreement and before the making of the credit or refund, plus the amount that could have been properly credited or refunded under the provisions of section 6511(b)(2) if a claim had been filed on the date of the execution of the agreement.

(d) *Effective date of agreement.* The agreement referred to in this section shall become effective when signed by the taxpayer and the appropriate TTB officer.

(26 U.S.C. 6511)

[T.D. ATF–251, 52 FR 19314, May 22, 1987. Redesignated by T.D. ATF–301, 55 FR 47606, Nov. 14, 1990]

§ 70.264 Time return deemed filed and tax considered paid.

For purposes of section 6511 of the Internal Revenue Code, a return filed before the last day prescribed by law or regulations for the filing thereof shall be considered as filed on such last day. For purposes of section 6511(b) (2) and (c), payment of any portion of the tax made before the last day prescribed for payment shall be considered made on such last day. An extension of time for filing a return or for paying any tax shall not be given any effect in determining under this section the last day prescribed for filing a return or paying any tax.

(26 U.S.C. 6513)

[T.D. ATF–251, 52 FR 19314, May 22, 1987. Redesignated by T.D. ATF–301, 55 FR 47606, Nov. 14, 1990]

§ 70.265 Credits or refunds after period of limitation.

(a) A refund of any portion of any internal revenue tax (or any interest, additional amount, addition to the tax, or assessable penalty) shall be considered erroneous and a credit of any such portion shall be considered void:

(1) If made after the expiration of the period of limitation prescribed by section 6511 of the Internal Revenue Code for filing claim therefor, unless prior to the expiration of such period claim was filed, or

(2) In the case of a timely claim, if the credit or refund was made after the expiration of the period of limitation prescribed by section 6532(a) for the filing of suit, unless prior to the expiration of such period, suit was begun.

(b) For procedure by the United States to recover erroneous refunds, see sections 6532(b) and 7405 of the Internal Revenue Code.

(26 U.S.C. 6514)

[T.D. ATF–251, 52 FR 19314, May 22, 1987. Redesignated by T.D. ATF–301, 55 FR 47606, Nov. 14, 1990]

§ 70.266 Credit against barred liability.

Any credit against a liability in respect of any taxable year shall be void if the collection of such liability would be barred by the applicable statute of limitations at the time such credit is made.

(26 U.S.C. 6514)

[T.D. ATF–251, 52 FR 19314, May 22, 1987. Redesignated by T.D. ATF–301, 55 FR 47606, Nov. 14, 1990]

TRANSFEREES

§ 70.271 Procedure in the case of transferred assets.

(a) *Method of collection.* (1) The liability, at law or in equity, of a transferee of property of any person liable in respect of any tax imposed under provisions of 26 U.S.C. enforced and administered by the Bureau, in any case where the liability of the transferee arises on the liquidation of a corporation or partnership, or a corporate reorganization within the meaning of 26 U.S.C. 368(a), shall be assessed against such transferee and paid and collected in the same manner and subject to the same provisions and limitations as in the case of the tax with respect to which such liability is incurred, except as hereinafter provided.

(2) *Applicable provisions.* The provisions of 26 U.S.C. made applicable by 26 U.S.C. 6901(a) to the liability of a transferee referred to in paragraph (a)(1) of this section, include the provisions relating to:

(i) Delinquency in payment after notice and demand and the amount of interest attaching because of such delinquency;

(ii) The authorization of distraint and proceedings in court for collection; and

(iii) The prohibition of claims and suits for refund.

For detailed provisions relating to assessments, collections, and refunds, see 26 U.S.C. chapters 63, 64, and 65, respectively.

(b) *Definition of transferee.* As used in this section, the term "transferee" includes the shareholder of a dissolved corporation, the assignee or donee of an insolvent person, the successor of a corporation, a party to a reorganization as defined in 26 U.S.C. 368, and all other classes of distributees.

(c) *Period of limitations on assessment.* The period of limitations for assessment of the liability of a transferee is as follows:

(1) *Initial transferee.* In the case of the liability of an initial transferee, 1 year after the expiration of the period of limitations for assessment against the transferor.

(2) *Transferee of transferee.* In the case of the liability of a transferee of a transferee, 1 year after the expiration of the period of limitations for assessment against the preceding transferee, or 3 years after the expiration of the period of limitations for assessment against the taxpayer, whichever of such periods first expires.

(3) *Court proceeding against taxpayer or last preceding transferee.* If, before the expiration of the period specified in paragraph (c)(1) or (2) of this section, (whichever is applicable), a court proceeding against the taxpayer or last preceding transferee for the collection of the tax or liability in respect thereof, respectively, has been begun within the period of limitation for the commencement of such proceeding, then within 1 year after the return of execution in such proceeding.

(d) *Extension by agreement*—(1) *Extension of time for assessment.* The time prescribed by 26 U.S.C. 6901 for the assessment of the liability of a transferee may, prior to the expiration of such time, be extended for any period of time agreed upon in writing by the transferee and the appropriate TTB officer. The extension shall become effective when the agreement has been executed by both parties. The period agreed upon may be extended by subsequent agreements in writing made before the expiration of the period previously agreed upon.

(2) *Extension of times for credit or refund.* (i) For the purposes of determining the period of limitations on credit or refund to the transferee of overpayments made by such transferee or overpayments made by the taxpayer to which such transferee may be legally entitled to credit or refund, an agreement and any extension thereof referred to in paragraph (d)(1) of this section, shall be deemed an agreement and extension thereof for purposes of 26 U.S.C. 6511(c) (relating to limitations on credit or refund in case of extension of time by agreement).

(ii) For the purpose of determining the limit specified in 26 U.S.C. 6511(c)(2) on the amount of the credit or refund, if the agreement is executed after the expiration of the period of limitations for assessment against the taxpayer with reference to whom the liability of such transferee arises, the periods specified in 26 U.S.C. 6511(b)(2) shall be increased by the period from the date of such expiration to the date the agreement is executed.

(e) *Period of assessment against taxpayer.* For the purpose of determining the period of limitations for assessment against a transferee, if the taxpayer is deceased, or, in the case of a corporation, has terminated its existence, the period of limitations for assessment against the taxpayer shall be the period that would be in effect had the termination of existence not occurred.

(26 U.S.C. 6901)

[T.D. ATF–301, 55 FR 47648, Nov. 14, 1990]

BONDS

§ 70.281 Form of bond and security required.

(a) *In general.* Any person required to furnish a bond under the provisions of this part shall execute such bond:

(1) On the appropriate form prescribed by the Bureau and

(2) With satisfactory surety.

For provisions as to what will be considered "satisfactory surety", see paragraph (b) of this section. The bonds referred to in this paragraph shall be drawn in favor of the United States.

(b) *Satisfactory surety*—(1) *Approved surety company or bonds or notes of the United States.* For purposes of paragraph (a) of this section, a bond shall be considered executed with satisfactory surety if:

(i) It is executed by a surety company holding a certificate of authority from the Secretary as an acceptable surety on Federal bonds; or

(ii) It is secured by bonds or notes of the United States as provided in by 31 U.S.C. 9303.

(2) *Other surety.* Unless otherwise expressly provided in 26 U.S.C. or this part, a bond may, in the discretion of the appropriate TTB officer, be considered executed with satisfactory surety if, in lieu of being executed or secured as provided in paragraph (b)(1) of this section, it is:

(i) Executed by a corporate surety (other than a surety company) provided such corporate surety establishes that it is within its corporate powers to act as surety for another corporation or an individual;

(ii) Executed by two or more individual sureties, provided such individual sureties meet the conditions contained in paragraph (b)(3) of this section;

(iii) Secured by a mortgage on real or personal property;

(iv) Secured by a certified, cashier's, or treasurer's check drawn on any bank or trust company incorporated under the laws of the United States or any State, Territory, or possession of the United States, or by a U.S. postal, bank, express or telegraph money order;

(v) Secured by corporate bonds or stocks, or by bonds issued by a State or political subdivision thereof, of recognized stability; or

(vi) Secured by any other acceptable collateral. Collateral shall be deposited with the appropriate TTB officer or, in that officer's discretion, with a responsible financial institution acting as escrow agent.

(3) *Conditions to be met by individual sureties.* If a bond is executed by two or more individual sureties, the following conditions must be met by each such individual surety:

(i) The surety must reside within the State in which the principal place of business or legal residence of the primary obligor is located;

(ii) The surety must have property subject to execution of a current market value, above all encumbrances, equal to at least the penalty of the bond;

(iii) All real property which the surety offers as security must be located in the State in which the principal place of business or legal residence of the primary obligor is located;

(iv) The surety must agree not to mortgage, or otherwise encumber, any property offered as security while the bond continues in effect without first securing the permission of the officer with whom the bond is filed; and

(v) The surety must file with the bond, and annually thereafter so long as the bond continues in effect, an affidavit as to the adequacy of the security, executed on the appropriate form furnished by the appropriate TTB officer.

Partners may not act as sureties upon bonds of their partnership. Stockholders of a corporate principal may be accepted as sureties provided their qualifications as such are independent of their holdings of the stock of the corporation.

(4) *Adequacy of surety.* No surety or security shall be accepted if it does not adequately protect the interest of the United States.

(26 U.S.C. 7101)

[T.D. ATF-301, 55 FR 47649, Nov. 14, 1990, as amended by T.D. ATF-450, 66 FR 29028, May 29, 2001]

§ 70.282 Single bond in lieu of multiple bonds.

In the case of bonds required under this part, a single bond will not be accepted in lieu of two or more bonds.

(26 U.S.C. 7102)

[T.D. ATF-301, 55 FR 47650, Nov. 14, 1990]

MISCELLANEOUS PROVISIONS

SOURCE: Sections 70.301 through 70.306 added by T.D. ATF-301, 55 FR 47650, Nov. 14, 1990, unless otherwise noted.

§ 70.301 Reproduction of returns and other documents.

(a) *In general.* The appropriate TTB officer may contract with any Federal agency or any person to have such agency or person process films and other photoimpressions of any return, statement, document, or of any card, record, or other matter required under the provisions of 26 U.S.C. enforced and administered by the Bureau, and make reproductions from such films and photoimpressions.

(b) *Safeguards*—(1) *By private contractor.* Any person entering into a contract with the Bureau for the performance of any of the services described in paragraph (a) of this section shall agree to comply, and to assume responsibility for compliance by that person's employees, with the following requirements:

(i) The films or photoimpressions, and reproductions made therefrom, shall be used only for the purpose of carrying out the provisions of the contract, and information contained in such material shall be treated as confidential and shall not be divulged or made known in any manner to any person except as may be necessary in the performance of the contract;

(ii) All the services shall be performed under the supervision of the person with whom the contract is made or that person's responsible employees;

(iii) All material received for processing and all processed and reproduced material shall be kept in a locked and fireproof compartment in a secure place when not being worked upon;

(iv) All spoilage of reproductions made from the film or photoimpressions supplied to the contractor shall be destroyed, and a statement under the penalties of perjury shall be submitted to the Bureau that such destruction has been accomplished; and

(v) All film, photoimpressions, and reproductions made therefrom, shall be transmitted to the Bureau by personal delivery, first-class mail, parcel post, or express.

(2) *By Federal agency.* Any Federal agency entering into a contract with the Bureau for the performance of any services described in paragraph (a) of this section, shall treat as confidential

all material processed or reproduced pursuant to such contract.

(3) *Inspection.* The Bureau shall have the right to send its officers and employees into the office and plants of Federal agencies and other contractors for inspection of the facilities and operations provided for the performance of any work contracted or to be contracted for under this section.

(4) *Criminal sanctions.* For penalty provisions relating to the unauthorized use and disclosure of information in violation of the provisions of this section, *see* 26 U.S.C. 7213(c).

(26 U.S.C. 7513)

§ 70.302 Fees and costs for witnesses.

(a) *Introduction.* Title 26 U.S.C. 7610 provides that the Bureau may make payments to certain persons who are summoned to give information to the Bureau under 26 U.S.C. 7602 and § 70.22 of this part. Under 26 U.S.C. 7610 witnesses generally will not be reimbursed for actual expenses incurred but instead will be paid in accordance with the payment rates established by regulations. Paragraph (b) of this section contains elaborations of certain terms found in 26 U.S.C. 7610 and definitions of other terms used in the regulations under 26 U.S.C. 7610 (a) and (b); and paragraphs (c) and (d) of this section contain rules and rates applicable to payments under 26 U.S.C. 7610.

(b) *Definitions*—(1) *Directly incurred costs.* Directly incurred costs are costs incurred solely, immediately, and necessarily as a consequence of searching for, reproducing, or transporting records in order to comply with a summons. They do not include a proportionate allocation of fixed costs, such as overhead, equipment depreciation, etc. However, where a third party's records are stored at an independent storage facility that charges the third party a search fee to search for, reproduce, or transport particular records requested, these fees are considered to be directly incurred by the summoned third party.

(2) *Reproduction cost.* Reproduction costs are costs incurred in making copies or duplicates of summoned documents, transcripts, and other similar material.

(3) *Search costs.* Search costs include only the total cost of personnel time directly incurred in searching for records or information and the cost of retrieving information stored by computer. Salaries of persons locating and retrieving summoned material are not included in search costs. Also, search costs do not include salaries, fees, or similar expenditures for analysis of material or for managerial or legal advice, expertise, or research, or time spent for these activities.

(4) *Third party.* A third party is any person served with a summons, other than a person with respect to whose liability a summons is issued, or an officer, employee, agent, accountant, or attorney of that person.

(5) *Third party records.* Third party records are books, papers, records, or other data in which the person with respect to whose liability a summons is issued does not have a proprietary interest at the time the summons is served.

(6) *Transportation costs.* Transportation costs include only costs incurred to transport personnel to search for records or information requested and costs incurred solely by the need to transport the summoned material to the place of examination. These costs do not include the cost of transporting the summoned witness for appearance at the place of examination. See paragraph (c)(2) of this section for payment of travel expenses.

(c) *Conditions and rates of payments*—(1) *Basis for payment.* Payment for search, reproduction, and transportation costs will be made only to third parties served with a summons to produce third party records or information and only for material requested by the summons. Payment will be made only for those costs both directly incurred and reasonably necessary. No payment will be made until the third party has satisfactorily complied with the summons and has submitted an itemized bill or invoice showing specific details concerning the costs to the Bureau employee before whom the third party was summoned. If a third party charges any other person for any cost for which the third party is seeking payment from the Bureau, the amount charged to the other person must be subtracted from the amount the Bureau must pay.

(2) *Payment rates.* The following rates are established.

(i) *Search costs.* (A) For the total amount of personnel time required to locate records or information, $8.50 per person hour.

(B) For retrieval of information stored by computer in the format in which it is normally produced, actual costs, based on computer time and necessary supplies, except that personnel time for computer search is payable only under paragraph (c)(2)(i)(A) of this section.

(ii) *Reproduction costs.* (A) For copies of documents $.20 per page.

(B) For photographers, films and other materials, actual cost, except that personnel time is payable only under paragraph (a)(2)(i)(A) of this section.

(iii) *Transportation costs.* For transportation costs, actual cost, except that personnel time is payable only under paragraph (c)(2)(i)(A) of this section.

(d) *Appearance fees and allowances*—(1) *In general.* Under 26 U.S.C. 7610(a)(1) and this paragraph, the Bureau shall pay a summoned person certain fees and allowances. No payments will be made until after the party summoned appears and has submitted any necessary receipts or other evidence of costs to the Bureau employee before whom the person was summoned.

(2) *Attendance fees.* A summoned person shall be paid an attendance fee for each day's attendance. A summoned person shall also be paid the attendance fee for the time necessarily occupied in going to and returning from the place of attendance at the beginning and end of the attendance or at any time during the attendance. The attendance fee is the higher of $30 per day or the amount paid under 28 U.S.C. 1821(b) to witnesses in attendance at courts of the United States at the time of the summoned person's appearance.

(3) *Travel allowances.* A summoned person who travels by common carrier shall be paid for the actual expenses of travel on the basis of the means of transportation reasonably utilized and the distance necessarily traveled to and from the summoned person's residence by the shortest practical route in going to and returning from the place of attendance. Such a summoned person shall utilize a common carrier at the most economical rate reasonably available. A receipt or other evidence of actual cost shall be furnished. A travel allowance equal to the mileage allowance which the Administrator of General Services has prescribed, under 5 U.S.C. 5704, for official travel of employees of the Federal Government shall be paid to each summoned person who travels by privately owned vehicle. Computation of mileage under this paragraph shall be made on the basis of a uniform table of distances adopted by the Administrator of General Services. Toll charges for toll roads, bridges, tunnels and ferries, taxicab fares between places of lodging and carrier terminals, and parking fees (upon presentation of a valid parking receipt) shall be paid in full to a summoned person incurring those expenses.

(4) *Subsistence allowances.* A subsistence allowance shall be paid to a summoned person (other than a summoned person who is incarcerated) when an overnight stay is required at the place of attendance because the place is so far removed from the residence of the summoned person as to prohibit return thereto from day to day. A subsistence allowance for a summoned person shall be paid in an amount not to exceed the maximum allowance prescribed by the Administrator of General Services, under 5 U.S.C. 5702(a), for official travel in the area of attendance by employees of the Federal Government. An alien who has been paroled into the United States by the Attorney General, under 8 U.S.C. 1182(d)(5)(A), or an alien who either has admitted belonging to a class of aliens who are deportable or has been determined under 8 U.S.C. 1252(b) to be deportable, shall be ineligible to receive the fees or allowances provided for under 26 U.S.C. 7610(a)(1).

(26 U.S.C. 7610)

§ 70.303 Rules and regulations.

(a) *Issuance.* The Administrator, with the approval of the Secretary, shall prescribe all needful rules and regulations for the enforcement of provisions of 26 U.S.C. enforced and administered by the Bureau (except where this authority is expressly given by 26 U.S.C. to any other person other than an officer or employee of the Treasury Department), including all rules and regulations as may be necessary by reason of any alteration of law in relation to taxes within the Administrator's jurisdiction.

(b) *Retroactivity.* The Administrator, with the approval of the Secretary, may prescribe the extent, if any, to which any regulation or Treasury decision relating to the laws within the Administrator's jurisdiction shall be applied without retroactive effect. The Administrator may prescribe the extent, if any, to which any ruling relating to the laws within the Administrator's jurisdiction, issued by or pursuant to authorization from the Administrator, shall be applied without retroactive effect.

(c) *Preparation and distribution of regulations, forms, stamps, and other matters.* The Administrator, under the direction of the Secretary, shall prepare and distribute all the instructions, regulations, directions, forms, blanks, stamps, and other matters pertaining to the assessment and collection of taxes within the Administrator's jurisdiction.

(26 U.S.C. 7805)

§ 70.304 Place for filing documents other than returns.

(a) If a document, other than a return, is required to be filed with a TTB office, such document may be hand delivered to such office.

(b) For purposes of this section, a return or document will be considered to be hand carried if it is brought to a TTB supervisor of the TTB office by the person required to file the return or other document, or by the person's agent. Examples of persons who will be considered to be agents, for purposes of the preceding sentence, are: Members of the taxpayer's family, an employee of the taxpayer, the taxpayer's attorney, accountant, or tax advisor, and messengers employed by the taxpayer. A return or document will not be considered to be hand carried if it is sent to the Bureau through the U.S. Mail.

(26 U.S.C. 6091)

[T.D. ATF–305, 55 FR 47650, Nov. 14, 1990, as amended by T.D. ATF–450, 66 FR 29028, May 29, 2001]

§ 70.305 Timely mailing treated as timely filing.

(a) *General rule.* Title 26 U.S.C. 7502 provides that, if the requirements of such section are met, a document shall be deemed to be filed on the date of the postmark stamped on the cover in which such document was mailed. Thus, if the cover containing such document bears a timely postmark, the document will be considered filed timely although it is received after the last date, or the last day of the period, prescribed for filing such document. Title 26 U.S.C. 7502 is applicable only to those documents which come within the definition of such term provided by paragraph (b) of this section and only if the document is mailed in accordance with paragraph (c) of this section and is delivered in accordance with paragraph (d) of this section.

(b) *Document defined.* The term *document,* as used in this section, means any return, claim, statement, or other document required to be filed within a prescribed period or on or before a prescribed date under authority of any provisions of 26 U.S.C. enforced and administered by the Bureau.

(c) *Mailing requirements.* (1) Title 26 U.S.C. 7502 is not applicable unless the document is mailed in accordance with the following requirements:

(i) The document must be contained in an envelope or other appropriate wrapper, properly addressed to the agency, officer, or office with which the document is required to be filed.

(ii) The document must be deposited within the prescribed time in the mail in the United States with sufficient postage prepaid. For this purpose, a document is deposited in the mail in the United States when it is deposited with the domestic mail service of the U.S. Postal Service, as defined by the postal regulations (39 CFR Part 2). Title 26 U.S.C. 7502 does not apply to any document which is deposited with the mail service of any other country.

(iii)(A) If the postmark on the envelope or wrapper is made by the U.S. Postal Service, such postmark must bear a date on or before the last date, or the last day of the period, prescribed for filing the document. If the postmark does not bear a date on or before the last date, or the last day of the period, prescribed for filing the document, the document will be considered not to be filed timely, regardless of when the document is deposited in the mail. Accordingly, the sender who relies upon the applicability of 26 U.S.C. 7502 assumes the risk that the postmark will bear a date on or before the last date, or the last day of the period, prescribed for filing the document, but see paragraph (c)(2) of this section, with respect to the use of registered mail or certified mail to avoid this risk. If the postmark on the envelope or wrapper is not legible, the person who is required to file the document has the burden of proving the time when the postmark was made. Furthermore, in case the cover containing a document bearing a timely postmark made by the U.S. Postal Service is received after the time when a document postmarked and mailed at such time would ordinarily be received, the sender may be required to prove that it was timely mailed.

(B) If the postmark on the envelope or wrapper is made other than by the U.S. Postal Service, the postmark so made must bear a date on or before the last date, or the last day of the period, prescribed for filing the document, and the document must be received by the agency, officer, or office with which it is required to be filed not later than the time when a document contained in an envelope or other appropriate wrapper which is properly addressed and mailed and sent by the same class of mail would ordinarily be received if it were postmarked at the same point of origin by the U.S. Postal Service on the last date, or the last day of the period, prescribed for filing the document. However, in case the document is received after the time when a document so mailed and so postmarked by the U.S. Postal Service would ordinarily be received, such document will be treated as having been received at the time when a document so mailed and so postmarked would ordinarily be received, if the person who is required to file the document establishes that it was actually deposited in the mail before the last collection of the mail from the place of deposit which was postmarked (except for the metered mail) by the U.S. Postal Service on or before the last date, or the last day of the period, prescribed for filing the document, that the delay in receiving the document was due to a delay in the transmission of the mail, and the cause of such delay. If the envelope has a postmark made by the U.S. Postal Service in addition to the postmark not so made, the postmark which was not made by the U.S. Postal Service shall be disregarded, and whether the envelope was mailed in accordance with this section shall be determined solely by applying the rules of paragraph (c)(1)(iii)(A) of this section.

(2) If the document is sent by U.S. registered mail, the date of registration of the document shall be treated as the postmark date. If the document is sent by U.S. certified mail and the sender's receipt is postmarked by the postal employee to whom such document is presented, the date of the U.S. postmark on such receipt shall be treated as the postmark date of the document. Accordingly, the risk that the document will not be postmarked on the day that it is deposited in the mail may be overcome by the use of registered mail or certified mail.

(3) As used in this section, the term "the last date, or the last day of the period, prescribed for filing the document" includes any extension of time granted for such filing. Except as provided in 26 U.S.C. 5061 for the filing of returns and payment of a tax under 26 U.S.C. subtitle E, when the last date, or the last day of the period, prescribed for filing the document falls on a Saturday, Sunday, or legal holiday, 26 U.S.C. 7503 is also applicable, so that, in applying the rules of this paragraph, the next succeeding day which is not a Saturday, Sunday, or legal holiday, shall be treated as the last date, or the last day of the period, prescribed for filing the document.

(d) *Delivery.* (1) Title 26 U.S.C. 7502 is not applicable unless the document is delivered by U.S. mail to the agency, officer, or office with which it is required to be filed. However, if the document is sent by registered mail or certified mail, proof that the document was properly registered or that a postmarked certified mail sender's receipt was properly issued therefor, and that the envelope or wrapper was properly addressed to such agency, officer or office shall constitute prima facie evidence that the document was delivered to such agency, officer or office.

(2) Title 26 U.S.C. 7502 is applicable only when the document is delivered after the last date, or the last day of the period, prescribed for filing the document.

(e) *Exceptions.* This section shall not apply with respect to:

(1) The filing of a document in, or the making of a payment to, any court,

(2) Currency or other medium of payment unless actually received and accounted for, or

(3) Returns, claims, statements, or other documents, or payments, which are required under any provision of 26 U.S.C. enforced and administered by the Bureau or the regulations thereunder to be delivered by any method other than by mailing.

(26 U.S.C. 5061 and 7503)

§ 70.306 Time for performance of acts other than payment of tax or filing of any return when the last day falls on Saturday, Sunday, or legal holiday.

(a) *In general.* Title 26 U.S.C. 7503 provides that when the last day prescribed under provisions of 26 U.S.C. enforced and administered by the Bureau, for the performance of any act falls on a Saturday, Sunday, or legal holiday, such act shall be considered performed timely if performed on the next succeeding day which is not a Saturday, Sunday, or legal holiday. For this purpose, any authorized extension of time shall be included in the determining of the last day for performance of any act. Title 26 U.S.C. 7503 is not applicable to the filing of returns and payment of tax under 26 U.S.C. subtitle E. Title 26 U.S.C. 7503 is applicable only in case an act is required under authority of any provisions of 26 U.S.C. enforced and administered by the Bureau to be performed on or before a prescribed date or within a prescribed period. Title 26 U.S.C. 7503 applies to acts to be performed by the taxpayer (such as the filing of a claim for credit or refund of tax) and acts to be performed by the appropriate TTB officer, (such as, the giving of any notice with respect to, or making any demand for the payment of, any tax; the assessment or collection of any tax). For rules concerning the payment of any tax or the filing of any return required under the authority of 26 U.S.C. 4181 and 4182 relating to firearms and ammunition or subtitle E relating to alcohol, tobacco products, and cigarette papers and tubes, see 26 U.S.C. 5061, 5703, and 6302 and the regulations covering the specific commodity.

(b) *Legal holidays.* (1) For the purpose of 26 U.S.C. 7503, the term "legal holiday" includes the legal holidays in the District of Columbia. Such legal holidays found in 5 U.S.C. 6103(a), as enacted and made effective by the Act of November 2, 1983 (97 Stat. 917), are:

(i) January 1, New Year's Day,

(ii) Third Monday in January, Birthday of Martin Luther King, Jr.,

(iii) January 20, when such day is Inauguration Day,

(iv) Third Monday in February, Washington's Birthday,

(v) Last Monday in May, Memorial Day,

(vi) July 4, Independence Day,

(vii) First Monday in September, Labor Day,

(viii) Second Monday in October, Columbus Day,

(ix) November 11, Veterans' Day,

(x) Fourth Thursday in November, Thanksgiving Day, and

(xi) December 25, Christmas Day.

When a legal holiday in the District of Columbia falls on a Sunday, the next day is a legal holiday in the District of Columbia. For the purpose of 26 U.S.C. 7503, when a legal holiday in the District of Columbia (other than Inauguration Day) falls on a Saturday it shall be treated as falling on the preceding Friday.

(2) In the case of any statement or other document required to be filed, or any other act required under the authority of provisions of 26 U.S.C. enforced and administered by the Bureau

to be performed at any office of the Bureau or any other office or agency of the United States, located outside the District of Columbia, the term "legal holiday" includes, in addition to the legal holidays enumerated in paragraph (b)(1) of this section, any statewide legal holiday of the State where the act is required to be performed. If the act is performed in accordance with law at an office of the Bureau or any other office or agency of the United States located in a Territory or possession of the United States, the term "legal holiday" includes, in addition to the legal holidays described in paragraph (b)(1) of this section, any legal holiday which is recognized throughout the Territory or possession in which the office is located.

(26 U.S.C. 5061 and 7503)

[T.D. ATF–6, 38 FR 32445, Nov. 26, 1973, as amended by T.D. ATF–365, 60 FR 33674, June 28, 1995; T.D. ATF–450, 66 FR 29028, May 29, 2001; T.D. TTB–89, 76 FR 3515, Jan. 20, 2011; T.D. TTB–91, 76 FR 5481, Feb. 1, 2011]

GENERAL PROVISIONS RELATING TO STAMPS, MARKS OR LABELS

§ 70.311 Authority for establishment, alteration, and distribution of stamps, marks, or labels.

The appropriate TTB officer may establish, and from time to time alter, renew, replace, or change the form, style, character, material, and device of any stamp, mark, or label under any provision of the law relating to Subtitle E of the Internal Revenue Code (or to any provision of Subtitle F which relates to Subtitle E).

(26 U.S.C. 6801)

[T.D. ATF–251, 52 FR 19314, May 22, 1987. Redesignated by T.D. ATF–301, 55 FR 47606, Nov. 14, 1990]

REGISTRATION

§ 70.321 Registration of persons paying a special tax.

(a) *Persons required to register.* Every person engaged in a trade or business in respect of which a special tax is imposed by one of the following sections of the Internal Revenue Code is required to register with the Alcohol and Tobacco Tax and Trade Bureau.

(1)–(5) [Reserved]

(6) Section 5731 (relating to special tax on manufacturers of tobacco products, manufacturers of cigarette papers and tubes, and export warehouse proprietors); or

(7) Section 5802 (relating to importers, manufacturers and dealers of National Firearms Act weapons).

(b) *Procedure for registration.* The registration required of a person by reason of the person being engaged in a trade or business, in respect of which one of the special taxes listed in paragraph (a) of this section is imposed, shall be accomplished by timely executing and filing, in accordance with the instructions relating thereto, TTB Form 5630.5, Special Tax Registration and Return.

(26 U.S.C. 5802, 7011)

[T.D. ATF–6, 38 FR 32445, Nov. 26, 1973, as amended by T.D. ATF–271, 53 FR 17549, May 17, 1988. Redesignated and amended by T.D. ATF–301, 55 FR 47606, 47653, Nov. 14, 1990; T.D. ATF–379, 61 FR 31426, June 20, 1996; T.D. TTB–79, 74 FR 37424, July 28, 2009]

CRIMES, OTHER OFFENSES AND FORFEITURES

SOURCE: Sections 70.331 through 70.333 added by T.D. ATF–301, 55 FR 47653, Nov. 14, 1990, unless otherwise noted.

§ 70.331 Fraudulent returns, statements, or other documents.

Any person who willfully delivers or discloses to any officer or employee of the Bureau any list, return, account, statement, or other document, known by him to be fraudulent or to be false as to any material matter, shall be fined not more than $10,000 ($50,000 in the case of a corporation) or imprisoned not more than 1 year, or both.

(26 U.S.C. 7207)

§ 70.332 Unauthorized use or sale of stamps.

Any person who buys, sells, offers for sale, uses, transfers, takes or gives in exchange, or pledges or gives in pledge, except as authorized in the Internal Revenue Code or in regulations made pursuant thereto, any stamp, coupon, ticket, book, or other device prescribed by the Administrator under provisions of 26 U.S.C. enforced and administered by the Bureau for the collection or payment of any tax imposed thereunder, shall, upon conviction thereof, be fined not more than $1,000, or imprisoned not more than 6 months, or both.

(26 U.S.C. 7209)

§ 70.333 Offenses by officers and employees of the United States.

Any officer or employee of the United States acting in connection with any provisions of 26 U.S.C. enforced and administered by the Bureau required to make a written report under the provisions of 26 U.S.C. 7214(a)(8) shall submit such report to the appropriate TTB officer.

(26 U.S.C. 7214)

[T.D. ATF–301, 55 FR 47653, Nov. 14, 1990, as amended by T.D. ATF–450, 66 FR 29028, May 29, 2001]

Subpart E—Procedural Rules Relating to Alcohol, Tobacco, Firearms, and Explosives

SOURCE: T.D. ATF–251, 52 FR 19325, May 22, 1987, unless otherwise noted. Redesignated by T.D. ATF–301, 55 FR 47653, Nov. 14, 1990.

PROVISIONS RELATING TO DISTILLED SPIRITS, WINES, AND BEER

§ 70.411 Imposition of taxes, qualification requirements, and regulations.

(a) *Imposition of taxes.* Subchapter A of Chapter 51 of the IRC imposes taxes on distilled spirits (including alcohol), wine and beer.

(b) *Qualification requirements.* Distillers, winemakers, brewers, warehousemen, rectifiers, bottlers, dealers in specially denatured alcohol, users of tax-free and specially denatured alcohol, and wholesalers and importers of liquors, are required to qualify with TTB usually by filing notice or application and bond with, and procuring permit from, the appropriate TTB officer. Dealers in alcohol products fit for beverage use and manufacturers of nonbeverage products who claim drawback under section 5114 of the Internal Revenue Code must register. Detailed information respecting such qualification and registration, including the forms to be used and the procedure to be followed, is contained in the respective regulations described in paragraph (c) of this section.

(c) *Regulations.* The procedural requirements with respect to matters relating to distilled spirits, wines, and beer which are within the jurisdiction of TTB are published in the regulations described in this paragraph. These regulations contain full information as to the general course and method by which the functions concerning liquors are channeled and determined, including the nature and requirements of formal and informal procedures, the forms, records, reports, and other documents required, and the contents of applications, notices, registrations, permits, bonds, and other documents. Forms prescribed by this part are available as provided in § 70.2(b). The following is a brief description of the several regulations arranged according to the principal subjects and operations concerned:

(1) *Establishment and operation of distilled spirits plants.* Part 19 of title 27 CFR contains the regulations relating to the location, qualification, construction, arrangement, equipment, and operations (including activities incident thereto) of distilled spirits plants for the production and/or warehousing (including denaturation), and bottling (including bottling in bond) of distilled spirits. Part 19 also contains the regulations relating to distilled spirits for fuel use and the production of vinegar by the vaporizing process.

(2) *Miscellaneous liquor transactions.* Part 29 of 27 CFR contains miscellaneous regulations relative to the manufacture, removal, and use of stills and condensers, and to the notice, registration, and recordkeeping requirements therefor.

(3) [Reserved]

(4) *Gauging of distilled spirits.* Part 30 of title 27 CFR contains the regulations that. prescribe the gauging instruments, and methods or techniques to be used in measuring distilled spirits (including denatured spirits). Tables are provided for use in making the necessary computation from gauge data.

(5) *Rules of practice in permit proceedings.* Part 71 of title 27 CFR contains the rules governing the procedure and practice in connection with the

disapproval of applications for basic permits, and for the issuance of citations for the suspension, revocation, and annulment of such permits under sections 3 and 4 of the Federal Alcohol Administration Act (27 U.S.C. 201 *et seq.*), and disapproval, suspension, and revocation of industrial use, operating, withdrawal, and tobacco permits under the Internal Revenue Code. Such rules also govern, insofar as applicable, any adversary proceeding involving adjudication required by statute to oe determined on the record, after opportunity for hearing, under laws administered by the Alcohol and Tobacco Tax and Trade Bureau.

(6) *Basic permit requirements under the Federal Alcohol Administration Act.* 27 CFR part 1, subpart C, issued pursuant to the Federal Alcohol Administration Act, as amended, contains the requirements relative to the issuance under the Act of basic permits to producers, rectifiers, blenders, bottlers, warehousemen, importers, and wholesalers of distilled spirits, wine, or beer, and the amendment, duration, revocation, suspension, or annulment of such permits.

(7) *Bulk sales and bottling of distilled spirits.* 27 CFR part 1, subpart E, issued under the Federal Alcohol Administration Act, as amended, contains the requirements relative to bulk sales and bottling of distilled spirits under the Federal Alcohol Administration Act, including the terms of warehouse receipts for distilled spirits in bulk.

(8) *Labeling and advertising of distilled spirits.* 27 CFR part 5, issued under the Federal Alcohol Administration Act, as amended, contains the requirements relative to the labeling and advertising of distilled spirits under the Federal Alcohol Administration Act, including standards of identity for distilled spirits, standards of fill for bottles of distilled spirits, withdrawal of bottled imported distilled spirits from customs custody, and the issuance of certificates of label approval and certificates of exemption from label approval.

(9) *American viticultural areas.* Part 9 of title 27 CFR contains the regulations that relate to American viticultural areas. The viticultural areas described in these regulations are approved for use as appellations of origin in accordance with 27 CFR part 4.

(10) *Production and removal of wine.* Part 24 of title 27 CFR contains the regulations relative to the establishment and operation of bonded wine cellars, including bonded wineries, for the production, cellar treatment, and storage of wines, including amelioration, sweetening, addition of volatile fruit flavor concentrates, addition of wine spirits (including distillates containing aldehydes), blending, and other cellar treatment; removals; taxpayment; return of taxpaid wine; use of wine for distilling material and manufacture of vinegar; and record and report requirements.

(11) *Bottling or Packaging of taxpaid wine.* Part 24 of title 27 CFR contains the regulations relative to the establishment, qualification, and operations of taxpaid wine bottling houses on premises other than those of a plant operated under part 19 of title 27 CFR, and to the bottling and packaging of taxpaid United States and foreign wines at such premises.

(12) *Nonindustrial use of distilled spirits and wine.* 27 CFR part 1, subpart D, issued under the Federal Alcohol Administration Act, as amended, specifies what uses of distilled spirits and wine are considered "nonindustrial," as that term is used in section 17 of the Federal Alcohol Administration Act.

(13) *Labeling and advertising of wine.* 27 CFR part 4, issued under the Federal Alcohol Administration Act, as amended, contains the requirements relative to the labeling and advertising of wine under the Federal Alcohol Administration Act, including standards of identity for wine, standards of fill for containers of wine, the withdrawal of imported wine from customs custody, and the issuance of certificates of label approval and certificates of exemption from label approval.

(14) *Establishment and operations of breweries and experimental breweries.* Part 25 of title 27 CFR contains the regulations relating to the production (including concentration and reconstitution incident thereto) and removal of beer and cereal beverages. The regulations cover the location, construction, equipment, and operations of breweries; and the qualification of such

establishments, including the ownership, control, and management thereof, and the establishment and operations of experimental breweries.

(15) *Labeling and advertising of malt beverages.* 27 CFR part 7, issued under the Federal Alcohol Administration Act, as amended, contains the requirements relative to the labeling and advertising of malt beverages (beer) under the Federal Alcohol Administration Act, including withdrawal of imported malt beverages from customs custody, and the issuance of certificates of label approval.

(16) *Liquor dealers.* Part 31 of title 27 CFR contains the regulations relative to the registration requirement imposed on wholesale and retail dealers in liquors and wholesale and retail dealers in beer; restrictions on purchases of distilled spirits; reuse or refilling of liquor bottles; sale or possession of refilled or used liquor bottles; repackaging of alcohol for industrial use; recordkeeping and reporting requirements; and provisions relating to entry of premises and inspection of records.

(17) *Drawback of tax on spirits used in nonbeverage products.* Part 17 of title 27 CFR contains the regulations which relate to obtaining drawback of internal revenue tax on distilled spirits used in the manufacture or production of medicines, medicinal preparations, food products, flavors, or flavoring extracts, which are unfit for beverage purposes.

(18) *Production of volatile fruit-flavor concentrates.* Part 18 of title 27 CFR contains the regulations relating to the manufacture, removal, sale, storage, transfer in bond, transportation, recordkeeping and reporting requirements, and use of volatile fruit flavor concentrates. It includes provisions regarding the location, qualification, use, and operations of concentrate plants.

(19) *Tied-House.* 27 CFR part 6, issued under the Federal Alcohol Administration Act, as amended, specifies practices which are prohibited by subsection (b) of section 5 of the Act and provides the exception to these prohibitions. This part applies only to transactions between industry members and retailers.

(20) *Exclusive outlets.* 27 CFR part 8, issued under the Federal Alcohol Administration Act, as amended, specifies practices which are prohibited by subsection (a) of section 5 of the Act. This part applies only to transactions between industry members and retailers.

(21) *Commercial bribery.* 27 CFR part 10, issued under the Federal Alcohol Administration Act, as amended, specifies practices which are prohibited by subsection (c) of section 5 of the Act. This part applies to transactions between industry members and employees, officers, or representatives of trade buyers.

(22) *Consignment sales.* 27 CFR part 11, issued under the Federal Alcohol Administration Act, as amended, specifies sales arrangements prohibited by subsection (d) of section 5 of the Act and contains guidelines concerning the return of distilled spirits, wines, and malt beverages from a trade buyer. The regulations in this part apply to transactions between industry members and trade buyers.

(23) *Distribution and use of denatured alcohol and rum.* Part 20 of title 27 CFR contains the regulations relating to the procurement, use, disposition, and recovery of denatured alcohol, specially denatured rum, and articles containing denatured spirits; and includes requirements in respect to industrial use and withdrawal permits; and the packaging, labeling, sales, rebottling, and reprocessing of articles containing specially denatured spirits.

(24) *Formulas for denatured alcohol and rum.* Part 21 of title 27 CFR contains the regulations relating to the formulation of completely denatured alcohol, specially denatured alcohol, and specially denatured rum; to the use of specially denatured spirits; and to the specifications for denaturants. The procedural requirements relative to the production of denatured alcohol and specially denatured rum are prescribed in part 19 of title 27 CFR, and those relative to the distribution and use of denatured alcohol and specially denatured rum are prescribed in part 20 of title 27 CFR.

(25) *Distribution and use of tax-free alcohol.* Part 22 of title 27 CFR contains the regulations relating to tax-free alcohol and covers the procurement,

storage, use, and recovery of such alcohol; and included requirements in respect to industrial use and withdrawal permits.

(26) *Liquors and articles from Puerto Rico and the Virgin Islands.* Part 26 of title 27 CFR contains the regulations relating to the production, bonded warehousing, and withdrawal of distilled spirits, and denatured spirits, and the manufacture of articles in Puerto Rico and the Virgin Islands to be brought into the United States free of tax and the collection of internal revenue taxes on taxable alcoholic products coming into the United States from Puerto Rico and the Virgin Islands. Regulations respecting spirits produced in Puerto Rico or the Virgin Islands and brought into the United States and transferred from customs custody to internal revenue bond are also contained in this part.

(27) *Importation of liquors.* Part 27 of title 27 CFR contains the substantive and procedural requirements relative to the importation of distilled spirits, wines, and beer into the United States from foreign countries including commodity taxes, permits, marking, branding, and labeling of containers and packages.

(28) *Exportation of liquors.* Part 28 of title 27 CFR contains the regulations relating to exportation including, where applicable, lading for use on vessels and aircraft, transfer to a foreign-trade zone, or transfer to a manufacturing bonded warehouse, Class 6, of distilled spirits (including specially denatured spirits), beer (including beer concentrate), and wine, and transfer of distilled spirits and wine for deposit in a customs bonded warehouse, whether without payment of tax, free of tax, or with benefit of drawback. It includes requirements with respect to removal, shipment, lading, deposit, evidence of exportation, losses, claims, and bonds.

[T.D. ATF-251, 52 FR 19325, May 22, 1987]

EDITORIAL NOTE: For FEDERAL REGISTER citations affecting § 70.411, see the List of CFR Sections Affected, which appears in the Finding Aids section of the printed volume and at *www.fdsys.gov*.

§ 70.412 Excise taxes.

(a) *Collection.* Taxes on distilled spirits, wines, and beer are paid by returns. If the person responsible for paying the taxes has filed a proper bond to defer payment, that person may be eligible to file semimonthly or quarterly returns, with proper remittances, to cover the taxes incurred on distilled spirits, wines, and beer during the semimonthly or quarterly period. Payment must accompany the return unless required to be made by electronic fund transfer (EFT). If the taxpayer is not qualified to defer taxpayment, or has been placed on a prepayment basis, the taxpayer must prepay the tax on the distilled spirits, wines, or beer. Distilled spirits, wines, and beer tax returns are filed in accordance with the instruction on the return forms, which are furnished to industry members by TTB. Detailed information respecting the payment of tax on liquors, including the forms to be used and procedures to be followed, is contained in the respective regulations described in § 70.411(c).

(b) *Assessment.* If additional or delinquent tax liability is disclosed by an investigation, or by an examination of records, of a qualified plant or permittee, a notice (except where delay may jeopardize collection of the tax, or where the amount involved is nominal or the result of an evident mathematical error) is sent to the taxpayer advising of the basis and amount of the liability and affording the taxpayer an opportunity to submit a protest, with supporting facts, or to request a conference.

[T.D. ATF-251, 52 FR 19325, May 22, 1987, as amended by T.D. ATF-271, 53 FR 17549, May 17, 1988. Redesignated and amended by T.D. ATF-301, 55 FR 47606, 47653, Nov. 14, 1990; T.D. ATF-450, 66 FR 29028, May 29, 2001; T.D. TTB-41, 71 FR 5605, Feb. 2, 2006; T.D. TTB-79, 74 FR 37424, July 28, 2009; T.D. TTB-89, 76 FR 3515, Jan. 20, 2011]

§ 70.413 Claims.

(a) *Claims for remission.* When distilled spirits (including distilling material and denatured spirits), wine, or beer on which the tax has not been paid or determined is lost, and the person liable for payment of the tax thereon desires to be relieved from such liability, such person may file claim on Form 5620.8 for remission of tax on the quantity that was lost. The appropriate TTB officer may, in any event, require such a claim to be filed, and will require it if circumstances indicate that the loss was caused by theft or, in the case of distilled spirits (including distilling material), unauthorized voluntary destruction. On receipt of a claim the appropriate TTB officer makes a factual determination, and notifies the claimant of allowance or rejection of the claim. If the claim is rejected, and circumstances so warrant, the appropriate TTB officer will take appropriate steps to collect the tax.

(b) *Claims for abatement.* When the tax on distilled spirits, wines, or beer is assessed and the taxpayer thinks that the tax is not due under the law, such taxpayer may file a claim for abatement of the tax on TTB Form 5620.8 with the officer who made demand for the tax. Such officer may call upon the taxpayer to file a bond in double the amount of the tax in order to insure collection of the tax if the claim is rejected. When the claim is acted upon, the taxpayer is notified of the allowance or rejection of the claim. If the claim is rejected, such officer, will initiate action to collect the tax.

(c) *Claims for refund*—(1) *Taxes illegally, erroneously, or excessively collected.* A claim for refund of taxes illegally, erroneously, or excessively collected may be filed by the taxpayer with the officer who collected the tax. Such claim must be filed within three years (two years under certain circumstances) after the date of payment of the tax. If the claim is rejected, the taxpayer is notified of the rejection by registered or certified mail, and the taxpayer may then bring suit in the U.S. District Court or the Court of Claims for recovery of the tax. Such suits must be filed generally within two years from the date of mailing of the rejection notice. If the claim is allowed, a check for the amount of the refund and allowable interest is forwarded to the taxpayer; however, if there are other unpaid taxes outstanding against the taxpayer, the overpayment may be applied to the outstanding taxes and the balance, if any, refunded.

(2) *Taxes on liquors lost, destroyed, returned to bond, or taken as samples by the United States.* A taxpayer may, subject to the conditions in the appropriate regulations, file claim on Form 5620.8 for refund of tax paid on:

(i) Spirits returned to bonded premises, lost by accident or disaster, or taken as samples by the United States, or

(ii) Wine returned to bond or lost by disaster, or

(iii) Beer returned to a brewery or voluntarily destroyed, or lost, whether by theft or otherwise, or destroyed or otherwise rendered unmerchantable by fire, casualty, or act of God. If the claim is allowed, a check for the amount of the refund is forwarded to the claimant; except, that where there are any unpaid taxes outstanding against the claimant, the refund may be applied to the outstanding taxes and a check for the balance, if any, forwarded to the claimant. If the claim is rejected, a copy of the claim giving the reasons for rejection is forwarded to the claimant.

(d) *Claims for allowance, credit, or relief.* A qualified permittee, manufacturer, or proprietor may, subject to the conditions in the appropriate regulations, file claim on Form 5620.8 for allowance of loss, credit of tax, or relief from tax liability, as applicable, on

(1) Spirits returned to bonded premises, lost or destroyed on bonded premises, or in transit thereto, or lost by accident or disaster;

(2) Wine lost or destroyed on bonded premises or in transit thereto and wine returned to bond;

(3) Beer returned to a brewery or voluntarily destroyed, or lost, whether by theft or otherwise, or destroyed or otherwise rendered unmerchantable by fire, casualty, or act of God;

(4) Denatured spirits lost or destroyed in bond, or lost on the premises of a qualified dealer or user or in transit to such premises; and

(5) Tax-free spirits lost on the premises of a qualified user or in transit to such premises.

(e) *Claims for payment-disaster losses.* When distilled spirits, wines, rectified products, or beer held or intended for sale is lost, rendered unmarketable, or condemned by a duly authorized official by reason of a "major disaster" as determined by the President of the

United States, the person holding such product for sale at that time may, subject to the conditions in the appropriate regulations, file a claim on form TTB F 5620.8 for payment of an amount equal to the internal revenue taxes paid or determined and any customs duties paid thereon. Claims must be filed within 6 months from the date on which the President makes the determination that the disaster has occurred. The determination date is construed to mean the date the Director, Office of Emergency Preparedness, identifies the specific disaster area.

(Approved by the Office of Management and Budget under control number 1513–0030)

[T.D. ATF–251, 52 FR 19325, May 22, 1987. Redesignated and amended by T.D. ATF–301, 55 FR 47606, 47653, Nov. 14, 1990; T.D. ATF–450, 66 FR 29028, May 29, 2001; T.D. TTB–91, 76 FR 5481, Feb. 1, 2011; T.D. TTB–130, 80 FR 55249, Sept. 15, 2015]

§ 70.414 Preparation and filing of claims.

(a) *Distilled spirits at distilled spirits plants.* Procedural instructions in respect of claims for remission, abatement, credit, or refund of tax on spirits (including denatured spirits) lost or destroyed on or lost in transit to, or on spirits returned to, the premises of a distilled spirits plant are contained in Part 19 of Title 27 CFR. It is not necessary to file a claim for credit of tax on taxpaid samples taken by appropriate TTB officers from distilled spirits plants, as the appropriate TTB officer will allow credit, without claim, for tax on such samples.

(b) *Specially denatured spirits.* Procedural instructions in respect of claims for allowance of loss on specially denatured spirits lost on the premises of a bonded dealer or user, or while in transit to such premises, are contained in part 20 of title 27 CFR.

(c) *Tax-free alcohol.* Procedural instructions in respect of claims for allowance of loss on tax-free alcohol lost on the premises of a qualified user, or while in transit to such premises, are contained in part 22 of title 27 CFR.

(d) *Wine spirits and wine at bonded wine cellar.* Procedural instructions in respect of claims for:

(1) Remission of tax on wine spirits lost on the premises of a bonded wine cellar or in transit thereto,

(2) Allowance of losses of wine in bond, and

(3) Credit or refund of tax paid on wine returned to bond are contained in part 24 of title 27 CFR.

(e) *Beer.* Procedural instructions in respect of claims for refund or credit of tax which has been paid (or allowance, credit, or relief of tax liability if the tax has not been paid) on domestic beer returned to a brewery or voluntarily destroyed; or lost, whether by theft or otherwise, or destroyed or otherwise rendered unmerchantable by fire, casualty, or act of God are contained in part 25 of title 27 CFR.

(f) *Distilled spirits, wines, or beer for export.* Procedural instructions in respect of claims for:

(1) Drawback of internal revenue tax on distilled spirits, wines, or beer for export, use as supplies on certain vessels or aircraft, or deposit in a foreign-trade zone, or deposit of distilled spirits or wine in a customs bonded warehouse, and

(2) Remission of tax on distilled spirits, specially denatured spirits, wines, or beer, withdrawn without payment or free of tax and lost during transportation to the port of export, customs bonded warehouse (distilled spirits and wine only), manufacturing bonded warehouse, vessel or aircraft, or foreign-trade zone, as applicable, are contained in part 28 of title 27 CFR. Procedural instructions as to claims respecting export with benefit of drawback of tax on domestic distilled spirits products containing spirits from Puerto Rico or the Virgin Islands are contained in parts 19 and 28 of title 27 CFR.

(g) *Miscellaneous.* Procedural instructions are contained in 27 CFR Part 70, subparts F and G in respect of claims for—

(1) Refund or credit of tax on distilled spirits, wines or beer where such refund or credit is claimed on the grounds that tax was assessed or collected erroneously, illegally, without authority, or in any manner wrongfully, or on the grounds that such amount was excessive, and where such refund or credit is subject to the limitations imposed by

section 6423 of the Internal Revenue Code.

(2) Payment of an amount equal to the internal revenue tax paid or determined and customs duties paid on distilled spirits, wines, rectified products, and beer previously withdrawn, which were lost, rendered unmarketable, or condemned by a duly authorized official by reason of a major disaster occurring in the United States after June 30, 1959.

(h) [Reserved]

(i) *Low wines at vinegar plants.* Procedural instructions in respect of claims for remission of tax on low wines (distilled spirits) lost at vinegar plants producing vinegar by the vaporizing process are contained in part 19 of title 27 CFR.

(j) *Distilled spirits used in nonbeverage products.* Procedural instructions in respect of claims for drawback of excise tax, submitted by persons using distilled spirits in the manufacture of medicines, medicinal preparations, food products, flavors, flavoring extracts, or perfume, which are unfit for beverage purposes, are contained in part 17 of title 27 CFR.

(k) *Reopening claims.* A claimant who wishes to have a rejected claim reopened must, within the applicable statutory period of limitations, submit a written application to the officer who originally rejected the claim for reconsideration of the claim. Such application must show that the additional evidence to be presented is new and material, and that such evidence was unknown to the claimant, or unobtainable by the claimant, when the claim was previously under consideration.

(l) *Claimant's rights under law and regulations.* Before final action has been taken on a claim, a claimant who, by reason of an oversight, misunderstanding of law and regulations, miscalculation, or other cause, did not claim the full amount of abatement, refund, credit, or drawback, as the case may be, of tax to which the claimant is legitimately entitled, may amend a valid claim, and statements filed in support thereof, in instances where such a claim is deficient in establishing the claimants eligibility to the rights extended to such claimant under law and regulations.

[T.D. ATF–251, 52 FR 19325, May 22, 1987]

EDITORIAL NOTE: For FEDERAL REGISTER citations affecting § 70.414, see the List of CFR Sections Affected, which appears in the Finding Aids section of the printed volume and at *www.fdsys.gov.*

§ 70.415 Offers in compromise.

Procedure in the case of offers in compromise of liabilities under 26 U.S.C. chapter 51 and of penalties for violation of the Federal Alcohol Administration Act, is set forth in §§ 70.482 through 70.484.

[T.D. ATF–301, 55 FR 47654, Nov. 14, 1990]

§ 70.416 Application for approval of interlocking directors and officers under section 8 of the Federal Alcohol Administration Act.

Any person who is an officer or director of a corporation now engaged in business as a distiller, rectifier, or blender of distilled spirits, or of an affiliate thereof, who desires to take office in other companies similarly engaged, must obtain permission to do so from the appropriate TTB officer. Applications for such permission to take office must be prepared and filed in accordance with instructions available from the appropriate TTB officer.

[T.D. ATF–450, 66 FR 29029, May 29, 2001]

§ 70.417 Rulings.

The procedure for rulings in alcohol tax matters is set forth in § 70.471.

[T.D. ATF–301, 55 FR 47654, Nov. 14, 1990]

§ 70.418 Conferences.

Any person desiring a conference with TTB, relative to any matter arising in connection with such person's operations, will be accorded such a conference upon request. No formal requirements are prescribed for such conference.

[T.D. ATF–450, 66 FR 29029, May 29, 2001]

§ 70.419 Representatives.

Title 31 CFR part 8 is applicable to all representatives of the taxpayer, for any conference with TTB.

[T.D. ATF–450, 66 FR 29029, May 29, 2001]

§70.420 Forms.

For forms to be used, *see* §70.411(c).

[T.D. ATF-301, 55 FR 47654, Nov. 14, 1990]

§70.421 Alcohol dealer registration.

Every person who sells, or offers for sale, any alcohol product (distilled spirits, wines, or beer) fit for beverage use must register with the Alcohol and Tobacco Tax and Trade Bureau. The specific requirements are contained in the following regulations:

(a) For proprietors of distilled spirits plants, parts 19 and 31 of this chapter;

(b) For bonded wineries, bonded wine cellars, bonded wine warehouses, and taxpaid wine bottling houses, parts 24 and 31 of this chapter;

(c) For brewers, parts 25 and 31 of this chapter;

(d) For persons bringing distilled spirits, wines, or beer from Puerto Rico and the Virgin Islands to the United States, parts 26 and 31 of this chapter;

(e) For importers of distilled spirits, wines, or beer, parts 27 and 31 of this chapter; and

(f) For wholesalers and retailers of distilled spirits, wines, or beer, part 31 of this chapter.

[T.D. TTB-79, 74 FR 37424, July 28, 2009]

§70.422 Registration of manufacturers of nonbeverage products.

For provisions regarding the registration of persons claiming drawback on distilled spirits used in the manufacture of certain nonbeverage products, see part 17 of this chapter.

[T.D. TTB-79, 74 FR 37424, July 28, 2009]

PROVISIONS RELATING TO TOBACCO PRODUCTS, AND CIGARETTE PAPERS AND TUBES

§70.431 Imposition of taxes; regulations.

(a) *Taxes.* Subchapter A of chapter 52 of the IRC imposes taxes on tobacco products, and cigarette papers and tubes manufactured in or imported into the United States. Occupational taxes are imposed by manufacturers of tobacco products, manufacturers of cigarette papers and tubes, and export warehouse proprietors. Subchapter D of chapter 78 of the Internal Revenue Code imposes a tax (equal to the internal revenue tax imposed in the United States upon the like articles of merchandise of domestic manufacture) on tobacco products, and cigarette papers and tubes of Puerto Rican and Virgin Islands manufacture brought into the United States and withdrawn for consumption or sale.

(b) *Regulations.* The procedural requirements with respect to matters relating to tobacco products, cigarette papers and tubes, and processed tobacco are contained in the regulations listed below:

(1) Part 71 of title 27 CFR relates to the procedure and practice in connection with the disapproval of applications for permits, and the suspension and revocation of permits, under chapter 52 of the Internal Revenue Code.

(2) Part 40 of title 27 CFR relates to the manufacture of tobacco products, cigarette papers and tubes, and processed tobacco, the payment of internal revenue taxes imposed by chapter 52 of the Internal Revenue Code on manufacturers of tobacco products and of cigarette papers and tubes, and the qualification of and operations by manufacturers of tobacco products, cigarette papers and tubes, and processed tobacco.

(3) Part 41 of title 27 CFR relates to tobacco products, cigarette papers and tubes, and processed tobacco imported into the United States from a foreign country or brought into the United States from Puerto Rico, the Virgin Islands, or a possession of the United States; the removal of cigars from a customs bonded manufacturing warehouse, Class 6; and the release of tobacco products, and cigarette papers and tubes from customs custody, without payment of internal revenue tax or customs duty attributable to the internal revenue tax.

(4) [Reserved]

(5) Part 44 of title 27 CFR relates to the exportation (including supplies for vessels and aircraft and transfers to a foreign-trade zone) of tobacco products, and cigarette papers and tubes, without payment of tax, or with benefit of drawback of tax, and the qualification of and operations by export warehouse proprietors.

(6) Part 45 of title 27 CFR relates to the removal of tobacco products, and

cigarette papers and tubes, without payment of tax, for use of the United States.

(7) Part 46 of title 27 CFR relates to the provisions of a miscellaneous nature or not of continuing application. Included are regulations relating to:

(i) Limitations imposed by section 6423 of the Internal Revenue Code on the refund or credit of tax paid or collected on tobacco products, and cigarette papers and tubes;

(ii) Losses of tobacco products, and cigarette papers and tubes caused by disasters occurring in the United States on or after September 3, 1958;

(iii) Purchase, receipt, possession, offering for sale, or sale or other disposition of tobacco products by dealers in such products; and

(iv) Liability for special (occupational) tax, filing special tax returns, issuance and examination of special tax stamps, and notification of changes to special tax stamps.

(Approved by the Office of Management and Budget under control number 1512–0472)

[T.D. ATF–251, 52 FR 19325, May 22, 1987]

EDITORIAL NOTE: For FEDERAL REGISTER citations affecting § 70.431, see the List of CFR Sections Affected, which appears in the Finding Aids section of the printed volume and at *www.fdsys.gov*.

§ 70.432 Qualification and bonding requirements.

(a) *Manufacturers of tobacco products and proprietors of export warehouses.* Every person, before commencing business as a manufacturer of tobacco products or as a proprietor of an export warehouse, is required to qualify with the Alcohol and Tobacco Tax and Trade Bureau by making application for a permit and filing bond and other required documents and obtaining a permit.

(b) *Manufacturers of cigarette papers and tubes.* Every person, before commencing business as a manufacturer of cigarette papers and tubes, is required to qualify with the Alcohol and Tobacco Tax and Trade Bureau by filing bond and other required documents.

(c) *Puerto Rican manufacturers of tobacco products.* Every manufacturer of tobacco products in Puerto Rico who desires to defer payment in Puerto Rico of the internal revenue tax imposed by section 7652(a) of the Internal Revenue Code on tobacco products of Puerto Rican manufacture coming into the United States must file a bond with the appropriate TTB officer. Such bond is conditioned on the principal's paying, at the time and in the manner prescribed in the regulations, the full amount of tax computed on the tobacco products which are released for shipment to the United States. No bond is required if the tax is prepaid.

(d) *Proprietors of customs warehouses.* Every proprietor of a customs bonded manufacturing warehouse, Class 6, who desires to remove under part 44 tax-exempt cigars for exportation (including supplies for vessels and aircraft), or for delivery for subsequent exportation, is required to file a bond. However, removal of cigars for sale or consumption in the United States is subject to customs regulations.

(e) *Drawback of tax.* Taxpaid tobacco products, and cigarette papers and tubes may be exported with benefit of drawback of tax. Drawback may be allowed only to the person who paid the tax on such articles and who files a claim and otherwise complies with the provisions contained in the applicable regulations referred to in § 70.431. As a condition precedent to the allowance of any drawback claim, the claimant is required to file a bond in an amount not less than the amount of tax covered in the claim.

(f) *General.* Detailed information relating to the qualification and bonding requirements, including the forms to be used and the procedure to be followed, is fully set forth in the regulations referred to in § 70.431.

[T.D. ATF–251, 52 FR 19325, May 22, 1987. Redesignated and amended by T.D. ATF–301, 55 FR 47606, 47654, Nov. 14, 1990; T.D. ATF–450, 66 FR 29029, May 29, 2001; T.D. ATF–464, 66 FR 43480, Aug. 20, 2001]

§ 70.433 Collection of taxes.

(a) *Tobacco products.* Taxes on tobacco products are paid by the manufacturer on the basis of a return. If the manufacturer has filed a proper bond, such manufacturer may defer payment at the time of removal and file semimonthly returns to cover the taxes. If the manufacturer has not filed such a bond or if the manufacturer has defaulted in any way in paying the taxes, the manufacturer is required to file a prepayment return prior to removal of such products, and to continue so doing until the appropriate TTB officer finds that the revenue will not be jeopardized by deferred payment. Tax returns, with remittances, are filed by the domestic manufacturer in accordance with instructions on the appropriate TTB form. Taxes on cigars produced in a customs bonded manufacturing warehouse, Class 6, are paid on the basis of a return to the director of customs in accordance with customs procedures and regulations. Taxes on tobacco products imported or brought into the United States from a foreign country, Puerto Rico, the Virgin Islands, or a possession of the United States are paid by the importer to the director of customs on the basis of a return made on the customs form by which release from customs custody is to be effected. However, taxes on tobacco products manufactured in Puerto Rico and brought into the United States may be prepaid in Puerto Rico on the basis of a return. If a Puerto Rican manufacturer has filed a proper bond, such manufacturer may defer payment at the time of release for shipment to the United States and file a semimonthly return to cover the taxes. If the manufacturer has not filed such a bond or if such manufacturer has defaulted in any way in payment of taxes, the manufacturer must file a prepayment return prior to removal of such products for shipment to the United States, and continue to do so until the appropriate TTB officer finds that the revenue will not be jeopardized by deferred payment. Tax returns, with remittances, are filed by the domestic manufacturer in accordance with instructions on the appropriate TTB form.

(b) *Cigarette papers and tubes.* Taxes on cigarette papers and tubes are paid by the manufacturer on the basis of a semimonthly return. Such returns, with remittances, are filed in accordance with the instructions on the appropriate TTB form. Taxes on cigarette papers and tubes imported or brought into the United States from a foreign country, Puerto Rico, the Virgin Islands, or a possession of the United States are paid to the director of customs before removal on the basis of a return made on the customs form by which release from customs custody is effected. However, taxes on cigarette papers and tubes of Puerto Rican manufacture which are to be shipped to the United States may be prepaid in Puerto Rico on the basis of a return.

(c) *Special tax.* Special (occupational) taxes are paid by manufacturers of tobacco products, manufacturers of cigarette papers and tubes, and export warehouse proprietors on the basis of a return. Special tax stamps are issued to denote the payment of special (occupational) taxes.

(d) *General.* Detailed information about the payment of taxes on tobacco products, and cigarette papers and tubes, including the forms to be used, records to be kept, and reports and inventories to be filed, is contained in the respective regulations referred to in § 70.431.

(Approved by the Office of Management and Budget under control number 1512–0472)

[T.D. ATF–251, 52 FR 19325, May 22, 1987, as amended by T.D. ATF–271, 53 FR 17549, May 17, 1988. Redesignated and amended by T.D. ATF–301, 55 FR 47606, 47654, Nov. 14, 1990; T.D. ATF–450, 66 FR 29029, May 29, 2001]

§ 70.434 Assessments.

When additional or delinquent tax liability on tobacco products, and cigarette papers and tubes is disclosed by an investigation or by an examination of the taxpayer's records, a notice (except where delay may jeopardize collection of the tax, or where the amount is nominal or the result of an evident mathematical error) is forwarded to the taxpayer indicating the basis for, and amount of, the liability and affording the taxpayer an opportunity to show cause, in writing, against assessment.

[T.D. ATF–251, 52 FR 19325, May 22, 1987. Redesignated by T.D. ATF–301, 55 FR 47606, Nov. 14, 1990]

§ 70.435 Claims.

(a) *General.* Detailed requirements, including the procedure to be followed in the filing of a claim, the form to be used, the supporting documents which must be submitted, the time within which a claim must be filed, and any other limitations or instructions are contained in the applicable regulations referred to in § 70.431.

(b) *Abatement of assessment.* Abatement of the unpaid portion of an assessment of any tax on tobacco products, and cigarette papers and tubes, or any liability in respect thereof, may be allowed to the extent that such assessment is excessive in amount, is assessed after expiration of the applicable period of limitation, or is erroneously or illegally assessed.

(c) *Allowance of tax.* Relief from the payment of tax on tobacco products, and cigarette papers and tubes may be extended to a manufacturer by approval of a claim for allowance where such articles, after removal from the factory upon determination of tax and prior to the time for payment of such tax, are lost (otherwise than by theft) or destroyed by fire, casualty, or act of God, while in the possession or ownership of the manufacturer who removed such articles, or are withdrawn by the manufacturer from the market.

(d) *Remission of tax liability.* Remission of the tax liability on tobacco products, and cigarette papers and tubes may be extended to a manufacturer or export warehouse proprietor liable for the tax, where such articles in bond are lost (otherwise than by theft) or destroyed by fire, casualty, or act of God, while in the possession or ownership of the manufacturer or export warehouse proprietor.

(e) *Refund of tax.* Taxes paid on tobacco products, cigarette papers and tubes lost (otherwise than by theft) or destroyed by fire, casualty, or act of God, while in the possession or ownership of the manufacturer, importer, or export warehouse proprietor, or withdrawn from the market, may be refunded. Refunds may also be made within certain limitations for overpayments of tax on tobacco products, and cigarette papers and tubes.

(f) *Losses caused by disaster.* Payment of an amount equal to the amount of internal revenue taxes paid or determined and customs duties paid on tobacco products, and cigarette papers and tubes removed from the factory or released from customs custody, which are lost, rendered unmarketable, or condemned by a duly authorized official by reason of a "major disaster" as determined by the President of the United States may be made only if, at the time of the disaster, such articles were being held for sale by the claimant. Claims must be filed within 6 months from the date on which the President makes the determination that the disaster has occurred. The determination date is construed to mean the date the Director, Office of Emergency Preparedness, identifies the specific disaster area.

(g) *Drawback of tax.* Drawback may be allowed to the person who paid the tax on tobacco products, and cigarette papers and tubes which are shipped to a foreign country, Puerto Rico, the Virgin Islands, or a possession of the United States.

(h) *Credit of tax.* Taxes paid on tobacco products, and cigarette papers and tubes lost (otherwise than by theft) or destroyed by fire, casualty, or act of God, while in the possession or ownership of the manufacturer, or withdrawn from the market, may be credited upon approval of a claim.

(i) *Reopening claims.* A claimant who wishes to have a rejected claim reopened must, within the applicable statutory period of limitations, submit a written application to the appropriate TTB officer for reconsideration of the claim. Such application must show that the additional evidence to be presented is new and material, and that such evidence was unknown to the claimant, or unobtainable by the claimant, when the claim was previously under consideration.

(j) *Claimant's rights under law and regulations.* Before final action has been taken on a claim, a claimant who, by reason of an oversight, misunderstanding of law and regulations, miscalculation, or other cause, did not claim the full amount of abatement, refund, credit, or drawback, as the case may be, of tax to which the claimant is legitimately entitled, may amend a valid claim, and statements filed in support thereof, in instances where such a claim is deficient in establishing the claimants eligibility to rights extended under law and regulations.

[T.D. ATF-251, 52 FR 19325, May 22, 1987. Redesignated and amended by T.D. ATF-301, 55 FR 47606, 47654, Nov. 14, 1990]

§ 70.436 Offers in compromise.

Procedure in the case of offers in compromise of liabilities under 26 U.S.C. chapter 52 is set forth in §§ 70.482 through 70.484.

[T.D. ATF-301, 55 FR 47654, Nov. 14, 1990]

§ 70.437 Rulings.

The procedure for rulings in tobacco tax matters is set forth in § 70.471.

[T.D. ATF-301, 55 FR 47654, Nov. 14, 1990]

§ 70.438 Forms.

Detailed information as to all forms prescribed for use in connection with tobacco taxes is contained in the regulations referred to in § 70.431(b).

[T.D. ATF-251, 52 FR 19325, May 22, 1987. Redesignated by T.D. ATF-301, 55 FR 47653, Nov. 14, 1990, as amended by T.D. ATF-450, 66 FR 29029, May 29, 2001]

Provisions Relating to Firearms, Shells and Cartridges, and Explosives

§ 70.441 Applicable laws.

(a) Chapter 53 of the Internal Revenue Code (26 U.S.C. 5801–5872), the provisions of which are derived from the National Firearms Act Amendments of 1968 (82 Stat. 1227), imposes a tax on the making and transfer in the United States of machine guns, destructive devices, and certain other types of firearms, and an occupational tax upon every importer and manufacturer of, and dealer in, such firearms. Section 1(b) (2) of the act of August 9, 1939 (52 Stat. 1291; 49 U.S.C. 781–788), makes provision for the seizure and forfeiture of vessels, vehicles, and aircraft which are used to transport, carry, or possess, or to facilitate the same, any firearms with respect to which there has been committed any violation of the National Firearms Act or any regulations issued pursuant thereto.

(b) Title I, State Firearms Control Assistance (18 U.S.C., Chapter 44), of the Gun Control Act of 1968 (82 Stat. 1213), as amended by Pub. L. 99–308 (100 Stat. 449), Pub. L. 99–360 (100 Stat. 766) and Pub. L. 99–408 (100 Stat. 920), provides for the licensing of manufacturers and importers of firearms and ammunition, collectors of firearms, and dealers in firearms, and establishes controls for firearms and ammunition acquisitions and dispositions.

(c) Title I, State Firearms Control Assistance (18 U.S.C. Chapter 44), of the Gun Control Act of 1968 (82 Stat. 1213) as amended by Pub. L. 99–308 (100 Stat. 449) and Pub. L. 99–360 (100 Stat. 766), provides that no person may ship or transport any firearms or ammunition in interstate or foreign commerce, or receive any firearms or ammunition which has been shipped or transported in interstate or foreign commerce, or possess any firearms or ammunition in or affecting commerce, who (1) has been convicted of a crime punishable by imprisonment for a term exceeding 1 year, (2) is a fugitive from justice, (3) is an unlawful user of or addicted to any controlled substance (as defined in section 102 of the Controlled Substances Act, 21 U.S.C. 802), (4) has been adjudicated as a mental defective or has been committed to a mental institution, (5) is an alien illegally or unlawfully in the United States, (6) has been discharged from the Armed Forces under dishonorable conditions, or (7) having been a citizen of the United States, has renounced citizenship.

(d) Section 38 of the Arms Export Control Act (22 U.S.C. 2778) and regulations thereunder and 27 CFR part 447 are applicable to the registration and licensing of persons engaged in the business of manufacturing, importing or exporting arms, ammunition, or implements of war. The Secretary of the Treasury is authorized to control, in furtherance of world peace and the security and foreign policy of the United States, the import of articles enumerated on the U.S. Munitions Import List.

(e) Title XI, Regulation of Explosives (18 U.S.C. chapter 40) of the Organized Crime Control Act of 1970 (84 Stat. 922) provides for the licensing of manufacturers, importers, and limited manufacturers of, and dealers in, explosives in interstate or foreign commerce, and for issuance of permits for users who buy or transport explosives in interstate or foreign commerce.

(f) Chapter 32 of the Internal Revenue Code (26 U.S.C. 4181), imposes a tax upon the sale by the manufacturer, producer, or importer of pistols, revolvers, firearms (other than pistols and revolvers), and shells and cartridges.

[T.D. ATF–251, 52 FR 19325, May 22, 1987. Redesignated by T.D. ATF–301, 55 FR 47653, Nov. 14, 1990, as amended by T.D. ATF–331, 57 FR 40328, Sept. 3, 1992; T.D. TTB–91, 76 FR 5481, Feb. 1, 2011]

§ 70.442 Taxes relating to machine guns, destructive devices, and certain other firearms.

Part 479 of title 27 CFR contains the regulations relative to the:

(a) Payment of special (occupational) taxes by manufacturers and importers of and dealers in, machine guns, destructive devices, and certain other types of firearms,

(b) Payment of the tax on the making or transfer of such firearms,

(c) Registration, identification, importation, and exportation of such firearms,

(d) Keeping of books and records and rendering of returns, and

(e) The forfeiture and disposition of seized firearms under the provisions of the National Firearms Act.

[T.D. ATF–251, 52 FR 19325, May 22, 1987. Redesignated by T.D. ATF–301, 55 FR 47653, Nov. 14, 1990, as amended by T.D. TTB–91, 76 FR 5481, Feb. 1, 2011]

§ 70.443 Firearms and ammunition.

(a) *Commerce in firearms and ammunition.* (1) 27 CFR part 478 contains the regulations relative to:

(i) The licensing of importers and manufacturers of firearms and ammunition, collectors of firearms, and dealers in firearms,

(ii) The identification of firearms,

(iii) The acquisition and disposition of firearms and ammunition,

(iv) The records required to be kept by licensees, and

(v) The forfeiture and disposition of seized firearms and ammunition, under the provisions of title I of the Gun Control Act of 1968, as amended, and also

(vi) The restrictions regarding the receipt, possession, or transportation of firearms by certain persons.

(b) *Firearms and ammunition excise taxes.* (1) 27 CFR part 53 contains the regulations relative to:

(i) Payment of excise tax on the sale of pistols, revolvers, firearms (other than pistols and revolvers), shells and cartridges,

(ii) Establishing constructive sales price,

(iii) Registration for tax free sales,

(iv) Keeping of records and rendering of returns, and

(v) The exportation or use in further manufacture of tax-paid articles.

[T.D. ATF–331, 57 FR 40328, Sept. 3, 1992, as amended by T.D. TTB–91, 76 FR 5482, Feb. 1, 2011]

§ 70.444 Importation of arms, ammunition, and implements of war.

Part 447 of title 27 CFR implements Executive Order 11958 and supplements the import provisions contained in parts 478 and 479 of title 27 CFR. Part 447 establishes the U.S. Munitions Import List and contains the regulations relative to:

(a) The registration of importers in arms, ammunition, and implements of war,

(b) Import permit requirements,

(c) Import certification and verification,

(d) Import restrictions applicable to certain countries, and

(e) The forfeiture of seized arms, ammunition, and implements of war under the Arms Export Control Act.

[T.D. ATF–301, 55 FR 47616, Nov. 14, 1990, as amended by T.D. TTB–91, 76 FR 5482, Feb. 1, 2011]

§ 70.445 Commerce in explosives.

Part 555 of title 27 CFR contains the regulations relative to:

(a) Licensing of manufacturers, importers, and limited manufacturers of, and dealers in, explosives,

(b) Permits for users who buy or transport explosives in interstate or foreign commerce,

(c) Construction of different types of storage facilities for three classes of explosive material,

(d) The identification of explosives,

(e) The acquisition and disposition of explosives,

(f) The records required to be kept by licensees and permittees,

(g) The forfeiture and disposition of seized explosive material, under the provision of Title XI of the Organized Crime Control Act of 1970,

(h) Operations by licensees or permittees and hearings procedure after denial or revocation of license or permit, and also

(i) Restrictions regarding the receipt, possession, or transportation of explosives by certain persons under the provisions of Title XI of the Organized Crime Control Act of 1970.

[T.D. ATF–301, 55 FR 47616, Nov. 14, 1990, as amended by T.D. TTB–91, 76 FR 5482, Feb. 1, 2011]

§ 70.446 Rulings.

The procedure for rulings in the firearms and explosives area is set forth in § 70.471.

[T.D. ATF–301, 55 FR 47654, Nov. 14, 1990]

§ 70.447 Assessments.

Where the evidence disclosed by investigation establishes that additional or delinquent tax liability has been incurred and not paid, the appropriate TTB officer will list the tax as an assessment. Notification and demand for payment of assessed taxes will be issued to the taxpayer by the appropriate TTB officer.

[T.D. ATF–301, 55 FR 47654, Nov. 14, 1990]

§ 70.448 Claims.

(a) The procedures applicable to the filing of claims under chapter 53 of the Internal Revenue Code are set forth below:

(1) Claims for refund of the making and transfer taxes, and of occupational taxes, whether paid pursuant to assessment or voluntarily paid, and claims for redemption of "National Firearms Act" stamps, are prepared and filed in accordance with the procedures set forth in 27 CFR part 479.

(2) Claims for abatement of making and transfer taxes, and claims for abatement of occupational taxes and penalties erroneously assessed, are prepared and filed in accordance with the procedures set forth in § 70.413(b).

(3) Claims may be reopened or amended in accordance with the provisions of § 70.414 (k) and (l).

(b) The procedures applicable to the filing of claims relating to the tax imposed by section 4181 of the Internal Revenue Code are set forth below:

(1) Claims for credit or refund of manufacturers taxes, whether paid pursuant to assessment of voluntarily paid, are prepared and filed in accordance with the procedures set forth in § 70.123 and 27 CFR 53.171 through 53.186. For regulations under section 6416 of the Internal Revenue Code, relating to conditions to allowance and other procedural requirements, see 27 CFR 53.172 through 53.186.

(2) Claims for abatement of manufacturers taxes are to be prepared and filed in accordance with § 70.125.

(3) Claims may be reopened or amended in accordance with the provisions of § 70.414 (k) and (l).

[T.D. ATF–331, 57 FR 40328, Sept. 3, 1992, as amended by T.D. TTB–91, 76 FR 5482, Feb. 1, 2011]

§ 70.449 Offers in compromise.

The procedures in the case of offers in compromise of liabilities under 26 U.S.C. 4181 and chapter 53 are set forth in §§ 70.482 and 70.484.

[T.D. ATF–331, 57 FR 40329, Sept. 3, 1992]

SEIZED PROPERTY

§ 70.450 Seizure and forfeiture of personal property.

Part 72 of title 27 CFR contains the regulations relative to the personal property seized by officers of the Bureau of Alcohol, Tobacco and Firearms as subject to forfeiture as being used, or intended to be used, to violate certain Federal laws; the remission or mitigation of such forfeiture; and the administrative sale or other disposition, pursuant to forfeiture, of such seized property other than firearms seized under the National Firearms Act and firearms and ammunition seized under Title I of the Gun Control Act of 1968, as amended. For disposal of firearms under the National Firearms Act, see 26 U.S.C. 5872(b). For disposal of firearms and ammunition under Title I of the Gun Control Act of 1968, see 18 U.S.C. 924(d). For disposal of explosives under Title XI of Organized Crime Control Act of 1970, see 18 U.S.C. 844(c).

POSSESSIONS

§ 70.461 Shipments to the United States.

For regulations under 26 U.S.C. 7652, see 27 CFR part 26 relating to liquors and articles from Puerto Rico and the Virgin Islands; and 27 CFR part 41 relating to cigars, cigarettes, and cigarette papers and tubes.

(68A Stat. 907, as amended (26 U.S.C. 7652))

[T.D. ATF–6, 38 FR 32445, Nov. 26, 1973, as amended by T.D. ATF–249, 52 FR 5961, Feb. 27, 1987. Redesignated by T.D. ATF–301, 55 FR 47606, Nov. 14, 1990, as amended by T.D. ATF–459, 66 FR 38550, July 25, 2001; T.D. TTB–16, 69 FR 52423, Aug. 26, 2004]

§ 70.462 Shipments from the United States.

For regulations under 26 U.S.C. 7653, see 27 CFR part 28 relating to exportation of liquors; and 27 CFR part 44, relating to exportation of cigars, cigarettes, and cigarette papers and tubes.

(68A Stat. 908, as amended; (26 U.S.C. 7653))

[T.D. ATF–6, 38 FR 32445, Nov. 26, 1973, as amended by T.D. ATF–249, 52 FR 5961, Feb. 27, 1987. Redesignated by T.D. ATF–301, 55 FR 47606, Nov. 14, 1990; T.D. ATF–464, 66 FR 43480, Aug. 20, 2001; T.D. TTB–8, 69 FR 3830, Jan. 27, 2004; T.D. TTB–91, 76 FR 5482, Feb. 1, 2011]

RULINGS

§ 70.471 Rulings.

(a) *Requests for rulings.* Any person who is in doubt as to any matter arising in connection with the following may request a ruling thereon by addressing a letter to the appropriate TTB officer:

(1) Operations or transactions in the alcohol tax area (26 U.S.C. chapter 51), the Federal Alcohol Administration Act (27 U.S.C. chapter 8, including the Alcohol Beverage Labeling Act of 1988), or the Webb-Kenyon Act (27 U.S.C. 122);

(2) Operations or transactions in the tobacco tax area (26 U.S.C. chapter 52);

(3) Operations or transactions in the firearms and ammunition manufacturers excise tax area (26 U.S.C. 4181–4182);

(4) Subchapters F and G of chapter 32 of the IRC insofar as they relate to activities administered and enforced with respect to sections 4181 and 4182 of the IRC; and

(5) Subtitle F of the IRC insofar as it relates to any of the foregoing.

(b) *Routine requests for information.* Routine requests for information should be addressed to the appropriate TTB officer.

(c) *Matters under ATF jurisdiction.* For rulings on matters under the jurisdiction of the Bureau of Alcohol, Tobacco, Firearms and Explosives (Department of Justice), contact the Bureau of Alcohol, Tobacco, Firearms and Explosives, Office of Public and Governmental Affairs, 99 New York Avenue, NE., Washington, DC 20226, or view the contact information posted online at *http://www.atf.gov/contact/.*

[T.D. TTB–91, 76 FR 5482, Feb. 1, 2011]

ADMINISTRATIVE REMEDIES

§ 70.481 Agreements for payment of liability in installments.

(a) *Authorization of agreements.* The appropriate TTB officer, is authorized to enter into written agreements with any taxpayer under which such taxpayer is allowed to satisfy liability for payment of any tax in installment payments if the appropriate TTB officer determines that such agreement will facilitate collection of such liability.

(b) *Extent to which agreements remain in effect*—(1) *In general.* Except as otherwise provided in this paragraph (b), any agreement under paragraph (a) of this section shall remain in effect for the term of the agreement.

(2) *Inadequate information or jeopardy.* The officer who entered into an installment agreement under paragraph (a) of this section may terminate such agreement if:

(i) Information which the taxpayer provided prior to the date such agreement was entered into was inaccurate or incomplete, or

(ii) The appropriate TTB officer believes that collection of any tax to which an agreement under this section relates is in jeopardy.

(3) *Subsequent change in financial conditions*—(i) *In general.* If the officer who entered into an installment agreement under paragraph (a) of this section makes a determination that the financial condition of the taxpayer has significantly changed, the officer may

alter, modify, or terminate such agreement.

(ii) *Notice.* Action may be taken by the appropriate TTB officer under paragraph (b)(3)(i) of this section only if:

(A) Notice of such determination is provided to the taxpayer no later than 30 days prior to the date of such action, and

(B) Such notice includes the reasons why the officer believes a significant change in the financial condition of the taxpayer has occurred.

(4) *Failure to pay an installment or any other tax liability when due or to provide requested financial information.* The officer who entered into an installment agreement under paragraph (a) of this section may alter, modify, or terminate such agreement in the case of the failure of the taxpayer:

(i) To pay an installment at the time such installment payment is due under such agreement,

(ii) To pay any other tax liability at the time such liability is due, or

(iii) To provide a financial condition update as requested by the appropriate TTB officer.

(26 U.S.C. 6159)

[T.D. ATF–301, 55 FR 47655, Nov. 14, 1990, as amended by T.D. ATF–450, 66 FR 29029, May 29, 2001]

§ 70.482 Offers in compromise of liabilities (other than forfeiture) under 26 U.S.C.

(a) *In general.* The appropriate TTB officer may compromise any civil or criminal liability arising under the provisions of 26 U.S.C. enforced and administered by TTB prior to reference of a case involving such liability to the Department of Justice for prosecution or defense. (For compromise of forfeiture liability, see § 70.484 of this part.) Any such liability may be compromised only upon one or both of the following two grounds:

(1) Doubt as to liability; or

(2) Doubt as to collectibility.

No such liability will be compromised if the liability has been established by a valid judgment or is certain, and there is no doubt as to the ability of the Government to collect the amounts owing with respect to such liability.

(b) *Scope of compromise agreement.* A compromise agreement may relate to civil or criminal liability for taxes, interest, ad valorem penalties, or specific penalties. However, a criminal liability may be compromised only if it involves a violation of a regulatory provision of 26 U.S.C., or a related statute, and then only if such violation was not deliberately committed with an intent to defraud.

(c) *Effect of compromise agreement.* A compromise agreement relates to the entire liability of the taxpayer (including taxes, ad valorem penalties, and interest) with respect to which the offer in compromise is submitted and all questions of such liability are conclusively settled thereby. Specific penalties, however, shall be compromised separately and not in connection with taxes, interest, or ad valorem penalties. Neither the taxpayer nor the Government shall, upon acceptance of an offer in compromise, be permitted to reopen the case except by reason of falsification or concealment of assets by the taxpayer, or mutual mistake of a material fact sufficient to cause a contract to be reformed or set aside. However, acceptance of an offer in compromise of a civil liability does not remit a criminal liability, nor does acceptance of an offer in compromise of a criminal liability remit a civil liability.

(d) *Procedure with respect to offers in compromise*—(1) *Submission of offers.* (i) Offers in compromise under this section shall be submitted on TTB Form 5640.1, along with any additional information required by the officer authorized to accept or reject the offer. If the offer in compromise is based on inability to pay, the proponent must submit any financial statement required by such officer.

(ii) The offer should generally be accompanied by a remittance representing the amount of the compromise offer or a deposit if the offer provides for future installment payments. When final action has been taken, the proponent is notified of the acceptance or rejection of the offer.

(2) *Stay of collection.* The submission of an offer in compromise shall not automatically operate to stay the collection of any tax liability. However,

enforcement of collection may be deferred if the interests of the United States will not be jeopardized thereby.

(3) *Acceptance.* An offer in compromise shall be considered accepted only when the proponent thereof is so notified in writing. As a condition to accepting an offer in compromise, the taxpayer may be required to enter into any collateral agreement or to post any security which is deemed necessary for the protection of the interests of the United States. If the final payment on an accepted offer is contingent upon the immediate or simultaneous release of a tax lien in whole or in part, such payment must be in cash, or in the form of a certified, cashier's, or treasurer's check drawn on any bank or trust company incorporated under the laws of the United States or any State, Territory, or possession of the United States, or by a U.S. postal, bank, express, or telegraph money order.

(4) *Withdrawal or rejection.* An offer in compromise may be withdrawn by the proponent at any time prior to its acceptance. In the event an offer is rejected, the proponent shall be promptly notified in writing. Frivolous offers or offers submitted for the purpose of delaying the collection of tax liabilities shall be immediately rejected. If an offer in compromise is withdrawn or rejected, the amount tendered with the offer, including all installments paid, shall be refunded without interest, unless the taxpayer has stated or agreed that the amount tendered may be applied to the liability with respect to which the offer was submitted.

(e) *Record.* Except as otherwise provided in this paragraph, if an offer in compromise is accepted, there shall be placed on file the opinion of counsel for the Bureau with respect to such compromise, with the reason therefor, and including a statement of:

(1) The amount of tax assessed,

(2) The amount of interest, additional amount, addition to the tax, or assessable penalty, imposed by law on the person against whom the tax is assessed, and

(3) The amount actually paid in accordance with the terms of the compromise.

However, no such opinion shall be required with respect to the offer in compromise of any civil case in which the unpaid amount of tax assessed (including any interest, additional amount, addition to the tax, or assessable penalty is less than $50,000. However, such compromise shall be subject to continuing quality review by the Secretary.

(f) *Requirement with respect to statute of limitations.* No offer in compromise shall be accepted unless the taxpayer waives the running of the statutory period of limitations on both or either assessment or collection of the tax liability involved for the period during which the offer is pending, or the period during which any installment remains unpaid, and for one year thereafter.

(g) *Inspection with respect to accepted offers in compromise.* For provisions relating to the inspection of returns and accepted offers in compromise, *see* 26 U.S.C. 6103(k)(1).

(26 U.S.C. 7122)

(Approved by the Office of Management and Budget under control number 1512–0472)

[T.D. ATF–301, 55 FR 47655, Nov. 14, 1990, as amended by T.D. ATF–331, 57 FR 40329, Sept. 3, 1992; T.D. ATF–450, 66 FR 29029, May 29, 2001]

§ 70.483 Offers in compromise of violations of Federal Alcohol Administration Act.

The Federal Alcohol Administration Act provides penalties for violations of its provisions. The appropriate TTB officer is authorized to compromise such liabilities. Persons desiring to submit offers in compromise may submit such offers on Form 5640.2. When the offer is acted upon, the proponent is notified of the acceptance or rejection of the offer. If the offer is rejected, the sum submitted with the offer in compromise is returned to the proponent. If the offer is accepted, the proponent is notified and the case is closed.

[T.D. ATF–450, 66 FR 29029, May 29, 2001]

§ 70.484 Offers in compromise of forfeiture liabilities.

The appropriate TTB officer is authorized to compromise liabilities to administrative forfeiture of personal property seized under the laws administered and enforced by the Bureau. Persons desiring to submit offers in compromise of such liabilities may submit such offers on Form 656–E to the appropriate TTB officer. When the offer is acted upon, the proponent is notified of the acceptance or rejection of the offer. If the offer is rejected, the sum submitted with the offer in compromise is returned to the proponent. If the offer is accepted, the proponent is notified and the case is closed. Acceptance of an offer in compromise of civil liabilities does not remit criminal liabilities, nor does acceptance of an offer in compromise of criminal liabilities remit civil liabilities.

[T.D. ATF–301, 55 FR 47655, Nov. 14, 1990, as amended by T.D. ATF–450, 66 FR 29030, May 29, 2001]

§ 70.485 Closing agreements.

(a) *In general.* The appropriate TTB officer may enter into a written agreement with any person relating to the liability of such person (or of the person or estate for whom the person acts) in respect of any tax imposed under the provisions of 26 U.S.C. enforced and administered by the Bureau for any taxable period ending prior or subsequent to the date of such agreement. A closing agreement may be entered into in any case in which there appears to be an advantage in having the case permanently and conclusively closed, or if good and sufficient reasons are shown by the taxpayer for desiring a closing agreement and it is determined by the appropriate TTB officer that the United States will sustain no disadvantage through consummation of such an agreement.

(b) *Scope of closing agreement*—(1) *In general.* A closing agreement may be executed even though under the agreement the taxpayer is not liable for any tax for the period to which the agreement relates. There may be a series of closing agreements relating to the tax liability for a single period.

(2) *Taxable periods ended prior to date of closing agreement.* Closing agreements with respect to taxable periods which ended prior to the date of the agreement may relate to the total tax liability of the taxpayer or to one or more separate items affecting the tax liability of the taxpayer.

(3) *Taxable periods ending subsequent to date of closing agreement.* Closing agreements with respect to taxable periods ending subsequent to the date of the agreement may relate to one or more separate items affecting the tax liability of the taxpayer.

(c) *Finality.* A closing agreement which is approved within such time as may be stated in such agreement, or later agreed to, shall be final and conclusive, and, except upon a showing of fraud or malfeasance, or misrepresentation of a material fact:

(1) The case shall not be reopened as to the matters agreed upon or the agreement modified by any officer, employee, or agent of the United States, and

(2) In any suit, action, or proceeding, such agreement, or any determination, assessment, collection, payment, abatement, refund, or credit made in accordance therewith, shall not be annulled, modified, set aside, or disregarded.

However, a closing agreement with respect to a taxable period ending subsequent to the date of the agreement is subject to any change in, or modification of, the law enacted subsequent to the date of the agreement and made applicable to such taxable period, and each closing agreement shall so recite.

(d) *Procedure with respect to closing agreements*—(1) *Submission of request.* A request for a closing agreement which relates to a prior taxable period may be submitted at any time before a case with respect to the tax liability involved is filed with a court of the United States. The procedure with respect to requests for closing agreements shall be under such rules as may be prescribed from time to time by the Administrator in accordance with the regulations under this section.

(2) *Collection, credit, or refund.* Any tax or deficiency in tax determined pursuant to a closing agreement shall be assessed and collected, and any overpayment determined pursuant thereto shall be credited or refunded,

in accordance with the applicable provisions of law.

(26 U.S.C. 7121)

[T.D. ATF–301, 55 FR 47655, Nov. 14, 1990]

§ 70.486 Managerial review.

If at any step in the collection process a taxpayer does not agree with a TTB employee under the authority of the appropriate TTB officer, the taxpayer has the right to discuss the matter with the employee's immediate supervisor. The TTB employee will give the taxpayer the name and telephone number of the person to be contacted.

[T.D. ATF–301, 55 FR 47655, Nov. 14, 1990, as amended by T.D. TTB–91, 76 FR 5482, Feb. 1, 2011]

Subpart F—Application of Section 6423, Internal Revenue Code of 1954, as Amended, to Refund or Credit of Tax on Distilled Spirits, Wines, and Beer

SOURCE: T.D. ATF–376, 61 FR 31031, June 19, 1996, unless otherwise noted.

GENERAL

§ 70.501 Meaning of terms.

When used in this subpart, where not otherwise distinctly expressed or manifestly incompatible with the intent thereof, terms shall have the meaning ascribed in this section.

Article. The commodity in respect to which the amount claimed was paid or collected as a tax.

Claimant. Any person who files a claim for a refund or credit of tax under this subpart.

District director of customs. The district director of customs at a headquarters port of the district (except the district of New York, N.Y.); the area directors of customs in the district of New York, N.Y.; and the port director at a port not designated as a headquarters port.

I.R.C. Internal Revenue Code of 1986, as amended.

Owner. A person who, by reason of a proprietary interest in the article, furnished the amount claimed to the claimant for the purpose of paying the tax.

Person. An individual, a trust, estate, partnership, association, company, or corporation.

Tax. Any tax imposed by 26 U.S.C. 5001–5066, or by any corresponding provision of prior internal revenue laws, and in the case of any commodity of a kind subject to a tax under any such sections, any tax equal to any such tax, any additional tax, or any floor stocks tax. The term includes an extraction denominated a "tax", and any penalty, addition to tax, additional amount, or interest applicable to any such tax.

§ 70.502 Applicability to certain credits or refunds.

The provisions of this subpart apply only where the credit or refund is claimed on the grounds that an amount of tax was assessed or collected erroneously, illegally, without authority, or in any manner wrongfully, or on the grounds that such amount was excessive. This subpart does not apply to:

(a) Any claim for drawback,

(b) Any claim made in accordance with any law expressly providing for credit or refund where an article is withdrawn from the market, returned to bond, or lost or destroyed, and

(c) Any claim based solely on errors in computation of the quantity of an article subject to tax or on mathematical errors in computation of the amount of the tax due, or to any claim in respect of tax collected or paid on an article seized and forfeited, or destroyed, as contraband.

§ 70.503 Ultimate burden.

For the purposes of this subpart, the claimant, or owner, shall be treated as having borne the ultimate burden of an amount of tax only if:

(a) The claimant or owner has not, directly or indirectly, been relieved of such burden or shifted such burden to any other person,

(b) No understanding or agreement exists for any such relief or shifting, and

(c) If the claimant or owner has neither sold nor contracted to sell the articles involved in such claim, such claimant or owner agrees that there will be no such relief or shifting.

§ 70.504 Conditions to allowance of credit or refund.

No credit or refund to which this subpart is applicable shall be allowed or made, pursuant to a court decision or otherwise, of any amount paid or collected as a tax unless a claim therefor has been filed, as provided in this subpart, by the person who paid the tax and the claimant, in addition to establishing that such claimant is otherwise legally entitled to credit or refund of the amount claimed, establishes:

(a) That the claimant bore the ultimate burden of the amount claimed, or

(b) That the claimant has unconditionally repaid the amount claimed to the person who bore the ultimate burden of such amount, or

(c) That:

(1) The owner of the article furnished the claimant the amount claimed for payment of the tax;

(2) The claimant has filed with the appropriate TTB officer the written consent of such owner to the allowance to the claimant of the credit or refund; and

(3) Such owner satisfies the requirements of paragraph (a) or (b) of this section.

§ 70.505 Requirements on persons intending to file claim.

Any person who, having paid the tax with respect to an article, desires to claim refund or credit of any amount of such tax to which the provisions of this subpart are applicable must:

(a) File a claim, as provided in § 70.506, and

(b) Comply with any other provisions of law or regulations which may apply to the claim.

CLAIM PROCEDURE

§ 70.506 Execution and filing of claim.

Claims to which this subpart is applicable must be executed on Form 2635 (5620.8) in accordance with the instructions on the form. (For provisions relating to handcarried documents, see 27 CFR 70.304). Claims for credit or refund of taxes collected by district directors of customs, to which the provisions of section 6423, I.R.C., are applicable and which Customs regulations (19 CFR Part 24—Customs Financial and Accounting Procedure) require to be filed with the appropriate TTB officer, must be executed and filed in accordance with applicable Customs regulations and this subpart. The claim must set forth each ground upon which the claim is made in sufficient detail to apprise the appropriate TTB officer of the exact basis therefor. Allegations pertaining to the bearing of the ultimate burden relate to additional conditions which must be established for a claim to be allowed and are not in themselves legal grounds for allowance of a claim. There shall also be attached to the form and made part of the claim the supporting data required by § 70.507. All evidence relied upon in support of such claim shall be clearly set forth and submitted with the claim.

[T.D.ATF-376, 61 FR 31031, June 19, 1996, as amended by T.D. ATF-450, 66 FR 29030, May 29, 2001]

§ 70.507 Data to be shown in claim.

Claims to which this subpart is applicable, in addition to the requirements of § 70.506 must set forth or contain the following:

(a) A statement that the claimant paid the amount claimed as a "tax" as defined in this subpart.

(b) Full identification (by specific reference to the form number, the date of filing, the place of filing, and the amount paid on the basis of the particular form or return) of the tax forms or returns covering the payments for which refund or credit is claimed.

(c) The written consent of the owner to the allowance of the refund or credit to the claimant (where the owner of the article in respect of which the tax was paid furnished the claimant the amount claimed for the purpose of paying the tax).

(d) If the claimant (or owner, as the case may be) has neither sold nor contracted to sell the articles involved in the claim, a statement that the claimant (or owner, as the case may be) agrees not to shift, directly or indirectly in any manner whatsoever, the burden of the tax to any other person.

(e) If the claim is for refund of a floor stocks tax, or of an amount resulting from an increase in rate of tax applicable to an article, a statement as to whether the price of the article was increased on or following the effective date of such floor stocks tax or rate increase, and if so, the date of the increase, together with full information as to the amount of such price increase.

(f) Specific evidence (such as relevant records, invoices, or other documents, or affidavits of individuals having personal knowledge of pertinent facts) which will satisfactorily establish the conditions to allowance set forth in § 70.504.

(g) The appropriate TTB officer may require the claimant to furnish as a part of the claim such additional information as may be deemed necessary.

§ 70.508 Time for filing claim.

No credit or refund of any amount of tax to which the provisions of this subpart apply shall be made unless the claimant files a claim therefor within the time prescribed by law and in accordance with the provisions of this subpart.

PENALTIES

§ 70.509 Penalties.

It is an offense punishable by fine and imprisonment for anyone to make or cause to be made any false or fraudulent claim upon the United States, or to make any false or fraudulent statements, or representations, in support of any claim, or to falsely or fraudulently execute any documents required by the provisions of the internal revenue laws, or any regulations made in pursuance thereof.

Subpart G—Losses Resulting From Disaster, Vandalism, or Malicious Mischief

DEFINITIONS

SOURCE: T.D. ATF–376, 61 FR 31033, June 19, 1996, unless otherwise noted.

§ 70.601 Meaning of terms.

When used in this subpart, terms are defined as follows in this section. Words in the plural shall include the singular, and vice versa, and words indicating the masculine gender shall include the feminine. The terms "includes" and "including" do not exclude other things not named which are in the same general class or are otherwise within the scope of the term defined.

Alcoholic liquors or liquors. Distilled spirits, wines, and beer lost, made unmarketable, or condemned, as provided in this subpart.

Beer. Beer, ale, porter, stout, and other similar fermented beverages (including sake, or other similar products) of any name or description containing one-half of 1 percent or more of alcohol by volume on which the internal revenue tax has been paid or determined, and if imported, on which duties have been paid.

Claimant. The person who held the liquors for sale at the time of the disaster or other specified cause of loss and who files a claim under this subpart.

Commissioner of Customs. The Commissioner of Customs, U.S. Customs Service, the Department of the Treasury, Washington, DC.

Distilled spirits, or spirits. Ethyl alcohol and other distillates such as whisky, brandy, rum, gin, vodka, in any form (including all dilutions and mixtures thereof, from whatever source or by whatever process produced), on which the internal revenue tax has been paid or determined and, if imported, on which duties have been paid.

Duly authorized official. Any Federal, State or local government official who is authorized to condemn liquors on which a claim is filed under this subpart.

Duty or duties. Any duty or duties paid under the customs laws of the United States.

Major Disaster. A flood, fire, hurricane, earthquake, storm, or other catastrophe defined as a "major disaster" under the Disaster Relief Act (42 U.S.C. 5122(2)), which occurs in any part of the United States and which the President has determined causes sufficient damage to warrant "major disaster" assistance under that Act.

Tax. (1) With respect to distilled spirits, "tax" means the internal revenue tax that is paid or determined on spirits.

(2) With respect to wines, "tax" means the internal revenue tax that is paid or determined on the wine.

(3) With respect to beer, "tax" means the internal revenue tax that is paid or determined on the beer.

United States. When used in a geographical sense includes only the States and the District of Columbia.

Wines. All still wines, effervescent wines, and flavored wines, on which internal revenue wine tax has been paid or determined, and if imported, on which duty has been paid.

[T.D. ATF–376, 61 FR 31033, June 19, 1996, as amended by T.D. ATF–450, 66 FR 29030, May 29, 2001]

PAYMENTS

§ 70.602 Circumstances under which payment may be made.

(a) *Major disasters.* The appropriate TTB officer shall allow payment (without interest) of an amount equal to the tax paid or determined, and the Commissioner of Customs shall allow payment (without interest) of an amount equal to the duty paid, on distilled spirits, wines, and beer previously withdrawn, if the liquors are lost, made unmarketable, or condemned by a duly authorized official as the result of a major disaster (as defined in § 70.601).

(b) *Other causes of loss*—(1) *Payment.* The appropriate TTB officer shall allow payment (without interest) of an amount equal to the tax paid or determined, and the Commissioner of Customs shall allow payment (without interest) of an amount equal to the duty paid, on distilled spirits, wines, and beer previously withdrawn, if the liquors are lost, made unmarketable, or condemned by a duly authorized official as a result of:

(i) Fire, flood, casualty, or other disaster; or

(ii) Breakage, destruction, or other damage (excluding theft) resulting from vandalism or malicious mischief.

(2) *Minimum claim.* No claim of less than $250 will be allowed for losses resulting from any disaster or damage described in paragraph (b)(1) of this section.

(c) *General.* Payment under this section may be made only if:

(1) The disaster or other specified cause of loss occurred in the United States;

(2) At the time of the disaster or other specified cause of loss, the liquors were being held for sale by the claimant;

(3) Refund or credit of the amount claimed, or any part of the amount claimed, has not or will not be claimed for the same liquors under any other law or regulations; and

(4) The claimant was not indemnified by any valid claim of insurance or otherwise for the tax and/or duty on the liquors covered by the claim.

CLAIMS PROCEDURES

§ 70.603 Execution and filing of claim.

(a) *General.* (1) Claims under this subpart must be filed on Form 2635 (5620.8).

(2) The claim shall include all the facts on which the claim is based, and be accompanied by a record of inventory of the liquors lost, made unmarketable, or condemned. (See § 70.604.)

(3) The claim shall contain a statement that no other claim for refund or credit of the amount claimed, or for any part of the amount claimed, has been or will be filed under any other law or regulations.

(b) *Major disasters.* Claims for refund of tax and/or duty on liquors which were lost, became unmarketable, or were condemned as a result of a major disaster must be filed not later than 6 months from the day on which the President determines that a major disaster has occurred.

(c) *Other causes of loss.* (1) Claims for amounts of $250 or more for refund of tax and/or duty on liquors which were lost, became unmarketable, or were condemned as the result of:

(i) Fire, flood, casualty, or other disaster; or

(ii) Damage (excluding theft) resulting from vandalism or malicious mischief, must be filed within 6 months after the date on which the disaster or damage occurred.

(2) Claims for amounts less than $250 will not be allowed.

[T.D. ATF–376, 61 FR 31033, June 19, 1996, as amended by T.D. ATF–450, 66 FR 29030, May 29, 2001]

§ 70.604 Record of inventory to support claims.

(a) *Claims relating to distilled spirits.* The record of inventory of distilled spirits lost, made unmarketable, or condemned, which is required to support claims filed under § 70.603, shall show the following information:

(1) Name and business address of claimant (as shown on claim, Form 2635 (5620.8)).

(2) Address where the spirits were lost, became unmarketable, or were condemned, if different from the business address.

(3) Kind of spirits.

(4) Brand name.

(5) For full cases, show:

(i) Number of cases;

(ii) Serial numbers;

(iii) Bottles per case;

(iv) Size of bottles;

(v) Wine gallons per case;

(vi) Proof; and

(vii) Proof gallons.

(6) For bottles not in cases, show:

(i) Total number;

(ii) Size of bottles;

(iii) Wine gallons;

(iv) Proof; and

(v) Total proof gallons.

(7) Total proof gallons for all items.

(b) *Claims relating to wines.* The record of inventory of wines lost, made unmarketable, or condemned, which is required to support claims filed under § 70.603, shall show the following information:

(1) Name and business address of claimant (as shown on claim, Form 2635 (5620.8)).

(2) Address where the wines were lost, became unmarketable, or were condemned, if different from the business address.

(3) Kind of wine.

(4) Percent of alcohol by volume.

(5) Number of barrels or kegs.

(6) Kind and number of other bulk containers.

(7) Number of full cases and bottles per case.

(8) Size of bottles.

(9) Number of bottles not in cases and wine gallons.

(10) Total wine gallons.

(c) *Claims relating to beer.* The record of inventory of beer lost, made unmarketable, or condemned, which is required to support claims filed under § 70.603, shall show the following information:

(1) Name and business address of claimant (as shown on claim, Form 2635 (5620.8)).

(2) Address where the beer was lost, became unmarketable, or was condemned, if different from the business address.

(3) Number and size of barrels.

(4) *For full cases, show:*

(i) Number of cases;

(ii) Bottles or cans per case; and

(iii) Size (in ounces) of bottles or cans.

(5) Number and size of bottles and cans not in cases.

(6) Quantity in terms of 31-gallon barrels.

(7) Total quantity.

(d) *Special instructions.* (1) Inventories of domestic liquors, imported liquors, and liquors manufactured in the Virgin Islands shall be reported separately.

(2) Liquors manufactured in Puerto Rico may not be included in claims filed under this subpart. Claims for losses of Puerto Rican liquors shall be filed with the Secretary of the Treasury of Puerto Rico under the laws of Puerto Rico.

§ 70.605 Claims relating to imported, domestic, and Virgin Islands liquors.

(a) Claims involving taxes on domestic liquors, imported liquors, and liquors manufactured in the Virgin Islands must show the quantities of each separately in the claim.

(b) A separate claim on Form 2635 (5620.8) must be filed for customs duties.

§ 70.606 Claimant to furnish proof.

The claimant shall furnish proof to the satisfaction of the appropriate TTB officer regarding the following:

(a) That the tax on the liquors, or the tax and duty if imported, was fully paid; or the tax, if not paid, was fully determined.

(b) That the liquors were lost, made unmarketable, or condemned by a duly authorized official, by reason of damage sustained as a result of a disaster or other cause of loss specified in this subpart.

(c) The type and date of occurrence of the disaster or other specified cause of loss, and the location of the liquors at the time.

(d) That the claimant was not indemnified by a valid claim of insurance or otherwise for the tax, or tax and duty, on the liquors covered by the claim.

(e) That the claimant is entitled to payment under this subpart.

§70.607 Supporting evidence.

(a) The claimant shall support the claim with any evidence (such as inventories, statements, invoices, bills, records, labels, formulas, stamps) that is available to submit, relating to the quantities and identities of the liquors, on which duty has been paid or tax has been paid or determined, that were on hand at the time of the disaster or other specified cause of loss and alleged to have been lost, made unmarketable, or condemned as a result of it.

(b) If the claim is for refund of duty, the claimant shall furnish, if possible:

(1) The customs number;

(2) The date of entry; and

(3) The name of the port of entry.

§70.608 Action on claims.

The appropriate TTB officer shall date stamp and examine each claim filed under this subpart and will determine the validity of the claim. Claims and supporting data involving customs duties will be forwarded to the Commissioner of Customs with a summary statement by the appropriate TTB officer regarding his or her findings.

DESTRUCTION OF LIQUORS

§70.609 Supervision.

When allowance has been made under this subpart for the tax and/or duty on liquors condemned by a duly authorized official or made unmarketable, the liquors shall be destroyed by suitable means under supervision satisfactory to the appropriate TTB officer, unless the liquors were previously destroyed under supervision satisfactory to the appropriate TTB officer. The Commissioner of Customs will notify the appropriate TTB officer as to allowance under this subpart of claims for duty on unmarketable or condemned liquors.

PENALTIES

§70.610 Penalties.

(a) Penalties are provided in 26 U.S.C. 7206 for making any false or fraudulent statement under the penalties of perjury in support of any claim.

(b) Penalties are provided in 26 U.S.C. 7207 for filing any false or fraudulent document under this subpart.

(c) All laws and regulations, including penalties, which apply to internal revenue taxes on liquors shall, when appropriate, apply to payments made under this subpart the same as if the payments were actual refunds of internal taxes on liquors.

Subpart H—Rules, Regulations and Forms

§70.701 Rules and regulations.

(a) *Formulation.* (1) Alcohol, tobacco, and firearms rules take various forms. The most important rules are issued as Treasury decisions, prescribed by the Administrator, and approved by the Secretary. Other rules may be issued over the signature of the Administrator or the signature of any appropriate TTB officer. The channeling of rules varies with the circumstances. Treasury decisions are prepared within the appropriate TTB offices. After approval by the Administrator, Treasury decisions are forwarded to the Secretary for further consideration and final approval.

(2) Where required by 5 U.S.C. 553, the Administrator publishes in the FEDERAL REGISTER general notice of proposed rules unless all persons subject thereto are named and either personally served or otherwise have actual notice thereof in accordance with law. Notice may also be published in the FEDERAL REGISTER in such other instances as may be desirable. This notice includes (i) a statement of the time, place, and nature of public rulemaking proceedings; (ii) reference to the authority under which the rule is proposed; and (iii) either the terms or substance of the proposed rule or a description of the subjects and issues involved. Interested persons may participate in the rulemaking by submitting written data, views, or arguments. Persons may also submit requests for a

public hearing. However, the Bureau reserves the right to determine, in the light of all circumstances, whether a public hearing should be held.

(3) If the Bureau determines that the public good will be served thereby, it may hold a public hearing for discussion of the issues raised by the proposed regulations. Such a hearing is announced by a notice in the FEDERAL REGISTER, stating the time and place where the hearing is to be held. The following rules govern the conduct of the public hearing only if incorporated by reference in the notice announcing the hearing:

(i) A person wishing to make oral comments at a public hearing shall submit, within the time prescribed in the notice of hearing, an outline of the topics he wishes to discuss, and the time he wishes to devote to each topic. Ordinarily, a period of 10 minutes is the time allotted to each person for making his oral comments.

(ii) A person making oral comments should be prepared to answer questions not only on the topics listed in his outline but also on matters relating to any written comments which he has submitted.

(iii) At the conclusion of the presentation of comments of persons listed in the agenda, to the extent time permits, other comments will be received.

(iv) Written comments submitted prior to the hearing shall be available at the hearing for inspection. Any request for copies of such written comments is treated as a request for records under 27 CFR 70.802(g).

(v) To the extent resources permit, the public hearings to which this paragraph applies may be transcribed.

(vi) In unusual circumstances or for good cause shown, the application of rules contained in this paragraph may be waived.

(b) *Comments on proposed rules.* Interested persons may submit data, views, or arguments with respect to a notice of proposed rulemaking published pursuant to 5 U.S.C. 553. Procedures are provided in § 70.802(g) for members of the public to inspect and obtain copies of written comments submitted in response to proposed rules. All such comments are open in their entirety to public inspection. Therefore, the Bureau does not recognize any designation of material in comments as confidential or not to be disclosed, and any material that the commenter considers to be confidential or inappropriate for disclosure to the public should not be included in his comments. The name of any person submitting comments or requesting a public hearing, the issues which may be discussed at the hearing, and outlines relating to the hearing are open to public disclosure. (See paragraph (a)(3) of this section for rules relating to hearing outlines.)

(c) *Petition to change rules.* Interested persons may petition for the issuance, amendment, or repeal of a rule. A petition for the issuance of a rule shall identify the section or sections of law involved; and a petition for the amendment or repeal of a rule shall set forth the section or sections of the regulations involved. The petition shall set forth the reasons for the requested action. Such petitions shall be given careful consideration, and the petitioner shall be advised of the action taken thereon. Petitions must be addressed to the Alcohol and Tobacco Tax and Trade Bureau, Washington, DC 20220. A petition to establish a new American viticultural area or to modify an existing American viticultural area is subject to the rules in part 9 of this chapter.

(d) *Publication of rules and regulations*—(1) *General.* All Alcohol and Tobacco Tax and Trade Bureau regulations and amendments thereto are published as Treasury Decisions which appear in the FEDERAL REGISTER, the Code of Federal Regulations, and the quarterly Alcohol and Tobacco Tax and Trade Bureau (TTB) Bulletin. The TTB Bulletin is the authoritative instrument of the Bureau for announcing Treasury decisions, legislation, administrative matters, and other items of general interest. The Bulletin incorporates, into one publication, all matters of the Bureau which are of public record. It is the policy of the Bureau to publish in the Bulletin all substantive rulings necessary to promote a uniform application of all laws administered by the Bureau as well as rulings that supersede, revoke, modify, or amend any of those previously published in the Bulletin (including those published prior to July 1, 1972, in the Internal Revenue Bulletin). Procedures relating solely to matters of internal management are not published; however, regulations appearing in internal management documents and statements of internal practices and procedures that affect the rights and duties of the public are published. Rulings and procedures reported in the Bulletin do not have the force and effect of Department of the Treasury Regulations, but they may be used as precedents. In applying published rulings and procedures, the effect of subsequent legislation, regulations, court decisions, rulings, and procedures must be considered. Concerned parties are cautioned against reaching the same conclusion in other cases unless the facts and circumstances are substantially the same. The Bulletin is published quarterly and may be obtained, on a subscription basis, from the Superintendent of Documents, U.S. Government Printing Office, Washington, DC 20402.

(2) *Objectives and standards for publication of TTB Rulings and TTB Procedures in the Alcohol, Tobacco and Firearms Bulletin.* (i)(A) A "TTB Ruling" is an official interpretation by the Bureau that has been published in the Bulletin for the information and guidance of taxpayers, Bureau officers, and others concerned. TTB Rulings represent the conclusions of the Bureau on the application of the law to the entire state of facts involved. In those that are based on positions taken in rulings to industry members or technical advice to Bureau field offices, identifying details and confidential information are deleted to prevent unwarranted invasions of privacy and to comply with statutory requirements concerning disclosure of information obtained from the public.

(B) A "TTB Procedure" is a statement of procedure that affects the rights or duties of taxpayers or other members of the public under law and regulations administered by the Bureau or information that, although not necessarily affecting the rights and duties of the public, should be a matter of public knowledge. TTB Procedures establish methods for performing operations in compliance with the requirements of law and regulations. It is Bureau practice to publish as much of the internal management document or communication as is necessary for an understanding of the procedure. TTB Procedures may also be based on internal management documents which should be a matter of public knowledge even though not necessarily affecting the rights or duties of the public.

(ii) It is the policy of the Bureau to publish in the Bulletin all rulings and other communications to members of the public or to Bureau field offices involving substantive law, procedures affecting taxpayer's rights or duties, or industry regulations, except those involving:

(A) Issues specifically and clearly covered by statute or regulations;

(B) Issues specifically covered by rulings, procedures, opinions, or court decisions previously published in the Bulletin;

(C) Issues not likely to arise again because of unique or specific facts;

(D) Determinations of fact rather than interpretations of law;

(E) Acceptability under the law and regulations of containers, labels, and advertising involving alcoholic beverages;

(F) Tobacco operations, such as the disposition of abandoned, seized, or condemned tobacco products;

(G) Informers and informers' rewards; or

(H) Disclosure of secret formulas, processes, business practices, and other similar information.

(iii)(A) It is the practice of the Bureau to publish as much of the ruling or communication as is necessary for an understanding of the position stated. However, in order to prevent unwarranted invasions of personal privacy and to comply with statutory provisions, such as 18 U.S.C. 1905 and 26 U.S.C 6103 and 7213, dealing with disclosure of information obtained from members of the public, identifying details, including the names and addresses of persons involved, and information of a confidential nature are deleted from the ruling.

(B) TTB Rulings published in the Bulletin do not have the force and effect of Department of the Treasury Regulations (including amendatory Treasury decisions) but are published to provide precedents to be used in the disposition of other cases, and may be cited and relied upon for that purpose. No unpublished ruling or decision may be relied on, used, or cited by any officer or employee of the Bureau as a precedent in the disposition of other cases.

(C) Concerned persons generally may rely upon TTB Rulings published in the Bulletin in determining the Bureau treatment of their own transactions and need not request specific rulings applying the principles of a published TTB Ruling to the facts of their particular cases. However, since each TTB Ruling represents the conclusion of the Bureau as to the application of the law to the entire state of facts involved, taxpayers, Bureau personnel, and others concerned are cautioned against reaching the same conclusion in other cases unless the facts and circumstances are substantially the same. They should consider the effect of subsequent legislation, regulations, court decisions and TTB Rulings.

(D) Comments and suggestions from taxpayers or other concerned persons on TTB Rulings being prepared for publication in the Bulletin may be solicited, if justified by special circumstances. Conferences on TTB Rulings being prepared for publication will not be granted except where the Bureau determines that such action is justified by special circumstances.

(iv)(A) The appropriate TTB officer is responsible for administering the program for the publication of TTB Rulings and TTB Procedures in the Bulletin including the standards for style and format.

(B) In accordance with the standards set forth in paragraph (d)(2)(ii) of this section, each appropriate TTB officer is responsible for the preparation and appropriate referral for publication of TTB Rulings reflecting interpretations of substantive law made by his office and communicated in writing to members of the public or field offices. In this connection, the Chief Counsel is responsible for the referral to the appropriate TTB officer, for consideration for publication as TTB rulings, of interpretations of substantive law made by his office.

(C) In accordance with the standards set forth in paragraph (d)(2)(ii) of this section, the appropriate TTB officers and the Chief Counsel are responsible for determining whether procedures established by an office under their jurisdiction should be published as TTB Procedures and for the initiation, content, and appropriate referral for publication of such TTB Procedures.

[T.D. ATF–47, 43 FR 10687, Mar. 15, 1978, as amended by T.D. ATF–201, 50 FR 12533, Mar. 29, 1985; T.D. ATF–249, 52 FR 5962, Feb. 27, 1987; Redesignated and amended by T.D. ATF–378, 61 FR 29955, June 13, 1996; T.D. ATF–432, 65 FR 69253, Nov. 16, 2000; T.D. ATF–450, 66 FR 29030, May 29, 2001; TTB–90, 76 FR 3502, Jan. 20, 2011; T.D. TTB–91, 76 FR 5482, Feb. 1, 2011]

§ 70.702 Forms and instructions.

(a) *Tax return forms and instructions.* Tax forms and instructions are developed by the Bureau to explain the requirements of Chapters 32, 51, 52, and 53 of Title 26 of the United States Code or regulations issued thereunder, and are issued for the assistance of taxpayers in exercising their rights and discharging their duties under such laws and regulations. The tax return forms are the instruments through which taxes are collected.

(b) *Other forms and instructions.* The Bureau provides other necessary or appropriate forms for assisting the public in complying with the technical requirements of the laws and regulations administered by the Bureau. The material contained in the forms and instructions, and the arrangement thereof, is carefully considered and is designed to lead the preparer step-by-step through an orderly accumulation of data to an accurate report of the information required.

(c) *Procurement of forms and instructions.* Forms prescribed by this part are available as provided in § 70.2(b).

[T.D. ATF–47, 43 FR 10687, Mar. 15, 1978, as amended by T.D. ATF–92, 46 FR 46914, Sept. 23, 1981; T.D. ATF–249, 52 FR 5962, Feb. 27, 1987; T.D. 372, 61 FR 20724, May 8, 1996. Redesignated and amended by T.D. ATF–378, 61 FR 29955, June 13, 1996]

Subpart I—Disclosure

§ 70.801 Publicity of information.

For information relating to the disclosure of records that is not contained in this Subpart I, see 31 CFR Part 1 and the Appendix of that Part relating to the Bureau of Alcohol, Tobacco and Firearms. Direct further questions to the Alcohol and Tobacco Tax and Trade Bureau, Washington, DC 20220, (202) 927–8210.

[T.D. ATF–378, 61 FR 29955, June 13, 1996, as amended by T.D. ATF–450, 66 FR 29030, May 29, 2001]

§ 70.802 Rules for disclosure of certain specified matters.

(a) *Accepted offers in compromise.* For each offer in compromise submitted and accepted pursuant to 26 U.S.C. 7122 in any case arising under Chapter 32 (relating to firearms and ammunition excise taxes) and Subtitle E (relating to alcohol, tobacco, and certain other excise taxes) of Title 26 of the United States Code, under section 107 of the Federal Alcohol Administration Act (27 U.S.C. 207) in any case arising under that Act, or in connection with property seized under Title I of the Gun Control Act of 1968 (18 U.S.C., Chapter 44) or title XI of the Organized Crime Control Act of 1970 (18 U.S.C., Chapter 40), a copy of the abstract and statement relating to the offer shall be kept available for public inspection, for a period of 1 year from the date of acceptance, with the appropriate ATF officer, Bureau of Alcohol, Tobacco and Firearms, Washington, DC 20226. Information may not be disclosed, however, concerning any trade secrets, processes, operations, style of work, apparatus, confidential data, or any other matter within the prohibition of 18 U.S.C. 1905. "Return information" (defined at 26 U.S.C. 6103 (b)) may not be disclosed except as provided by 26 U.S.C. 6103 (k) (1).

(b) *Information regarding liquor permits*—(1) *Applications for permits.* Information with respect to the handling of applications for basic permits under the Federal Alcohol Administration Act (27 U.S.C. 204) is maintained for public inspection until the expiration of 1 year following final action on these applications. See § 1.59 of this chapter for more details.

(c) *List of plants and permittees.* Upon request, the appropriate TTB officer shall furnish a list of any type of qualified proprietor or permittee if the disclosure is not prohibited by law.

(d) *Information relating to certificates of label approval for distilled spirits, wine, and malt beverages.* Upon written request, the appropriate TTB officer, Alcohol and Tobacco Tax and Trade Bureau, Washington, DC 20220, shall furnish information as to the issuance, pursuant to section 105(e) of the Federal Alcohol Administration Act (27 U.S.C. 205(e)) and Part 4, 5, or 7 of this chapter, of certificates of label approval, or of exemption from label approval, for distilled spirits, wine, or malt beverages. The request must identify the class and type and brand name of the product and the name and address of the bottler or importer thereof or of the person to whom the certificate was issued. The person making the request may obtain reproductions or certified copies of such certificates upon payment of the established fees prescribed by 31 CFR 1.7. Information will not be disclosed, however, concerning any trade secrets, processes, operations, style of work, apparatus, confidential data, or any other matter prohibited by statutes such as but not limited to 18 U.S.C. 1905 or 26 U.S.C. 6103.

(e) *True identity of companies authorized to use trade names.* Information regarding the true identity (name and address) of companies authorized to use trade names is available from the appropriate TTB officer, for disclosure upon request to any member of the public.

(f) *Information relating to the tax classification of a roll of tobacco wrapped in reconstituted tobacco.* Upon written request, the appropriate TTB officer, Alcohol and Tobacco Tax and Trade Bureau, Washington, DC 20220, shall furnish information as to a Bureau determination of the tax classification of a roll of tobacco wrapped in reconstituted tobacco. The request must identify the brand name of the product and the name and address of the manufacturer or importer. Information may not be disclosed, however, concerning any trade secrets, processes, operations, apparatus, confidential data, or any other matter prohibited by statutes such as but not limited to 26 U.S.C. 6103 or 18 U.S.C. 1905.

(g) *Comments received in response to a notice of proposed rulemaking.* (1) The Bureau will post written comments received in response to a notice of proposed rulemaking to the appropriate rulemaking docket on the Regulations.gov Web site at *http://www.regulations.gov.* The Bureau reserves the right not to post lengthy paper comments or attachments requiring scanning, although a notice regarding the receipt of any such non-posted comments or attachments will be made to Regulations.gov. TTB will not post duplicate or anonymous comments to Regulations.gov.

(2) All comments and attachments received in response to a notice of proposed rulemaking may be inspected by any person in the Bureau's public reading room by appointment during normal business hours. Copies of comments (or portions therefore) also may be obtained. Appointment and copy requests may be addressed to the appropriate TTB officer in writing to the Alcohol and Tobacco Tax and Trade Bureau, Washington, DC 20220, or by telephone at 202–453–2270. A person requesting copies should allow a reasonable time for processing the request. The provisions of 31 CFR 1.7, relating to fees, apply to requests made in accordance with this paragraph.

(27 U.S.C. 205; 22 U.S.C. 2778; 26 U.S.C. 7602; 5 U.S.C. 301)

[T.D. ATF–47, 43 FR 10687, Mar. 15, 1978, as amended by T.D. ATF–57, 44 FR 20794, May 9, 1979; T.D. ATF–201, 50 FR 12533, Mar. 29, 1985; T.D. ATF–249, 52 FR 5961, Feb. 27, 1987. Redesignated and amended by T.D. ATF–378, 61 FR 29955, 29956, June 13, 1996; T.D. ATF–450, 66 FR 29030, May 29, 2001; T.D. TTB–91, 76 FR 5482, Feb. 1, 2011]

§ 70.803 Requests or demands for disclosure in testimony and in related matters.

(a) *Authority.* The provisions of this section are prescribed under the authority of 5 U.S.C. 301; section 2 of Reorganization Plan No. 26 of 1950 (64 Stat. 1280); 12 U.S.C. 3412; 18 U.S.C. 1905; section 2(g) of the Federal Alcohol Administration Act (27 U.S.C. 202(c)); and sections 5274, 6103, 7213, 7803 and 7805 of the Internal Revenue Code of 1954 (26 U.S.C. 5274, 6103, 7213, 7803 and 7805).

(b) *Definitions.* The following definitions apply whenever the defined terms appear in this section.

(1) *TTB officer or employee.* The terms *TTB officer* and *TTB employee* mean all officers and employees of the United States, engaged in the administration and enforcement of laws administered by the Alcohol and Tobacco Tax and Trade Bureau, and appointed or employed by, or subject to the directions, instructions or orders of, the Secretary of the Treasury or his delegate.

(2) *TTB records or information.* The terms *TTB records* and *TTB information* mean any records (including copies thereof) or information, made or obtained by, furnished to, or coming to the knowledge of, any TTB officer or employee while acting in his official capacity, or because of his official status, with respect to the administration of laws administered by or concerning the Alcohol and Tobacco Tax and Trade Bureau.

(3) *Demand.* The term *demand* means any subpoena, notice of deposition either upon oral examination or written interrogatory, or other order, of any court, administrative agency, or other authority.

(c) *Disclosure of TTB records or information prohibited without prior approval of the appropriate TTB officer.* The disclosure, including the production, of TTB records or information to any person outside the Department of the Treasury or to any court, administrative agency, or other authority, in response to any request or demand for the disclosure of such records or information shall be made only with the prior approval of the appropriate TTB officer. However, nothing in this section restricts the disclosure of TTB records or information for which the appropriate TTB officer has determined that the disclosure is authorized under any provision of statute, Executive order, or regulations, or for which a procedure has been established by the Administrator. For example, this section does not restrict the disclosure of TTB records or information under

§ 71.22, nor does it restrict the disclosure of TTB records or information which is requested by U.S. attorneys or attorneys of the Department of Justice for use in cases which arise under the laws administered by or concerning the Alcohol and Tobacco Tax and Trade Bureau and which are referred by the Department of the Treasury to the Department of Justice for prosecution or defense.

(d) *Delegation of authority to determine disclosure and establish procedures.* The appropriate TTB officer is hereby authorized to determine whether or not TTB officers and employees will be permitted to disclose TTB records or information in response to:

(1) A request by any court, administrative agency, or other authority, or by any person, for the disclosure of such records or information; or

(2) A demand for the disclosure of such records or information.

(3) The Administrator is also authorized to establish such other procedures as he or she may deem necessary with respect to the disclosure of TTB records or information by TTB officers and employees. Any determination by the appropriate TTB officer as to whether TTB records or information will be disclosed, or any procedure established by the Administrator in connection therewith, must be made in accordance with applicable statutes, Executive orders, regulations, and any instructions that may be issued by the Secretary. Notwithstanding the preceding provisions of this paragraph, the appropriate TTB officer shall, where either the Secretary or such officer deems it appropriate, refer the opposing of a request or demand for disclosure of TTB records or information to the Secretary.

(e) *Procedure in the event of a request or demand for TTB records or information*—(1) *Request procedure.* Any TTB officer or employee who receives a request for TTB records or information, the disposition of which is not covered by a procedure established by the Administrator, must promptly communicate the contents of the request to the appropriate TTB officer. The officer or employee must await instructions from the appropriate TTB officer concerning the response to the request.

(2) *Demand procedure.* Any TTB officer or employee who is served with a demand for TTB records or information, the disposition of which is not covered by a procedure established by the Administrator, must promptly, and without awaiting appearance before the court, administrative agency, or other authority, communicate the contents of the demand to the appropriate TTB officer. The TTB officer or employee must await instructions from the appropriate TTB officer concerning the response to the demand. If it is determined by the appropriate TTB officer that the demand should be opposed, the U.S. attorney, his or her assistant, or other appropriate legal representative shall be requested to respectfully inform the court, administrative agency, or other authority that the appropriate TTB officer has instructed the TTB officer or employee to refuse to disclose the TTB records or information sought. If instructions have not been received from the appropriate TTB officer at the time when the TTB officer or employee is required to appear before the court, administrative agency, or other authority in response to the demand, the U.S. attorney, his or her assistant, or other appropriate legal representative must be requested to appear with the TTB officer or employee upon whom the demand has been served and request additional time in which to receive such instructions. In the event the court, administrative agency, or other authority rules adversely with respect to the refusal to disclose the records or information pursuant to the instructions of the appropriate TTB officer, or declines to defer a ruling until instructions from the appropriate TTB officer have been received, the TTB officer or employee upon whom the demand has been served must, pursuant to this section, respectfully decline to disclose the TTB records or information sought.

(3) *Affidavit required for testimony.* If testimony of an TTB officer or employee is sought by a request or demand on behalf of a party other than a State in any case or matter in which the United States is not a party, an affidavit, or if that is not feasible, a statement shall be submitted. The affidavit or statement shall be prepared by

the party (or party's attorney) seeking the testimony, and shall set forth a summary of the testimony sought and its relevance to the proceedings. The affidavit or statement must be submitted before permission to testify may be granted. The appropriate TTB officer may, upon request and for good cause shown, waive the requirement of this paragraph.

(4) *Time limit for serving request or demand.* The request or demand, together with the affidavit or statement (if required by paragraph (e)(3) of this section), must be served at least 5 working days prior to the scheduled date of testimony or disclosure of records, in order to ensure that the appropriate TTB officer has adequate time to consider whether to grant the request or demand. The appropriate TTB officer may, upon request and for good cause shown, waive the requirement of this paragraph.

(5) *Factors to be considered in determining whether a request or demand will be granted.* The appropriate TTB officer must consider whether granting the request or demand would be appropriate under the relevant rules of procedure and substantive law concerning privilege. Among the requests or demands that will not be granted are those that would, if granted, result in—

(i) The violation of a statute, such as 26 U.S.C. 6103 or 7213, or a rule of procedure, such as the grand jury secrecy rule (F.R.Cr.P. Rule 6(e)), or a specific regulation;

(ii) The disclosure of classified information;

(iii) The disclosure of a confidential source or informant, unless the TTB officer or employee and the source or informant, have no objection;

(iv) The disclosure of investigative records compiled for law enforcement purposes if enforcement proceedings would thereby be impeded, or of investigative techniques and procedures whose effectiveness would thereby be impaired, unless the appropriate TTB officer determines that the administration of justice requires disclosure;

(v) The disclosure of trade secrets without the owner's consent; or

(vi) Testimony in a case in which TTB has no interest, records or other official information.

(f) *State cases.* The appropriate TTB officer, may, in the interest of Federal and State law enforcement, upon receipt of demands or requests of State authorities, and at the expense of the State, authorize employees under their supervision to attend trials and administrative hearings in liquor, tobacco, firearms, or explosives cases in which the State is a party or on behalf of the State in any criminal case, to produce records, and to testify as to facts coming to their knowledge in their official capacities. However, in cases where a defendant in a criminal case requests or demands testimony or the production of TTB records or information, authorization from the appropriate TTB officer is required. Production or testimony may not divulge information contrary to 26 U.S.C. 6103 and 7213, or 12 U.S.C. 3412. See also 18 U.S.C. 1905.

(g) *Penalties.* Any TTB officer or employee who disobeys the provisions of this section will be subject to dismissal and may incur criminal liability.

[T.D ATF–57, 44 FR 27094, May 9, 1979, as amended by T.D. ATF–302, 55 FR 47325, Nov. 13, 1990. Redesignated by T.D. ATF–378, 61 FR 29955, June 13, 1996, as amended by T.D. ATF–446a, 66 FR 19089, Apr. 13, 2001; T.D. ATF–450, 66 FR 29030, May 29, 2001; T.D. TTB–91, 76 FR 5482, Feb. 1, 2011]

PART 71—RULES OF PRACTICE IN PERMIT PROCEEDINGS

Subpart A—Scope and Construction of Regulations

Sec.

Subpart B—Definitions

Subpart C—General

TIME

RECORD

AUTHORITY: 26 U.S.C. 5271, 5181, 5712, 5713, 7805, 27 U.S.C. 204.

SOURCE: 21 FR 1441, Mar. 6, 1956, unless otherwise noted. Redesignated at 40 FR 16835, Apr. 15, 1975, and further redesignated by T.D. ATF–463, 66 FR 42734, Aug. 15, 2001.

EDITORIAL NOTE: Nomenclature changes to part 71 appear by T.D. ATF–414, 64 FR 49084, Sept. 10, 1999and T.D. ATF–463, 66 FR 42734, 42735, Aug. 15, 2001.

Subpart A—Scope and Construction of Regulations

§ 71.1 Scope of part.

The regulations in this part govern the procedure and practice in connection with the disapproval of applications for basic permits, and for the suspension, revocation and annulment of such permits under sections 3 and 4 of the Federal Alcohol Administration Act (27 U.S.C. 201 *et seq.*) and disapproval, suspension, and revocation of permits under title 26 of the U.S. Code. The regulations in this part shall also govern, insofar as applicable, any adversary proceeding involving adjudication required by statute to be determined on the record after opportunity for hearing, under laws administered by the Alcohol and Tobacco Tax and Trade Bureau.

[21 FR 1441, Mar. 6, 1956, as amended by T.D. 6389, 24 FR 4790, June 12, 1959. Redesignated at 40 FR 16835, Apr. 15, 1975]

EDITORIAL NOTE: For FEDERAL REGISTER citations affecting § 71.1, see the List of CFR Sections Affected, which appears in the Finding Aids section of the printed volume and at *www.fdsys.gov.*

§ 71.2 Liberal construction.

The regulations in this part shall be liberally contrued to secure just, expeditious, and efficient determination of the issues presented. The Rules of Civil Procedure for the U.S. District Courts (28 U.S.C. appendix), where applicable, shall be a guide in any situation not provided for or controlled by this part but shall be liberally construed or relaxed when necessary.

(5 U.S.C. 552(a) (80 Stat. 383, as amended))

[T.D. ATF–92, 46 FR 46917, Sept. 23, 1981]

§ 71.3 Forms prescribed.

(a) The appropriate TTB officer is authorized to prescribe all forms required by this part. All of the information called for in each form shall be furnished as indicated by the headings on the form and the instructions on or pertaining to the form. In addition, information called for in each form shall be furnished as required by this part.

(b) Forms prescribed by this part are available for printing through the TTB Web site (*http://www.ttb.gov*) or by mailing a request to the Alcohol and Tobacco Tax and Trade Bureau, National Revenue Center, 550 Main Street, Room 1516, Cincinnati, OH 45202.

(5 U.S.C. 552(a) (80 Stat. 383, as amended))

[T.D. ATF–92, 46 FR 46918, Sept. 23, 1981, as amended by T.D. ATF–372, 61 FR 20725, May 8, 1996; T.D. TTB–44, 71 FR 16964, Apr. 4, 2006]

§ 71.4 Delegations of the Administrator.

Most of the regulatory authorities of the Administrator contained in this part are delegated to appropriate TTB officers. These TTB officers are specified in TTB Order 1135.71, Delegation of the Administrator's Authorities in 27 CFR Part 71, Rules of Practice in Permit Proceedings. You may obtain a copy of this order by accessing the TTB Web site (*http://www.ttb.gov*) or by mailing a request to the Alcohol and Tobacco Tax and Trade Bureau, National Revenue Center, 550 Main Street, Room 1516, Cincinnati, OH 45202.

[T.D. TTB–44, 71 FR 16964, Apr. 4, 2006]

Subpart B—Definitions

§ 71.5 Meaning of terms.

When used in this part and in forms prescribed under this part, where not otherwise distinctly expressed or manifestly incompatible with the intent thereof, terms shall have the meaning ascribed in this subpart. Words in the plural form shall include the singular, and vice versa, and words importing the masculine gender shall include the feminine. The terms "include" and "including" do not exclude things not enumerated which are in the same general class.

Administrative law judge. The person appointed pursuant to 5 U.S.C. 3105, designated to preside over any administrative proceedings under this part.

Administrator. The Administrator, Alcohol and Tobacco Tax and Trade Bureau, Department of the Treasury, Washington, DC.

Applicant. Any person who has filed an initial application for a permit under the Federal Alcohol Administration Act or the Internal Revenue Code (26 U.S.C.).

Application. Any application for a permit under the Federal Alcohol Administration Act or the Internal Revenue Code (26 U.S.C.) for operations not covered by an existing permit.

Appropriate TTB officer. An officer or employee of the Alcohol and Tobacco Tax and Trade Bureau (TTB) authorized to perform any functions relating to the administration or enforcement of this part by TTB Order 1135.71, Delegation of the Administrator's Authorities in 27 CFR Part 71, Rules of Practice in Permit Proceedings.

Attorney for the Government. The attorney in the appropriate office of Chief Counsel authorized to represent the appropriate TTB officer in the proceeding.

CFR. The Code of Federal Regulations.

Citation. Includes any notice contemplating the disapproval of an application or any order to show cause why a permit should not be suspended, revoked or annulled.

Initial decision. The decision of the appropriate TTB officer or administrative law judge in a proceeding on the suspension, revocation or annulment of a permit.

Other term. Any other term defined in the Federal Alcohol Administration Act (27 U.S.C. 201), the Internal Revenue Code (26 U.S.C.) or the Administrative Procedure Act (5 U.S.C. 1001), where used in this part, shall have the meaning assigned to it therein.

Permit—(a) *Alcohol fuel permit.* The document issued under 26 U.S.C. 5181, authorizing the person named therein to engage in the business described therein.

(b) *Basic permit.* The document authorizing the person named therein to engage in a designated business or activity under the Federal Alcohol Administration Act.

(c) *Industrial use permit.* The document issued under 26 U.S.C. 5271(a), authorizing the person named therein to withdraw and use distilled spirits free of tax in accordance with part 22 of this chapter, or withdraw and deal in or use specially denatured spirits in accordance with part 20 of this chapter, as described therein.

(d) *Operating permit.* The document issued under 26 U.S.C. 5171, authorizing the person named therein to engage in the business described therein.

(e) *Tobacco permit.* The document issued under 26 U.S.C. 5713(a), authorizing the person named therein to engage in the business described therein.

Permittee. Any person holding a basic permit under the Federal Alcohol Administration Act or the Internal Revenue Code (26 U.S.C.).

Person. An individual, trust, estate, partnership, association, company, or corporation.

Recommended decision. The advisory decision of the administrative law judge in any proceeding on an initial application for a permit.

Respondent. Any person holding a permit against which an order has been issued to show cause why such permit should not be suspended, revoked or annulled.

[T.D. ATF-48, 43 FR 13543, Mar. 31, 1978; 44 FR 55845, Sept. 28, 1978, and amended by T.D. ATF-62, 44 FR 71696, Dec. 11, 1979; T.D. ATF-199, 50 FR 9196, Mar. 6, 1985; T.D ATF-244, 51 FR 45762, Dec. 22, 1986; T.D. ATF-374, 61 FR 29956, June 13, 1996; T.D. ATF-414, 64 FR 49084, Sept. 10, 1999; T.D. TTB-44, 71 FR 16964, Apr. 4, 2006]

Subpart C—General

§71.25 Communications and pleadings.

All communications to the Government regarding the procedures set forth in this part and all pleadings, such as answers, motions, requests, or other papers or documents required or permitted to be filed under this part, relating to a proceeding pending before an administrative law judge, shall be addressed to the administrative law judge, at his post of duty or to the administrative law judge, in care of the appropriate TTB officer to be forwarded to the examiner. Communications concerning proceedings not pending before an administrative law judge, should be addressed to the appropriate TTB officer or the Administrator, as the case may be. All pleadings should be filed in quadruplicate.

[21 FR 1441, Mar. 6, 1956. Redesignated at 40 FR 16835, Apr. 15, 1975, as amended by T.D. ATF–374, 61 FR 29957, June 13, 1996]

§ 71.26 Service on applicant or respondent.

All orders, notices, citations, motions and other formal documents, except subpoenas, required to be served under the regulations in this part may be served by mailing a signed duplicate original copy thereof to the permittee or applicant by registered mail, with request for return receipt card, at the address stated in his permit or application or at his last known address, or by delivery of such original copy to the permittee or applicant personally, or in the case of a corporation, partnership, or other unincorporated association, by delivering the same to an officer, or manager, or general agent thereof, or to its attorney of record. Such personal service may be made by any employee of the Alcohol and Tobacco Tax and Trade Bureau or by any employee of the Treasury Department designated by the Secretary. A certificate of mailing and the return receipt card, or certificate of service signed by the person making such service, shall be filed as a part of the record.

[21 FR 1441, Mar. 6, 1956. Redesignated at 40 FR 16835, Apr. 15, 1975, and amended by T.D. ATF–48, 44 FR 55846, Sept. 28, 1979]

§ 71.27 Service on the appropriate TTB officer or Administrator.

Pleadings, motions, notices, and other formal documents, except subpoenas, may be served, by registered mail or personally, on the appropriate TTB officer (or upon the attorney for the Government on behalf of the appropriate TTB officer, or on the Administrator, if the proceeding is before him for review on appeal).

[21 FR 1441, Mar. 6, 1956. Redesignated at 40 FR 16835, Apr. 15, 1975, as amended by T.D. ATF–374, 61 FR 29957, June 13, 1996; T.D. TTB–91, 76 FR 5482, Feb. 1, 2011]

TIME

§ 71.28 Computation.

In computing any period of time prescribed or allowed by this part, the day of the act, event or default after which the designated period of time is to run, is not to be included. The last day of the period to be computed is to be included, unless it be a Saturday, Sunday or legal holiday, in which event the period runs until the next day which is neither a Saturday, Sunday or legal holiday. Pleading, requests, or other papers or documents required or permitted to be filed under this part must be received for filing at the appropriate office within the time limits, if any, for such filing.

§ 71.29 Continuances and extensions.

For good cause shown, the administrative law judge, Administrator, or the appropriate TTB officer, as the case may be, may grant continuances and as to all matters pending before him extend any time limit prescribed by the regulations in this part (except where the time limit is statutory).

(26 U.S.C. 7805 (68A Stat. 917), 27 U.S.C. 205 (49 Stat. 981 as amended), 18 U.S.C. 926 (82 Stat. 959), and Sec. 38, Arms Export Control Act (22 U.S.C. 2778, 90 Stat. 744))

[21 FR 1441, Mar. 6, 1956. Redesignated at 40 FR 16835, Apr. 15, 1975, and amended by T.D. ATF–48, 43 FR 13531, Mar. 31, 1978; T.D. ATF–374, 61 FR 29957, June 13, 1996]

REPRESENTATION AT HEARINGS

§ 71.30 Personal representation.

Any individual or member of a partnership may after adequate identification, appear for himself, or such partnership, and a corporation or association may be represented by a bona fide officer of such corporation or association, upon showing of adequate authorization.

§71.31 Attorneys and other representatives.

A respondent or applicant may be represented by an attorney, certified public accountant, or other person enrolled to practice before the Alcohol and Tobacco Tax and Trade Bureau under 31 CFR part 8—Practice before the Alcohol and Tobacco Tax and Trade Bureau. The representative shall file in the proceeding a duly executed power of attorney to represent the applicant or respondent. See 26 CFR 601.501 through 601.527 (conference and practice requirements). The appropriate TTB officer shall be represented in proceedings under this part by the attorney for the Government who is authorize to execute and file motions, briefs, and other papers in the proceeding, on behalf of the appropriate TTB officer, in his own name as "Attorney for the Government".

(5 U.S.C. 552(a) (80 Stat. 383, as amended))

[T.D. ATF–48, 44 FR 55846, Sept. 28, 1979, as amended by T.D. ATF–92, 46 FR 46918, Sept. 23, 1981; T.D. ATF–374, 61 FR 29957, June 13, 1996]

Subpart D—Compliance and Settlement

§71.35 Opportunity for compliance.

Except in proceedings involving willfulness or those in which the public interest requires otherwise, and the appropriate TTB officer so alleges in his citation, stating his reasons therefor, no permit shall be suspended, revoked or annulled, unless, prior to the institution of proceedings, facts or conduct warranting such action shall have been called to the attention of the permittee by the appropriate TTB officer, in writing, and the permittee shall have been accorded an opportunity to demonstrate or achieve compliance with all lawful requirements, as set forth in section 9(b) of the Administrative Procedure Act. If the permittee fails to meet the requirements of the law and regulations within such reasonable time as may be specified by the appropriate TTB officer, proceedings for suspension, revocation or annulment of the permit shall be initiated.

[21 FR 1441, Mar. 6, 1956. Redesignated at 40 FR 16835, Apr. 15, 1975, and amended by T.D. ATF–199, 50 FR 9196, Mar. 6, 1985; T.D. ATF–374, 61 FR 29957, June 13, 1996]

INFORMAL SETTLEMENT

§71.36 General.

In all proceedings in which a permittee is cited to show cause why the permit should not be suspended, revoked or annulled, the permittee shall be afforded opportunity for the submission and consideration of facts, arguments, offers of settlement, or proposals of adjustment, where time, the nature of the proceeding, and the public interest permit. Such submittals should be made to the appropriate TTB officer, but may be made through the attorney for the Government. Where necessary, the date of the hearing may be postponed, pending consideration of such proposals, when they are made in good faith and not for the purpose of delay. If proposals of settlement are submitted, and they are considered unsatisfactory, the appropriate TTB officer may reject the proposals and may, either directly or through the attorney for the Government, inform the permittee of any conditions on which the alleged violations may be settled. If the proposals of settlement are considered satisfactory to the appropriate TTB officer, the permittee shall be notified thereof and the proceeding shall be dismissed, unless such proposals of settlement include a monetary offer in compromise considered satisfactory to the appropriate TTB officer, in which event the proceeding shall be held in abeyance pending final action on such monetary offer in compromise.

[T.D. ATF–244, 51 FR 45762, Dec. 22, 1986, as amended by T.D. ATF–374, 61 FR 29957, June 13, 1996]

§71.37 Notice of contemplated action.

Where the appropriate TTB officer believes that the matter may be settled informally, i.e., without formal administrative proceedings, he shall, in accordance with section 5 (b) of the Administrative Procedure Act, prior to the issuance of a citation, inform the permittee of the contemplated issuance of an order to show cause why his permit should not be suspended, revoked or annulled, and that he is being given an opportunity for the submission and consideration of facts, arguments, offers of settlement, or proposals of adjustment. The notice should inform the permittee of the charges on which the citation would be based, if issued, and afford him a period of 10 days from the date of the notice, or such longer period as the appropriate TTB officer deems necessary, in which to submit proposals of settlement to the appropriate TTB officer. Where informal settlement is not reached promptly because of inaction of the permittee or proposals are made for the purpose of delay, a citation shall be issued in accordance with §§ 71.55 and 71.56.

[21 FR 1441, Mar. 6, 1956. Redesignated at 40 FR 16835, Apr. 15, 1975, and amended by T.D. ATF–199, 50 FR 9196, Mar. 6, 1985; T.D. ATF–244, 51 FR 45763, Dec. 22, 1986; T.D. ATF–374, 61 FR 29957, June 13, 1996]

§ 71.38 Limitation on informal settlement.

Where the evidence is conclusive and the nature of the violation is such as to preclude any settlement short of suspension, revocation or annulment, or the violation is of a continuing character that necessitates immediate action to protect the public interest, or where the appropriate TTB officer believes that any informal settlement of the alleged violation will not insure future compliance with the laws and regulations, or in any similar case where the circumstances are such as to clearly preclude informal settlement, and the appropriate TTB officer so finds and states his reasons therefor as provided in § 71.35, he may restrict settlement to that provided in § 71.71.

[21 FR 1441, Mar. 6, 1956. Redesignated at 40 FR 16835, Apr. 15, 1975, and amended by T.D. ATF–199, 50 FR 9197, Mar. 6, 1985; T.D. ATF–374, 61 FR 29957, June 13, 1996]

Subpart E—Grounds for Citation

§ 71.45 Basic permits.

Whenever the appropriate TTB officer has reason to believe that any person has willfully violated any of the conditions of his basic permit, or has not in fact or in good faith engaged in the operations authorized by such permit for a period of more than two years, or that such permit was procured through fraud, misrepresentation or concealment of material facts, he shall issue a citation for the suspension, revocation or annulment of such permit, as the case may be.

[21 FR 1441, Mar. 6, 1956, as amended by T.D. 6389, 24 FR 4790, June 12, 1959. Redesignated at 40 FR 16835, Apr. 15, 1975, as amended by T.D. ATF–374, 61 FR 29957, June 13, 1996]

§ 71.46 Suspension and revocation of tobacco permits.

Whenever the appropriate TTB officer has reason to believe that any person has not in good faith complied with any of the provisions of 26 U.S.C. chapter 52 or regulations issued thereunder, or has not complied with any provision of 26 U.S.C. which involves intent to defraud, or has violated any of the conditions of his permit, or has failed to disclose any material information required, or has made any materially false statement, in the application for his permit, or has failed to maintain his premises in such manner as to protect the revenue, or is, by reason of previous or current legal proceedings involving a felony violation of any other provision of Federal criminal law relating to tobacco products, processed tobacco, cigarette paper, or cigarette tubes, not likely to maintain operations in compliance with 26 U.S.C. chapter 52, or has been convicted of a felony violation of any provision of Federal or State criminal law relating to tobacco products, processed tobacco, cigarette paper, or cigarette tubes, the appropriate TTB officer shall issue a citation for the revocation or suspension of such permit.

(72 Stat 1421, as amended; 26 U.S.C. 5713)

[T.D. TTB–75, 74 FR 14491, Mar. 31, 2009]

§ 71.48 Operating permits and industrial use permits.

Whenever the appropriate TTB officer has reason to believe that any person who has an operating permit or an industrial use permit:

(a) Has not in good faith complied with the provisions of 26 U.S.C. chapter 51 or enabling regulations; or

(b) Has violated the conditions of such permit; or

(c) Has made any false statement as to any material fact in his application therefor; or

(d) Has failed to disclose any material information required to be furnished; or

(e) Has violated or conspired to violate any law of the United States relating to intoxicating liquor or has been convicted of any offense under 26 U.S.C. punishable as a felony or of any conspiracy to commit such an offense; or

(f) Is (in the case of any person who has a permit to procure or use distilled spirits free of tax for nonbeverage purposes and not for resale or use in the manufacture of any product for sale, or to procure, deal in, or use specially denatured distilled spirits) by reason of his operations, no longer warranted in procuring or using the distilled spirits or specially denatured distilled spirits authorized by his permit; or

(g) Has, in the case of any person who has a permit to procure, deal in, or use specially denatured distilled spirits, manufactured articles which do not correspond to the descriptions and limitation prescribed by law and regulations; or

(h) Has not engaged in any of the operations authorized by the permit for a period of more than 2 years;

He may issue a citation for the revocation or suspension of such permit.

(72 Stat. 1349, 1370; 26 U.S.C. 5171, 5271)

[T.D. 6389, 24 FR 4790, June 12, 1959. Redesignated at 40 FR 16835, Apr. 15, 1975, and amended by T.D. ATF–48, 44 FR 55846, Sept. 28, 1979; T.D. ATF–199, 50 FR 9196, 9197, Mar. 6, 1985; T.D. ATF–374, 61 FR 29957, June 13, 1996]

§ 71.49 Applications for basic permits.

If, upon examination of any application (including a renewal application) for a basic permit, the appropriate TTB officer has reason to believe that the applicant is not entitled to such permit he shall issue a citation for the contemplated disapproval of the application.

[T.D. 6954, 33 FR 6814, May 4, 1968. Redesignated at 40 FR 16835, Apr. 15, 1975, as amended by T.D. ATF–374, 61 FR 29957, June 13, 1996]

§ 71.49a Applications for operating permits and industrial use permits.

If, on examination of an application for an operating permit or an industrial use permit, the appropriate TTB officer has reason to believe:

(a) In case of an application to withdraw and use distilled spirits free of tax, the applicant is not authorized by law or regulations issued pursuant thereto to withdraw or use such distilled spirits; or

(b) The applicant (including in the case of a corporation, any officer, Administrator, or principal stockholder and, in the case of a partnership, a partner) is, by reason of the applicant's business experience, financial standing, or trade connections, not likely to maintain operations in compliance with 26 U.S.C. chapter 51 or implementing regulations; or

(c) The applicant has failed to disclose any material information required, or has made any false statement as to any material fact, in connection with his application; or

(d) The premises on which the applicant proposes to conduct the business are not adequate to protect the revenue;

He may issue a citation for the contemplated disapproval of the application.

(72 Stat. 1349, 1370; 26 U.S.C. 5171, 5271)

[T.D. 6389, 24 FR 4791, June 12, 1959. Redesignated at 40 FR 16835, Apr. 15, 1975, and amended by T.D. ATF–48, 44 FR 55846, Sept. 28, 1979; T.D. ATF–199, 50 FR 9196, 9197, Mar. 6, 1985; T.D. ATF–374, 61 FR 29957, June 13, 1996]

§ 71.49b Denial of application for tobacco permit.

The appropriate TTB officer may issue a citation for the contemplated disapproval of an application for a tobacco permit provided for in 26 U.S.C. 5713, if the appropriate TTB officer on examination of the application has reason to believe—

(a) The premises on which it is proposed to conduct the business are not adequate to protect the revenue;

(b) The applicant for a permit does not meet the minimum manufacturing and activity requirements in §40.61 of this chapter; or

(c) The applicant (including, in the case of a corporation, any officer, administrator, or principal stockholder and, in the case of a partnership, a partner) is, by reason of his business experience, financial standing, or trade connections, or by reason of previous or current legal proceedings involving a felony violation of any other provision of Federal criminal law relating to tobacco products, processed tobacco, cigarette paper, or cigarette tubes, not likely to maintain operations in compliance with 26 U.S.C. chapter 52, or has been convicted of a felony violation of any provision of Federal or State criminal law relating to tobacco products, processed tobacco, cigarette paper, or cigarette tubes, or has failed to disclose any material information required or made any material false statement in the application.

(72 Stat. 1421, as amended; 26 U.S.C. 5712)

[T.D. TTB–75, 74 FR 14491, Mar. 31, 2009]

Subpart F—Hearing Procedure

CITATIONS

§71.55 Content.

(a) Citation for the suspension, revocation or annulment of a permit shall be issued by the appropriate TTB officer and shall set forth (1) the sections of law and regulations relied upon for authority and jurisdiction, (2) in separate paragraphs, the matters of fact constituting the violations specified, dates, places, section of law and regulations violated, and (3) the permittee has 15 days within which to request a hearing before an administrative law judge.

(b) Citations for the disapproval of an application for a permit shall set forth (1) the sections of law and regulations relied upon for authority and jurisdiction, (2) in separate paragraphs, the matters of fact and law relied upon for the contemplated disapproval of the application, and (3) that the application will be disapproved unless a hearing is requested within 15 days.

[T.D. ATF–244, 51 FR 45763, Dec. 22, 1986, as amended by T.D. ATF–374, 61 FR 29957, June 13, 1996]

§71.56 Form.

Citations shall be issued on the following forms:

(a) Form 5000.6. "Order To Show Cause", shall be used for all citations for the suspension, revocation, or annulment, as the case may be, of permits under the Internal Revenue Code or the Federal Alcohol Administration Act.

(b) Forms 5000.17. "Notice of Contemplated Disapproval of Application For Basic Permit," shall be used to issue notice of contemplated disapproval of applications for permit.

[21 FR 1441, Mar. 6, 1956]

EDITORIAL NOTE: For FEDERAL REGISTER citations affecting §71.56, see the List of CFR Sections Affected, which appears in the Finding Aids section of the printed volume and at *www.fdsys.gov.*

§71.57 Execution and disposition.

Forms 5000.6 and 5000.17 shall be executed in quintuplicate. A signed duplicated original shall be served on the permittee. If a hearing is requested, one copy shall be sent to the administrative law judge designated to conduct the hearing. The original copy containing the certificate of service shall be placed in the official record of the proceeding; and the remaining copies shall be retained by the appropriate TTB officer.

[T.D. ATF–244, 51 FR 45763, Dec. 22, 1986, as amended by T.D. ATF–374, 61 FR 29957, June 13, 1996]

§71.58 Designated place of hearing.

The designated place of hearing shall be such as meets the convenience and necessity of the parties.

[T.D. 6389, 24 FR 4791, June 12, 1959. Redesignated at 40 FR 16835, Apr. 15, 1975]

REQUEST FOR HEARING

§71.59 Application cases.

If the applicant for a permit desires a hearing, he shall file a request therefor, in writing, with the appropriate

TTB officer within fifteen days after receipt of notice of the contemplated disapproval, in whole or in part, of his application.

[21 FR 1441, Mar. 6, 1956. Redesignated at 40 FR 16835, Apr. 15, 1975, and amended by T.D. ATF-199, 50 FR 9197, Mar. 6, 1985; T.D. ATF-374, 61 FR 29957, June 13, 1996]

§ 71.60 Suspension, revocation, or annulment proceedings.

(a) If a hearing is desired, the respondent shall file a request, in writing, with the appropriate TTB officer within 15 days after receipt of the citation or within such time as the appropriate TTB officer may allow.

(b) Where a respondent requests a hearing, the appropriate TTB officer shall forward a copy of the request together with a copy of the citation to the Administrator for the assignment of an administrative law judge.

(c) After the Administrator notifies the appropriate TTB officer of the assignment of the administrative law judge, the appropriate TTB officer shall serve a notice of designation of the administrative law judge on the respondent.

(d) The administrative law judge shall set a time and place for a hearing and shall serve notice thereof on the parties at least 10 days in advance of the hearing date.

[T.D. ATF-244, 51 FR 45763, Dec. 22, 1986, as amended by T.D. ATF-374, 61 FR 29957, June 13, 1996]

§ 71.61 Notice of hearing.

In case a request for a hearing is filed by the applicant within the required time, the appropriate TTB officer shall refer the matter to the administrative law judge and the administrative law judge shall set a time and place for a hearing and shall serve notice thereof upon the parties at least ten days in advance of the hearing date.

[21 FR 1441, Mar. 6, 1956. Redesignated at 40 FR 16835, Apr. 15, 1975, as amended by T.D. ATF-374, 61 FR 29957, June 13, 1996]

NON-REQUEST FOR HEARING

§ 71.62 Application.

In the case of an application, if the applicant does not request a hearing within the time specified in § 71.59, or within such further time as the appropriate TTB officer may in his discretion allow, the appropriate TTB officer will by order, stating the findings upon which it is based, disapprove the application, and will serve signed duplicate original of such order on the applicant.

[21 FR 1441, Mar. 6, 1956. Redesignated at 40 FR 16835, Apr. 15, 1975, and amended by T.D. ATF-199, 50 FR 9197, Mar. 6, 1985; T.D. ATF-374, 61 FR 29957, June 13, 1996]

§ 71.63 Suspension, revocation, or annulment proceedings.

If the respondent does not request a hearing within the time specified in § 71.60, and does not file an answer as required in § 71.64, the appropriate TTB officer shall make the initial decision in the case in accordance with § 71.79.

[T.D. ATF-244, 51 FR 45763, Dec. 22, 1986, as amended by T.D. ATF-374, 61 FR 29957, June 13, 1996]

ANSWERS

§ 71.64 When required.

(a) Where the respondent requests a hearing in accordance with § 71.60, a written answer shall be filed with the administrative law judge and served on the appropriate TTB officer within 15 days after service of the designation of the administrative law judge.

(b) Where no hearing is requested, the respondent shall file a written answer with the appropriate TTB officer within 15 days after service of a citation.

(c) An answer shall contain a concise statement of the facts that constitute his grounds for defense. The hearing may be limited to the issues contained in the citation and the answer. The administrative law judge, or appropriate TTB officer as the case may be, may, as a matter of discretion, waive any requirement of this section.

(d) Answers need not be filed in application proceedings.

[T.D. ATF-244, 51 FR 45763, Dec. 22, 1986, as amended by T.D. ATF-374, 61 FR 29957, June 13, 1996]

§ 71.65 Answer admitting facts.

If the respondent desires to waive the hearing on the allegations of fact set forth in the order to show cause, and does not contest the facts, the answer may consist of a statement that the respondent admits all material allegations of fact charged in the citation to be true. The appropriate TTB officer shall thereupon base the decision on the citation and such answer although such an answer shall not affect the respondent's right to submit proposed findings of fact and conclusions of law, or the right to appeal.

[T.D. ATF–244, 51 FR 45763, Dec. 22, 1986, as amended by T.D. ATF–374, 61 FR 29957, June 13, 1996]

§71.66 Prehearing conferences.

In any proceeding the administrative law judge may, upon his own motion or upon the motion of one of the parties or their qualified representatives, in his discretion direct the parties or their qualified representatives to appear at a specified time and place for a conference to consider:

(a) The simplifications of the issues;

(b) The necessity of amendments to the pleadings;

(c) The possibility of obtaining stipulations, admissions of facts and of documents;

(d) The limitation of the number of expert witnesses; and

(e) Such other matters as may aid in the disposition of the proceeding. As soon as practicable after such conference, the administrative law judge shall issue an order which recites the action taken thereat, the amendments allowed to the pleadings and the agreements made by the parties or their qualified representatives as to any of the matters considered, and which limits the issues for hearing to those not disposed of by admission or agreement; and such order shall control the subsequent course of the proceedings, unless modified for good cause by a subsequent order.

FAILURE TO APPEAR

§71.67 Applications.

Where the applicant on an application for a permit has requested a hearing and does not appear at the appointed time and place, and evidence has not been offered to refute or explain the grounds upon which disapproval of the application is contemplated, this shall be construed as a waiver of the hearing, a default will be entered and the administrative law judge shall recommend disapproval of said application.

[21 FR 1441, Mar. 6, 1956. Redesignated at 40 FR 16835, Apr. 15, 1975, and amended by T.D. ATF–199, 50 FR 9197, Mar. 6, 1985]

§71.68 [Reserved]

§71.69 Suspension, revocation, or annulment.

If on the date set for the hearing respondent does not appear and no evidence has been offered, the attorney for the Government will proceed ex parte and offer for the record sufficient evidence to make a prima facie case. At such hearing, documents, statements and affidavits may be submitted in lieu of testimony of witnesses.

WAIVER OF HEARING

§71.70 Application proceedings.

At any time prior to final action thereon the applicant may, by filing written notice with the appropriate TTB officer, withdraw his application. If such a notice is filed after referral to the administrative law judge of a proceeding on an application for a permit and prior to issuance of his recommended decision or decision thereon, the appropriate TTB officer shall move the administrative law judge to dismiss the proceedings as moot. If such a notice is filed while the proceeding is before the appropriate TTB officer and prior to final action thereon, that is, either (a) after issuance of a notice of contemplated disapproval and before referral of the proceeding to the administrative law judge or (b) after issuance by the administrative law judge of his recommended decision and prior to the appropriate TTB officer's order disapproving the application, the appropriate TTB officer shall, by order, dismiss the proceeding.

[21 FR 1441, Mar. 6, 1956. Redesignated at 40 FR 16835, Apr. 15, 1975, and amended by T.D. ATF–199, 50 FR 9197, Mar. 6, 1985; T.D. ATF–374, 61 FR 29957, June 13, 1996]

§71.71 Adjudication based upon written submissions.

The respondent may waive the hearing before the administrative law judge, and stipulate that the matter will be adjudicated by the appropriate TTB officer based upon written submissions. Written submissions may include stipulations of law or facts, proposed findings of fact and conclusions of law, briefs, or any other documentary material. The pleadings together with the written submissions of both the attorneys for the Government and the respondent shall constitute the record on which the initial decision shall be based. The election to contest the citation without a hearing under this section does not affect the respondent's right to appeal.

[T.D. ATF-244, 51 FR 45763, Dec. 22, 1986, as amended by T.D. ATF-374, 61 FR 29957, June 13, 1996]

SURRENDER OF PERMIT

§71.72 Before citation.

If a respondent surrenders the permit before citation, the appropriate TTB officer may accept the surrender. But if the evidence, in the opinion of the appropriate TTB officer, warrants citation for suspension, revocation or annulment, the surrender shall be refused and the appropriate TTB officer shall issue the citation.

[T.D. ATF-244, 51 FR 45764, Dec. 22, 1986, as amended by T.D. ATF-374, 61 FR 29957, June 13, 1996]

§71.73 After citation.

If a respondent surrenders the permit after citation and prior to an initial decision, the appropriate TTB officer may accept the surrender of the permit and dismiss the proceeding as moot. If, however, in the opinion of the appropriate TTB officer, the evidence is such as to warrant suspension, revocation or annulment, as the case may be, the surrender of the permit shall be refused, and the proceeding shall continue.

[T.D. ATF-244, 51 FR 45764, Dec. 22, 1986, as amended by T.D. ATF-374, 61 FR 29957, June 13, 1996]

MOTIONS

§71.74 General.

All motions shall be made and addressed to the officer before whom the proceeding is pending, and copies of all motion papers shall be served upon the other party or parties. Such officer may dispose of any motion without oral argument, but he may, if he so desires, set it down for hearing and request argument. He may dispose of such motion prior to the hearing on the merits or he may postpone the disposition until the hearing on the merits. No appeal may be taken from any ruling on a motion until the whole record is certified for review. Examples of typical motions may be found in the Rules of Civil Procedure referred to in §71.2.

§71.75 Prior to hearing.

All motions which should be made prior to the hearing, such as motion directed to the sufficiency of the pleadings or of preliminary orders, shall be filed in writing with the appropriate TTB officer issuing the citation or the administrative law judge if the matter has been referred to him, and shall briefly state the order or relief applied for and the grounds for such motion, and shall be filed within 15 days after service of the citation.

[21 FR 1441, Mar. 6, 1956. Redesignated at 40 FR 16835, Apr. 15, 1975, as amended by T.D. ATF-374, 61 FR 29957, June 13, 1996]

§71.76 At hearing.

Motions at the hearing may be made in writing to the administrative law judge or stated orally on the record.

HEARING

§71.77 General.

If a hearing is requested, it shall be held at the time and place stated in the notice of hearing unless otherwise ordered by the administrative law judge.

[T.D. ATF-244, 51 FR 45764, Dec. 22, 1986]

§71.78 Applications.

The administrative law judge who presides at the hearing on applications shall recommend a decision to the appropriate TTB officer who shall make the initial decision as provided in §71.107. The applicant may be directed by the appropriate TTB officer to produce such records as may be deemed necessary for examination. All hearings on applications shall be open to the public subject to such restrictions and limitations as may be consistent with orderly procedure.

[21 FR 1441, Mar. 6, 1956. Redesignated at 40 FR 16835, Apr. 15, 1975, and amended by T.D. ATF–199, 50 FR 9197, Mar. 6, 1985; T.D. ATF–374, 61 FR 29957, June 13, 1996]

§71.79 Suspension, revocation, or annulment.

(a) The administrative law judge who presides at the hearing in proceedings for the suspension, revocation and annulment of permits shall make the initial decision.

(b) If no hearing is requested, the appropriate TTB officer shall make the initial decision.

[T.D. ATF–244, 51 FR 45764, Dec. 22, 1986, as amended by T.D. ATF–374, 61 FR 29957, June 13, 1996]

BURDEN OF PROOF

§71.80 Applications.

In hearings on the contemplated disapproval of applications there may be incorporated in the record sufficient testimony, reports, affidavits and other documents to be considered only for the limited purpose of establishing probable cause for the issuance of the notice of contemplated disapproval by showing that the appropriate TTB officer had reason to believe that the applicant is not entitled to a permit. The burden of proof shall be upon the applicant to produce evidence to show he is entitled to a permit. The appropriate TTB officer may, instead of following the aforementioned procedure, assume the burden of going forward.

[21 FR 1441, Mar. 6, 1956. Redesignated at 40 FR 16835, Apr. 15, 1975, and amended by T.D. ATF–199, 50 FR 9197, Mar. 6, 1985; T.D. ATF–374, 61 FR 29957, June 13, 1996]

§71.81 Suspension, revocation, or annulment.

In hearings on the suspension, revocation, or annulment of a permit, the burden of proof is on the Government.

[T.D. ATF–199, 50 FR 9197, Mar. 6, 1985]

GENERAL

§71.82 Stipulations at hearing.

If there has been no prehearing conference under §71.66, the administrative law judge shall at the beginning of the hearing, require that the parties attempt to arrive at such stipulations as will eliminate the necessity of taking evidence with respect to allegations of fact concerning which there is no substantial dispute. The administrative law judge should take similar action, where it appears appropriate, throughout the hearing and should call and conduct any conferences which he deems advisable with a view to the simplification, clarification, and disposition of any of the issues involved.

§71.83 Evidence.

Any evidence which would be admissible under the rules of evidence governing proceedings in matters not involving trial by jury in the Courts of the United States, shall be admissible and controlling as far as possible: *Provided,* That the administrative law judge may relax such rules in any hearing when in his judgment such relaxation would not impair the rights of either party and would more speedily conclude the hearing, or would better serve the ends of justice. Except as provided in §71.81, the proponent of an order shall have the burden of proof. Every party shall have the right to present his case or defense by oral or documentary evidence, depositions, duly authenticated copies of records and documents, to submit rebuttal evidence, and to conduct such reasonable cross-examination as may be required for a full and true disclosure of the facts. The administrative law judge shall have the right in his discretion to limit the number of witnesses whose testimony may be merely cumulative and shall, as a matter of policy, not only exclude irrelevant, immaterial, or unduly repetitious evidence but shall also limit the cross-examination of witnesses to reasonable bounds so as not to unnecessarily prolong the hearing and unduly burden the record. Material and relevant evidence shall not be excluded, because it is not the best evidence, unless its authenticity is challenged, in which case reasonable time shall be given to establish its authenticity. When portions only of a document are to be relied upon, the offering party shall prepare the pertinent excerpts, adequately identified, and shall supply copies of such excerpts, together with a statement indicating the purpose for which such materials will be offered, to the administrative law judge and to the other parties. Only the excerpts, so prepared and submitted, shall be received in the record. However, the whole of the original document should be made available for examination and for use by opposing counsel for purposes of cross-examination. Compilations, charts, summaries of data and photostatic copies of documents may be admitted in evidence if the proceedings will thereby be expedited, and if the material upon which they are based is available for examination by the parties. Objections to the evidence shall be in short form, stating the grounds relied upon. The transcript shall not include argument or debate on objections, except as ordered by the administrative law judge, but shall include the rulings thereon.

§ 71.84 Closing of hearings; arguments, briefs and proposed findings.

Before closing a hearing, the administrative law judge shall inquire of each party whether he has any further evidence to offer, which inquiry and the response thereto shall be shown in the record. The administrative law judge may hear arguments of counsel and may limit the time of such arguments at his discretion, and may, in his discretion, allow briefs to be filed on behalf of either party but shall closely limit the time within which the briefs for both parties shall be filed, so as to avoid unreasonable delay. The administrative law judge shall also ascertain whether the parties desire to submit proposed findings and conclusions, together with supporting reasons, and if so a period of not more than 15 days (unless extended by the administrative law judge)—after the close of the hearing or receipt of a copy of the record, if one is requested—will be allowed for such purpose.

§ 71.85 Reopening of the hearing.

The Administrator, the appropriate TTB officer, or the administrative law judge, as the case may be, may, as to all matters pending before him, in his discretion reopen the hearing (a) in case of default where applicant failed to request a hearing or to appear after one was set, upon petition setting forth reasonable grounds for such failure, and (b) in case any party desires leave to adduce additional evidence upon petition summarizing such evidence, establishing its materiality and stating reasonable grounds why such party with due diligence was unable to produce such evidence at the hearing.

[21 FR 1441, Mar. 6, 1956. Redesignated at 40 FR 16835, Apr. 15, 1975, and amended by T.D. ATF-48, 43 FR 13531, Mar. 31, 1978; 44 FR 55846, Sept. 28, 1979; T.D. ATF-374, 61 FR 29957, June 13, 1996]

RECORD OF TESTIMONY

§ 71.86 Stenographic record.

A stenographic record shall be made of the testimony and proceedings, including stipulations and admissions of fact (but not arguments of counsel unless otherwise ordered by the administrative law judge) in all proceedings. A transcript of the evidence and proceedings at the hearing shall be made in all cases.

§ 71.87 Oath of reporter.

The reporter making the stenographic record shall subscribe an oath before the administrative law judge, to be filed in the record of the case, that he will truly and correctly report the oral testimony and proceedings at such hearing and accurately transcribe the same to the best of his ability.

Subpart G—Administrative Law Judges

§ 71.95 Responsibilities of administrative law judges.

Administrative law judges shall be under the administrative control of the Administrator. They shall be responsible for the conduct of hearings and shall render their decisions as soon as is reasonably possible after the hearing is closed. Administrative law judges shall also be responsible for the preparation, certification and forwarding of reports of hearings, and the administrative work relating thereto, and, by arrangement with the appropriate TTB officer and representatives of the Chief Counsel, shall have access to facilities and temporary use of personnel at such times and places as are needed in the prompt dispatch of official business.

[21 FR 1441, Mar. 6, 1956. Redesignated at 40 FR 16835, Apr. 15, 1975, and amended by T.D. ATF–48, 43 FR 13531, Mar. 31, 1978; 44 FR 55846, Sept. 28, 1979; T.D. ATF–374, 61 FR 29957, June 13, 1996]

§ 71.96 Disqualification.

An administrative law judge shall, at any time, withdraw from any proceeding if he deems himself disqualified; and upon the filing in good faith by the applicant or respondent, or by the attorney for the Government, of a timely and sufficient affidavit of facts showing personal bias or otherwise warranting the disqualification of any administrative law judge, the Administrator shall upon appeal as provided in § 71.115, if the administrative law judge fails to disqualify himself, determine the matter as a part of the record and decision in the proceeding. If he decides the administrative law judge should have declared himself disqualified, he will remand the record for hearing de novo before another administrative law judge. If the Administrator should decide against the disqualification of the administrative law judge, the proceeding will be reviewed on its merits.

§ 71.97 Powers.

Administrative law judges shall have authority to (a) administer oaths and affirmations; (b) issue subpoenas authorized by law; (c) rule upon offers of proof and receive relevant evidence; (d) take or cause depositions to be taken whenever the ends of justice would be served thereby; (e) regulate the course of the hearing; (f) hold conferences for the settlement or simplification of the issues by consent of the parties; (g) dispose of procedural requests or similar matters; (h) render recommended decisions in proceedings on applications for permits, and in suspension, revocation, or annulment proceedings against permits; (i) call, examine and cross-examine witnesses, including hostile or adverse witnesses when he deems such action to be necessary to a just disposition of the cause, and introduce into the record documentary or other evidence; and (j) take any other action authorized by rule of the Alcohol and Tobacco Tax and Trade Bureau consistent with the Administrative Procedure Act.

[21 FR 1441, Mar. 6, 1956. Redesignated at 40 FR 16835, Apr. 15, 1975, and amended by T.D. ATF–48, 44 FR 55846, Sept. 28, 1979; T.D. ATF–119, 50 FR 9197, Mar. 6, 1985]

§ 71.98 Separation of functions.

Administrative law judges shall perform no duties inconsistent with their duties and responsibilities as such. Administrative law judges may be assigned duties not inconsistent with the performance of their functions as administrative law judges. Save to the extent required for the disposition of ex parte matters as required by law, no administrative law judge shall consult any person or party as to any fact in issue unless upon notice and opportunity for all parties to participate. The functions of the administrative law judge shall be entirely separated from the general investigative functions of the agency. No officer, employee, or agent engaged in the performance of investigative or prosecuting functions in any proceeding shall, in that or a factually related proceeding, participate or advise in the administrative law judge's or Administrator's decision, or in the agency review on appeal, except as a witness or counsel in the proceedings. The administrative law judge may not informally obtain advice or opinions from the parties or their counsel, or from any officer or employee of the Alcohol and Tobacco Tax and Trade Bureau, as to the facts or the weight or interpretation to be given to the evidence. He may, however, informally obtain advice on matters of law from officers or employees who were not engaged in the performance of investigative or prosecuting functions in that or a factually related proceeding. This limitation does not apply to the Administrator, and the administrative law judge may, at any time, consult with and obtain instructions from him on questions of law and policy.

[21 FR 1441, Mar. 6, 1956. Redesignated at 40 FR 16835, Apr. 15, 1975, and amended by T.D. ATF–48, 43 FR 13531, Mar. 31, 1978; 44 FR 55846, Sept. 28, 1979]

§71.99 Conduct of hearing.

The administrative law judge is charged with the duty of conducting a fair and impartial hearing and of maintaining order in form and manner consistent with dignity. In the event that counsel or any person or witness in any proceeding shall refuse to obey the orders of the administrative law judge, or be guilty of disorderly or contemptuous language or conduct in connection with any hearing, the administrative law judge may, for good cause stated in the record, suspend the hearing, and, in the case of an attorney, recommend that the Administrator report the matter to the Administrator of Practice for disciplinary action. The refusal of a witness to answer any question which has been ruled to be proper shall be considered by the administrative law judge in determining the weight to be given all the testimony of that witness.

[21 FR 1441, Mar. 6, 1956. Redesignated at 40 FR 16835, Apr. 15, 1975, and amended by T.D. ATF–48, 43 FR 13531, Mar. 31, 1978; 44 FR 55846, Sept. 28, 1979]

§71.100 Unavailability of administrative law judge.

In the event that the administrative law judge designated to conduct a hearing becomes unavailable before the filing of his findings and decision or recommended decision, the Administrator may assign the case to another administrative law judge for the continuance of the proceeding, in accordance with the regulations in this part in the same manner as if he had been designated administrative law judge at the commencement of the proceeding.

[21 FR 1441, Mar. 6, 1956. Redesignated at 40 FR 16835, Apr. 15, 1975, and amended by T.D. ATF–48, 43 FR 13531, Mar. 31, 1978; 44 FR 55846, Sept. 28, 1979]

Subpart H—Decisions

§71.105 Administrative law judge's finding and decision or recommended decision.

Within a reasonable time after the conclusion of the hearing, and as expeditiously as possible, the administrative law judge shall render his decision or recommended decision, as the case may be. All decisions shall become a part of the record and, if proposed findings and conclusions have been filed, shall show the administrative law judge's ruling upon each of such proposed findings and conclusions. Decisions shall consist of (a) a brief statement of the issues of fact involved in the proceeding; (b) the administrative law judge's findings and conclusions, as well as the reasons or basis therefor with record references, upon all the material issues of fact, law or discretion presented on the record (including, when appropriate, comment as to the credibility and demeanor of the witnesses); and (c) the administrative law judge's determination or recommended determination on the record. Where the administrative law judge determines that the imposition of a period of suspension of the permit is appropriate, his decision shall state the length of such period of suspension, to commence at such time as the appropriate TTB officer shall specify.

[21 FR 1441, Mar. 6, 1956. Redesignated at 40 FR 16835, Apr. 15, 1975, as amended by T.D. ATF–374, 61 FR 29957, June 13, 1996]

§71.106 Certification and transmittal of record and decision.

After reaching his decision, the administrative law judge shall certify to the complete record of the proceeding before him and (a) in proceedings on an application, shall immediately forward the complete certified record together with four copies of his recommended decision to the appropriate TTB officer for initial decision, or (b) in revocation, suspension or annulment proceedings, shall immediately forward the complete certified record, together with two copies of his decision, to the appropriate TTB officer, serve one copy of his decision on the respondent or his counsel and transmit a copy of his decision to the attorney for the Government.

[21 FR 1441, Mar. 6, 1956. Redesignated at 40 FR 16835, Apr. 15, 1975, and amended by T.D. ATF–199, 50 FR 9197, Mar. 6, 1985; T.D. ATF–374, 61 FR 29957, June 13, 1996]

ACTION BY THE APPROPRIATE TTB OFFICER

§ 71.107 Application proceedings.

If, upon receipt of the record and the recommended decision of the administrative law judge, the appropriate TTB officer decides that the permit should be issued, he shall thereupon approve the application briefly stating, for the record, his reasons therefor, but if he contemplates the disapproval of the application he shall serve a copy of the administrative law judge's recommended decision on the applicant, informing the applicant of his contemplated action and affording the applicant not more than 10 days in which to submit proposed findings and conclusions or exceptions to the recommended decision with reasons in support thereof. If the appropriate TTB officer, after consideration of the record of the hearing and of any proposed findings, conclusions or exceptions filed with him by the applicant, approves the findings, conclusions and recommended decision of the administrative law judge, he shall by order approve or disapprove of the application in accordance therewith. If, after such consideration, he disapproves of the findings, conclusions and recommended decision of the administrative law judge, in whole or in part, he shall by order make such findings and conclusions as in his opinion are warranted by the law and facts in the record. Any decision of the appropriate TTB officer ordering the disapproval of an application for a permit shall state the findings and conclusions upon which it is based, including his ruling upon each proposed finding, conclusion and exception to the administrative law judge's recommended decision, together with a statement of his findings and conclusions, and reasons or basis therefor, upon all material issues of fact, law or discretion presented on the record. A signed duplicate original of the decision shall be served upon the applicant and the original copy containing certificate of service shall be placed in the official record of the proceeding.

[21 FR 1441, Mar. 6, 1956. Redesignated at 40 FR 16835, Apr. 15, 1975, and amended by T.D. ATF–199, 50 FR 9197, Mar. 6, 1985; T.D. ATF–374, 61 FR 29957, June 13, 1996]

§ 71.107a Appropriate TTB officer's decision.

(a) When the appropriate TTB officer issues an initial decision in accordance with § 71.79, the decision shall become a part of the record. The decision shall consist of

(1) A brief statement of the issues involved in the proceedings;

(2) The appropriate TTB officer's findings and conclusions, as well as the reasons therefor; and

(3) The appropriate TTB officer's determination on the record.

[T.D. ATF–244, 51 FR 45764, Dec. 22, 1986, as amended by T.D. ATF–374, 61 FR 29957, June 13, 1996]

§ 71.108 Suspension, revocation, or annulment proceedings.

(a) Upon receipt of the complete certified record of the hearing the appropriate TTB officer shall enter an order suspending, revoking, or annulling the permit (on TTB F 5000.5) or dismissing the proceedings in accordance with the administrative law judge's findings and decision, unless he disagrees with such findings and decision and files a petition with the Administrator, for review thereof, as provided in § 71.115. If the appropriate TTB officer files such petition, he shall withhold issuance of the order, pending the decision of the Administrator, upon receipt of which he shall issue the order in accordance therewith. A signed duplicate original of the order of the appropriate TTB officer shall be served upon the respondent and the original copy containing certificate of service shall be placed in the official record of the proceeding. In all proceedings in which a suspension is imposed, the appropriate TTB officer's order shall state the time when the suspension period set forth in the administrative law judge's decision shall commence and terminate.

(b) In a case where the initial decision is made by the appropriate TTB officer in accordance with § 71.79, the appropriate TTB officer will also issue an order suspending, revoking or annulling the permit (on Form 5000.5), or dismissing the proceedings in accordance with his initial decision. A signed duplicated original of the decision and order of the appropriate TTB officer shall be served upon the respondent and the original copy placed in the official record of the proceeding. In all proceedings in which a suspension is imposed, the appropriate TTB officer's order shall state the time when the suspension period set forth in the initial decision shall commence and terminate.

[21 FR 1441, Mar. 6, 1956. Redesignated at 40 FR 16835, Apr. 15, 1975, and amended by T.D. ATF-199, 50 FR 9196, 9197, Mar. 6, 1985; T.D. ATF-244, 51 FR 45764, Dec. 22, 1986; T.D. ATF-374, 61 FR 29957, June 13, 1996; T.D. TTB-91, 76 FR 5482, Feb. 1, 2011]

§71.109 Notice to Administrator.

When the appropriate TTB officer makes an order suspending, revoking or annulling a permit, he will furnish a copy of the order and of the decision on which it is based to the Administrator. Should such order be subsequently set aside on review by the courts, the appropriate TTB officer will so advise the Administrator.

[21 FR 1441, Mar. 6, 1956. Redesignated at 40 FR 16835, Apr. 15, 1975, and amended by T.D. ATF-199, 50 FR 9197, Mar. 6, 1985; T.D. ATF-374, 61 FR 29957, June 13, 1996]

Subpart I—Review

§71.115 Appeal on petition to the Administrator.

An appeal to the Administrator is required prior to application to the Federal courts for review. An appeal may be taken by the applicant or respondent or by the appropriate TTB officer. Such appeal shall be taken by filing a petition for review on appeal with the Administrator within 15 days of the service of the order disapproving an application for a permit or the initial decision suspending, revoking or annulling a permit. The petition must set forth facts tending to show action of an arbitrary nature, or action without reasonable warrant in fact, or action contrary to law and regulations. A copy of the petition shall be filed with the appropriate TTB officer or served on the respondent or applicant as the case may be. In the event of such appeal, the appropriate TTB officer shall immediately certify and forward the complete original record, by certified mail, to the Administrator, for his consideration and review.

[T.D. ATF-244, 51 FR 45764, Dec. 22, 1986, as amended by T.D. ATF-374, 61 FR 29957, June 13, 1996]

§71.116 Review by Administrator.

The Administrator, on appeal on petition for review, shall afford a reasonable opportunity for the submission of proposed findings, conclusions or exceptions with reasons in support thereof and an opportunity for oral argument. He may alter or modify any finding of the administrative law judge (or of the appropriate TTB officer in application proceedings) and may affirm, reverse, or modify the decision of the administrative law judge (or of the appropriate TTB officer in initial application proceedings), or he may remand the case for further hearing, but he shall not consider evidence which is not a part of the record. Appeals and petitions for review shall not be decided by the Administrator in any proceeding in which he has engaged in investigation or prosecution, and in such event he shall so state his disqualification in writing and refer the record to the Under Secretary for appropriate action. The Under Secretary may designate an Assistant Secretary or one of his principal aides to consider any proceeding instead of the Administrator. The original copy of the decision on review shall be placed in the official record of the proceeding, a signed duplicate original shall be served upon the applicant or respondent and a copy shall be transmitted to the appropriate TTB officer. When, on appeal, the Administrator affirms the decision of the appropriate TTB officer or the administrative law judge, as the case may be, disapproving an application or suspending, revoking or annulling a permit, such action shall not supersede the decision of the appropriate TTB officer or the administrative law judge and such decision shall be final.

(26 U.S.C. 7805 (68A Stat. 917), 27 U.S.C. 205 (49 Stat. 981 as amended), 18 U.S.C. 926 (82 Stat. 959), and Sec. 38, Arms Export Control Act (22 U.S.C. 2778, 90 Stat. 744))

[21 FR 1441, Mar. 6, 1956. Redesignated at 40 FR 16835, Apr. 15, 1975, and amended by T.D. ATF–48, 43 FR 13531, Mar. 31, 1978; T.D. ATF–199, 50 FR 9197, Mar. 6, 1985; T.D. ATF–374, 61 FR 29957, June 13, 1996]

§ 71.117 Permit privileges, exceptions.

Pending final determination of any timely appeal in revocation, suspension, or annulment proceeding to the Administrator, the permit involved shall continue in force and effect except that, in the case of industrial use permits, any time after a citation has been issued withdrawals of tax-free spirits or specially denatured spirits by such permittee may, in the discretion of the appropriate TTB officer or Administrator, be restricted to the quantity which, together with the quantity then on hand, is necessary to carry on legitimate operations under such permit. The appropriate TTB officer may, in restricting the permittee to his legitimate needs, refuse to issue any withdrawal permit.

[T.D. 6389, 24 FR 4791, June 12, 1959. Redesignated at 40 FR 16835, Apr. 15, 1975; T.D. ATF–199, 50 FR 9197, Mar. 6, 1985; T.D. ATF–374, 61 FR 29957, June 13, 1996]

§ 71.118 Court review.

If an applicant or respondent files an appeal in Federal court of the Administrator's decision, the Administrator, upon notification that an appeal has been taken, shall prepare the record for submission to the court in accordance with the applicable court rules.

[T.D. ATF–244, 51 FR 45764, Dec. 22, 1986]

§ 71.119 [Reserved]

Subpart J—Miscellaneous

§ 71.125 Depositions.

The administrative law judge may take or order the taking of depositions by either party to the proceeding at such time and place as he may designate before a person having the power to administer oaths, upon application therefor and notice to the parties to the action. The testimony shall be reduced to writing by the person taking the deposition, or under his direction, and the deposition shall be subscribed by the deponent unless subscribing thereof is waived in writing by the parties. Any person may be subpoenaed to appear and depose and to produce documentary evidence in the same manner as witnesses at hearings.

§ 71.126 Subpoenas.

On written application by a party to a proceeding, the attendance and testimony of any person, or the production of documentary evidence in proceedings instituted under this part may be required by personal subpoena (Form 5600.10) or by subpoena duces tecum (Form 5600.11). Application should be addressed to, and subpoenas should be issued by, the administrative law judge before whom the proceedings are pending, but may be issued by the appropriate TTB officer or by the Administrator, if the administrative law judge is unavailable. Both the application and the subpoena shall set forth the title of the proceedings, the name and address of the person whose attendance is required, the date and place of his attendance and, if documents are to be produced, a description thereof; and the application must have reasonable scope and specify as exactly as possible the documents required, if any, and show their general relevance. Subpoenas shall be served in person. When issued on behalf of the United States, service shall be made by an officer, employee, or agent of the Treasury Department; when issued on behalf of a permittee or applicant, service shall be made by any person who is not a party to the proceeding and is not less than 18 years of age.

(49 Stat. 977, 72 Stat. 1372; 27 U.S.C. 202, 26 U.S.C. 5274)

[21 FR 1441, Mar. 6, 1956, as amended by T.D. 6389, 24 FR 4791, June 12, 1959. Redesignated at 40 FR 16835, Apr. 15, 1975, and amended by T.D. ATF–244, 51 FR 45764, Dec. 22, 1986; T.D. ATF–374, 61 FR 29957, June 13, 1996]

§ 71.127 Witnesses and fees.

Witnesses summoned before the administrative law judge may be paid the same fees and mileage that are paid witnesses in the courts of the United States, and witnesses whose depositions are taken and the persons taking the same shall severally be entitled to the same fees as are paid for like services in the courts of the United States. Witness fees and mileage shall be paid by the party at whose instance the witnesses appear and the person taking the deposition shall be paid by the party at whose instance the deposition is taken.

RECORD

§ 71.128 What constitutes record.

The transcript of testimony, pleadings and exhibits, all papers and requests filed in the proceeding, together with all findings, decisions and orders, shall constitute the exclusive record. Where the decision rests on official notice of material fact not appearing in the record, the administrative law judge shall so state in his findings and any party shall, on timely request, be afforded an opportunity to show facts to the contrary.

§ 71.129 Availability.

A copy of the record shall be available for inspection by the parties to the proceedings during business hours at the office of the administrative law judge or the appropriate TTB officer or, pending administrative review, at the office of the Administrator. Copies of the record desired by the respondent or applicant may be purchased from the contract reporter or may be obtained in accordance with part 71 of this chapter.

(5 U.S.C. 552(a) (80 Stat. 383, as amended))

[21 FR 1441, Mar. 6, 1956. Redesignated at 40 FR 16835, Apr. 15, 1975, and amended by T.D. ATF–92, 46 FR 46918, Sept. 23, 1981; T.D. ATF–374, 61 FR 29957, June 13, 1996]

PART 72—DISPOSITION OF SEIZED PERSONAL PROPERTY

Subpart A—Scope of Regulations

Subpart B—Definitions

Subpart C—Seizures and Forfeitures

Subpart D—Remission or Mitigation of Forfeitures

Subpart E—Appraiser's Fees

Subpart F—Administrative Sale or Disposition of Personal Property

Subpart G—Disposal of Forfeited Firearms, Ammunition, Explosive Materials, or Contraband Cigarettes

AUTHORITY: 18 U.S.C. 921, 1261; 19 U.S.C. 1607, 1610, 1612, 1613, 1618; 26 U.S.C. 7101, 7322–7325, 7326, 7805; 31 U.S.C. 9301, 9303, 9304, 9306; 40 U.S.C. 304(k); 49 U.S.C. 784, 788.

SOURCE: T.D. ATF–9, 39 FR 9954, Mar. 15, 1974, unless otherwise noted.

Subpart A—Scope of Regulations

§ 72.1 Procedures relating to personal property and carriers.

Regulations in this part shall relate to personal property and carriers seized by alcohol, tobacco and firearms officers as subject to forfeiture as being involved, used, or intended to be used, as the case may be, in any violation of Federal laws.

§ 72.2 Forms prescribed.

(a) The Director is authorized to prescribe all forms required by this part, or necessary for its administration. All of the information called for in each form shall be furnished as indicated by the headings on the form and the instructions on or pertaining to the form. In addition, information called for in each form shall be furnished as required by this part.

(b) "Public Use Forms" (ATF Publication 1322.1) is a numerical listing of forms issued or used by the Bureau of Alcohol, Tobacco and Firearms. This publication is available from the Superintendent of Documents, U.S. Government Printing Office, Washington, DC 20402.

(c) Requests for forms should be mailed to the ATF Distribution Center, 7943 Angus Court, Springfield, Virginia 22153.

[T.D. ATF–92, 46 FR 46914, Sept. 23, 1981, as amended by T.D. ATF–249, 52 FR 5962, Feb. 27, 1987]

Subpart B—Definitions

§ 72.11 Meaning of terms.

As used in this part, unless the context otherwise requires, terms shall have the meanings ascribed in this section. Words in the plural form shall include the singular, and vice versa, and words importing the masculine gender shall include the feminine. The terms "includes" and "including" do not exclude things not enumerated which are in the same general class.

ATF Officer. An officer or employee of the Bureau of Alcohol, Tobacco, and Firearms (ATF) duly authorized to perform any function relating to the administration or enforcement of this part.

Appraised value. The value placed upon seized property or carriers by the appraiser or appraisers designated for the purpose of determining whether the property or carriers may be forfeited administratively.

Carrier. A vessel, vehicle, or aircraft seized under 49 U.S.C. Chapter 11 for having been used to transport, carry, or conceal a contraband firearm or contraband cigarettes. Vessels, vehicles, or aircraft seized under other provisions of applicable laws shall be considered personal property.

Commercial crimes. Any of the following types of crimes (Federal or State): Offenses against the revenue laws; burglary; counterfeiting; forgery; kidnapping; larceny; robbery; illegal sale or possession of deadly weapons; prostitution (including soliciting, procuring, pandering, white slaving, keeping house of ill fame, and like offenses); extortion; swindling and confidence games; and attempting to commit, conspiring to commit, or compounding any of the foregoing crimes. Addiction to narcotic drugs and use of marihuana will be treated as if such were commercial crime.

Contraband cigarettes. Any quantity of cigarettes in excess of 60,000, if:

(a) The cigarettes bear no evidence of the payment of applicable State cigarette taxes in the State where the cigarettes are found;

(b) The State in which the cigarettes are found requires a stamp, impression, or other indication to be placed on packages or other containers of cigarettes to evidence payment of cigarette taxes; and

(c) The cigarettes are in the possession of any person other than any person who is:

(1) Holding a permit issued under 26 U.S.C. Chapter 52 as a manufacturer of tobacco products or as an export warehouse proprietor;

(2) Operating a customs bonded warehouse under 19 U.S.C. 1311 or 1555;

(3) An agent of a tobacco products manufacturer, an export warehouse proprietor, or an operator of a customs bonded warehouse;

(4) A common or contract carrier transporting the cigarettes involved under a proper bill of lading or freight

bill which states the quantity, source, and destination of the cigarettes;

(5) Licensed or otherwise authorized by the State where the cigarettes are found to account for and pay cigarette taxes imposed by that State; and who has complied with the accounting and payment requirements relating to the license or authorization with respect to the cigarettes involved; or

(6) An agent of the United States, of an individual State, or of a political subdivision of a State and having possession of cigarettes in connection with the performance of official duties.

(7) Operating within a foreign-trade zone, established under 19 U.S.C. 81b, when the cigarettes involved have been entered into the foreign-trade zone under zone-restricted status or when foreign cigarettes have been admitted into the foreign-trade zone but have not been entered into the United States.

Contraband firearm. A firearm with respect to which there has been committed a violation of the National Firearms Act (26 U.S.C., Chapter 53) or any regulation issued thereunder.

Director. The Director, Bureau of Alcohol, Tobacco, and Firearms, the Department of the Treasury, Washington, DC.

Equity. As used in administrative action on petitions for remission or mitigation of forfeitures, shall mean that interest which a petitioner has in the personal property or carrier petitioned for at the time of final administrative action on the petition, but such interest shall not be considered to include any unearned finance charges from the date of seizure or the date of default, if later; any amount rebatable on account of paid insurance premiums; attorney's fees for collection; any amount identified as dealer's reserve; or any amount in the nature of liquidated damages that may have been agreed upon by the buyer and the petitioner.

Person. An individual, trust, estate, partnership, association, company or a corporation.

Re-appraisal. An up-to-date statutory appraisal to determine the present value of the property or carrier involved in a petition for remission or mitigation of forfeiture made in the same manner as the original appraisal, and performed at the written request of the petitioner whose petition in regard to the property or carrier has been allowed and who, for reasonable cause, is not satisfied that the original appraisal represents the present value of the property or carrier.

Region. A Bureau of Alcohol, Tobacco, and Firearms Region.

U.S.C. The United States Code.

[T.D. ATF-48, 43 FR 13535, Mar. 31, 1978; 44 FR 55841, Sept. 28, 1979, as amended by T.D. ATF-65, 45 FR 8593, Feb. 8, 1980; T.D. ATF-183, 49 FR 37061, Sept. 21, 1984]

Subpart C—Seizures and Forfeitures

§72.21 Personal property and carriers subject to seizure.

(a) Personal property may be seized by duly authorized ATF officers for forfeiture to the United States when involved, used, or intended to be used, in violation of the laws of the United States which ATF officers are empowered to enforce, including Title 18 U.S.C. Chapters 40 (explosives), 44 (firearms), 59 (liquor traffic), 114 (contraband cigarettes), 229 (liquor); Title 26 U.S.C. Chapters 51 (distilled spirits), 52 (tobacco), 53 (firearms); and Title 27 U.S.C. 206 (liquor). Carriers, as defined in §72.11, similarly may be seized when used in violation of Title 49 U.S.C. App., Chapter 11 (transportation, et cetera) of contraband firearms or contraband cigarettes.

(b) Any action or proceeding for the forfeiture of firearms or ammunition seized under 18 U.S.C. Chapter 44 shall be commenced within 120 days of such seizure.

(c) Upon acquittal of the owner or possessor, or the dismissal of the criminal charges against such person other than upon motion of the Government prior to trial, or lapse of or court termination of the restraining order to which such person is subject, firearms or ammunition seized or relinquished under 18 U.S.C. Chapter 44 shall be returned forthwith to the owner or possessor or to a person delegated by the owner or possessor unless the return of the firearms or ammunition would place the owner or possessor or his delegate in violation of law.

[T.D. ATF–270, 53 FR 10489, Mar. 31, 1988, as amended by T.D. ATF–363, 60 FR 17449, Apr. 6, 1995]

§ 72.22 Forfeiture of seized personal property and carriers.

(a) *Administrative forfeiture.* (1) Personal property seized as subject to forfeiture under Title 26 U.S.C. which has an appraised value of $100,000.00 or less, and any carrier appraised by the seizing officer at $100,000.00 or less under the customs laws, shall be forfeited to the United States in administrative or summary forfeiture proceedings.

(2) In respect of personal property seized as subject to forfeiture under title 26 U.S.C. which, in the opinion of the seizing officer, has an appraised value of $100,000.00 or less, such officer shall cause a list containing a particular description of the seized property to be prepared and an appraisement thereof to be made by three sworn appraisers, selected by the seizing officer, who shall be respectable and disinterested citizens of the United States residing within the internal revenue district wherein the seizure was made. Such list and appraisement shall be properly attested to by the seizing officer and such appraisers.

(3) In respect of personal property seized as subject to forfeiture under title 26 U.S.C. and found by the appraisers to have a value of $100,000.00 or less, the Director or his delegate shall publish a notice once a week for three consecutive weeks, in some newspaper of the judicial district where the seizure was made, describing the articles and stating the time, place, and cause of their seizure, and requiring any person claiming them to make such claim within 30 days from the date of the first publication of such notice.

(4) In respect of carriers seized as subject to forfeiture under the customs laws which, in the opinion of the seizing officer, have an appraised value of $100,000.00 or less, such officer shall cause a list containing a particular description of the seized carriers to be prepared and the seizing officer shall make the appraisement thereof. Such list and appraisement shall be properly attested to by the seizing officer.

(5) In respect of carriers seized as subject to forfeiture under the customs laws and appraised by the seizing officer as having a value of $100,000.00 or less, the Director or his delegate shall publish a notice of seizure in the same manner as required by paragraph (a)(3) of this section; provided that the time for making claim shall be within 20 days from the date of first publication. (19 U.S.C. 1608).

(6) Any person claiming the personal property or carrier so seized, within the time specified in the notice, may file with the Director a claim stating the interest in the articles or carrier seized, and may execute a bond to the United States, conditioned that, in case of condemnation of the articles or carrier so seized, the obligators shall pay all the costs and expenses of the proceedings to obtain such condemnation. The amount of the cost bond is $2,500.00, unless the seized property is a vehicle, vessel, or aircraft seized for a violation of 49 U.S.C. App., Chapter 11, in which case the cost bond shall be in the amount of $2,500 or ten percent of the value of the claimed property, whichever is lower, but not less than $250.00. Both the claim and the cost bond shall be executed in quadruplicate.

(b) *Judicial condemnation.* The Chief Counsel of the Bureau of Alcohol, Tobacco and Firearms, shall authorize institution of forfeiture proceedings in those instances where the appraised value of the seized personal property or carrier exceeds $100,000.00 or where a claim and cost bond are filed.

(Sec. 111, Pub. L. 95–410, 92 Stat. 897, as amended (19 U.S.C. 1607, 1610, 1612))

[T.D. ATF–9, 39 FR 9954, Mar. 15, 1974, as amended by T.D. ATF–65, 45 FR 8593, Feb. 8, 1980; T.D. ATF–183, 49 FR 37061, Sept. 21, 1984; T.D. ATF–241, 51 FR 39613, Oct. 29, 1986; T.D. ATF–270, 53 FR 10489, Mar. 31, 1988]

§ 72.23 Type and conditions of cost bond.

The cost bond delivered by a claimant to effect removal of the forfeiture status of the property or carrier claimed to the jurisdiction of the Federal court for adjudication shall be a corporate surety bond: *Provided, however,* That upon a showing to the satisfaction of the Director or his delegate that the claimant is unable to furnish a corporate surety bond such claimant may deliver a cost bond with individual sureties acceptable to the Director or his delegate: *Provided further*, That in lieu of a cost bond with corporate or individual sureties the claimant may deposit collateral as provided in § 72.25. The cost bond shall be conditioned that in the case of the condemnation of the property the obligators shall pay all costs and expenses of the proceedings to obtain such condemnation.

[T.D. ATF–9, 39 FR 9954, Mar. 15, 1974, as amended by T.D. ATF–183, 49 FR 37061, Sept. 21, 1984]

§ 72.24 Corporate surety bonds.

(a) Corporate surety bonds may be given only with surety companies holding certificates of authority from the Secretary of the Treasury as acceptable sureties on Federal bonds, subject to the limitations prescribed by Treasury Department Circular No. 570 (Companies Holding Certificates of Authority as Acceptable Sureties on Federal Bonds and as Acceptable Reinsuring Companies), and subject to such amendments as may be issued from time to time.

(b) Treasury Department Circular No. 570 is published in the FEDERAL REGISTER yearly as of the first workday of July. As they occur, interim revisions of the circular are published in the FEDERAL REGISTER. Copies may be obtained from the Audit Staff, Bureau of Government Financial Operations, Department of the Treasury, Washington, DC 20226.

(July 30, 1947, Ch. 390, 61 Stat. 648, as amended (6 U.S.C. 6, 7); Aug. 16, 1954, Ch. 736, 68A Stat. 847, as amended (26 U.S.C. 7101))

[T.D. ATF–92, 46 FR 46914, Sept. 23, 1981]

§ 72.25 Deposit of collateral.

(a) Bonds or notes of the United States, or other obligations which are unconditionally guaranteed as to both interest and principal by the United States, may be pledged and deposited by claimants as collateral security in lieu of corporate sureties in accordance with the provisions of Treasury Department Circular No. 154 (31 CFR Part 225—Acceptance of Bonds, Notes or Other Obligations Issued or Guaranteed by the United States as Security in Lieu of Surety or Sureties on Penal Bonds). Alternatively, cash, postal money orders, and certified or cashiers' or treasurers' checks may be furnished by claimants as collateral security in lieu of corporate sureties.

(b) Treasury Department Circular No. 154 is periodically revised and contains the provisions of 31 CFR Part 225 and the forms prescribed in 31 CFR Part 225. Copies of the circular may be obtained from the Audit Staff, Bureau of Government Financial Operations, Department of the Treasury, Washington, DC 20226.

(July 30, 1947, Ch. 390, 61 Stat. 650 (6 U.S.C. 15); Aug. 16, 1954, Ch. 736, 68A Stat. 847, as amended (26 U.S.C. 7101))

[T.D. ATF–92, 46 FR 46914, Sept. 23, 1981]

§ 72.26 Bond for return of seized perishable goods.

The proceedings to enforce forfeiture of perishable goods shall be in the nature of a proceeding in rem in the district court of the United States for the district wherein such seizure is made. Whenever such property is liable to perish or become greatly reduced in price or value by keeping, or when it cannot be kept without great expense, the Director or his delegate shall advise the owner, when known, of the seizure thereof. The owner may apply to the Director or his delegate to have the property examined any time prior to referral of the property to the U.S. Marshal for disposition, and if in the opinion of the Director or his delegate it shall be necessary to sell such property to prevent waste or expense, the Director or his delegate shall cause the property to be appraised. Thereupon the owner shall have the property returned to him upon giving a corporate surety bond (see § 72.24) in an amount equal to the appraised value of the property, which bond shall be conditioned to abide the final order, decree, or judgment of the court having cognizance of the case, and to pay the amount of the appraised value to the Director or his delegate, the U.S. Marshal, or otherwise, as may be ordered and directed by the court, which bond shall be filed by the Director or his delegate officer with the U.S. Attorney for the district in which the proceedings may be commenced. If the owner of such property neglects or refuses to give such bond within a reasonable time considering the condition of the property the Director or his delegate shall request the U.S. Marshal to proceed to sell the property at public sale as soon as practicable and to pay the proceeds of sale, less reasonable costs of the seizure and sale, to the court to abide its final order, decree, or judgment.

(68A Stat. 869, 870, as amended; 26 U.S.C. 7322, 7323, 7324)

[T.D. ATF–9, 39 FR 9954, Mar. 15, 1974, as amended by T.D. ATF–183, 49 FR 37061, Sept. 21, 1984]

§ 72.27 Summary destruction of explosives subject to forfeiture.

(a) Notwithstanding the provisions of § 55.166 of this Title, in the case of the seizure of any explosive materials for any offense for which the materials would be subject to forfeiture in which it would be impracticable or unsafe to remove the materials to a place of storage or would be unsafe to store them, the seizing officer may destroy the explosive materials forthwith. Any destruction under this paragraph shall be in the presence of at least 1 credible witness.

(b) Within 60 days after any destruction made pursuant to paragraph (a) of this section, the owner of the property and any other persons having an interest in the property so destroyed may make application to the Director for reimbursement of the value of the property in accordance with the instructions contained in ATF Publication 1850.1 (9–93), Information to Claimants. ATF P 1850.1 is available at no cost upon request from the ATF Distribution Center, P.O. Box 5950, Springfield, Virginia 22150–5950. The Director shall make an allowance to the claimant not exceeding the value of the property destroyed, if the claimant establishes to the satisfaction of the Director that—

(1) The property has not been used or involved in a violation of law; or

(2) Any unlawful involvement or use of the property was without the claimant's knowledge, consent, or willful blindness.

[T.D. ATF–363, 60 FR 17449, Apr. 6, 1995]

Subpart D—Remission or Mitigation of Forfeitures

§ 72.31 Laws applicable.

Remission or mitigation of forfeitures shall be governed by the applicable customs laws.

(Sec. 613, 618, 46 Stat. 756, as amended, 757, as amended, sec. 4, 53 Stat. 1292, sec. 7327, 68A Stat. 871; 19 U.S.C. 1613, 1618, 49 U.S.C. 784, 26 U.S.C. 7327)

§ 72.32 Interest claimed.

Any person claiming an interest in property, including carriers, seized by alcohol, tobacco and firearms officers as subject to administrative forfeiture may file a petition addressed to the Director, for remission or mitigation of the forfeiture of such property.

§ 72.33 Form of the petition.

There is no set or standardized form provided or required by the Department for use in filing a petition for remission or mitigation of forfeiture. However, it is preferable that the petition be typewritten on legal size paper; and it is necessary that the petition be executed under oath, prepared in triplicate and addressed to the Director, and that all copies of original documents submitted as exhibits in support of allegations of the petition be certified as true and accurate copies of originals. Each copy of the petition must contain a complete set of exhibits.

§ 72.34 Contents of the petition.

(a) *Description of the property.* The petition should contain such a description of the property or carrier and such facts of the seizure as will enable the alcohol, tobacco and firearms officers concerned to identify the property or carrier.

(b) *Statement regarding knowledge of seizure.* In the event the petition is filed for the restoration of the proceeds derived from sale of the property or carrier pursuant to summary forfeiture, it should also contain, or be supported by, satisfactory proof that the petitioner did not know of the seizure prior to the declaration or condemnation of forfeiture, and that he was in such circumstances as prevented him from knowing of the same. (See also § 72.35.)

(c) *Interest of petitioner.* The petitioner should state in clear and concise terms the nature and amount of the present interest of the petitioner in the property or carrier, and the facts relied upon to show that the forfeiture was incurred without willful negligence or without any intention upon the part of the petitioner to defraud the revenue or to violate the law, or such other mitigating circumstances as, in the opinion of the petitioner, would justify the remission or mitigation of the forfeiture.

(d) *Petitioner innocent party.* If the petitioner is not the one who in person committed the act which caused the seizure the petition should state how the property or carrier came into the possession of such other person, and that the petitioner had no knowledge or reason to believe, if such be the fact, that the property or carrier would be used in violation of law. If known to the petitioner, at the time the petition is filed, that such other person had either a record or a reputation, or both, as a violator in the field of commercial crime, the petition should state whether the petitioner had actual knowledge of such record or reputation, or both, before the petitioner acquired his interest in the property or carrier, before such other person acquired his right in the property or carrier, whichever occurred later. When personal property is seized for violation of the liquor laws, the determining factor will be whether the person dealt with by the petitioner had either a record or a reputation, or both, as a violator of the liquor laws.

(e) *Documents supporting claim.* The petition should also be accompanied by copies, certified by the petitioner under oath as correct, of contracts, bills of sale, chattel mortgages, reports of investigators or credit reporting agencies, affidavits, and any other papers or documents that would tend to support the claims made in the petition.

(f) *Costs.* The petition should also contain an undertaking to pay the costs, if costs are assessed as a condition of allowance of the petition. Costs shall include all the expenses incurred in seizing and storing the property or carrier; the costs borne or to be borne by the United States; the taxes, if any, payable by the petitioner or imposed in respect of the property or carrier to which the petition relates; the penalty, if any, asserted by the Director; and, if the property or carrier has been sold, or is in the course of being sold, the expenses so incurred.

§ 72.35 Time of filing petition.

A petition may be filed at any time prior to the sale or other disposition of the property or carrier involved pursuant to administrative forfeiture, but a petition in regard to property or a carrier which has already been sold or otherwise disposed of pursuant to administrative forfeiture must be filed within three months from the date of sale, and must contain the proof defined in § 72.34(b). Acquisition for official use is equivalent to sale so far as remission or mitigation of any forfeiture is concerned.

(Sec. 306, 49 Stat. 880; 40 U.S.C. 304k)

§ 72.36 Place of filing.

The petition should be filed in triplicate with the Director or his delegate for the region in which the seizure was made.

[T.D. ATF–9, 39 FR 9954, Mar. 15, 1974, as amended by T.D. ATF–183, 49 FR 37061, Sept. 21, 1984]

§ 72.37 Discontinuance of administrative proceedings.

If the petition is filed prior to administrative sale or retention for official use, proceedings to effect such sale or retention will be discontinued.

§ 72.38 Return of defective petition.

If the petition is defective in some correctable respect, the original of the petition will be returned by letter to the petitioner for his submission of a corrected petition, in triplicate, within a reasonable time.

§ 72.39 Final action.

(a) *Petitions for remission or mitigation of forfeiture.* (1) The Director shall take final action on any petition filed pursuant to these regulations. Such final action shall consist either of the allowance or denial of the petition. In the case of allowance, the Director shall state the conditions of the allowance.

(2) In the case of an allowed petition, the Director may order the property or carrier returned to the petitioner, sold for the account of the petitioner, or, pursuant to agreement, acquired for official use.

(3) The Director or his delegate shall notify the petitioner of the allowance or denial of the petition and, in the case of allowance, the terms and conditions under which the Director allowed the petition.

(b) *Offers in compromise of liability to forfeiture.* The Director or his delegate shall take final action on any offer in compromise of the liability to forfeiture of personal property, including carriers, seized as provided in § 72.21. Such action shall consist either of the acceptance or rejection of the offer.

[T.D. ATF–9, 39 FR 9954, Mar. 15, 1974, as amended by T.D. ATF–183, 49 FR 37061, Sept. 21, 1984]

§ 72.40 Acquisition for official use and sale for account of petitioner in allowed petitions.

(a) *Acquisition for official use.* The property or carrier may be purchased by the United States pursuant to agreement and retained for official use. Where the petitioner is the owner, the purchase price is the appraised value of the property or carrier less all costs. Where the petitioner is a creditor, the purchase price is whichever one of these amounts is the smaller: (1) The petitioner's equity, or (2) the appraised value of the property or carrier less the amount of all costs incident to the seizure and forfeiture.

(b) *Sale for account of petitioner.* The petitioner may elect not to comply with the condition on which the property or carrier may be returned. In this event, the Director or his delegate is authorized to sell it. Where the petitioner is the owner of the property or carrier, there is deducted from the proceeds of the sale all costs incident to the seizure, forfeiture, and sale, and the Director or his delegate pays to the petitioner, out of the proper appropriation, an amount equal to the balance, if any. Where the petitioner is a creditor, there is deducted from the proceeds of the sale all costs incident to the seizure, forfeiture, and sale, and the Director or his delegate pays to the petitioner, out of the proper appropriation, an amount equal to the balance, if any, of the selling price after deduction of all costs incident to the seizure, forfeiture, or sale: *Provided,* That if the amount of such balance exceeds the amount of the equity of the petitioner, only the latter amount is paid to the petitioner.

[T.D. ATF–9, 39 FR 9954, Mar. 15, 1974, as amended by T.D. ATF–183, 49 FR 37061, Sept. 21, 1984]

§ 72.41 Re-appraisal of property involved in an allowed petition.

In determining the nature and extent of the relief to be afforded a petitioner pursuant to allowance of his petition, the value of the property or carrier involved in the allowed petition shall be considered to mean the value placed on said property or carrier pursuant to official appraisal thereof immediately following seizure: *Provided, however,* That if the petitioner desires an up-to-date re-appraisal made of the property or carrier, after notification as to the terms of allowance of the petition, and makes written request therefor, undertaking in said request to pay, or to be liable for, the total costs of such re-appraisal, the property or carrier shall be re-appraised officially in the same manner in which the original appraisal was made, and the terms and conditions of allowance shall stand modified to the extent required by such re-appraisal.

Subpart E—Appraiser's Fees

§ 72.51 Rate of compensation.

Each appraiser selected under § 72.22(a)(2) shall receive compensation at a reasonable fee not to exceed $15.00 per hour or portion thereof for the performance of his or her duties in appraising property seized as subject to forfeiture under Title 26 U.S.C.

(Act of Aug. 16, 1954, Ch. 736, 68A Stat. 870, as amended; 26 U.S.C. 7325)

[T.D. ATF–8, 46 FR 18536, Mar. 25, 1981]

Subpart F—Administrative Sale or Disposition of Personal Property

§72.61 Alternative methods of sale.

(a) *Sale by auction or competitive bid.* When personal property or a carrier. When personal property or a carrier forfeited administratively may be sold, the Director or his delegate shall cause a notice of sale to be placed in a newspaper of general circulation published in the judicial district wherein the seizure was made. The sale shall not occur in less than 10 days from the date of the publication of the notice. At the discretion of the Director or his delegate based upon which method in his sound judgment is most advantageous to the best interests of the United States, the forfeited personal property or carrier may be advertised for sale, and sold, at public auction to the highest bidder on open, competitive bids, or to the highest bidder on sealed, competitive bids.

(b) *Sale by General Services Administration.* When a vessel, vehicle, or aircraft seized under 49 U.S.C. App., Chapter 11 is forfeited administratively, the Director may authorize the General Services Administration to conduct the sale pursuant to such conditions as the Director deems proper.

(68A Stat. 870, as amended; 26 U.S.C. 7325)

[T.D. ATF-9, 39 FR 9954, Mar. 15, 1974, as amended by T.D. ATF-183, 49 FR 37061, Sept. 21, 1984; T.D. ATF-241, 51 FR 39613, Oct. 29, 1986; T.D. ATF-270, 53 FR 10489, Mar. 31, 1988]

§72.62 All bids on unit basis.

All competitive bids, whether sealed or otherwise, shall be on a unit basis, i.e. if a number of forfeited automobiles are advertised for sale at the same date, hour and place, whether or not in the same notice of sale, there shall be a separate, individual bid required as to each automobile, and it shall not be permissible to accept one blanket bid to cover the entire group of cars offered for sale.

§72.63 Conditions of sale.

(a) *No recourse.* All personal property and carriers to be sold shall be offered for sale "as is" and without recourse against the United States.

(b) *No guarantee.* No guarantee or warranty, expressed or implied, shall be given or understood in respect of any forfeited property or carrier offered for sale.

(c) *No sale.* (1) The United States reserves the right to reject any and all bids received at public auction and in sealed, competitive bid sales.

(2) When "no sale" is declared for property other than cigars, cigarettes, and cigarette papers and tubes, the Director or his delegate shall re-advertise the property for sale.

(3) When "no sale" is declared for cigars, cigarettes, or cigarette papers or tubes, such property shall be destroyed or, if fit for human consumption, be given to a Federal or State hospital or institution.

(d) *One bid.* When only one bid is received for a single unit of property or a carrier offered at public auction or in a sealed, competitive bid sale, such bid shall be considered to be and treated as the highest bid received for that property or carrier.

[T.D. ATF-9, 39 FR 9954, Mar. 15, 1974, as amended by T.D. ATF-183, 49 FR 37061, Sept. 21, 1984]

§72.64 Terms of sale.

The terms of sale shall be cash, cashier's check, certified check, or postal money order, in the amount of the accepted bid.

§72.65 Sale of forfeited tobacco products and cigarette papers and tubes.

All tobacco products and cigarette papers and tubes forfeited under the internal revenue laws shall be sold at a price which will include the tax due and payable on those forfeited articles. Written, timely notice shall be given by the Director or his delegate to the manufacturer of any such forfeited articles offered for sale.

[T.D. ATF-9, 39 FR 9954, Mar. 15, 1974, as amended by T.D. ATF-65, 45 FR 8593, Feb. 8, 1980; T.D. ATF-183, 49 FR 37061, Sept. 21, 1984]

§72.66 Purchaser entitled to bill of sale.

Each purchaser of administratively forfeited property, including carriers, shall be entitled to receive a suitable and authentic bill of sale on a form to be provided for the purpose.

§ 72.67 Sale on open, competitive bids.

If the personal property or carrier is to be sold at public auction to the highest bidder on open, competitive bids, the notice of sale shall so specify, and state the date, hour, and place of sale.

§ 72.68 Sale on sealed, competitive bids.

If the property or carrier is to be sold to the highest bidder on sealed, competitive bids, the notice of sale shall so specify, and shall state the date, hour, and place of sale, and the date, hour, and place before the sale when and where the property, including carriers, may be viewed by prospective sealed bidders, and necessary information obtained. All sealed bids must be filed with the Director or his delegate before the sale. No bids will be accepted after the sale starts. At the appointed date, hour, and place of sale, all sealed bids timely filed shall be opened in the presence of all bidders attending the sale, who shall have the privilege of inspecting the bids if they so desire.

[T.D. ATF–9, 39 FR 9954, Mar. 15, 1974, as amended by T.D. ATF–183, 49 FR 37061, Sept. 21, 1984]

§ 72.69 Alternative disposition of seized carriers.

(a) *State or local proceedings.* The Director may discontinue forfeiture proceedings instituted under the Customs laws for seizures of carriers under 49 U.S.C. App., Chapter 11 in favor of the institution of forfeiture proceedings by State or local authorities under an appropriate State or local statute. If such forfeiture proceedings are discontinued or dismissed, the Director may transfer the seized property to the appropriate State or local official, and notice of discontinuance or dismissal shall be provided to all known interested parties.

(b) *Transfer to State or local law enforcement agency.* Any carrier forfeited under the Customs laws for seizures under 49 U.S.C. App., Chapter 11 may be transferred by the Director to any State or local law enforcement agency which participated directly in the seizure or forfeiture of the property.

(19 U.S.C. 1616)

[T.D. ATF–270, 53 FR 10489, Mar. 31, 1988]

Subpart G—Disposal of Forfeited Firearms, Ammunition, Explosive Materials, or Contraband Cigarettes

§ 72.81 Authority for disposal.

Forfeited firearms, aummunition, explosive materials, or contraband cigarettes, not the subject of an allowed petition, may only be disposed of in accordance with the provisions of 26 U.S.C. 5872(b).

[T.D. ATF–65, 45 FR 8593, Feb. 8, 1980]

PART 73—ELECTRONIC SIGNATURES; ELECTRONIC SUBMISSION OF FORMS

Sec.

Subpart D—Electronic Filing of Documents With Other Agencies

AUTHORITY: 26 U.S.C. 6011(f), 6061(b), 7502(c); 44 U.S.C. 3504 Note.

SOURCE: 68 FR 58601, Oct. 10, 2003, unless otherwise noted.

Subpart A—General Provisions

SCOPE

§73.1 What does this part do?

(a) This part provides the conditions under which we will allow you to:

(1) Use electronic signatures or digital signatures executed to electronic forms instead of traditional handwritten signatures executed on paper forms; and

(2) Electronically submit certain forms to TTB or, where applicable, to other agencies.

(b) This part does not require you to submit forms to us electronically.

[68 FR 58601, Oct. 10, 2003, as amended at 79 FR 17033, Mar. 27, 2014]

DEFINITIONS

§73.3 What terms must I know to understand this part?

You need to know the following terms to understand this part:

27 CFR. Title 27 of the Code of Federal Regulations, chapter I.

Biometrics. A method of verifying an individual's identity based on measurement of the individual's physical feature(s) or repeatable action(s) where those features and/or actions are both unique to that individual and measurable.

Digital signature. An electronic signature based upon cryptographic methods of originator authentication, computed by using a set of rules and a set of parameters such that the identity of the signer and the integrity of the data can be verified. A signer creates a digital signature by using public-key encryption to transform a message digest of an electronic message. If a recipient of the digital signature has an electronic message, message digest function, and the signer's public key, the recipient can verify:

(1) Whether the transformation was accomplished with the private key that corresponds to the signer's public key; and

(2) Whether the electronic message has been altered since the transformation was made.

Electronic document receiving system. Any set of apparatus, procedures, software, records, or documentation used to receive documents communicated to it via a telecommunications network.

Electronic signature. A computer data compilation of any symbol or series of symbols executed, adopted, or authorized by an individual to be the legally binding equivalent of the individual's handwritten signature, and that:

(1) Identifies and authenticates a particular person as the source of the electronic message; and

(2) Indicates such person's approval of the information contained in the electronic message.

Form(s). The term form(s), when used in this part, includes all documents required by 27 CFR, chapter I, to be submitted to TTB or any other agency.

Handwritten signature. The scripted name or legal mark of an individual handwritten by that individual and executed or adopted with the present intention to authenticate a writing in a permanent form. The act of signing with a writing or marking instrument such as a pen or stylus is preserved. The scripted name or legal mark, while conventionally applied to paper, may also be applied to other materials or devices that capture the name or mark.

Paper format. A paper document.

TTB. Refers to the Alcohol and Tobacco Tax and Trade Bureau within the Department of the Treasury.

You and I. "You" and "I" refer to the organization or person who must maintain records or submit documents to TTB to satisfy the requirements of 27 CFR, chapter I.

[68 FR 58601, Oct. 10, 2003, as amended at 79 FR 52199, Sept. 3, 2014]

Subpart B—Electronic Signatures

§73.10 What does subpart B cover?

This subpart provides the conditions under which TTB will allow you to use electronic signatures executed to electronic forms instead of traditional handwritten signatures executed on paper forms. Where electronic signatures and their associated electronic forms meet the requirements of this part, TTB will consider the electronic signatures to be the equivalent of full handwritten signatures, initials, and other general signings this chapter requires.

§ 73.11 What are the required components and controls for acceptable electronic signatures?

(a) *Electronic signatures not based on biometrics.* If you use electronic signatures that are not based upon biometrics you must:

(1) Employ at least two distinct identification components such as an identification code and a password;

(2) Use both identification components when executing an electronic signature to an electronic document; and

(3) Ensure that the electronic signature can only be used by the authorized user.

(b) *Electronic signatures based on biometrics.* If you use electronic signatures based upon biometrics, they must be designed to ensure that they cannot be used by anyone other than their genuine owners.

§ 73.12 What security controls must I use for identification codes and passwords?

If you use electronic signatures based upon use of identification codes in combination with passwords, you must employ controls to ensure their security and integrity. These controls must include:

(a) Maintaining the uniqueness of each combined identification code and password, such that no two individuals have the same combination of identification code and password;

(b) Ensuring that identification code and password issuances are periodically checked, recalled, or revised (*e.g.*, to cover such events as password aging);

(c) Following loss management procedures to electronically deauthorize lost, stolen, missing, or otherwise potentially compromised tokens, cards, or other devices that bear or generate identification code or password information, and to issue temporary or permanent replacements using suitable, rigorous controls;

(d) Using transaction safeguards to prevent unauthorized use of passwords and/or identification codes, and to detect and report in an immediate and urgent manner any attempts at their unauthorized use to the system security unit and, as appropriate, to organizational management; and

(e) Initial and periodic testing of devices, such as tokens or cards, that bear or generate identification code or password information to ensure that they function properly and have not been altered in any unauthorized manner.

Subpart C—Electronic Filing of Documents with TTB

§ 73.30 What does subpart C cover?

This subpart provides the conditions under which TTB will allow you to satisfy certain requirements to submit forms in this chapter by submitting forms electronically to TTB.

[79 FR 17033, Mar. 27, 2014]

§ 73.31 May I submit forms electronically to TTB?

Yes; to satisfy any requirement to submit forms in this chapter (including a requirement to submit an original form or copies), you may submit an electronic form or you may submit, by electronic means, a copy of an original form, but only if:

(a) You submit the form through an electronic document receiving system that TTB has designated for the receipt of that specific form and for which you have registered if so required; and

(b) The conditions in any one of the following paragraphs apply:

(1) It is an electronic form that bears valid electronic signatures, as provided in subpart B of this part, to the same extent that the paper submission for which it substitutes would bear handwritten signatures;

(2) It is a copy of an original form that requires the signature of a third party who is not the person required to submit the form (such as a bond form or a power of attorney form) or a corporate seal; you submit the copy of the

form electronically along with a certification that the copy is an exact copy of the original; the original bears all signatures of all required parties and any required corporate seal; and you maintain the original along with any other records required by TTB and make it available or submit it to TTB upon request; or

(3) It is a copy of a TTB form that is not available in an electronic format or it is a document other than a TTB form (that is, other than a document issued by TTB that bears an Office of Management and Budget control number) that is required to be submitted to TTB; you submit the copy electronically along with a certification that the copy is an exact copy of the original; and you maintain the original along with any other records required by TTB and make it available or submit it to TTB upon request.

[79 FR 17033, Mar. 27, 2014]

§73.32 May I electronically sign forms I submit electronically to TTB?

You may electronically sign the electronic form you submit to us if:

(a) You have registered with TTB to do so and have certified, prior to the time of such use, that the electronic signatures or digital signatures in your system are intended to be the legally binding equivalent of traditional handwritten signatures;

(b) The electronic or digital signature meets the standards of this part and is authorized by TTB in accordance with this part; and

(c) The electronic or digital signature is sufficiently trustworthy and reliable that the signing party may not repudiate the signature.

§73.33 Am I legally bound by a form I sign electronically?

Yes; by electronically signing a form you submit to us, you are agreeing to be legally bound to the same extent as if you applied a traditional handwritten signature on a paper document submitted to satisfy the same requirement. Persons using electronic signatures shall, upon TTB's request, provide additional certification or testimony that a specific electronic signature is the legally binding equivalent of the signer's handwritten signature.

[68 FR 58601, Oct. 10, 2003, as amended at 79 FR 17034, Mar. 27, 2014]

§73.34 When is an electronically submitted form considered timely filed?

If you submit a form to our electronic document receiving system, the document will be considered filed on the date of the electronic postmark given by that system.

[68 FR 58601, Oct. 10, 2003, as amended at 79 FR 17034, Mar. 27, 2014]

§73.35 Do I need to keep paper copies of forms I submit to TTB electronically?

Nothing in this part alters any other regulatory or statutory requirement that records be maintained in paper format. If the regulations in this chapter require you to keep paper copies of certain forms, you must continue to do so unless TTB otherwise authorizes you to maintain electronic copies of these documents through an approved alternate method or procedure.

[68 FR 58601, Oct. 10, 2003, as amended at 79 FR 17034, Mar. 27, 2014]

Subpart D—Electronic Filing of Documents With Other Agencies

§73.40 May I satisfy TTB requirements to submit forms to other agencies by submitting those forms electronically?

You may satisfy any requirement in the TTB regulations to submit a form (as that term is defined in §73.3) to another agency by submitting such form to such agency by electronic means, as long as the agency provides for, and authorizes, the electronic submission of such form and you satisfy any registration or related requirement by that agency for that electronic submission. The submission of a form electronically to another agency does not alter any requirement regarding copies you must maintain.

[79 FR 17034, Mar. 27, 2014, as amended at 79 FR 52199, Sept. 3, 2014]

SUBCHAPTERS G–L [RESERVED]

SUBCHAPTER M—ALCOHOL, TOBACCO AND OTHER EXCISE TAXES

PARTS 194–399 [RESERVED]

FINDING AIDS

A list of CFR titles, subtitles, chapters, subchapters and parts and an alphabetical list of agencies publishing in the CFR are included in the CFR Index and Finding Aids volume to the Code of Federal Regulations which is published separately and revised annually.

Table of CFR Titles and Chapters

(Revised as of April 1, 2016)

Title 1—General Provisions

Title 2—Grants and Agreements

Title 2—Grants and Agreements—Continued

Title 3—The President

Title 4—Accounts

Title 5—Administrative Personnel

Chap.	
XXIX	Federal Communications Commission (Parts 3900—3999)
XXX	Farm Credit System Insurance Corporation (Parts 4000—4099)
XXXI	Farm Credit Administration (Parts 4100—4199)
XXXIII	Overseas Private Investment Corporation (Parts 4300—4399)
XXXIV	Securities and Exchange Commission (Parts 4400—4499)
XXXV	Office of Personnel Management (Parts 4500—4599)
XXXVI	Department of Homeland Security (Parts 4600—4699)
XXXVII	Federal Election Commission (Parts 4700—4799)
XL	Interstate Commerce Commission (Parts 5000—5099)
XLI	Commodity Futures Trading Commission (Parts 5100—5199)
XLII	Department of Labor (Parts 5200—5299)
XLIII	National Science Foundation (Parts 5300—5399)
XLV	Department of Health and Human Services (Parts 5500—5599)
XLVI	Postal Rate Commission (Parts 5600—5699)
XLVII	Federal Trade Commission (Parts 5700—5799)
XLVIII	Nuclear Regulatory Commission (Parts 5800—5899)
XLIX	Federal Labor Relations Authority (Parts 5900—5999)
L	Department of Transportation (Parts 6000—6099)
LII	Export-Import Bank of the United States (Parts 6200—6299)
LIII	Department of Education (Parts 6300—6399)
LIV	Environmental Protection Agency (Parts 6400—6499)
LV	National Endowment for the Arts (Parts 6500—6599)
LVI	National Endowment for the Humanities (Parts 6600—6699)
LVII	General Services Administration (Parts 6700—6799)
LVIII	Board of Governors of the Federal Reserve System (Parts 6800—6899)
LIX	National Aeronautics and Space Administration (Parts 6900—6999)
LX	United States Postal Service (Parts 7000—7099)
LXI	National Labor Relations Board (Parts 7100—7199)
LXII	Equal Employment Opportunity Commission (Parts 7200—7299)
LXIII	Inter-American Foundation (Parts 7300—7399)
LXIV	Merit Systems Protection Board (Parts 7400—7499)
LXV	Department of Housing and Urban Development (Parts 7500—7599)
LXVI	National Archives and Records Administration (Parts 7600—7699)
LXVII	Institute of Museum and Library Services (Parts 7700—7799)
LXVIII	Commission on Civil Rights (Parts 7800—7899)
LXIX	Tennessee Valley Authority (Parts 7900—7999)
LXX	Court Services and Offender Supervision Agency for the District of Columbia (Parts 8000—8099)
LXXI	Consumer Product Safety Commission (Parts 8100—8199)
LXXIII	Department of Agriculture (Parts 8300—8399)
LXXIV	Federal Mine Safety and Health Review Commission (Parts 8400—8499)

Title 5—Administrative Personnel—Continued

Chap.	
LXXVI	Federal Retirement Thrift Investment Board (Parts 8600—8699)
LXXVII	Office of Management and Budget (Parts 8700—8799)
LXXX	Federal Housing Finance Agency (Parts 9000—9099)
LXXXIII	Special Inspector General for Afghanistan Reconstruction (Parts 9300—9399)
LXXXIV	Bureau of Consumer Financial Protection (Parts 9400—9499)
LXXXVI	National Credit Union Administration (Parts 9600—9699)
XCVII	Department of Homeland Security Human Resources Management System (Department of Homeland Security—Office of Personnel Management) (Parts 9700—9799)
XCVII	Council of the Inspectors General on Integrity and Efficiency (Parts 9800—9899)
XCIX	Military Compensation and Retirement Modernization Commission (Parts 9900—9999)
C	National Council on Disability (Partys 10000—10049)

Title 6—Domestic Security

I	Department of Homeland Security, Office of the Secretary (Parts 1—199)
X	Privacy and Civil Liberties Oversight Board (Parts 1000—1099)

Title 7—Agriculture

SUBTITLE A—OFFICE OF THE SECRETARY OF AGRICULTURE (PARTS 0—26)

SUBTITLE B—REGULATIONS OF THE DEPARTMENT OF AGRICULTURE

I	Agricultural Marketing Service (Standards, Inspections, Marketing Practices), Department of Agriculture (Parts 27—209)
II	Food and Nutrition Service, Department of Agriculture (Parts 210—299)
III	Animal and Plant Health Inspection Service, Department of Agriculture (Parts 300—399)
IV	Federal Crop Insurance Corporation, Department of Agriculture (Parts 400—499)
V	Agricultural Research Service, Department of Agriculture (Parts 500—599)
VI	Natural Resources Conservation Service, Department of Agriculture (Parts 600—699)
VII	Farm Service Agency, Department of Agriculture (Parts 700—799)
VIII	Grain Inspection, Packers and Stockyards Administration (Federal Grain Inspection Service), Department of Agriculture (Parts 800—899)
IX	Agricultural Marketing Service (Marketing Agreements and Orders; Fruits, Vegetables, Nuts), Department of Agriculture (Parts 900—999)
X	Agricultural Marketing Service (Marketing Agreements and Orders; Milk), Department of Agriculture (Parts 1000—1199)

Title 7—Agriculture—Continued

Chap.

Chap.	
XI	Agricultural Marketing Service (Marketing Agreements and Orders; Miscellaneous Commodities), Department of Agriculture (Parts 1200—1299)
XIV	Commodity Credit Corporation, Department of Agriculture (Parts 1400—1499)
XV	Foreign Agricultural Service, Department of Agriculture (Parts 1500—1599)
XVI	Rural Telephone Bank, Department of Agriculture (Parts 1600—1699)
XVII	Rural Utilities Service, Department of Agriculture (Parts 1700—1799)
XVIII	Rural Housing Service, Rural Business-Cooperative Service, Rural Utilities Service, and Farm Service Agency, Department of Agriculture (Parts 1800—2099)
XX	Local Television Loan Guarantee Board (Parts 2200—2299)
XXV	Office of Advocacy and Outreach, Department of Agriculture (Parts 2500—2599)
XXVI	Office of Inspector General, Department of Agriculture (Parts 2600—2699)
XXVII	Office of Information Resources Management, Department of Agriculture (Parts 2700—2799)
XXVIII	Office of Operations, Department of Agriculture (Parts 2800—2899)
XXIX	Office of Energy Policy and New Uses, Department of Agriculture (Parts 2900—2999)
XXX	Office of the Chief Financial Officer, Department of Agriculture (Parts 3000—3099)
XXXI	Office of Environmental Quality, Department of Agriculture (Parts 3100—3199)
XXXII	Office of Procurement and Property Management, Department of Agriculture (Parts 3200—3299)
XXXIII	Office of Transportation, Department of Agriculture (Parts 3300—3399)
XXXIV	National Institute of Food and Agriculture (Parts 3400—3499)
XXXV	Rural Housing Service, Department of Agriculture (Parts 3500—3599)
XXXVI	National Agricultural Statistics Service, Department of Agriculture (Parts 3600—3699)
XXXVII	Economic Research Service, Department of Agriculture (Parts 3700—3799)
XXXVIII	World Agricultural Outlook Board, Department of Agriculture (Parts 3800—3899)
XLI	[Reserved]
XLII	Rural Business-Cooperative Service and Rural Utilities Service, Department of Agriculture (Parts 4200—4299)

Title 8—Aliens and Nationality

I	Department of Homeland Security (Immigration and Naturalization) (Parts 1—499)

Title 8—Aliens and Nationality—Continued

Chap.	
V	Executive Office for Immigration Review, Department of Justice (Parts 1000—1399)

Title 9—Animals and Animal Products

I	Animal and Plant Health Inspection Service, Department of Agriculture (Parts 1—199)
II	Grain Inspection, Packers and Stockyards Administration (Packers and Stockyards Programs), Department of Agriculture (Parts 200—299)
III	Food Safety and Inspection Service, Department of Agriculture (Parts 300—599)

Title 10—Energy

I	Nuclear Regulatory Commission (Parts 0—199)
II	Department of Energy (Parts 200—699)
III	Department of Energy (Parts 700—999)
X	Department of Energy (General Provisions) (Parts 1000—1099)
XIII	Nuclear Waste Technical Review Board (Parts 1300—1399)
XVII	Defense Nuclear Facilities Safety Board (Parts 1700—1799)
XVIII	Northeast Interstate Low-Level Radioactive Waste Commission (Parts 1800—1899)

Title 11—Federal Elections

I	Federal Election Commission (Parts 1—9099)
II	Election Assistance Commission (Parts 9400—9499)

Title 12—Banks and Banking

I	Comptroller of the Currency, Department of the Treasury (Parts 1—199)
II	Federal Reserve System (Parts 200—299)
III	Federal Deposit Insurance Corporation (Parts 300—399)
IV	Export-Import Bank of the United States (Parts 400—499)
V	Office of Thrift Supervision, Department of the Treasury (Parts 500—599)
VI	Farm Credit Administration (Parts 600—699)
VII	National Credit Union Administration (Parts 700—799)
VIII	Federal Financing Bank (Parts 800—899)
IX	Federal Housing Finance Board (Parts 900—999)
X	Bureau of Consumer Financial Protection (Parts 1000—1099)
XI	Federal Financial Institutions Examination Council (Parts 1100—1199)
XII	Federal Housing Finance Agency (Parts 1200—1299)
XIII	Financial Stability Oversight Council (Parts 1300—1399)
XIV	Farm Credit System Insurance Corporation (Parts 1400—1499)

Title 12—Banks and Banking—Continued

Chap.	
XV	Department of the Treasury (Parts 1500—1599)
XVI	Office of Financial Research (Parts 1600—1699)
XVII	Office of Federal Housing Enterprise Oversight, Department of Housing and Urban Development (Parts 1700—1799)
XVIII	Community Development Financial Institutions Fund, Department of the Treasury (Parts 1800—1899)

Title 13—Business Credit and Assistance

I	Small Business Administration (Parts 1—199)
III	Economic Development Administration, Department of Commerce (Parts 300—399)
IV	Emergency Steel Guarantee Loan Board (Parts 400—499)
V	Emergency Oil and Gas Guaranteed Loan Board (Parts 500—599)

Title 14—Aeronautics and Space

I	Federal Aviation Administration, Department of Transportation (Parts 1—199)
II	Office of the Secretary, Department of Transportation (Aviation Proceedings) (Parts 200—399)
III	Commercial Space Transportation, Federal Aviation Administration, Department of Transportation (Parts 400—1199)
V	National Aeronautics and Space Administration (Parts 1200—1299)
VI	Air Transportation System Stabilization (Parts 1300—1399)

Title 15—Commerce and Foreign Trade

	SUBTITLE A—OFFICE OF THE SECRETARY OF COMMERCE (PARTS 0—29)
	SUBTITLE B—REGULATIONS RELATING TO COMMERCE AND FOREIGN TRADE
I	Bureau of the Census, Department of Commerce (Parts 30—199)
II	National Institute of Standards and Technology, Department of Commerce (Parts 200—299)
III	International Trade Administration, Department of Commerce (Parts 300—399)
IV	Foreign-Trade Zones Board, Department of Commerce (Parts 400—499)
VII	Bureau of Industry and Security, Department of Commerce (Parts 700—799)
VIII	Bureau of Economic Analysis, Department of Commerce (Parts 800—899)
IX	National Oceanic and Atmospheric Administration, Department of Commerce (Parts 900—999)
XI	Technology Administration, Department of Commerce (Parts 1100—1199)
XIII	East-West Foreign Trade Board (Parts 1300—1399)

Title 15—Commerce and Foreign Trade—Continued

Title 16—Commercial Practices

Title 17—Commodity and Securities Exchanges

Title 18—Conservation of Power and Water Resources

Title 19—Customs Duties

Title 20—Employees' Benefits

Title 21—Food and Drugs

Title 22—Foreign Relations

Title 23—Highways

Title 23—Highways—Continued

Chap.

Title 24—Housing and Urban Development

Title 25—Indians

Chap.

I Bureau of Indian Affairs, Department of the Interior (Parts 1—299)

II Indian Arts and Crafts Board, Department of the Interior (Parts 300—399)

III National Indian Gaming Commission, Department of the Interior (Parts 500—599)

IV Office of Navajo and Hopi Indian Relocation (Parts 700—799)

V Bureau of Indian Affairs, Department of the Interior, and Indian Health Service, Department of Health and Human Services (Part 900)

VI Office of the Assistant Secretary-Indian Affairs, Department of the Interior (Parts 1000—1199)

VII Office of the Special Trustee for American Indians, Department of the Interior (Parts 1200—1299)

Title 26—Internal Revenue

I Internal Revenue Service, Department of the Treasury (Parts 1—End)

Title 27—Alcohol, Tobacco Products and Firearms

I Alcohol and Tobacco Tax and Trade Bureau, Department of the Treasury (Parts 1—399)

II Bureau of Alcohol, Tobacco, Firearms, and Explosives, Department of Justice (Parts 400—699)

Title 28—Judicial Administration

I Department of Justice (Parts 0—299)

III Federal Prison Industries, Inc., Department of Justice (Parts 300—399)

V Bureau of Prisons, Department of Justice (Parts 500—599)

VI Offices of Independent Counsel, Department of Justice (Parts 600—699)

VII Office of Independent Counsel (Parts 700—799)

VIII Court Services and Offender Supervision Agency for the District of Columbia (Parts 800—899)

IX National Crime Prevention and Privacy Compact Council (Parts 900—999)

XI Department of Justice and Department of State (Parts 1100—1199)

Title 29—Labor

SUBTITLE A—OFFICE OF THE SECRETARY OF LABOR (PARTS 0—99)

SUBTITLE B—REGULATIONS RELATING TO LABOR

I National Labor Relations Board (Parts 100—199)

Title 29—Labor—Continued

Title 30—Mineral Resources

Title 31—Money and Finance: Treasury

Title 32—National Defense

Title 33—Navigation and Navigable Waters

Title 34—Education

Title 34—Education—Continued

Title 35 [Reserved]

Title 36—Parks, Forests, and Public Property

Title 37—Patents, Trademarks, and Copyrights

Title 38—Pensions, Bonuses, and Veterans' Relief

Title 39—Postal Service

Chap.	
I	United States Postal Service (Parts 1—999)
III	Postal Regulatory Commission (Parts 3000—3099)

Title 40—Protection of Environment

I	Environmental Protection Agency (Parts 1—1099)
IV	Environmental Protection Agency and Department of Justice (Parts 1400—1499)
V	Council on Environmental Quality (Parts 1500—1599)
VI	Chemical Safety and Hazard Investigation Board (Parts 1600—1699)
VII	Environmental Protection Agency and Department of Defense; Uniform National Discharge Standards for Vessels of the Armed Forces (Parts 1700—1799)
VIII	Gulf Coast Ecosystem Restoration Council (Parts 1800—1899)

Title 41—Public Contracts and Property Management

	SUBTITLE A—FEDERAL PROCUREMENT REGULATIONS SYSTEM [NOTE]
	SUBTITLE B—OTHER PROVISIONS RELATING TO PUBLIC CONTRACTS
50	Public Contracts, Department of Labor (Parts 50–1—50–999)
51	Committee for Purchase From People Who Are Blind or Severely Disabled (Parts 51–1—51–99)
60	Office of Federal Contract Compliance Programs, Equal Employment Opportunity, Department of Labor (Parts 60–1—60–999)
61	Office of the Assistant Secretary for Veterans' Employment and Training Service, Department of Labor (Parts 61–1—61–999)
62—100	[Reserved]
	SUBTITLE C—FEDERAL PROPERTY MANAGEMENT REGULATIONS SYSTEM
101	Federal Property Management Regulations (Parts 101–1—101–99)
102	Federal Management Regulation (Parts 102–1—102–299)
103—104	[Reserved]
105	General Services Administration (Parts 105–1—105–999)
109	Department of Energy Property Management Regulations (Parts 109–1—109–99)
114	Department of the Interior (Parts 114–1—114–99)
115	Environmental Protection Agency (Parts 115–1—115–99)
128	Department of Justice (Parts 128–1—128–99)
129—200	[Reserved]
	SUBTITLE D—OTHER PROVISIONS RELATING TO PROPERTY MANAGEMENT [RESERVED]
	SUBTITLE E—FEDERAL INFORMATION RESOURCES MANAGEMENT REGULATIONS SYSTEM [RESERVED]
	SUBTITLE F—FEDERAL TRAVEL REGULATION SYSTEM
300	General (Parts 300–1—300–99)
301	Temporary Duty (TDY) Travel Allowances (Parts 301–1—301–99)

Title 41—Public Contracts and Property Management—Continued

Title 42—Public Health

Title 43—Public Lands: Interior

Title 44—Emergency Management and Assistance

Title 45—Public Welfare

Title 46—Shipping

Title 47—Telecommunication

Title 48—Federal Acquisition Regulations System

Title 49—Transportation

Chap.

SUBTITLE A—OFFICE OF THE SECRETARY OF TRANSPORTATION (PARTS 1—99)

SUBTITLE B—OTHER REGULATIONS RELATING TO TRANSPORTATION

I Pipeline and Hazardous Materials Safety Administration, Department of Transportation (Parts 100—199)

II Federal Railroad Administration, Department of Transportation (Parts 200—299)

III Federal Motor Carrier Safety Administration, Department of Transportation (Parts 300—399)

IV Coast Guard, Department of Homeland Security (Parts 400—499)

V National Highway Traffic Safety Administration, Department of Transportation (Parts 500—599)

VI Federal Transit Administration, Department of Transportation (Parts 600—699)

VII National Railroad Passenger Corporation (AMTRAK) (Parts 700—799)

VIII National Transportation Safety Board (Parts 800—999)

X Surface Transportation Board, Department of Transportation (Parts 1000—1399)

XI Research and Innovative Technology Administration, Department of Transportation (Parts 1400—1499) [Reserved]

XII Transportation Security Administration, Department of Homeland Security (Parts 1500—1699)

Title 50—Wildlife and Fisheries

I United States Fish and Wildlife Service, Department of the Interior (Parts 1—199)

II National Marine Fisheries Service, National Oceanic and Atmospheric Administration, Department of Commerce (Parts 200—299)

III International Fishing and Related Activities (Parts 300—399)

IV Joint Regulations (United States Fish and Wildlife Service, Department of the Interior and National Marine Fisheries Service, National Oceanic and Atmospheric Administration, Department of Commerce); Endangered Species Committee Regulations (Parts 400—499)

V Marine Mammal Commission (Parts 500—599)

VI Fishery Conservation and Management, National Oceanic and Atmospheric Administration, Department of Commerce (Parts 600—699)

Alphabetical List of Agencies Appearing in the CFR

(Revised as of April 1, 2016)

Agency	CFR Title, Subtitle or Chapter
Administrative Committee of the Federal Register	1, I
Administrative Conference of the United States	1, III
Advisory Council on Historic Preservation	36, VIII
Advocacy and Outreach, Office of	7, XXV
Afghanistan Reconstruction, Special Inspector General for	5, LXXXIII
African Development Foundation	22, XV
Federal Acquisition Regulation	48, 57
Agency for International Development	2, VII; 22, II
Federal Acquisition Regulation	48, 7
Agricultural Marketing Service	7, I, IX, X, XI
Agricultural Research Service	7, V
Agriculture Department	2, IV; 5, LXXIII
Advocacy and Outreach, Office of	7, XXV
Agricultural Marketing Service	7, I, IX, X, XI
Agricultural Research Service	7, V
Animal and Plant Health Inspection Service	7, III; 9, I
Chief Financial Officer, Office of	7, XXX
Commodity Credit Corporation	7, XIV
Economic Research Service	7, XXXVII
Energy Policy and New Uses, Office of	2, IX; 7, XXIX
Environmental Quality, Office of	7, XXXI
Farm Service Agency	7, VII, XVIII
Federal Acquisition Regulation	48, 4
Federal Crop Insurance Corporation	7, IV
Food and Nutrition Service	7, II
Food Safety and Inspection Service	9, III
Foreign Agricultural Service	7, XV
Forest Service	36, II
Grain Inspection, Packers and Stockyards Administration	7, VIII; 9, II
Information Resources Management, Office of	7, XXVII
Inspector General, Office of	7, XXVI
National Agricultural Library	7, XLI
National Agricultural Statistics Service	7, XXXVI
National Institute of Food and Agriculture	7, XXXIV
Natural Resources Conservation Service	7, VI
Operations, Office of	7, XXVIII
Procurement and Property Management, Office of	7, XXXII
Rural Business-Cooperative Service	7, XVIII, XLII
Rural Development Administration	7, XLII
Rural Housing Service	7, XVIII, XXXV
Rural Telephone Bank	7, XVI
Rural Utilities Service	7, XVII, XVIII, XLII
Secretary of Agriculture, Office of	7, Subtitle A
Transportation, Office of	7, XXXIII
World Agricultural Outlook Board	7, XXXVIII
Air Force Department	32, VII
Federal Acquisition Regulation Supplement	48, 53
Air Transportation Stabilization Board	14, VI
Alcohol and Tobacco Tax and Trade Bureau	27, I
Alcohol, Tobacco, Firearms, and Explosives, Bureau of	27, II
AMTRAK	49, VII
American Battle Monuments Commission	36, IV
American Indians, Office of the Special Trustee	25, VII

Agency	CFR Title, Subtitle or Chapter
Animal and Plant Health Inspection Service	7, III; 9, I
Appalachian Regional Commission	5, IX
Architectural and Transportation Barriers Compliance Board	36, XI
Arctic Research Commission	45, XXIII
Armed Forces Retirement Home	5, XI
Army Department	32, V
Engineers, Corps of	33, II; 36, III
Federal Acquisition Regulation	48, 51
Bilingual Education and Minority Languages Affairs, Office of	34, V
Blind or Severely Disabled, Committee for Purchase from People Who Are	41, 51
Broadcasting Board of Governors	22, V
Federal Acquisition Regulation	48, 19
Career, Technical and Adult Education, Office of	34, IV
Census Bureau	15, I
Centers for Medicare & Medicaid Services	42, IV
Central Intelligence Agency	32, XIX
Chemical Safety and Hazardous Investigation Board	40, VI
Chief Financial Officer, Office of	7, XXX
Child Support Enforcement, Office of	45, III
Children and Families, Administration for	45, II, III, IV, X
Civil Rights, Commission on	5, LXVIII; 45, VII
Civil Rights, Office for	34, I
Council of the Inspectors General on Integrity and Efficiency	5, XCVIII
Court Services and Offender Supervision Agency for the District of Columbia	5, LXX
Coast Guard	33, I; 46, I; 49, IV
Coast Guard (Great Lakes Pilotage)	46, III
Commerce Department	2, XIII; 44, IV; 50, VI
Census Bureau	15, I
Economic Analysis, Bureau of	15, VIII
Economic Development Administration	13, III
Emergency Management and Assistance	44, IV
Federal Acquisition Regulation	48, 13
Foreign-Trade Zones Board	15, IV
Industry and Security, Bureau of	15, VII
International Trade Administration	15, III; 19, III
National Institute of Standards and Technology	15, II
National Marine Fisheries Service	50, II, IV
National Oceanic and Atmospheric Administration	15, IX; 50, II, III, IV, VI
National Telecommunications and Information Administration	15, XXIII; 47, III, IV
National Weather Service	15, IX
Patent and Trademark Office, United States	37, I
Productivity, Technology and Innovation, Assistant Secretary for	37, IV
Secretary of Commerce, Office of	15, Subtitle A
Technology Administration	15, XI
Technology Policy, Assistant Secretary for	37, IV
Commercial Space Transportation	14, III
Commodity Credit Corporation	7, XIV
Commodity Futures Trading Commission	5, XLI; 17, I
Community Planning and Development, Office of Assistant Secretary for	24, V, VI
Community Services, Office of	45, X
Comptroller of the Currency	12, I
Construction Industry Collective Bargaining Commission	29, IX
Consumer Financial Protection Bureau	5, LXXXIV; 12, X
Consumer Product Safety Commission	5, LXXI; 16, II
Copyright Royalty Board	37, III
Corporation for National and Community Service	2, XXII; 45, XII, XXV
Cost Accounting Standards Board	48, 99
Council on Environmental Quality	40, V
Court Services and Offender Supervision Agency for the District of Columbia	5, LXX; 28, VIII
Customs and Border Protection	19, I
Defense Contract Audit Agency	32, I

Agency	CFR Title, Subtitle or Chapter
Defense Department	2, XI; 5, XXVI; 32, Subtitle A; 40, VII
Advanced Research Projects Agency	32, I
Air Force Department	32, VII
Army Department	32, V; 33, II; 36, III; 48, 51
Defense Acquisition Regulations System	48, 2
Defense Intelligence Agency	32, I
Defense Logistics Agency	32, I, XII; 48, 54
Engineers, Corps of	33, II; 36, III
National Imagery and Mapping Agency	32, I
Navy Department	32, VI; 48, 52
Secretary of Defense, Office of	2, XI; 32, I
Defense Contract Audit Agency	32, I
Defense Intelligence Agency	32, I
Defense Logistics Agency	32, XII; 48, 54
Defense Nuclear Facilities Safety Board	10, XVII
Delaware River Basin Commission	18, III
District of Columbia, Court Services and Offender Supervision Agency for the	5, LXX; 28, VIII
Drug Enforcement Administration	21, II
East-West Foreign Trade Board	15, XIII
Economic Analysis, Bureau of	15, VIII
Economic Development Administration	13, III
Economic Research Service	7, XXXVII
Education, Department of	2, XXXIV; 5, LIII
Bilingual Education and Minority Languages Affairs, Office of	34, V
Career, Technical and Adult Education, Office of	34, IV
Civil Rights, Office for	34, I
Educational Research and Improvement, Office of	34, VII
Elementary and Secondary Education, Office of	34, II
Federal Acquisition Regulation	48, 34
Postsecondary Education, Office of	34, VI
Secretary of Education, Office of	34, Subtitle A
Special Education and Rehabilitative Services, Office of	34, III
Career, Technical, and Adult Education, Office of	34, IV
Educational Research and Improvement, Office of	34, VII
Election Assistance Commission	2, LVIII; 11, II
Elementary and Secondary Education, Office of	34, II
Emergency Oil and Gas Guaranteed Loan Board	13, V
Emergency Steel Guarantee Loan Board	13, IV
Employee Benefits Security Administration	29, XXV
Employees' Compensation Appeals Board	20, IV
Employees Loyalty Board	5, V
Employment and Training Administration	20, V
Employment Standards Administration	20, VI
Endangered Species Committee	50, IV
Energy, Department of	2, IX; 5, XXIII; 10, II, III, X
Federal Acquisition Regulation	48, 9
Federal Energy Regulatory Commission	5, XXIV; 18, I
Property Management Regulations	41, 109
Energy, Office of	7, XXIX
Engineers, Corps of	33, II; 36, III
Engraving and Printing, Bureau of	31, VI
Environmental Protection Agency	2, XV; 5, LIV; 40, I, IV, VII
Federal Acquisition Regulation	48, 15
Property Management Regulations	41, 115
Environmental Quality, Office of	7, XXXI
Equal Employment Opportunity Commission	5, LXII; 29, XIV
Equal Opportunity, Office of Assistant Secretary for	24, I
Executive Office of the President	3, I
Environmental Quality, Council on	40, V
Management and Budget, Office of	2, Subtitle A; 5, III, LXXVII; 14, VI; 48, 99

Agency	CFR Title, Subtitle or Chapter
Forest Service	36, II
General Services Administration	5, LVII; 41, 105
Contract Appeals, Board of	48, 61
Federal Acquisition Regulation	48, 5
Federal Management Regulation	41, 102
Federal Property Management Regulations	41, 101
Federal Travel Regulation System	41, Subtitle F
General	41, 300
Payment From a Non-Federal Source for Travel Expenses	41, 304
Payment of Expenses Connected With the Death of Certain Employees	41, 303
Relocation Allowances	41, 302
Temporary Duty (TDY) Travel Allowances	41, 301
Geological Survey	30, IV
Government Accountability Office	4, I
Government Ethics, Office of	5, XVI
Government National Mortgage Association	24, III
Grain Inspection, Packers and Stockyards Administration	7, VIII; 9, II
Gulf Coast Ecosystem Restoration Council	2, LIX; 40, VIII
Harry S. Truman Scholarship Foundation	45, XVIII
Health and Human Services, Department of	2, III; 5, XLV; 45, Subtitle A,
Centers for Medicare & Medicaid Services	42, IV
Child Support Enforcement, Office of	45, III
Children and Families, Administration for	45, II, III, IV, X
Community Services, Office of	45, X
Family Assistance, Office of	45, II
Federal Acquisition Regulation	48, 3
Food and Drug Administration	21, I
Human Development Services, Office of	45, XIII
Indian Health Service	25, V
Inspector General (Health Care), Office of	42, V
Public Health Service	42, I
Refugee Resettlement, Office of	45, IV
Homeland Security, Department of	2, XXX; 5, XXXVI; 6, I; 8, I
Coast Guard	33, I; 46, I; 49, IV
Coast Guard (Great Lakes Pilotage)	46, III
Customs and Border Protection	19, I
Federal Emergency Management Agency	44, I
Human Resources Management and Labor Relations Systems	5, XCVII
Immigration and Customs Enforcement Bureau	19, IV
Transportation Security Administration	49, XII
HOPE for Homeowners Program, Board of Directors of	24, XXIV
Housing and Urban Development, Department of	2, XXIV; 5, LXV; 24, Subtitle B
Community Planning and Development, Office of Assistant Secretary for	24, V, VI
Equal Opportunity, Office of Assistant Secretary for	24, I
Federal Acquisition Regulation	48, 24
Federal Housing Enterprise Oversight, Office of	12, XVII
Government National Mortgage Association	24, III
Housing—Federal Housing Commissioner, Office of Assistant Secretary for	24, II, VIII, X, XX
Housing, Office of, and Multifamily Housing Assistance Restructuring, Office of	24, IV
Inspector General, Office of	24, XII
Public and Indian Housing, Office of Assistant Secretary for	24, IX
Secretary, Office of	24, Subtitle A, VII
Housing—Federal Housing Commissioner, Office of Assistant Secretary for	24, II, VIII, X, XX
Housing, Office of, and Multifamily Housing Assistance Restructuring, Office of	24, IV
Human Development Services, Office of	45, XIII
Immigration and Customs Enforcement Bureau	19, IV
Immigration Review, Executive Office for	8, V

Agency	CFR Title, Subtitle or Chapter
Independent Counsel, Office of	28, VII
Independent Counsel, Offices of	28, VI
Indian Affairs, Bureau of	25, I, V
Indian Affairs, Office of the Assistant Secretary	25, VI
Indian Arts and Crafts Board	25, II
Indian Health Service	25, V
Industry and Security, Bureau of	15, VII
Information Resources Management, Office of	7, XXVII
Information Security Oversight Office, National Archives and Records Administration	32, XX
Inspector General	
Agriculture Department	7, XXVI
Health and Human Services Department	42, V
Housing and Urban Development Department	24, XII, XV
Institute of Peace, United States	22, XVII
Inter-American Foundation	5, LXIII; 22, X
Interior Department	2, XIV
American Indians, Office of the Special Trustee	25, VII
Endangered Species Committee	50, IV
Federal Acquisition Regulation	48, 14
Federal Property Management Regulations System	41, 114
Fish and Wildlife Service, United States	50, I, IV
Geological Survey	30, IV
Indian Affairs, Bureau of	25, I, V
Indian Affairs, Office of the Assistant Secretary	25, VI
Indian Arts and Crafts Board	25, II
Land Management, Bureau of	43, II
National Indian Gaming Commission	25, III
National Park Service	36, I
Natural Resource Revenue, Office of	30, XII
Ocean Energy Management, Bureau of	30, V
Reclamation, Bureau of	43, I
Safety and Enforcement Bureau, Bureau of	30, II
Secretary of the Interior, Office of	2, XIV; 43, Subtitle A
Surface Mining Reclamation and Enforcement, Office of	30, VII
Internal Revenue Service	26, I
International Boundary and Water Commission, United States and Mexico, United States Section	22, XI
International Development, United States Agency for	22, II
Federal Acquisition Regulation	48, 7
International Development Cooperation Agency, United States	22, XII
International Joint Commission, United States and Canada	22, IV
International Organizations Employees Loyalty Board	5, V
International Trade Administration	15, III; 19, III
International Trade Commission, United States	19, II
Interstate Commerce Commission	5, XL
Investment Security, Office of	31, VIII
James Madison Memorial Fellowship Foundation	45, XXIV
Japan–United States Friendship Commission	22, XVI
Joint Board for the Enrollment of Actuaries	20, VIII
Justice Department	2, XXVIII; 5, XXVIII; 28, I, XI; 40, IV
Alcohol, Tobacco, Firearms, and Explosives, Bureau of	27, II
Drug Enforcement Administration	21, II
Federal Acquisition Regulation	48, 28
Federal Claims Collection Standards	31, IX
Federal Prison Industries, Inc.	28, III
Foreign Claims Settlement Commission of the United States	45, V
Immigration Review, Executive Office for	8, V
Independent Counsel, Offices of	28, VI
Prisons, Bureau of	28, V
Property Management Regulations	41, 128
Labor Department	2, XXIX; 5, XLII
Employee Benefits Security Administration	29, XXV
Employees' Compensation Appeals Board	20, IV

Agency	CFR Title, Subtitle or Chapter
National Park Service	36, I
National Railroad Adjustment Board	29, III
National Railroad Passenger Corporation (AMTRAK)	49, VII
National Science Foundation	2, XXV; 5, XLIII; 45, VI
Federal Acquisition Regulation	48, 25
National Security Council	32, XXI
National Security Council and Office of Science and Technology Policy	47, II
National Telecommunications and Information Administration	15, XXIII; 47, III, IV
National Transportation Safety Board	49, VIII
Natural Resources Conservation Service	7, VI
Natural Resource Revenue, Office of	30, XII
Navajo and Hopi Indian Relocation, Office of	25, IV
Navy Department	32, VI
Federal Acquisition Regulation	48, 52
Neighborhood Reinvestment Corporation	24, XXV
Northeast Interstate Low-Level Radioactive Waste Commission	10, XVIII
Nuclear Regulatory Commission	2, XX; 5, XLVIII; 10, I
Federal Acquisition Regulation	48, 20
Occupational Safety and Health Administration	29, XVII
Occupational Safety and Health Review Commission	29, XX
Ocean Energy Management, Bureau of	30, V
Oklahoma City National Memorial Trust	36, XV
Operations Office	7, XXVIII
Overseas Private Investment Corporation	5, XXXIII; 22, VII
Patent and Trademark Office, United States	37, I
Payment From a Non-Federal Source for Travel Expenses	41, 304
Payment of Expenses Connected With the Death of Certain Employees	41, 303
Peace Corps	2, XXXVII; 22, III
Pennsylvania Avenue Development Corporation	36, IX
Pension Benefit Guaranty Corporation	29, XL
Personnel Management, Office of	5, I, XXXV; 5, IV; 45, VIII
Human Resources Management and Labor Relations Systems, Department of Homeland Security	5, XCVII
Federal Acquisition Regulation	48, 17
Federal Employees Group Life Insurance Federal Acquisition Regulation	48, 21
Federal Employees Health Benefits Acquisition Regulation	48, 16
Pipeline and Hazardous Materials Safety Administration	49, I
Postal Regulatory Commission	5, XLVI; 39, III
Postal Service, United States	5, LX; 39, I
Postsecondary Education, Office of	34, VI
President's Commission on White House Fellowships	1, IV
Presidential Documents	3
Presidio Trust	36, X
Prisons, Bureau of	28, V
Privacy and Civil Liberties Oversight Board	6, X
Procurement and Property Management, Office of	7, XXXII
Productivity, Technology and Innovation, Assistant Secretary	37, IV
Public Contracts, Department of Labor	41, 50
Public and Indian Housing, Office of Assistant Secretary for	24, IX
Public Health Service	42, I
Railroad Retirement Board	20, II
Reclamation, Bureau of	43, I
Refugee Resettlement, Office of	45, IV
Relocation Allowances	41, 302
Research and Innovative Technology Administration	49, XI
Rural Business-Cooperative Service	7, XVIII, XLII
Rural Development Administration	7, XLII
Rural Housing Service	7, XVIII, XXXV
Rural Telephone Bank	7, XVI
Rural Utilities Service	7, XVII, XVIII, XLII

Agency	CFR Title, Subtitle or Chapter
Safety and Environmental Enforcement, Bureau of	30, II
Saint Lawrence Seaway Development Corporation	33, IV
Science and Technology Policy, Office of	32, XXIV
Science and Technology Policy, Office of, and National Security Council	47, II
Secret Service	31, IV
Securities and Exchange Commission	5, XXXIV; 17, II
Selective Service System	32, XVI
Small Business Administration	2, XXVII; 13, I
Smithsonian Institution	36, V
Social Security Administration	2, XXIII; 20, III; 48, 23
Soldiers' and Airmen's Home, United States	5, XI
Special Counsel, Office of	5, VIII
Special Education and Rehabilitative Services, Office of	34, III
State Department	2, VI; 22, I; 28, XI
Federal Acquisition Regulation	48, 6
Surface Mining Reclamation and Enforcement, Office of	30, VII
Surface Transportation Board	49, X
Susquehanna River Basin Commission	18, VIII
Technology Administration	15, XI
Technology Policy, Assistant Secretary for	37, IV
Tennessee Valley Authority	5, LXIX; 18, XIII
Thrift Supervision Office, Department of the Treasury	12, V
Trade Representative, United States, Office of	15, XX
Transportation, Department of	2, XII; 5, L
Commercial Space Transportation	14, III
Contract Appeals, Board of	48, 63
Emergency Management and Assistance	44, IV
Federal Acquisition Regulation	48, 12
Federal Aviation Administration	14, I
Federal Highway Administration	23, I, II
Federal Motor Carrier Safety Administration	49, III
Federal Railroad Administration	49, II
Federal Transit Administration	49, VI
Maritime Administration	46, II
National Highway Traffic Safety Administration	23, II, III; 47, IV; 49, V
Pipeline and Hazardous Materials Safety Administration	49, I
Saint Lawrence Seaway Development Corporation	33, IV
Secretary of Transportation, Office of	14, II; 49, Subtitle A
Surface Transportation Board	49, X
Transportation Statistics Bureau	49, XI
Transportation, Office of	7, XXXIII
Transportation Security Administration	49, XII
Transportation Statistics Bureau	49, XI
Travel Allowances, Temporary Duty (TDY)	41, 301
Treasury Department	2, X;5, XXI; 12, XV; 17, IV; 31, IX
Alcohol and Tobacco Tax and Trade Bureau	27, I
Community Development Financial Institutions Fund	12, XVIII
Comptroller of the Currency	12, I
Customs and Border Protection	19, I
Engraving and Printing, Bureau of	31, VI
Federal Acquisition Regulation	48, 10
Federal Claims Collection Standards	31, IX
Federal Law Enforcement Training Center	31, VII
Financial Crimes Enforcement Network	31, X
Fiscal Service	31, II
Foreign Assets Control, Office of	31, V
Internal Revenue Service	26, I
Investment Security, Office of	31, VIII
Monetary Offices	31, I
Secret Service	31, IV
Secretary of the Treasury, Office of	31, Subtitle A
Thrift Supervision, Office of	12, V
Truman, Harry S. Scholarship Foundation	45, XVIII
United States and Canada, International Joint Commission	22, IV
United States and Mexico, International Boundary and Water Commission, United States Section	22, XI

Agency	CFR Title, Subtitle or Chapter
U.S. Copyright Office	37, II
Utah Reclamation Mitigation and Conservation Commission	43, III
Veterans Affairs Department	2, VIII; 38, I
Federal Acquisition Regulation	48, 8
Veterans' Employment and Training Service, Office of the Assistant Secretary for	41, 61; 20, IX
Vice President of the United States, Office of	32, XXVIII
Wage and Hour Division	29, V
Water Resources Council	18, VI
Workers' Compensation Programs, Office of	20, I, VII
World Agricultural Outlook Board	7, XXXVIII

List of CFR Sections Affected

All changes in this volume of the Code of Federal Regulations (CFR) that were made by documents published in the FEDERAL REGISTER since January 1, 2011 are enumerated in the following list. Entries indicate the nature of the changes effected. Page numbers refer to FEDERAL REGISTER pages. The user should consult the entries for chapters, parts and subparts as well as sections for revisions.

For changes to this volume of the CFR prior to this listing, consult the annual edition of the monthly List of CFR Sections Affected (LSA). The LSA is available at *www.fdsys.gov*. For changes to this volume of the CFR prior to 2001, see the "List of CFR Sections Affected, 1949–1963, 1964–1972, 1973–1985, and 1986–2000" published in 11 separate volumes. The "List of CFR Sections Affected 1986–2000" is available at *www.fdsys.gov*.

2011

27 CFR

76 FR Page

27 CFR—Continued

76 FR Page

27 CFR—Continued

76 FR Page

2012

27 CFR

77 FR Page

27 CFR—Continued

77 FR Page

27 CFR—Continued

77 FR Page

27 CFR—Continued

77 FR Page

2013

27 CFR

78 FR Page

27 CFR—Continued

78 FR Page

2014

27 CFR

79 FR Page

27 CFR—Continued

79 FR Page

2015

27 CFR

81 FR Page

2016

(No regulations published)